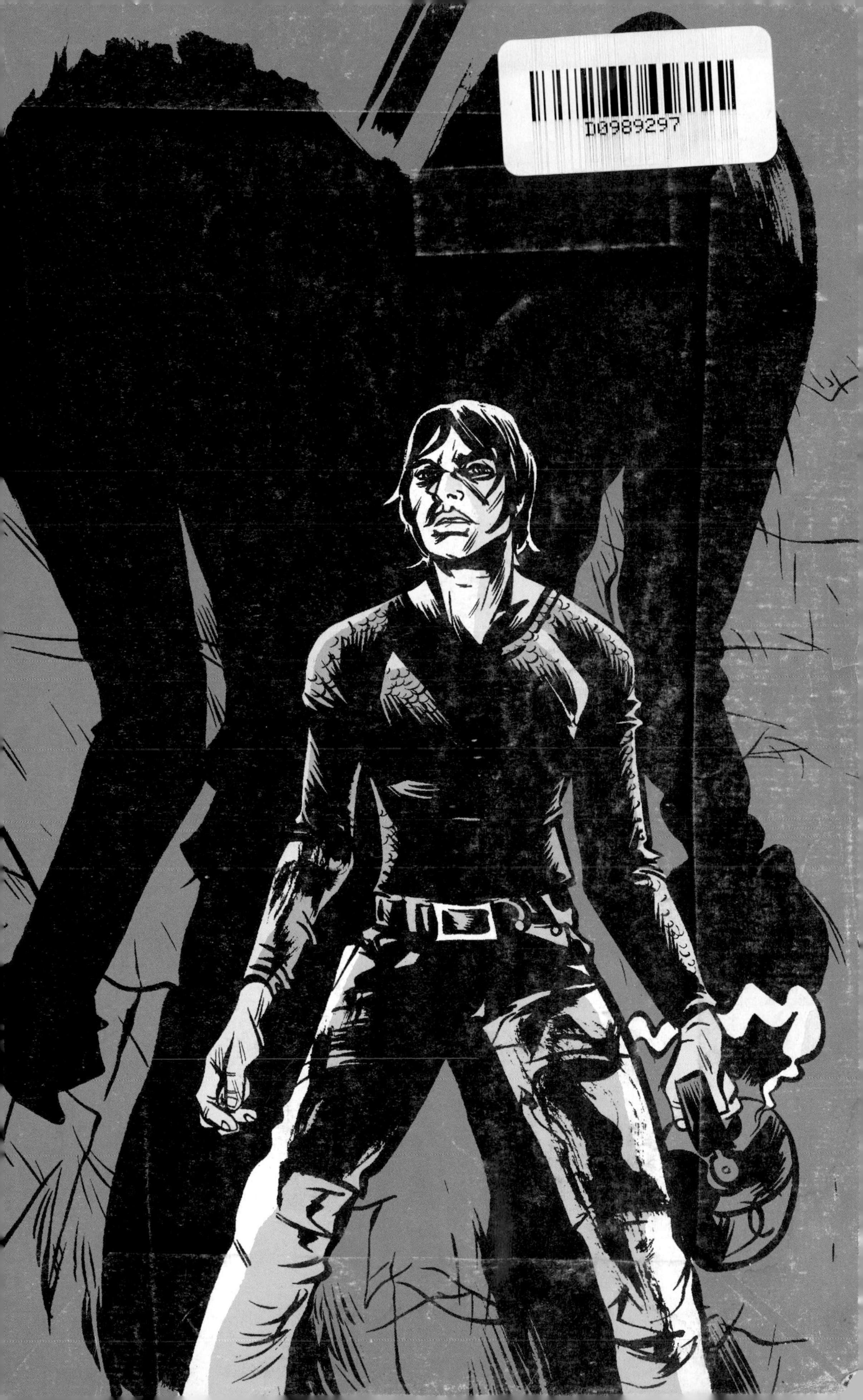

dramatis personae

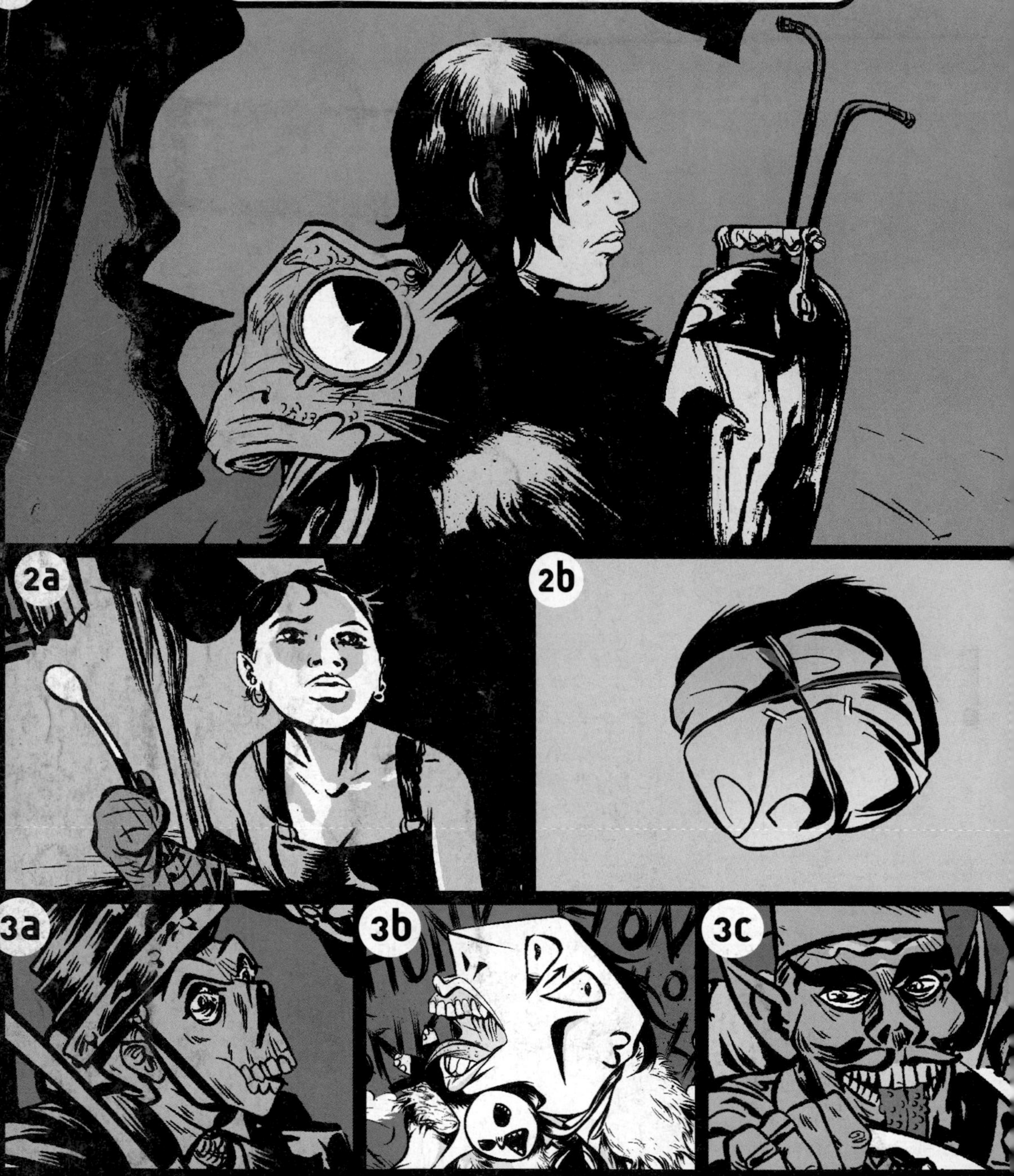
1a
2a
2b
3a
3b
3c

a few worms in the big apple:

1a: **call him "s."** "S" for the Stooge. Why have a name when a letter will do? A hard-boiled dandy or a noir-lizard king. He'll be in two places at once and cast no shadow. Aren't you tired of anti-heroes? So is "S."

2a: **luna.** Poor kid. By the time you've figured out how it all works, you've already lost about everything you'd hoped to keep. But a smile is a frown turned upside down. Can you still smile?

2b: **the stuff.** A bizarre metallic substance that's like lava at room temperature. As heavy as a barbell, corrosive to the core—what is this stuff? Where did it come from? What's it supposed to be for?

3a: **crunchy.** 3b: **kip.** 3c: **drophead.** Three tough guys who work for a shadowy crime syndicate. They want to flush "S"'s head down a toilet. In their weird costumes, they blend in with all the other holiday goofs out on the street celebrating St. Huck's day.

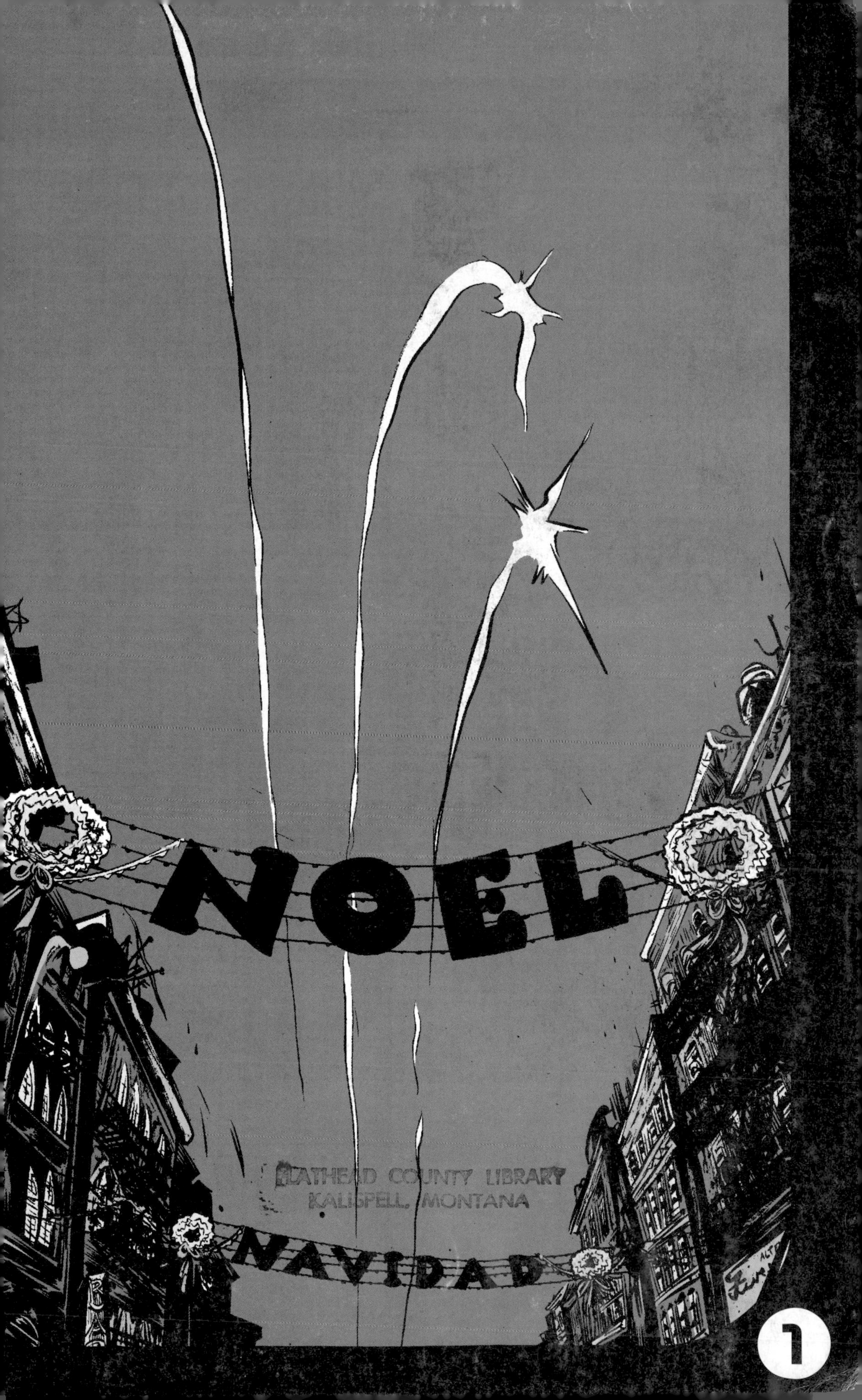
NOEL
NAVIDAD

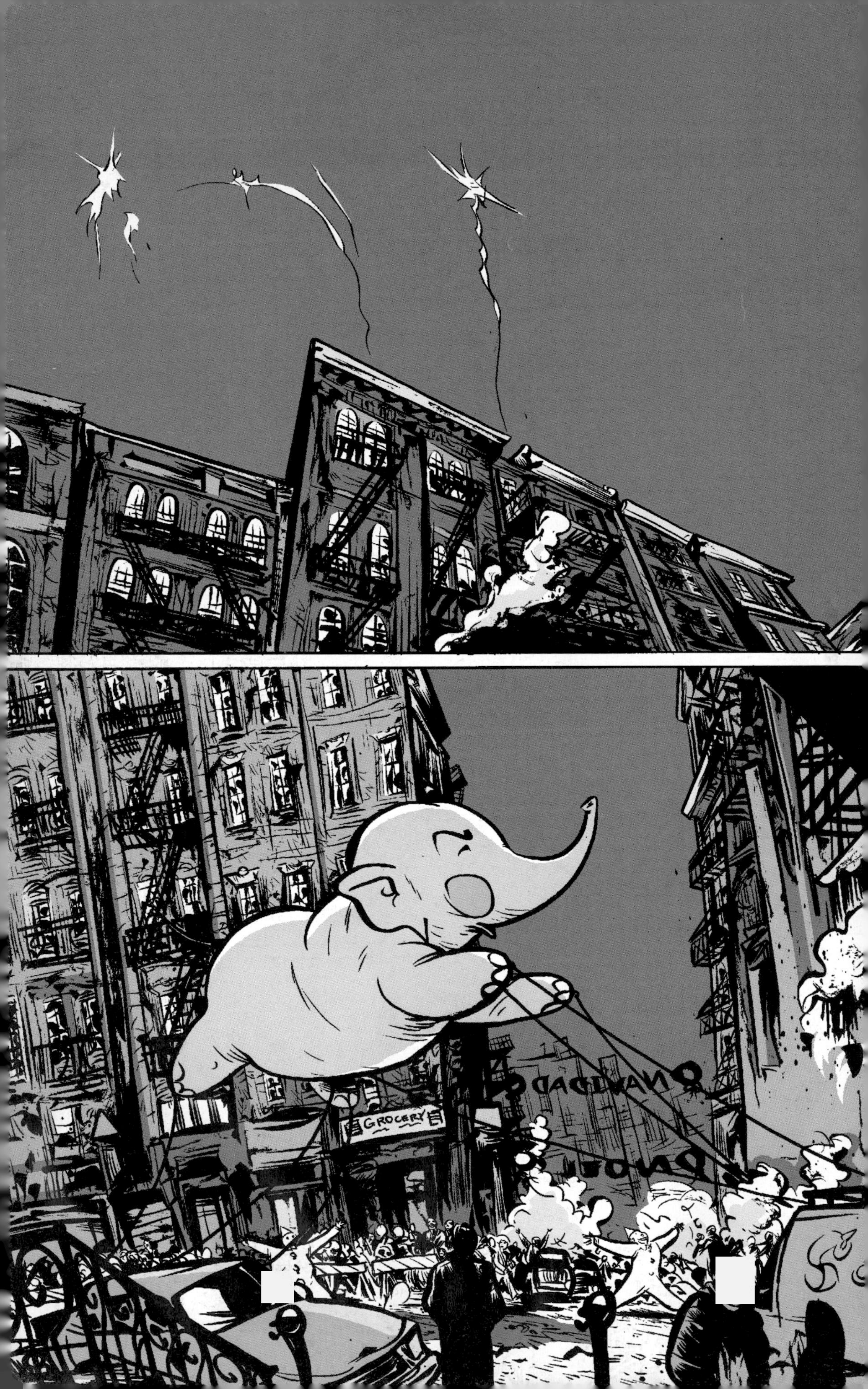
GROCERY

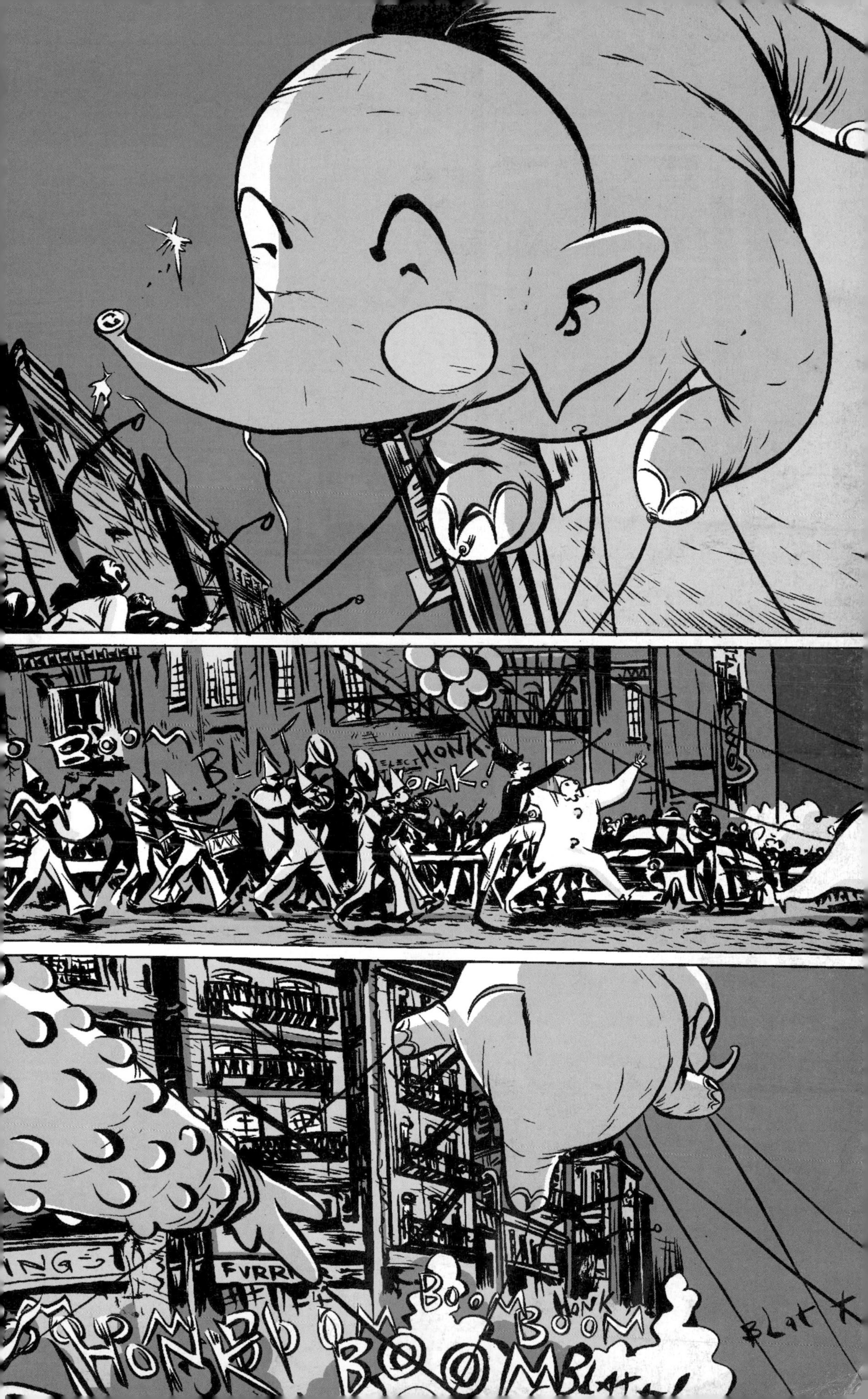
BOOM
BLAT
ELECT
HONK! HONK!
BOOM HONK BOOM
BLAT
HONK
BOOM
BOOM

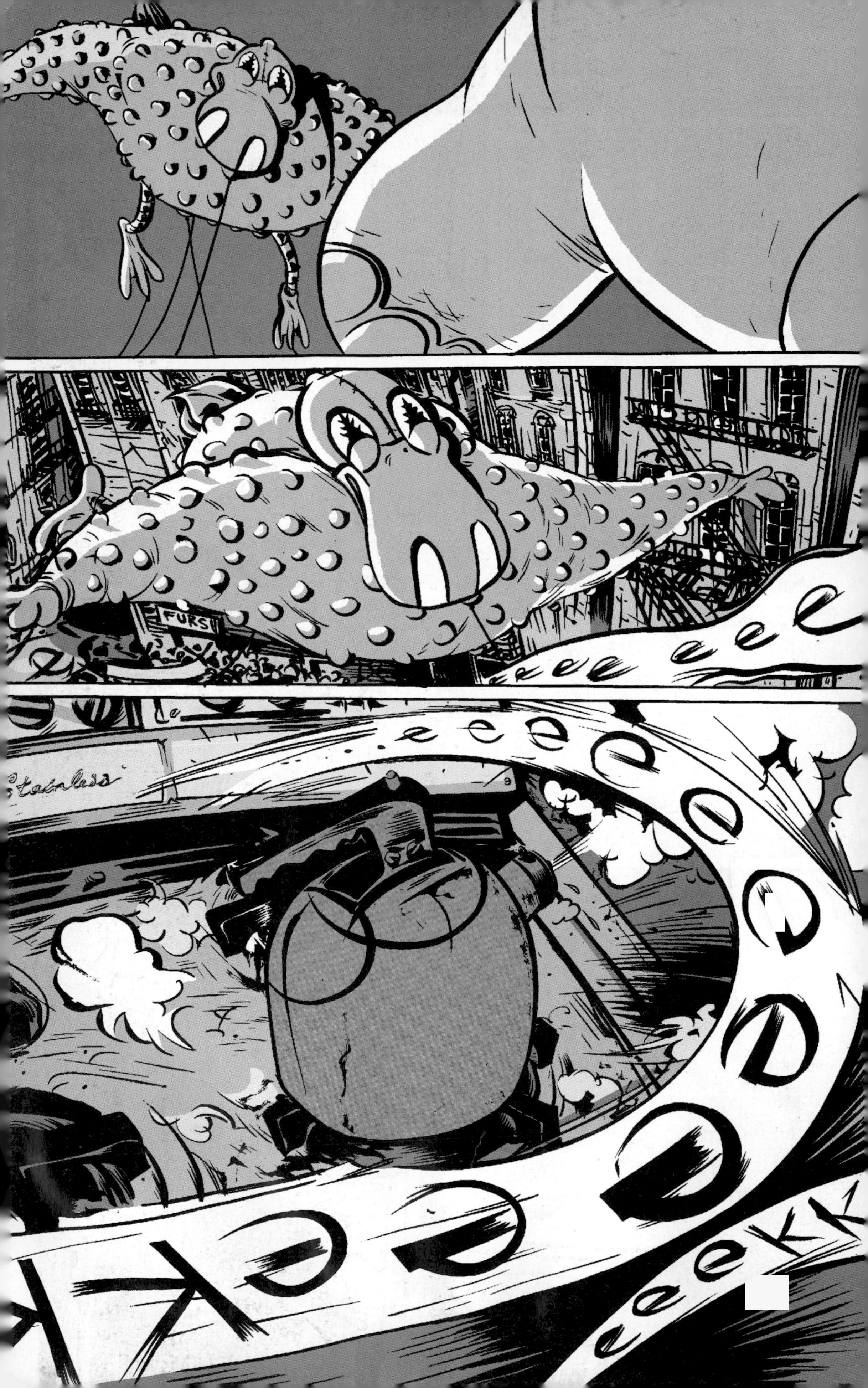
FURS
Stainless

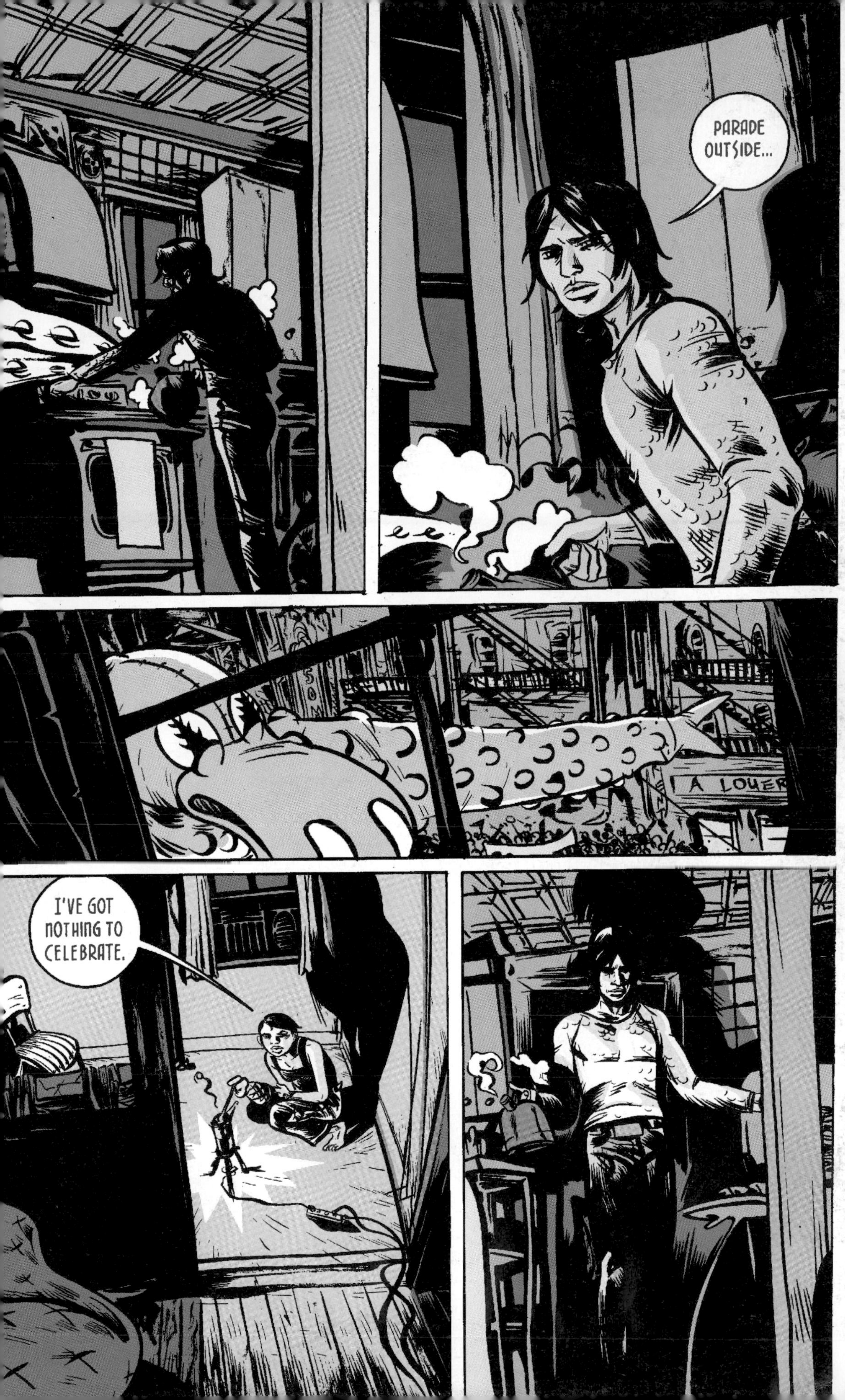
PARADE OUTSIDE...
A LOUER
I'VE GOT NOTHING TO CELEBRATE.

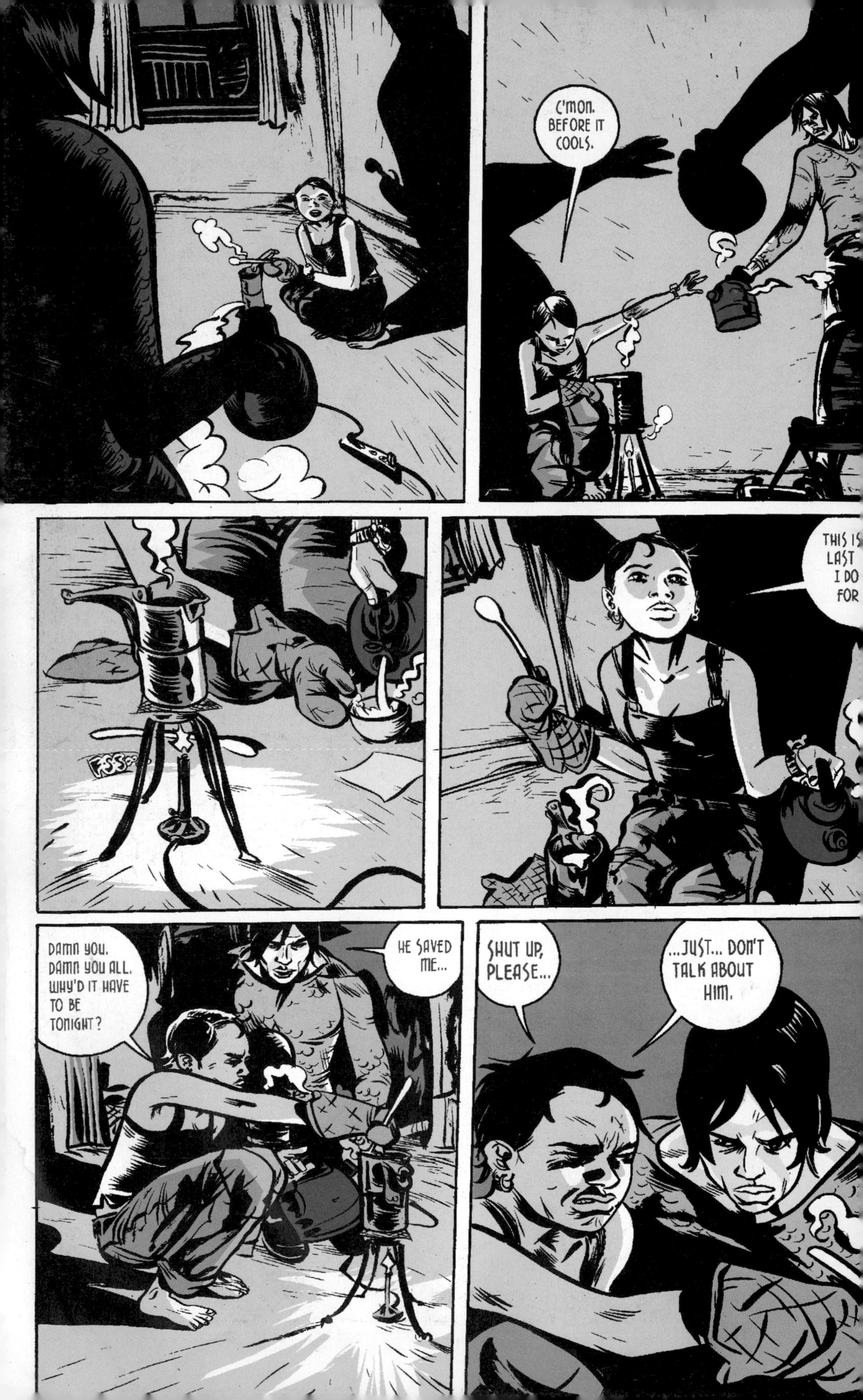
C'MON. BEFORE IT COOLS.
THIS IS LAST I DO FOR
DAMN YOU. DAMN YOU ALL. WHY'D IT HAVE TO BE TONIGHT?
HE SAVED ME...
SHUT UP, PLEASE...
...JUST... DON'T TALK ABOUT HIM.

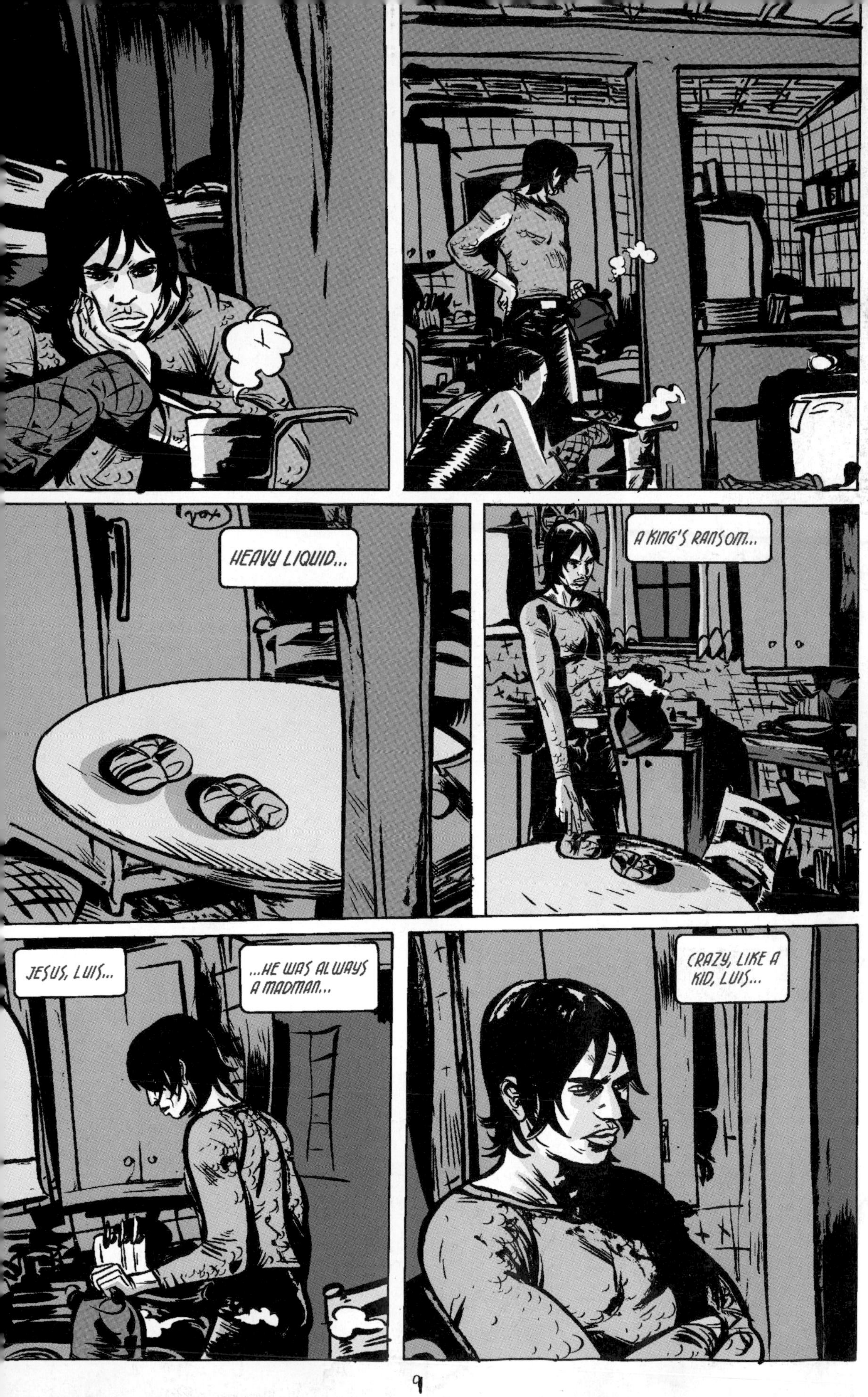
HEAVY LIQUID...
A KING'S RANSOM...
JESUS, LUIS...
...HE WAS ALWAYS A MADMAN...
CRAZY, LIKE A KID, LUIS...

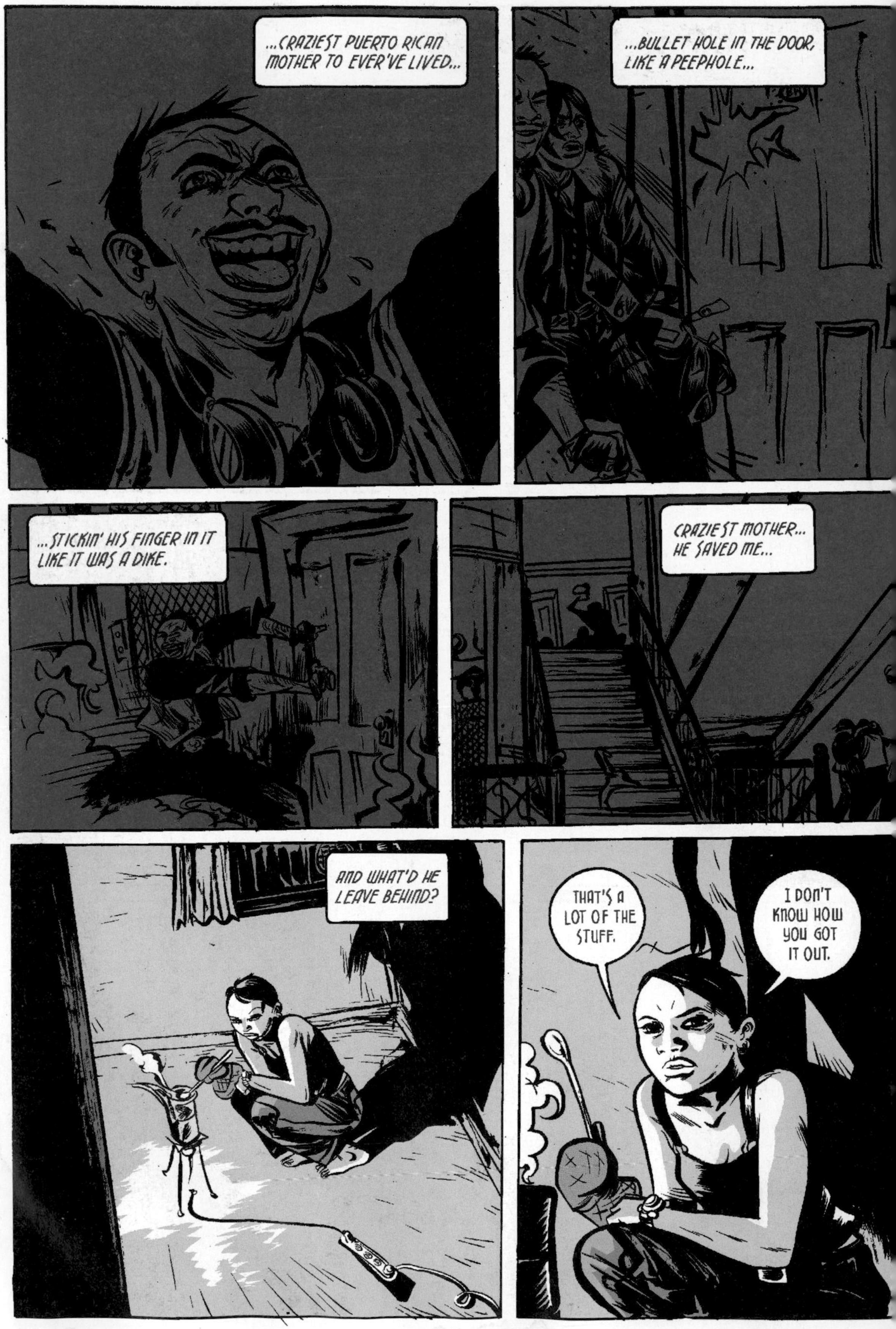
...CRAZIEST PUERTO RICAN MOTHER TO EVER'VE LIVED...
...BULLET HOLE IN THE DOOR, LIKE A PEEPHOLE...
...STICKIN' HIS FINGER IN IT LIKE IT WAS A DIKE.
CRAZIEST MOTHER... HE SAVED ME...
AND WHAT'D HE LEAVE BEHIND?
THAT'S A LOT OF THE STUFF.
I DON'T KNOW HOW YOU GOT IT OUT.

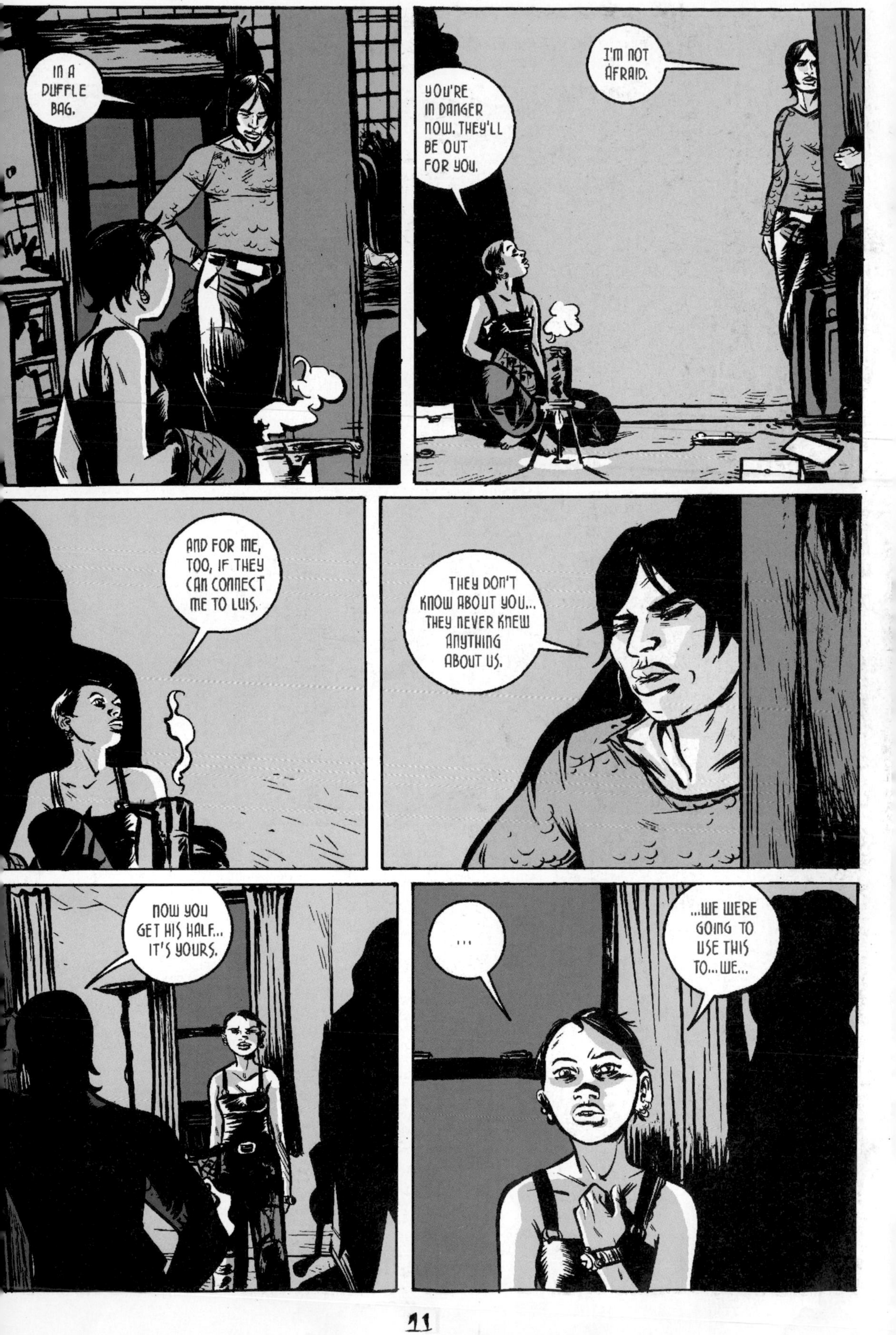

IN A DUFFLE BAG.
I'M NOT AFRAID.
YOU'RE IN DANGER NOW. THEY'LL BE OUT FOR YOU.
AND FOR ME, TOO, IF THEY CAN CONNECT ME TO LUIS.
THEY DON'T KNOW ABOUT YOU... THEY NEVER KNEW ANYTHING ABOUT US.
NOW YOU GET HIS HALF... IT'S YOURS.
...
...WE WERE GOING TO USE THIS TO... WE...

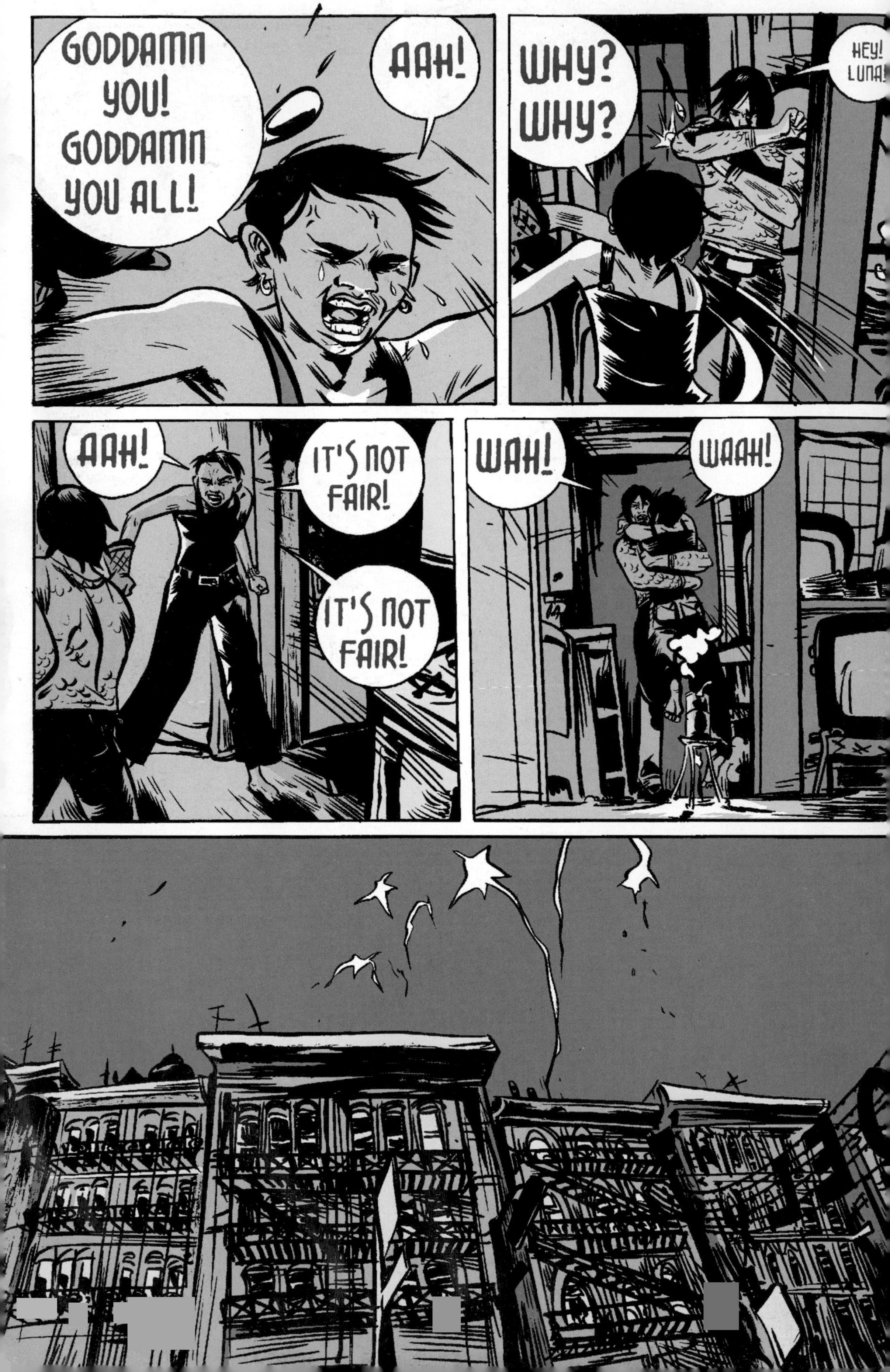
GODDAMN YOU! GODDAMN YOU ALL!
AAH!
WHY? WHY?
HEY! LUNA!
AAH!
IT'S NOT FAIR!
IT'S NOT FAIR!
WAH!
WAAH!

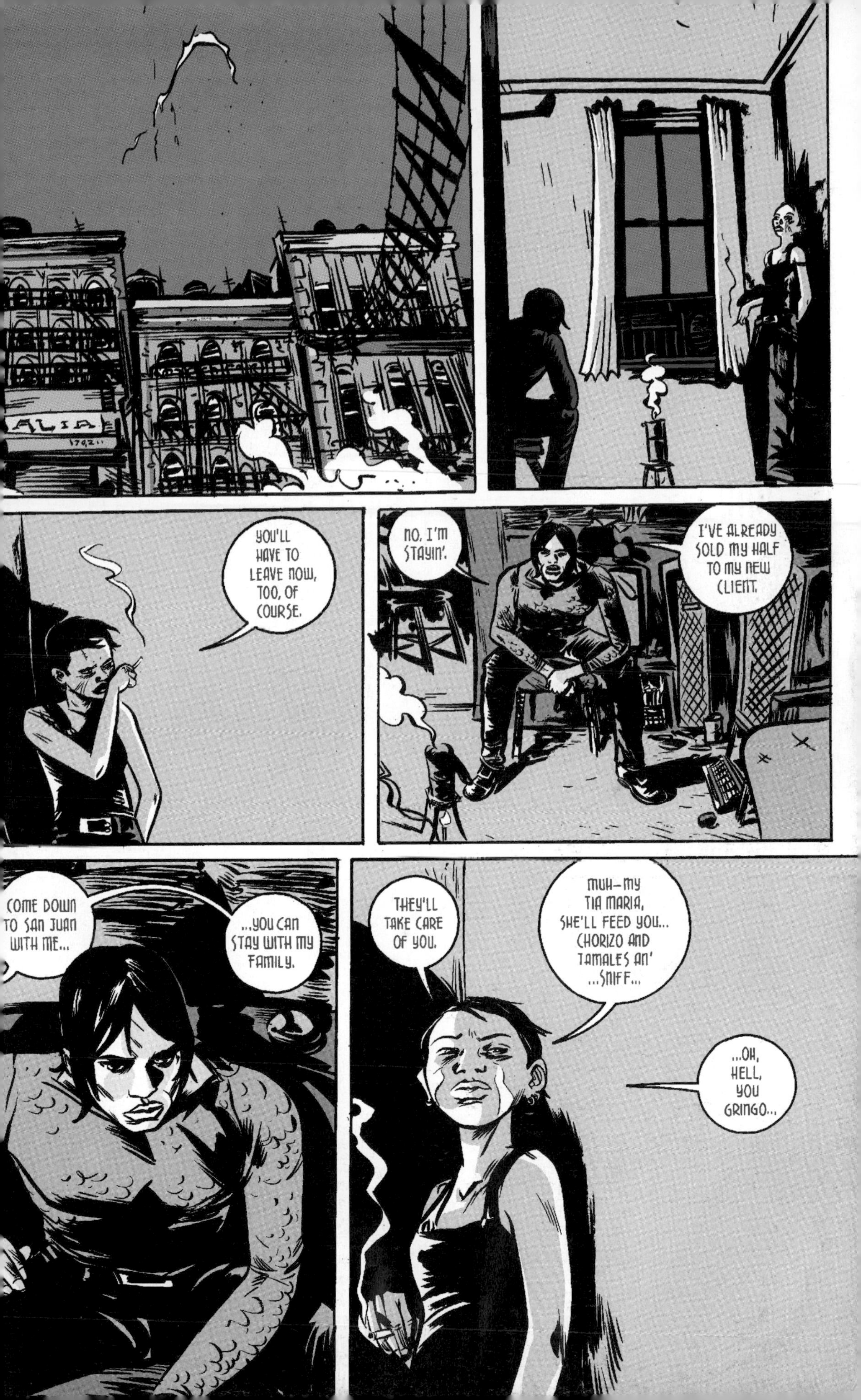
YOU'LL HAVE TO LEAVE NOW, TOO, OF COURSE.
NO, I'M STAYIN'.
I'VE ALREADY SOLD MY HALF TO MY NEW CLIENT.
COME DOWN TO SAN JUAN WITH ME...
...YOU CAN STAY WITH MY FAMILY.
THEY'LL TAKE CARE OF YOU.
MUH-MY TIA MARIA, SHE'LL FEED YOU... CHORIZO AND TAMALES AN' ...SNIFF...
...OH, HELL, YOU GRINGO...

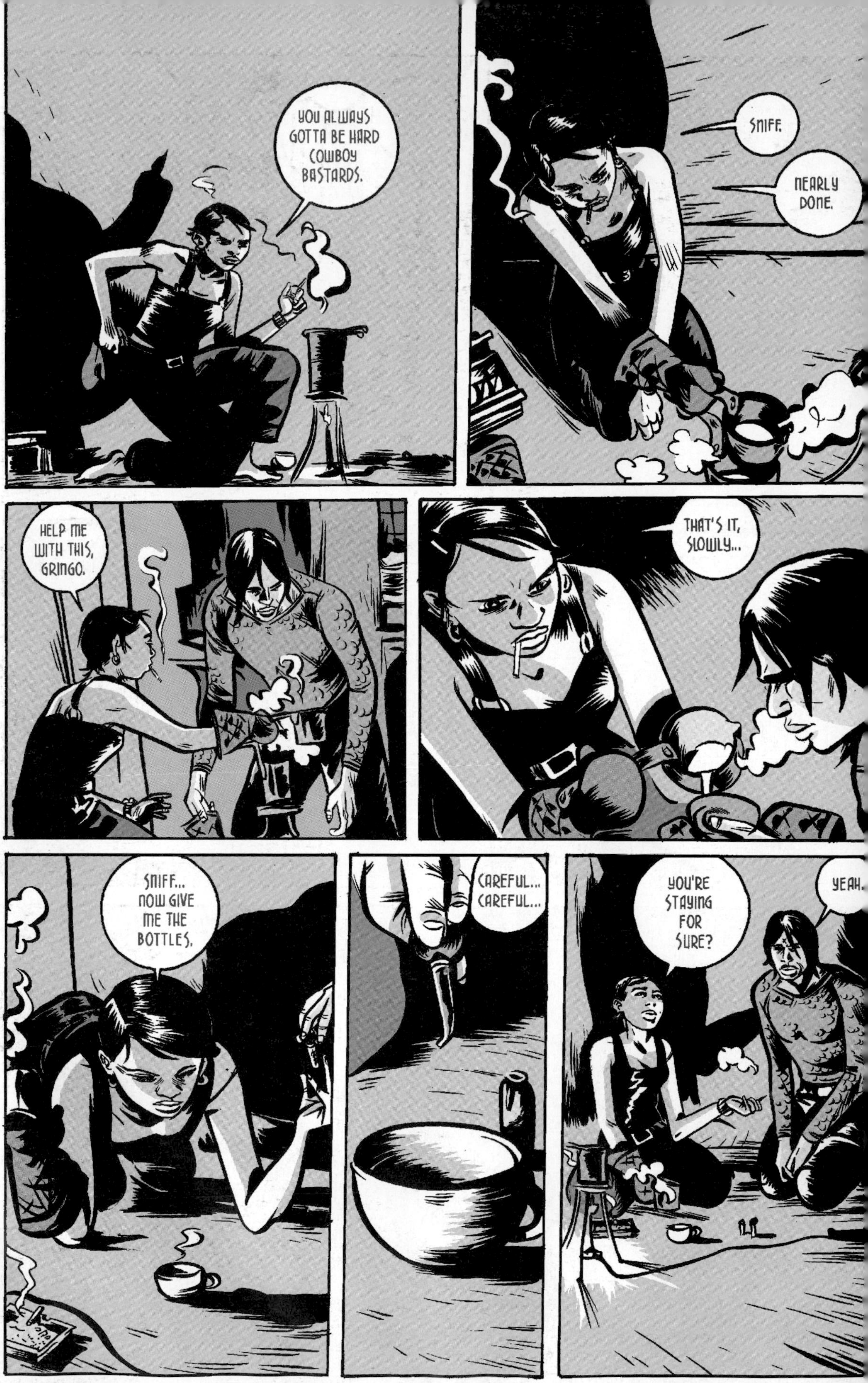
YOU ALWAYS GOTTA BE HARD COWBOY BASTARDS.
SNIFF.
NEARLY DONE.
HELP ME WITH THIS, GRINGO.
THAT'S IT, SLOWLY...
SNIFF... NOW GIVE ME THE BOTTLES.
CAREFUL... CAREFUL...
YOU'RE STAYING FOR SURE?
YEAH.

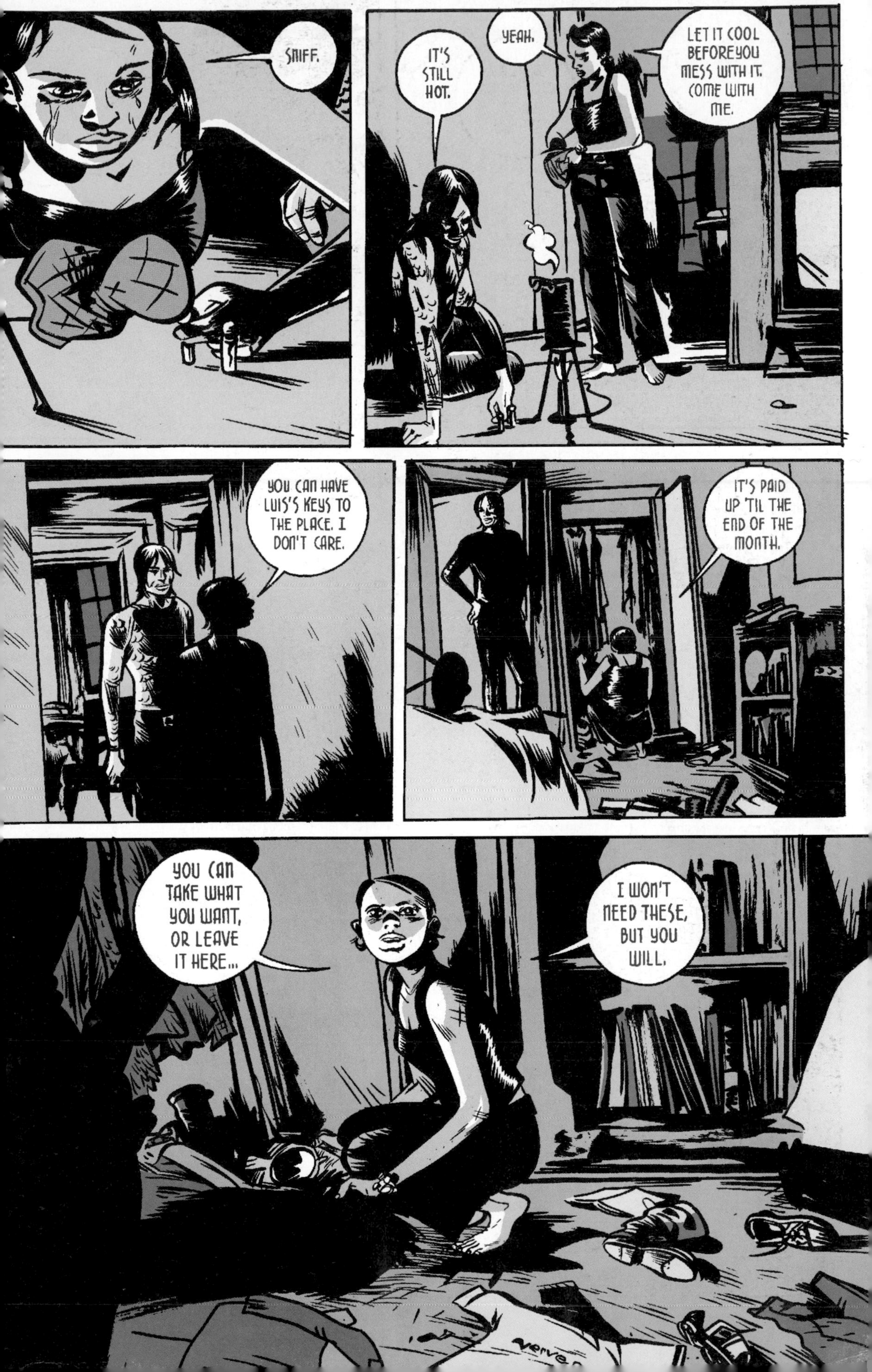
SNIFF.
YEAH.
IT'S STILL HOT.
LET IT COOL BEFORE YOU MESS WITH IT. COME WITH ME.
YOU CAN HAVE LUIS'S KEYS TO THE PLACE. I DON'T CARE.
IT'S PAID UP 'TIL THE END OF THE MONTH.
YOU CAN TAKE WHAT YOU WANT, OR LEAVE IT HERE...
I WON'T NEED THESE, BUT YOU WILL.
vertigo

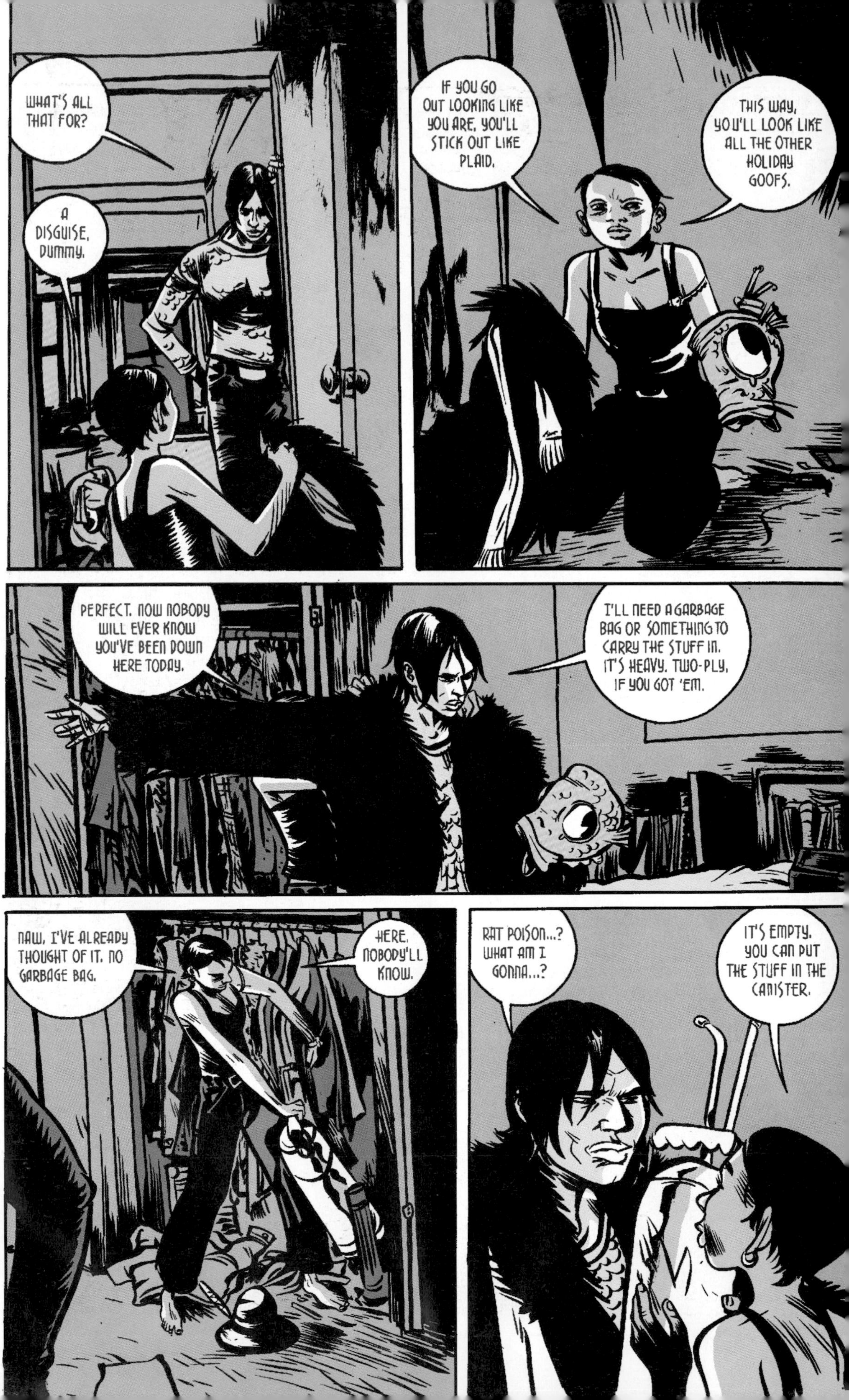
WHAT'S ALL THAT FOR?
A DISGUISE, DUMMY.
IF YOU GO OUT LOOKING LIKE YOU ARE, YOU'LL STICK OUT LIKE PLAID.
THIS WAY, YOU'LL LOOK LIKE ALL THE OTHER HOLIDAY GOOFS.
PERFECT. NOW NOBODY WILL EVER KNOW YOU'VE BEEN DOWN HERE TODAY.
I'LL NEED A GARBAGE BAG OR SOMETHING TO CARRY THE STUFF IN. IT'S HEAVY. TWO-PLY, IF YOU GOT 'EM.
NAW, I'VE ALREADY THOUGHT OF IT. NO GARBAGE BAG.
HERE. NOBODY'LL KNOW.
RAT POISON...? WHAT AM I GONNA...?
IT'S EMPTY. YOU CAN PUT THE STUFF IN THE CANISTER.

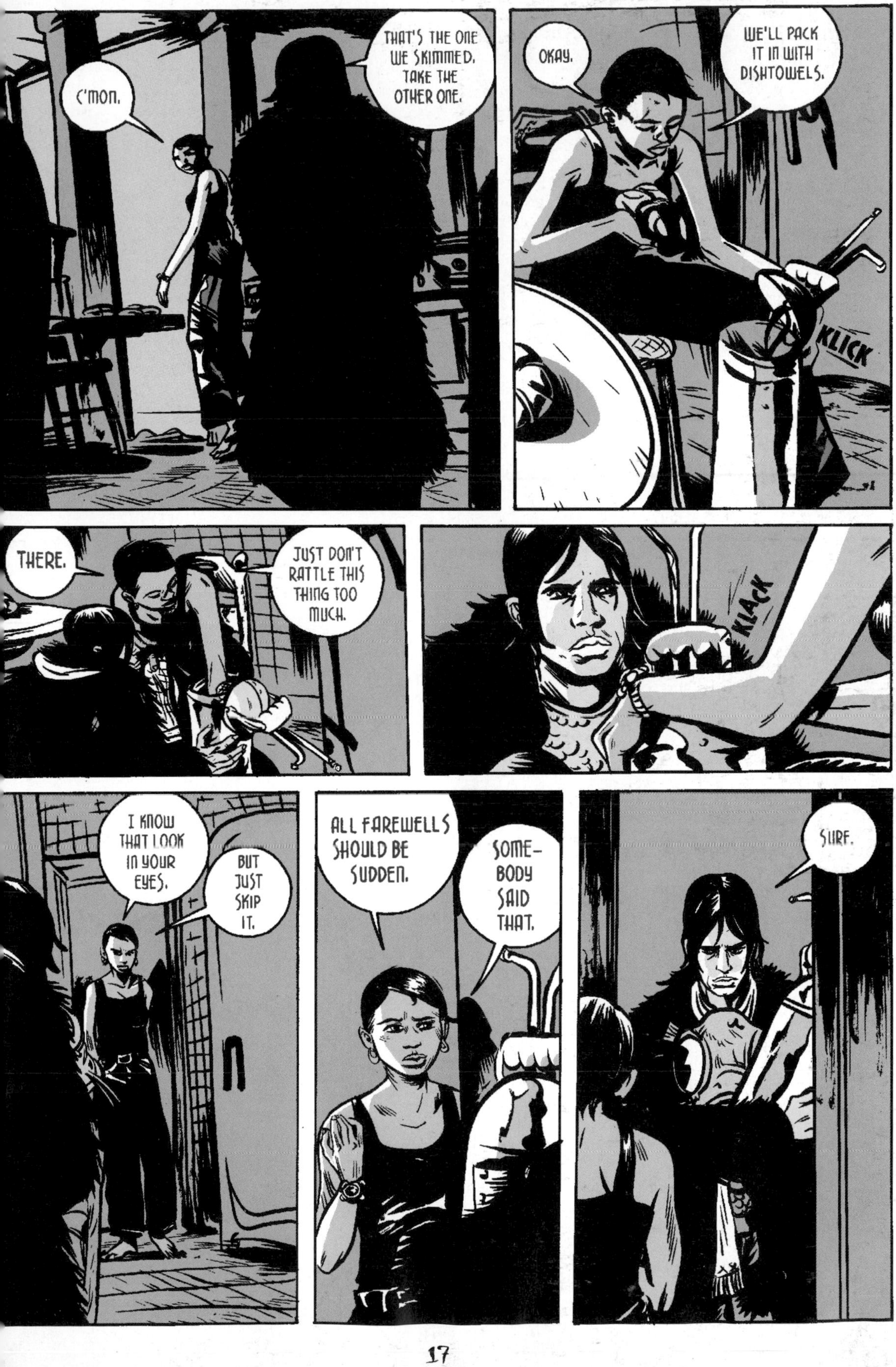
C'MON.
THAT'S THE ONE WE SKIMMED. TAKE THE OTHER ONE.
OKAY.
WE'LL PACK IT IN WITH DISHTOWELS.
KLICK
THERE.
JUST DON'T RATTLE THIS THING TOO MUCH.
KLACK
I KNOW THAT LOOK IN YOUR EYES.
BUT JUST SKIP IT.
ALL FAREWELLS SHOULD BE SUDDEN.
SOME-BODY SAID THAT.
SURF.

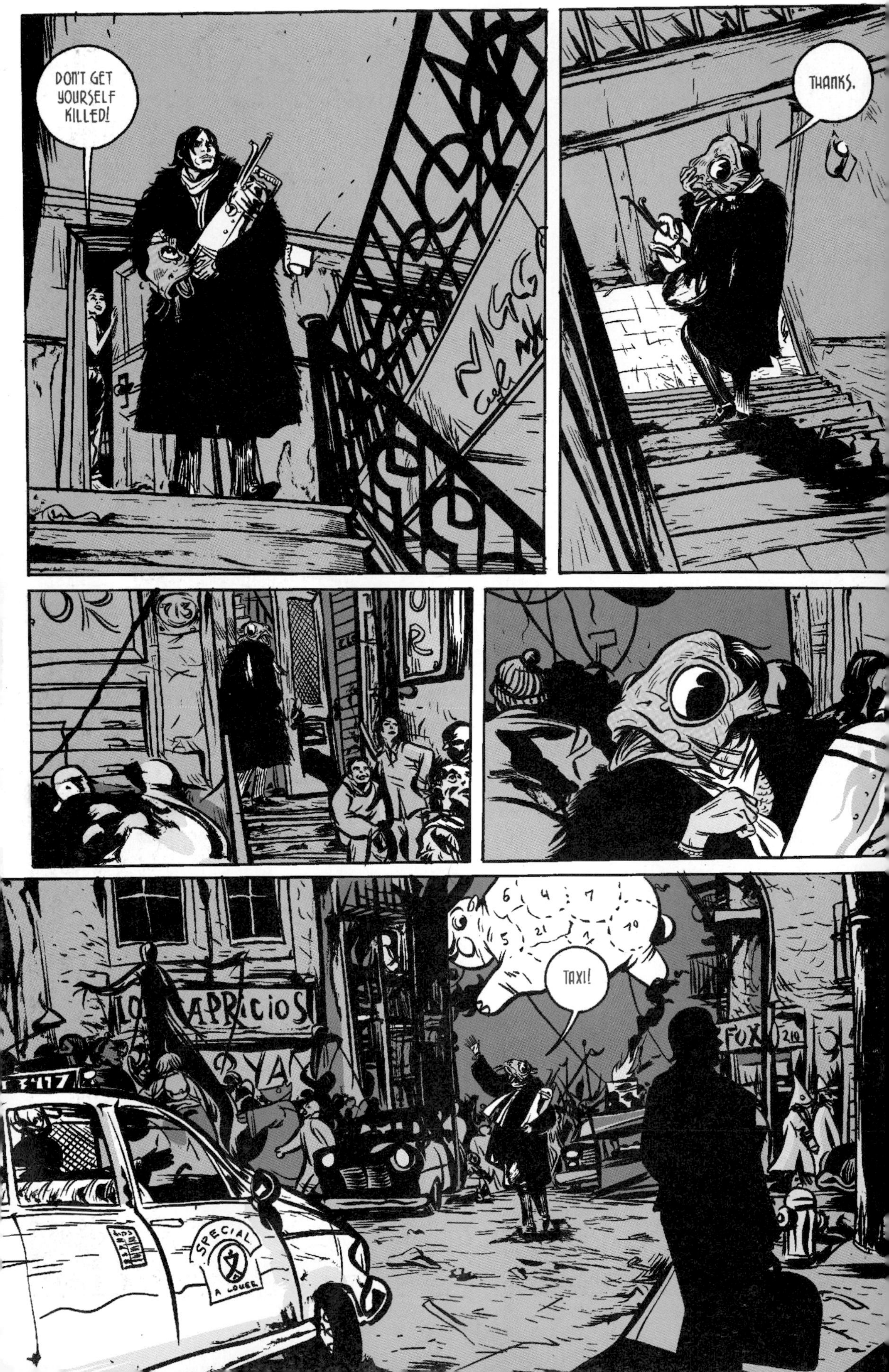
DON'T GET YOURSELF KILLED!
THANKS.
TAXI!
FOX
210
SPECIAL
A LOUER

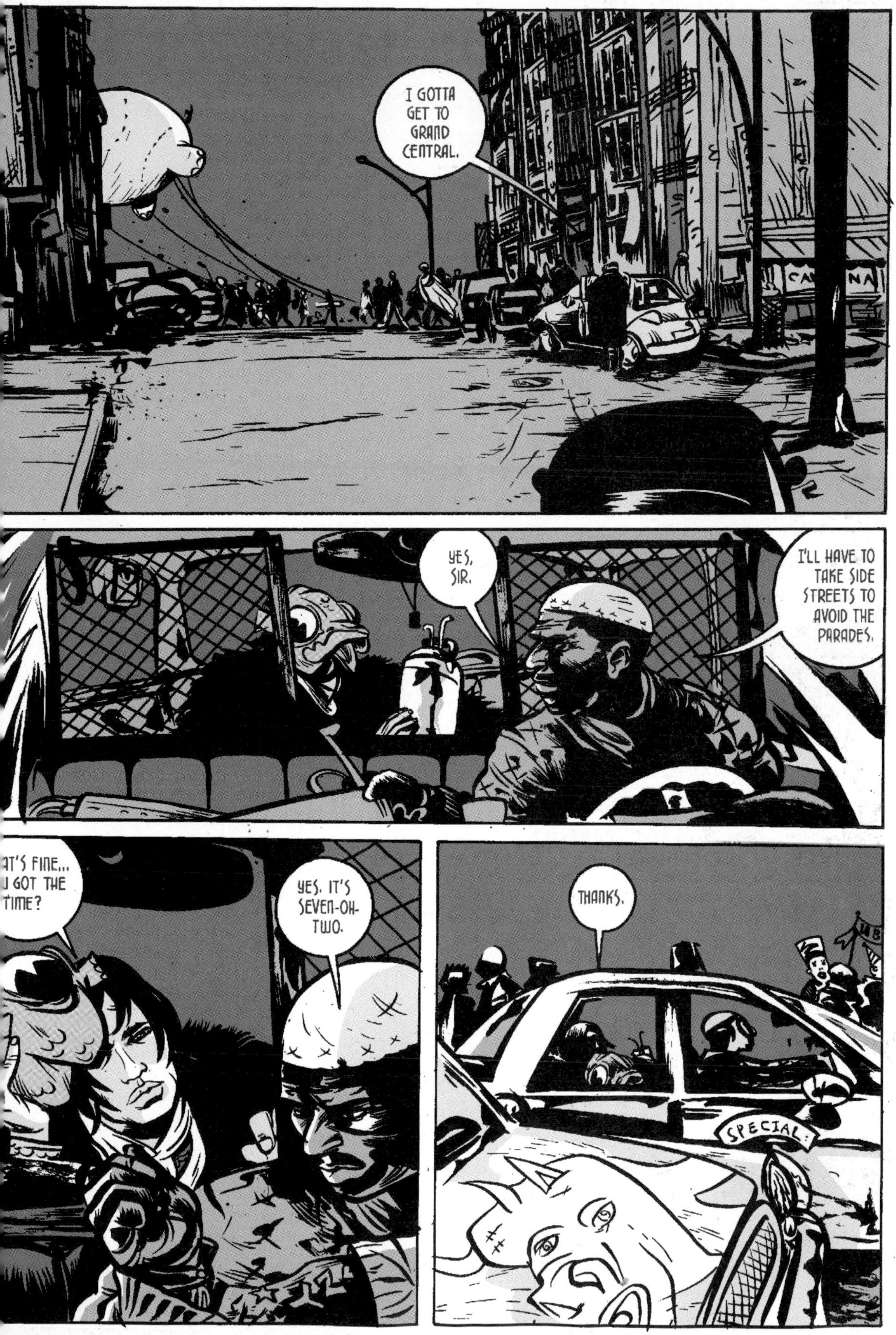
I GOTTA GET TO GRAND CENTRAL.
YES, SIR.
I'LL HAVE TO TAKE SIDE STREETS TO AVOID THE PARADES.
AT'S FINE... U GOT THE TIME?
YES. IT'S SEVEN-OH-TWO.
THANKS.
SPECIAL

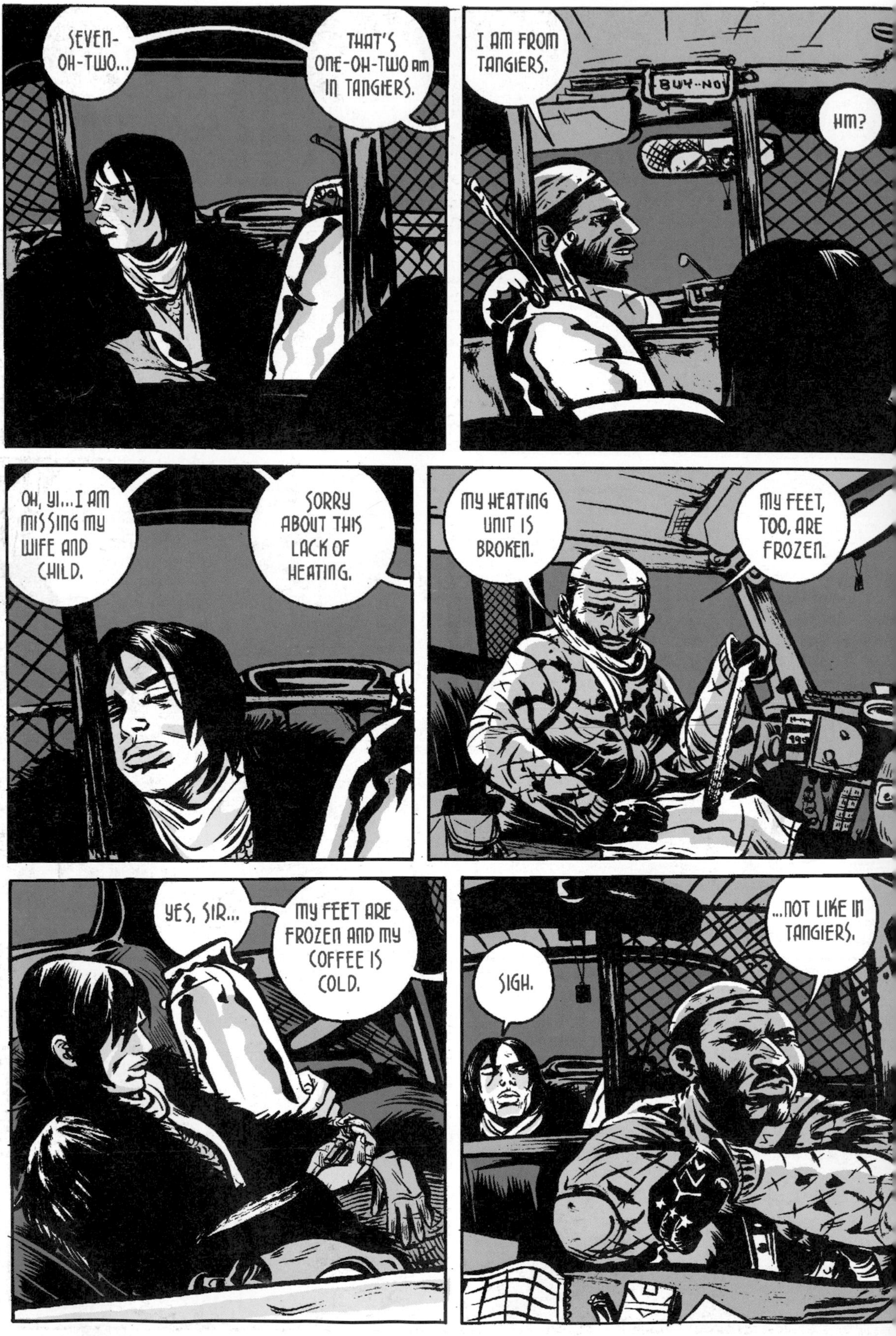
SEVEN-OH-TWO...
THAT'S ONE-OH-TWO am IN TANGIERS.
I AM FROM TANGIERS.
BUY-NO
HM?
OH, YI...I AM MISSING MY WIFE AND CHILD.
SORRY ABOUT THIS LACK OF HEATING.
MY HEATING UNIT IS BROKEN.
MY FEET, TOO, ARE FROZEN.
YES, SIR...
MY FEET ARE FROZEN AND MY COFFEE IS COLD.
...NOT LIKE IN TANGIERS.
SIGH.

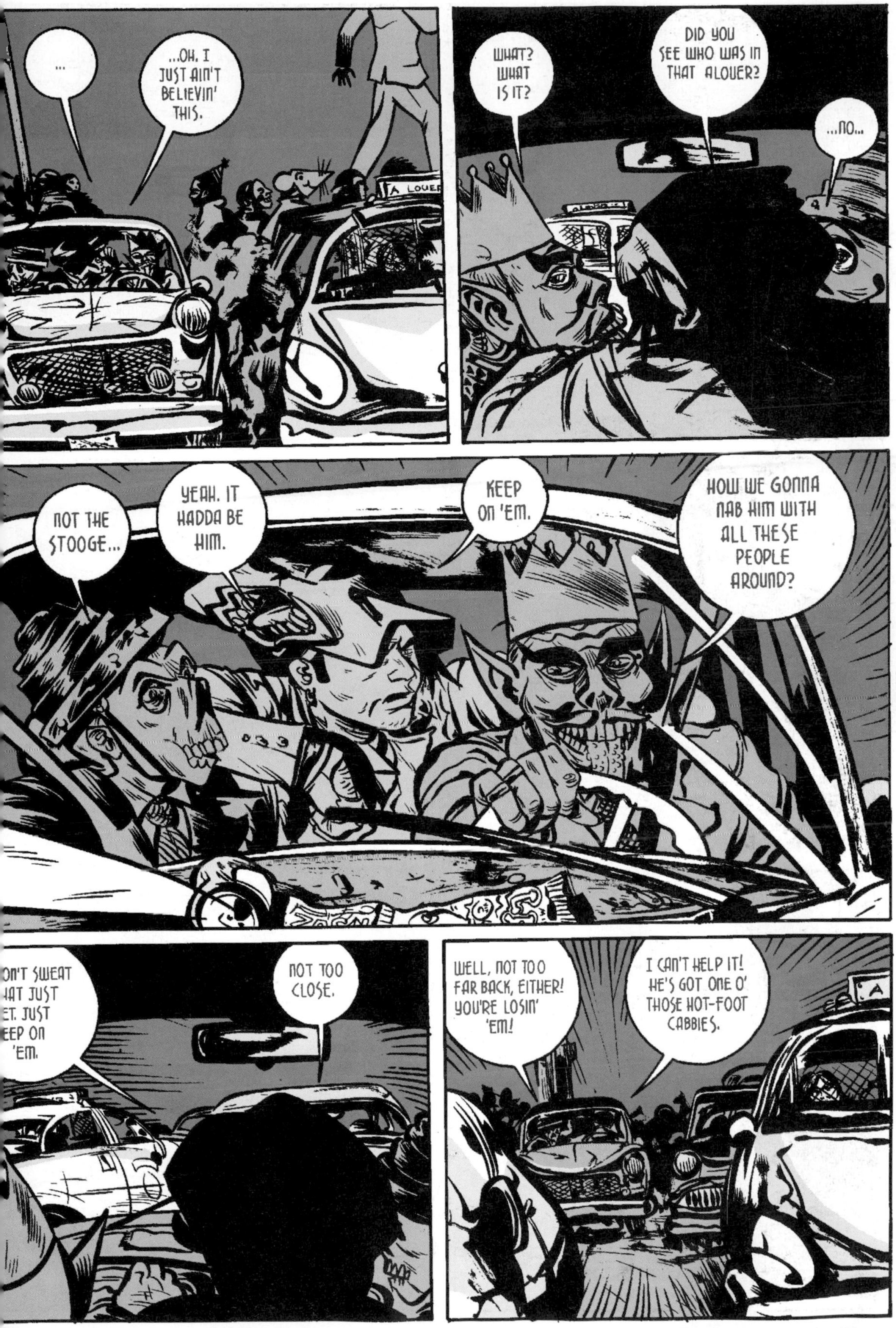
...
...OH. I JUST AIN'T BELIEVIN' THIS.
WHAT? WHAT IS IT?
DID YOU SEE WHO WAS IN THAT ALOUER?
...NO...
NOT THE STOOGE...
YEAH. IT HADDA BE HIM.
KEEP ON 'EM.
HOW WE GONNA NAB HIM WITH ALL THESE PEOPLE AROUND?
NOT TOO CLOSE.
WELL, NOT TOO FAR BACK, EITHER! YOU'RE LOSIN' 'EM!
I CAN'T HELP IT! HE'S GOT ONE O' THOSE HOT-FOOT CABBIES.

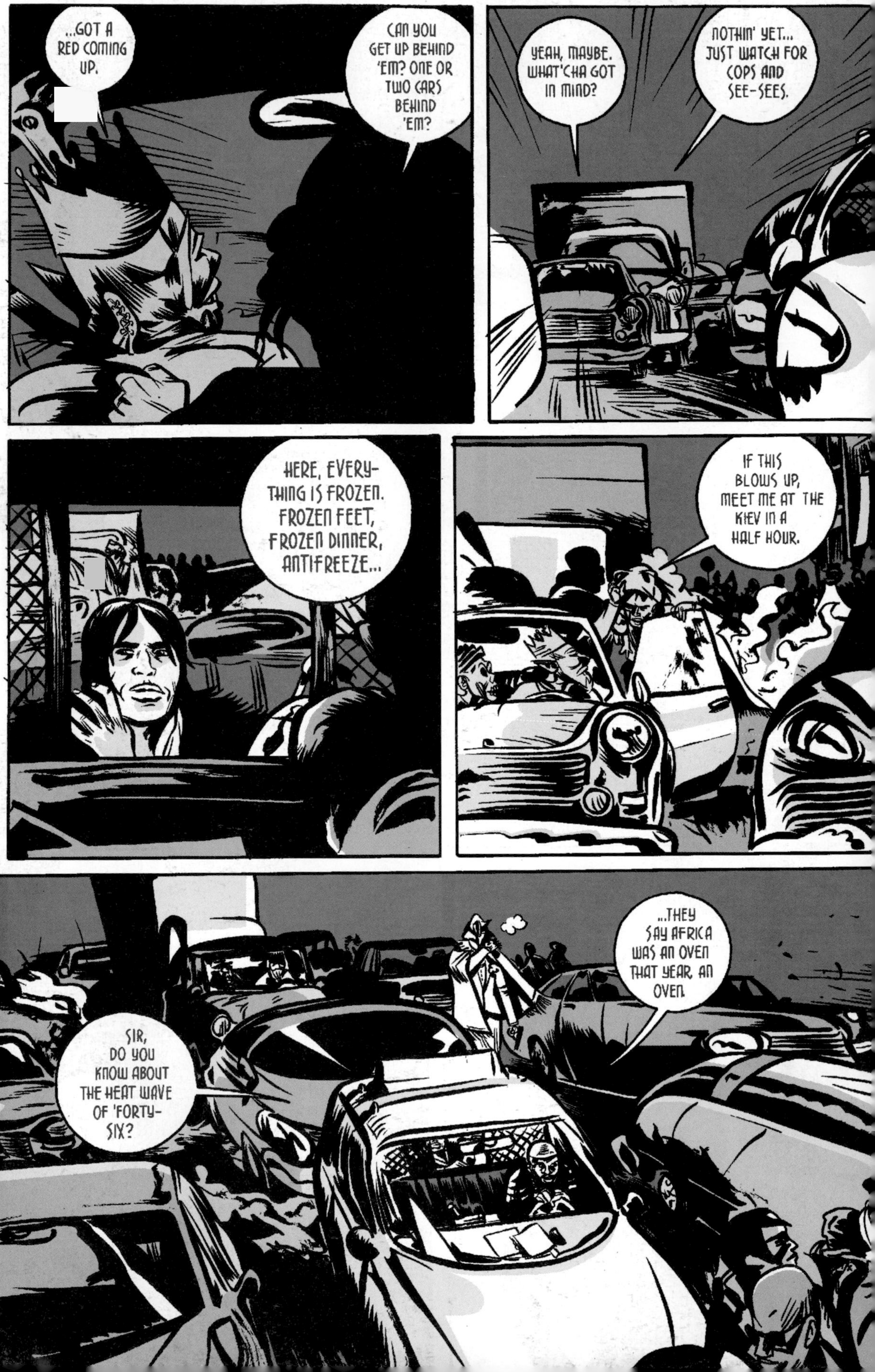
...GOT A RED COMING UP.
CAN YOU GET UP BEHIND 'EM? ONE OR TWO CARS BEHIND 'EM?
YEAH, MAYBE. WHAT'CHA GOT IN MIND?
NOTHIN' YET... JUST WATCH FOR COPS AND SEE-SEES.
HERE, EVERYTHING IS FROZEN. FROZEN FEET, FROZEN DINNER, ANTIFREEZE...
IF THIS BLOWS UP, MEET ME AT THE KIEV IN A HALF HOUR.
SIR, DO YOU KNOW ABOUT THE HEAT WAVE OF 'FORTY-SIX?
...THEY SAY AFRICA WAS AN OVEN THAT YEAR, AN OVEN.

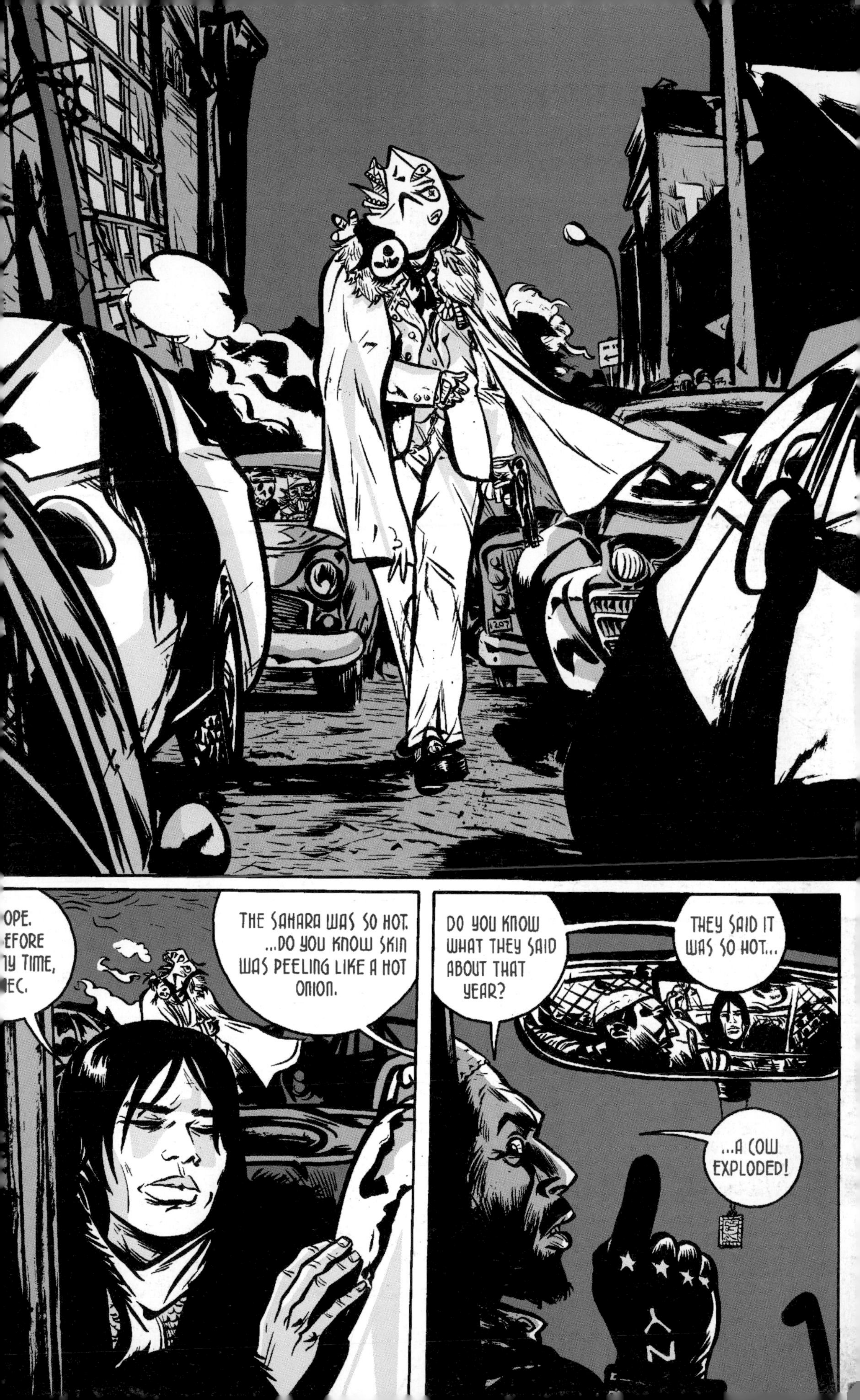

OPE. EFORE IY TIME, IEC.
THE SAHARA WAS SO HOT. ...DO YOU KNOW SKIN WAS PEELING LIKE A HOT ONION.
DO YOU KNOW WHAT THEY SAID ABOUT THAT YEAR?
THEY SAID IT WAS SO HOT...
...A COW EXPLODED!

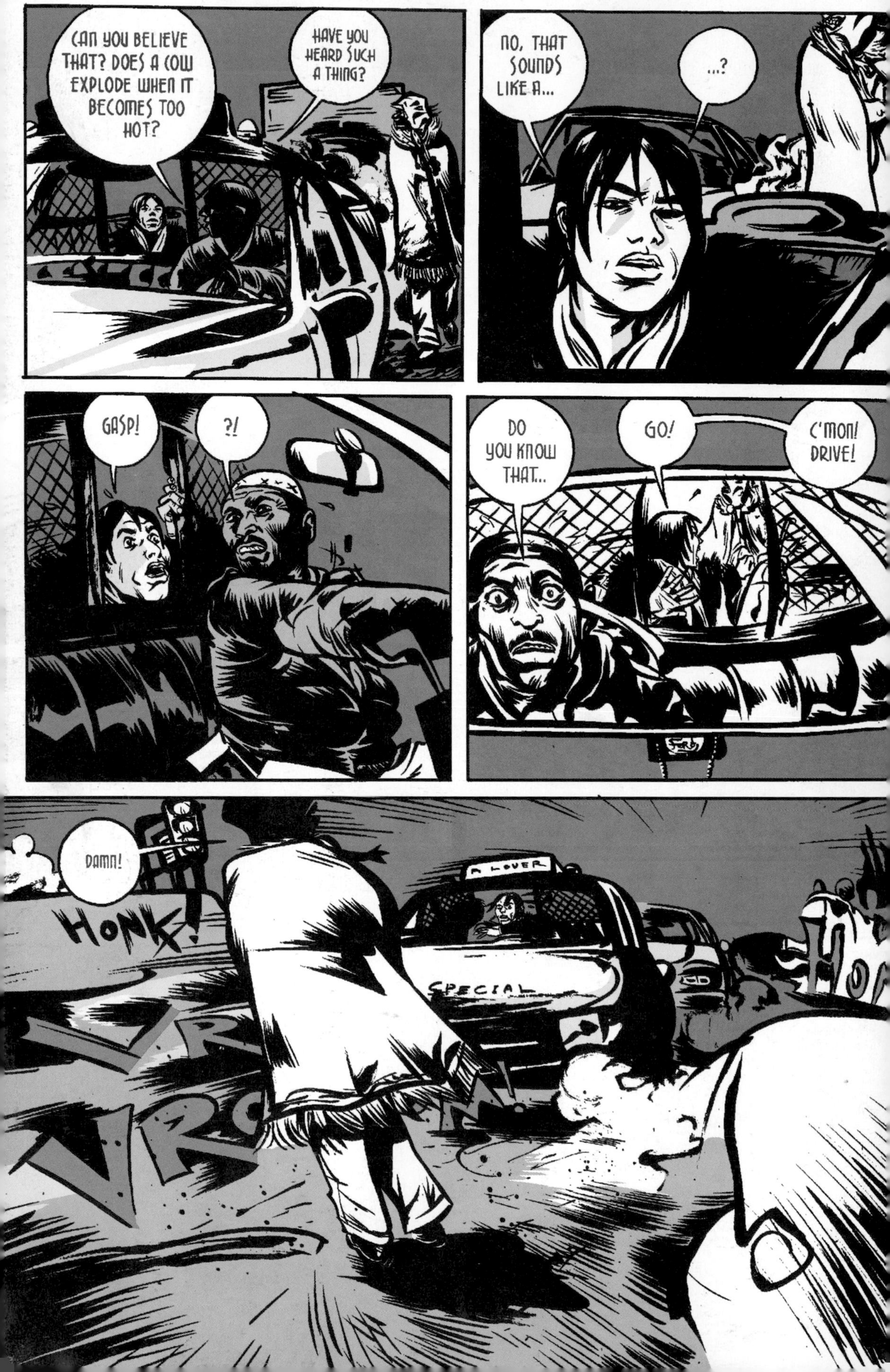
CAN YOU BELIEVE THAT? DOES A COW EXPLODE WHEN IT BECOMES TOO HOT?
HAVE YOU HEARD SUCH A THING?
NO, THAT SOUNDS LIKE A...
...?
GASP!
?!
DO YOU KNOW THAT...
GO!
C'MON! DRIVE!
DAMN!
A LOVER
HONK
SPECIAL

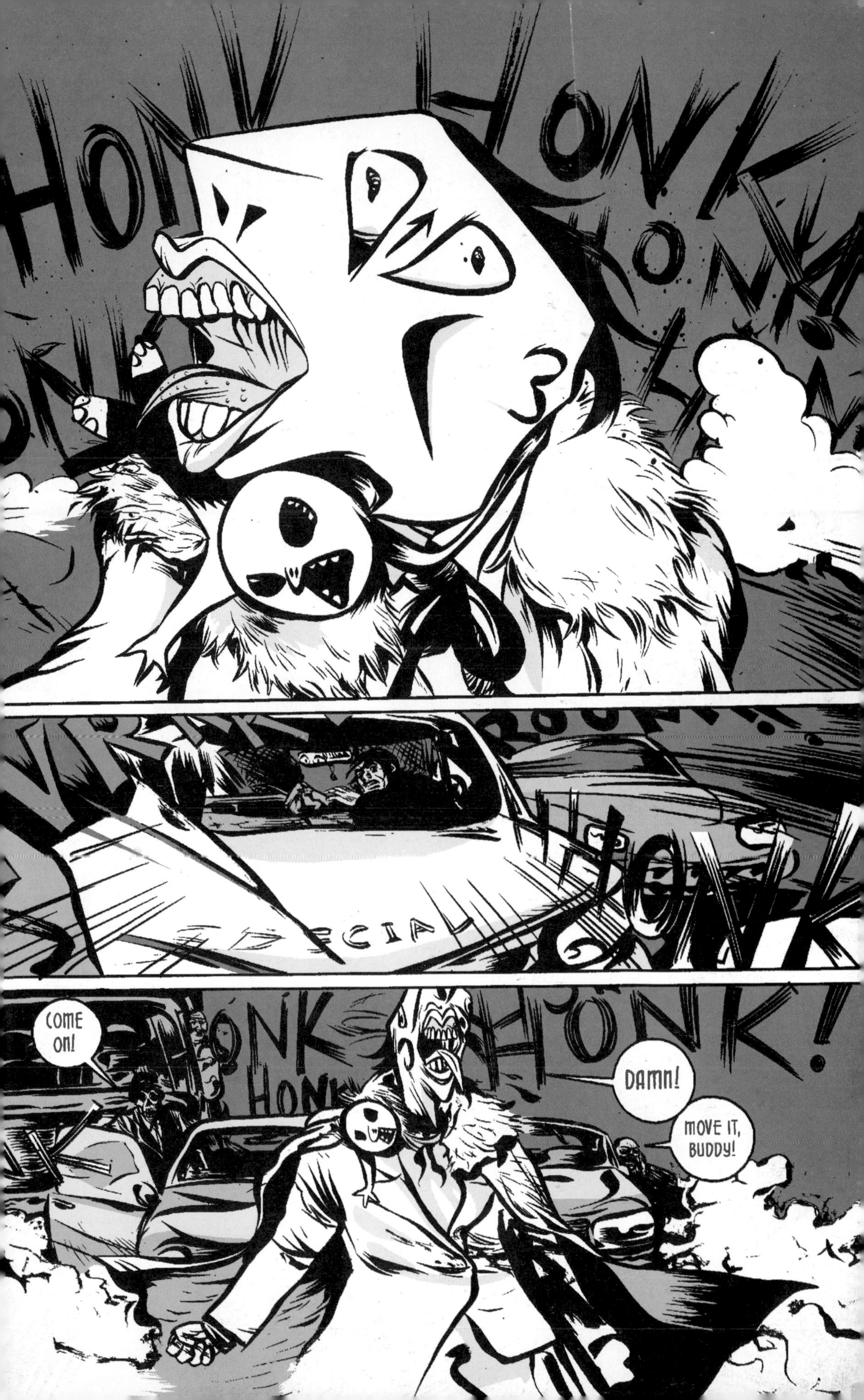
HONK
HONK!
COME ON!
HONK
DAMN!
MOVE IT, BUDDY!

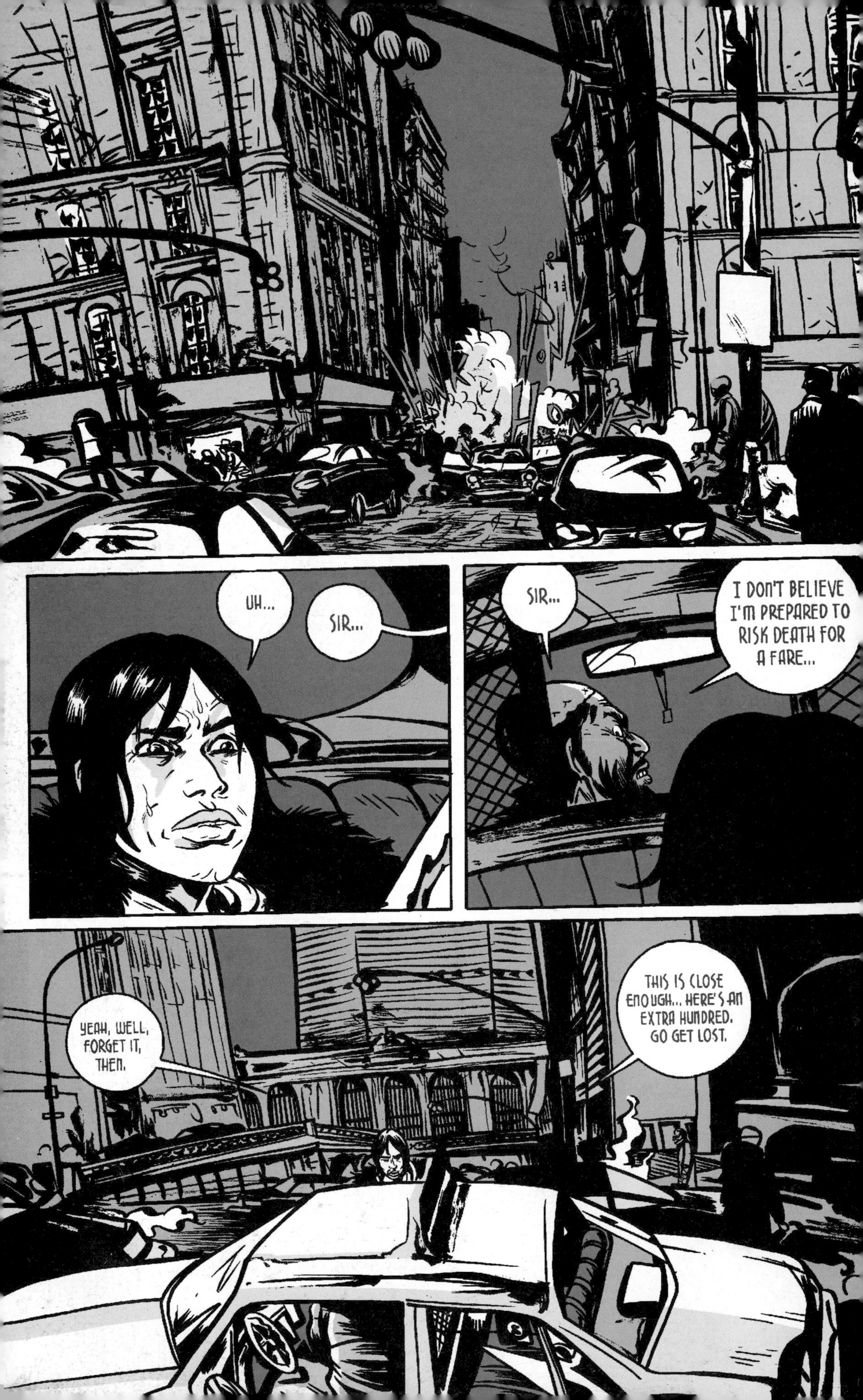
UH...
SIR...
SIR...
I DON'T BELIEVE I'M PREPARED TO RISK DEATH FOR A FARE...
THIS IS CLOSE ENOUGH... HERE'S AN EXTRA HUNDRED. GO GET LOST.
YEAH, WELL, FORGET IT, THEN.

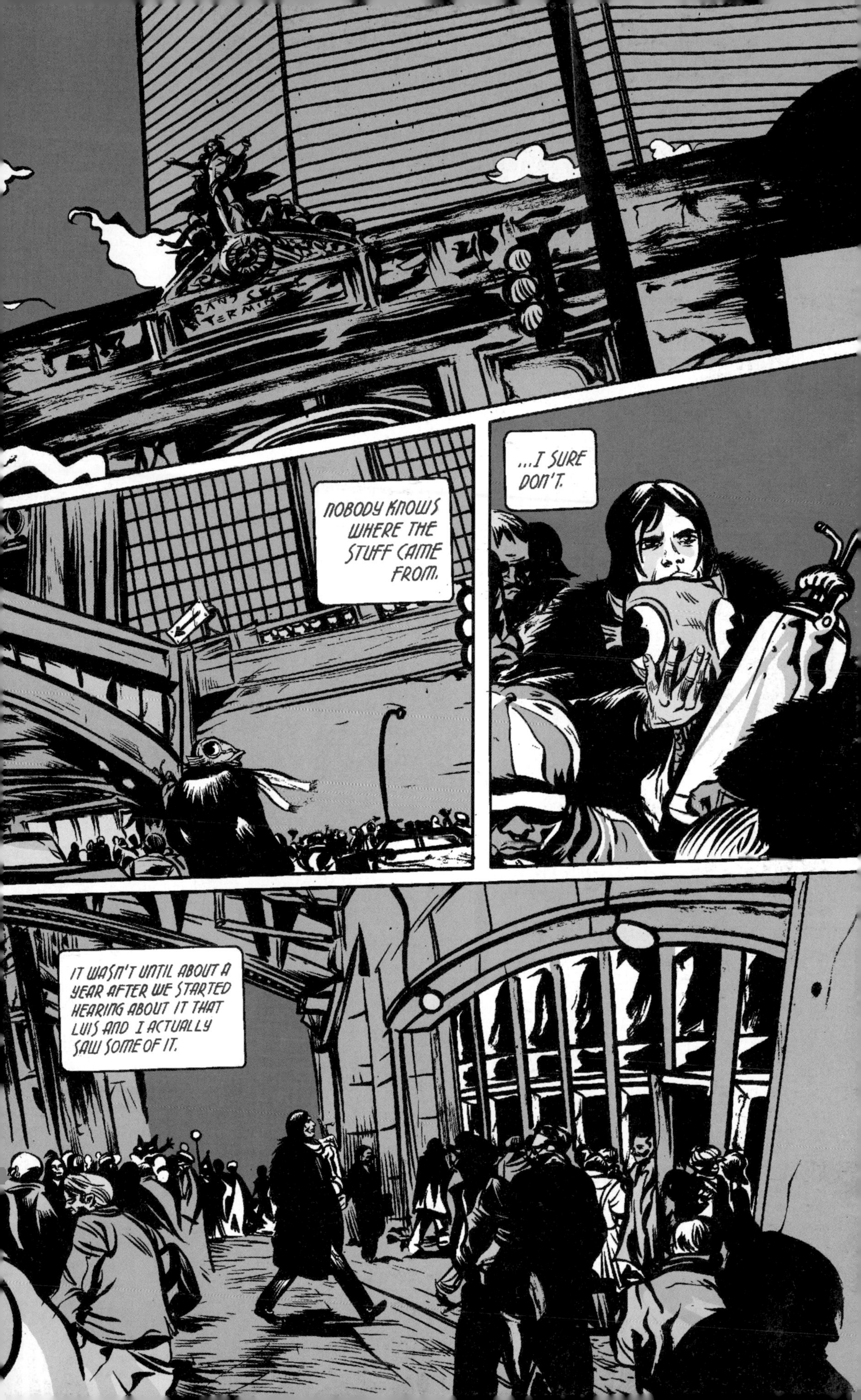

NOBODY KNOWS WHERE THE STUFF CAME FROM.
...I SURE DON'T.
IT WASN'T UNTIL ABOUT A YEAR AFTER WE STARTED HEARING ABOUT IT THAT LUIS AND I ACTUALLY SAW SOME OF IT.

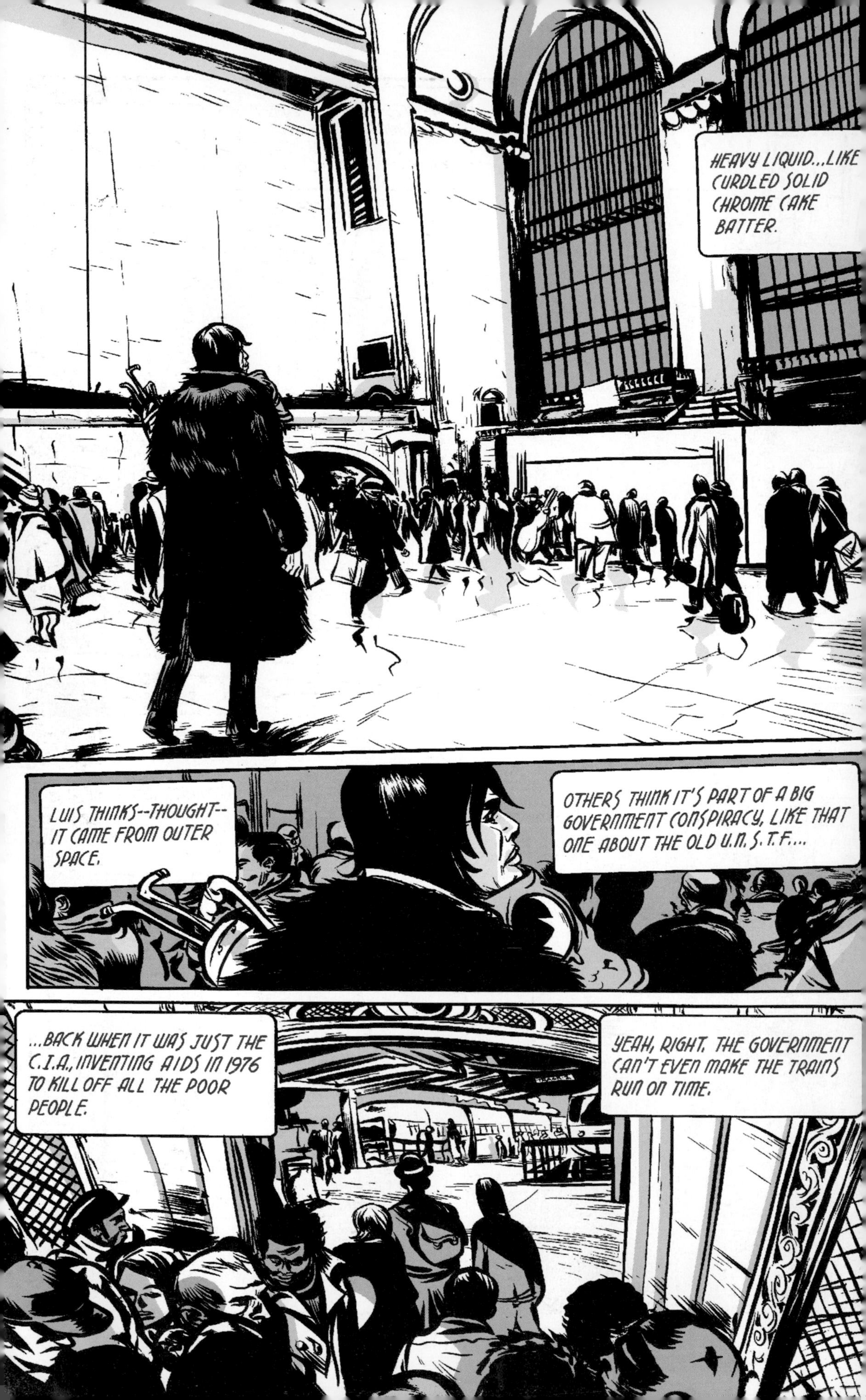
HEAVY LIQUID...LIKE CURDLED SOLID CHROME CAKE BATTER.
LUIS THINKS--THOUGHT-- IT CAME FROM OUTER SPACE.
OTHERS THINK IT'S PART OF A BIG GOVERNMENT CONSPIRACY, LIKE THAT ONE ABOUT THE OLD U.N.S.T.F....
...BACK WHEN IT WAS JUST THE C.I.A., INVENTING AIDS IN 1976 TO KILL OFF ALL THE POOR PEOPLE.
YEAH, RIGHT. THE GOVERNMENT CAN'T EVEN MAKE THE TRAINS RUN ON TIME.

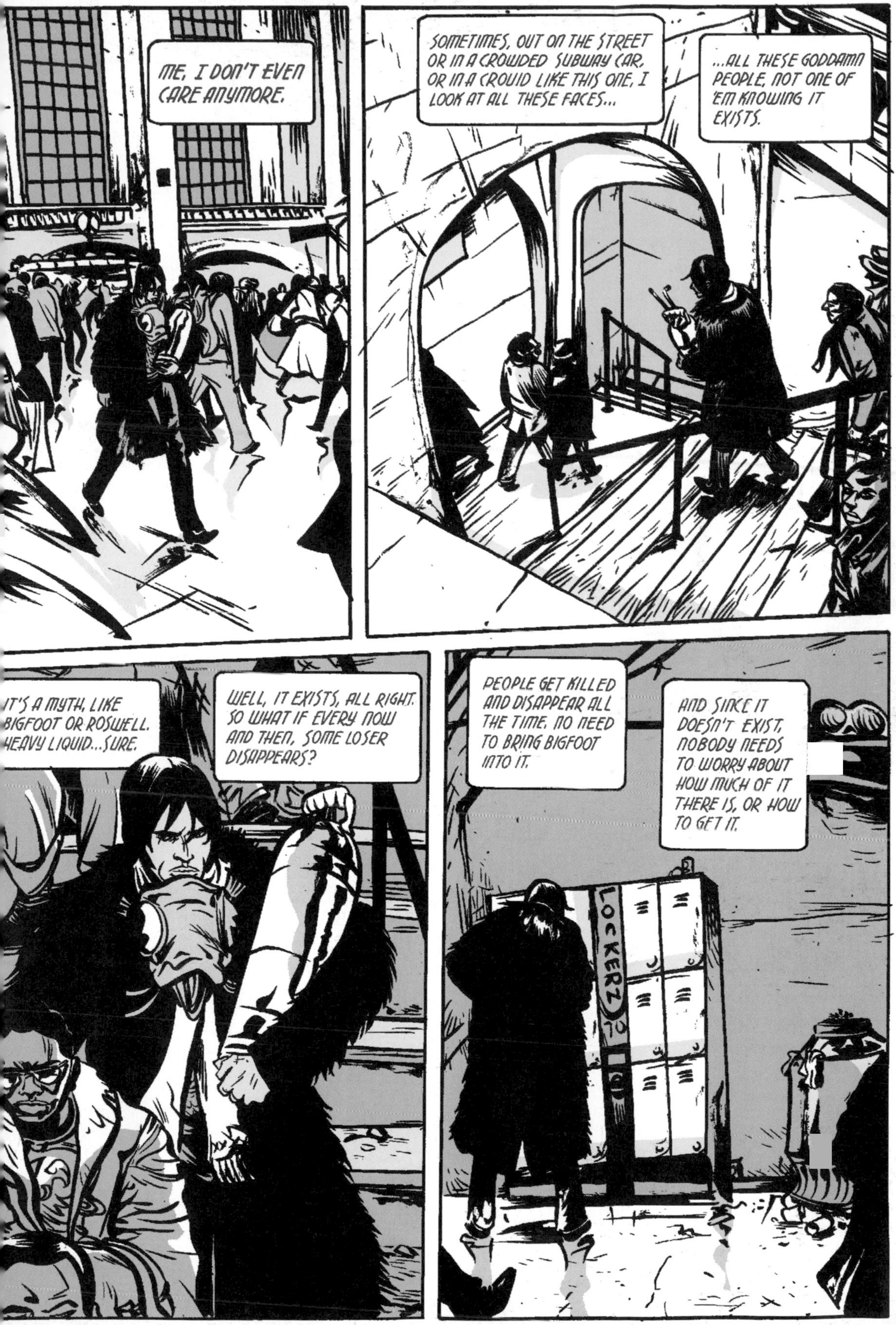
ME, I DON'T EVEN CARE ANYMORE.
SOMETIMES, OUT ON THE STREET OR IN A CROWDED SUBWAY CAR, OR IN A CROWD LIKE THIS ONE, I LOOK AT ALL THESE FACES...
...ALL THESE GODDAMN PEOPLE, NOT ONE OF 'EM KNOWING IT EXISTS.
IT'S A MYTH, LIKE BIGFOOT OR ROSWELL. HEAVY LIQUID...SURE.
WELL, IT EXISTS, ALL RIGHT. SO WHAT IF EVERY NOW AND THEN, SOME LOSER DISAPPEARS?
PEOPLE GET KILLED AND DISAPPEAR ALL THE TIME. NO NEED TO BRING BIGFOOT INTO IT.
AND SINCE IT DOESN'T EXIST, NOBODY NEEDS TO WORRY ABOUT HOW MUCH OF IT THERE IS, OR HOW TO GET IT.
LOCKERZ

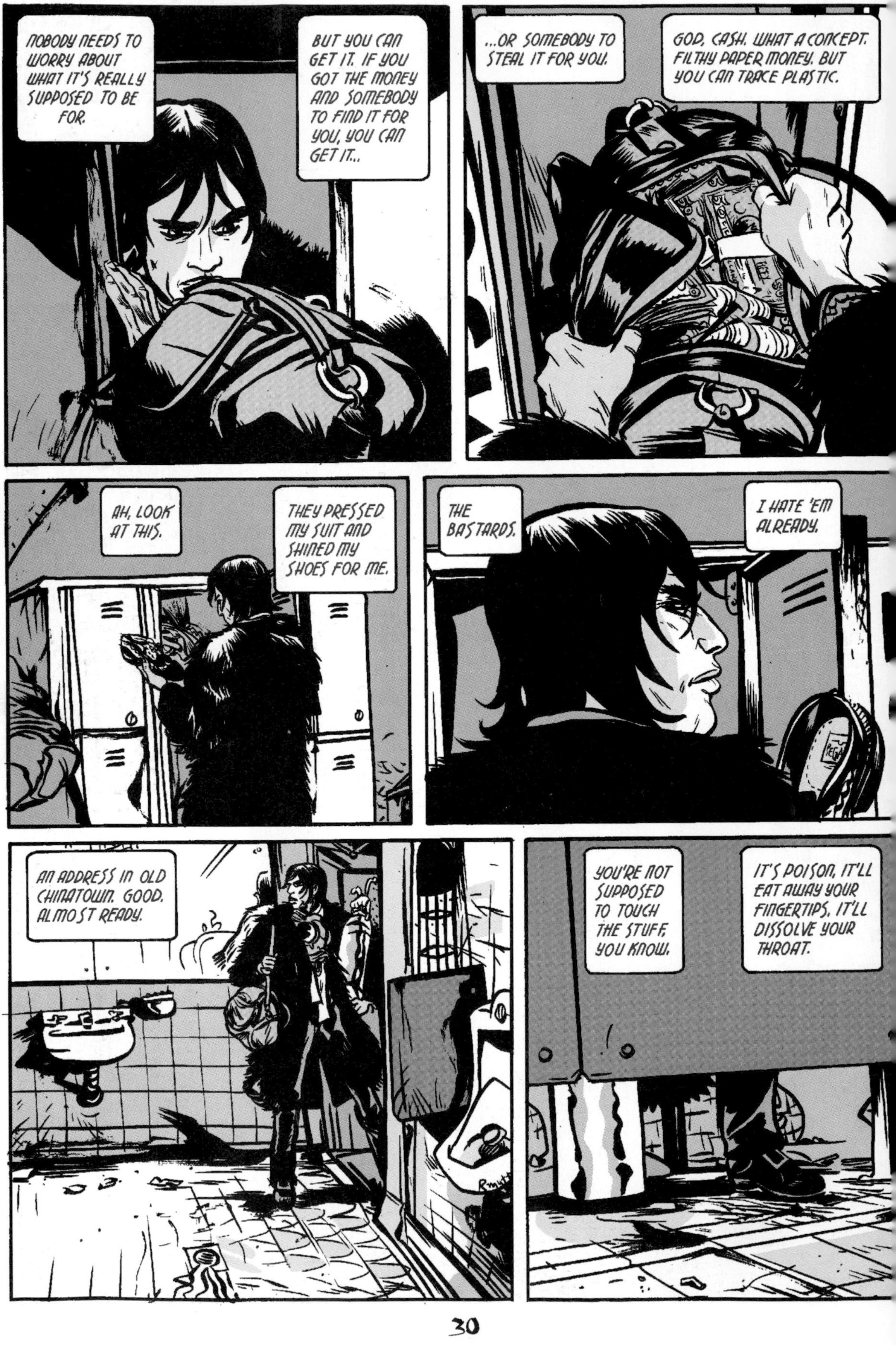
NOBODY NEEDS TO WORRY ABOUT WHAT IT'S REALLY SUPPOSED TO BE FOR.
BUT YOU CAN GET IT. IF YOU GOT THE MONEY AND SOMEBODY TO FIND IT FOR YOU, YOU CAN GET IT...
...OR SOMEBODY TO STEAL IT FOR YOU.
GOD, CASH. WHAT A CONCEPT. FILTHY PAPER MONEY. BUT YOU CAN TRACE PLASTIC.
AH, LOOK AT THIS.
THEY PRESSED MY SUIT AND SHINED MY SHOES FOR ME.
THE BASTARDS.
I HATE 'EM ALREADY.
AN ADDRESS IN OLD CHINATOWN. GOOD. ALMOST READY.
YOU'RE NOT SUPPOSED TO TOUCH THE STUFF, YOU KNOW.
IT'S POISON, IT'LL EAT AWAY YOUR FINGERTIPS, IT'LL DISSOLVE YOUR THROAT.

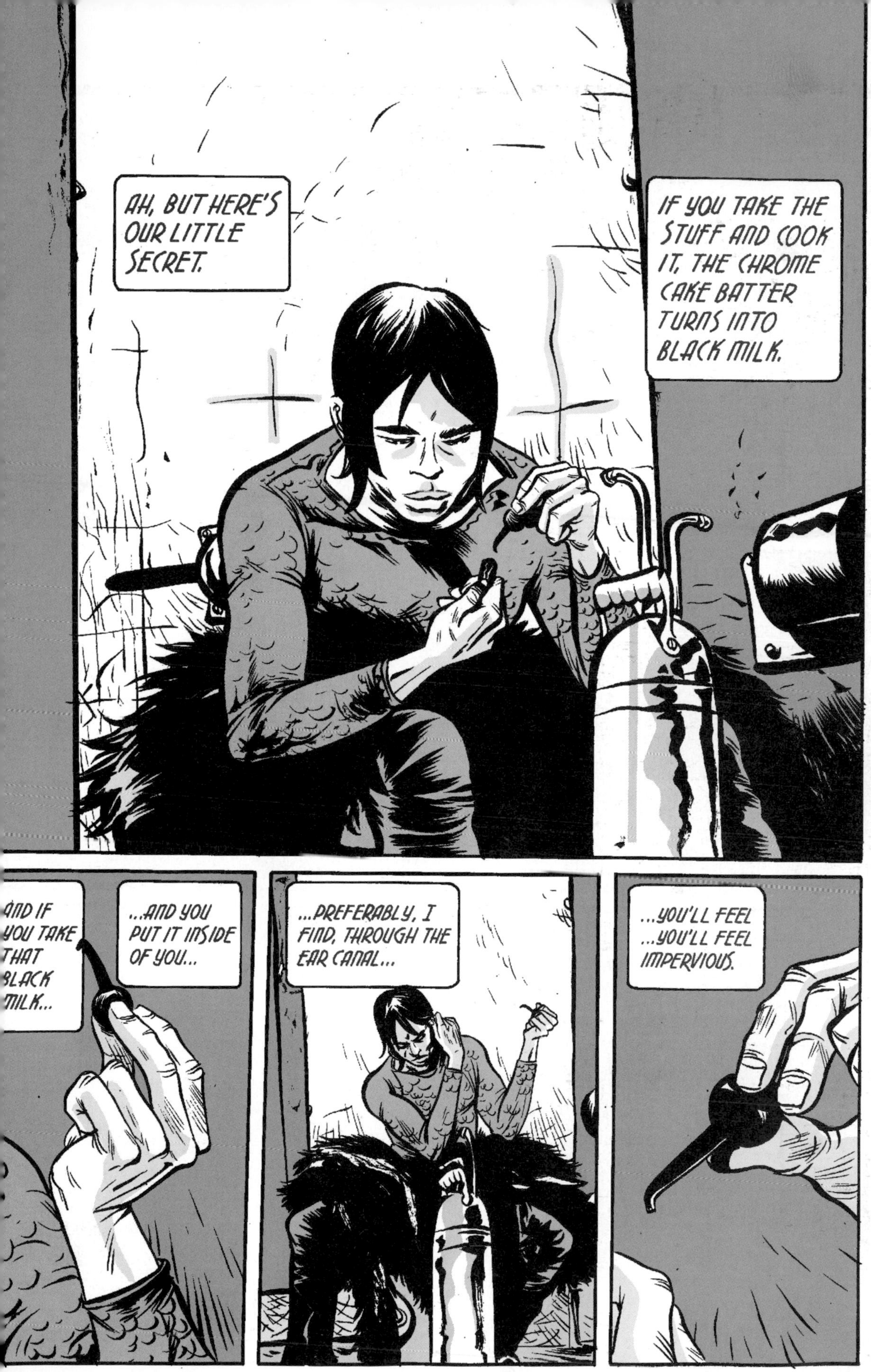
AH, BUT HERE'S OUR LITTLE SECRET.
IF YOU TAKE THE STUFF AND COOK IT, THE CHROME CAKE BATTER TURNS INTO BLACK MILK.
AND IF YOU TAKE THAT BLACK MILK...
...AND YOU PUT IT INSIDE OF YOU...
...PREFERABLY, I FIND, THROUGH THE EAR CANAL...
...YOU'LL FEEL ...YOU'LL FEEL IMPERVIOUS.

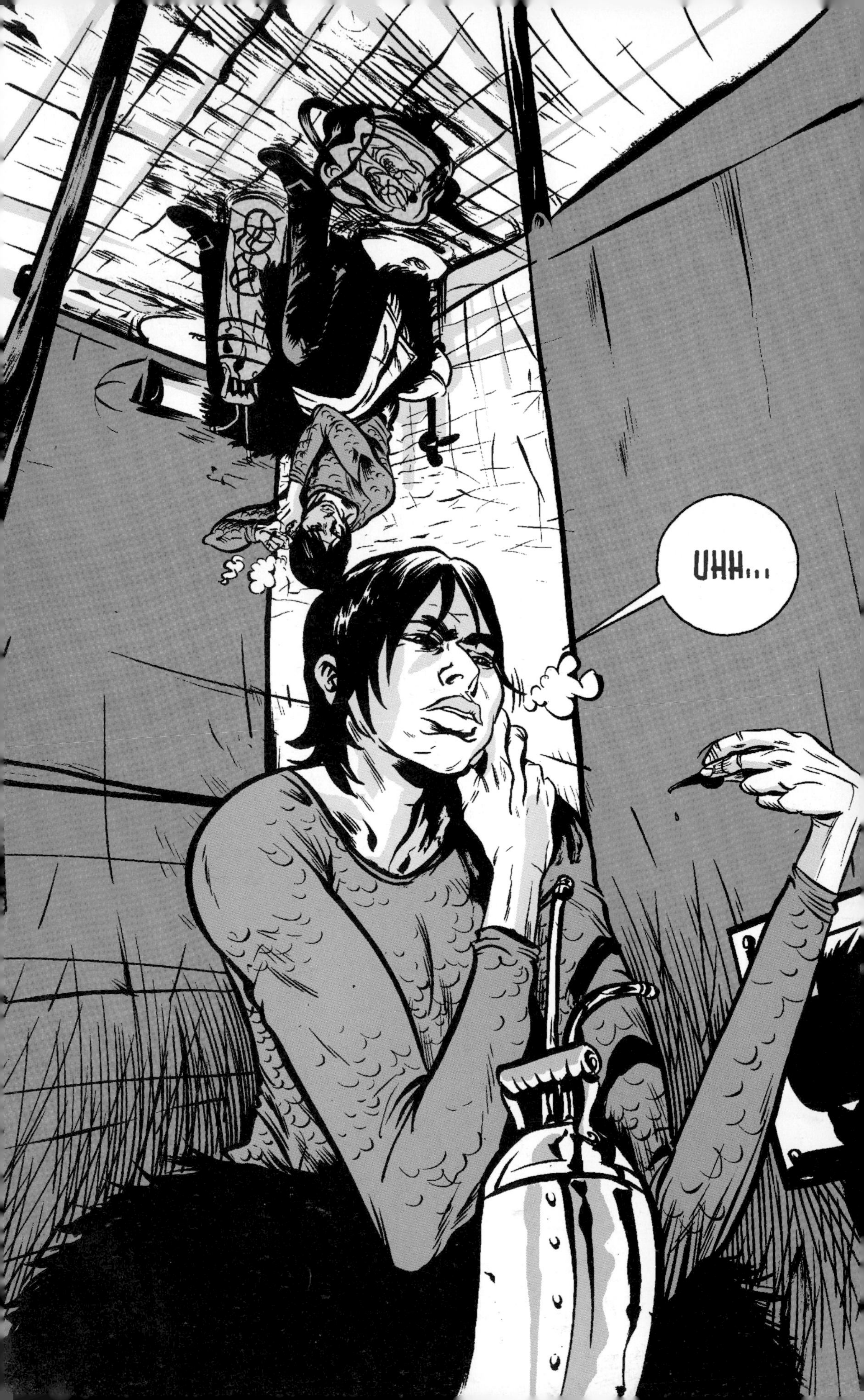
UHH...

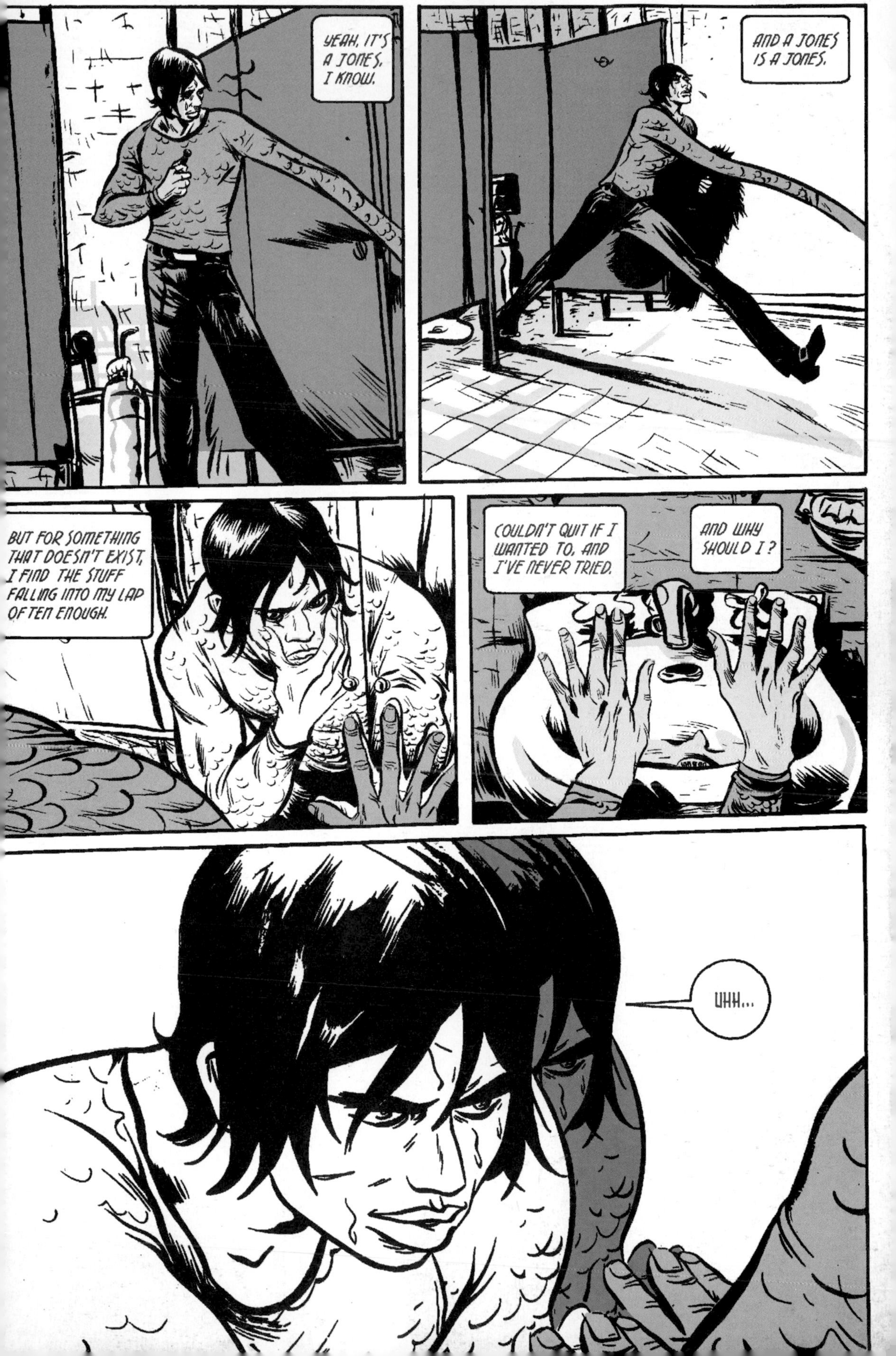
YEAH, IT'S A JONES, I KNOW.
AND A JONES IS A JONES.
BUT FOR SOMETHING THAT DOESN'T EXIST, I FIND THE STUFF FALLING INTO MY LAP OFTEN ENOUGH.
COULDN'T QUIT IF I WANTED TO, AND I'VE NEVER TRIED.
AND WHY SHOULD I?
UHH...

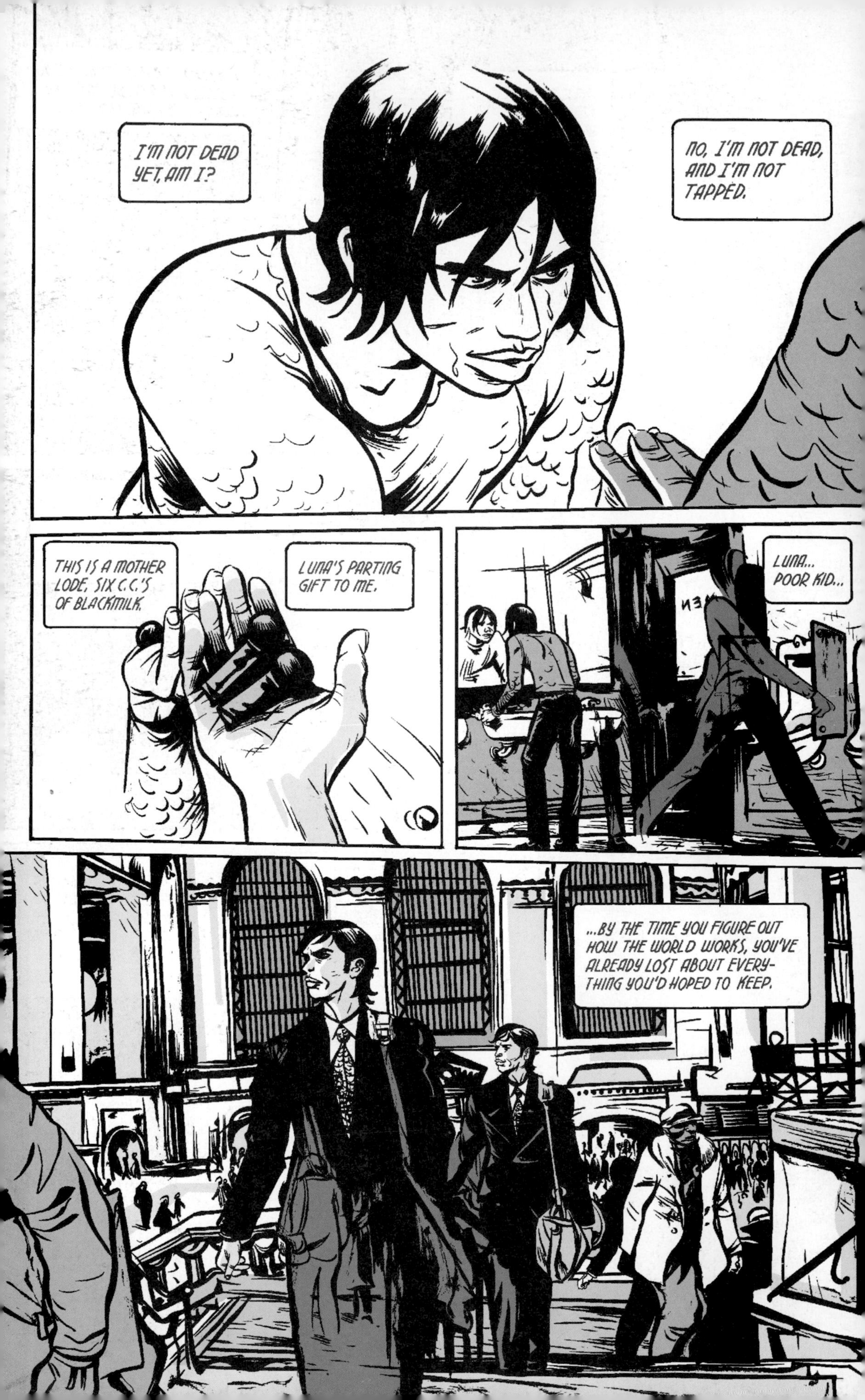
I'M NOT DEAD YET, AM I?
NO, I'M NOT DEAD, AND I'M NOT TAPPED.
THIS IS A MOTHER LODE, SIX C.C.'S OF BLACKMILK.
LUNA'S PARTING GIFT TO ME.
LUNA... POOR KID...
...BY THE TIME YOU FIGURE OUT HOW THE WORLD WORKS, YOU'VE ALREADY LOST ABOUT EVERY-THING YOU'D HOPED TO KEEP.

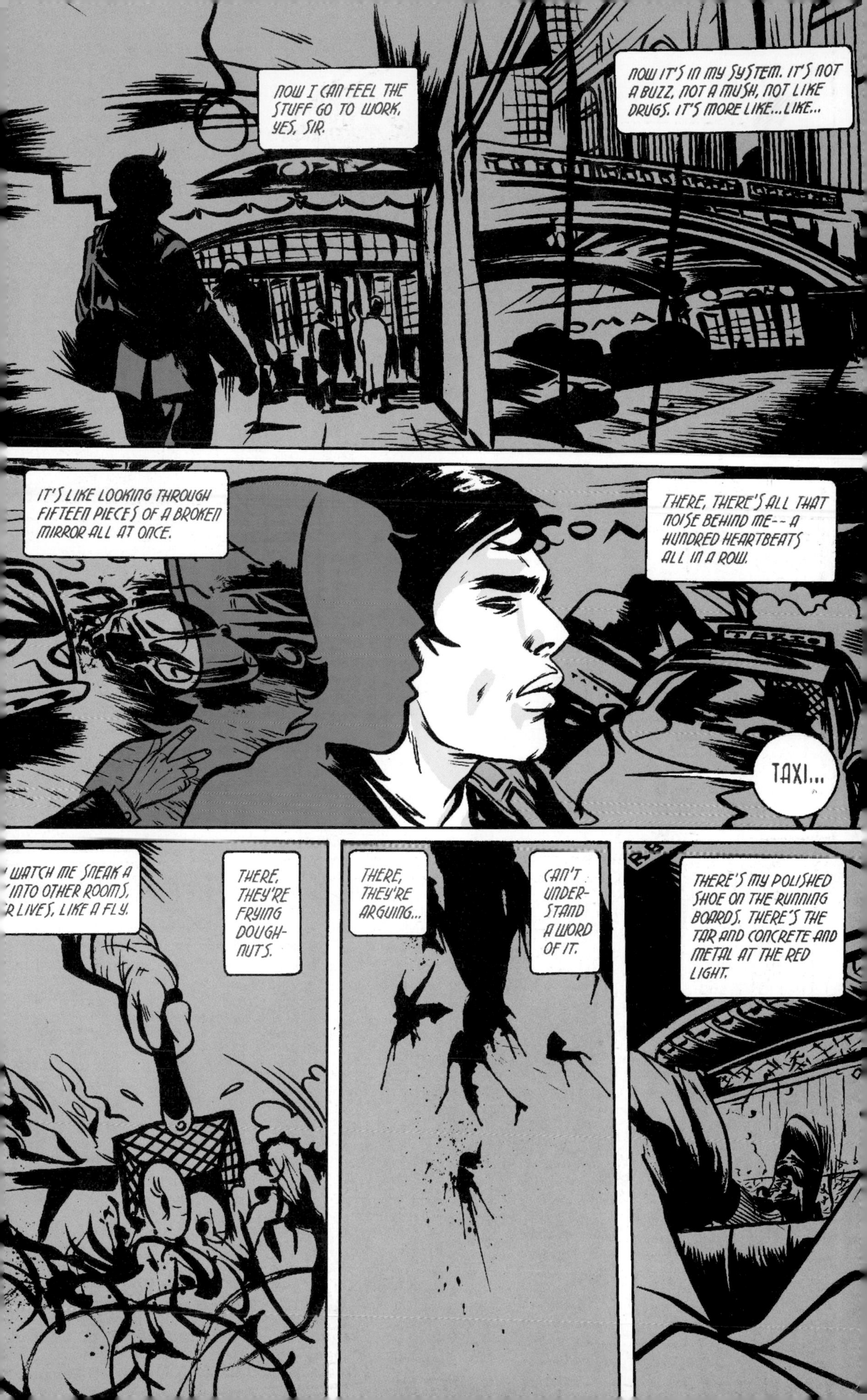
NOW I CAN FEEL THE STUFF GO TO WORK, YES, SIR.
NOW IT'S IN MY SYSTEM. IT'S NOT A BUZZ, NOT A MUSH, NOT LIKE DRUGS. IT'S MORE LIKE... LIKE...
IT'S LIKE LOOKING THROUGH FIFTEEN PIECES OF A BROKEN MIRROR ALL AT ONCE.
THERE, THERE'S ALL THAT NOISE BEHIND ME-- A HUNDRED HEARTBEATS ALL IN A ROW.
TAXI...
WATCH ME SNEAK A
INTO OTHER ROOMS,
LIVES, LIKE A FLY.
THERE, THEY'RE FRYING DOUGH-NUTS.
THERE, THEY'RE ARGUING...
CAN'T UNDER-STAND A WORD OF IT.
THERE'S MY POLISHED SHOE ON THE RUNNING BOARDS. THERE'S THE TAR AND CONCRETE AND METAL AT THE RED LIGHT.

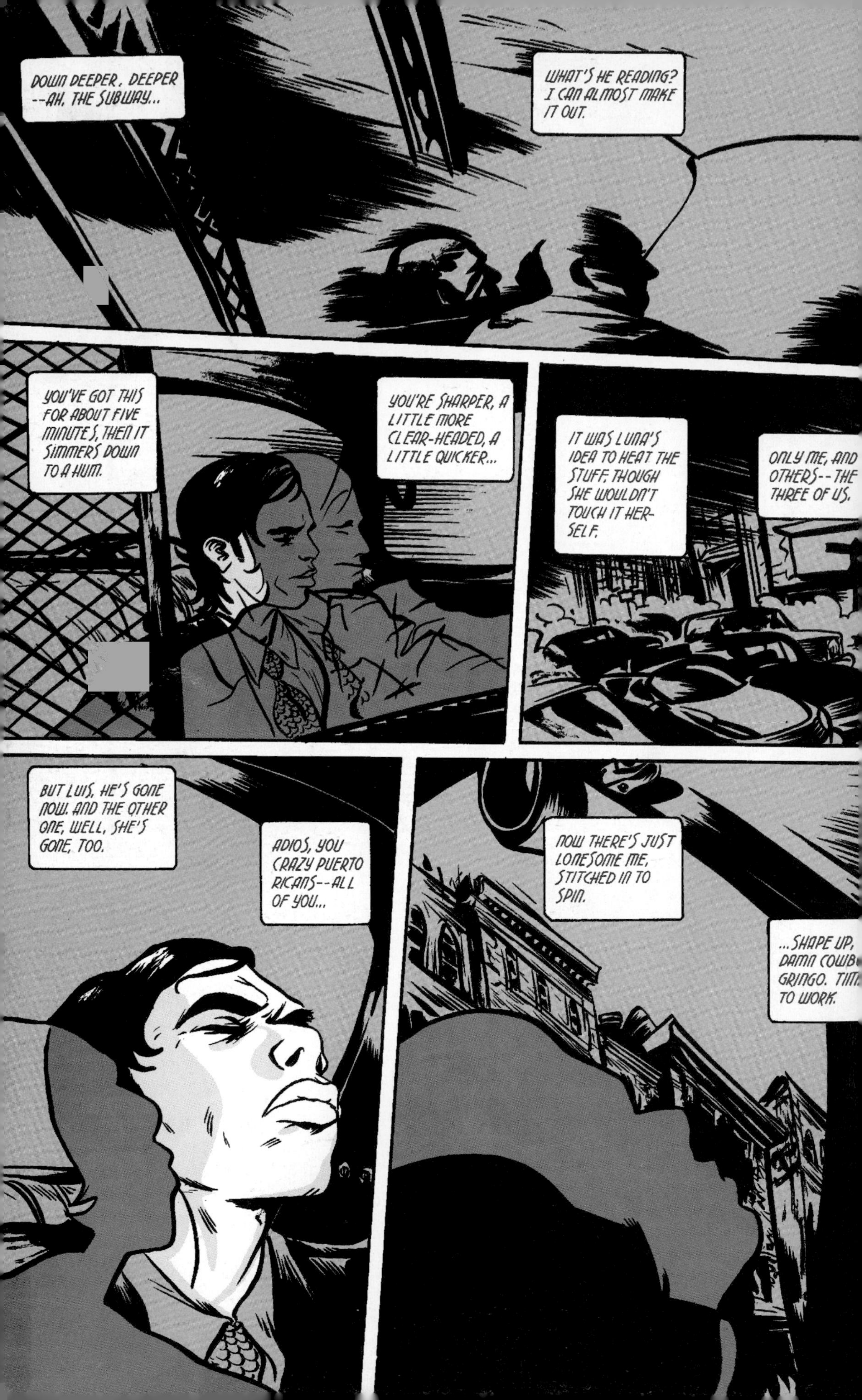
DOWN DEEPER. DEEPER --AH, THE SUBWAY...
WHAT'S HE READING? I CAN ALMOST MAKE IT OUT.
YOU'VE GOT THIS FOR ABOUT FIVE MINUTES, THEN IT SIMMERS DOWN TO A HUM.
YOU'RE SHARPER, A LITTLE MORE CLEAR-HEADED, A LITTLE QUICKER...
IT WAS LUNA'S IDEA TO HEAT THE STUFF, THOUGH SHE WOULDN'T TOUCH IT HER-SELF.
ONLY ME, AND OTHERS-- THE THREE OF US.
BUT LUIS, HE'S GONE NOW. AND THE OTHER ONE, WELL, SHE'S GONE, TOO.
ADIOS, YOU CRAZY PUERTO RICANS--ALL OF YOU...
NOW THERE'S JUST LONESOME ME, STITCHED IN TO SPIN.
...SHAPE UP,
DAMN COWB
GRINGO. TIM
TO WORK.

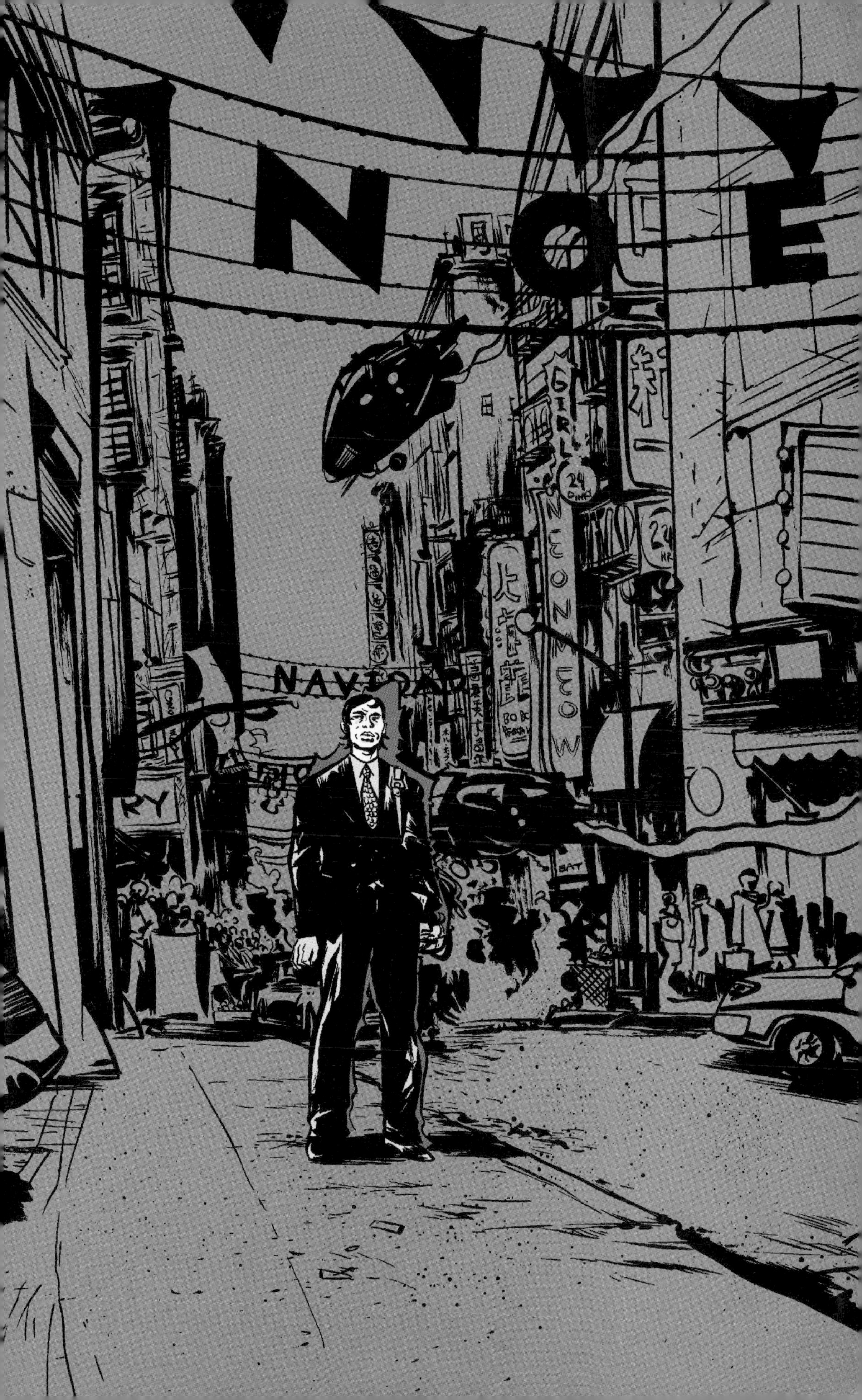
N O E
GIRL
NEON MEOW
24 HR
NAVIDAD
RY

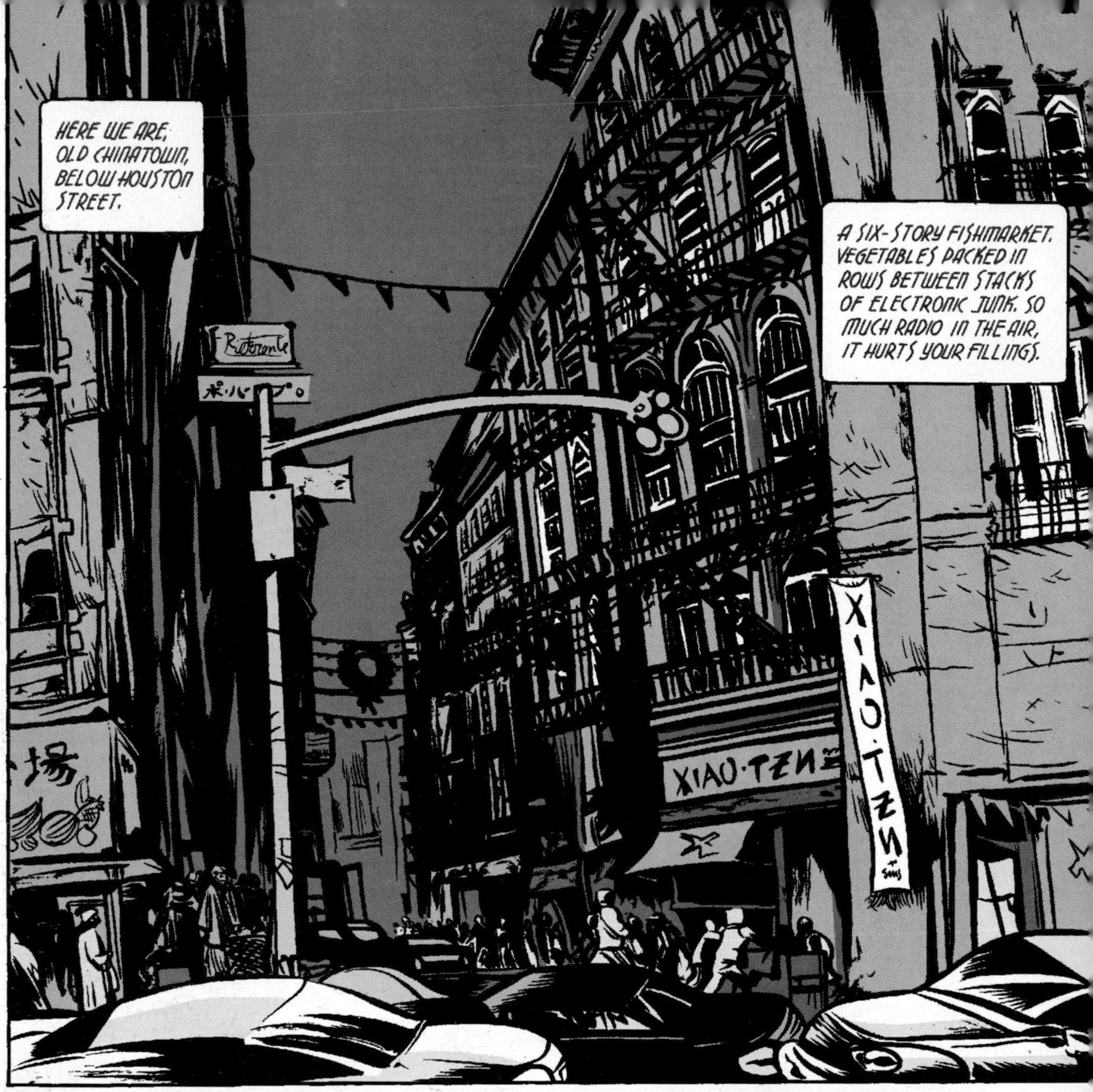
HERE WE ARE; OLD CHINATOWN, BELOW HOUSTON STREET.
A SIX-STORY FISHMARKET. VEGETABLES PACKED IN ROWS BETWEEN STACKS OF ELECTRONIC JUNK. SO MUCH RADIO IN THE AIR, IT HURTS YOUR FILLINGS.

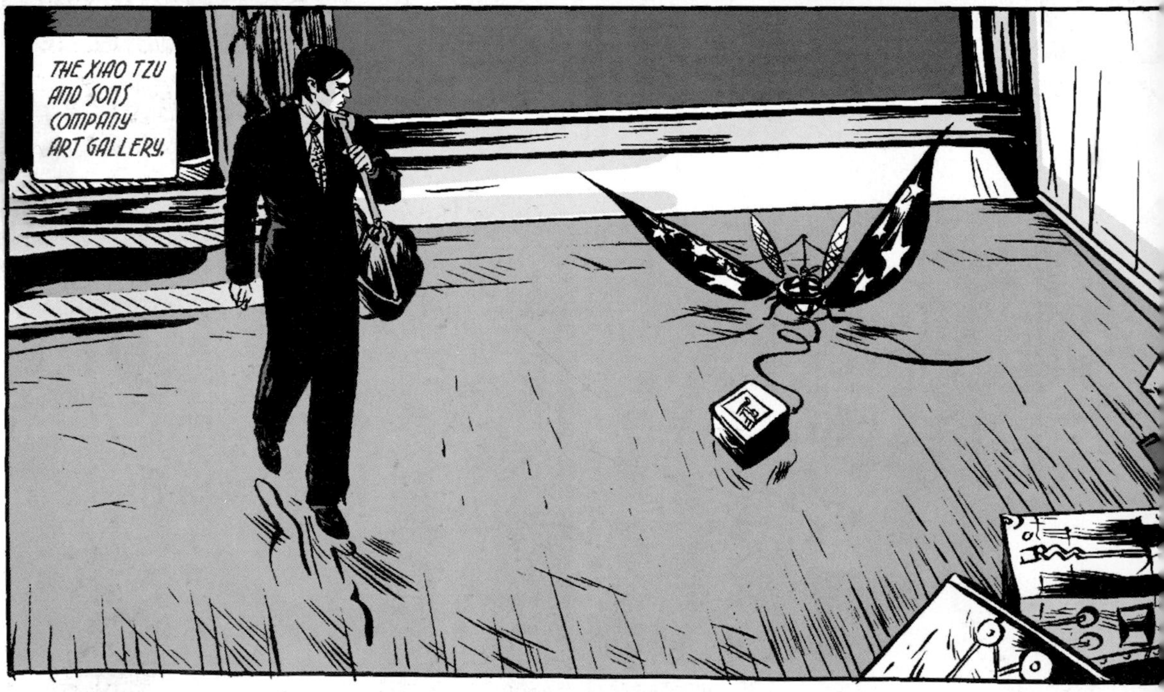
THE XIAO TZU AND SONS COMPANY ART GALLERY.

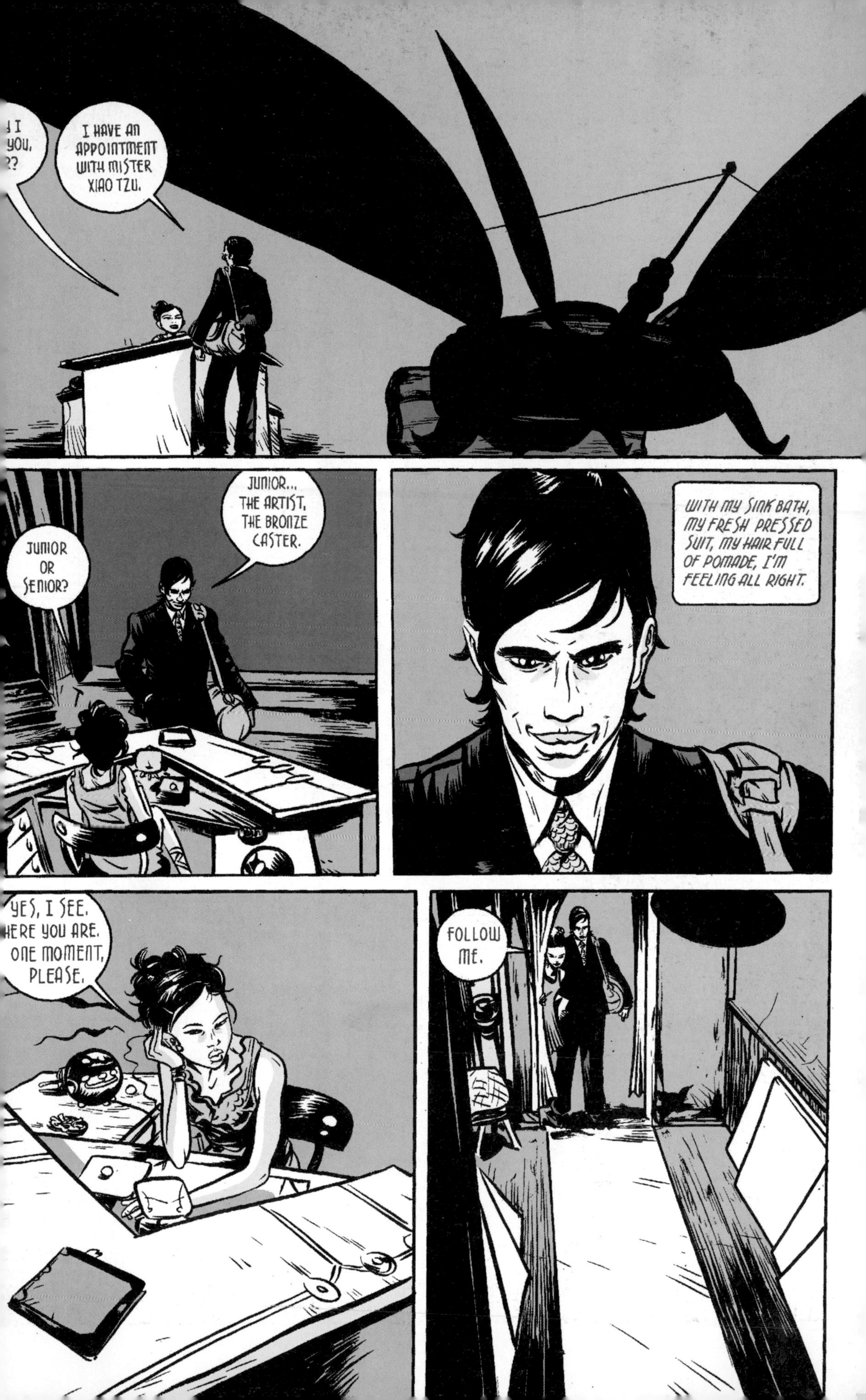
I HAVE AN APPOINTMENT WITH MISTER XIAO TZU.
JUNIOR OR SENIOR?
JUNIOR... THE ARTIST, THE BRONZE CASTER.
WITH MY SINK BATH, MY FRESH PRESSED SUIT, MY HAIR FULL OF POMADE, I'M FEELING ALL RIGHT.
YES, I SEE. HERE YOU ARE. ONE MOMENT, PLEASE.
FOLLOW ME.

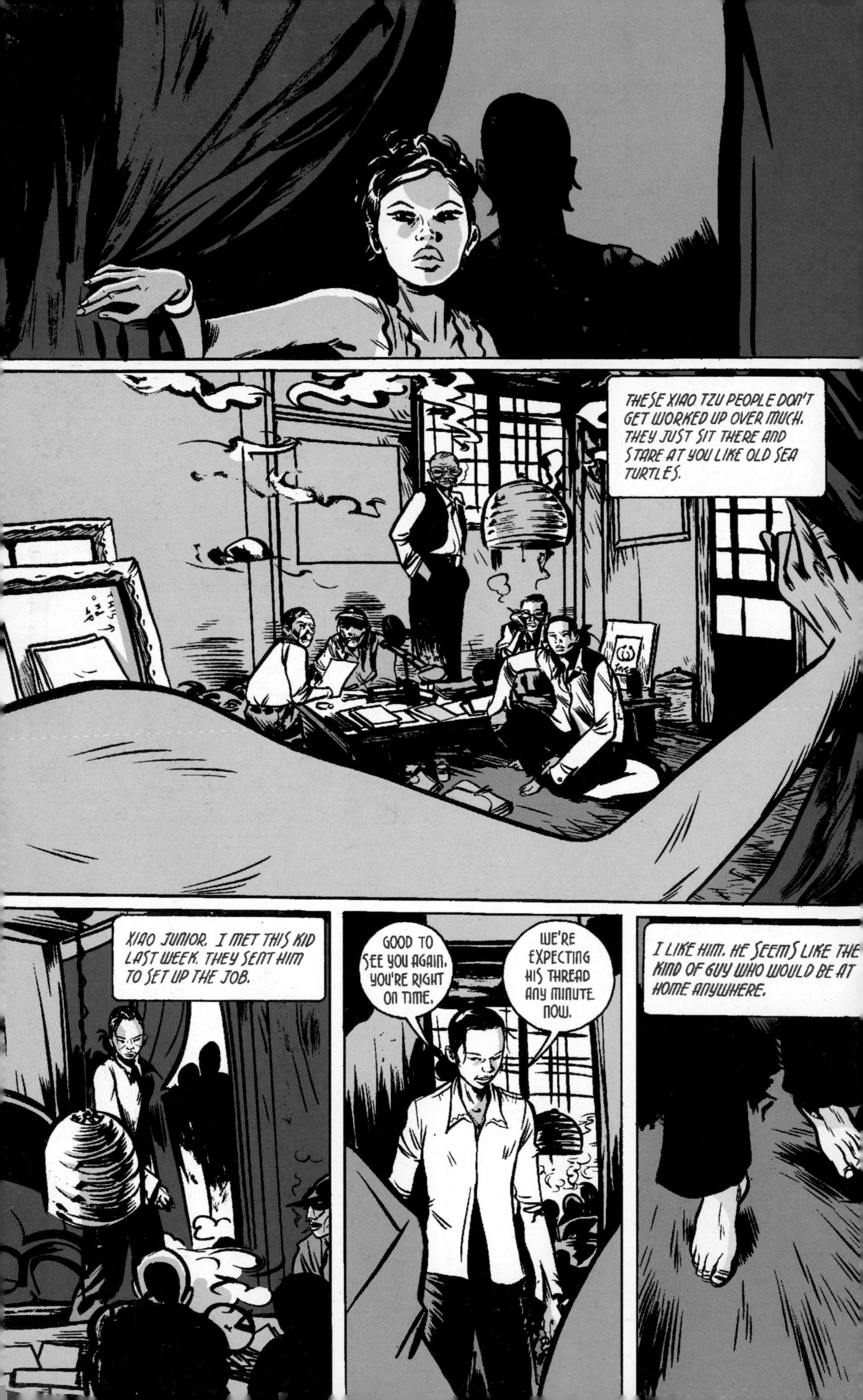
THESE XIAO TZU PEOPLE DON'T GET WORKED UP OVER MUCH. THEY JUST SIT THERE AND STARE AT YOU LIKE OLD SEA TURTLES.
XIAO JUNIOR. I MET THIS KID LAST WEEK. THEY SENT HIM TO SET UP THE JOB.
GOOD TO SEE YOU AGAIN. YOU'RE RIGHT ON TIME.
WE'RE EXPECTING HIS THREAD ANY MINUTE NOW.
I LIKE HIM. HE SEEMS LIKE THE KIND OF GUY WHO WOULD BE AT HOME ANYWHERE.

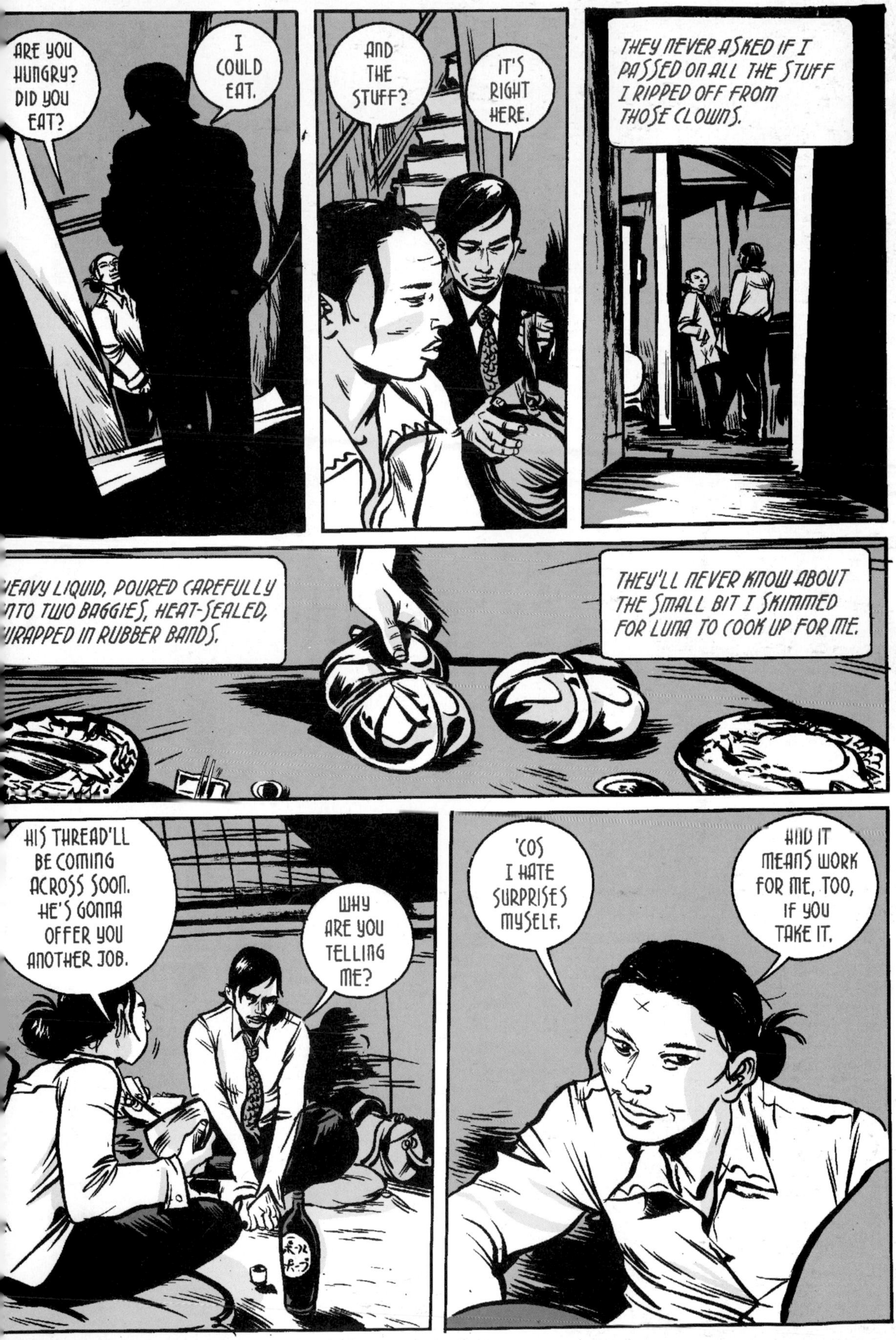
ARE YOU HUNGRY? DID YOU EAT?
I COULD EAT.
AND THE STUFF?
IT'S RIGHT HERE.
THEY NEVER ASKED IF I PASSED ON ALL THE STUFF I RIPPED OFF FROM THOSE CLOWNS.
EAVY LIQUID, POURED CAREFULLY NTO TWO BAGGIES, HEAT-SEALED, RAPPED IN RUBBER BANDS.
THEY'LL NEVER KNOW ABOUT THE SMALL BIT I SKIMMED FOR LUNA TO COOK UP FOR ME.
HIS THREAD'LL BE COMING ACROSS SOON. HE'S GONNA OFFER YOU ANOTHER JOB.
WHY ARE YOU TELLING ME?
'COS I HATE SURPRISES MYSELF.
AND IT MEANS WORK FOR ME, TOO, IF YOU TAKE IT.

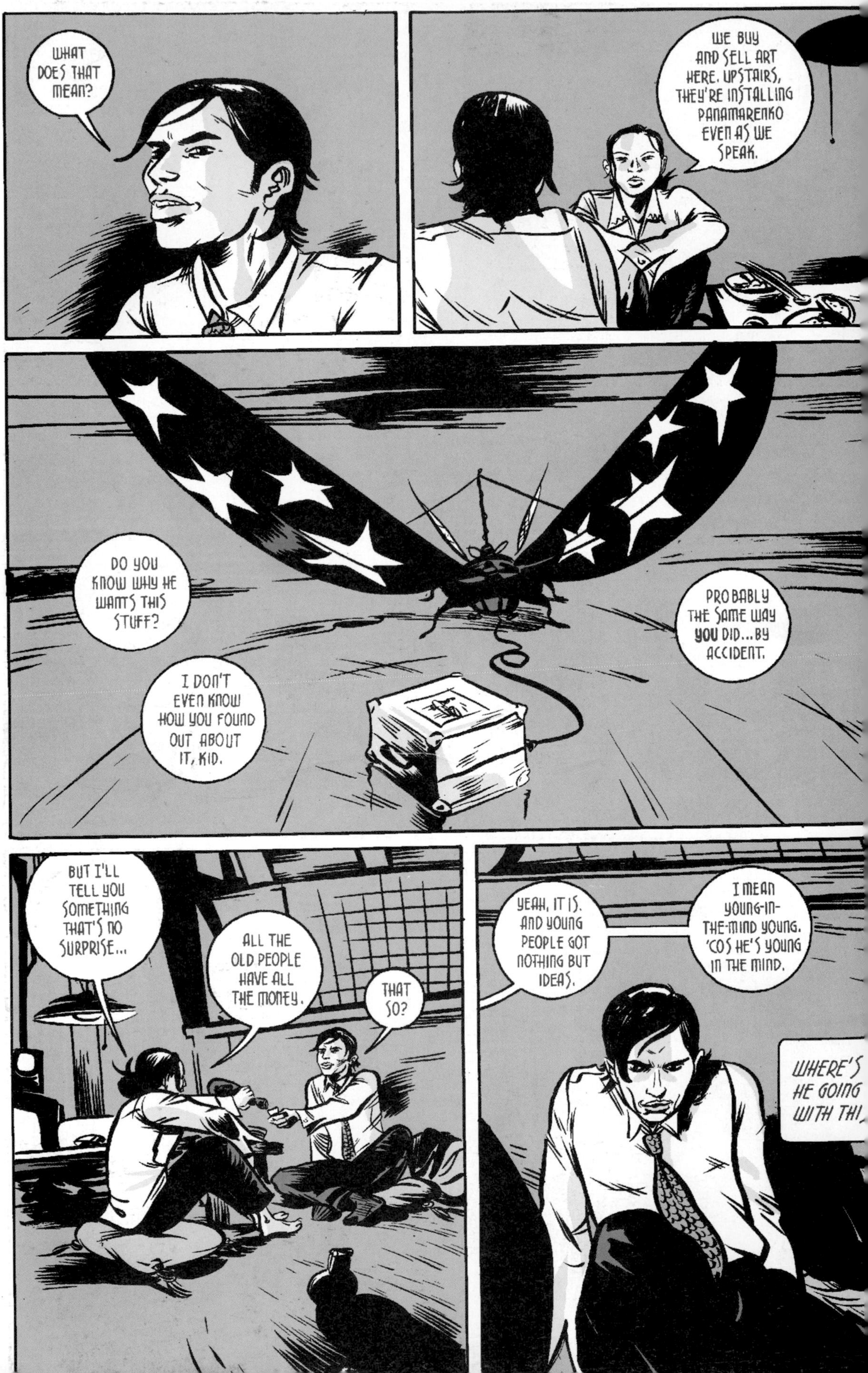
WHAT DOES THAT MEAN?
WE BUY AND SELL ART HERE. UPSTAIRS, THEY'RE INSTALLING PANAMARENKO EVEN AS WE SPEAK.
DO YOU KNOW WHY HE WANTS THIS STUFF?
PROBABLY THE SAME WAY **YOU** DID...BY ACCIDENT.
I DON'T EVEN KNOW HOW YOU FOUND OUT ABOUT IT, KID.
BUT I'LL TELL YOU SOMETHING THAT'S NO SURPRISE...
ALL THE OLD PEOPLE HAVE ALL THE MONEY.
THAT SO?
YEAH, IT IS. AND YOUNG PEOPLE GOT NOTHING BUT IDEAS.
I MEAN YOUNG-IN-THE-MIND YOUNG. 'COS HE'S YOUNG IN THE MIND.
WHERE'S HE GOING WITH THI

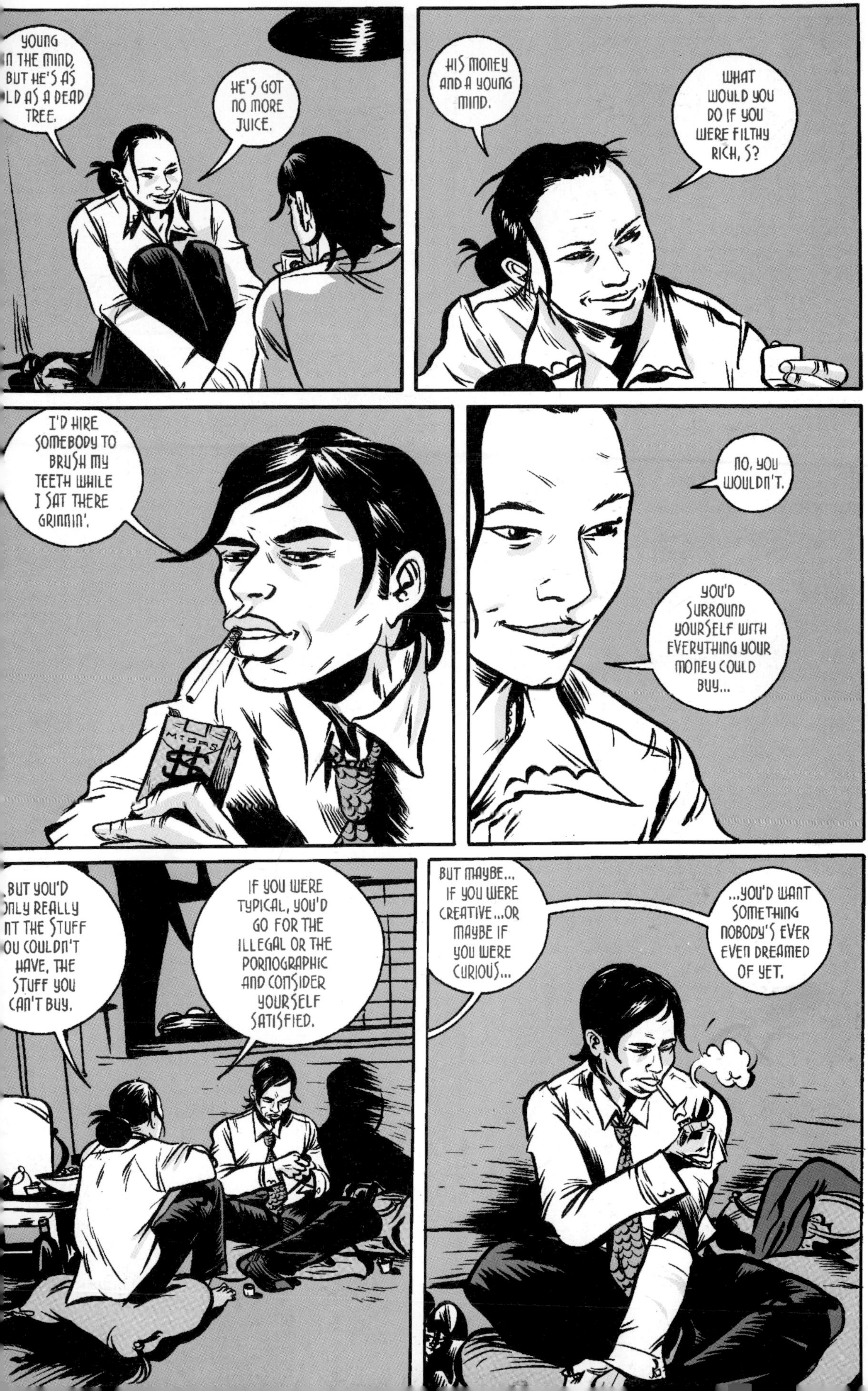
YOUNG N THE MIND, BUT HE'S AS LD AS A DEAD TREE.
HE'S GOT NO MORE JUICE.
HIS MONEY AND A YOUNG MIND.
WHAT WOULD YOU DO IF YOU WERE FILTHY RICH, S?
I'D HIRE SOMEBODY TO BRUSH MY TEETH WHILE I SAT THERE GRINNIN'.
NO, YOU WOULDN'T.
YOU'D SURROUND YOURSELF WITH EVERYTHING YOUR MONEY COULD BUY...
BUT YOU'D NLY REALLY NT THE STUFF OU COULDN'T HAVE, THE STUFF YOU CAN'T BUY.
IF YOU WERE TYPICAL, YOU'D GO FOR THE ILLEGAL OR THE PORNOGRAPHIC AND CONSIDER YOURSELF SATISFIED.
BUT MAYBE... IF YOU WERE CREATIVE...OR MAYBE IF YOU WERE CURIOUS...
...YOU'D WANT SOMETHING NOBODY'S EVER EVEN DREAMED OF YET.

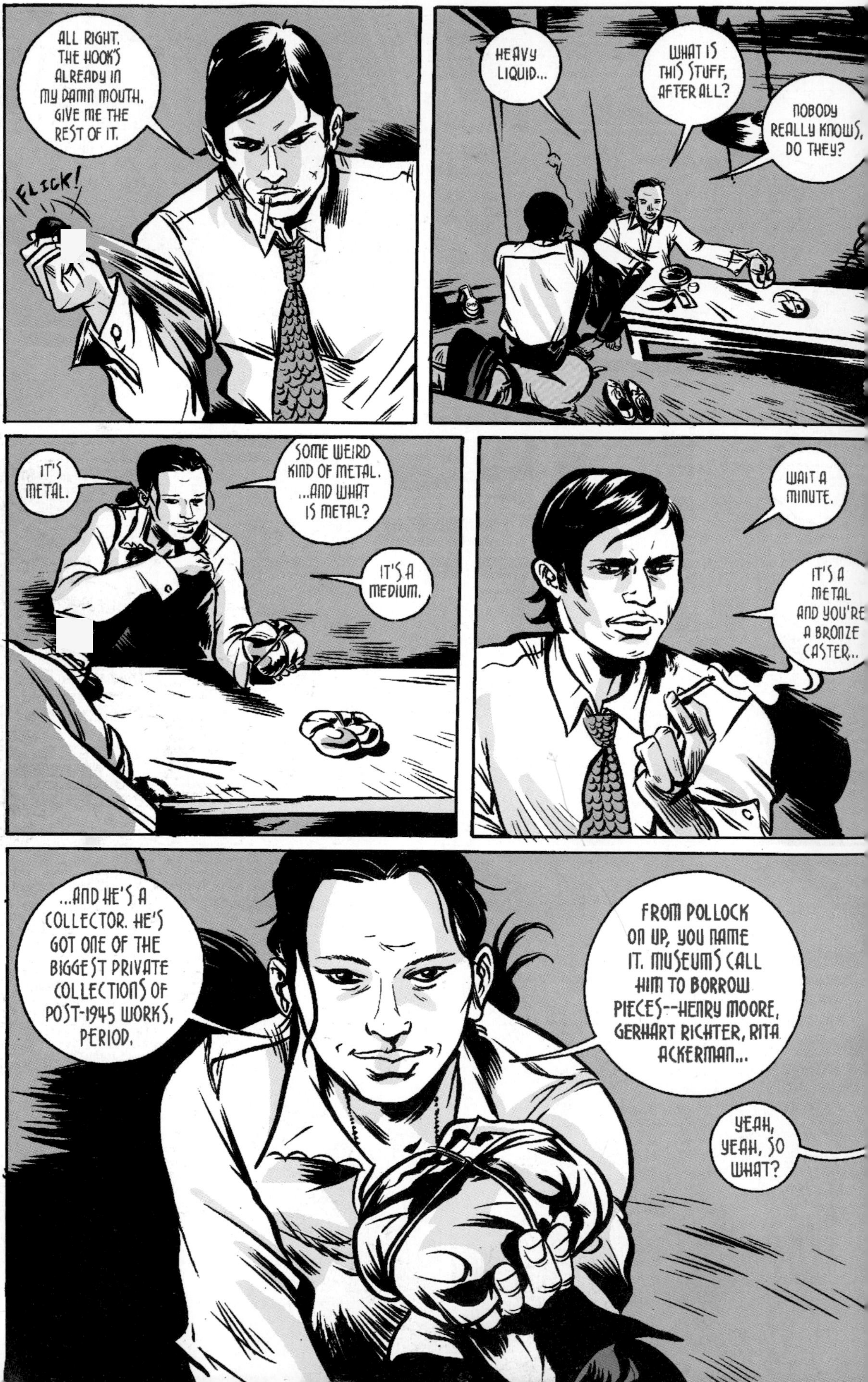
ALL RIGHT. THE HOOK'S ALREADY IN MY DAMN MOUTH. GIVE ME THE REST OF IT.
FLICK!
HEAVY LIQUID...
WHAT IS THIS STUFF, AFTER ALL?
NOBODY REALLY KNOWS, DO THEY?
IT'S METAL.
SOME WEIRD KIND OF METAL. ...AND WHAT IS METAL?
IT'S A MEDIUM.
WAIT A MINUTE.
IT'S A METAL AND YOU'RE A BRONZE CASTER...
...AND HE'S A COLLECTOR. HE'S GOT ONE OF THE BIGGEST PRIVATE COLLECTIONS OF POST-1945 WORKS, PERIOD.
FROM POLLOCK ON UP, YOU NAME IT. MUSEUMS CALL HIM TO BORROW PIECES--HENRY MOORE, GERHART RICHTER, RITA ACKERMAN...
YEAH, YEAH, SO WHAT?

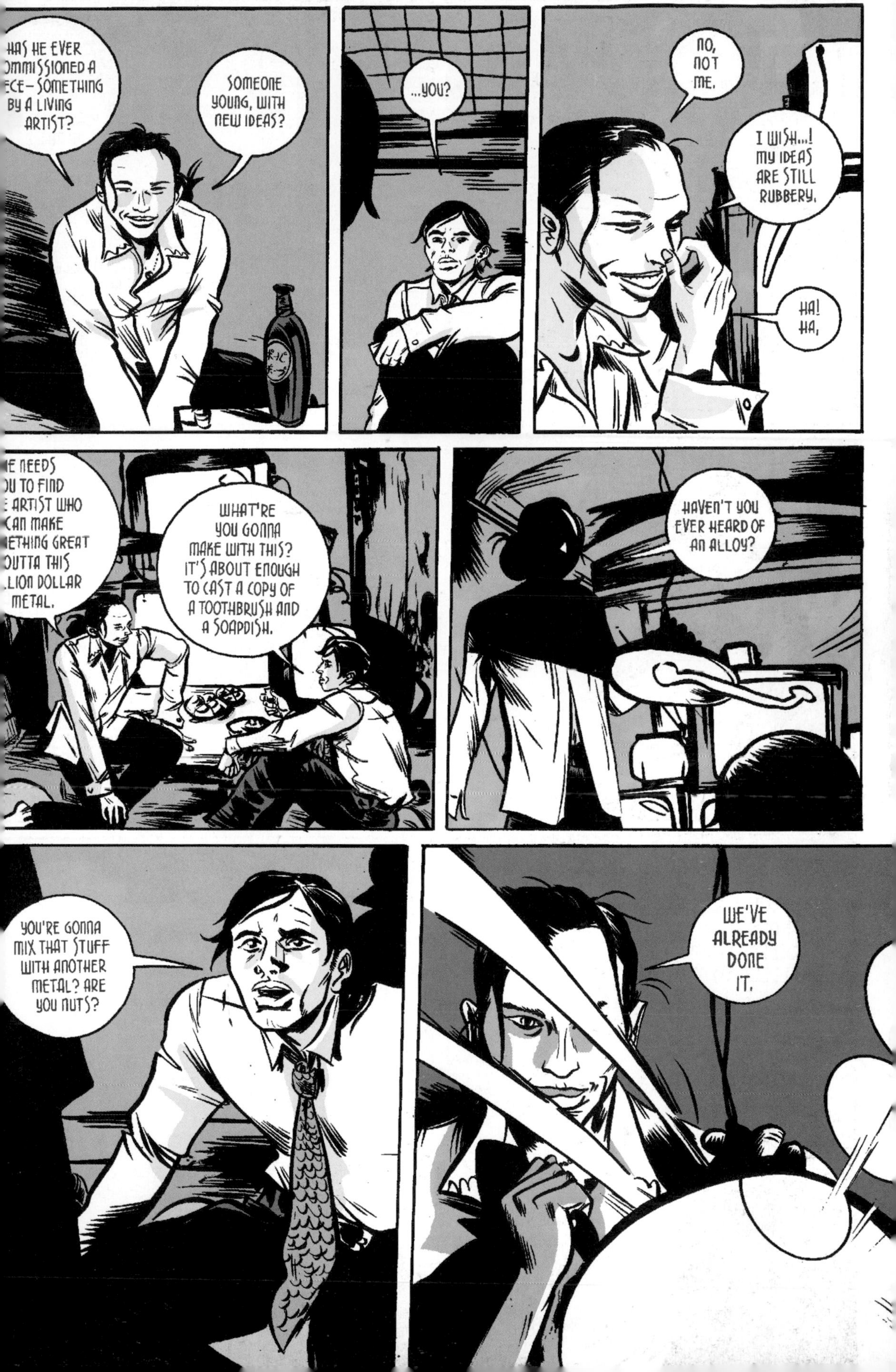
HAS HE EVER OMMISSIONED A ECE—SOMETHING BY A LIVING ARTIST?
SOMEONE YOUNG, WITH NEW IDEAS?
...YOU?
NO, NOT ME.
I WISH...! MY IDEAS ARE STILL RUBBERY.
HA! HA,
E NEEDS U TO FIND ARTIST WHO CAN MAKE ETHING GREAT OUTTA THIS LION DOLLAR METAL.
WHAT'RE YOU GONNA MAKE WITH THIS? IT'S ABOUT ENOUGH TO CAST A COPY OF A TOOTHBRUSH AND A SOAPDISH.
HAVEN'T YOU EVER HEARD OF AN ALLOY?
YOU'RE GONNA MIX THAT STUFF WITH ANOTHER METAL? ARE YOU NUTS?
WE'VE ALREADY DONE IT.

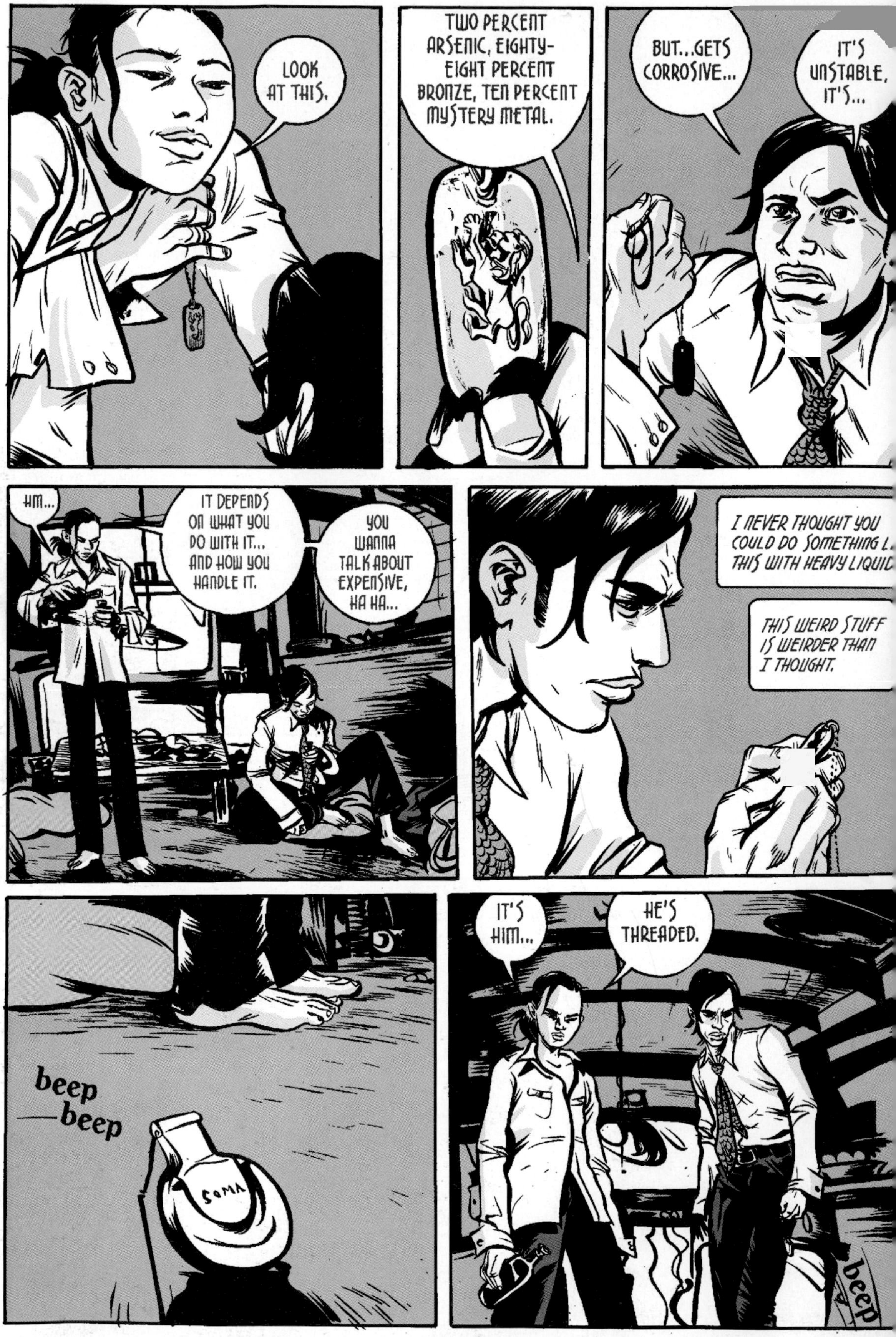

LOOK AT THIS.
TWO PERCENT ARSENIC, EIGHTY-EIGHT PERCENT BRONZE, TEN PERCENT MYSTERY METAL.
BUT...GETS CORROSIVE...
IT'S UNSTABLE, IT'S...
HM...
IT DEPENDS ON WHAT YOU DO WITH IT... AND HOW YOU HANDLE IT.
YOU WANNA TALK ABOUT EXPENSIVE, HA HA...
I NEVER THOUGHT YOU COULD DO SOMETHING L THIS WITH HEAVY LIQUI
THIS WEIRD STUFF IS WEIRDER THAN I THOUGHT.
beep beep
SOMA
IT'S HIM...
HE'S THREADED.
beep

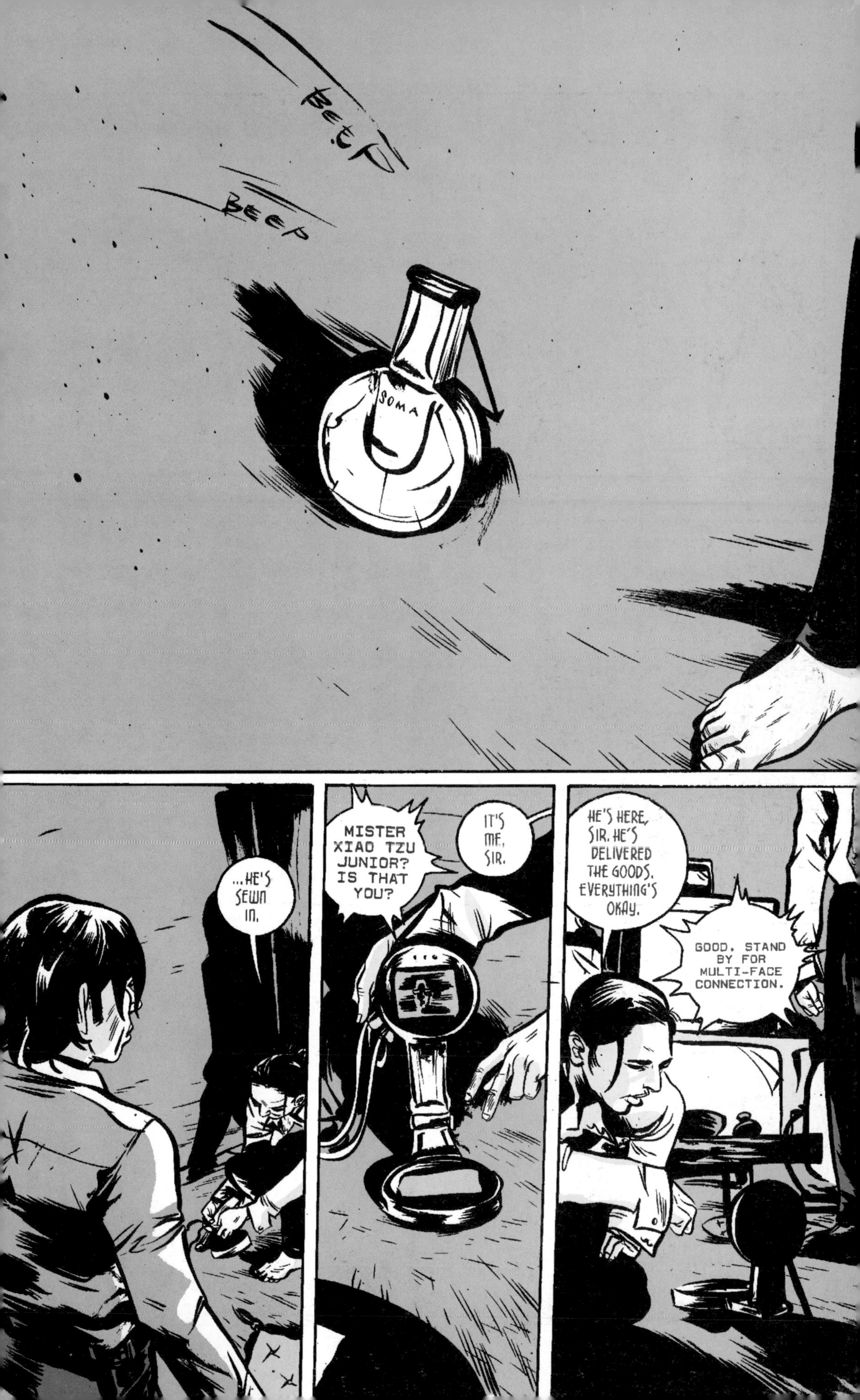
BEEP
BEEP
SOMA
...HE'S SEWN IN.
MISTER XIAO TZU JUNIOR? IS THAT YOU?
IT'S ME, SIR.
HE'S HERE, SIR. HE'S DELIVERED THE GOODS. EVERYTHING'S OKAY.
GOOD. STAND BY FOR MULTI-FACE CONNECTION.

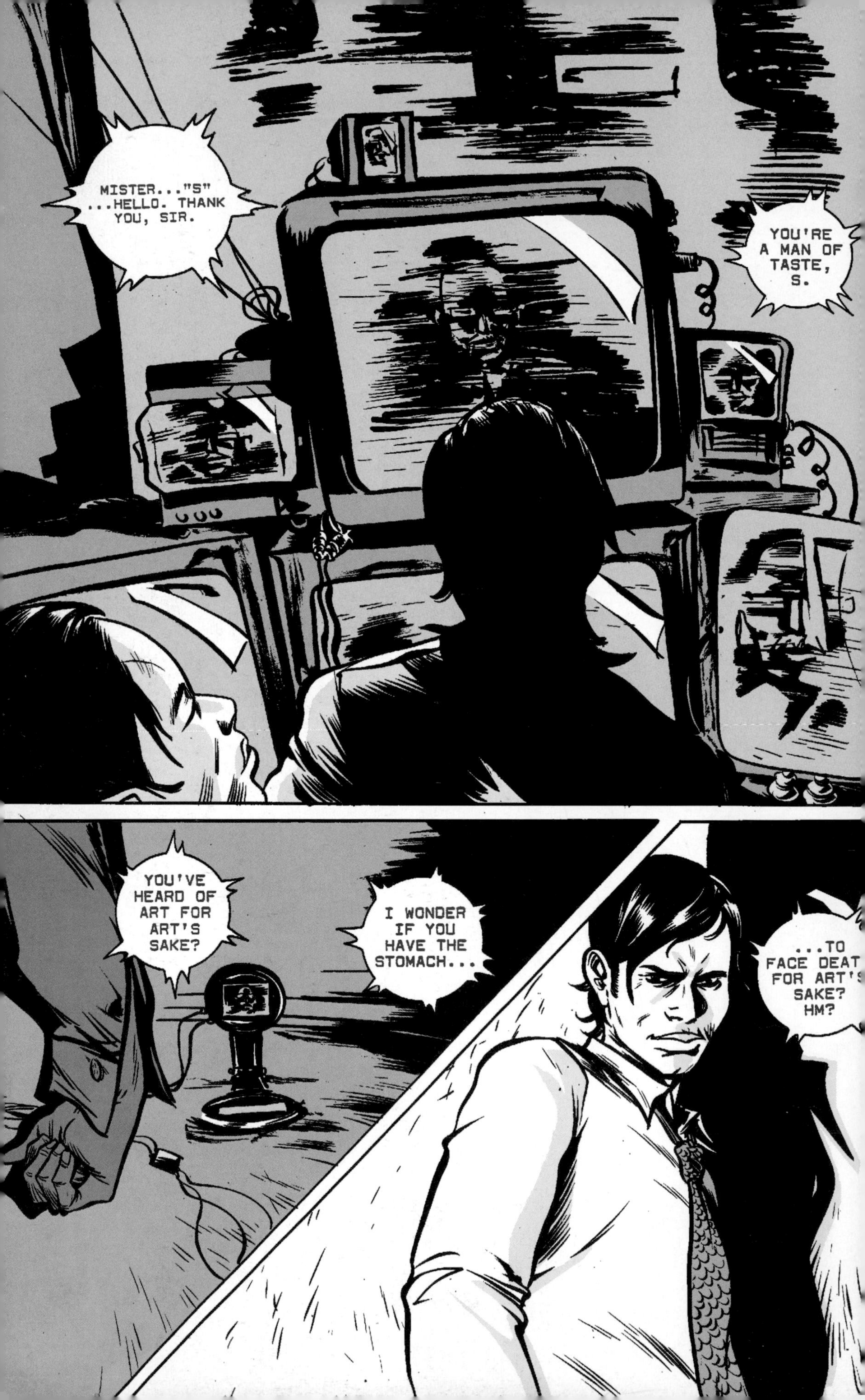
MISTER..."S" ...HELLO. THANK YOU, SIR.
YOU'RE A MAN OF TASTE, S.
YOU'VE HEARD OF ART FOR ART'S SAKE?
I WONDER IF YOU HAVE THE STOMACH...
...TO FACE DEAT FOR ART'S SAKE? HM?

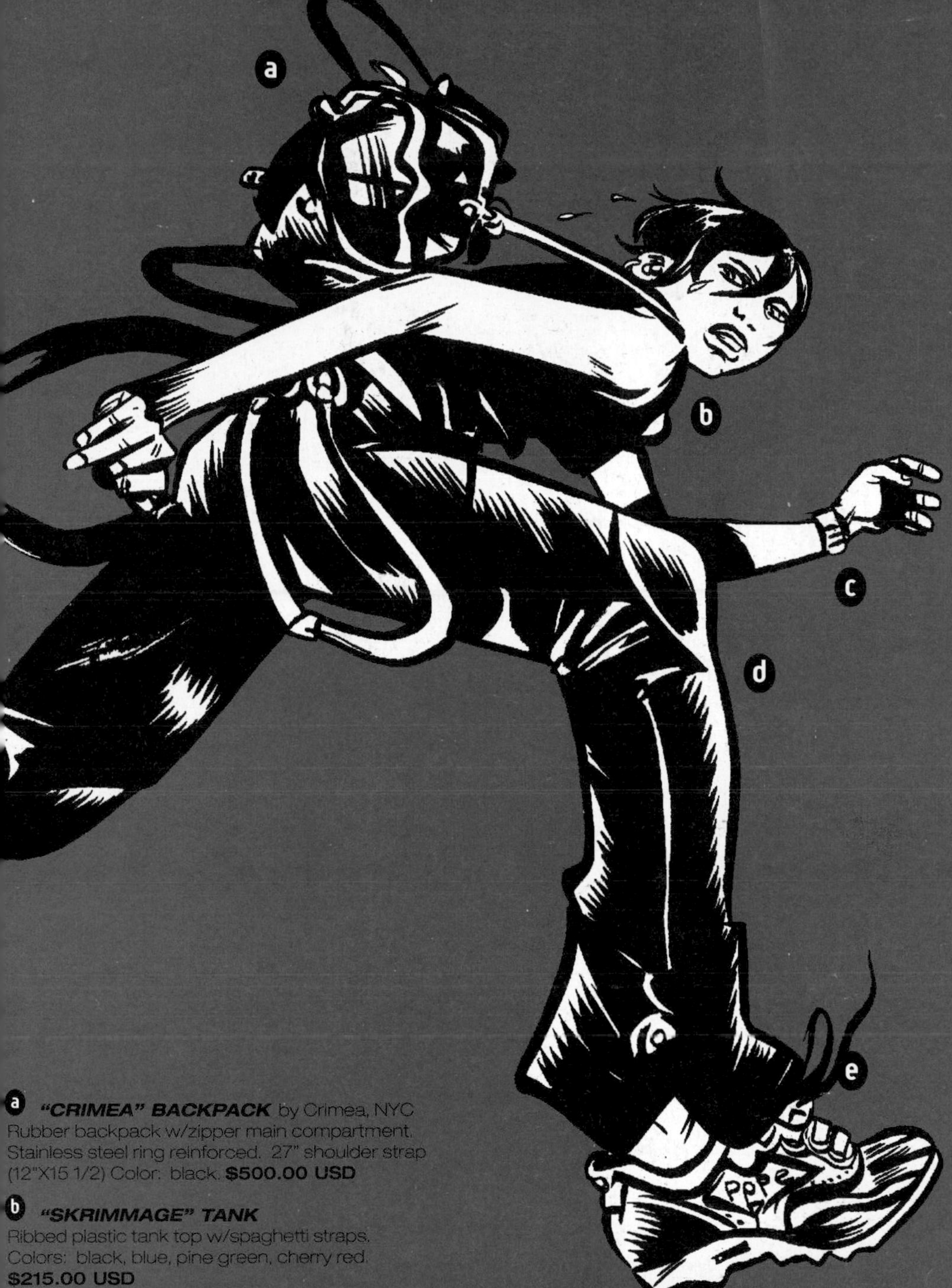
a
b
c
d
e

a **"CRIMEA" BACKPACK** by Crimea, NYC
Rubber backpack w/zipper main compartment. Stainless steel ring reinforced. 27" shoulder strap (12"X15 1/2) Color: black. **$500.00 USD**

b **"SKRIMMAGE" TANK**
Ribbed plastic tank top w/spaghetti straps. Colors: black, blue, pine green, cherry red. **$215.00 USD**

c **WRIST-COM**
Standard personal digital assistant. Log book, clock, databank, calculator, dub. Typical 2070's model. Not fancy. **$899.99 USD**

d **WISE-LEG JEANS**
Cotton denim jeans w/PVC varnish. Rivets on front pockets. Water-resistant, button fly. Colors: dark blue w/white stitching. note: size 7/8 has 32" inseam. **$1485.56 USD**

e **SNAP-SNEAKER**
Runner-style sneaker w/mesh-nylon body and suede-reinforced toe, "snap" logo on tongue and heel, "pope" on sides. Cushioned insole. Color: all red. women's whole + half sizes. **$653.00 USD**

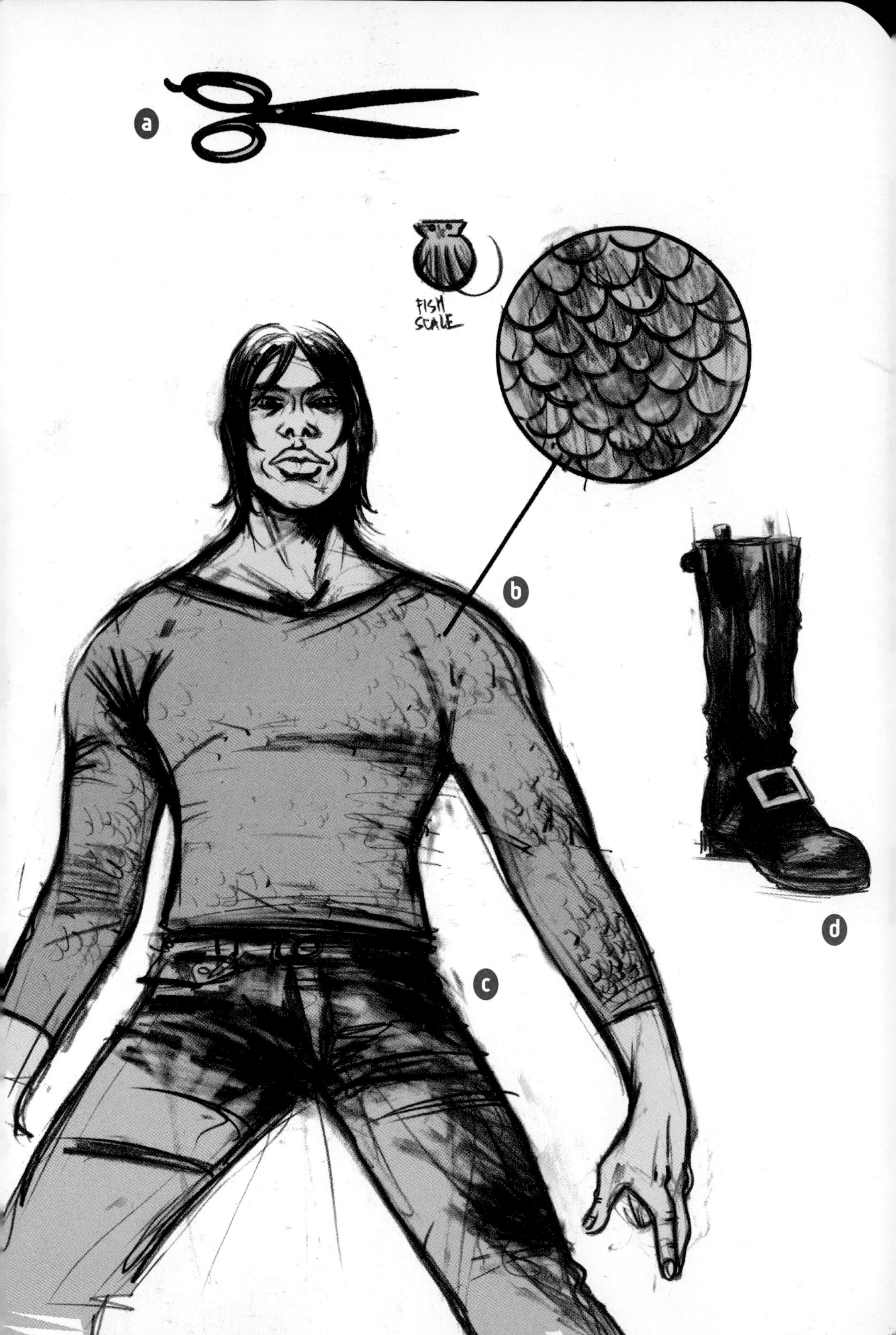
a
FISH SCALE
b
c
d

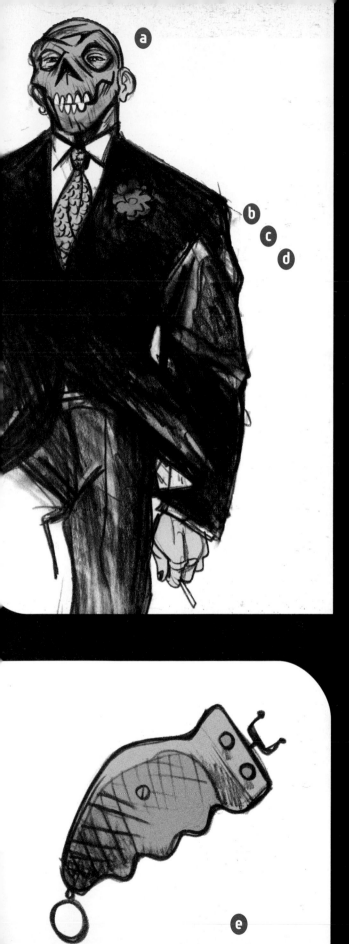

(PREVIOUS PAGE)

a *"THE JAGGER"* razorcut by Bumble Bee, NYC: **$225.00 USD**

b *QUIRBEY "FISHSCALE" SHIRT* HI-DENZ™ plastic and lambswool. Designed for warmth and comfort. Thin lambswool sweater woven with plastic "fishscale" chain mail exterior. Outer layer either slightly iridescent or matte (choose one). Colors: "aqua" green w/orange stitch or "American" blue w/green stitch: **$1760.25 USD.**

c *LEATHER JEANS* Vintage (2016) leather jeans, black, reinforced stitching at stress points. Felt lining in crotch and knees. Slight flare at cuff. Handtailored in Chicago, IL: **$1057.00 USD**

d *"COLONIAL" BOOT* to commemorate USA's 300th anniversary, the front buckle returns. Black leather with lug rubber sole, 1 1/2" heel. Midcalf with adjustable brass buckle: **$699.95 USD**

(THIS PAGE)

a *SKULL FACE* mask in molded HI-DENZ™ plastic w/leather interior harness + strap. Colors: bone white, red, glow-in-the-dark. **(inquire for price)** info: (Sugarman, NYC)

b *DULCET TONE CASHMERE WOOL 3UIT*, two-piece, in black. Silk lining: **$3000.00 USD**

c *SILK TIE* by Quirbey. "Fish" pattern. Colors: crimson, pink, orange, ocean, silver: **$600.00 USD**

d *TEN-BUTTON SILK SHIRT* by Glass, NYC: **$1050.00 USD**

e *WELDHAMMAR® POCKET CUTTER.* Hand-held 800° torch. Electric w/battery-cel adapter. Kiegal. Not for sale in continental U.S.

PAUL POPE HEAVY LIQUID

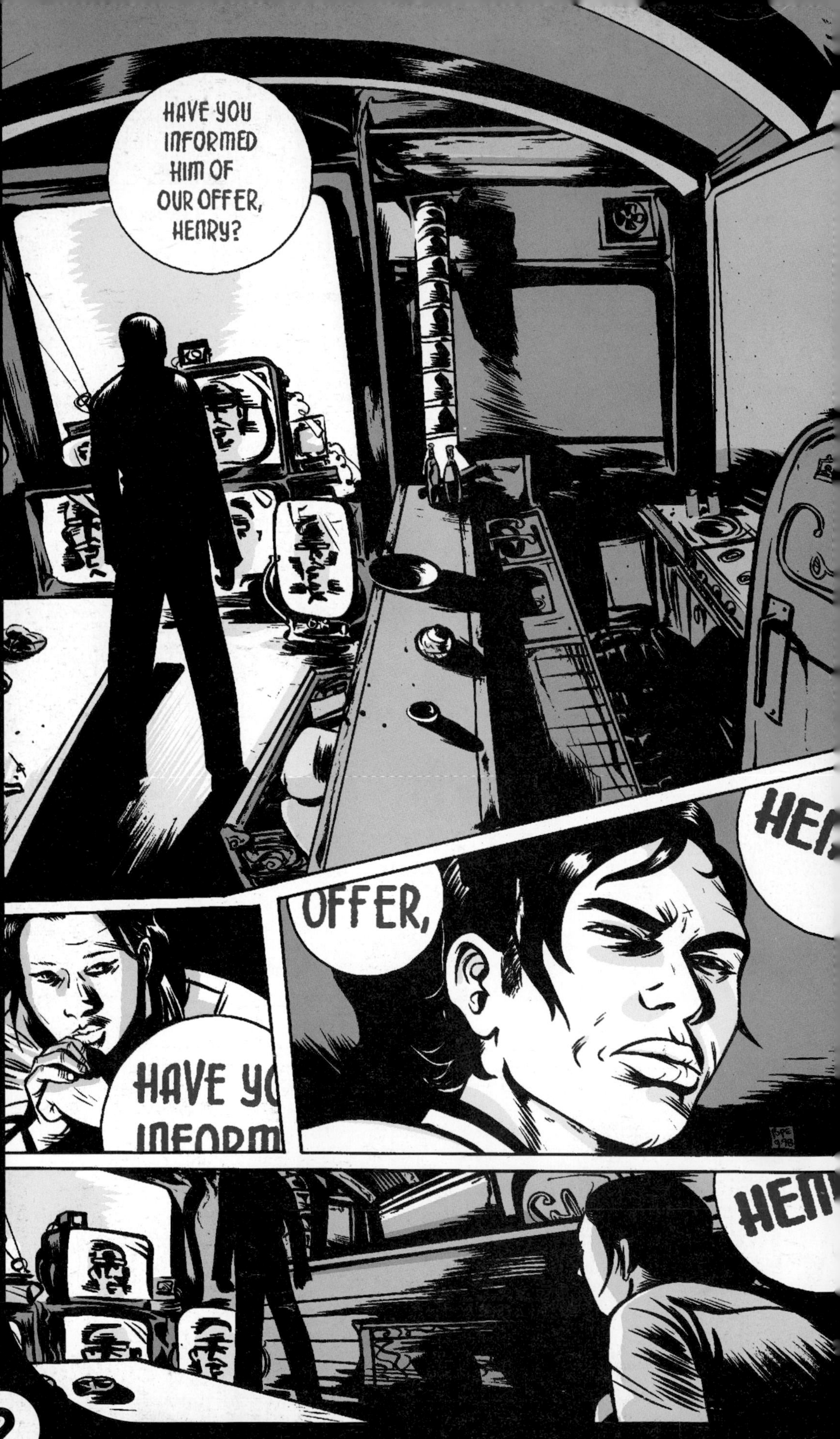
HAVE YOU INFORMED HIM OF OUR OFFER, HENRY?
HAVE YO
OFFER,
HEN
HEN

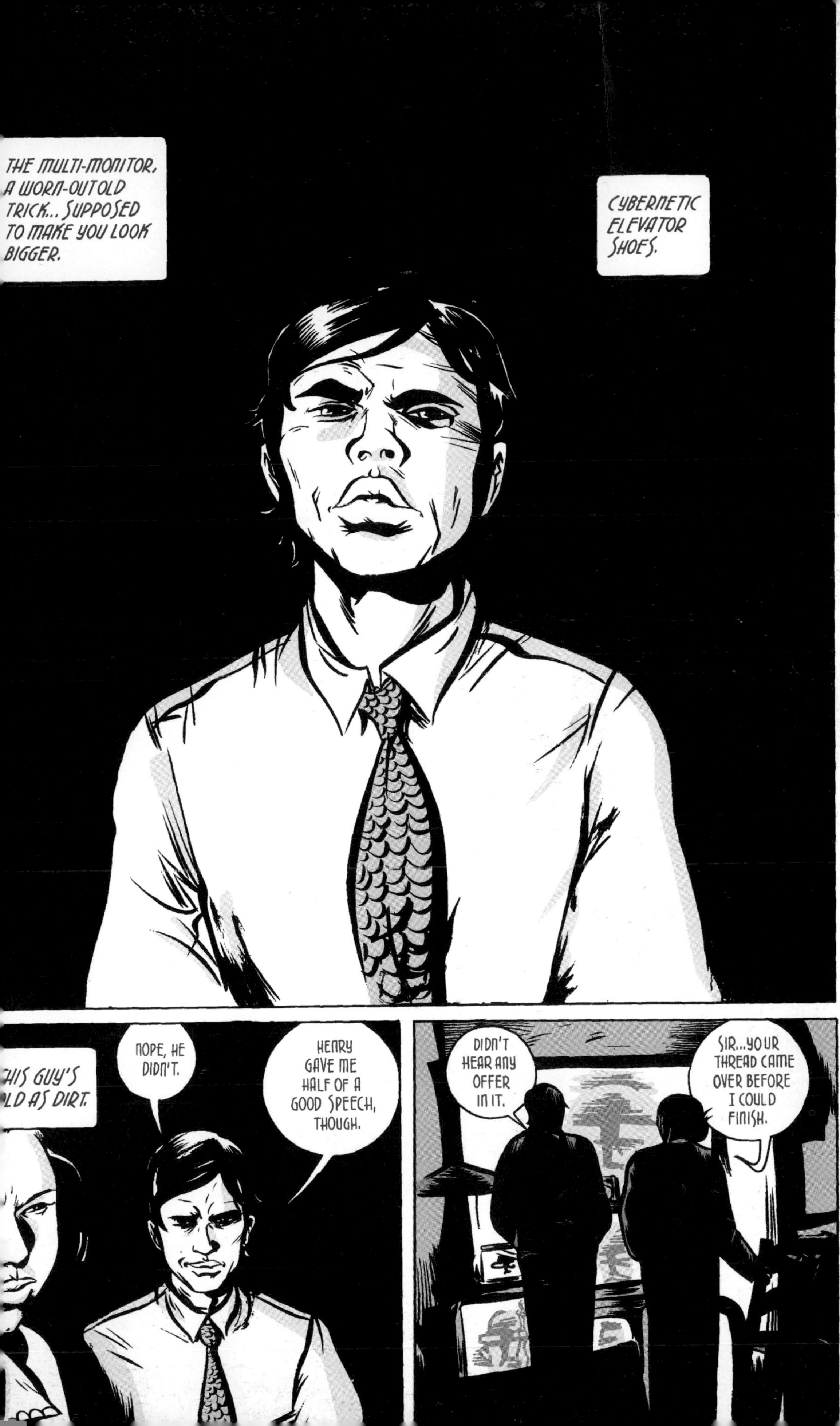
THE MULTI-MONITOR, A WORN-OUT OLD TRICK... SUPPOSED TO MAKE YOU LOOK BIGGER.
CYBERNETIC ELEVATOR SHOES.
HIS GUY'S LD AS DIRT.
NOPE, HE DIDN'T.
HENRY GAVE ME HALF OF A GOOD SPEECH, THOUGH.
DIDN'T HEAR ANY OFFER IN IT.
SIR...YOUR THREAD CAME OVER BEFORE I COULD FINISH.

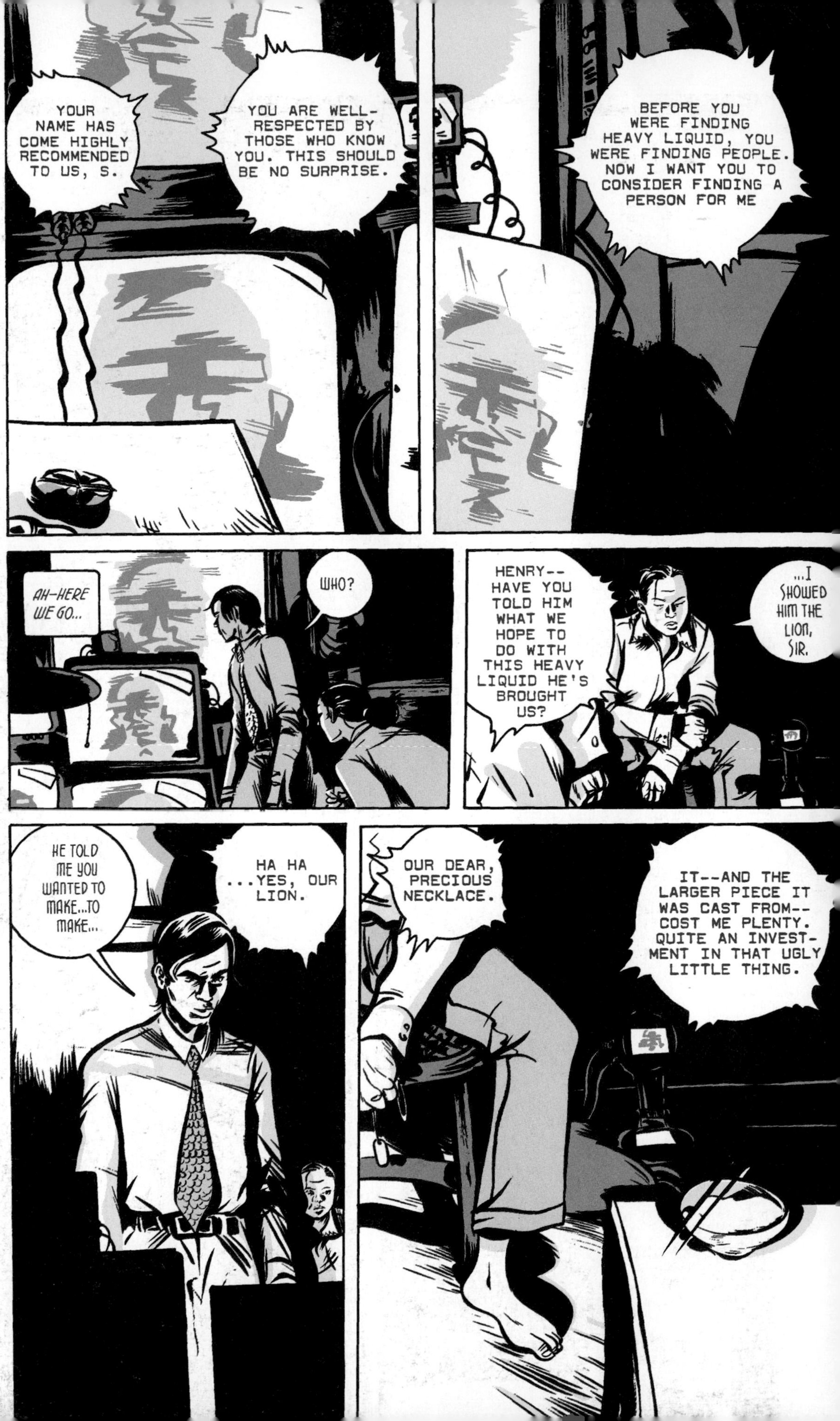
YOUR NAME HAS COME HIGHLY RECOMMENDED TO US, S.
YOU ARE WELL-RESPECTED BY THOSE WHO KNOW YOU. THIS SHOULD BE NO SURPRISE.
BEFORE YOU WERE FINDING HEAVY LIQUID, YOU WERE FINDING PEOPLE. NOW I WANT YOU TO CONSIDER FINDING A PERSON FOR ME
AH--HERE WE GO...
WHO?
HENRY-- HAVE YOU TOLD HIM WHAT WE HOPE TO DO WITH THIS HEAVY LIQUID HE'S BROUGHT US?
...I SHOWED HIM THE LION, SIR.
HE TOLD ME YOU WANTED TO MAKE...TO MAKE...
HA HA ...YES, OUR LION.
OUR DEAR, PRECIOUS NECKLACE.
IT--AND THE LARGER PIECE IT WAS CAST FROM--COST ME PLENTY. QUITE AN INVESTMENT IN THAT UGLY LITTLE THING.

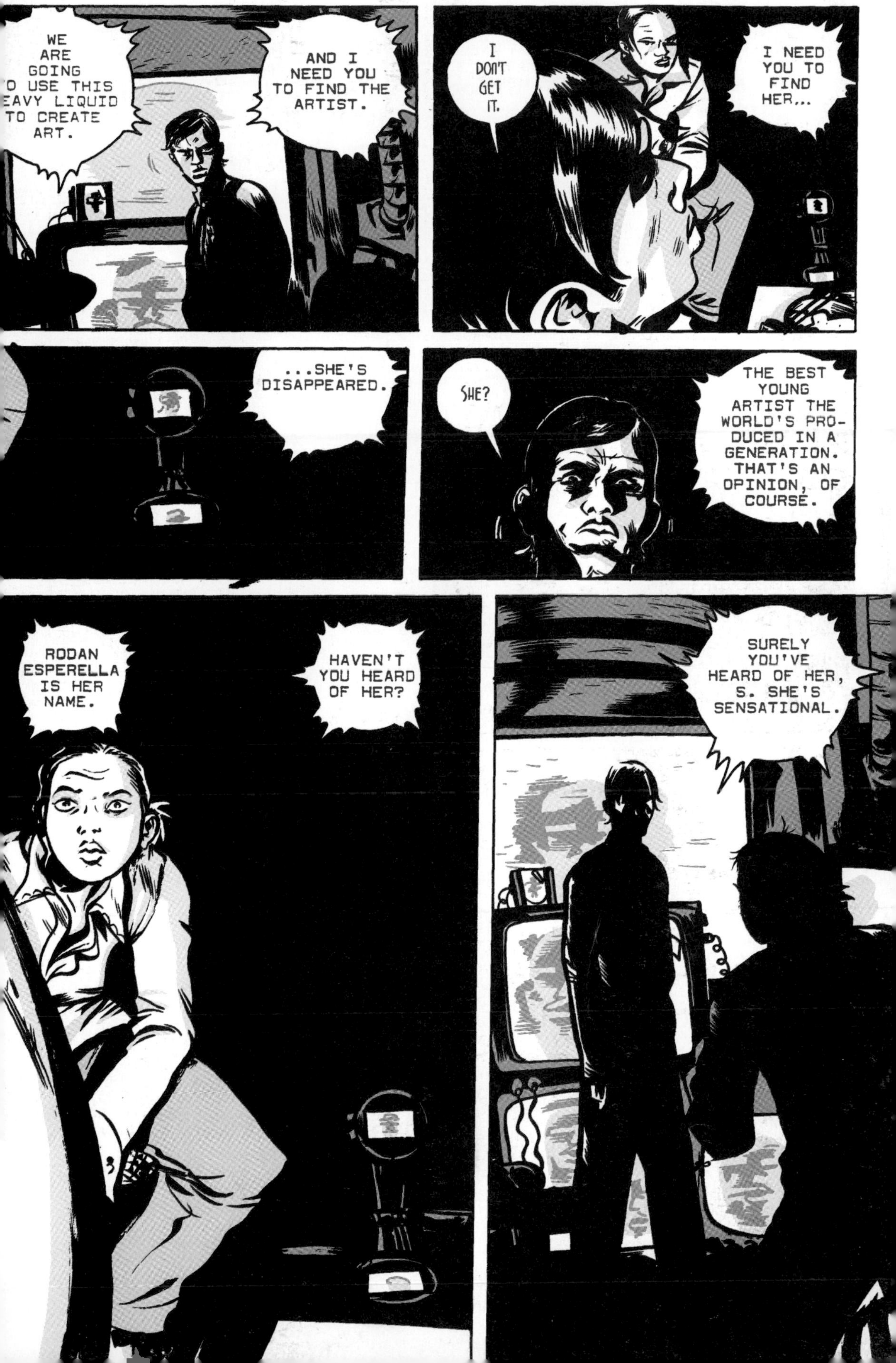
WE ARE GOING 'O USE THIS EAVY LIQUID TO CREATE ART.
AND I NEED YOU TO FIND THE ARTIST.
I DON'T GET IT.
I NEED YOU TO FIND HER...
...SHE'S DISAPPEARED.
SHE?
THE BEST YOUNG ARTIST THE WORLD'S PRO-DUCED IN A GENERATION. THAT'S AN OPINION, OF COURSE.
RODAN ESPERELLA IS HER NAME.
HAVEN'T YOU HEARD OF HER?
SURELY YOU'VE HEARD OF HER, S. SHE'S SENSATIONAL.

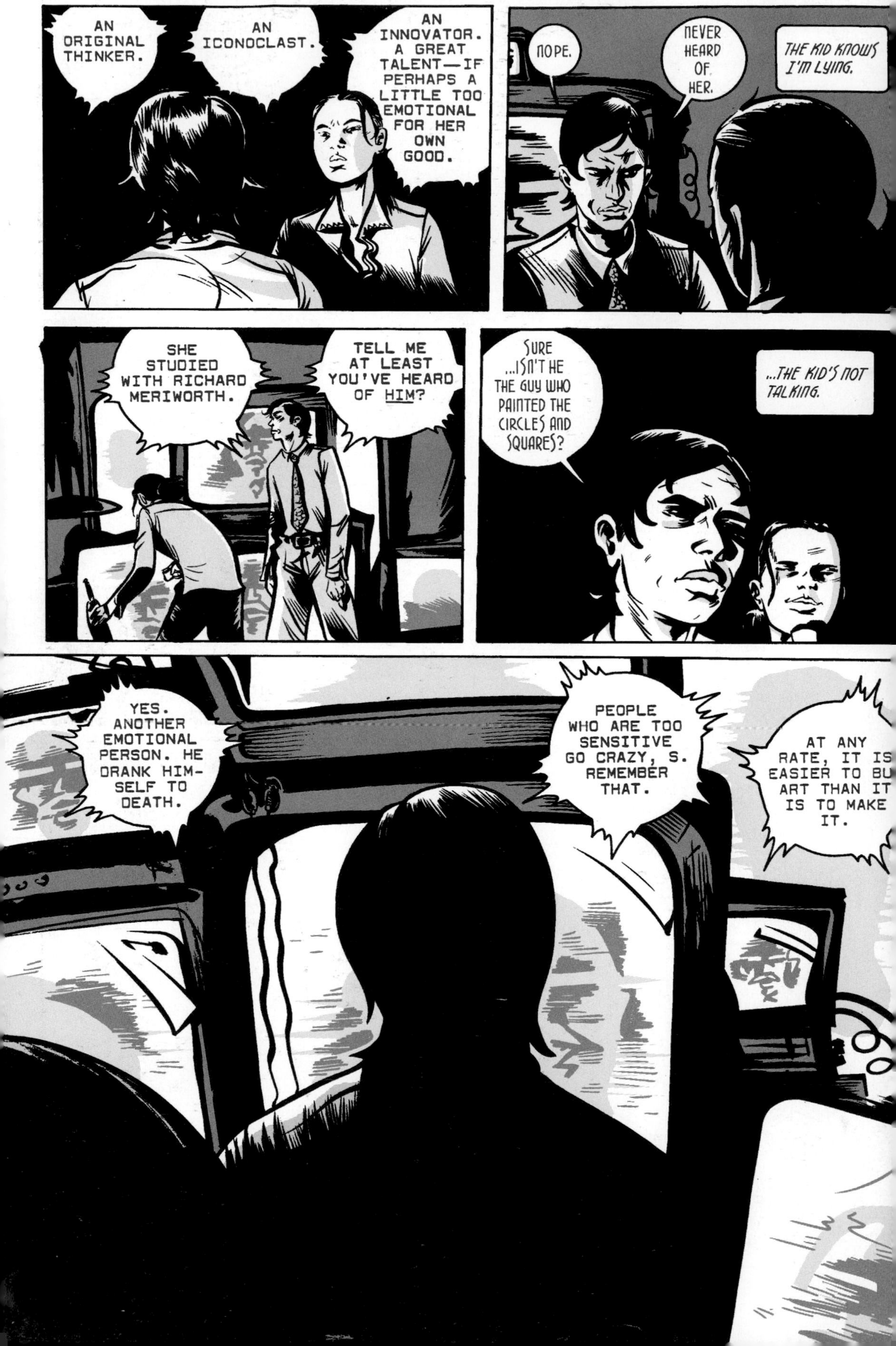
AN ORIGINAL THINKER.
AN ICONOCLAST.
AN INNOVATOR. A GREAT TALENT—IF PERHAPS A LITTLE TOO EMOTIONAL FOR HER OWN GOOD.
NOPE.
NEVER HEARD OF HER.
THE KID KNOWS I'M LYING.
SHE STUDIED WITH RICHARD MERIWORTH.
TELL ME AT LEAST YOU'VE HEARD OF HIM?
SURE ...ISN'T HE THE GUY WHO PAINTED THE CIRCLES AND SQUARES?
...THE KID'S NOT TALKING.
YES. ANOTHER EMOTIONAL PERSON. HE DRANK HIM-SELF TO DEATH.
PEOPLE WHO ARE TOO SENSITIVE GO CRAZY, S. REMEMBER THAT.
AT ANY RATE, IT IS EASIER TO BU ART THAN IT IS TO MAKE IT.

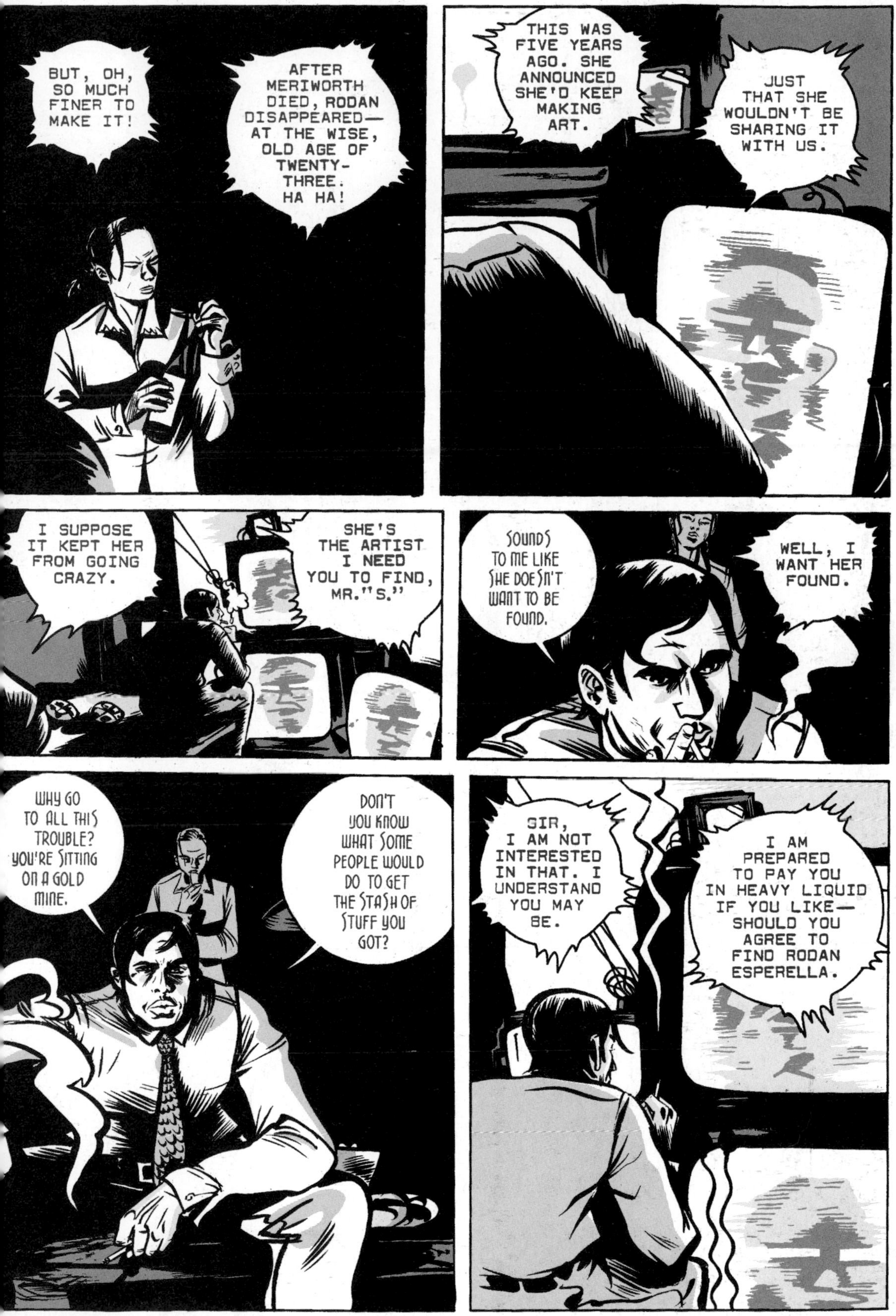
BUT, OH, SO MUCH FINER TO MAKE IT!
AFTER MERIWORTH DIED, RODAN DISAPPEARED— AT THE WISE, OLD AGE OF TWENTY-THREE. HA HA!
THIS WAS FIVE YEARS AGO. SHE ANNOUNCED SHE'D KEEP MAKING ART.
JUST THAT SHE WOULDN'T BE SHARING IT WITH US.
I SUPPOSE IT KEPT HER FROM GOING CRAZY.
SHE'S THE ARTIST I NEED YOU TO FIND, MR. "S."
SOUNDS TO ME LIKE SHE DOESN'T WANT TO BE FOUND.
WELL, I WANT HER FOUND.
WHY GO TO ALL THIS TROUBLE? YOU'RE SITTING ON A GOLD MINE.
DON'T YOU KNOW WHAT SOME PEOPLE WOULD DO TO GET THE STASH OF STUFF YOU GOT?
SIR, I AM NOT INTERESTED IN THAT. I UNDERSTAND YOU MAY BE.
I AM PREPARED TO PAY YOU IN HEAVY LIQUID IF YOU LIKE— SHOULD YOU AGREE TO FIND RODAN ESPERELLA.

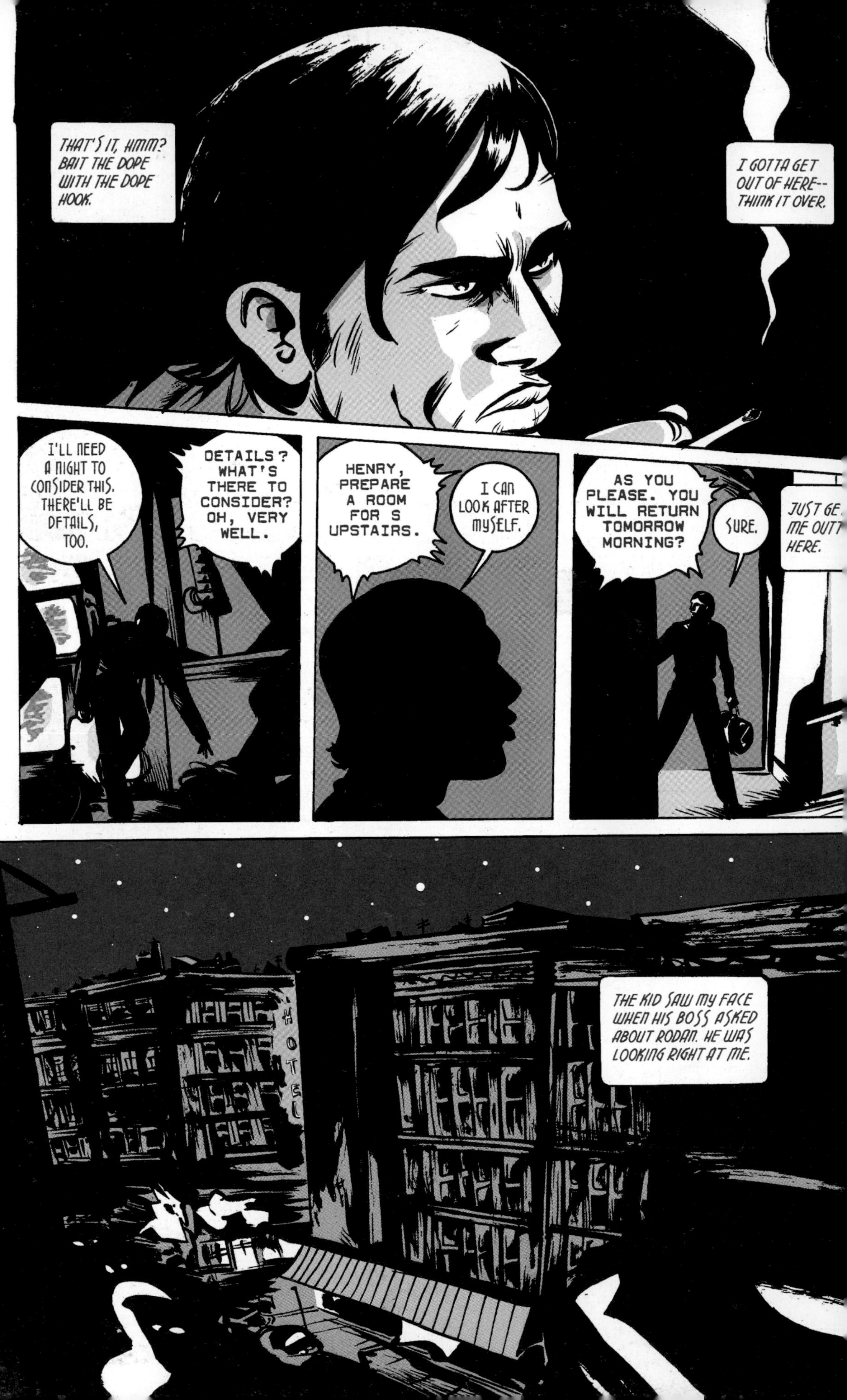
THAT'S IT, HMM? BAIT THE DOPE WITH THE DOPE HOOK.
I GOTTA GET OUT OF HERE-- THINK IT OVER.
I'LL NEED A NIGHT TO CONSIDER THIS. THERE'LL BE DETAILS, TOO.
DETAILS? WHAT'S THERE TO CONSIDER? OH, VERY WELL.
HENRY, PREPARE A ROOM FOR S UPSTAIRS.
I CAN LOOK AFTER MYSELF.
AS YOU PLEASE. YOU WILL RETURN TOMORROW MORNING?
SURE.
JUST GE ME OUT HERE.
HOTEL
THE KID SAW MY FACE WHEN HIS BOSS ASKED ABOUT RODAN. HE WAS LOOKING RIGHT AT ME.

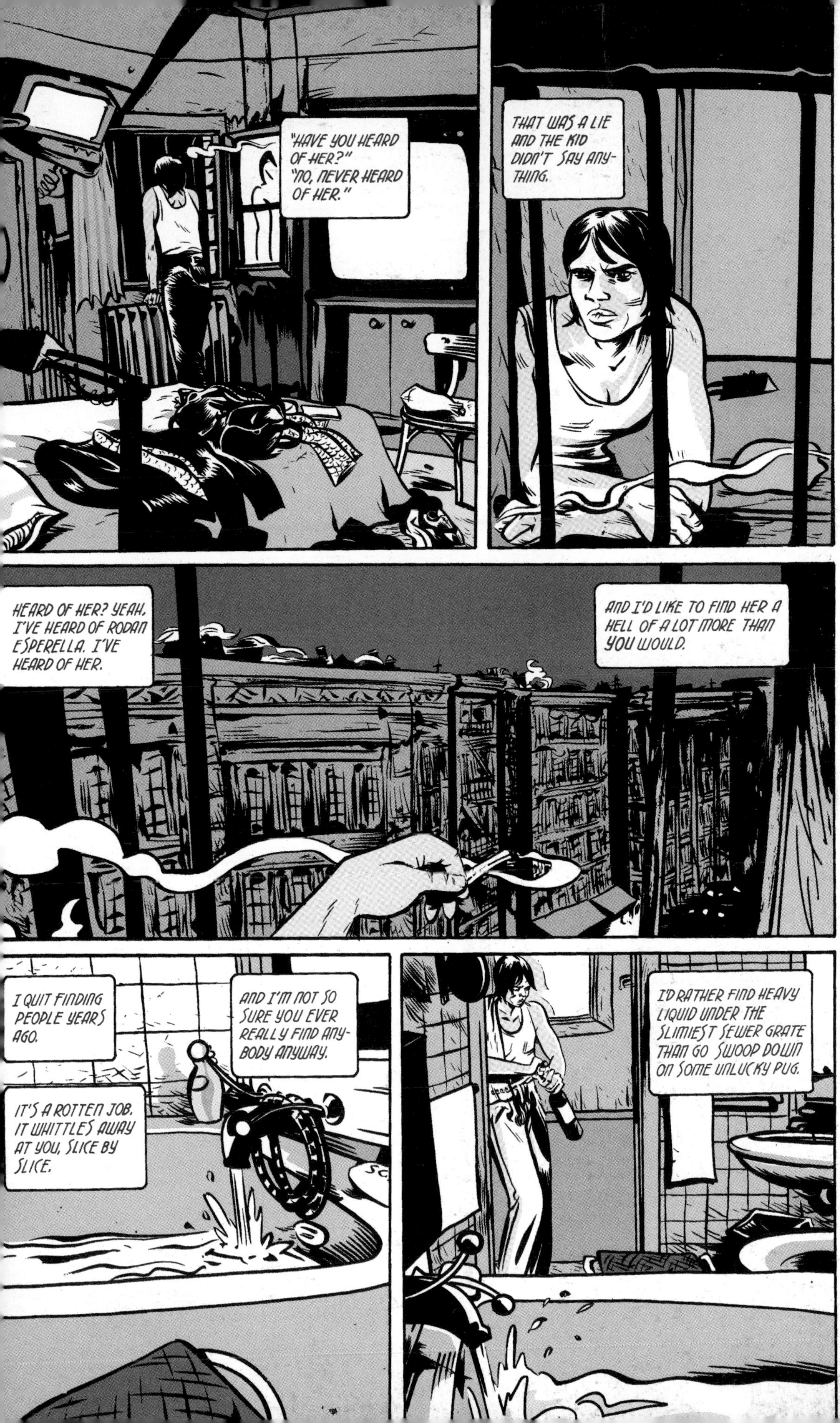
"HAVE YOU HEARD OF HER?"
"NO, NEVER HEARD OF HER."
THAT WAS A LIE AND THE KID DIDN'T SAY ANYTHING.
HEARD OF HER? YEAH, I'VE HEARD OF RODAN ESPERELLA. I'VE HEARD OF HER.
AND I'D LIKE TO FIND HER A HELL OF A LOT MORE THAN YOU WOULD.
I QUIT FINDING PEOPLE YEARS AGO.
AND I'M NOT SO SURE YOU EVER REALLY FIND ANYBODY ANYWAY.
IT'S A ROTTEN JOB. IT WHITTLES AWAY AT YOU, SLICE BY SLICE.
I'D RATHER FIND HEAVY LIQUID UNDER THE SLIMIEST SEWER GRATE THAN GO SWOOP DOWN ON SOME UNLUCKY PUG.

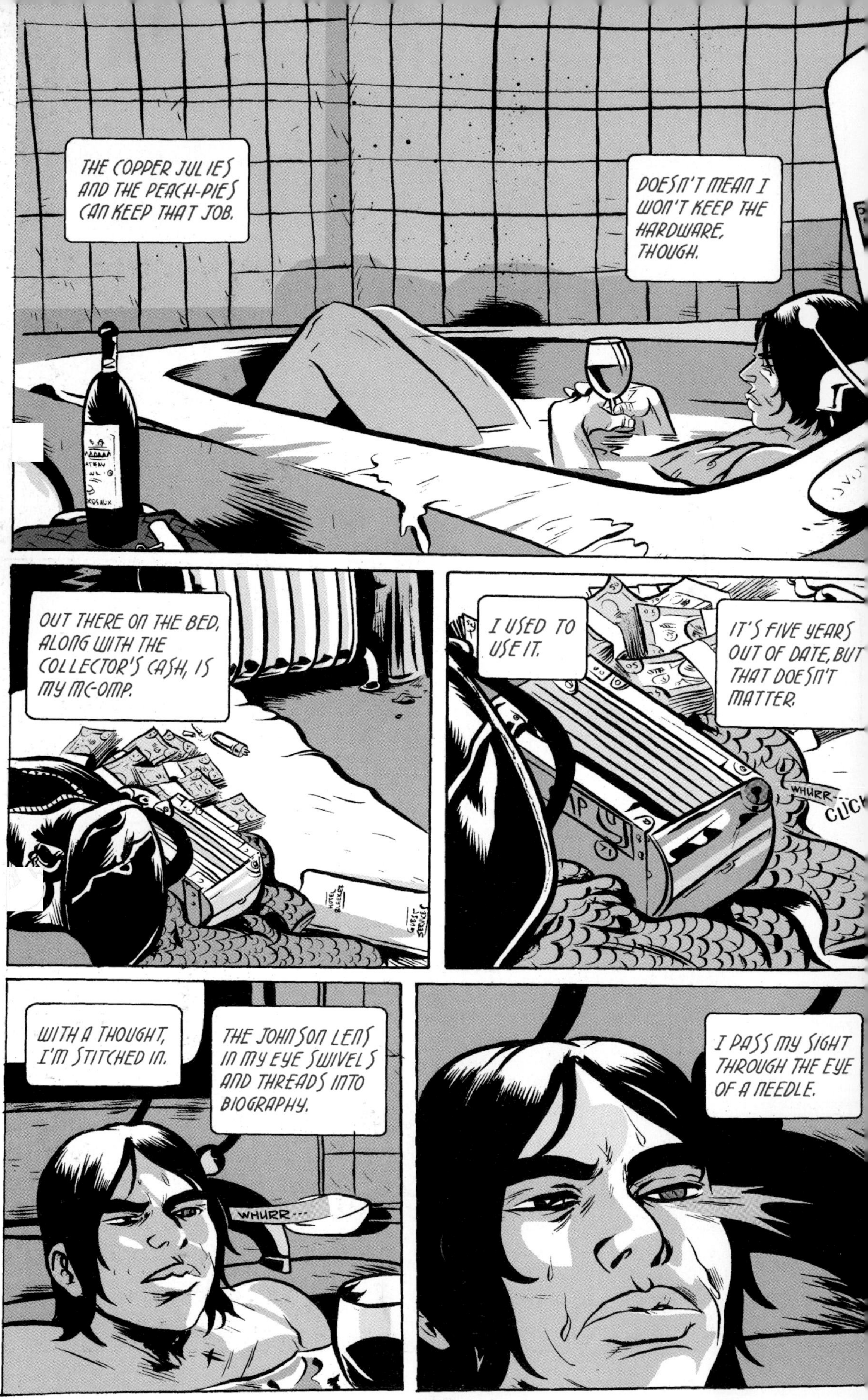
THE COPPER JULIES AND THE PEACH-PIES CAN KEEP THAT JOB.
DOESN'T MEAN I WON'T KEEP THE HARDWARE, THOUGH.
OUT THERE ON THE BED, ALONG WITH THE COLLECTOR'S CASH, IS MY MC-OMP.
HOTEL BLEEKER
GUEST SERVICES
I USED TO USE IT.
IT'S FIVE YEARS OUT OF DATE, BUT THAT DOESN'T MATTER.
WHURR---
WITH A THOUGHT, I'M STITCHED IN.
THE JOHNSON LENS IN MY EYE SWIVELS AND THREADS INTO BIOGRAPHY.
WHURR---
I PASS MY SIGHT THROUGH THE EYE OF A NEEDLE.

LKSDJFOIWEFWEMFOSDI9FIW
YLKDJF8IWEJIIFOWEKFOWEK
REORV,LDSGG[AVL;IL'A0GAEGEGL'ALA;G7WBDP
A:WAGJHOGKLFJGIFDJGDILUGIERGJG
GKLFJGIFDJ

THERE I AM,
SUCH A SUCKER.

STITCHING INTO THE
PROMPT I'VE STITCHED
INTO A MILLION TIMES
BEFORE.

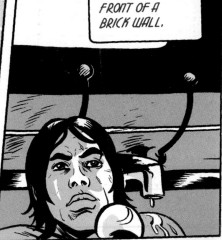

A PARAGRAPH AND
A BLOOD TYPE IN
FRONT OF A
BRICK WALL.

RODAN ESPERELLA-
BORN, STATE OF
PUERTO RICO, NINE-
TWO-FORTY-SIX.

FAMILY RAN A
SUCCESSFUL SUGAR
FARM ON THE
SOUTH COAST.

ACCEPTED INTO S.V.A.
IN SAN JUAN, TRANS-
FERRED TO COOPER
UNION IN SIXTY-
SEVEN.

BLAH-BLAH-BLAH
..."RETIRED" IN
SEVENTY, C.W.U.
--CURRENT
WHEREABOUTS
UNKNOWN.

THAT'S ABOUT ALL
YOU CAN PASS
THROUGH A NEEDLE
WITH STANDARD
HARDWARE.

TRY MY BIO, AND
YOU WON'T FIND
ANYTHING--NOT
WITH HOUSEHOLD
HARDWARE.

THAT'S HOW EASY IT IS
TO WASH YOURSELF
OFF THESE LAUNDRY
LISTS.

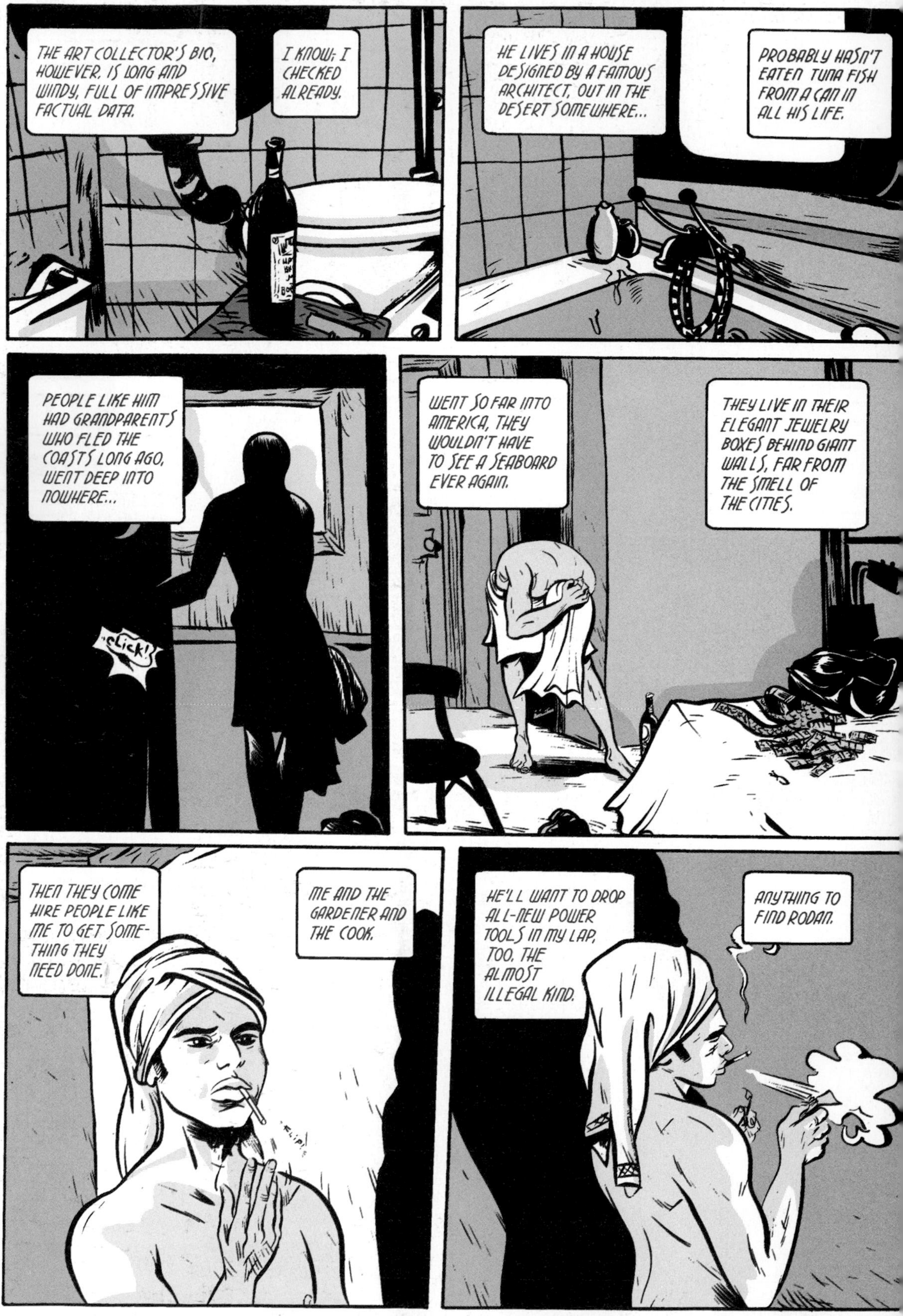
THE ART COLLECTOR'S BIO, HOWEVER, IS LONG AND WINDY, FULL OF IMPRESSIVE FACTUAL DATA.
I KNOW; I CHECKED ALREADY.
HE LIVES IN A HOUSE DESIGNED BY A FAMOUS ARCHITECT, OUT IN THE DESERT SOMEWHERE...
PROBABLY HASN'T EATEN TUNA FISH FROM A CAN IN ALL HIS LIFE.
PEOPLE LIKE HIM HAD GRANDPARENTS WHO FLED THE COASTS LONG AGO, WENT DEEP INTO NOWHERE...
CLICK!
WENT SO FAR INTO AMERICA, THEY WOULDN'T HAVE TO SEE A SEABOARD EVER AGAIN.
THEY LIVE IN THEIR ELEGANT JEWELRY BOXES BEHIND GIANT WALLS, FAR FROM THE SMELL OF THE CITIES.
THEN THEY COME HIRE PEOPLE LIKE ME TO GET SOMETHING THEY NEED DONE.
ME AND THE GARDENER AND THE COOK.
FLIP!
HE'LL WANT TO DROP ALL-NEW POWER TOOLS IN MY LAP, TOO. THE ALMOST ILLEGAL KIND.
ANYTHING TO FIND RODAN.

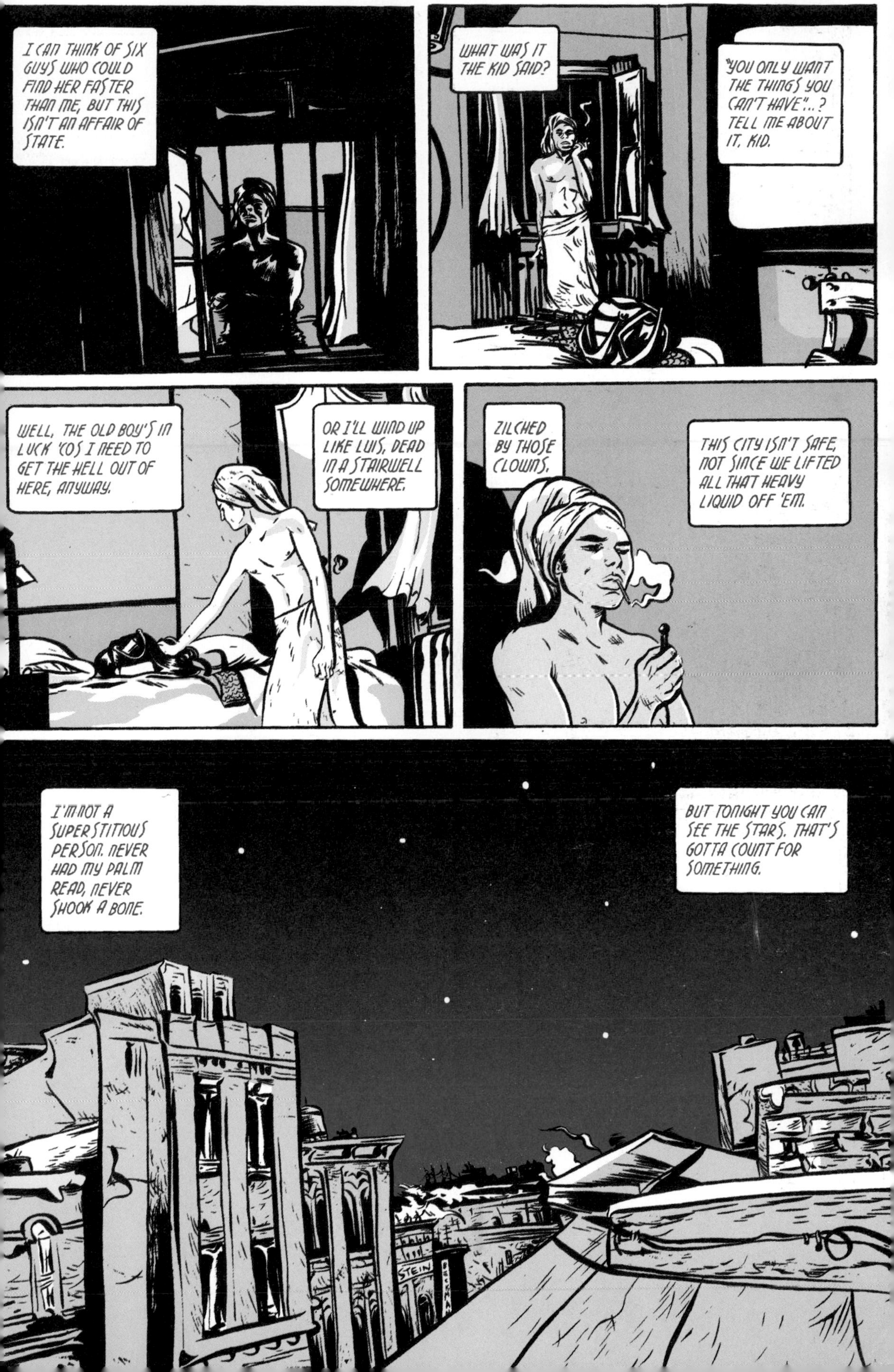
I CAN THINK OF SIX GUYS WHO COULD FIND HER FASTER THAN ME, BUT THIS ISN'T AN AFFAIR OF STATE.
WHAT WAS IT THE KID SAID?
"YOU ONLY WANT THE THINGS YOU CAN'T HAVE"...? TELL ME ABOUT IT, KID.
WELL, THE OLD BOY'S IN LUCK 'COS I NEED TO GET THE HELL OUT OF HERE, ANYWAY.
OR I'LL WIND UP LIKE LUIS, DEAD IN A STAIRWELL SOMEWHERE.
ZILCHED BY THOSE CLOWNS.
THIS CITY ISN'T SAFE, NOT SINCE WE LIFTED ALL THAT HEAVY LIQUID OFF 'EM.
I'M NOT A SUPERSTITIOUS PERSON. NEVER HAD MY PALM READ, NEVER SHOOK A BONE.
BUT TONIGHT YOU CAN SEE THE STARS. THAT'S GOTTA COUNT FOR SOMETHING.
STEIN

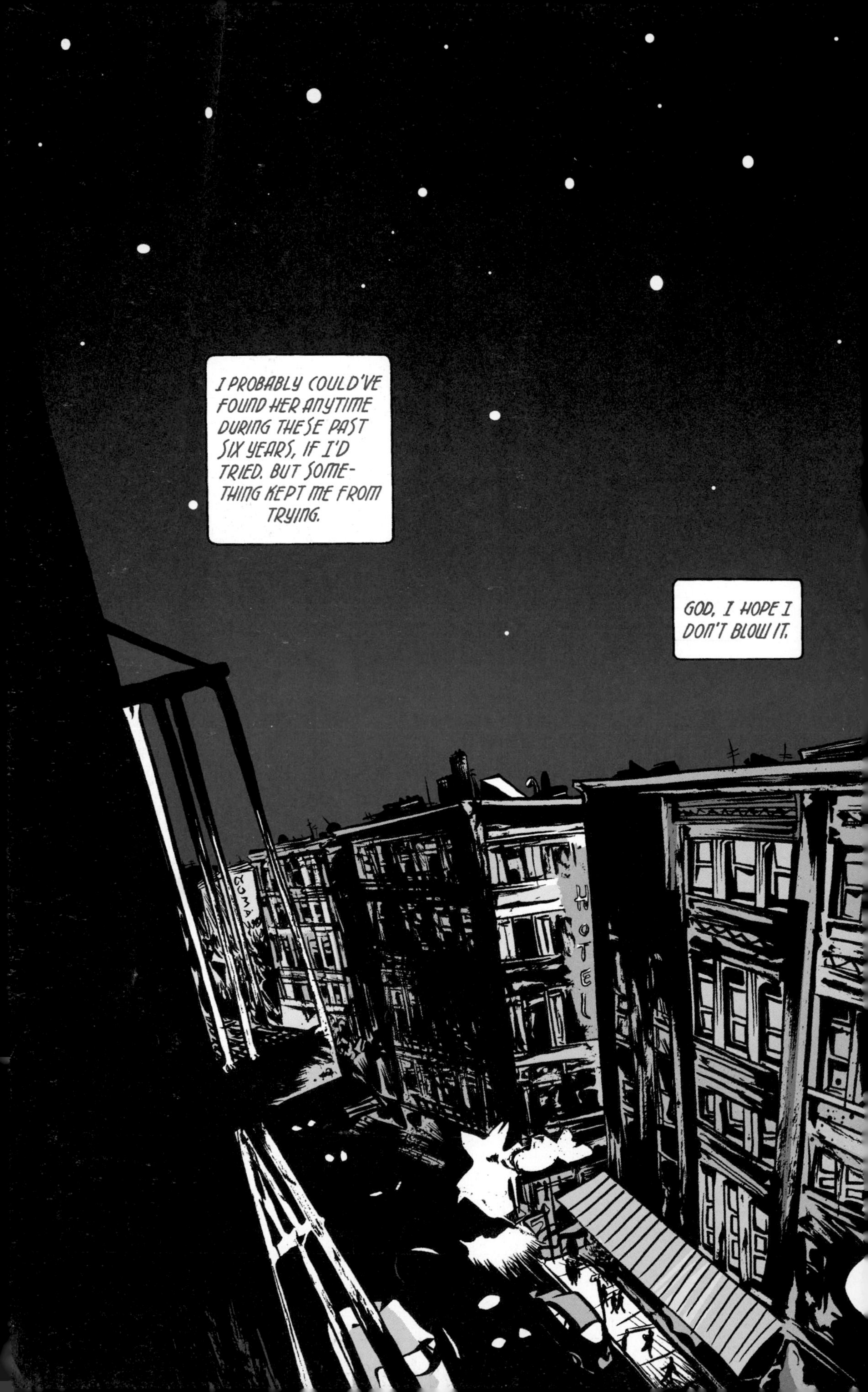
I PROBABLY COULD'VE FOUND HER ANYTIME DURING THESE PAST SIX YEARS, IF I'D TRIED. BUT SOME-THING KEPT ME FROM TRYING.
GOD, I HOPE I DON'T BLOW IT.
HOTEL

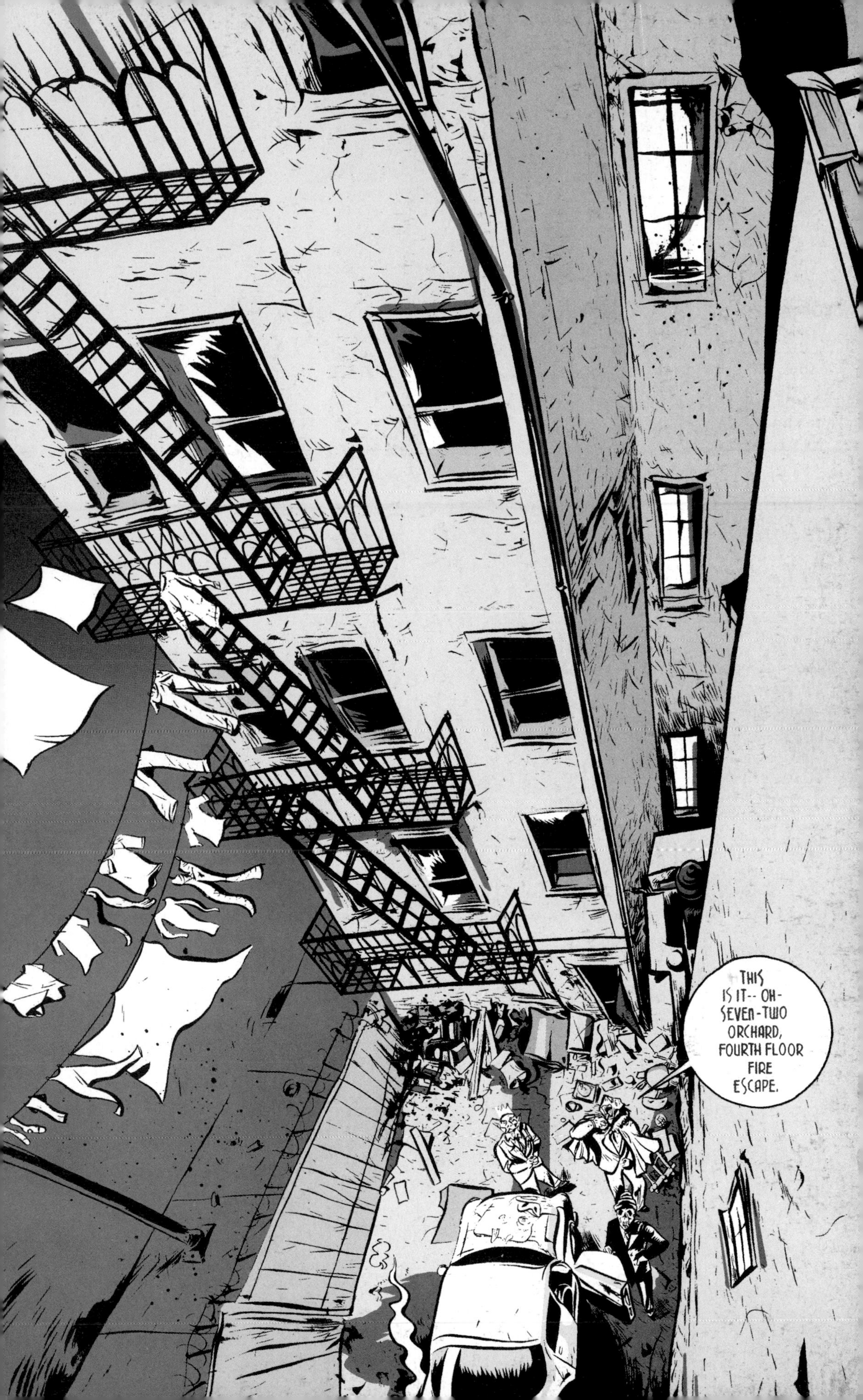
THIS IS IT-- OH-SEVEN-TWO ORCHARD, FOURTH FLOOR FIRE ESCAPE.

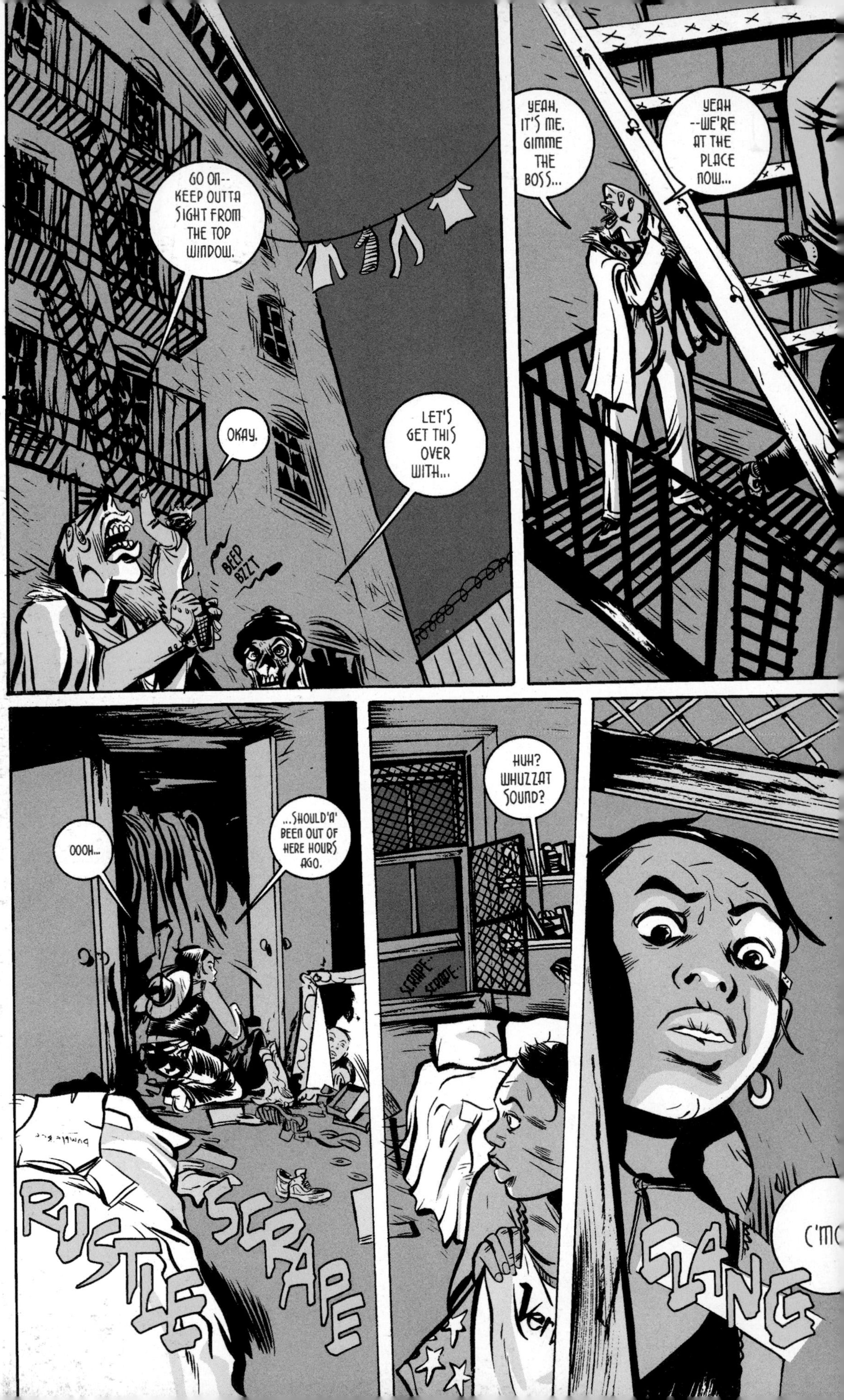
GO ON--
KEEP OUTTA
SIGHT FROM
THE TOP
WINDOW.
OKAY.
BEEP
BZZT
LET'S
GET THIS
OVER
WITH...
YEAH,
IT'S ME.
GIMME
THE
BOSS...
YEAH
--WE'RE
AT THE
PLACE
NOW...
OOOH...
...SHOULD'A'
BEEN OUT OF
HERE HOURS
AGO.
RUSTLE
SCRAPE
HUH?
WHUZZAT
SOUND?
SCRAPE
SCRAPE
CLANG
C'MO

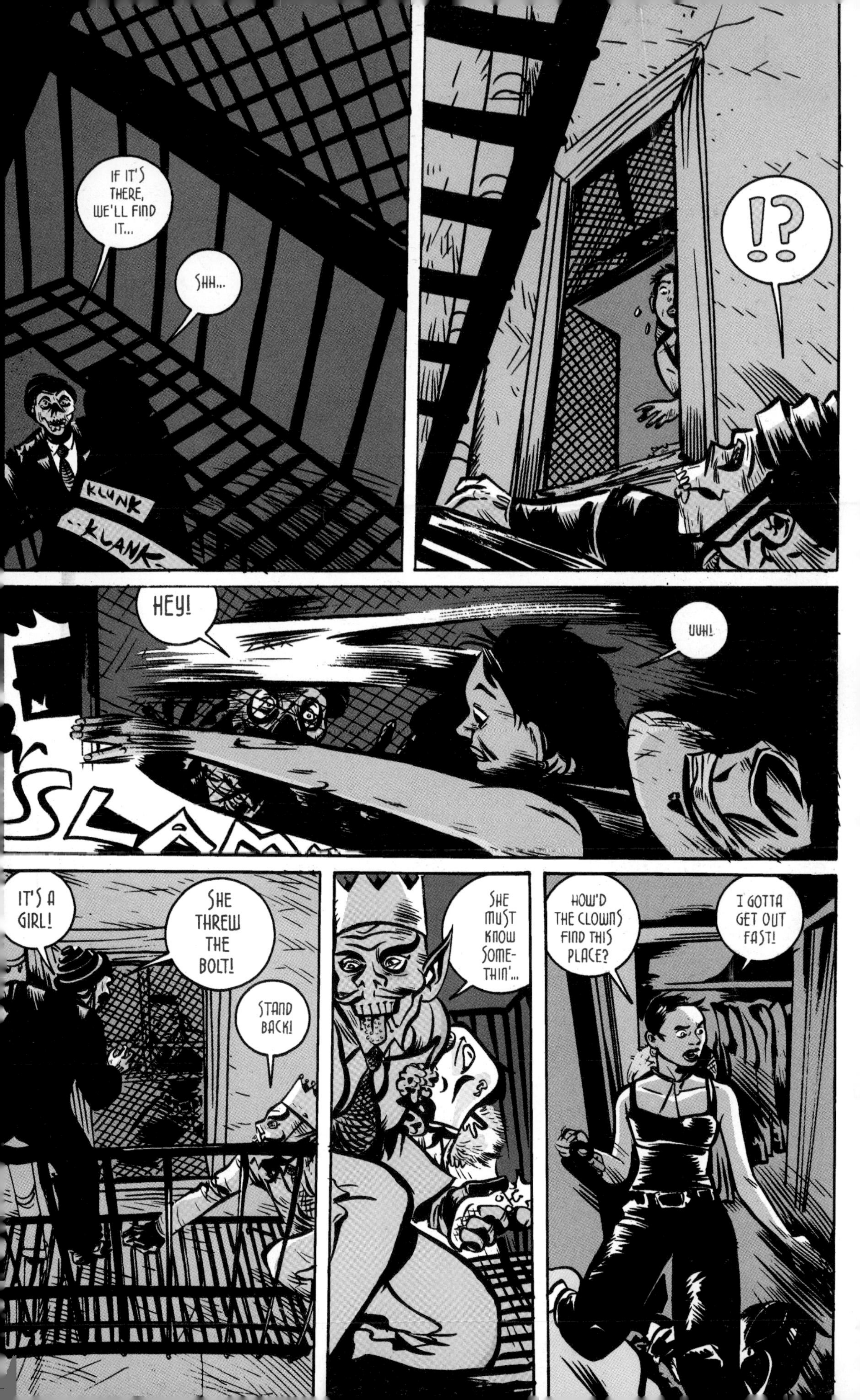

IF IT'S THERE, WE'LL FIND IT...
SHH...
KLUNK
..KLANK
!?
HEY!
UUH!
IT'S A GIRL!
SHE THREW THE BOLT!
STAND BACK!
SHE MUST KNOW SOME-THIN'...
HOW'D THE CLOWNS FIND THIS PLACE?
I GOTTA GET OUT FAST!

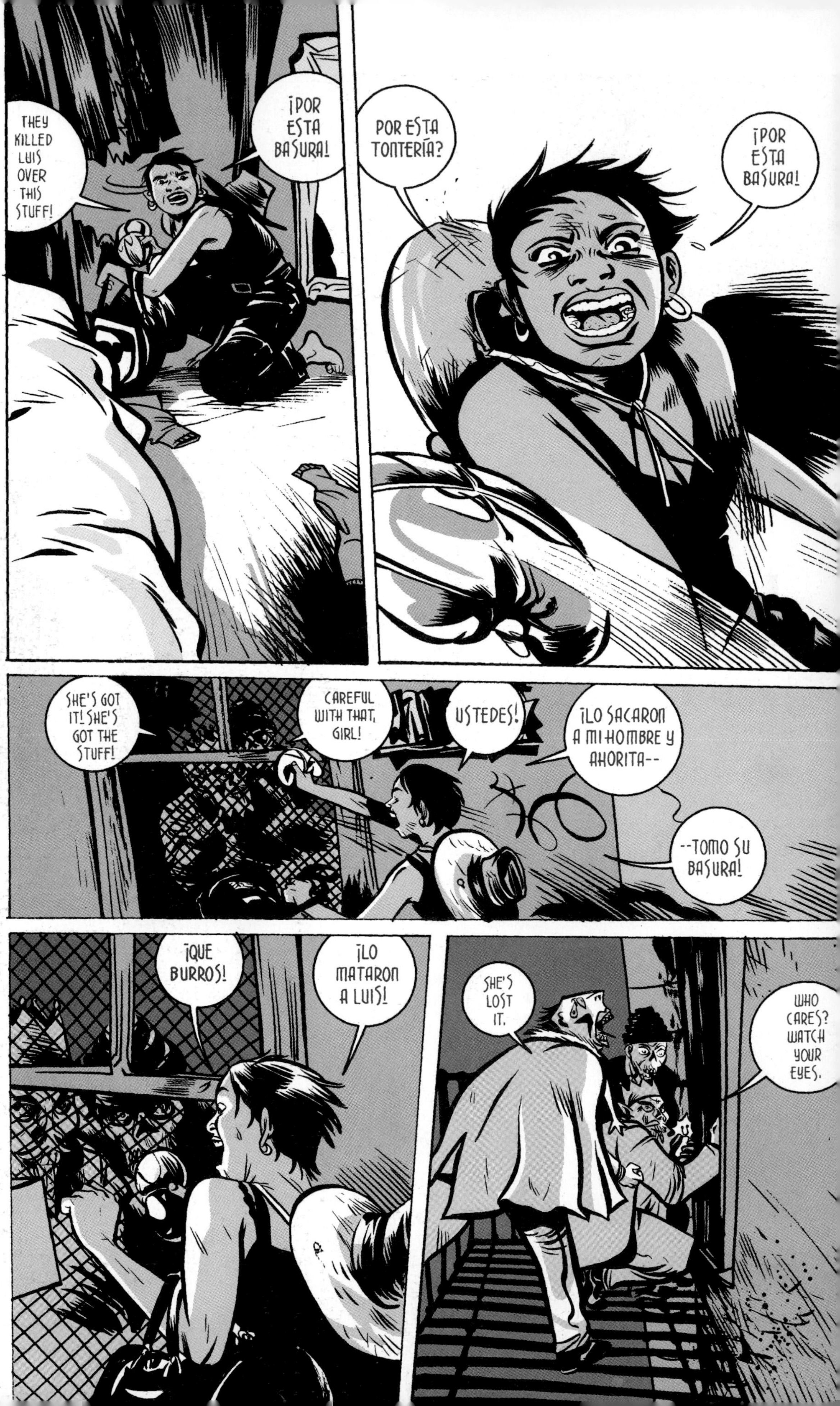
THEY KILLED LUIS OVER THIS STUFF!
¡POR ESTA BASURA!
POR ESTA TONTERÍA?
¡POR ESTA BASURA!
SHE'S GOT IT! SHE'S GOT THE STUFF!
CAREFUL WITH THAT, GIRL!
USTEDES!
¡LO SACARON A MI HOMBRE Y AHORITA--
--TOMO SU BASURA!
¡QUE BURROS!
¡LO MATARON A LUIS!
SHE'S LOST IT.
WHO CARES? WATCH YOUR EYES.

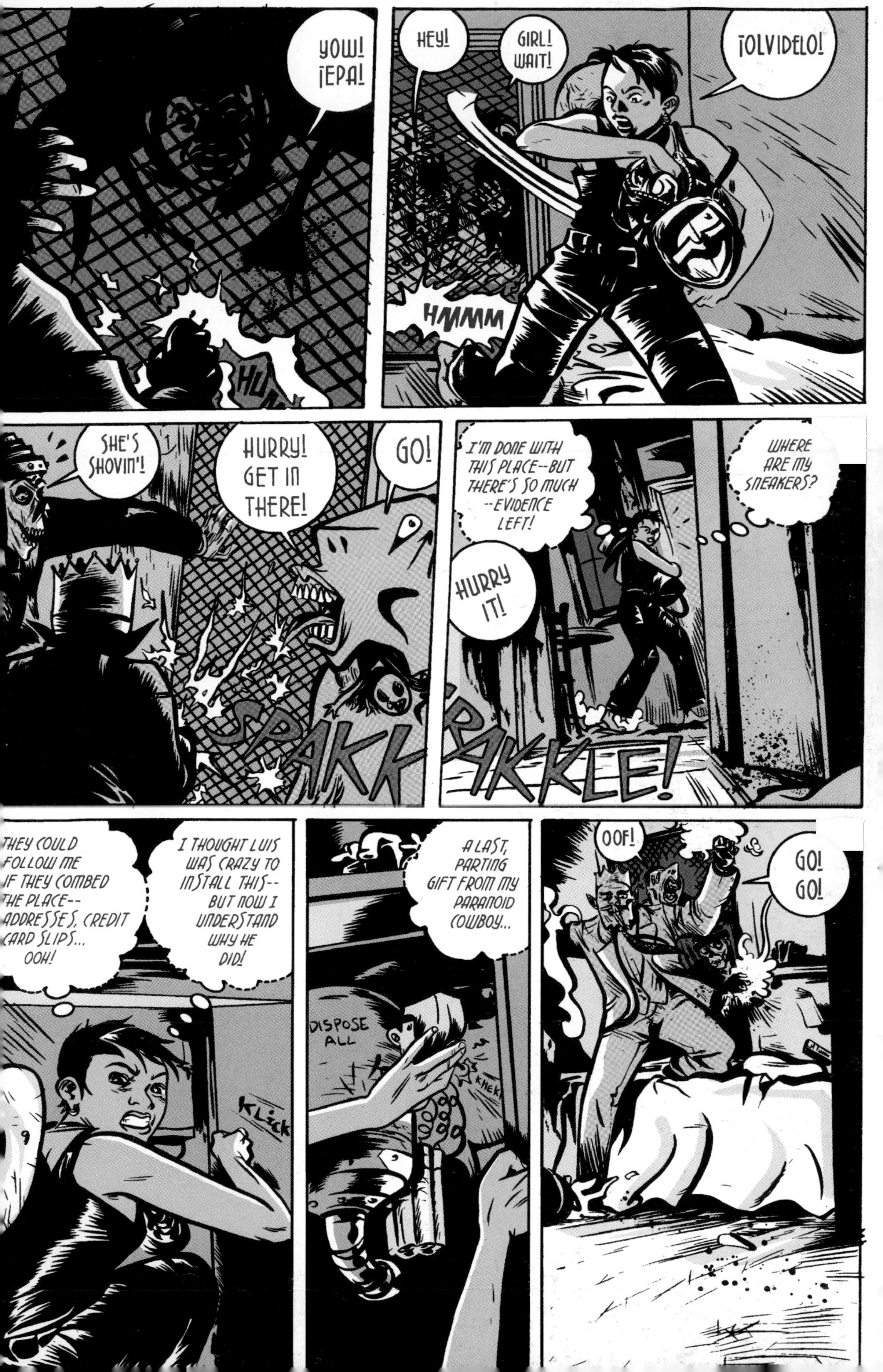
YOW! ¡EPA!
HU
HEY!
GIRL! WAIT!
¡OLVIDELO!
HMMM
SHE'S SHOVIN'!
HURRY! GET IN THERE!
GO!
I'M DONE WITH THIS PLACE--BUT THERE'S SO MUCH --EVIDENCE LEFT!
WHERE ARE MY SNEAKERS?
HURRY IT!
SPAKK KRAKKLE!
THEY COULD FOLLOW ME IF THEY COMBED THE PLACE-- ADDRESSES, CREDIT CARD SLIPS... OOH!
I THOUGHT LUIS WAS CRAZY TO INSTALL THIS-- BUT NOW I UNDERSTAND WHY HE DID!
KLICK
A LAST, PARTING GIFT FROM MY PARANOID COWBOY...
DISPOSE ALL
KHEK
OOF!
GO! GO!

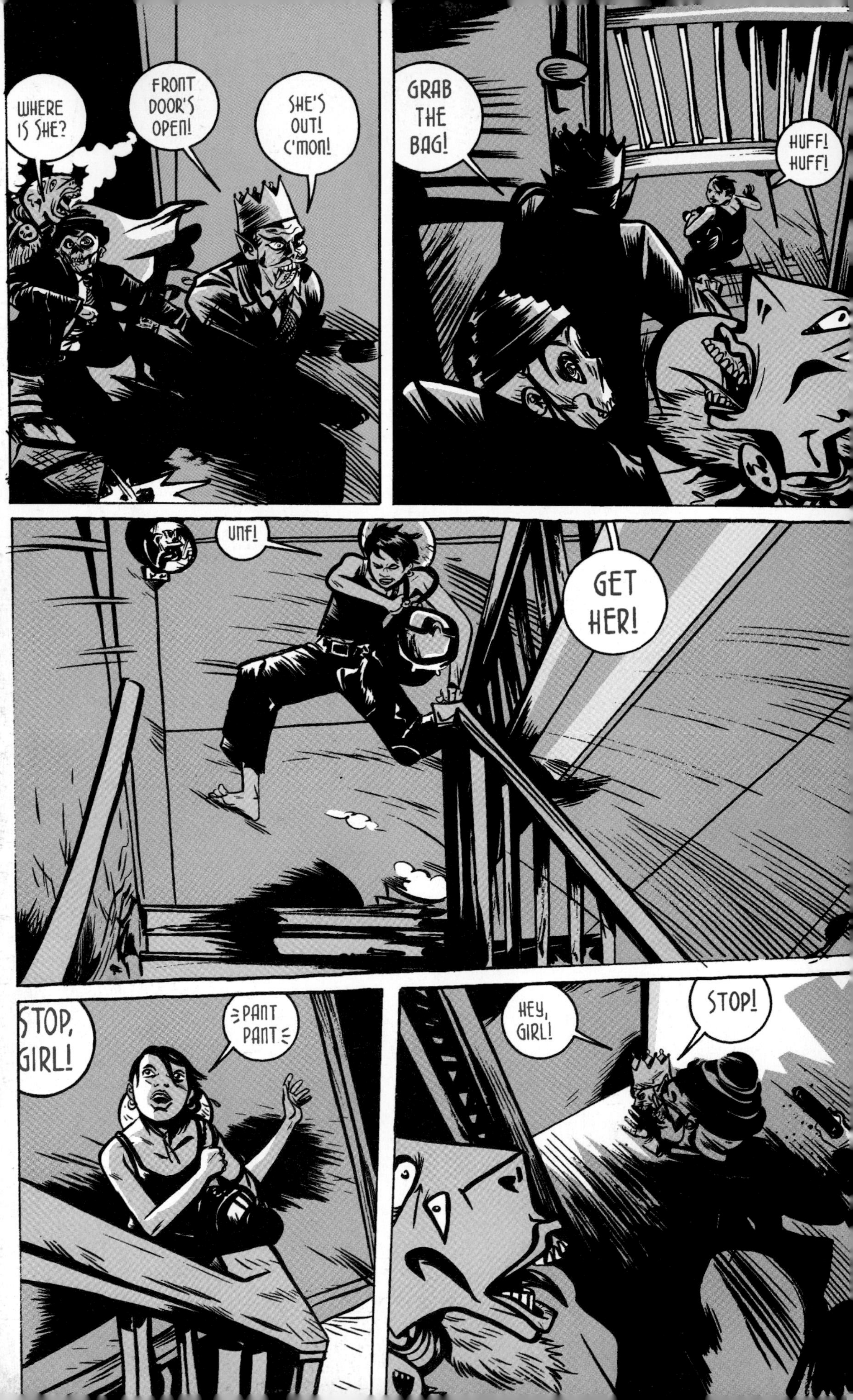
WHERE IS SHE?
FRONT DOOR'S OPEN!
SHE'S OUT! C'MON!
GRAB THE BAG!
HUFF! HUFF!
UNF!
GET HER!
STOP, GIRL!
PANT PANT
HEY, GIRL!
STOP!

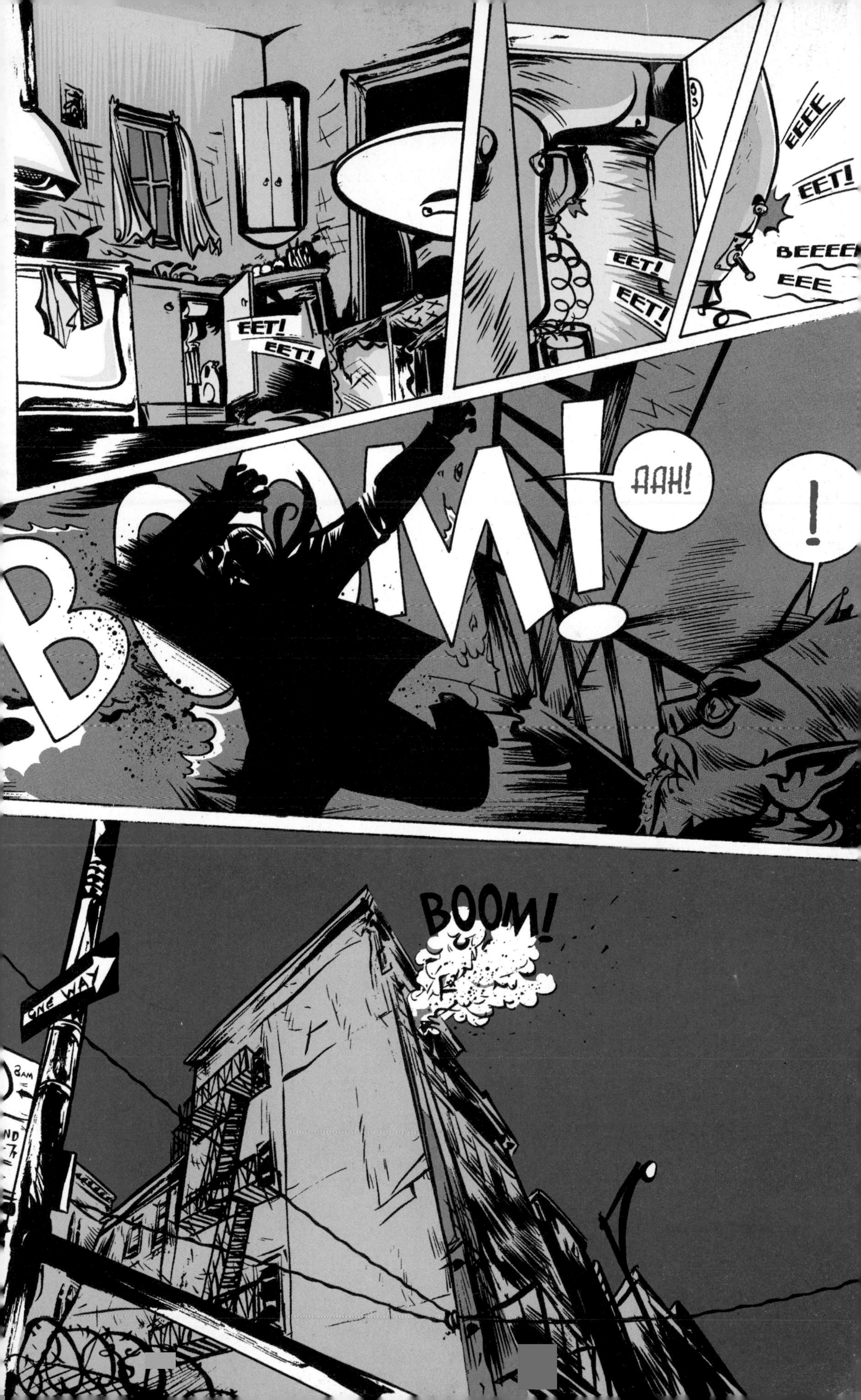
EET!
EET!
EET!
EET!
EEEE
EET!
BEEEE
EEE
BOOM!
AAH!
!
BOOM!
ONE WAY
8AM

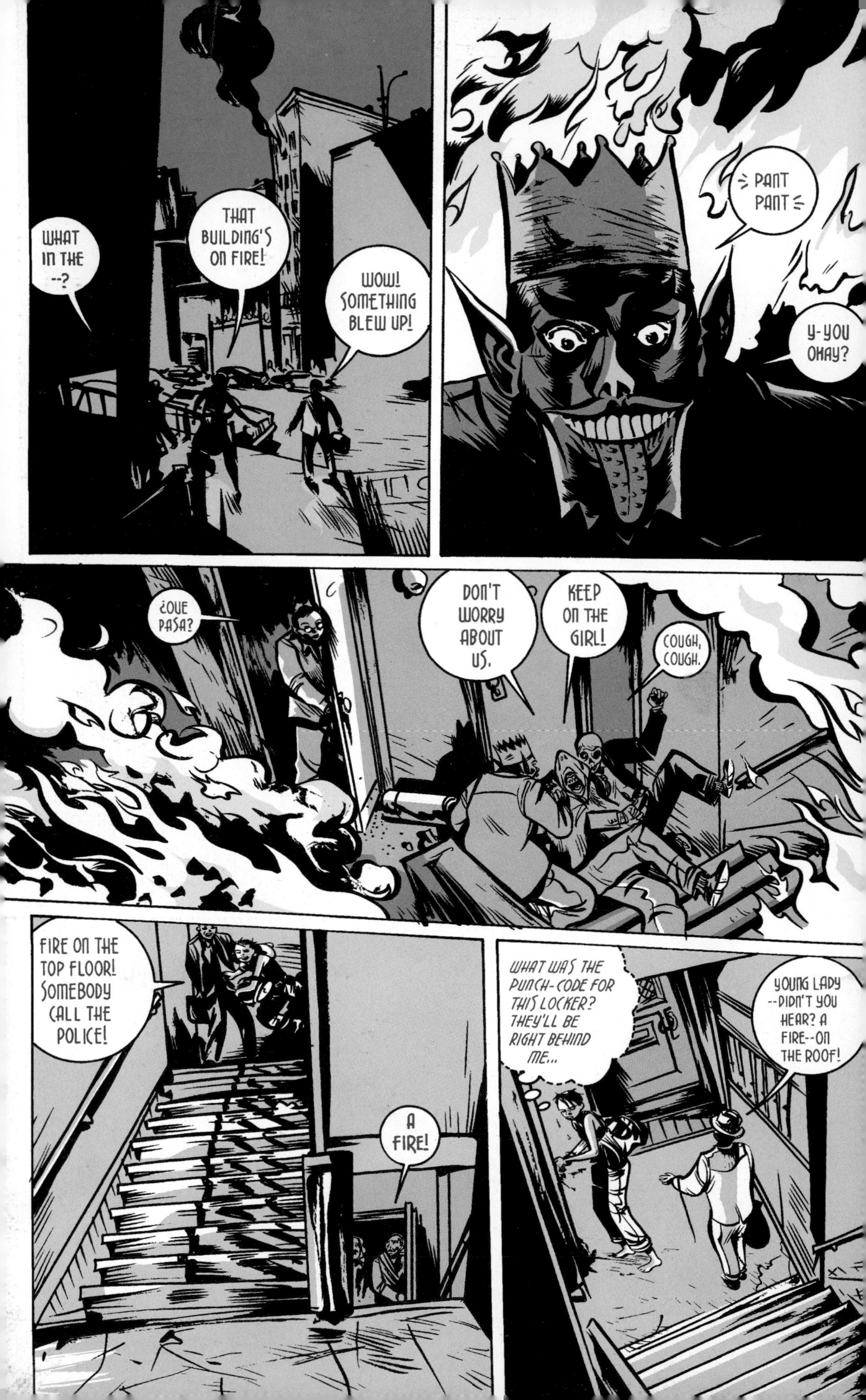
WHAT IN THE --?
THAT BUILDING'S ON FIRE!
WOW! SOMETHING BLEW UP!
PANT PANT
Y-YOU OKAY?
¿QUE PASA?
DON'T WORRY ABOUT US.
KEEP ON THE GIRL!
COUGH, COUGH.
FIRE ON THE TOP FLOOR! SOMEBODY CALL THE POLICE!
A FIRE!
WHAT WAS THE PUNCH-CODE FOR THIS LOCKER? THEY'LL BE RIGHT BEHIND ME...
YOUNG LADY --DIDN'T YOU HEAR? A FIRE--ON THE ROOF!

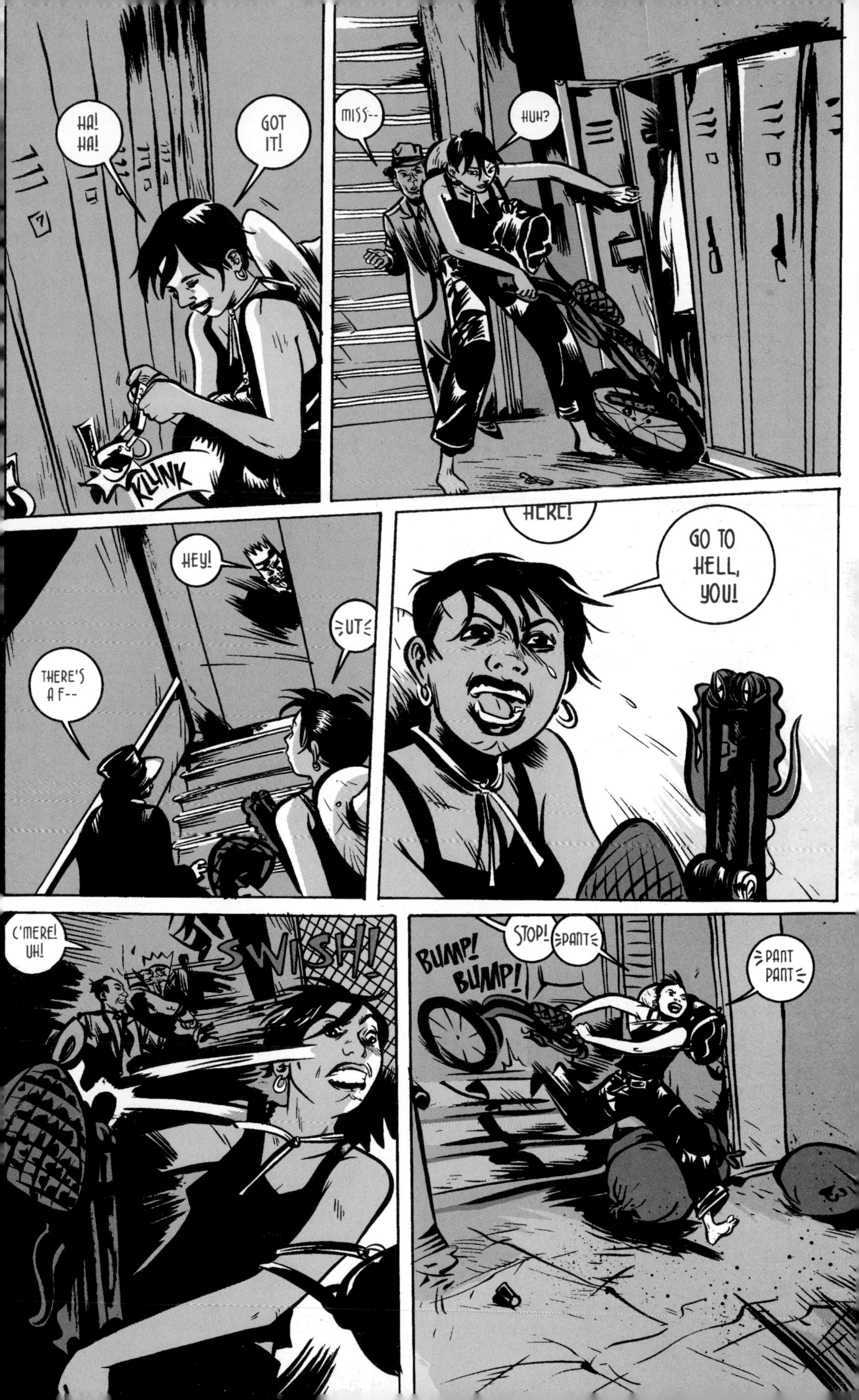
HA! HA!
GOT IT!
KLUNK
MISS--
HUH?
HEY!
THERE'S A F--
UT
HERE!
GO TO HELL, YOU!
C'MERE! UH!
SWISH!
BUMP! BUMP!
STOP!
PANT
PANT PANT

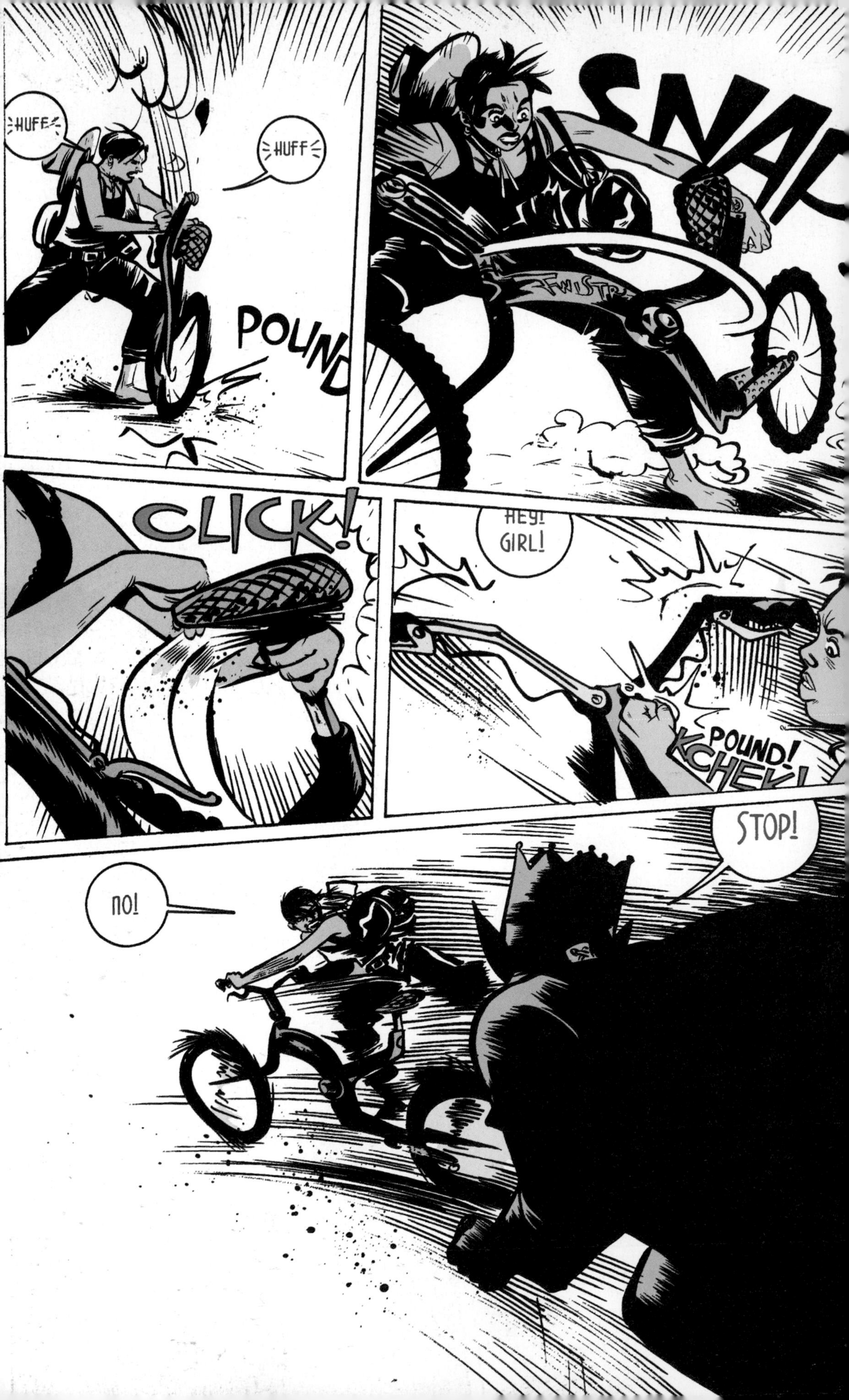
HUFF
HUFF
POUND
SNA
CLICK!
HEY! GIRL!
POUND!
KCHEK!
STOP!
NO!

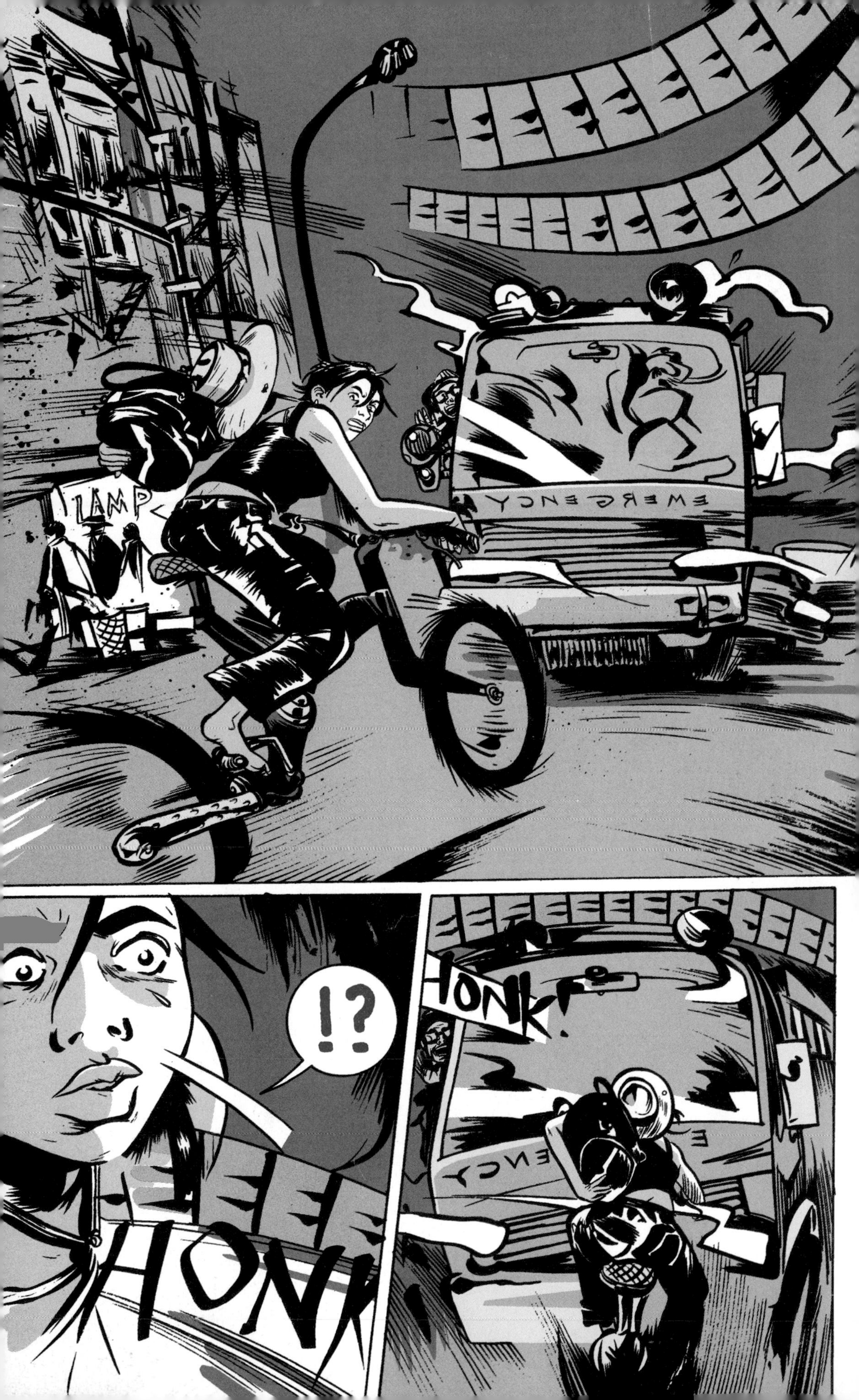
LAMP
!?
HONK!
HONK

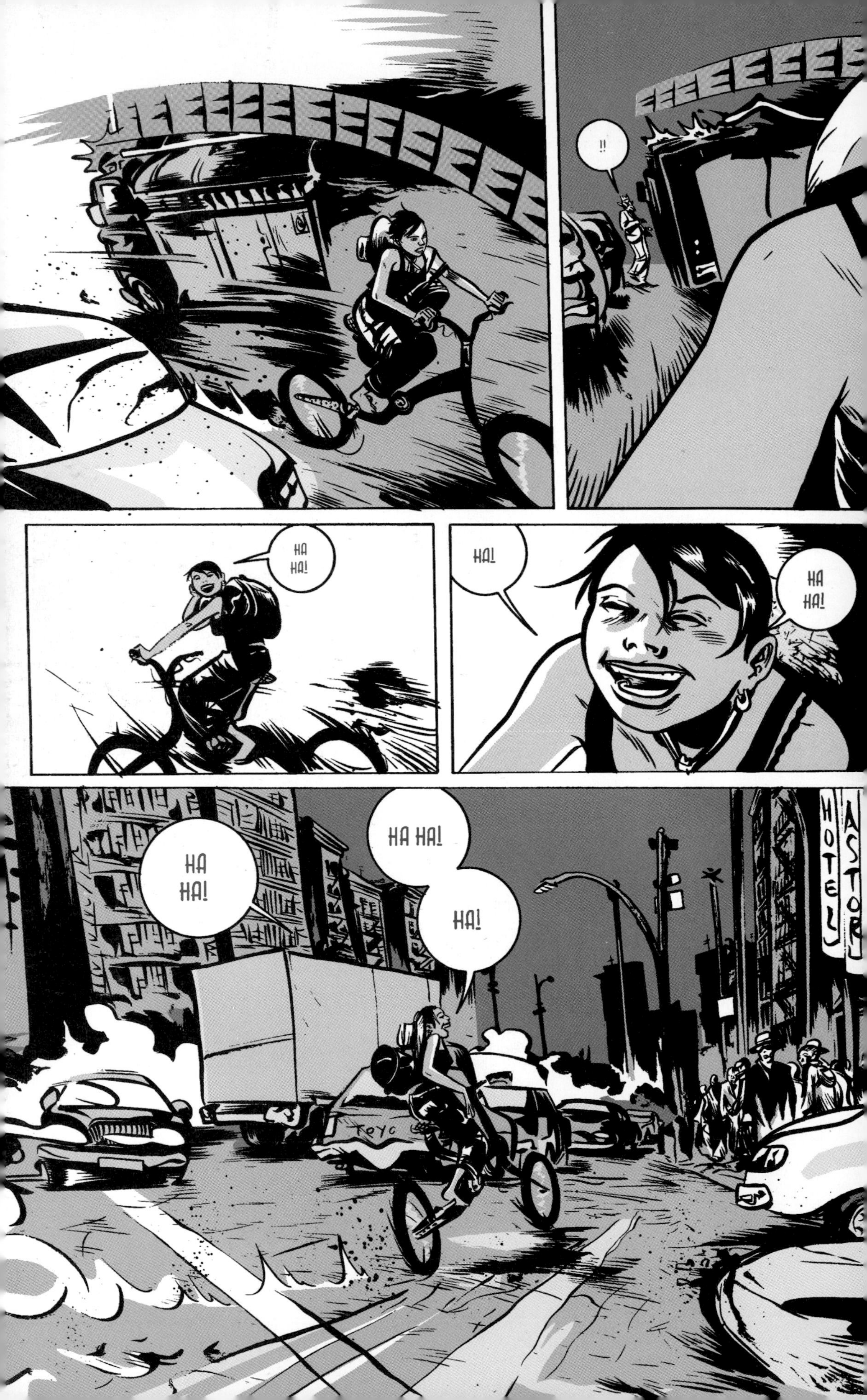

EEEEEEEEEEEEEE
EEEEEEEE
!!
HA
HA!
HA!
HA
HA!
HA
HA!
HA HA!
HA!
HOTEL
ASTOR

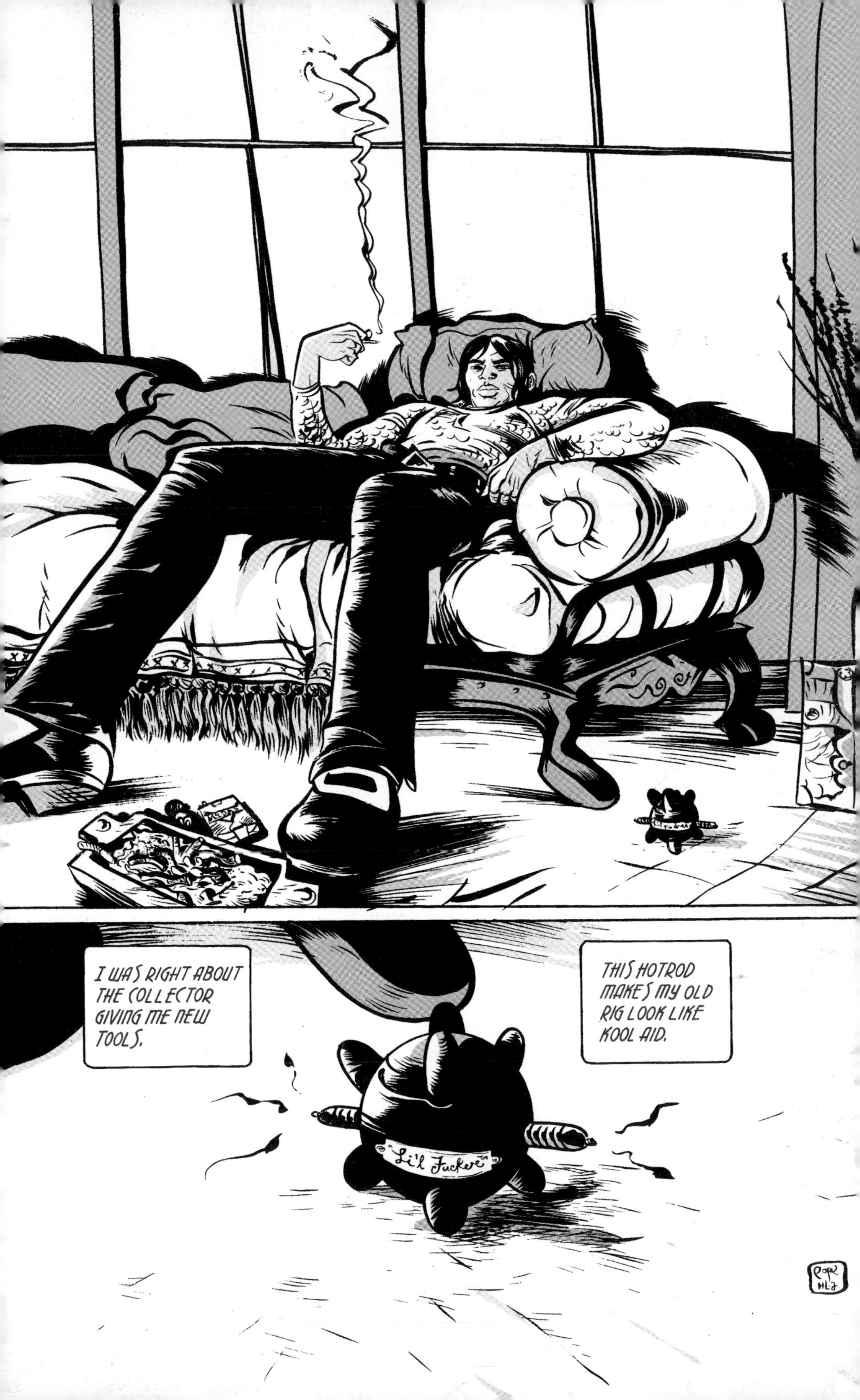
I WAS RIGHT ABOUT THE COLLECTOR GIVING ME NEW TOOLS.
THIS HOTROD MAKES MY OLD RIG LOOK LIKE KOOL AID.
"Li'l Fucker"

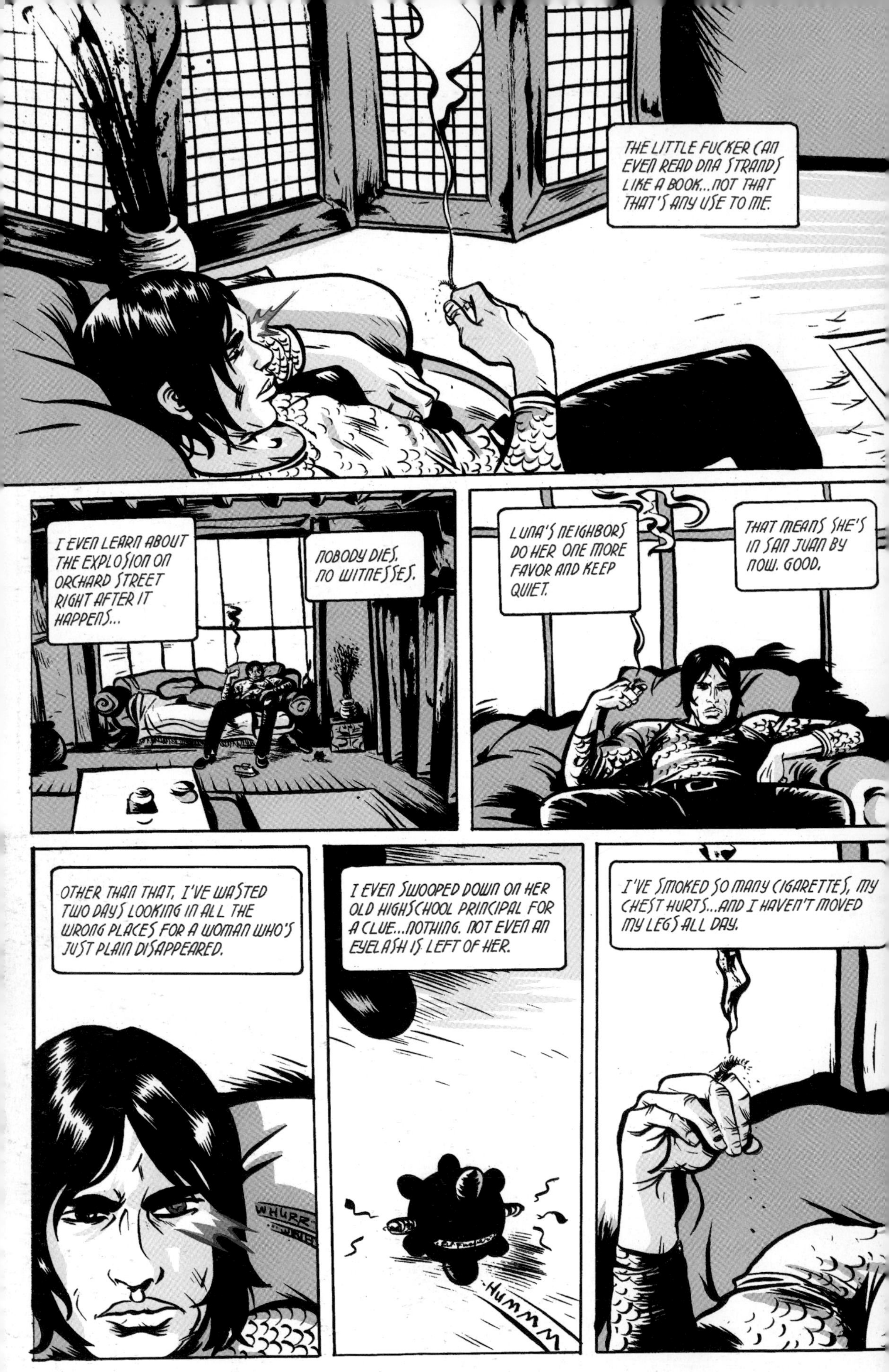
THE LITTLE FUCKER CAN EVEN READ DNA STRANDS LIKE A BOOK...NOT THAT THAT'S ANY USE TO ME.
I EVEN LEARN ABOUT THE EXPLOSION ON ORCHARD STREET RIGHT AFTER IT HAPPENS...
NOBODY DIES, NO WITNESSES.
LUNA'S NEIGHBORS DO HER ONE MORE FAVOR AND KEEP QUIET.
THAT MEANS SHE'S IN SAN JUAN BY NOW. GOOD.
OTHER THAN THAT, I'VE WASTED TWO DAYS LOOKING IN ALL THE WRONG PLACES FOR A WOMAN WHO'S JUST PLAIN DISAPPEARED.
I EVEN SWOOPED DOWN ON HER OLD HIGHSCHOOL PRINCIPAL FOR A CLUE...NOTHING. NOT EVEN AN EYELASH IS LEFT OF HER.
I'VE SMOKED SO MANY CIGARETTES, MY CHEST HURTS...AND I HAVEN'T MOVED MY LEGS ALL DAY.

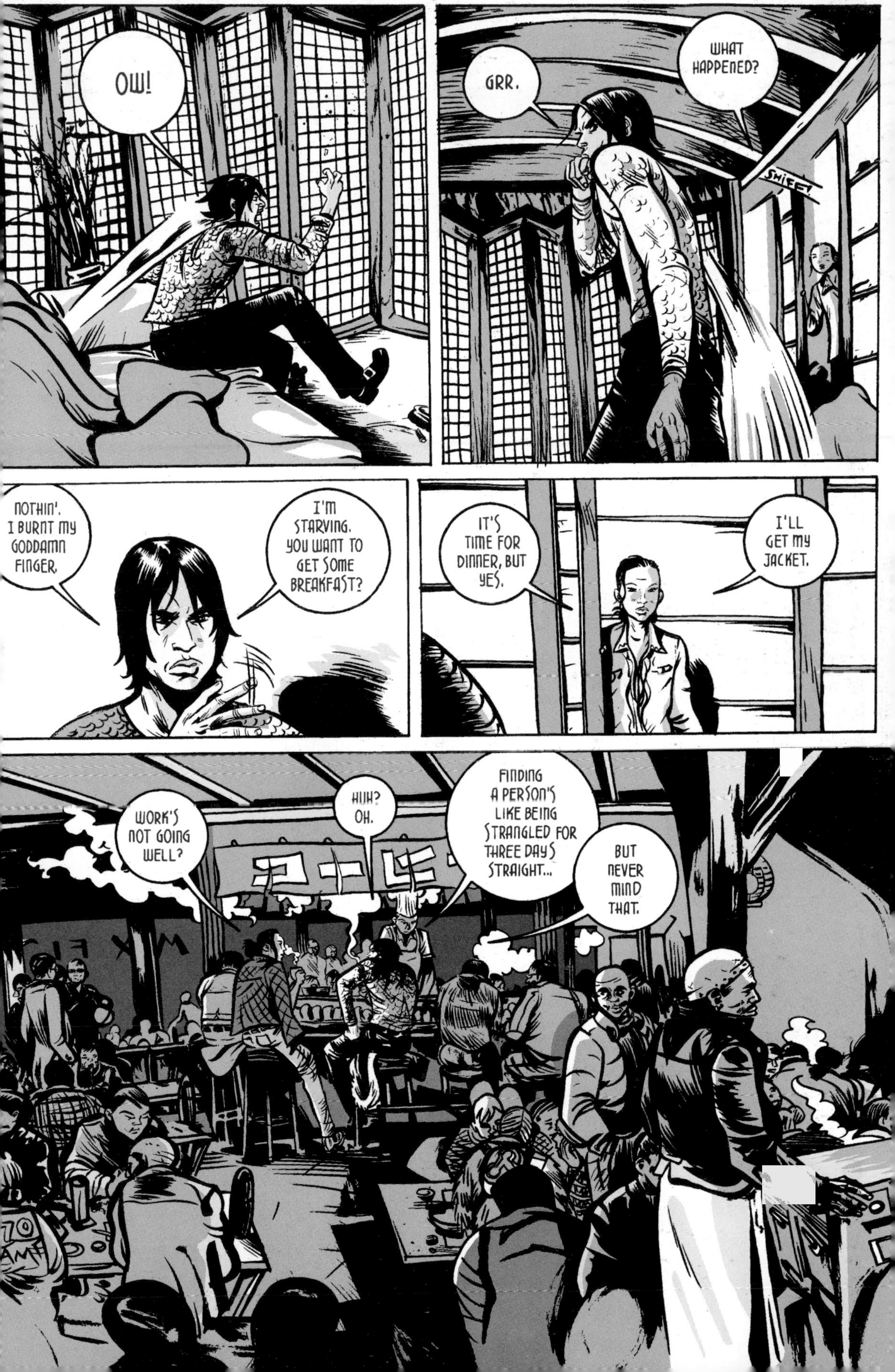
OW!
GRR.
WHAT HAPPENED?
SHIFF!
NOTHIN'. I BURNT MY GODDAMN FINGER.
I'M STARVING. YOU WANT TO GET SOME BREAKFAST?
IT'S TIME FOR DINNER, BUT YES.
I'LL GET MY JACKET.
WORK'S NOT GOING WELL?
HUH? OH.
FINDING A PERSON'S LIKE BEING STRANGLED FOR THREE DAYS STRAIGHT...
BUT NEVER MIND THAT.

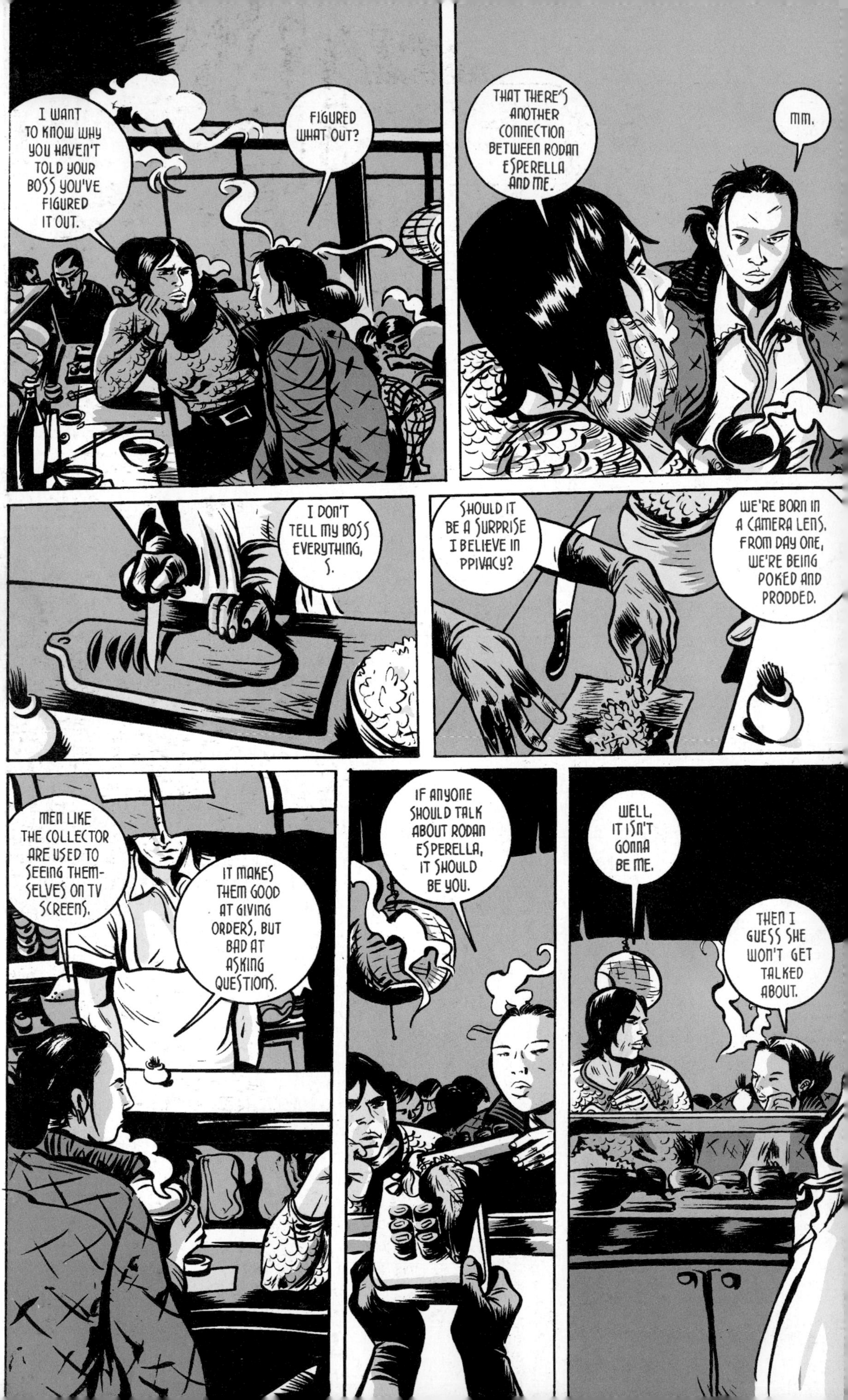

I WANT TO KNOW WHY YOU HAVEN'T TOLD YOUR BOSS YOU'VE FIGURED IT OUT.
FIGURED WHAT OUT?
THAT THERE'S ANOTHER CONNECTION BETWEEN RODAN ESPERELLA AND ME.
MM.
I DON'T TELL MY BOSS EVERYTHING, S.
SHOULD IT BE A SURPRISE I BELIEVE IN PPIVACY?
WE'RE BORN IN A CAMERA LENS. FROM DAY ONE, WE'RE BEING POKED AND PRODDED.
MEN LIKE THE COLLECTOR ARE USED TO SEEING THEM-SELVES ON TV SCREENS.
IT MAKES THEM GOOD AT GIVING ORDERS, BUT BAD AT ASKING QUESTIONS.
IF ANYONE SHOULD TALK ABOUT RODAN ESPERELLA, IT SHOULD BE YOU.
WELL, IT ISN'T GONNA BE ME.
THEN I GUESS SHE WON'T GET TALKED ABOUT.

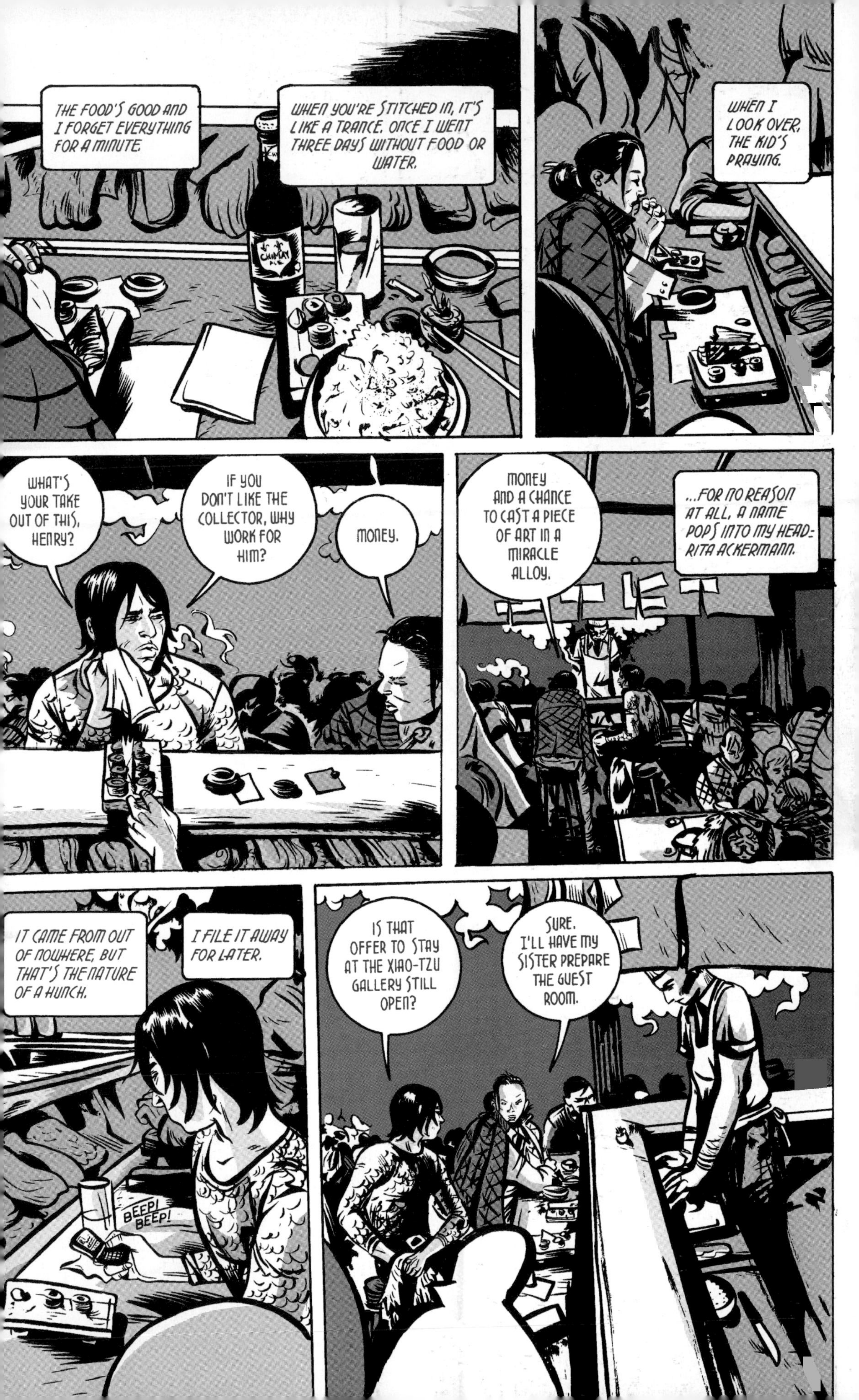
THE FOOD'S GOOD AND I FORGET EVERYTHING FOR A MINUTE.
WHEN YOU'RE STITCHED IN, IT'S LIKE A TRANCE. ONCE I WENT THREE DAYS WITHOUT FOOD OR WATER.
CHIMAY
WHEN I LOOK OVER, THE KID'S PRAYING.
WHAT'S YOUR TAKE OUT OF THIS, HENRY?
IF YOU DON'T LIKE THE COLLECTOR, WHY WORK FOR HIM?
MONEY.
MONEY AND A CHANCE TO CAST A PIECE OF ART IN A MIRACLE ALLOY.
...FOR NO REASON AT ALL, A NAME POPS INTO MY HEAD-- RITA ACKERMANN.
IT CAME FROM OUT OF NOWHERE, BUT THAT'S THE NATURE OF A HUNCH.
I FILE IT AWAY FOR LATER.
BEEP! BEEP!
IS THAT OFFER TO STAY AT THE XIAO-TZU GALLERY STILL OPEN?
SURE. I'LL HAVE MY SISTER PREPARE THE GUEST ROOM.

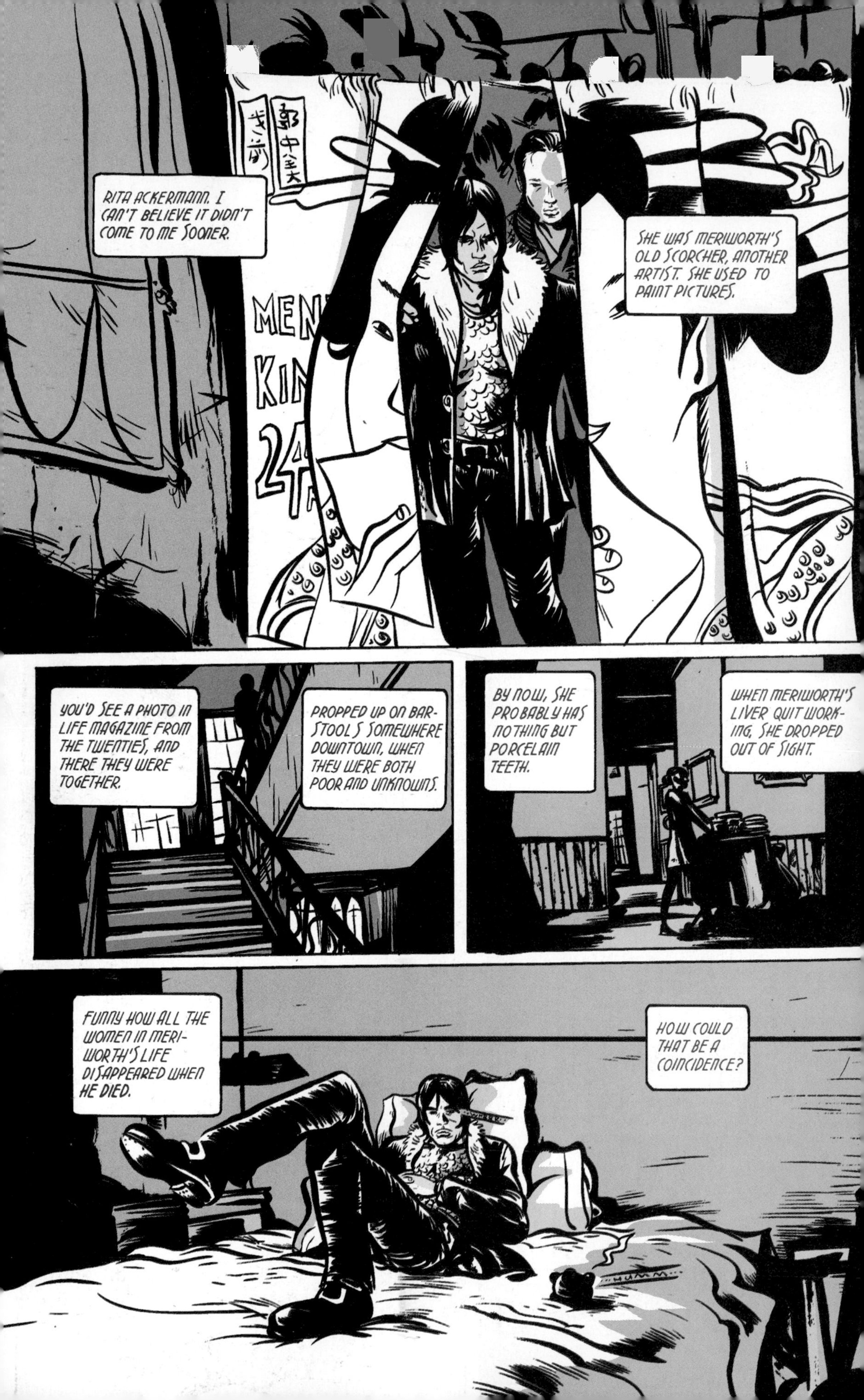
RITA ACKERMANN. I CAN'T BELIEVE IT DIDN'T COME TO ME SOONER.
SHE WAS MERIWORTH'S OLD SCORCHER, ANOTHER ARTIST. SHE USED TO PAINT PICTURES.
YOU'D SEE A PHOTO IN LIFE MAGAZINE FROM THE TWENTIES, AND THERE THEY WERE TOGETHER.
PROPPED UP ON BAR-STOOLS SOMEWHERE DOWNTOWN, WHEN THEY WERE BOTH POOR AND UNKNOWNS.
BY NOW, SHE PROBABLY HAS NOTHING BUT PORCELAIN TEETH.
WHEN MERIWORTH'S LIVER QUIT WORKING, SHE DROPPED OUT OF SIGHT.
FUNNY HOW ALL THE WOMEN IN MERIWORTH'S LIFE DISAPPEARED WHEN HE DIED.
HOW COULD THAT BE A COINCIDENCE?
...HUMM...

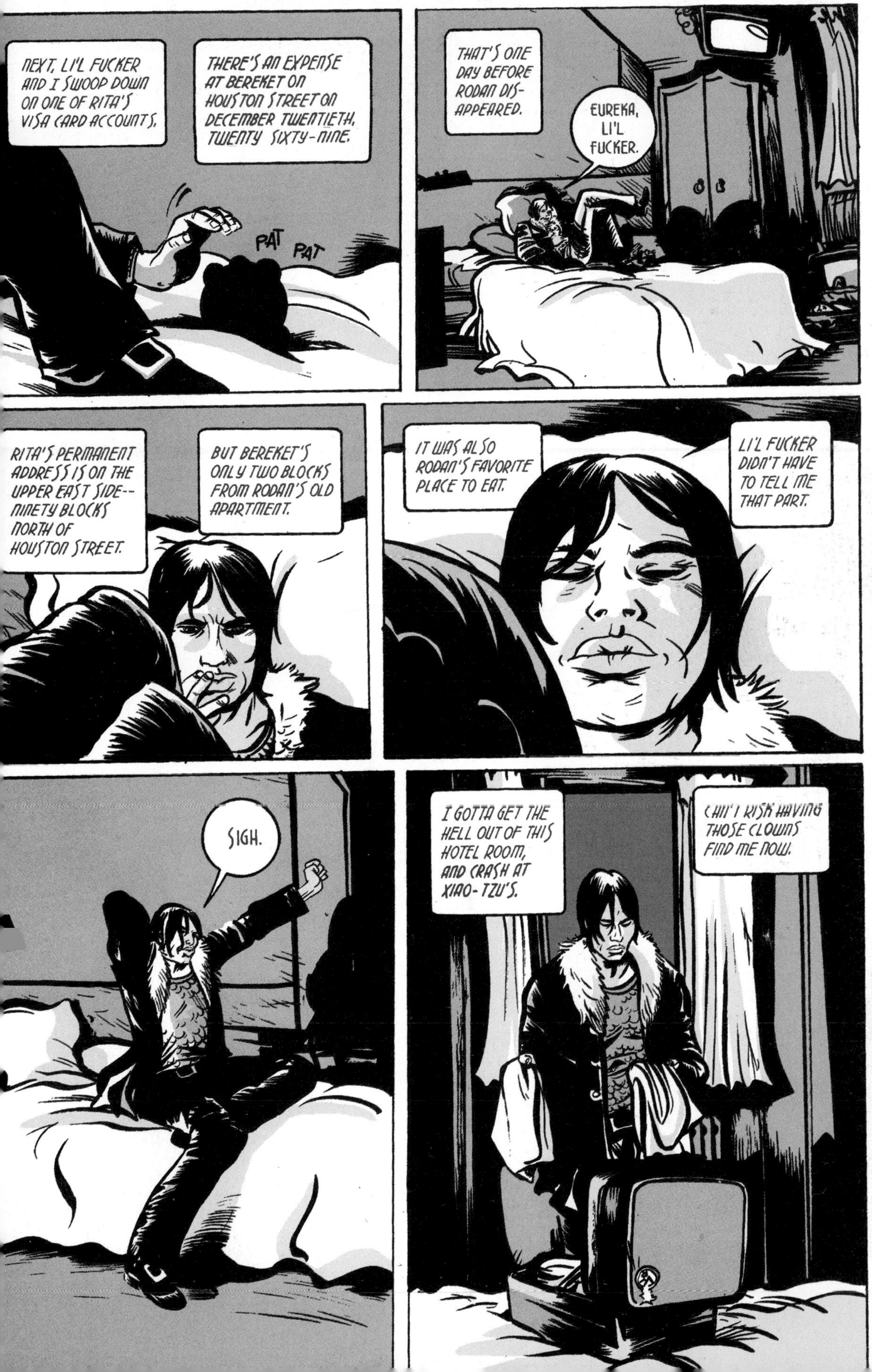
NEXT, LI'L FUCKER AND I SWOOP DOWN ON ONE OF RITA'S VISA CARD ACCOUNTS.
THERE'S AN EXPENSE AT BEREKET ON HOUSTON STREET ON DECEMBER TWENTIETH, TWENTY SIXTY-NINE.
PAT PAT
THAT'S ONE DAY BEFORE RODAN DIS-APPEARED.
EUREKA, LI'L FUCKER.
RITA'S PERMANENT ADDRESS IS ON THE UPPER EAST SIDE-- NINETY BLOCKS NORTH OF HOUSTON STREET.
BUT BEREKET'S ONLY TWO BLOCKS FROM RODAN'S OLD APARTMENT.
IT WAS ALSO RODAN'S FAVORITE PLACE TO EAT.
LI'L FUCKER DIDN'T HAVE TO TELL ME THAT PART.
SIGH.
I GOTTA GET THE HELL OUT OF THIS HOTEL ROOM, AND CRASH AT XIAO-TZU'S.
CAN'T RISK HAVING THOSE CLOWNS FIND ME NOW.

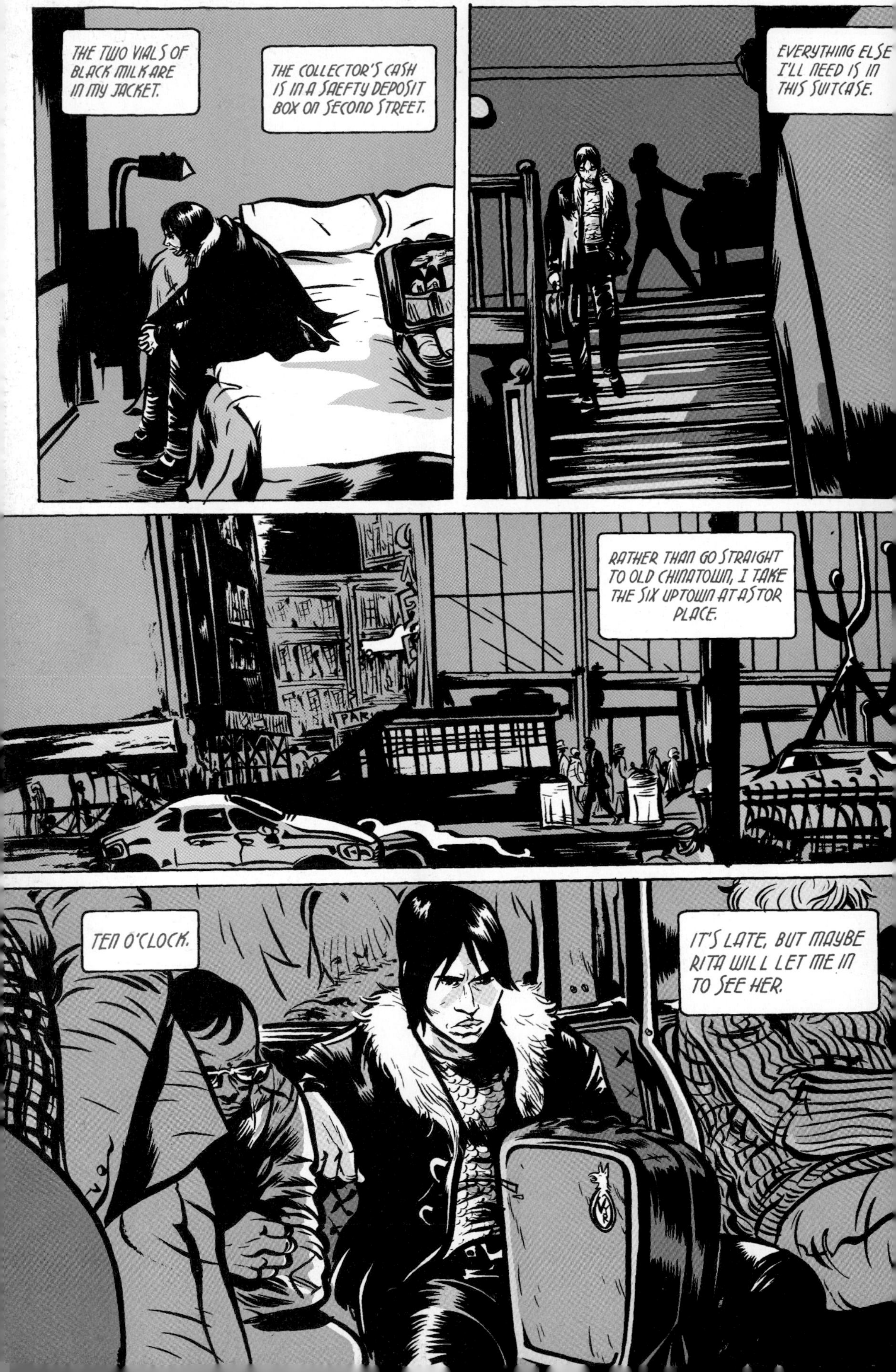
THE TWO VIALS OF BLACK MILK ARE IN MY JACKET.
THE COLLECTOR'S CASH IS IN A SAEFTY DEPOSIT BOX ON SECOND STREET.
EVERYTHING ELSE I'LL NEED IS IN THIS SUITCASE.
RATHER THAN GO STRAIGHT TO OLD CHINATOWN, I TAKE THE SIX UPTOWN AT ASTOR PLACE.
TEN O'CLOCK.
IT'S LATE, BUT MAYBE RITA WILL LET ME IN TO SEE HER.

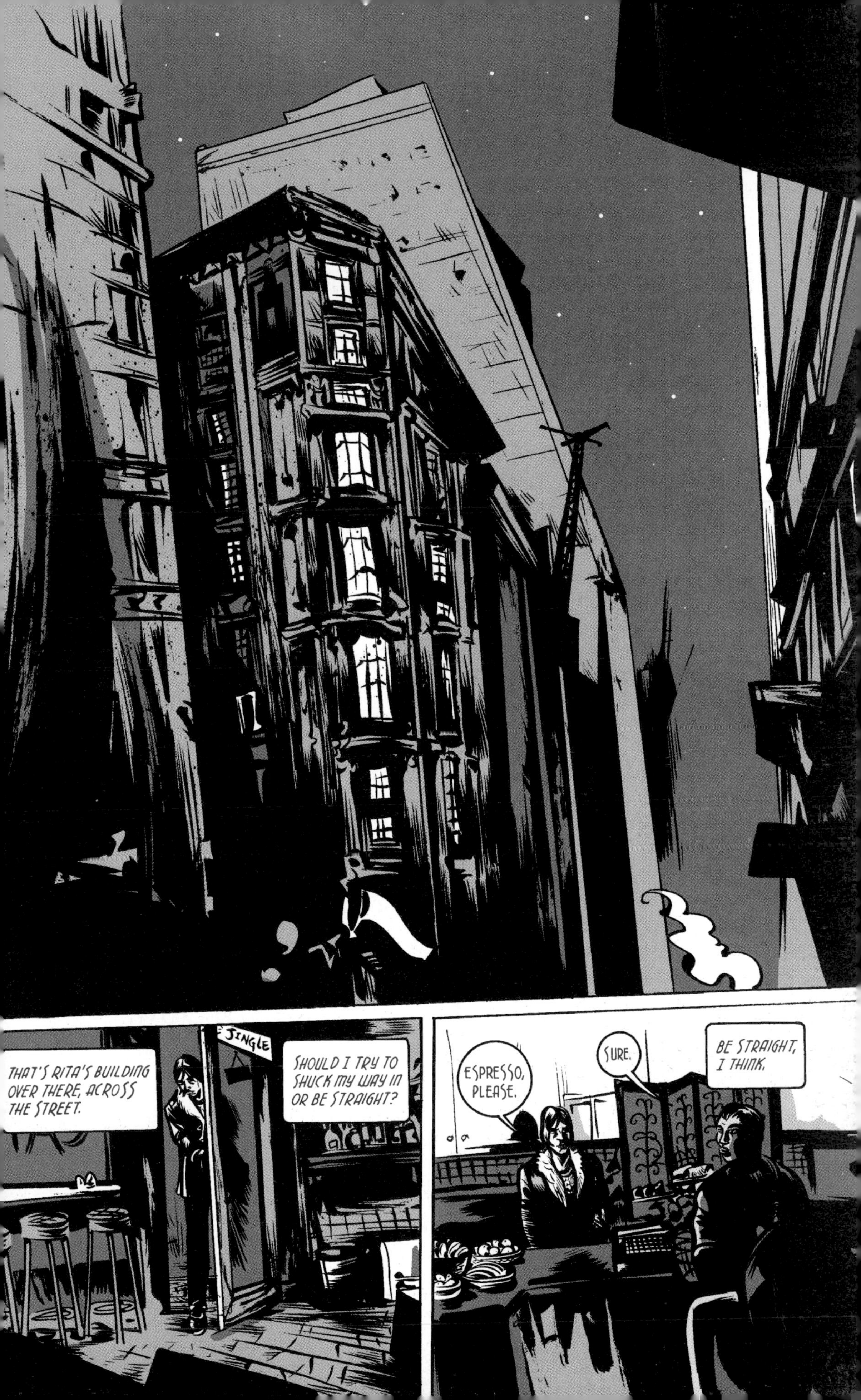

THAT'S RITA'S BUILDING OVER THERE, ACROSS THE STREET.
JINGLE
SHOULD I TRY TO SHUCK MY WAY IN OR BE STRAIGHT?
ESPRESSO, PLEASE.
SURE.
BE STRAIGHT, I THINK.

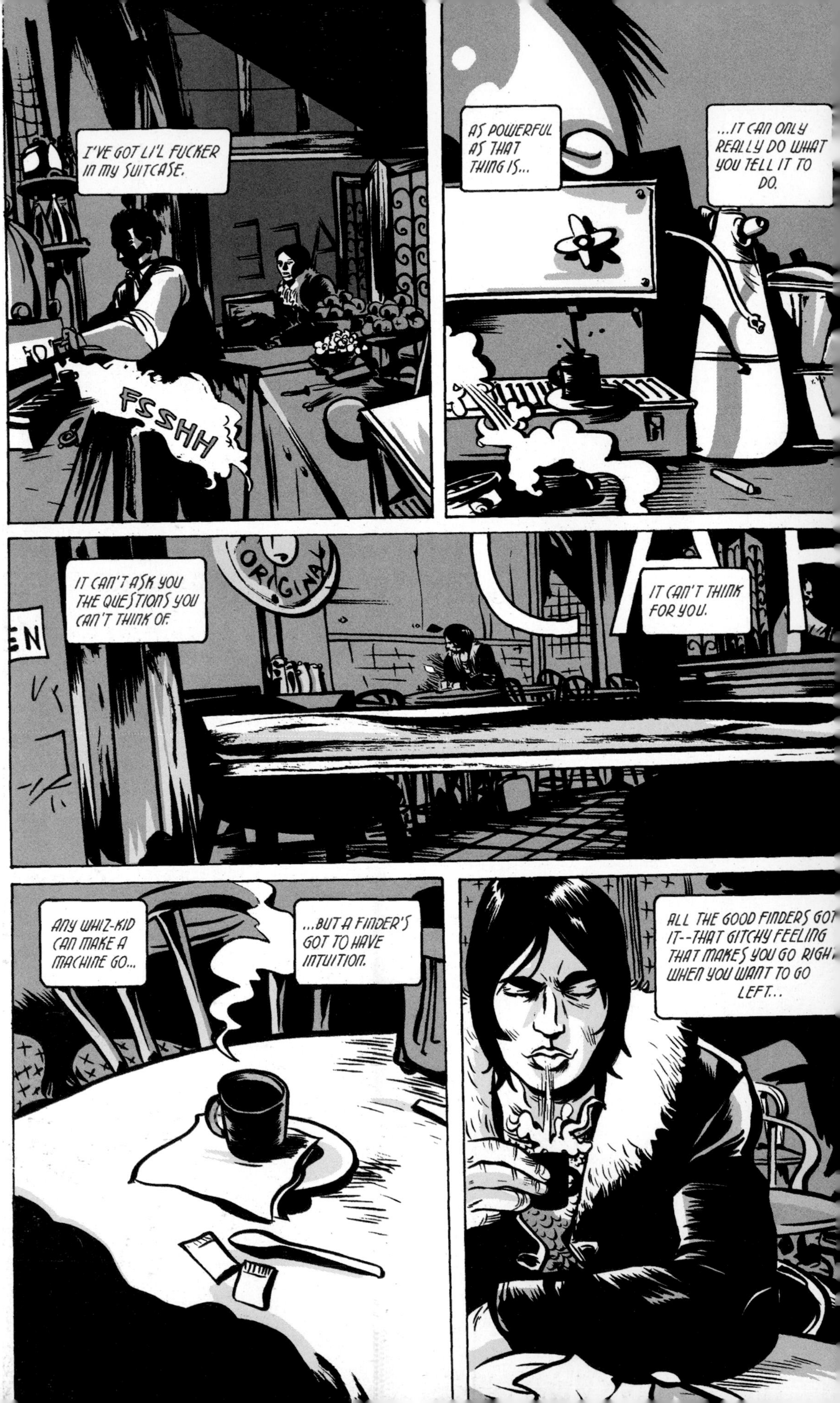
I'VE GOT LI'L FUCKER IN MY SUITCASE.
FSSHH
AS POWERFUL AS THAT THING IS...
...IT CAN ONLY REALLY DO WHAT YOU TELL IT TO DO.
ORIGINAL
IT CAN'T ASK YOU THE QUESTIONS YOU CAN'T THINK OF.
IT CAN'T THINK FOR YOU.
ANY WHIZ-KID CAN MAKE A MACHINE GO...
...BUT A FINDER'S GOT TO HAVE INTUITION.
ALL THE GOOD FINDERS GOT IT--THAT GITCHY FEELING THAT MAKES YOU GO RIGHT WHEN YOU WANT TO GO LEFT...

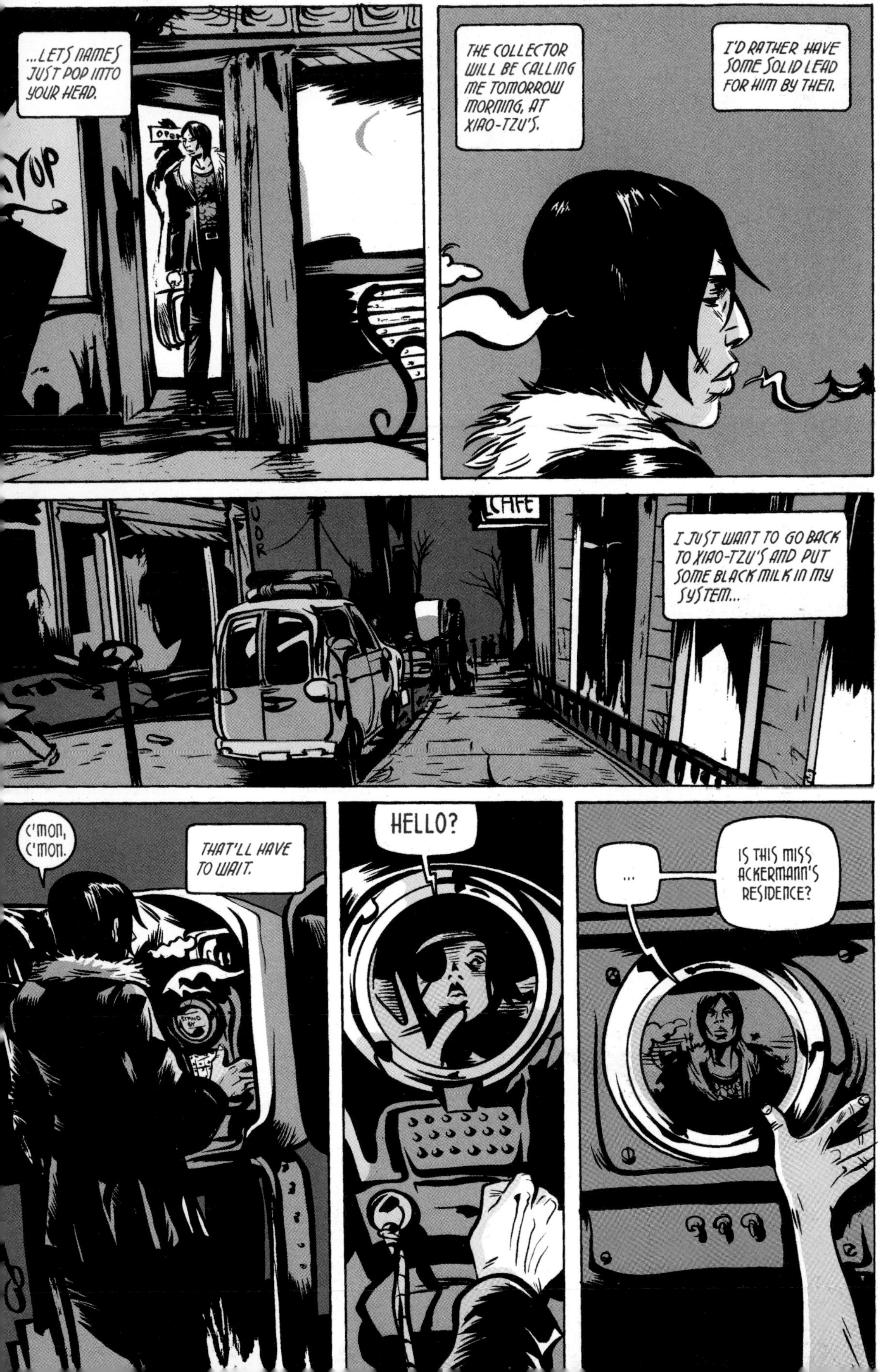
...LETS NAMES JUST POP INTO YOUR HEAD.
OPEN
THE COLLECTOR WILL BE CALLING ME TOMORROW MORNING, AT XIAO-TZU'S.
I'D RATHER HAVE SOME SOLID LEAD FOR HIM BY THEN.
CAFE
I JUST WANT TO GO BACK TO XIAO-TZU'S AND PUT SOME BLACK MILK IN MY SYSTEM...
C'MON, C'MON.
THAT'LL HAVE TO WAIT.
HELLO?
...
IS THIS MISS ACKERMANN'S RESIDENCE?

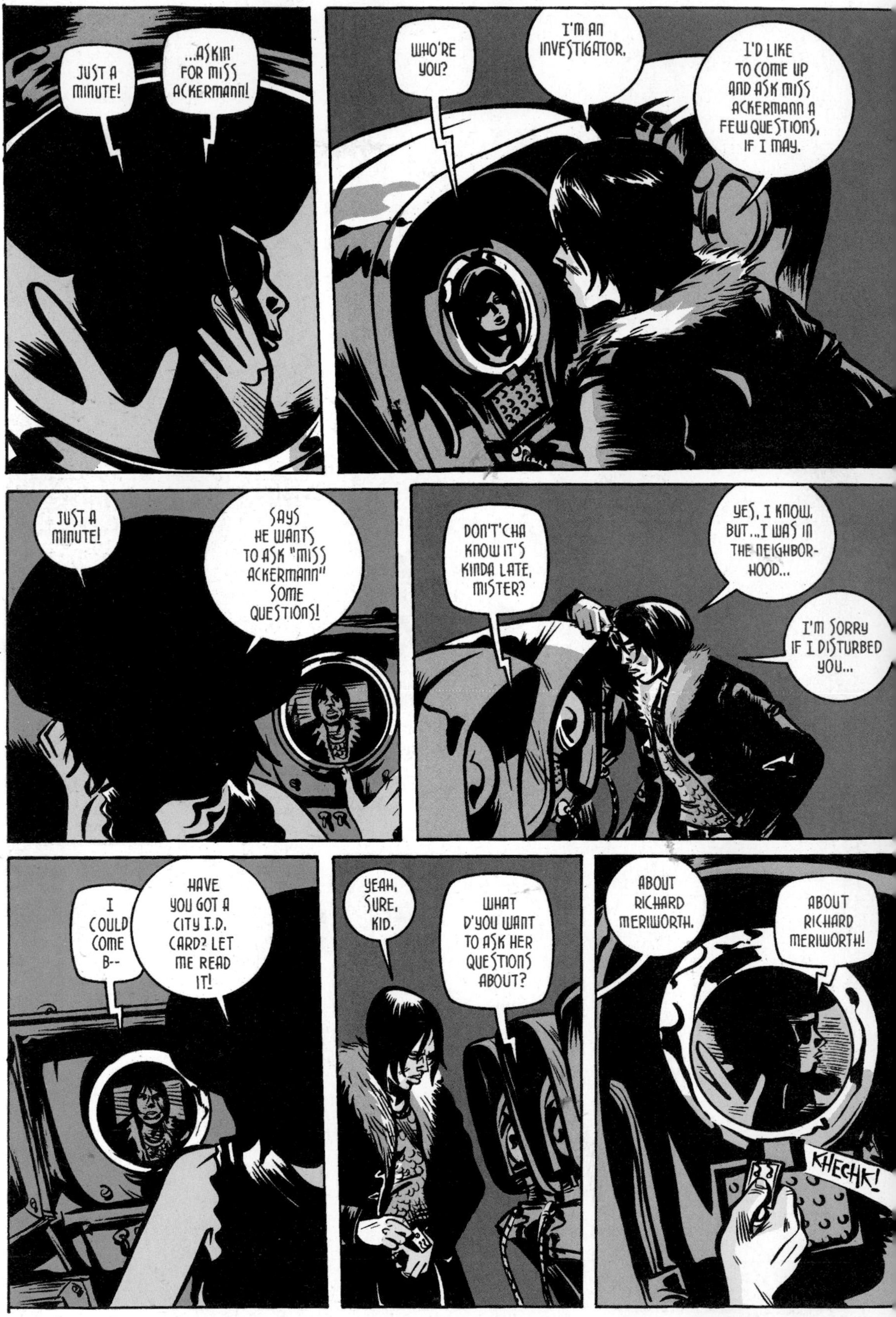
JUST A MINUTE!
...ASKIN' FOR MISS ACKERMANN!
WHO'RE YOU?
I'M AN INVESTIGATOR.
I'D LIKE TO COME UP AND ASK MISS ACKERMANN A FEW QUESTIONS, IF I MAY.
JUST A MINUTE!
SAYS HE WANTS TO ASK "MISS ACKERMANN" SOME QUESTIONS!
DON'T'CHA KNOW IT'S KINDA LATE, MISTER?
YES, I KNOW. BUT...I WAS IN THE NEIGHBOR-HOOD...
I'M SORRY IF I DISTURBED YOU...
I COULD COME B--
HAVE YOU GOT A CITY I.D. CARD? LET ME READ IT!
YEAH, SURE, KID.
WHAT D'YOU WANT TO ASK HER QUESTIONS ABOUT?
ABOUT RICHARD MERIWORTH.
ABOUT RICHARD MERIWORTH!
KHECHK!

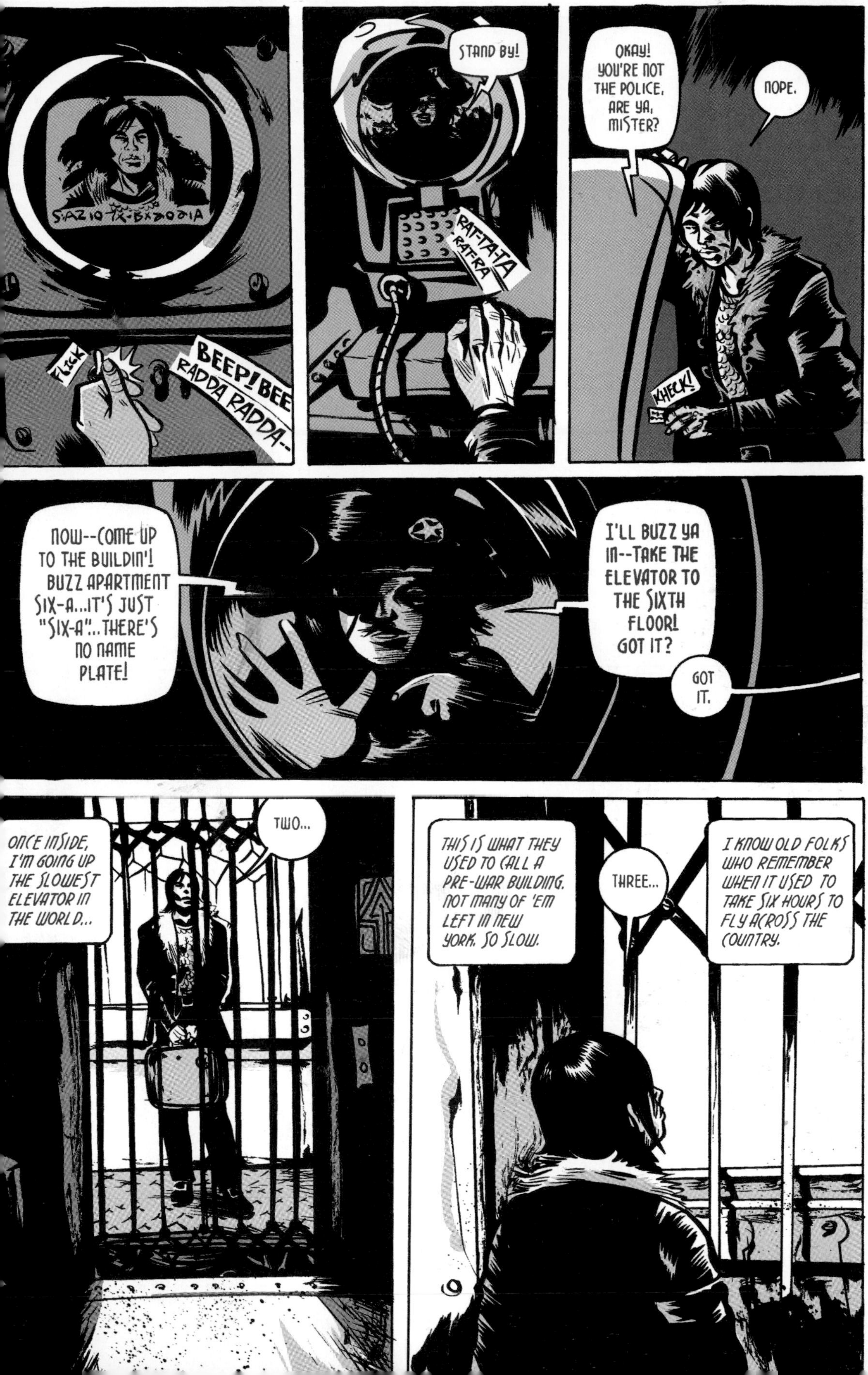
FLICK
BEEP! BEE
RADDA RADDA--
STAND BY!
RAT-TA-TA
RAT-RA
OKAY! YOU'RE NOT THE POLICE, ARE YA, MISTER?
NOPE.
KHECK!
NOW--COME UP TO THE BUILDIN'! BUZZ APARTMENT SIX-A...IT'S JUST "SIX-A"...THERE'S NO NAME PLATE!
I'LL BUZZ YA IN--TAKE THE ELEVATOR TO THE SIXTH FLOOR! GOT IT?
GOT IT.
ONCE INSIDE, I'M GOING UP THE SLOWEST ELEVATOR IN THE WORLD...
TWO...
THIS IS WHAT THEY USED TO CALL A PRE-WAR BUILDING. NOT MANY OF 'EM LEFT IN NEW YORK. SO SLOW.
THREE...
I KNOW OLD FOLKS WHO REMEMBER WHEN IT USED TO TAKE SIX HOURS TO FLY ACROSS THE COUNTRY.

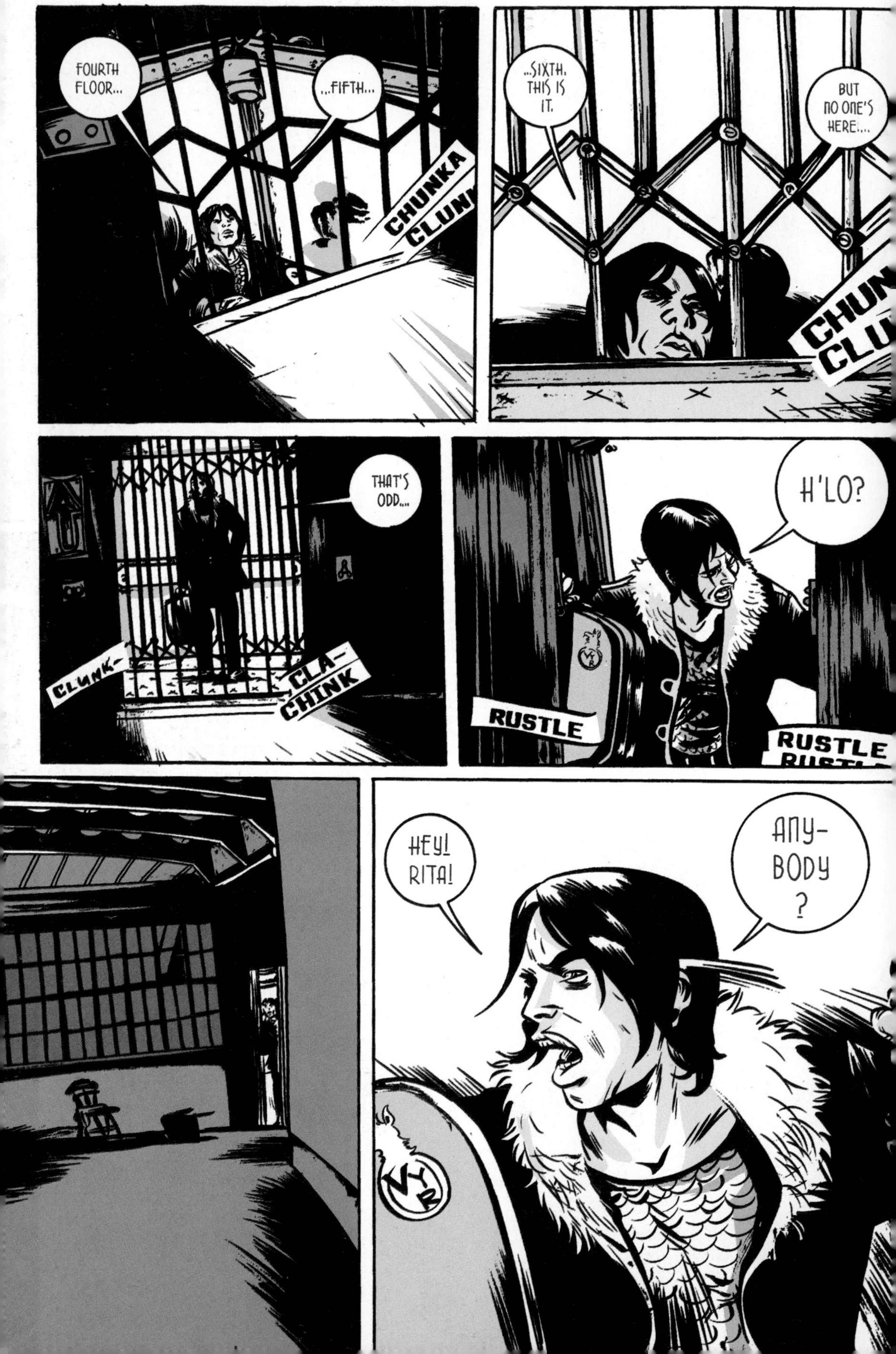
FOURTH FLOOR...
...FIFTH...
CHUNKA CLUNK
...SIXTH, THIS IS IT.
BUT NO ONE'S HERE...
CHUNKA CLUNK
THAT'S ODD...
CLUNK-
CLA-CHINK
H'LO?
RUSTLE
RUSTLE RUSTLE
HEY! RITA!
ANY-BODY?

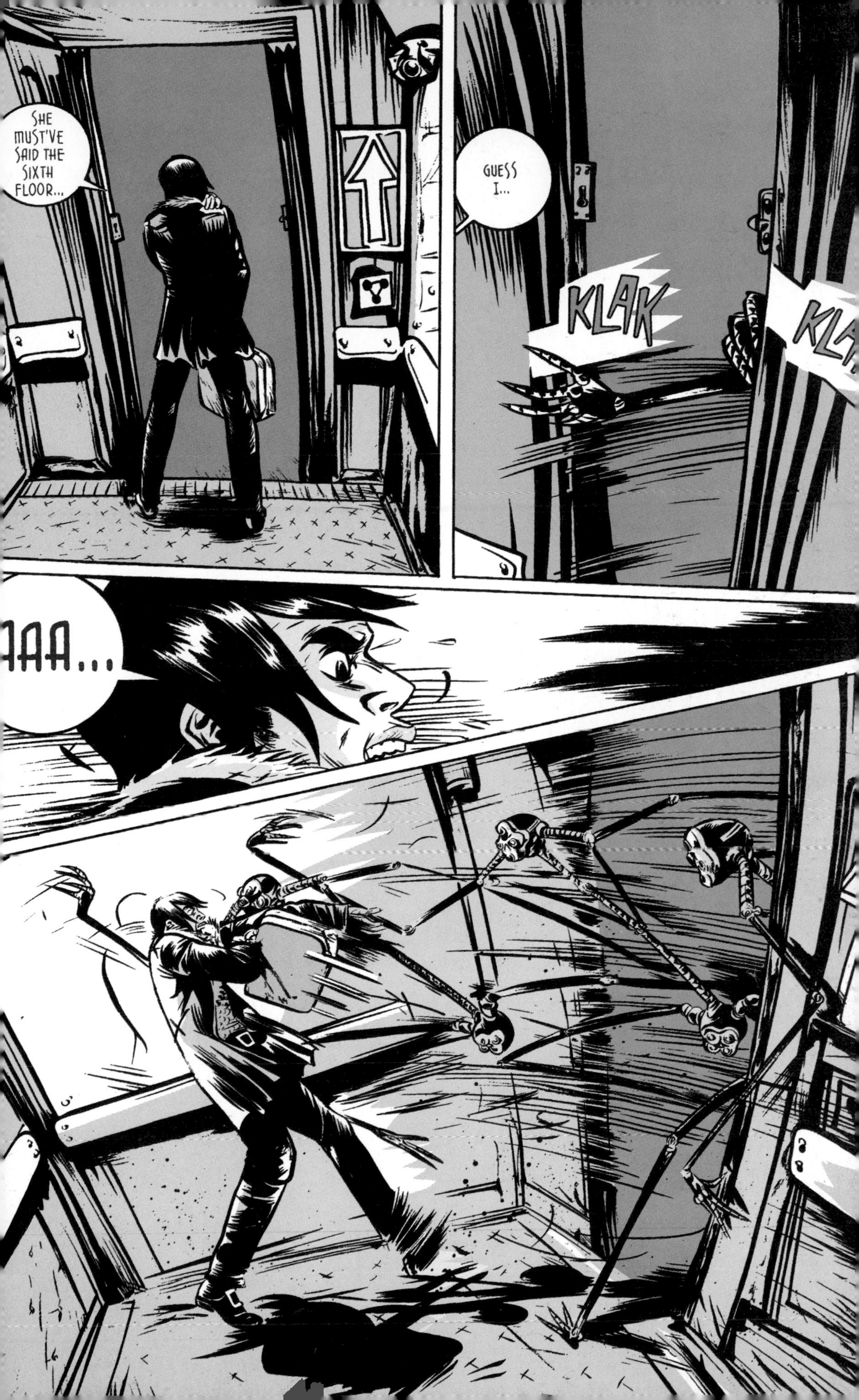
SHE MUST'VE SAID THE SIXTH FLOOR...
GUESS I...
KLAK
AAA...

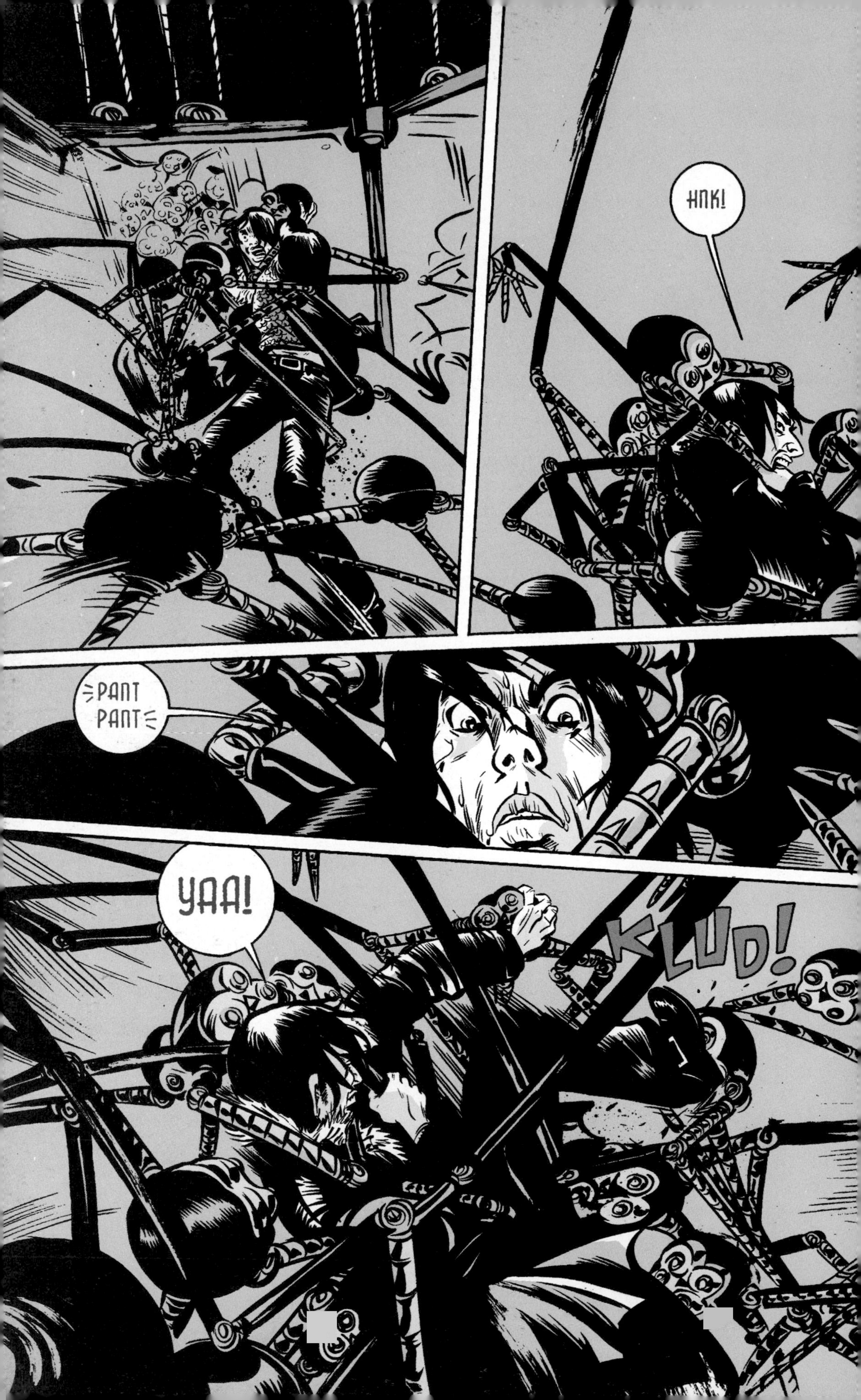
HNK!
PANT
PANT
YAA!
KLUD!

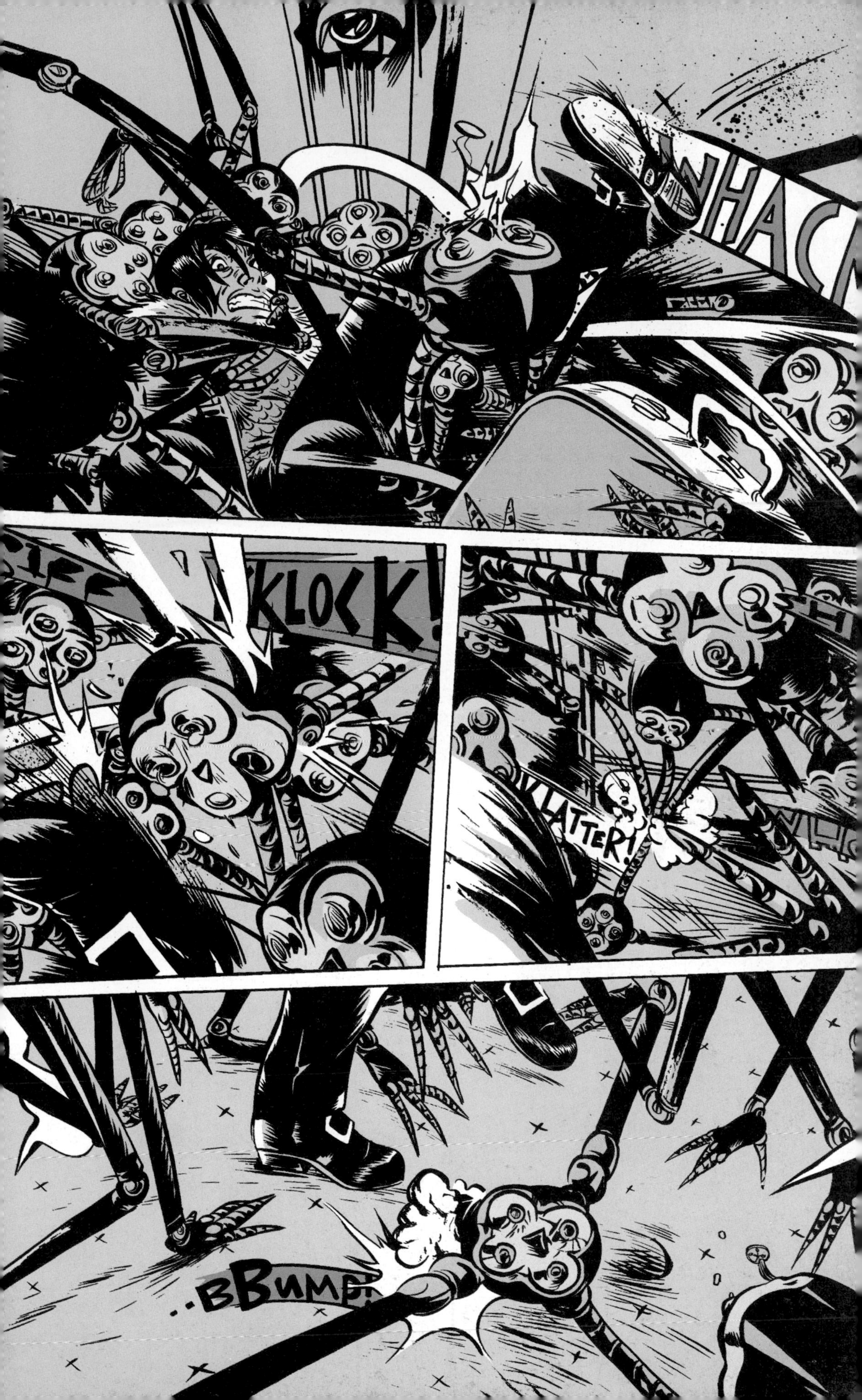
WHACK
KLOCK!
KLATTER!
..BBUMP!

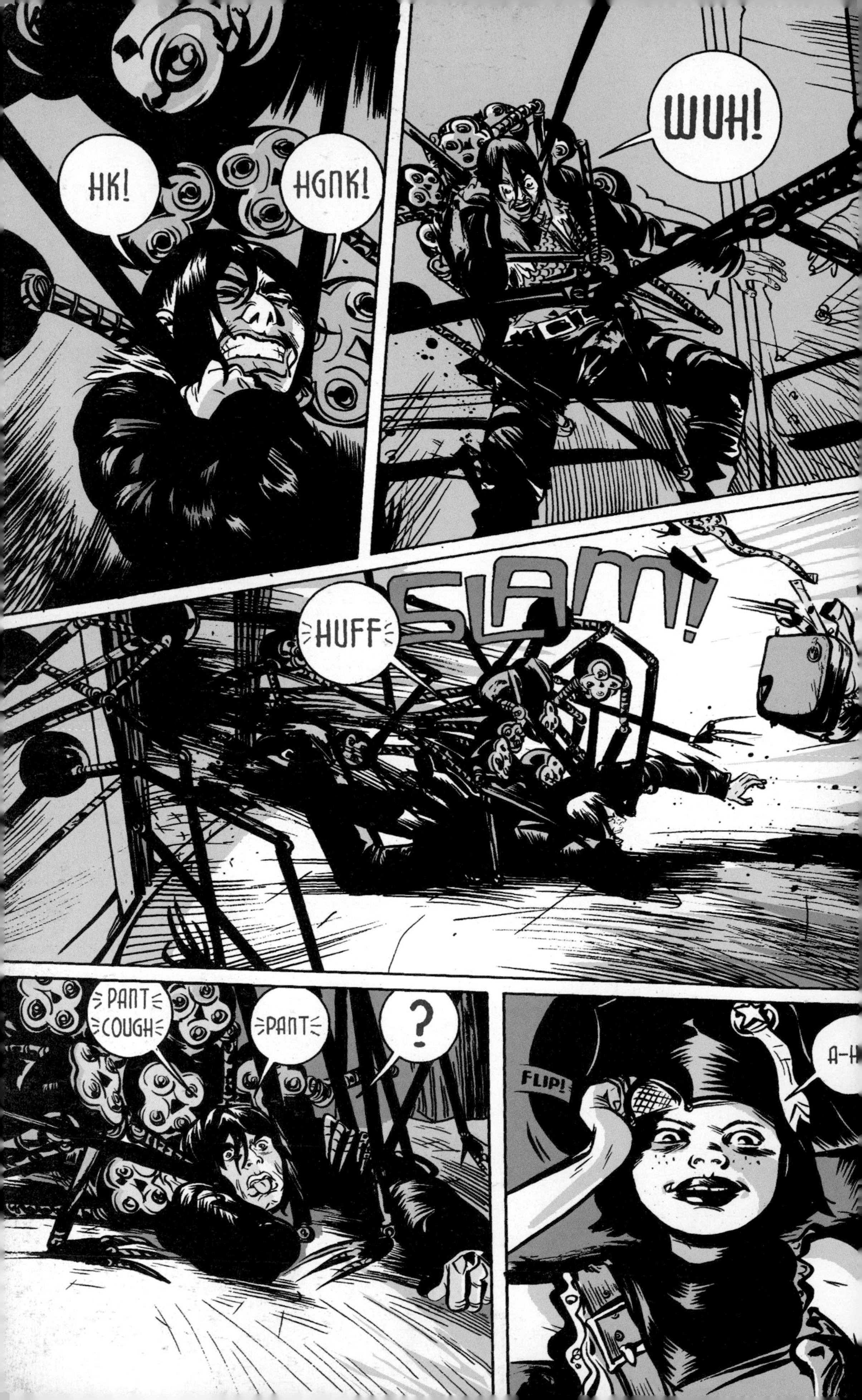
HK!
HGNK!
WUH!
SLAM!
HUFF
PANT
COUGH
PANT
?
FLIP!
A-H

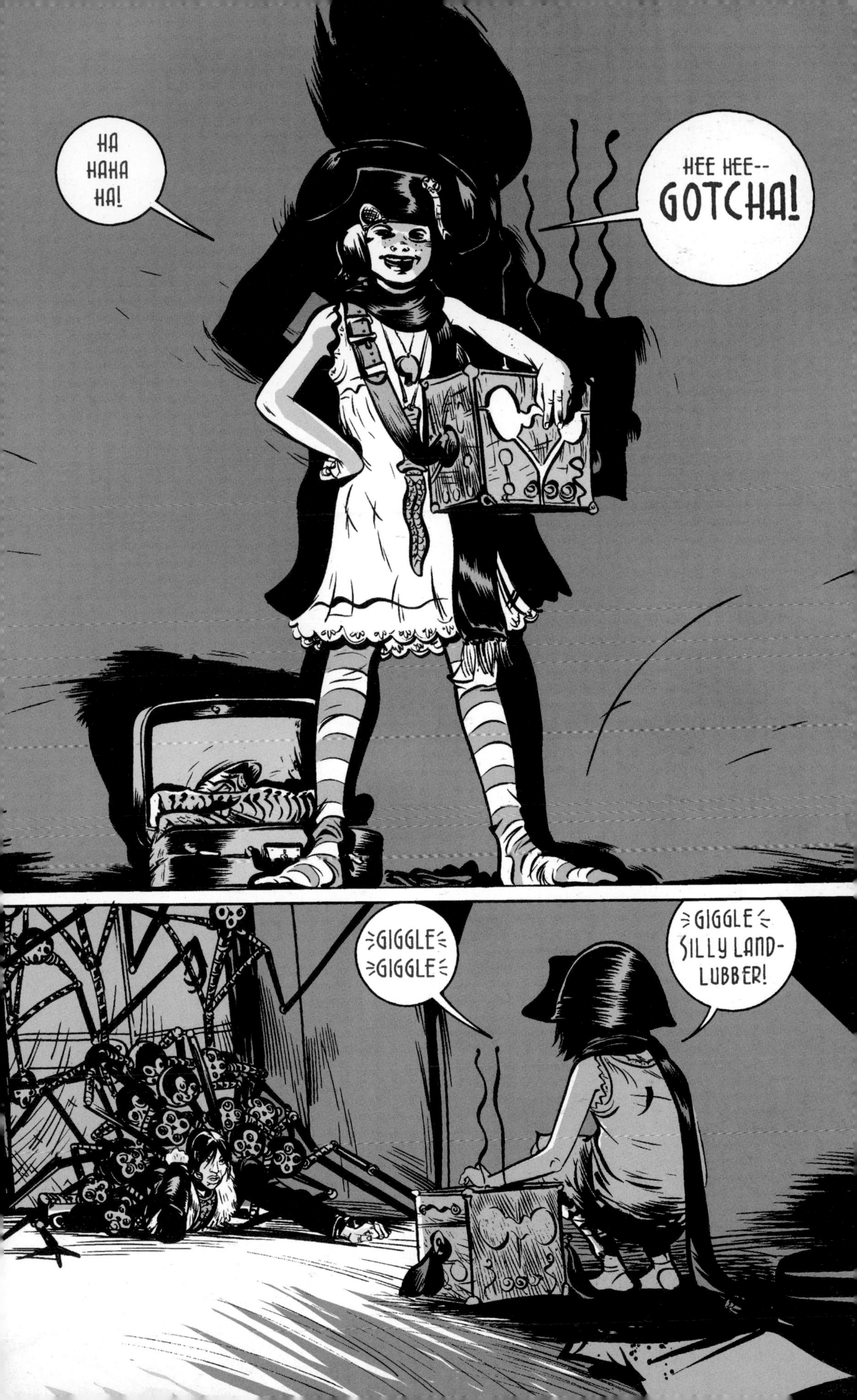
HA HAHA HA!
HEE HEE-- GOTCHA!
GIGGLE GIGGLE
GIGGLE SILLY LAND-LUBBER!

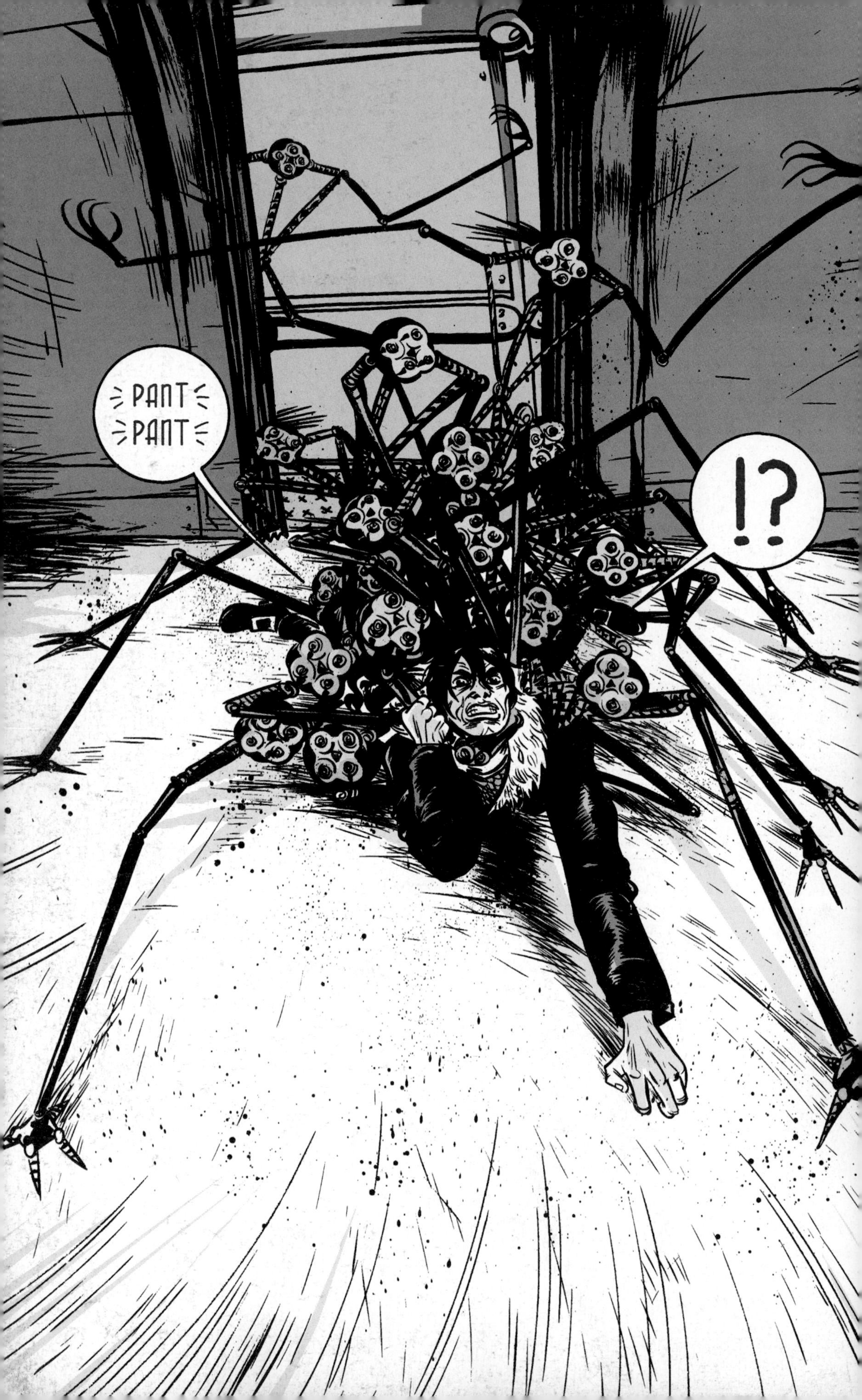
PANT PANT
!?

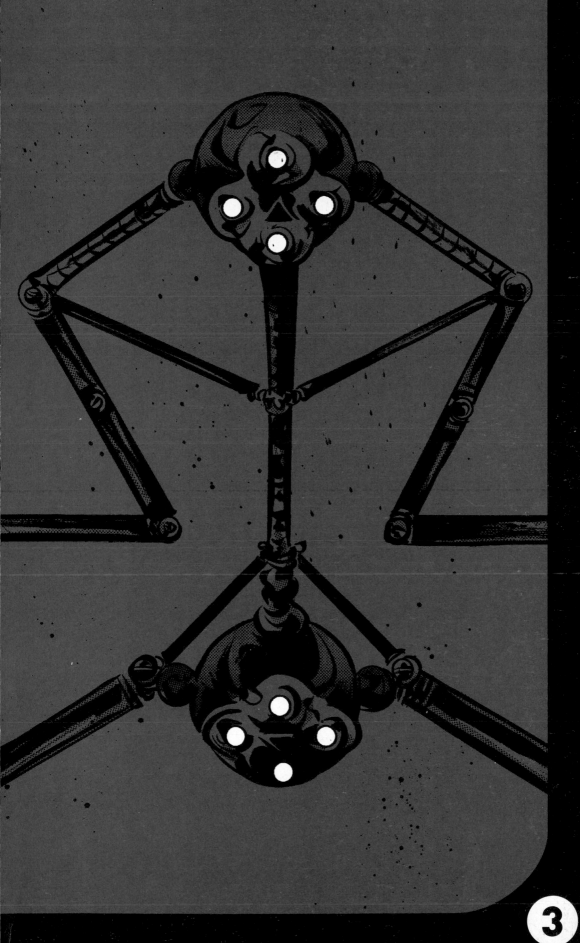

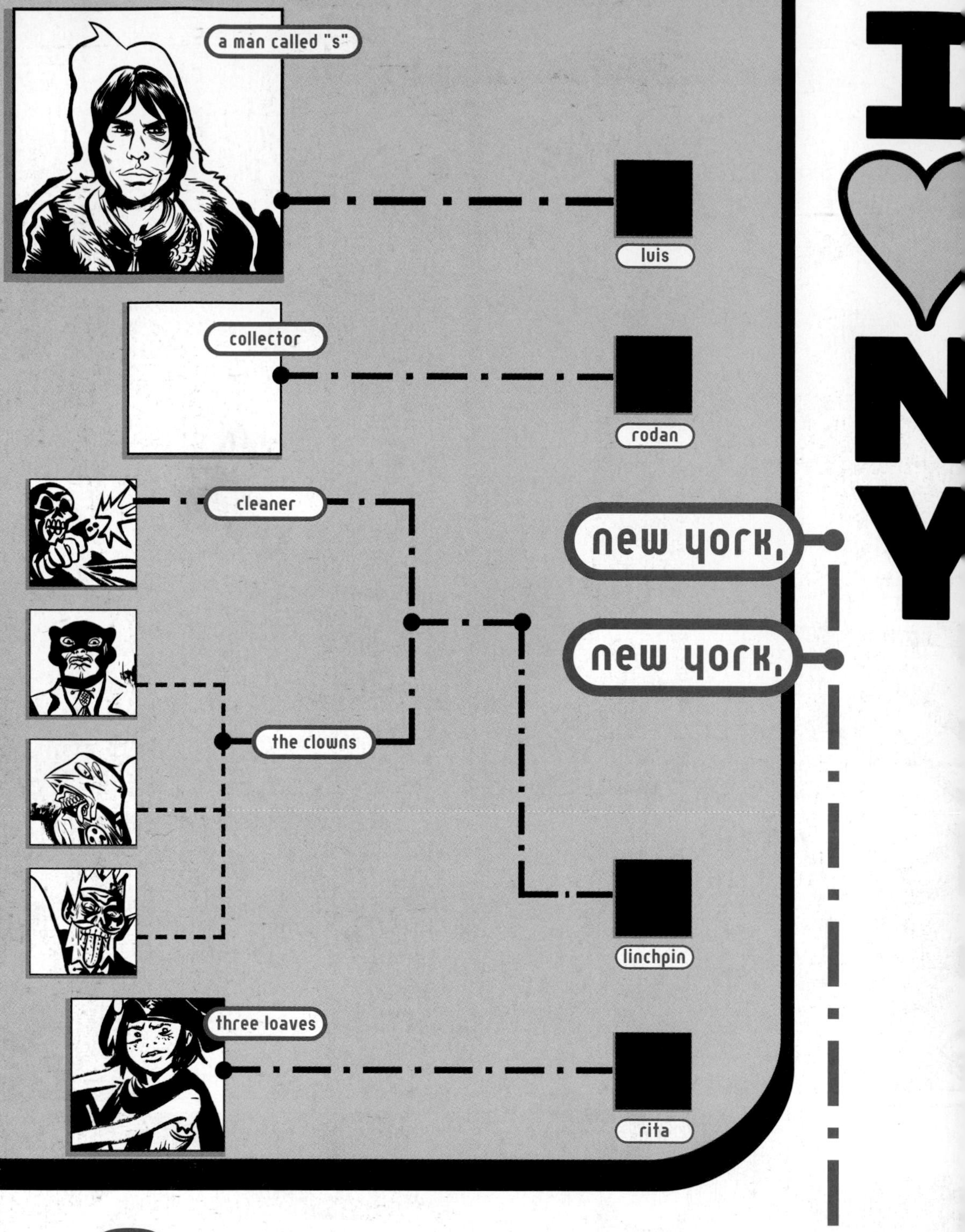
a man called "s"
luis
collector
rodan
cleaner
new york,
new york,
the clowns
linchpin
three loaves
rita
I
NY

S, a clever devil, works for the ***collector***, a mean old cuss. He's been hired to find an artist ***rodan***, who fell off the face of the earth five years back.

"***S***" and his now-dead partner, ***luis***, stole a big batch of the strange Heavy Liquid from a shadowy crime sync who, in turn, have sent three ***clowns*** and a ***cleaner*** to mop up the tiles with "S"'s face.

three loaves, a 6-year-old rascal, believes she's a pirate on the Jolly Roger, and that her caretaker ***rita*** captain. Rita, for her part, is 103 years old, having been born in 1972, and has six replacement organs and two various other prosthetics. She is blind in one eye, despite the organi-gene computer she had implanted in 2066 pays $9218 USD a month in rent.

** NOTE: "The Goose," America's most popular VI2-JAK for three prime time seasons in a row, is "on" at 9 PM on chanr in New York City, with nightly repeats at 1 AM. The broadcast features 51 minutes of rapid digi-splice images of exploding ships interspersed with close-ups of engorged human genitalia, followed by 9 minutes of white noise accompanied by a pink color field. Sub/audio/visual advertising plays continuously throughout the VI2-JAK, although never more than is a by FCC regulations. (see: NY state code #3121-2074/sub.set.B)*

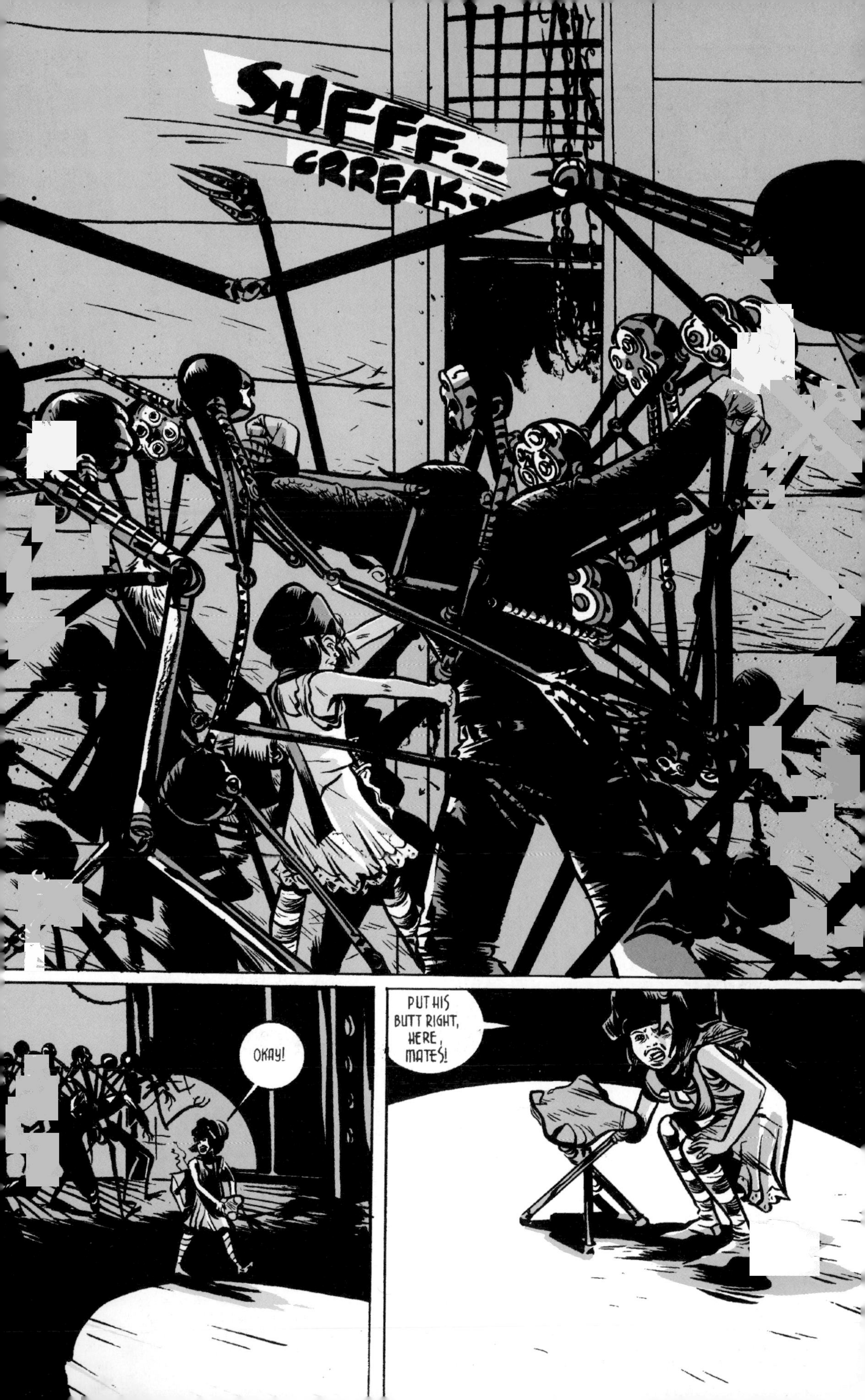
SHFFF--
CRREAK--
OKAY!
PUT HIS BUTT RIGHT, HERE, MATES!

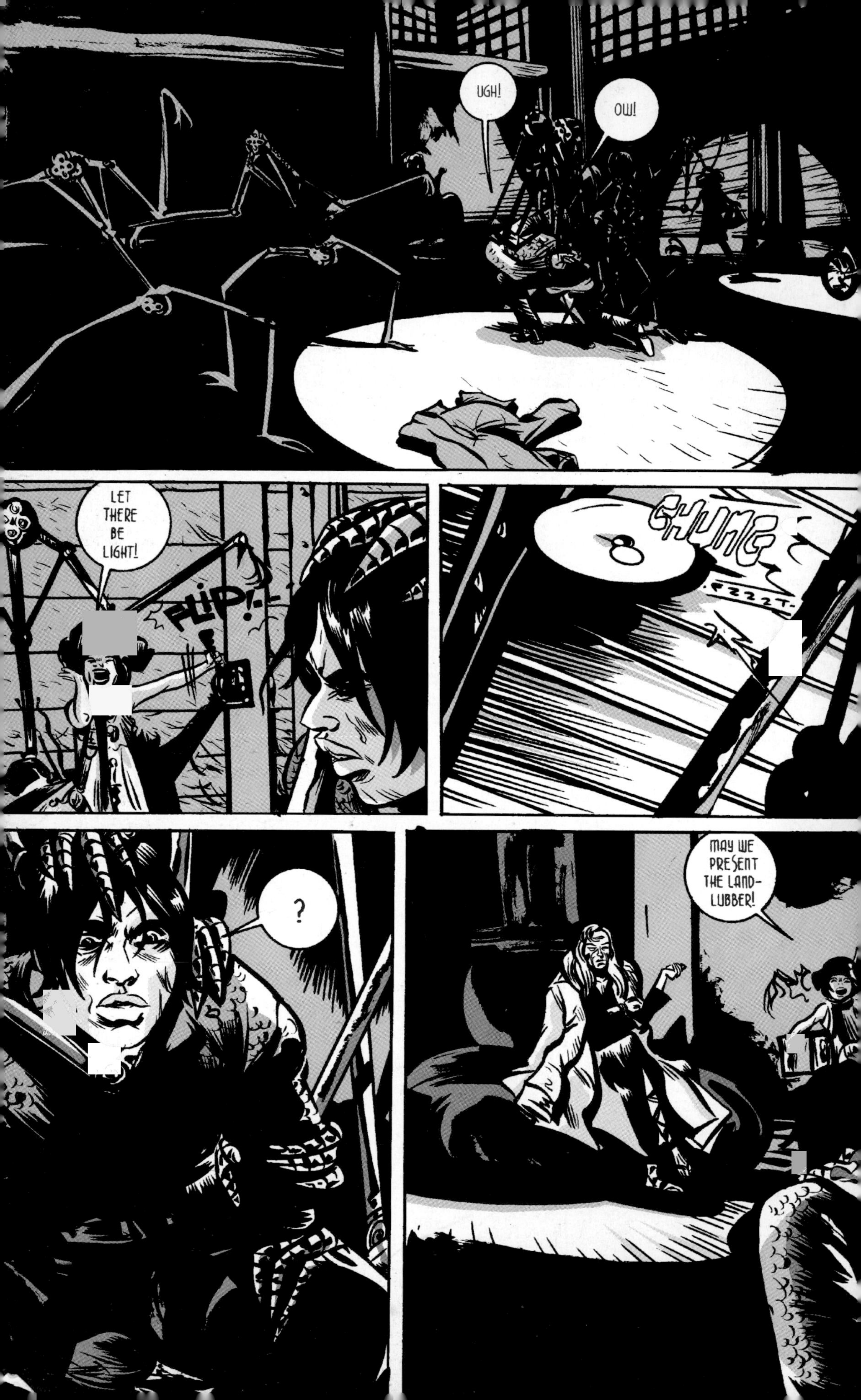
UGH!
OW!
LET THERE BE LIGHT!
FLIP!
CHUNG
FZZZZT
?
MAY WE PRESENT THE LAND-LUBBER!

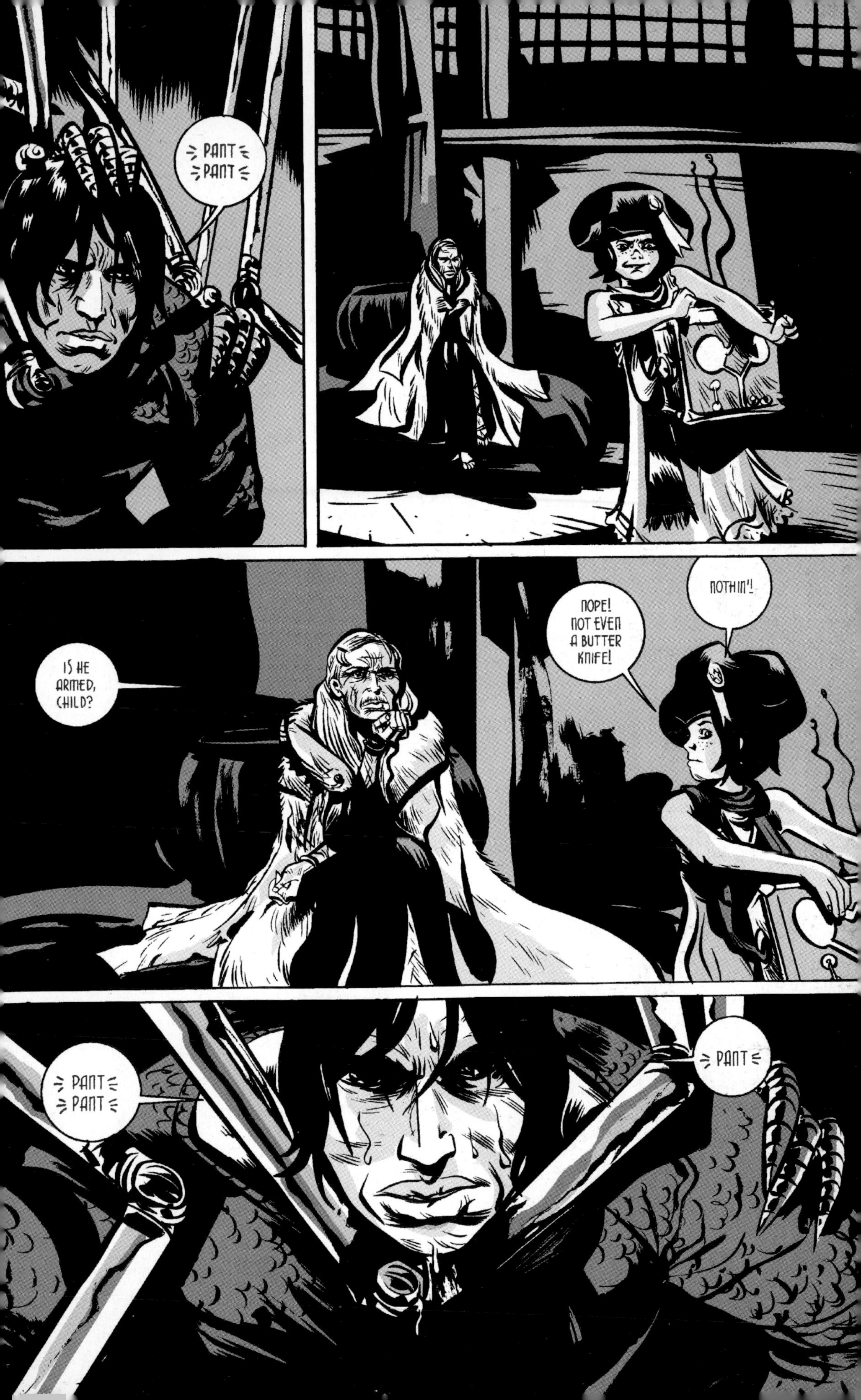
PANT
PANT
IS HE ARMED, CHILD?
NOPE! NOT EVEN A BUTTER KNIFE!
NOTHIN'!
PANT
PANT
PANT

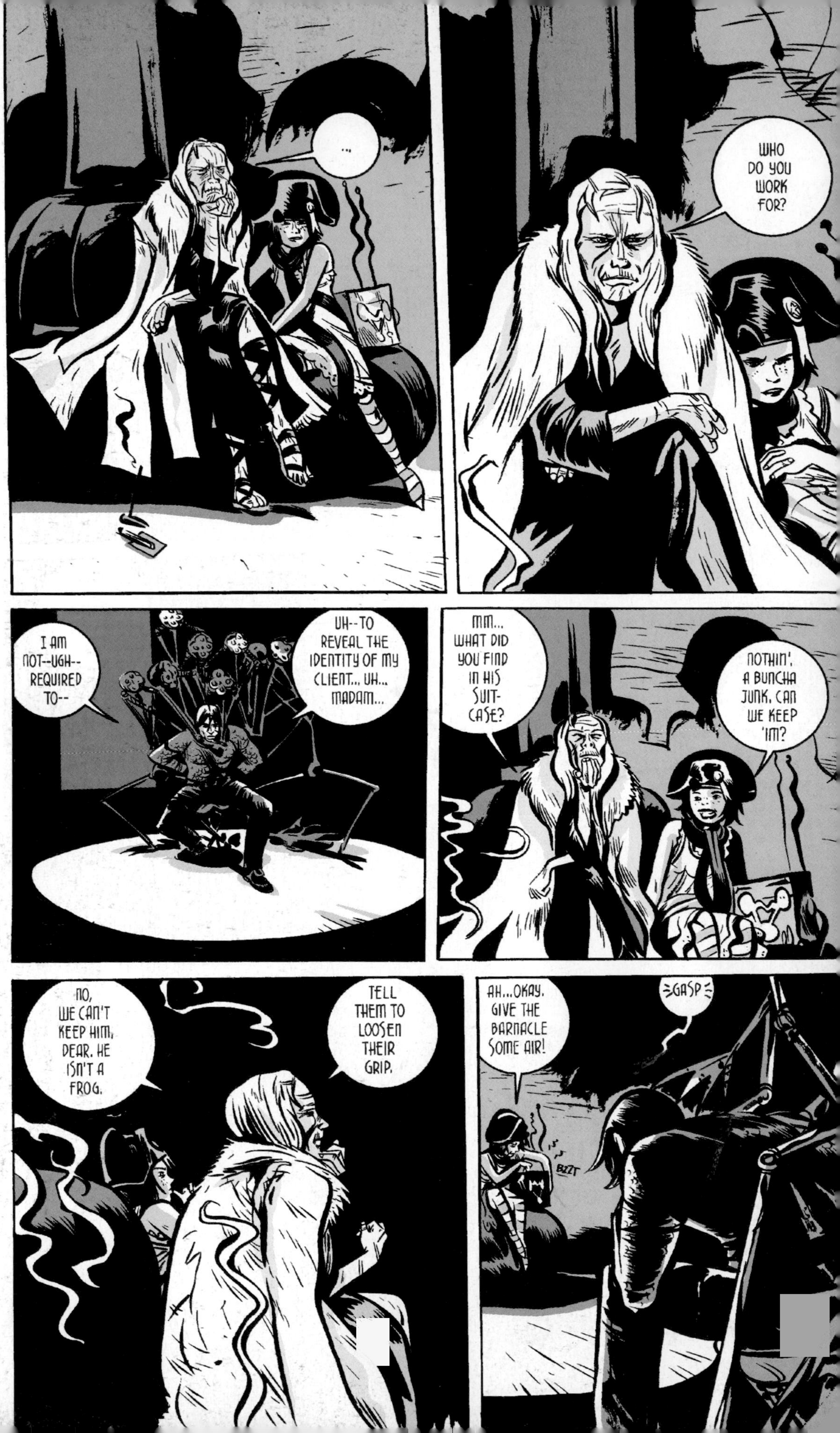
...
WHO DO YOU WORK FOR?
I AM NOT--UGH--REQUIRED TO--
UH--TO REVEAL THE IDENTITY OF MY CLIENT... UH... MADAM...
MM... WHAT DID YOU FIND IN HIS SUIT-CASE?
NOTHIN'. A BUNCHA JUNK. CAN WE KEEP 'IM?
NO, WE CAN'T KEEP HIM, DEAR. HE ISN'T A FROG.
TELL THEM TO LOOSEN THEIR GRIP.
AH...OKAY. GIVE THE BARNACLE SOME AIR!
GASP
BZZT

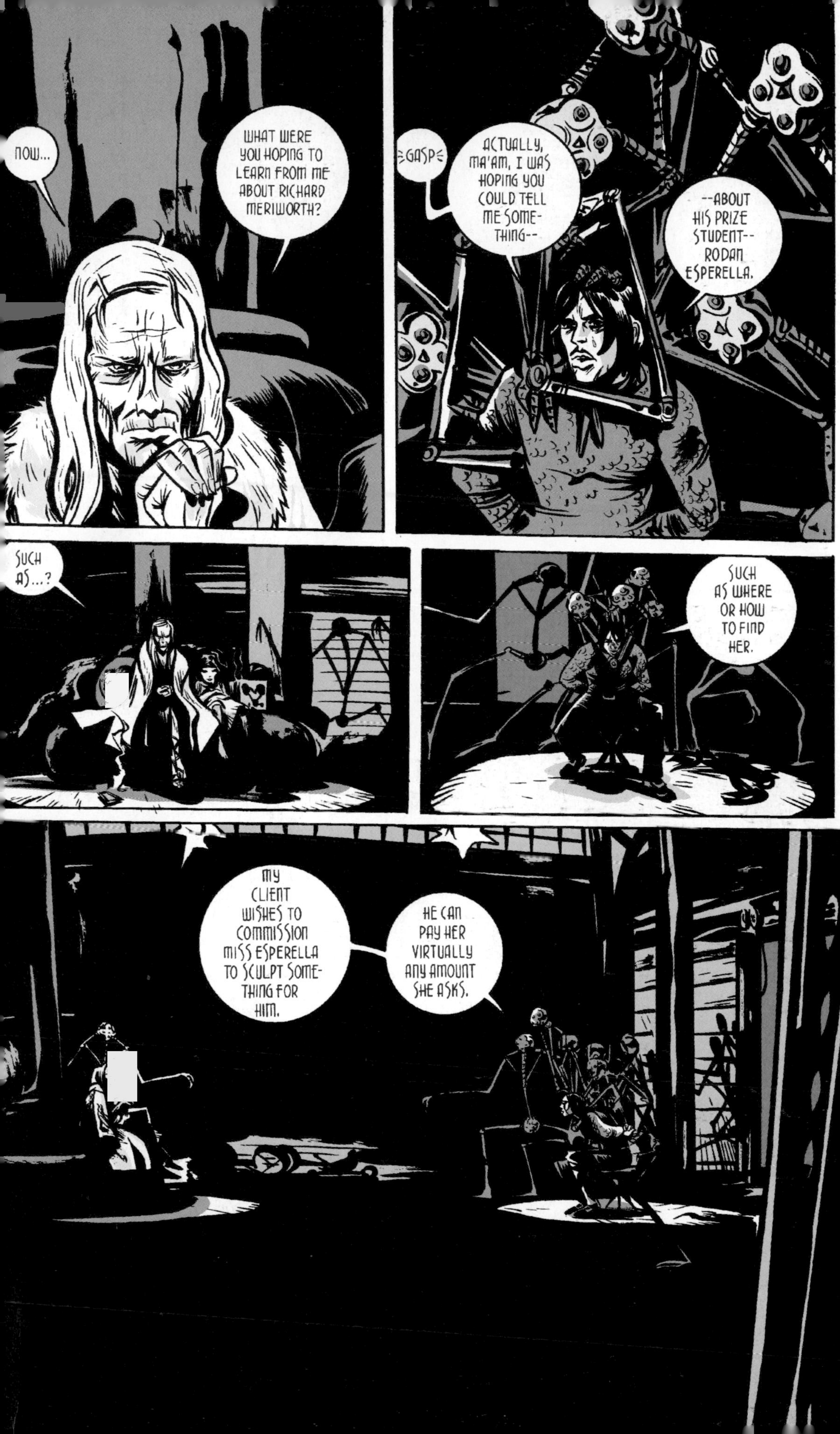
NOW...
WHAT WERE YOU HOPING TO LEARN FROM ME ABOUT RICHARD MERIWORTH?
GASP
ACTUALLY, MA'AM, I WAS HOPING YOU COULD TELL ME SOME-THING--
--ABOUT HIS PRIZE STUDENT--RODAN ESPERELLA.
SUCH AS...?
SUCH AS WHERE OR HOW TO FIND HER.
MY CLIENT WISHES TO COMMISSION MISS ESPERELLA TO SCULPT SOME-THING FOR HIM.
HE CAN PAY HER VIRTUALLY ANY AMOUNT SHE ASKS.

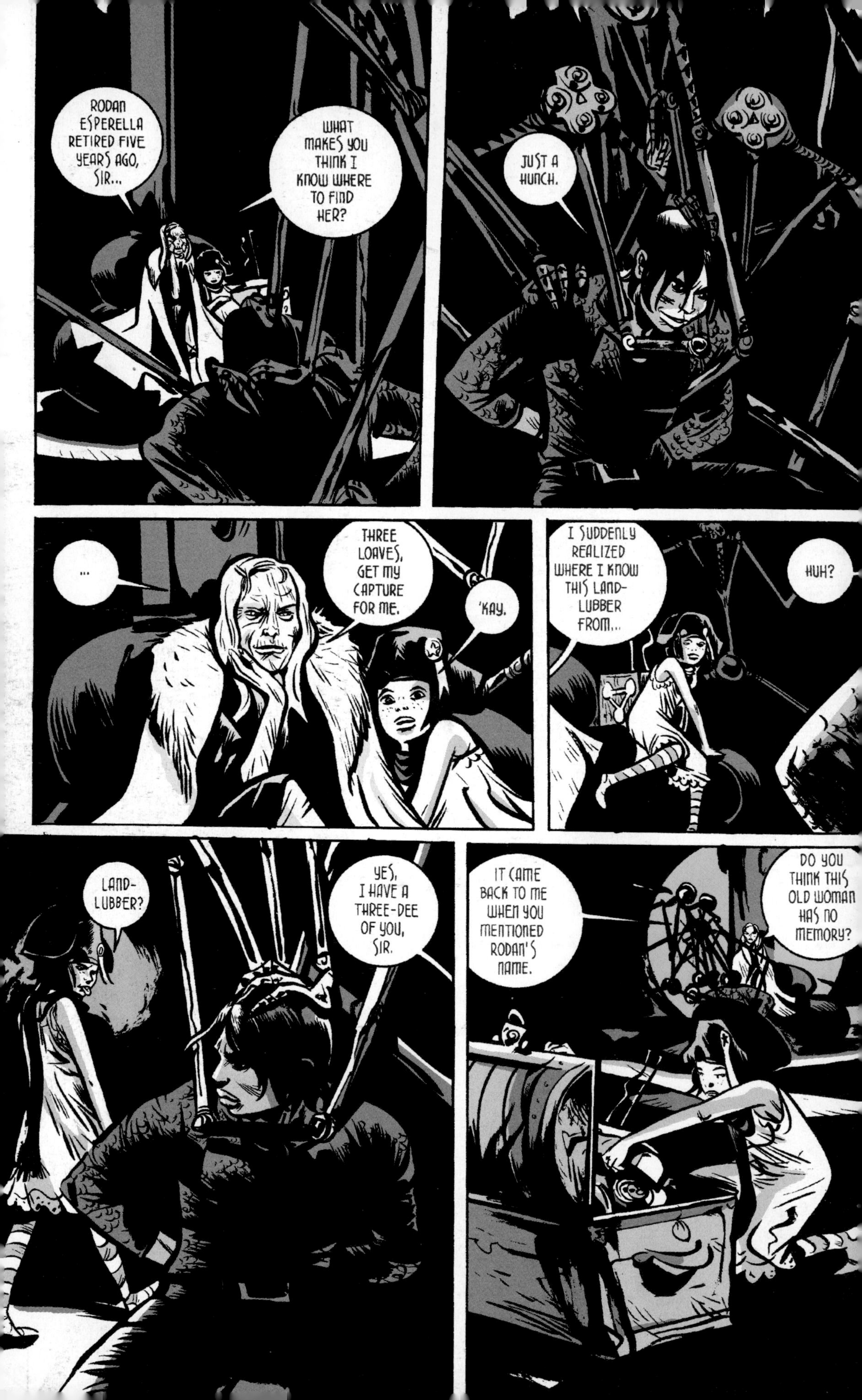
RODAN ESPERELLA RETIRED FIVE YEARS AGO, SIR...
WHAT MAKES YOU THINK I KNOW WHERE TO FIND HER?
JUST A HUNCH.
...
THREE LOAVES, GET MY CAPTURE FOR ME.
'KAY.
I SUDDENLY REALIZED WHERE I KNOW THIS LAND-LUBBER FROM...
HUH?
LAND-LUBBER?
YES, I HAVE A THREE-DEE OF YOU, SIR.
IT CAME BACK TO ME WHEN YOU MENTIONED RODAN'S NAME.
DO YOU THINK THIS OLD WOMAN HAS NO MEMORY?

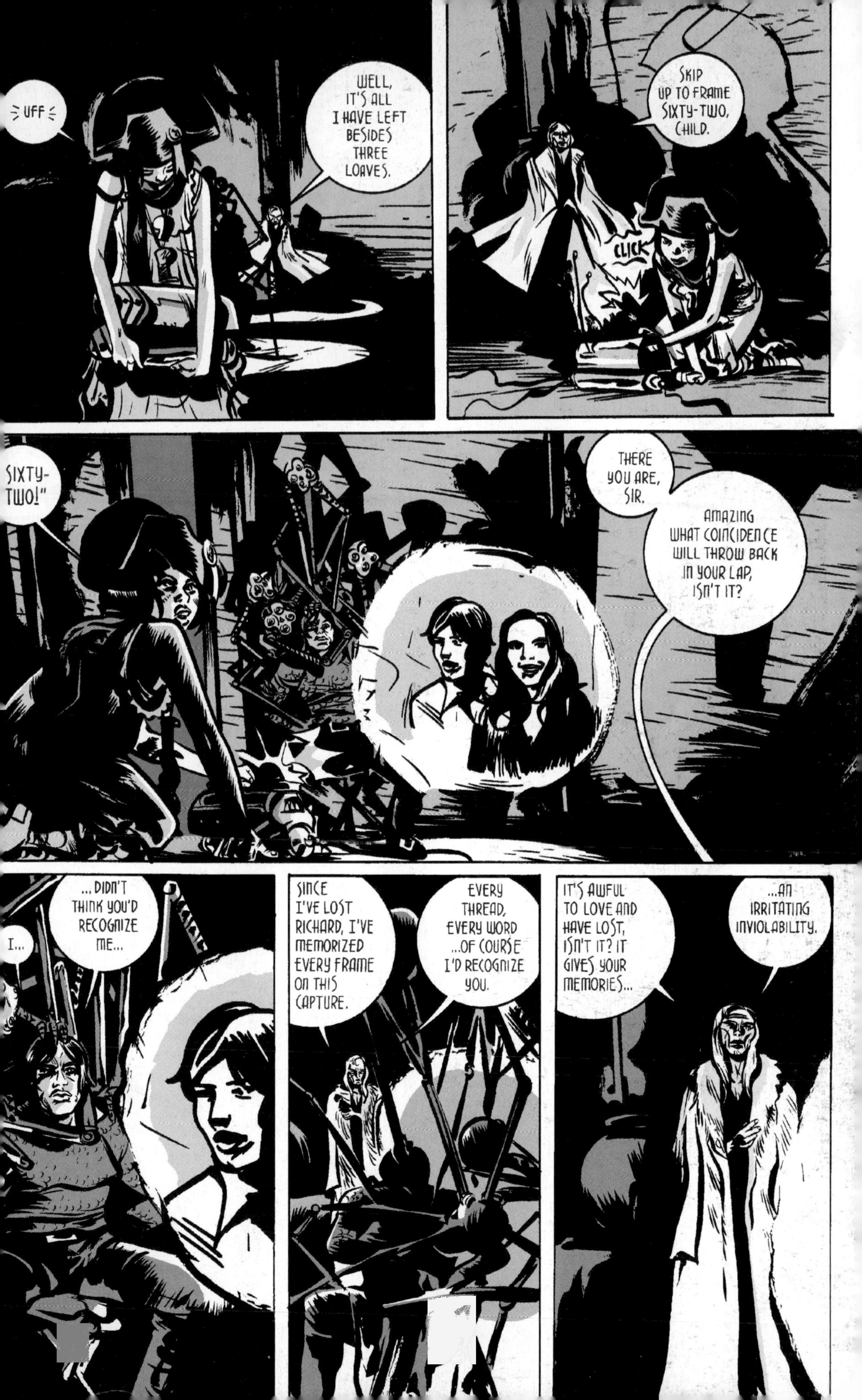
UFF
WELL, IT'S ALL I HAVE LEFT BESIDES THREE LOAVES.
SKIP UP TO FRAME SIXTY-TWO, CHILD.
CLICK
SIXTY-TWO!"
THERE YOU ARE, SIR.
AMAZING WHAT COINCIDENCE WILL THROW BACK IN YOUR LAP, ISN'T IT?
I...
...DIDN'T THINK YOU'D RECOGNIZE ME...
SINCE I'VE LOST RICHARD, I'VE MEMORIZED EVERY FRAME ON THIS CAPTURE.
EVERY THREAD, EVERY WORD ...OF COURSE I'D RECOGNIZE YOU.
IT'S AWFUL TO LOVE AND HAVE LOST, ISN'T IT? IT GIVES YOUR MEMORIES...
...AN IRRITATING INVIOLABILITY.

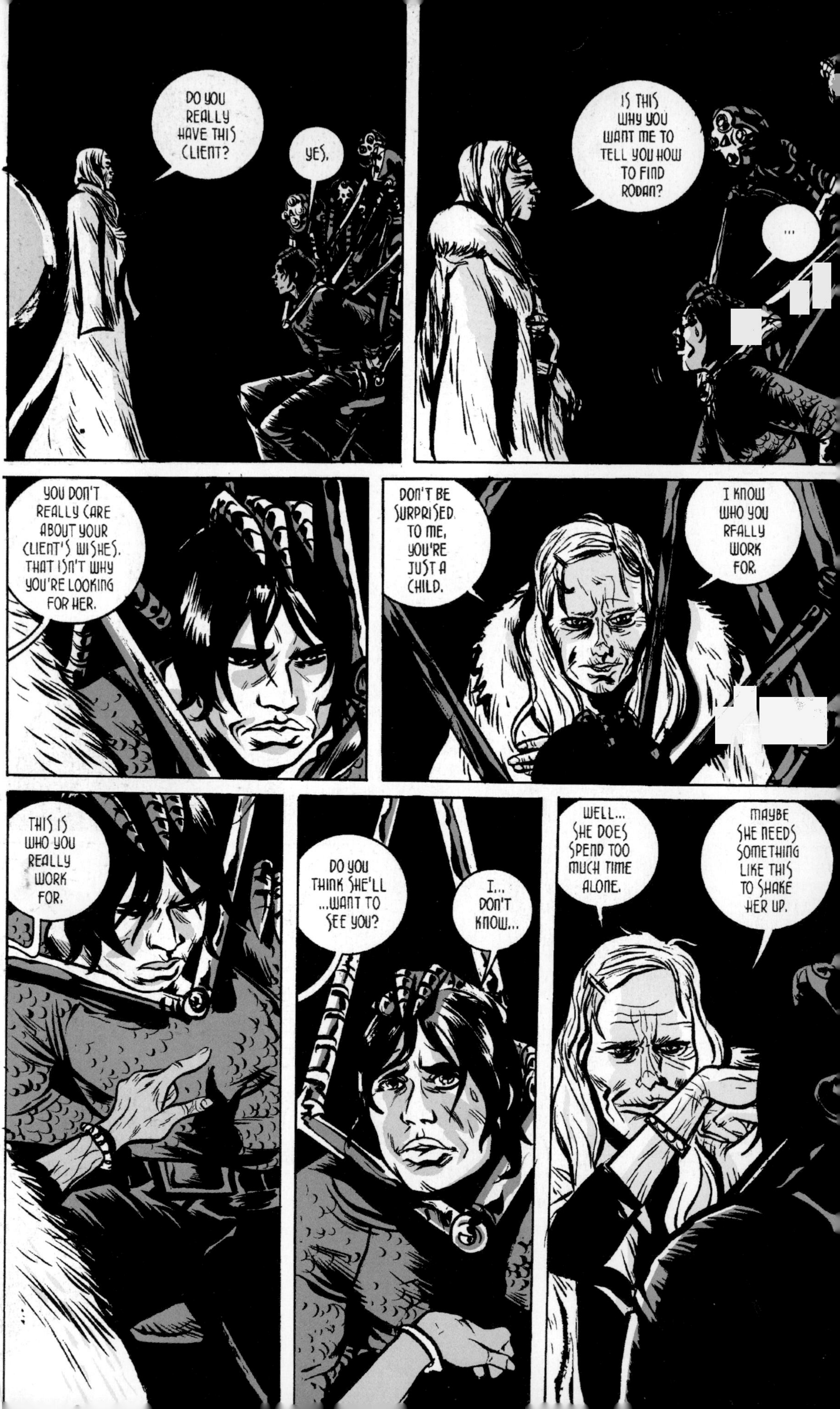
DO YOU REALLY HAVE THIS CLIENT?
YES.
IS THIS WHY YOU WANT ME TO TELL YOU HOW TO FIND RODAN?
...
YOU DON'T REALLY CARE ABOUT YOUR CLIENT'S WISHES. THAT ISN'T WHY YOU'RE LOOKING FOR HER.
DON'T BE SURPRISED. TO ME, YOU'RE JUST A CHILD.
I KNOW WHO YOU REALLY WORK FOR.
THIS IS WHO YOU REALLY WORK FOR.
DO YOU THINK SHE'LL ...WANT TO SEE YOU?
I... DON'T KNOW...
WELL... SHE DOES SPEND TOO MUCH TIME ALONE.
MAYBE SHE NEEDS SOMETHING LIKE THIS TO SHAKE HER UP.

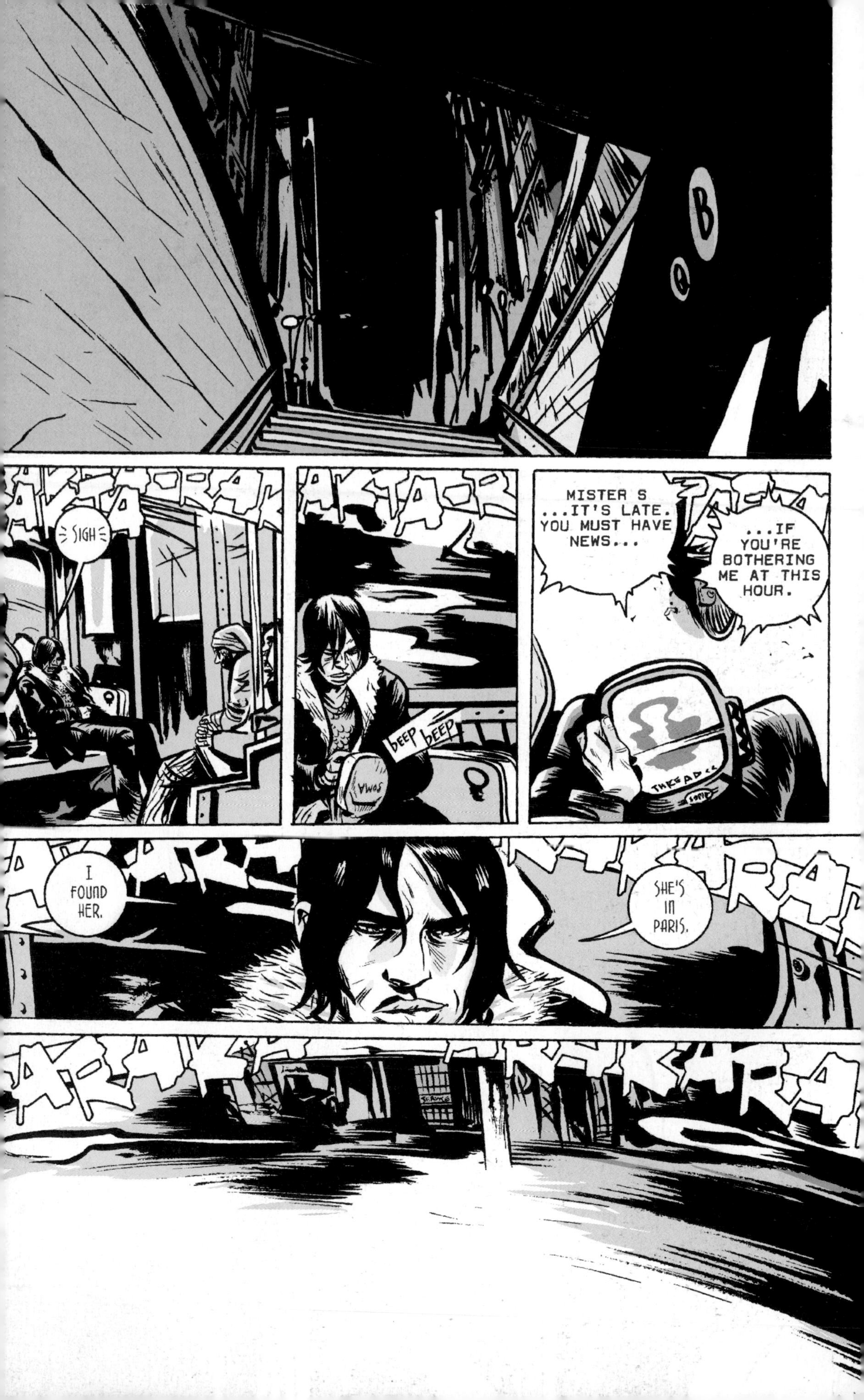
SIGH
beep beep
MISTER S ...IT'S LATE. YOU MUST HAVE NEWS...
...IF YOU'RE BOTHERING ME AT THIS HOUR.
I FOUND HER.
SHE'S IN PARIS.

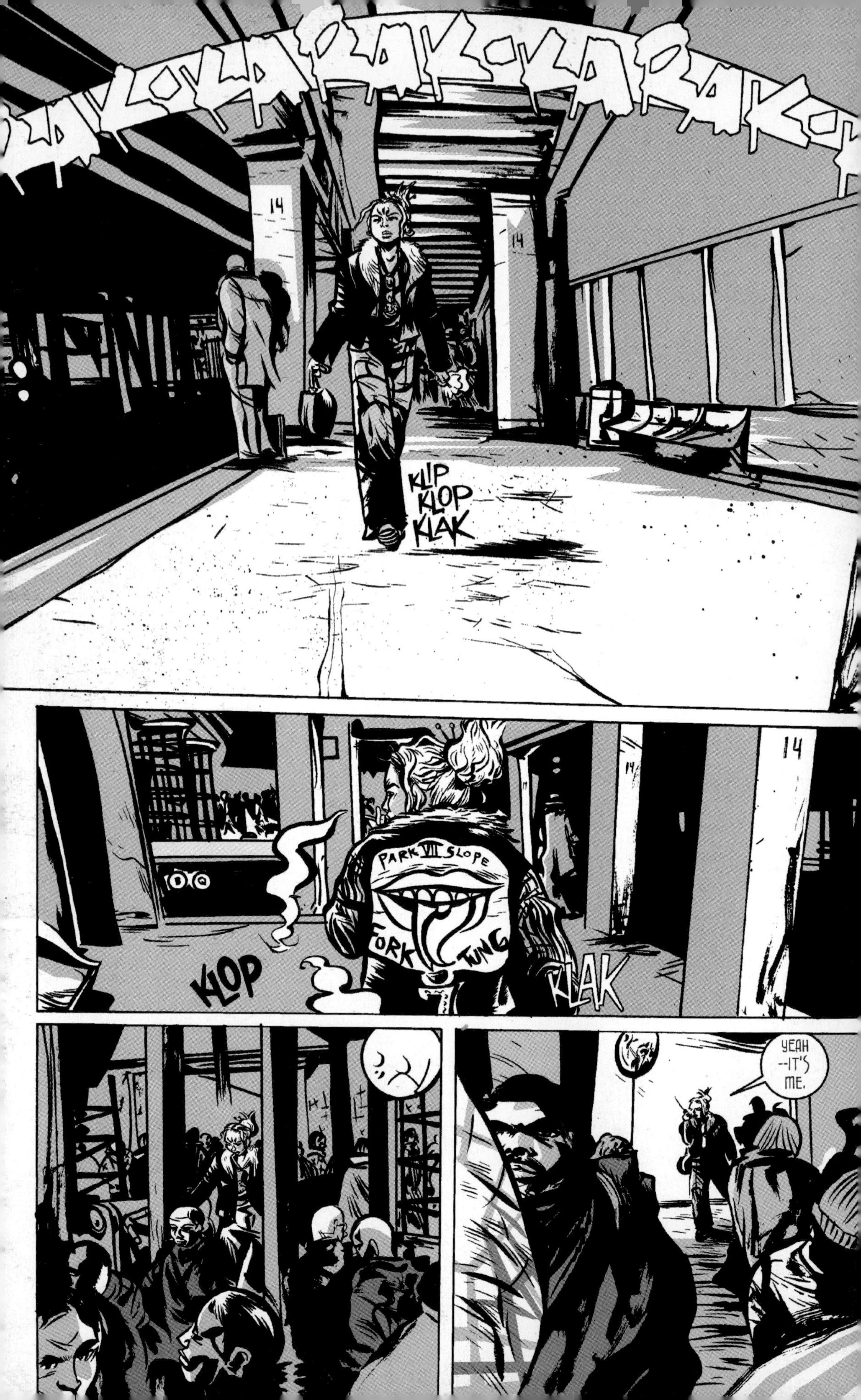
KLIP
KLOP
KLAK
14
14
PARK VII SLOPE
FORK TUNG
KLOP
KLAK
YEAH
--IT'S
ME.

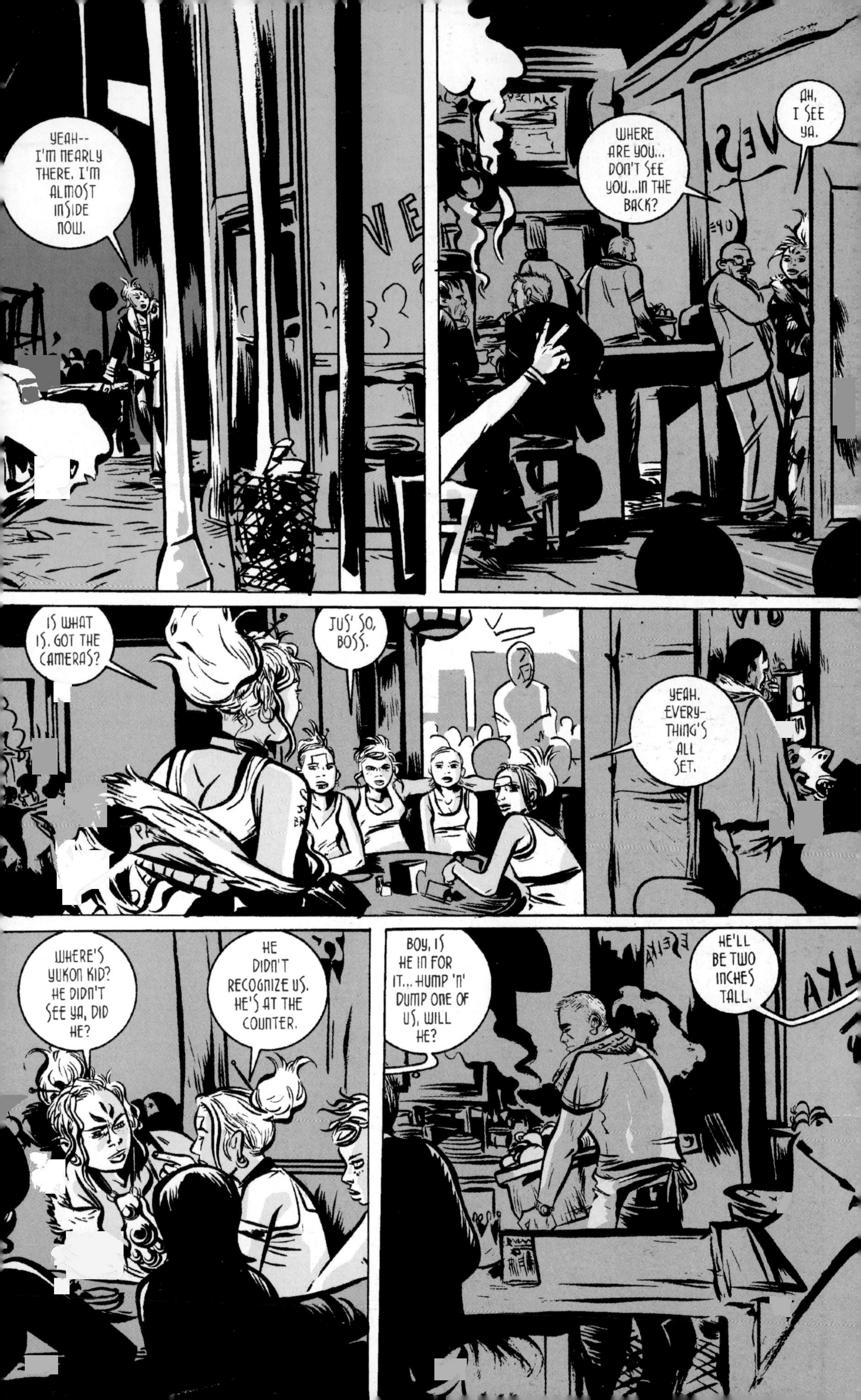
YEAH-- I'M NEARLY THERE. I'M ALMOST INSIDE NOW.
WHERE ARE YOU... DON'T SEE YOU...IN THE BACK?
AH, I SEE YA.
IS WHAT IS. GOT THE CAMERAS?
JUS' SO, BOSS.
YEAH. EVERYTHING'S ALL SET.
WHERE'S YUKON KID? HE DIDN'T SEE YA, DID HE?
HE DIDN'T RECOGNIZE US. HE'S AT THE COUNTER.
BOY, IS HE IN FOR IT... HUMP 'N' DUMP ONE OF US, WILL HE?
HE'LL BE TWO INCHES TALL.

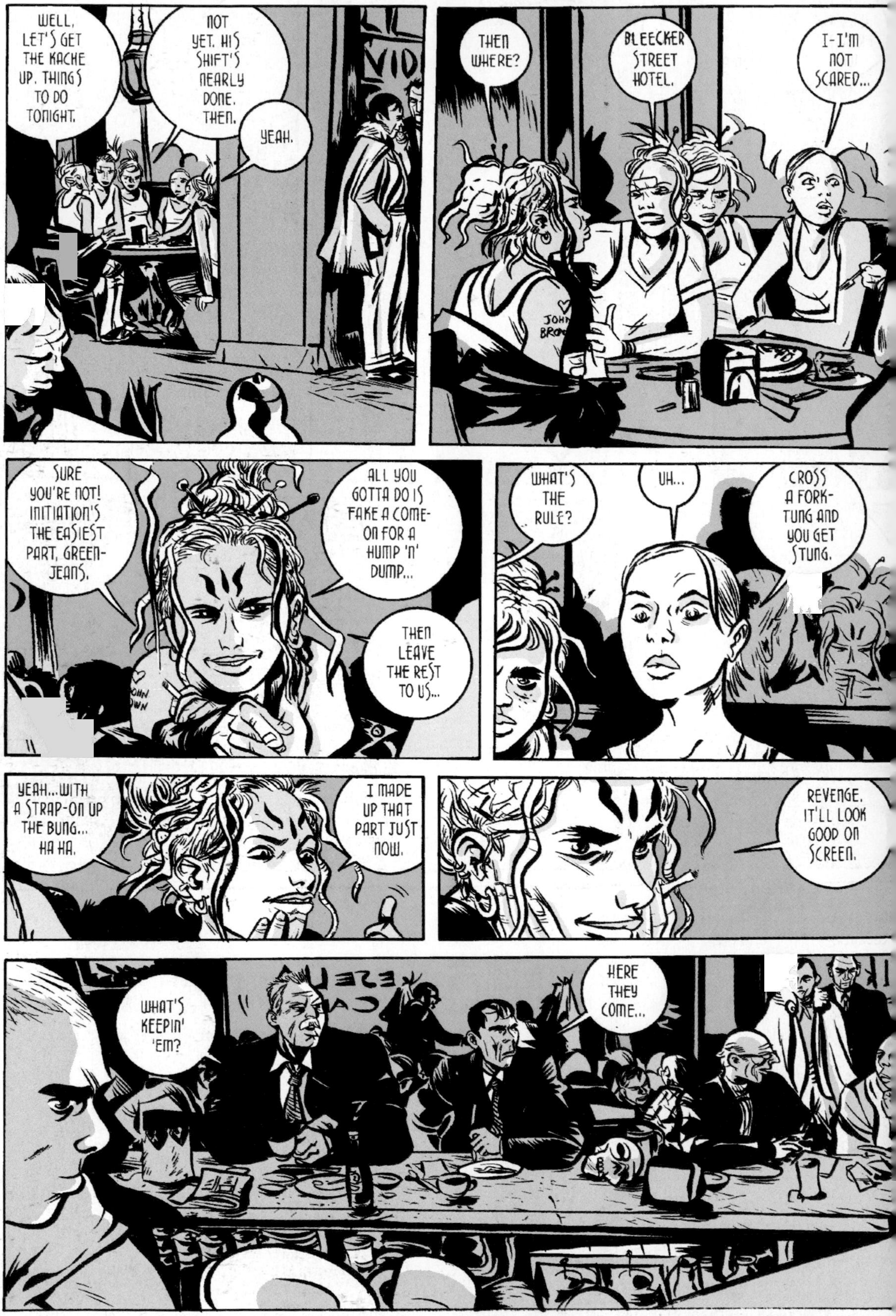
WELL, LET'S GET THE KACHE UP. THINGS TO DO TONIGHT.
NOT YET. HIS SHIFT'S NEARLY DONE. THEN.
YEAH.
THEN WHERE?
BLEECKER STREET HOTEL.
I-I'M NOT SCARED...
SURE YOU'RE NOT! INITIATION'S THE EASIEST PART, GREEN-JEANS.
ALL YOU GOTTA DO IS FAKE A COME-ON FOR A HUMP 'N' DUMP...
THEN LEAVE THE REST TO US...
WHAT'S THE RULE?
UH...
CROSS A FORK-TUNG AND YOU GET STUNG.
YEAH...WITH A STRAP-ON UP THE BUNG... HA HA.
I MADE UP THAT PART JUST NOW.
REVENGE. IT'LL LOOK GOOD ON SCREEN.
WHAT'S KEEPIN' 'EM?
HERE THEY COME...

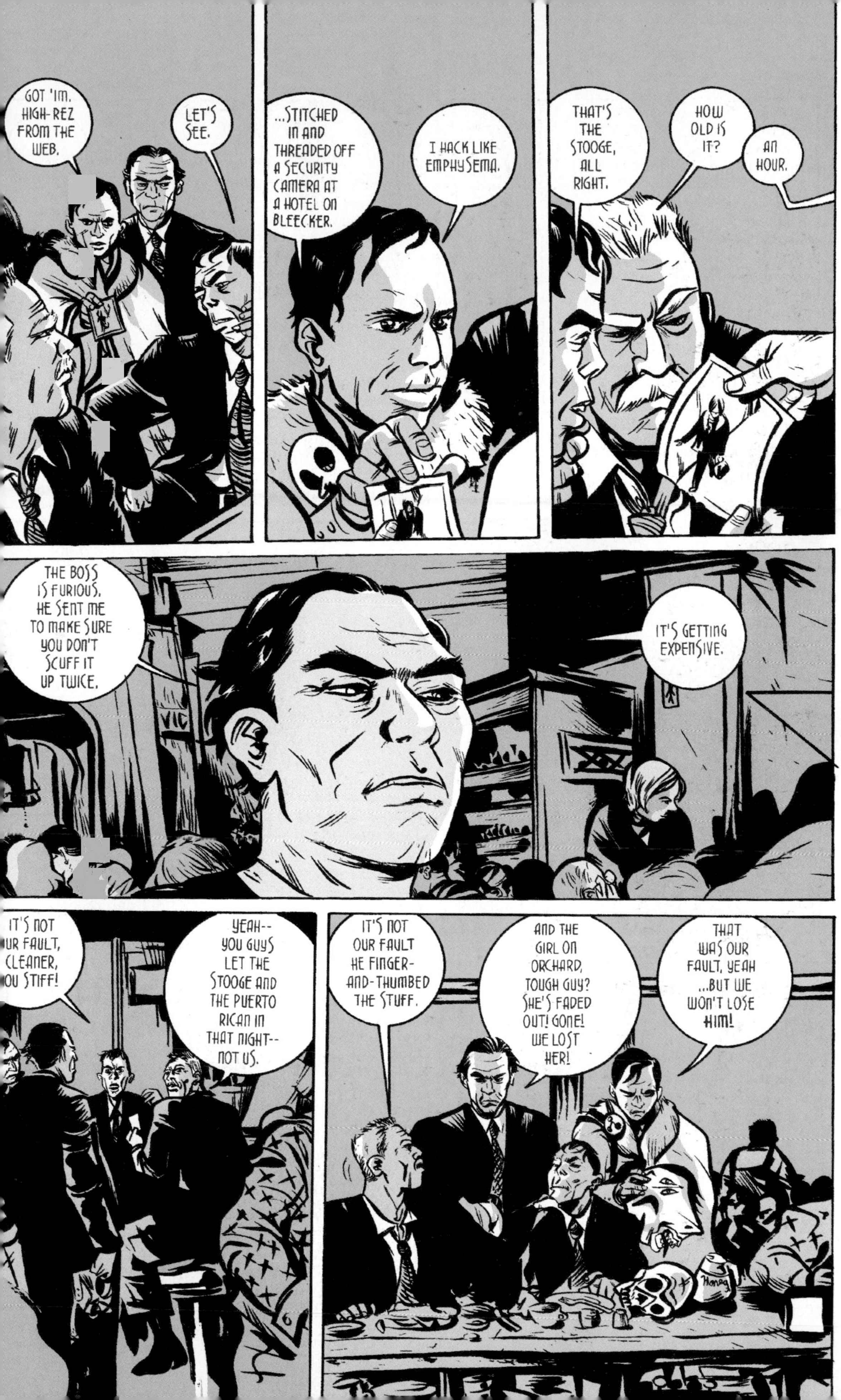
GOT 'IM. HIGH-REZ FROM THE WEB.
LET'S SEE.
...STITCHED IN AND THREADED OFF A SECURITY CAMERA AT A HOTEL ON BLEECKER.
I HACK LIKE EMPHYSEMA.
THAT'S THE STOOGE, ALL RIGHT.
HOW OLD IS IT?
AN HOUR.
THE BOSS IS FURIOUS. HE SENT ME TO MAKE SURE YOU DON'T SCUFF IT UP TWICE.
IT'S GETTING EXPENSIVE.
IT'S NOT UR FAULT, CLEANER, OU STIFF!
YEAH-- YOU GUYS LET THE STOOGE AND THE PUERTO RICAN IN THAT NIGHT-- NOT US.
IT'S NOT OUR FAULT HE FINGER-AND-THUMBED THE STUFF.
AND THE GIRL ON ORCHARD, TOUGH GUY? SHE'S FADED OUT! GONE! WE LOST HER!
THAT WAS OUR FAULT, YEAH ...BUT WE WON'T LOSE **HIM!**

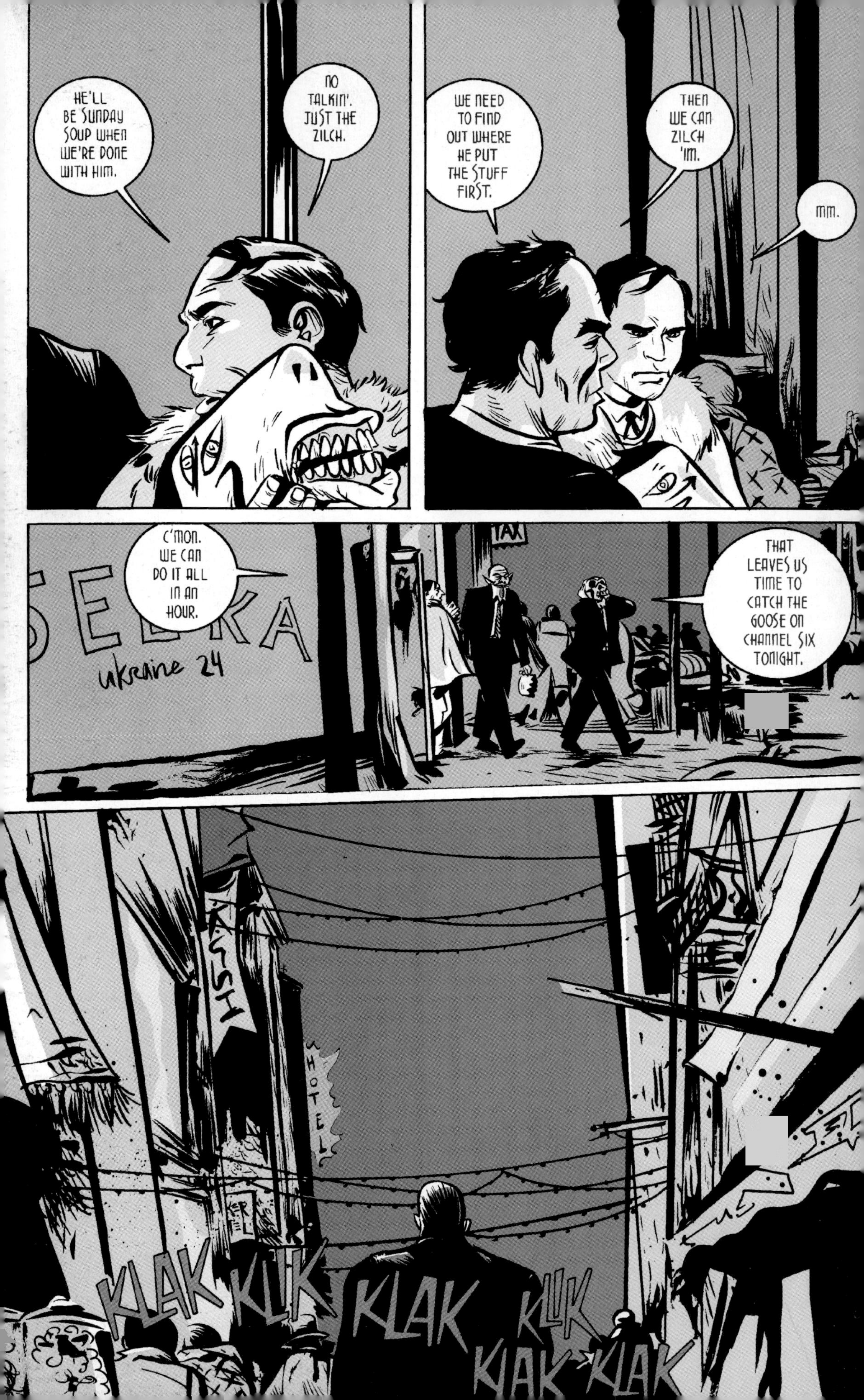
HE'LL BE SUNDAY SOUP WHEN WE'RE DONE WITH HIM.
NO TALKIN'. JUST THE ZILCH.
WE NEED TO FIND OUT WHERE HE PUT THE STUFF FIRST.
THEN WE CAN ZILCH 'IM.
MM.
C'MON. WE CAN DO IT ALL IN AN HOUR.
ukraine 24
TAX
THAT LEAVES US TIME TO CATCH THE GOOSE ON CHANNEL SIX TONIGHT.
HOTEL
KLAK KLIK KLAK KLIK
KLAK KLAK

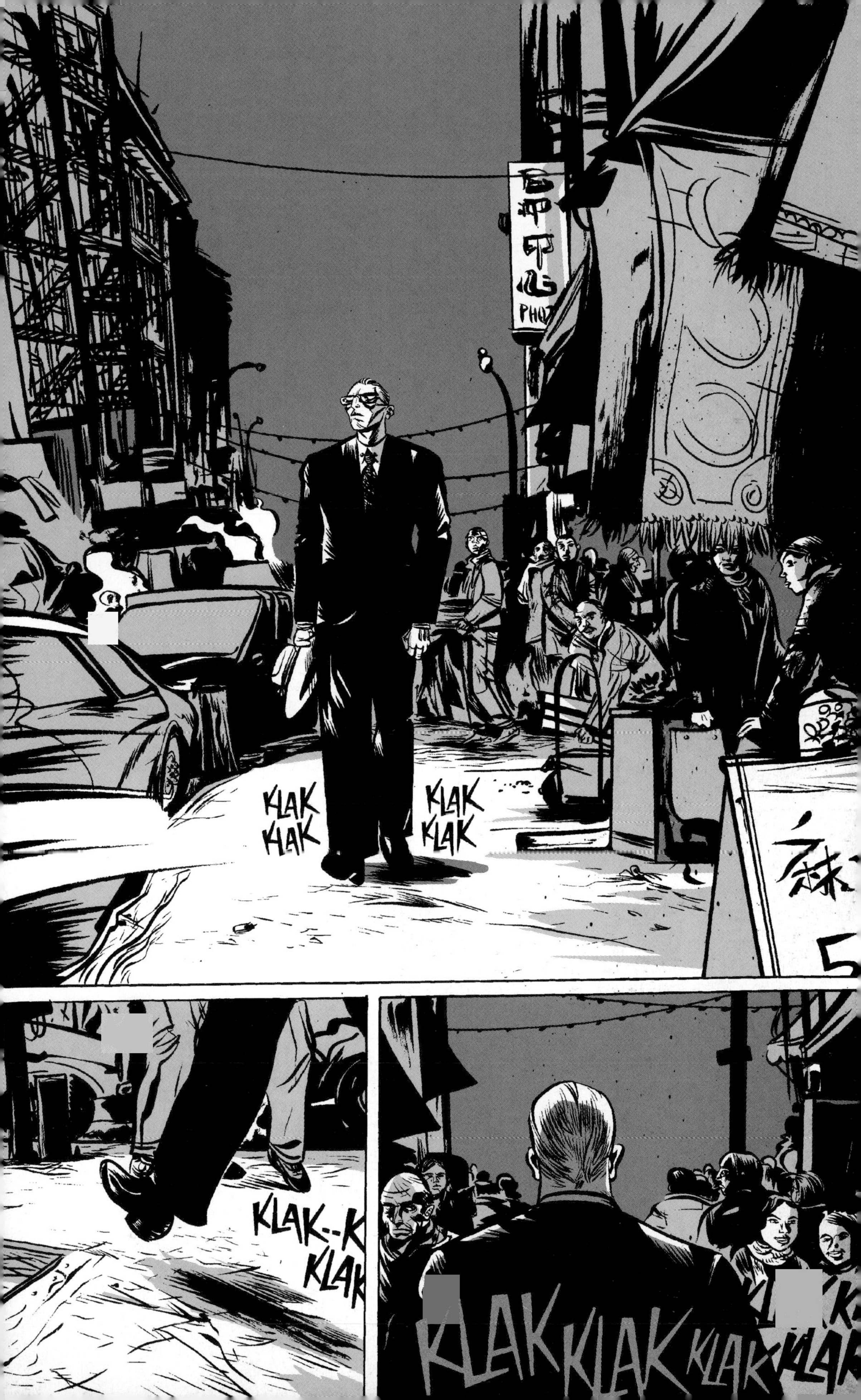
KLAK
KLAK
KLAK
KLAK
KLAK--K
KLAK
KLAK KLAK KLAK

SWSHH!

GOOD EVENING, SIR. WILL YOU BE NEEDING A ROOM?

I'M IN SEVEN-TEN, I'M HERE TO CHECK IN.

YES, I SEE IT HERE...YOUR ARRANGEMENTS HAVE ALREADY BEEN TAKEN CARE OF.

NO BAGS, SIR?

NO.

WOULD YOU LIKE TO SIGN OUR GUEST BOOK?

OF COURSE.

BREAKFAST IS SERVED FROM SEVEN 'TIL ELEVEN.

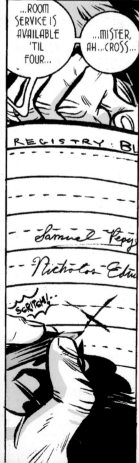

...ROOM SERVICE IS AVAILABLE 'TIL FOUR...

...MISTER, AH...CROSS...

REGISTRY: BU

Samuel Pepys

Nicholas Edm

SCRITCH!

KLIK- KLAK

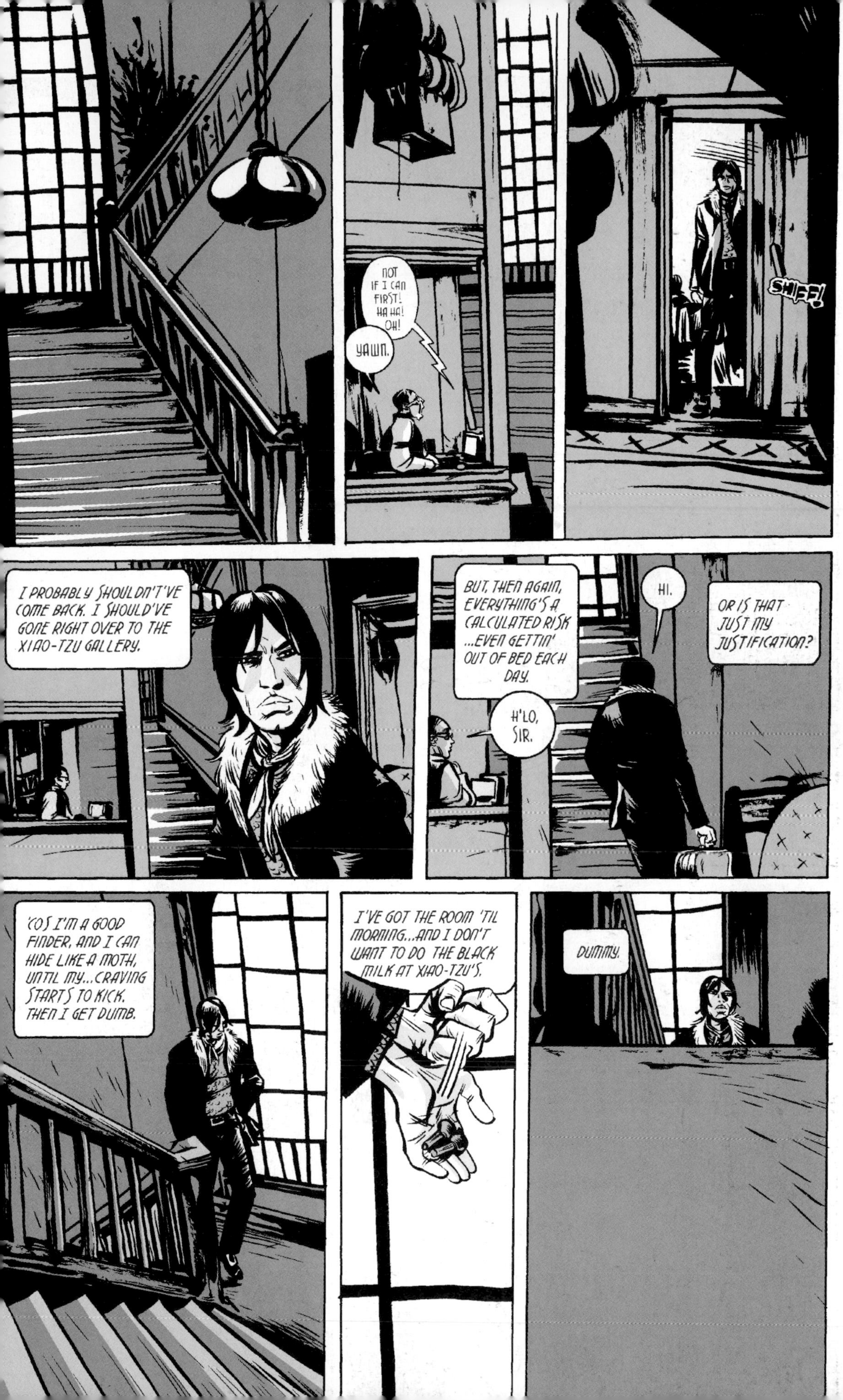
NOT IF I CAN FIRST! HA HA! OH!
YAWN.
SHIFF!
I PROBABLY SHOULDN'T'VE COME BACK. I SHOULD'VE GONE RIGHT OVER TO THE XIAO-TZU GALLERY.
BUT, THEN AGAIN, EVERYTHING'S A CALCULATED RISK ...EVEN GETTIN' OUT OF BED EACH DAY.
HI.
H'LO, SIR.
OR IS THAT JUST MY JUSTIFICATION?
'COS I'M A GOOD FINDER, AND I CAN HIDE LIKE A MOTH, UNTIL MY...CRAVING STARTS TO KICK. THEN I GET DUMB.
I'VE GOT THE ROOM 'TIL MORNING...AND I DON'T WANT TO DO THE BLACK MILK AT XIAO-TZU'S.
DUMMY.

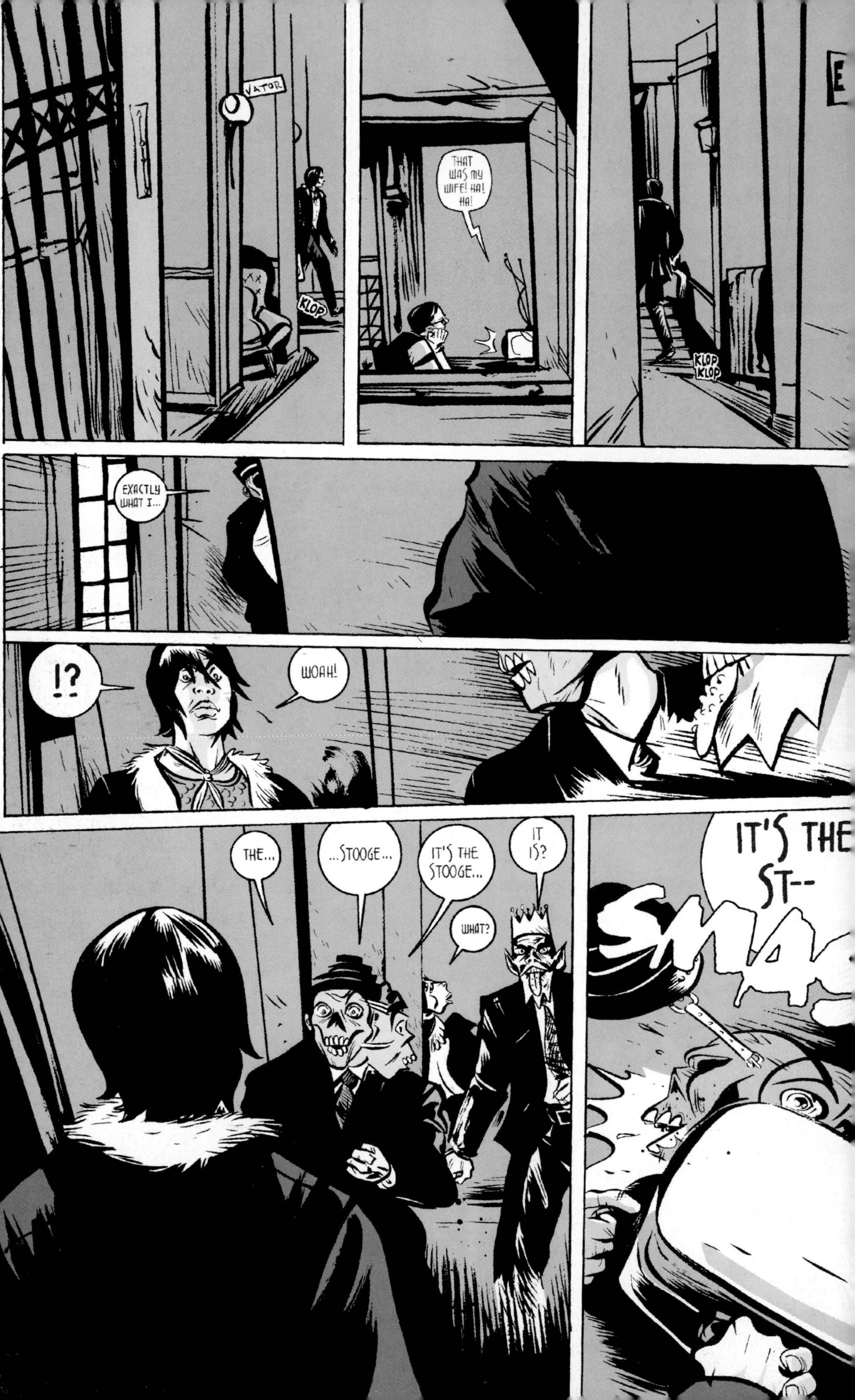
VATOR
KLOP
THAT WAS MY WIFE! HA! HA!
KLOP KLOP
E
EXACTLY WHAT I...
!?
WOAH!
THE...
...STOOGE...
IT'S THE STOOGE...
WHAT?
IT IS?
IT'S THE ST--

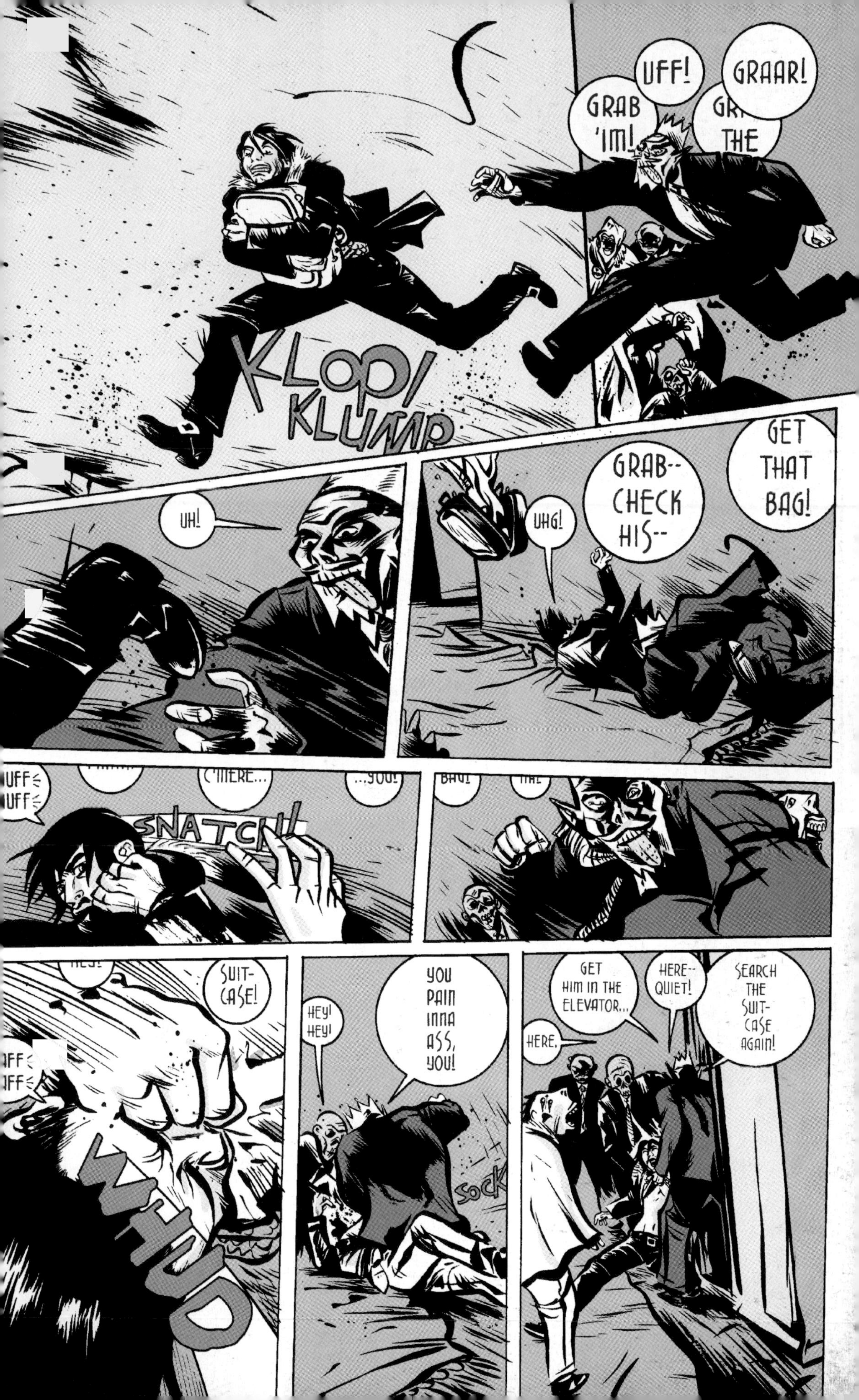
GRAB 'IM!
UFF!
GRAAR!
KLOP! KLUMP
UH!
UHG!
GRAB-- CHECK HIS--
GET THAT BAG!
UFF UFF
C'MERE...
...YOU!
SNATCH!!
SUIT-CASE!
WHUD
HEY! HEY!
YOU PAIN INNA ASS, YOU!
SOCK
HERE.
GET HIM IN THE ELEVATOR...
HERE-- QUIET!
SEARCH THE SUIT-CASE AGAIN!

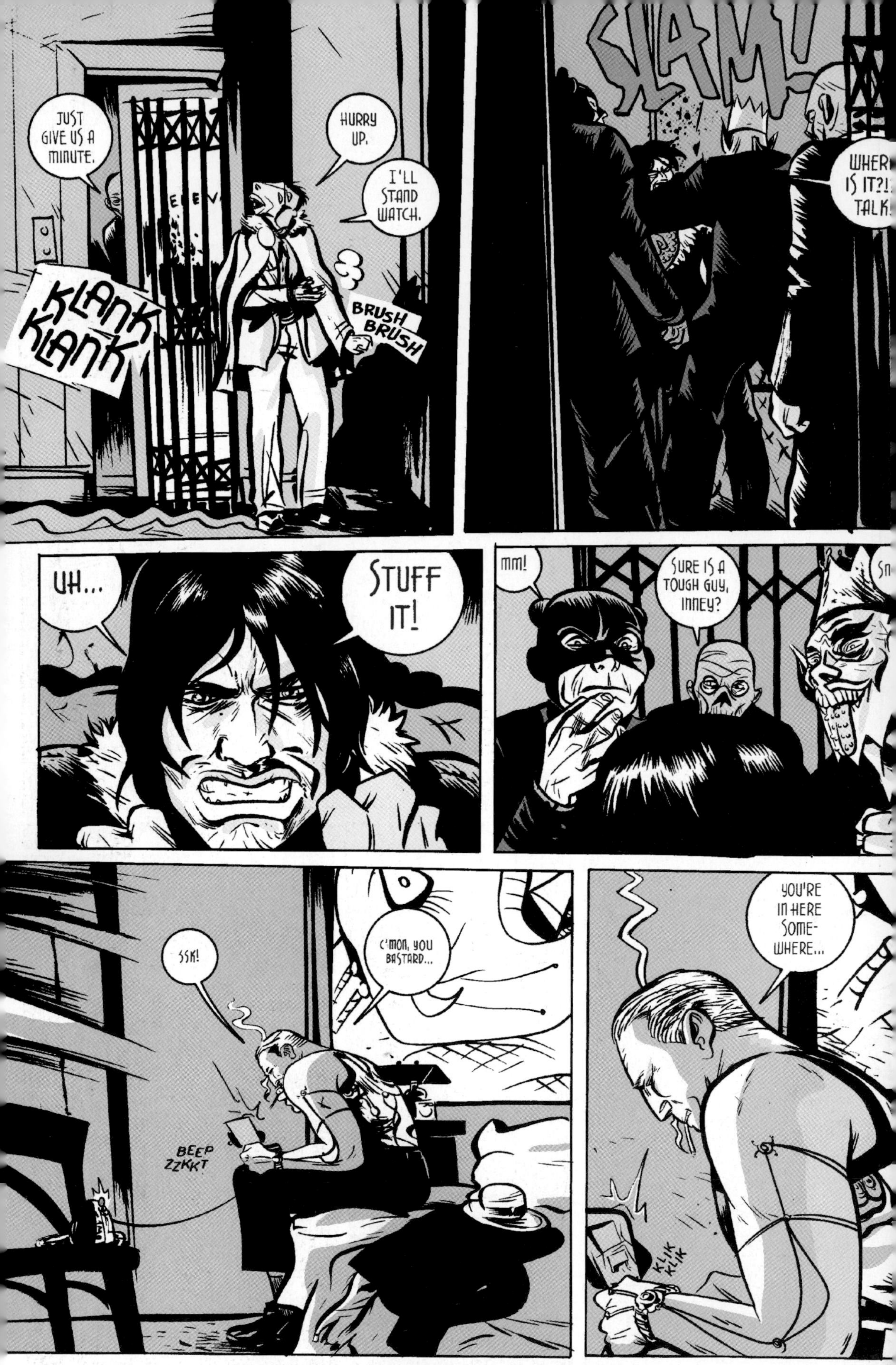
JUST GIVE US A MINUTE.
HURRY UP.
I'LL STAND WATCH.
KLANK KLANK
BRUSH BRUSH
WHER IS IT?!! TALK!
UH...
STUFF IT!
MM!
SURE IS A TOUGH GUY, INNEY?
SSK!
C'MON, YOU BASTARD...
BEEP ZZKKT
YOU'RE IN HERE SOME-WHERE...
KLIK KLIK

BZZT

SSK.

IT! BEEP STUFF IT!

VWOS BZZT KLIKK

WHH--

SURE IS A TOUGH GUY, INNEY!

IT'S HIM!

SNORT

DOESN'T MAKE A BIT OF DIFFERE DAMN!

LEMME HIT 'IM, TOO, DROPHEAD!

COUGH

GASP- GASP-

KAFF--

WELL, HURRY UP, THEN!

WA

WAIT! HANG ON! LET ME THROUGH TO 'IM--

NO, I WANT IT--

LET GO, CLEANER

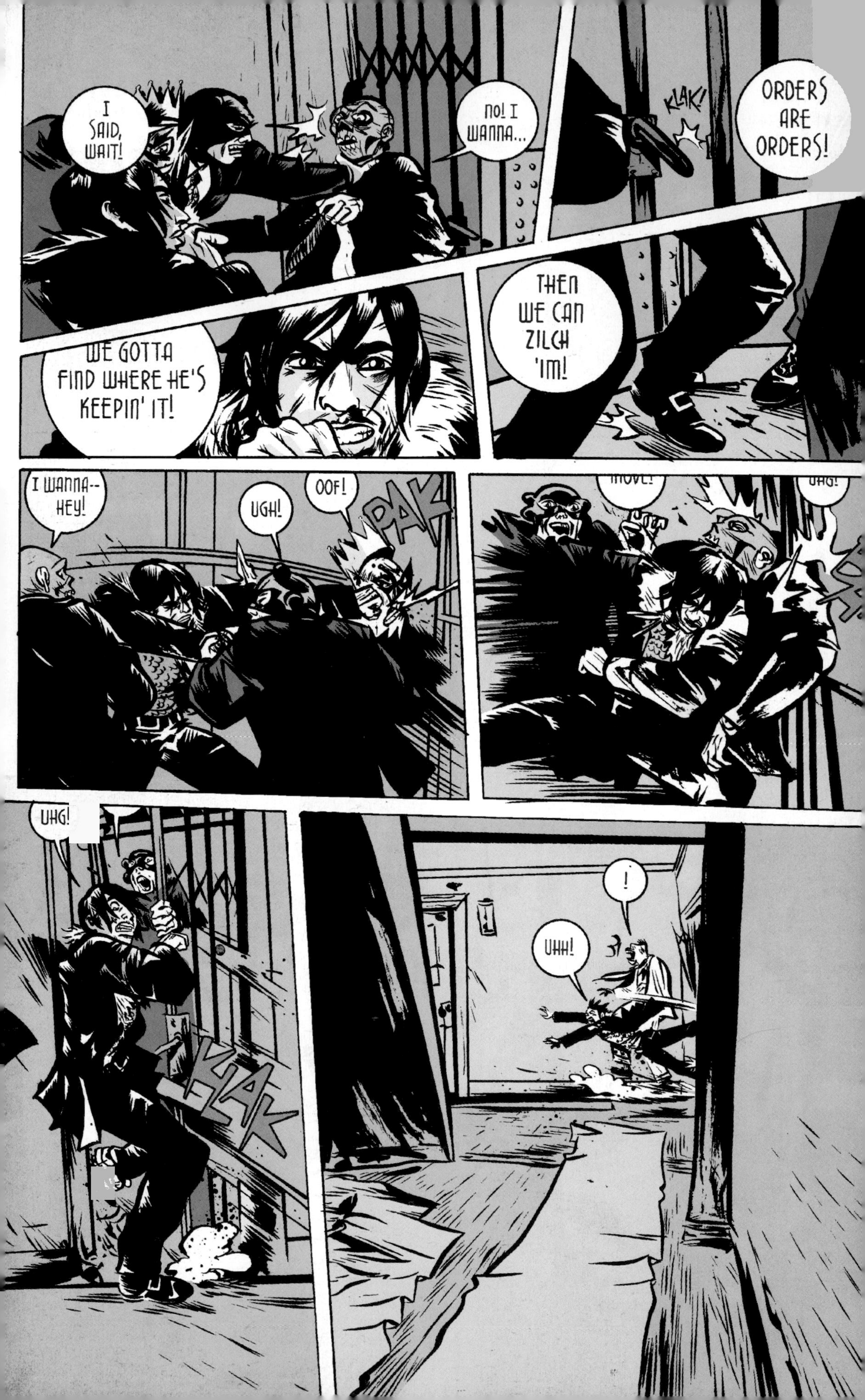
I SAID, WAIT!
NO! I WANNA...
KLAK!
ORDERS ARE ORDERS!
WE GOTTA FIND WHERE HE'S KEEPIN' IT!
THEN WE CAN ZILCH 'IM!
I WANNA-- HEY!
UGH!
OOF!
PAK
UHG!
KLAK
!
UHH!

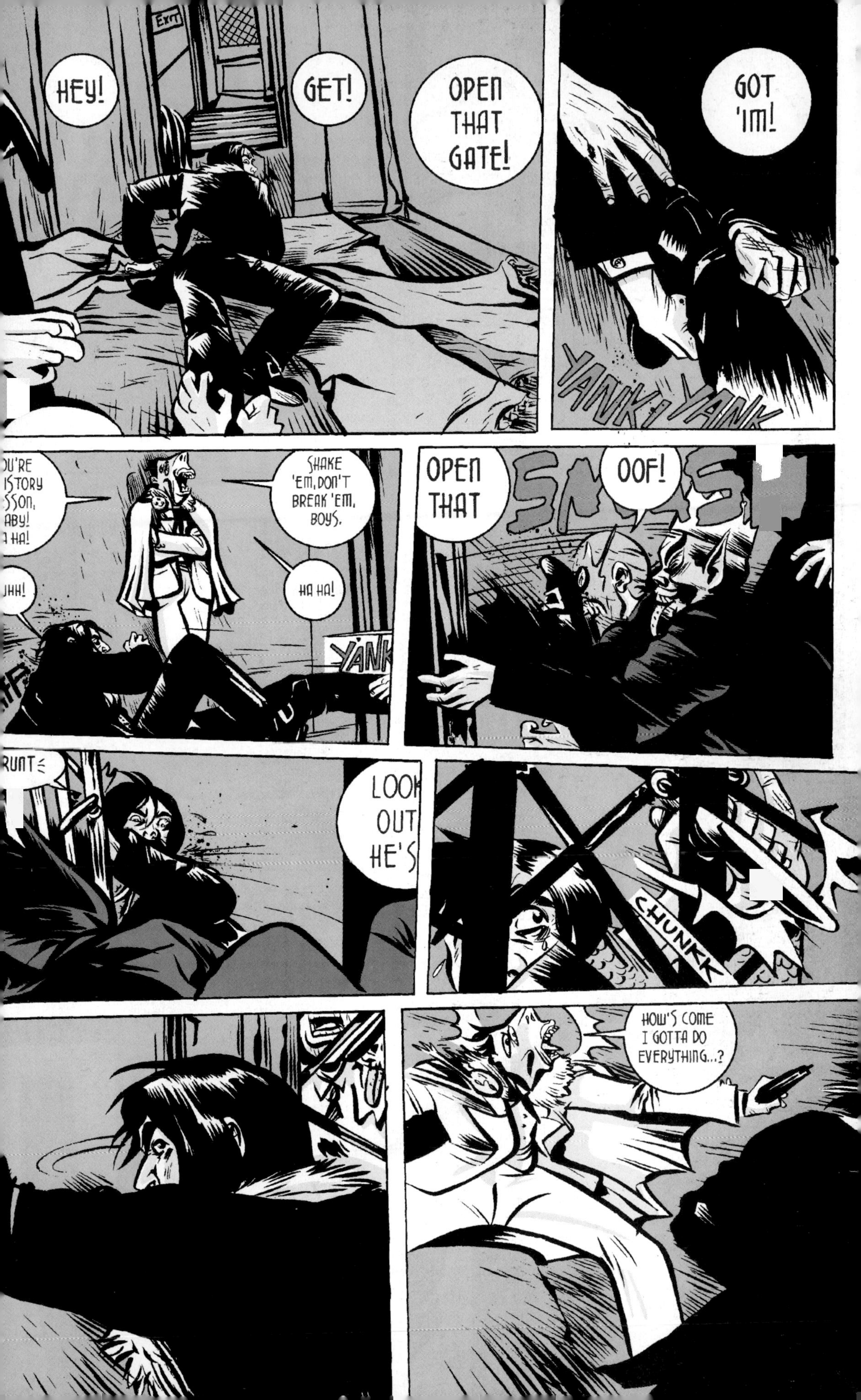
EXIT
HEY!
GET!
OPEN THAT GATE!
GOT 'IM!
YANK! YANK
OU'RE ISTORY SSON, ABY! A HA!
SHAKE 'EM, DON'T BREAK 'EM, BOYS.
UHH!
HA HA!
YANK
OPEN THAT
OOF!
RUNT
LOOK OUT HE'S
CHUNKK
HOW'S COME I GOTTA DO EVERYTHING...?

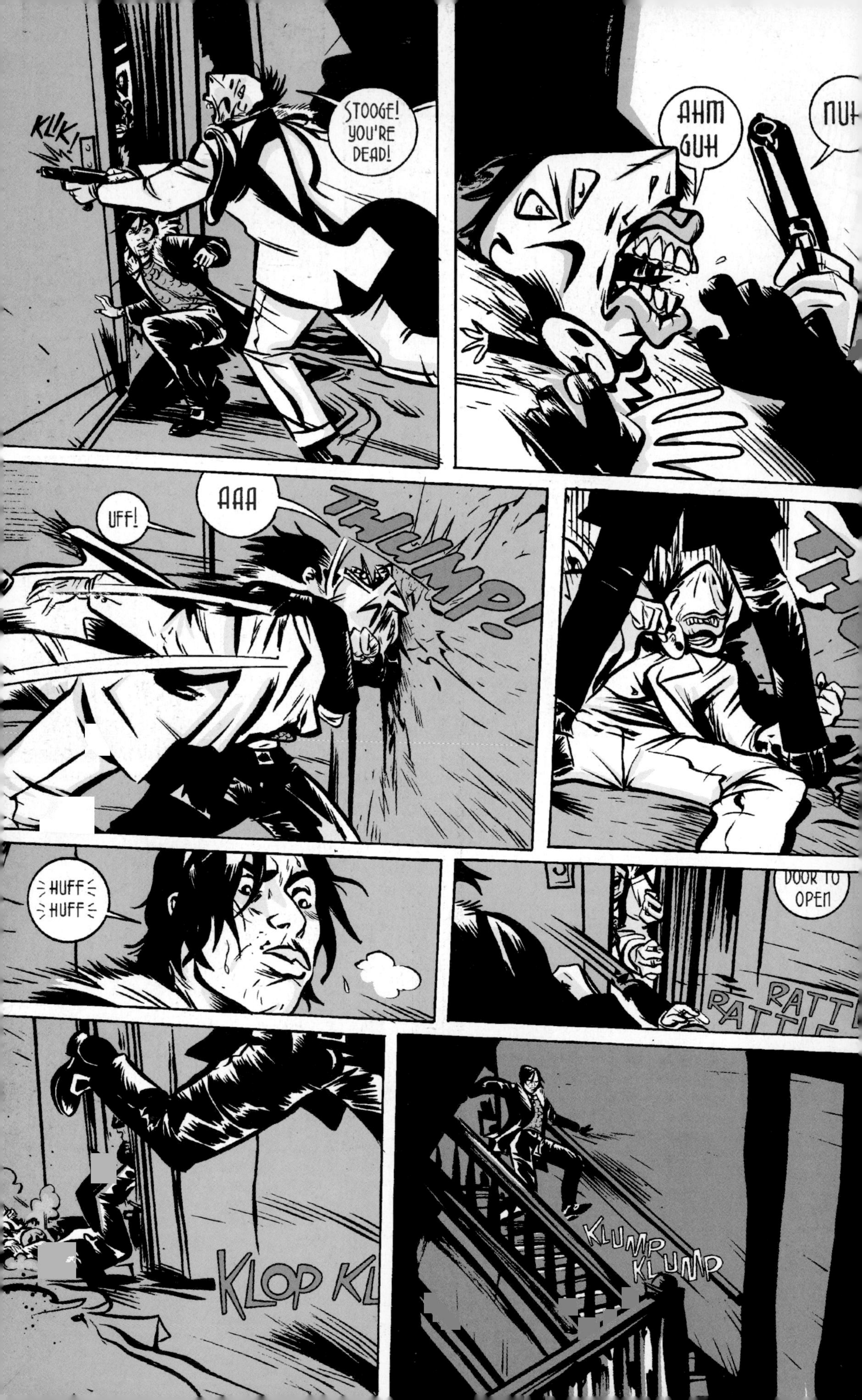
KLIK!
STOOGE! YOU'RE DEAD!
AHM GUH
NUH
UFF!
AAA
THUMP!
HUFF HUFF
DOOR TO OPEN
RATT
RATTLE
KLOP KL
KLUMP KLUMP

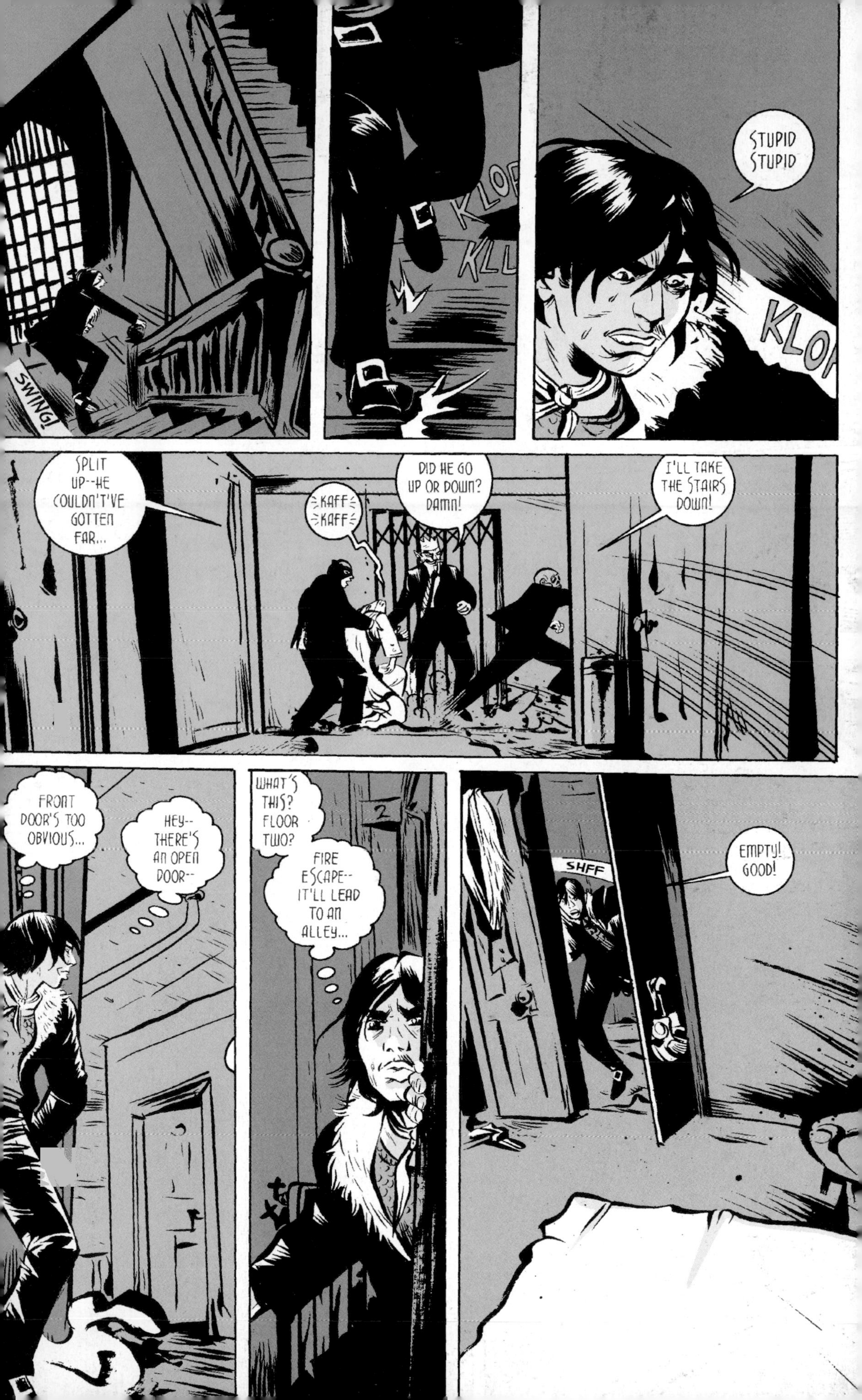
SWING!
KLOP
KLL
STUPID STUPID
KLOP
SPLIT UP--HE COULDN'T'VE GOTTEN FAR...
KAFF KAFF
DID HE GO UP OR DOWN? DAMN!
I'LL TAKE THE STAIRS DOWN!
FRONT DOOR'S TOO OBVIOUS...
HEY-- THERE'S AN OPEN DOOR--
WHAT'S THIS? FLOOR TWO?
2
FIRE ESCAPE-- IT'LL LEAD TO AN ALLEY...
SHFF
EMPTY! GOOD!

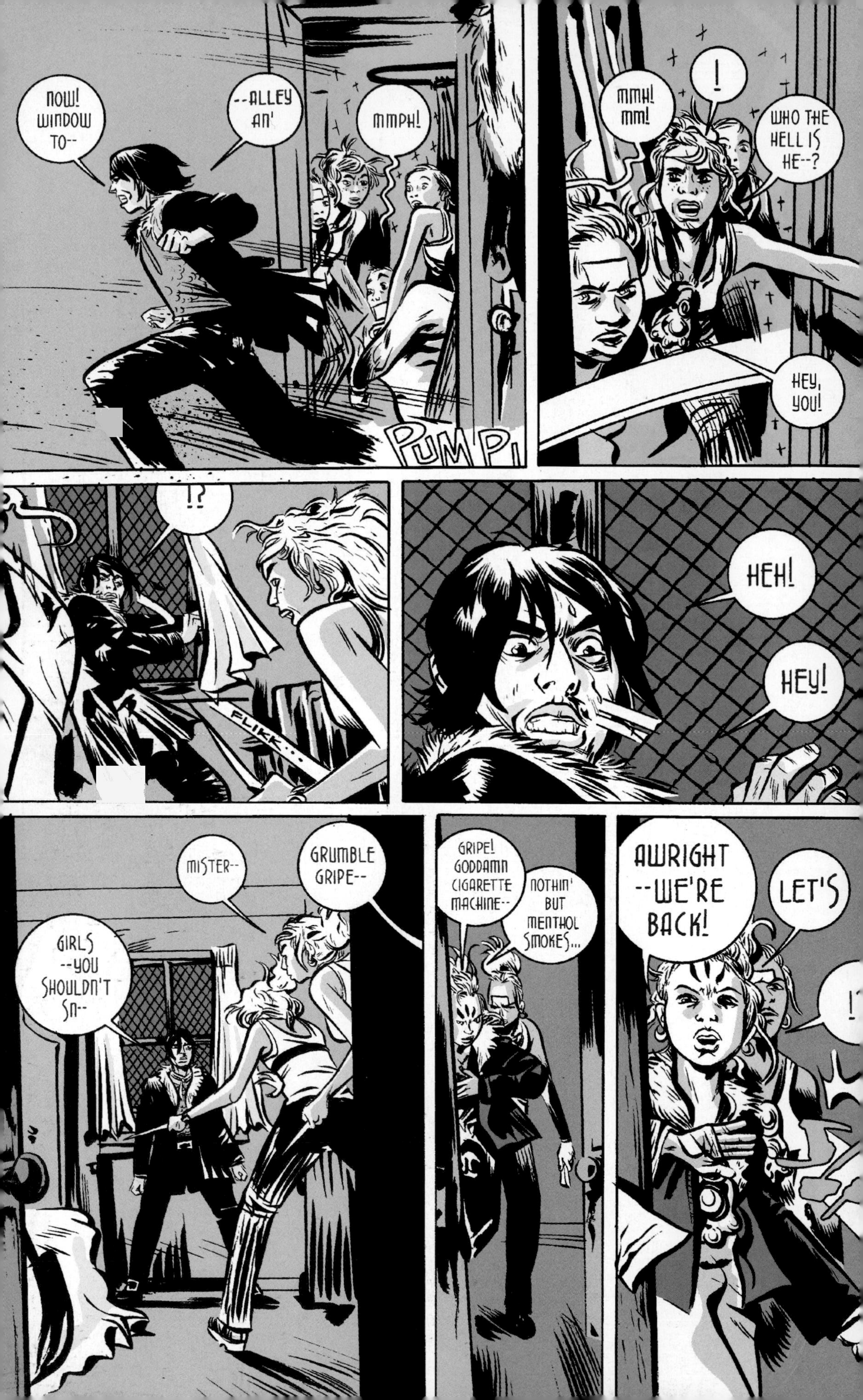
NOW! WINDOW TO--
--ALLEY AN'
MMPH!
PUMP!
MMH! MM!
!
WHO THE HELL IS HE--?
HEY, YOU!
!?
FLIKK
HEH!
HEY!
MISTER--
GRUMBLE GRIPE--
GIRLS --YOU SHOULDN'T SN--
GRIPE! GODDAMN CIGARETTE MACHINE--
NOTHIN' BUT MENTHOL SMOKES...
AWRIGHT --WE'RE BACK!
LET'S
!

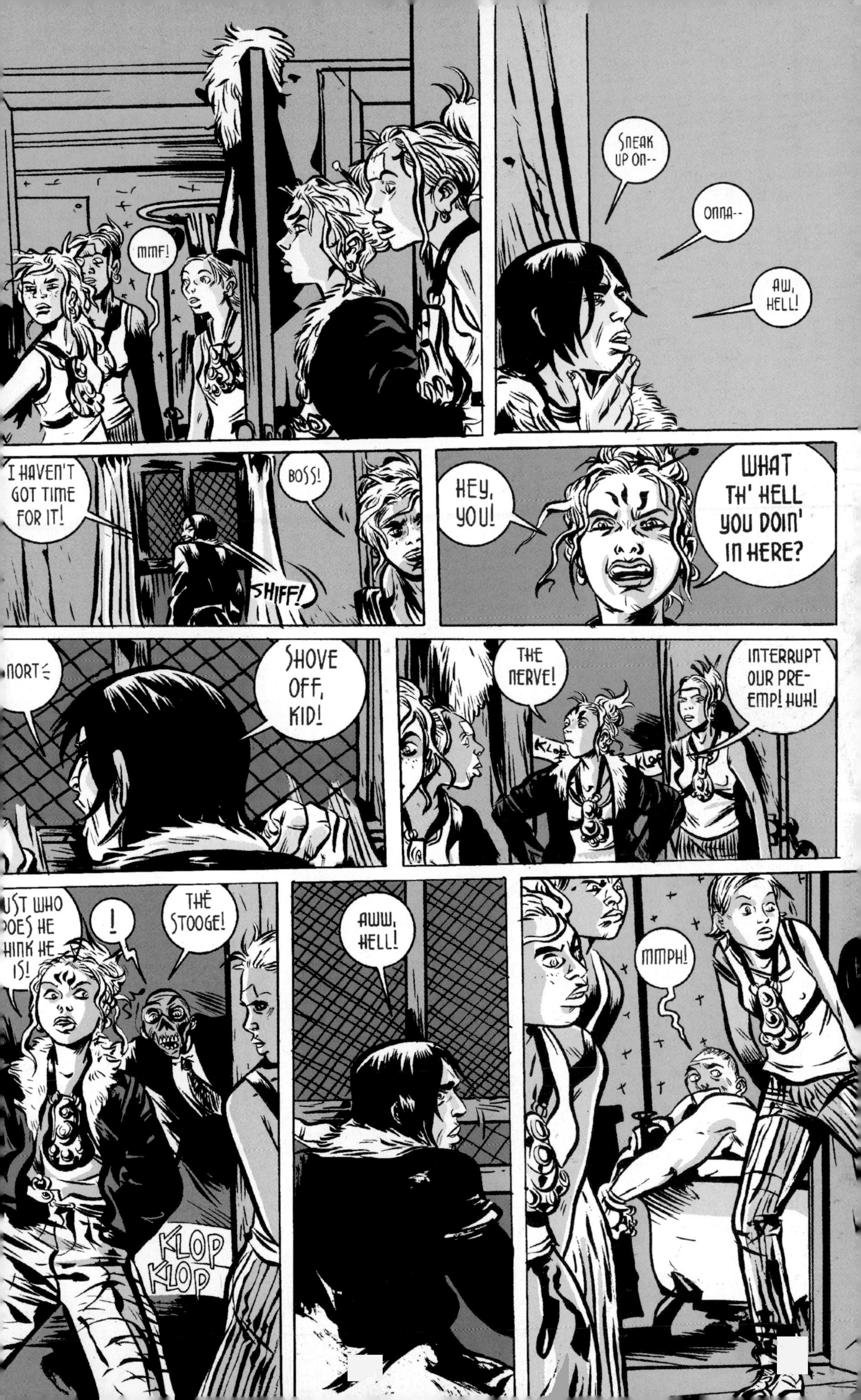
MMF!
SNEAK UP ON--
ONNA--
AW, HELL!
I HAVEN'T GOT TIME FOR IT!
BOSS!
SHIFF!
HEY, YOU!
WHAT TH' HELL YOU DOIN' IN HERE?
NORT
SHOVE OFF, KID!
THE NERVE!
INTERRUPT OUR PRE-EMP! HUH!
KLOP
KLOP
UST WHO OES HE HINK HE IS!
!
THE STOOGE!
KLOP KLOP
AWW, HELL!
MMPH!

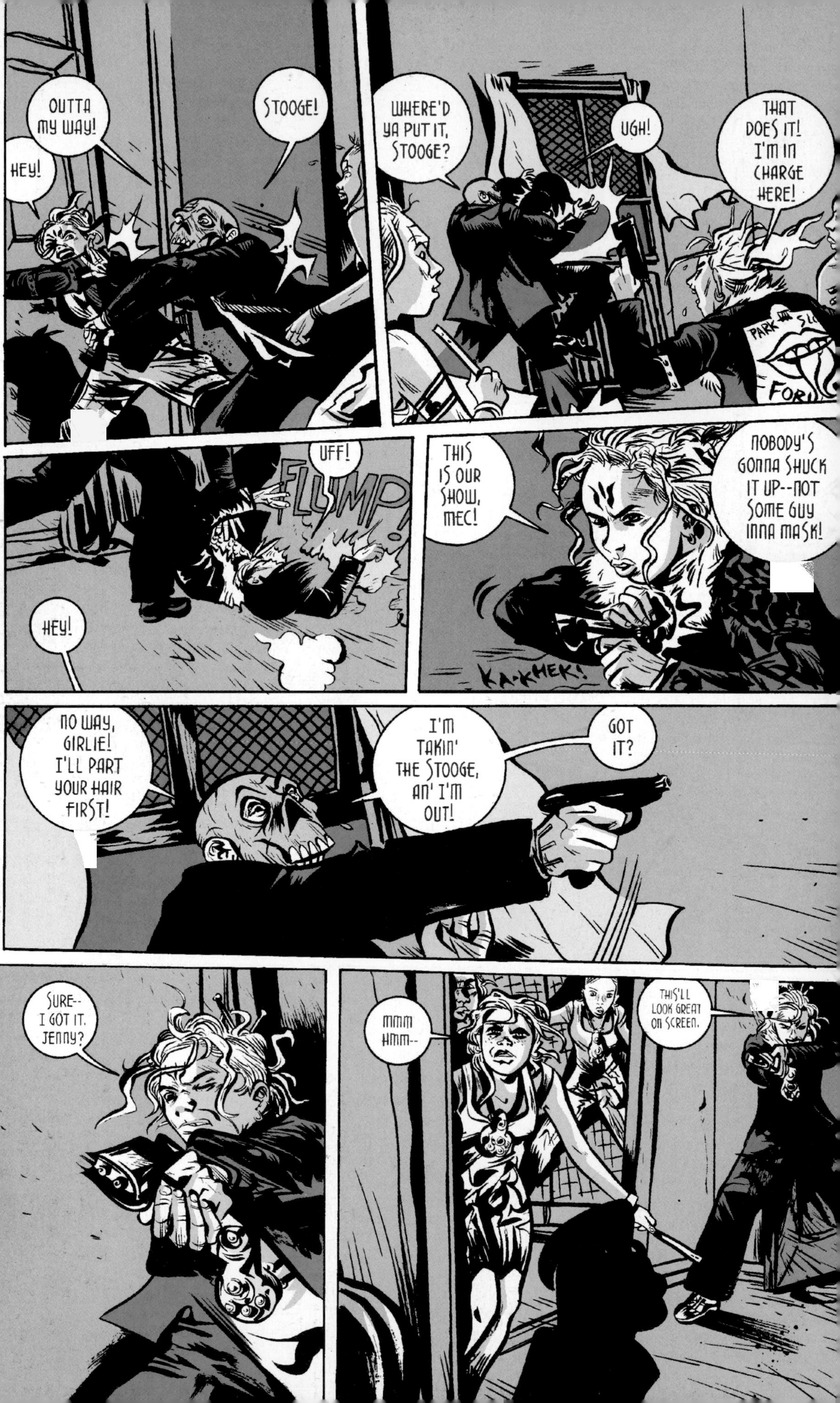
OUTTA MY WAY!
HEY!
STOOGE!
WHERE'D YA PUT IT, STOOGE?
UGH!
THAT DOES IT! I'M IN CHARGE HERE!
PARK SL
FOR
UFF!
FLUMP!
HEY!
THIS IS OUR SHOW, MEC!
NOBODY'S GONNA SHUCK IT UP--NOT SOME GUY INNA MASK!
KA-KHEK!
NO WAY, GIRLIE! I'LL PART YOUR HAIR FIRST!
I'M TAKIN' THE STOOGE, AN' I'M OUT!
GOT IT?
SURE-- I GOT IT. JENNY?
MMM HMM--
THIS'LL LOOK GREAT ON SCREEN.

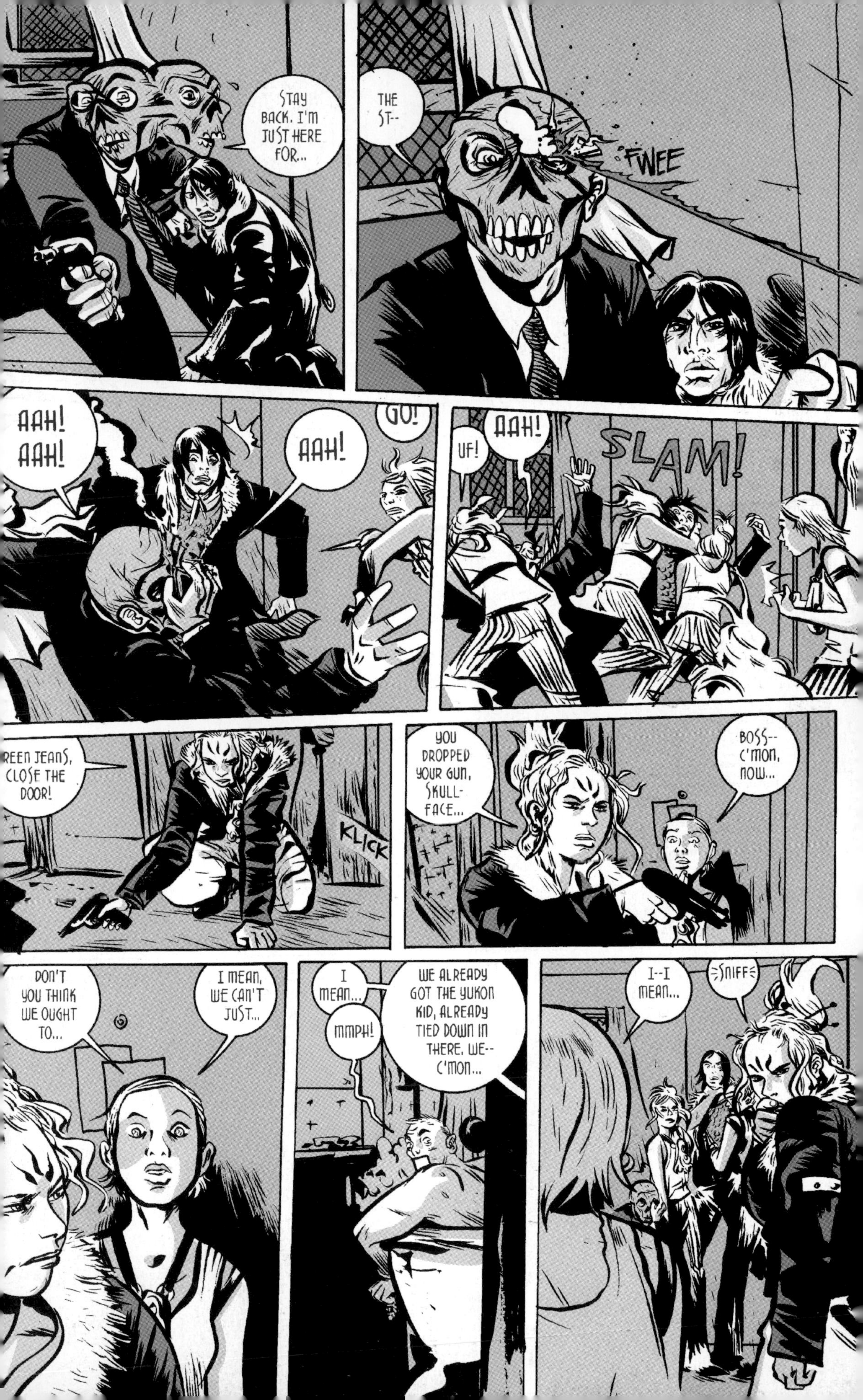
STAY BACK. I'M JUST HERE FOR...
THE ST--
FWEE
AAH! AAH!
AAH!
GO!
UF!
AAH!
SLAM!
REEN JEANS, CLOSE THE DOOR!
KLICK
YOU DROPPED YOUR GUN, SKULL-FACE...
BOSS-- C'MON, NOW...
DON'T YOU THINK WE OUGHT TO...
I MEAN, WE CAN'T JUST...
I MEAN...
MMPH!
WE ALREADY GOT THE YUKON KID, ALREADY TIED DOWN IN THERE. WE-- C'MON...
I--I MEAN...
SNIFF

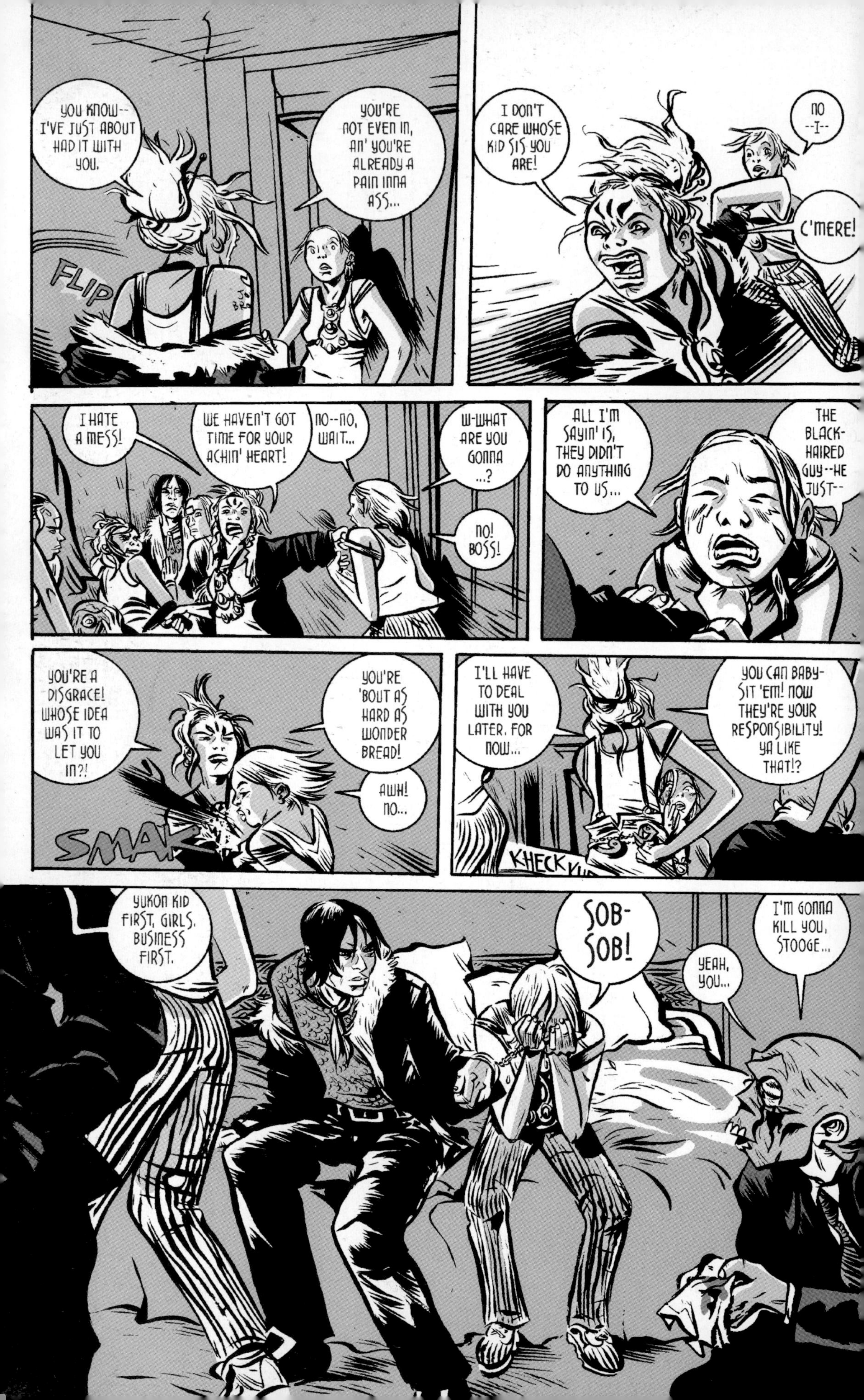
YOU KNOW-- I'VE JUST ABOUT HAD IT WITH YOU.
FLIP
YOU'RE NOT EVEN IN, AN' YOU'RE ALREADY A PAIN INNA ASS...
I DON'T CARE WHOSE KID SIS YOU ARE!
NO --I--
C'MERE!
I HATE A MESS!
WE HAVEN'T GOT TIME FOR YOUR ACHIN' HEART!
NO--NO, WAIT...
W-WHAT ARE YOU GONNA ...?
NO! BOSS!
ALL I'M SAYIN' IS, THEY DIDN'T DO ANYTHING TO US...
THE BLACK-HAIRED GUY--HE JUST--
YOU'RE A DISGRACE! WHOSE IDEA WAS IT TO LET YOU IN?!
YOU'RE 'BOUT AS HARD AS WONDER BREAD!
AWH! NO...
SMAK
I'LL HAVE TO DEAL WITH YOU LATER. FOR NOW...
YOU CAN BABY-SIT 'EM! NOW THEY'RE YOUR RESPONSIBILITY! YA LIKE THAT!?
YUKON KID FIRST, GIRLS. BUSINESS FIRST.
SOB-SOB!
YEAH, YOU...
I'M GONNA KILL YOU, STOOGE...

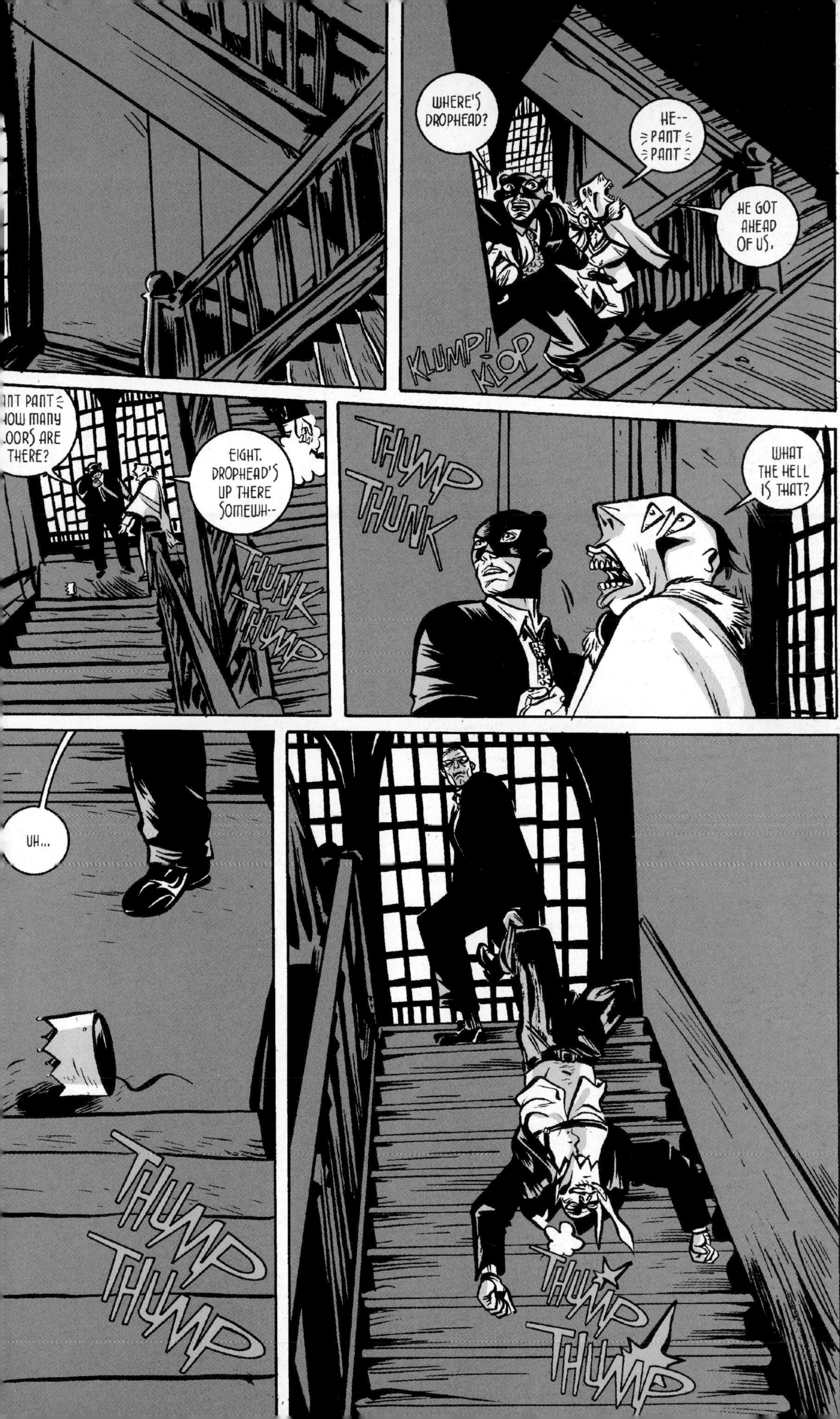
WHERE'S DROPHEAD?
HE-- PANT PANT
HE GOT AHEAD OF US.
KLUMP! KLOP
ANT PANT HOW MANY LOORS ARE THERE?
EIGHT. DROPHEAD'S UP THERE SOMEWH--
THUNK THUMP
THUMP THUNK
WHAT THE HELL IS THAT?
UH...
THUMP THUMP
THUMP THUMP

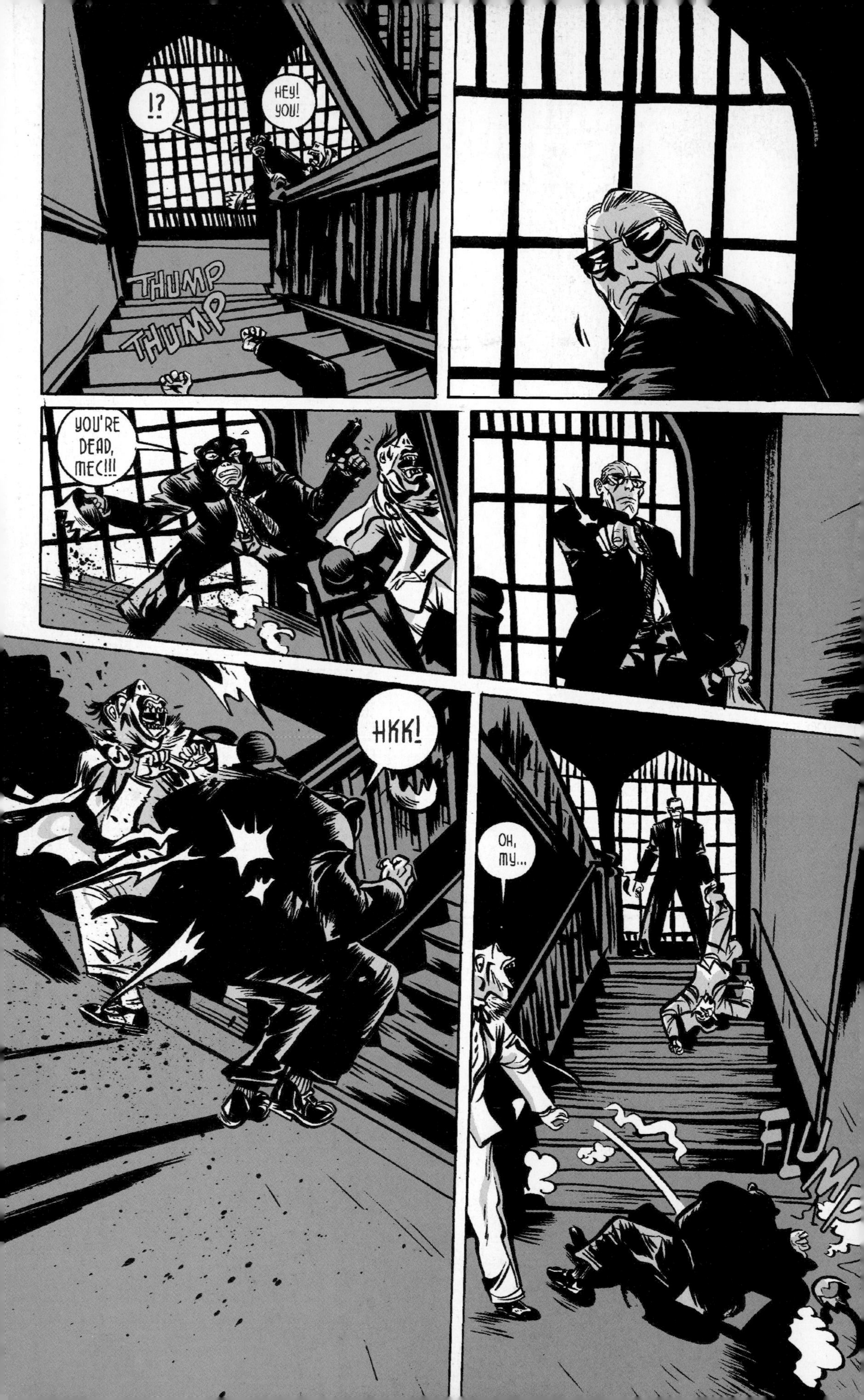
!?
HEY! YOU!
THUMP
THUMP
YOU'RE DEAD, MEC!!!
HKK!
OH, MY...

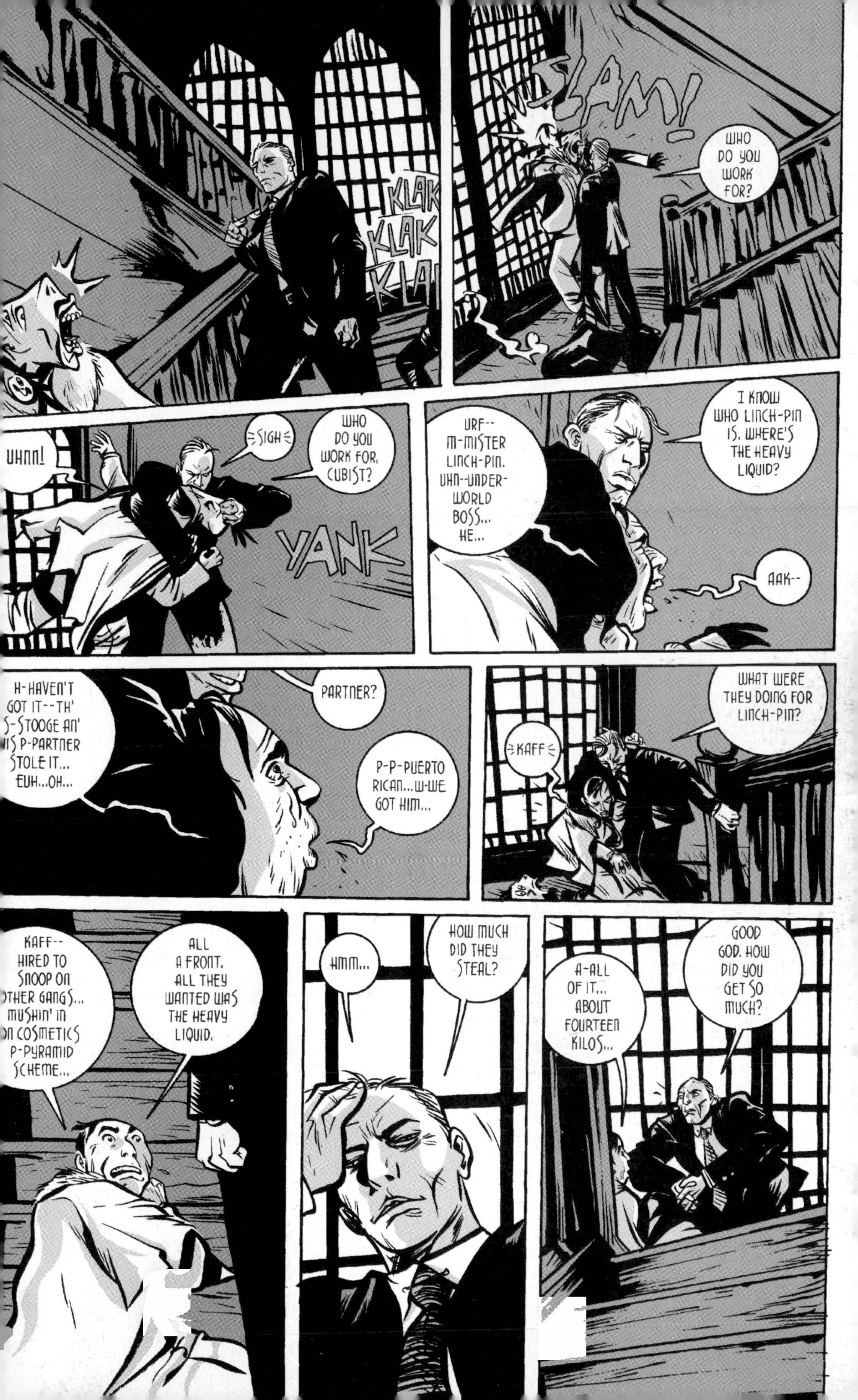
SPLATCH
KLAK
KLAK
KLAK
SLAM!
WHO DO YOU WORK FOR?
UHNN!
SIGH
WHO DO YOU WORK FOR, CUBIST?
YANK
URF-- M-MISTER LINCH-PIN. UHN--UNDER-WORLD BOSS... HE...
I KNOW WHO LINCH-PIN IS. WHERE'S THE HEAVY LIQUID?
AAK--
H-HAVEN'T GOT IT--TH' S-STOOGE AN' HIS P-PARTNER STOLE IT... EUH...OH...
PARTNER?
P-P-PUERTO RICAN...W-WE GOT HIM...
KAFF
WHAT WERE THEY DOING FOR LINCH-PIN?
KAFF-- HIRED TO SNOOP ON OTHER GANGS... MUSHIN' IN ON COSMETICS P-PYRAMID SCHEME...
ALL A FRONT. ALL THEY WANTED WAS THE HEAVY LIQUID.
HMM...
HOW MUCH DID THEY STEAL?
A-ALL OF IT... ABOUT FOURTEEN KILOS...
GOOD GOD. HOW DID YOU GET SO MUCH?

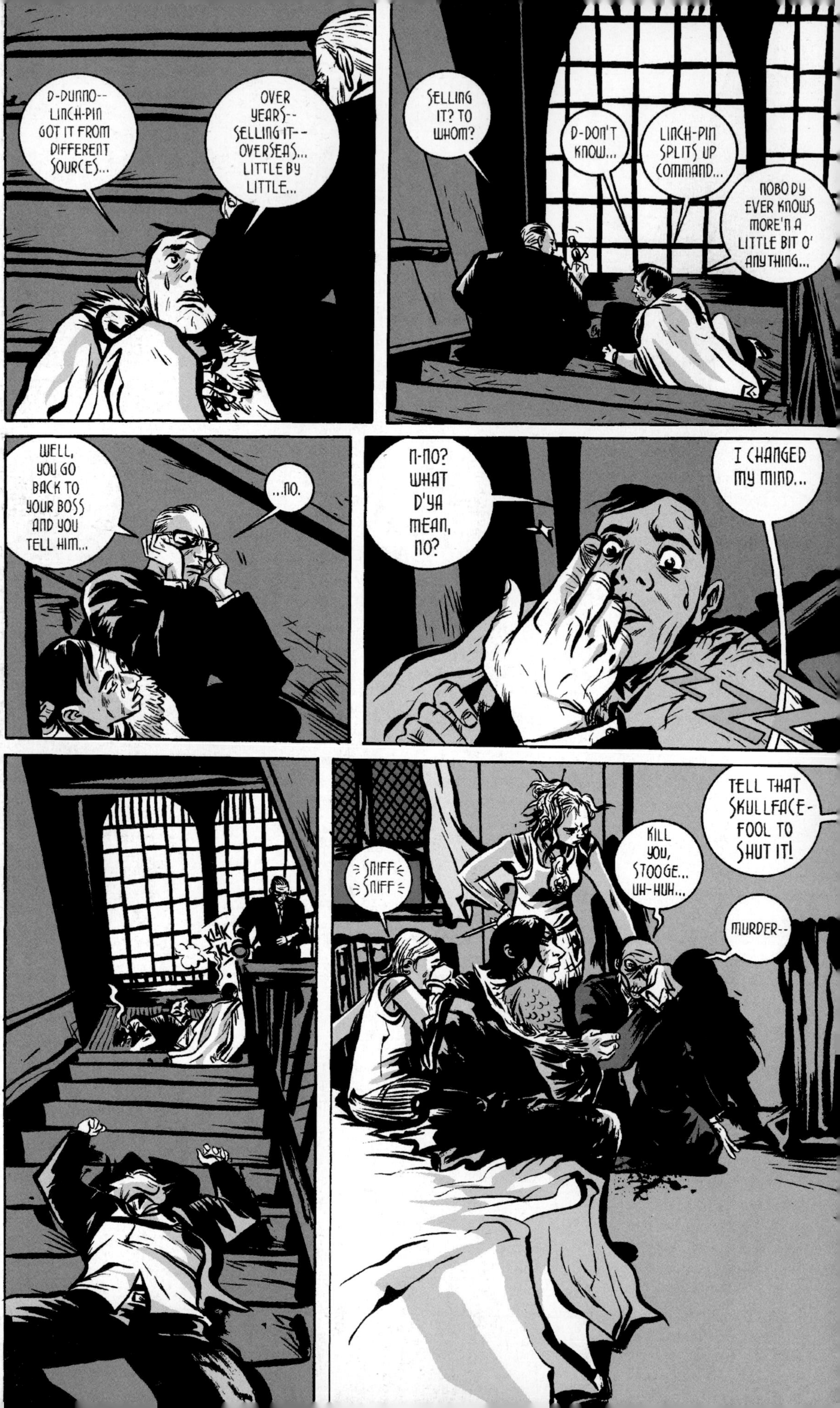
D-DUNNO-- LINCH-PIN GOT IT FROM DIFFERENT SOURCES...
OVER YEARS-- SELLING IT-- OVERSEAS... LITTLE BY LITTLE...
SELLING IT? TO WHOM?
D-DON'T KNOW...
LINCH-PIN SPLITS UP COMMAND...
NOBODY EVER KNOWS MORE'N A LITTLE BIT O' ANYTHING...
WELL, YOU GO BACK TO YOUR BOSS AND YOU TELL HIM...
...NO.
N-NO? WHAT D'YA MEAN, NO?
I CHANGED MY MIND...
KLAK
SNIFF SNIFF
KILL YOU, STOOGE... UH-HUH...
TELL THAT SKULLFACE-FOOL TO SHUT IT!
MURDER--

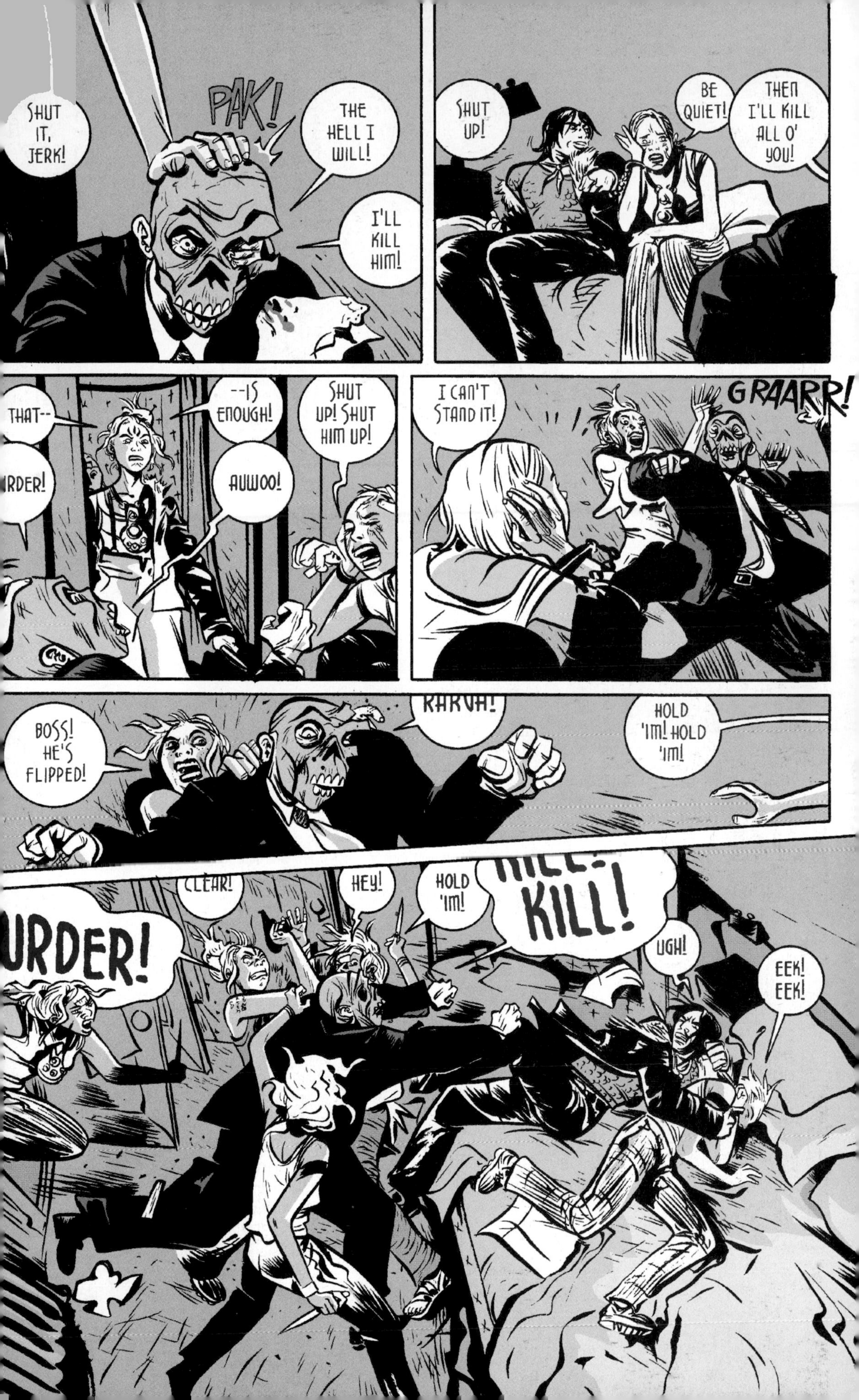
SHUT IT, JERK!
PAK!
THE HELL I WILL!
I'LL KILL HIM!
SHUT UP!
BE QUIET!
THEN I'LL KILL ALL O' YOU!
THAT--
--IS ENOUGH!
RDER!
AUWOO!
SHUT UP! SHUT HIM UP!
I CAN'T STAND IT!
GRAARR!
BOSS! HE'S FLIPPED!
RARGH!
HOLD 'IM! HOLD 'IM!
URDER!
CLEAR!
HEY!
HOLD 'IM!
KILL!
UGH!
EEK! EEK!

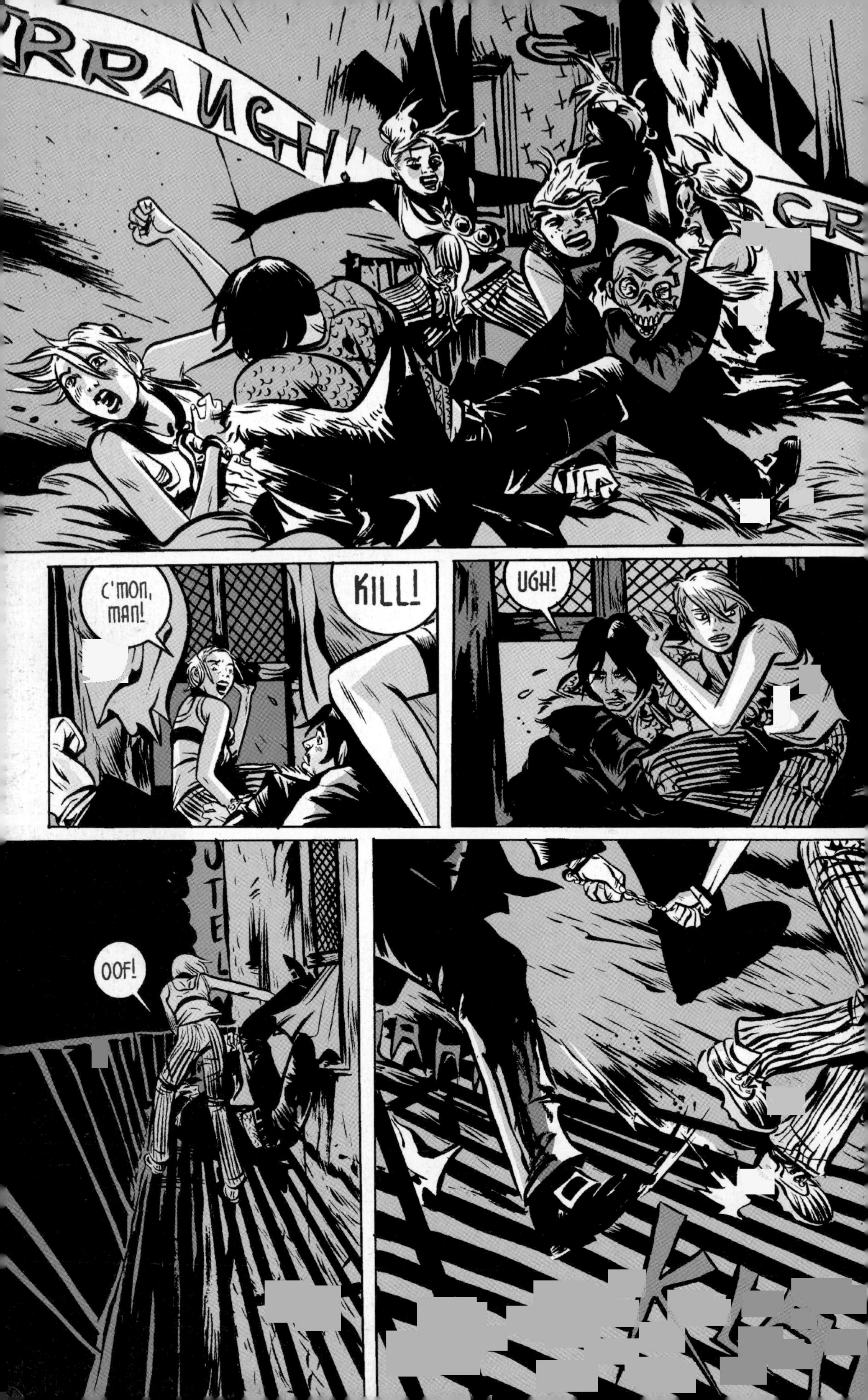
RRAUGH!
CR
C'MON, MAN!
KILL!
UGH!
OOF!

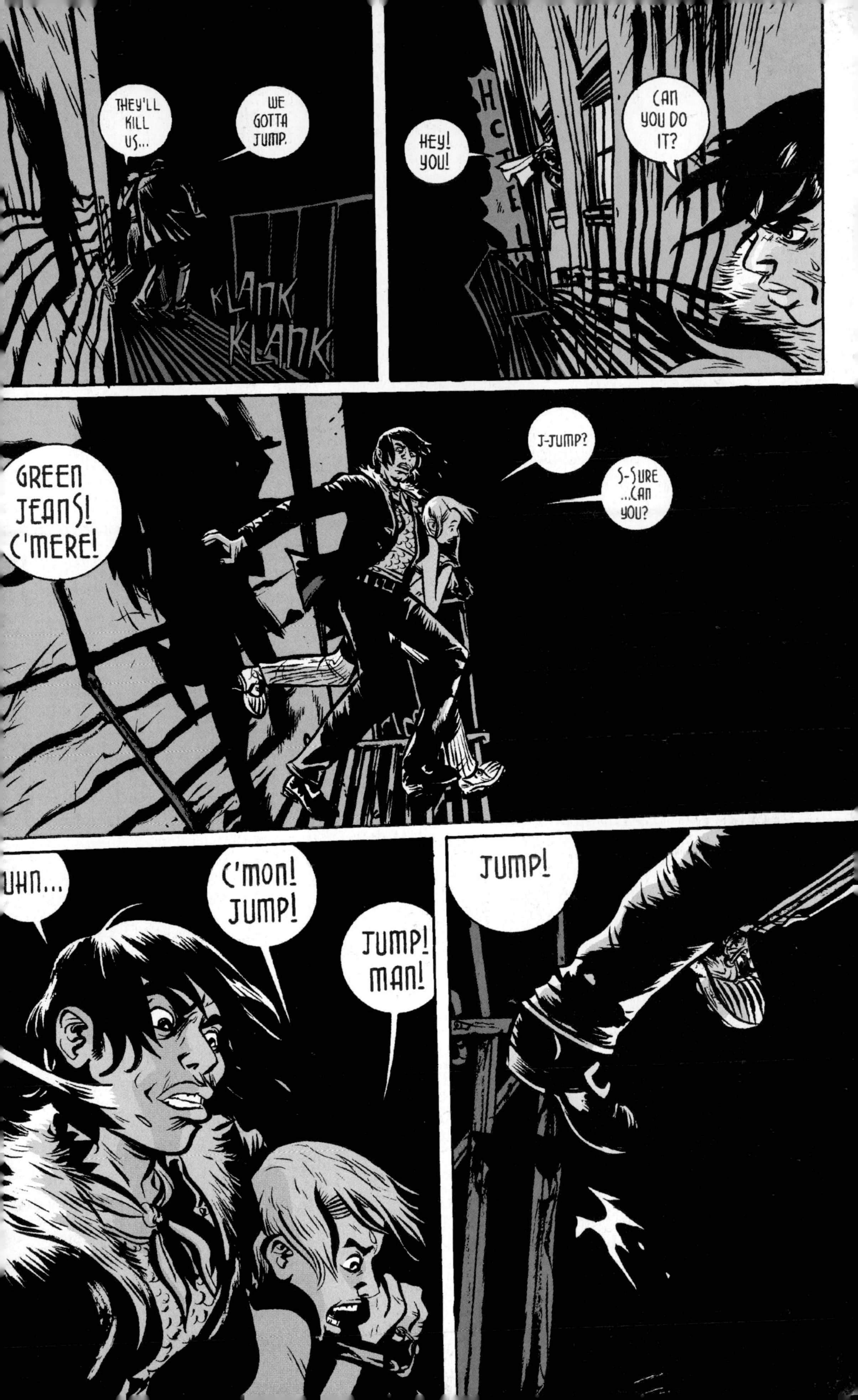
THEY'LL KILL US...
WE GOTTA JUMP.
KLANK KLANK
HEY! YOU!
HOTEL
CAN YOU DO IT?
GREEN JEANS! C'MERE!
J-JUMP?
S-SURE ...CAN YOU?
UHN...
C'MON! JUMP!
JUMP! MAN!
JUMP!

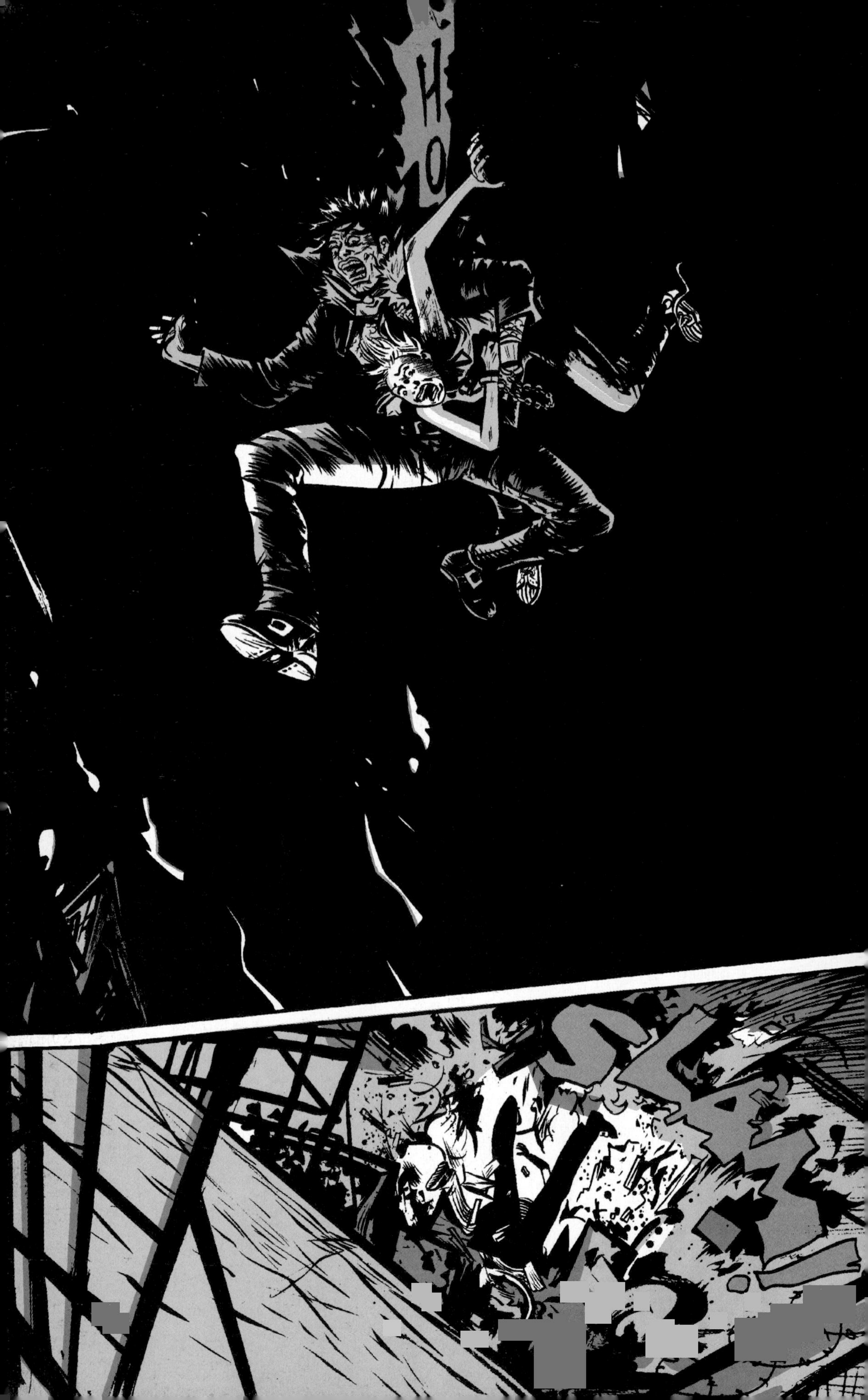
HO

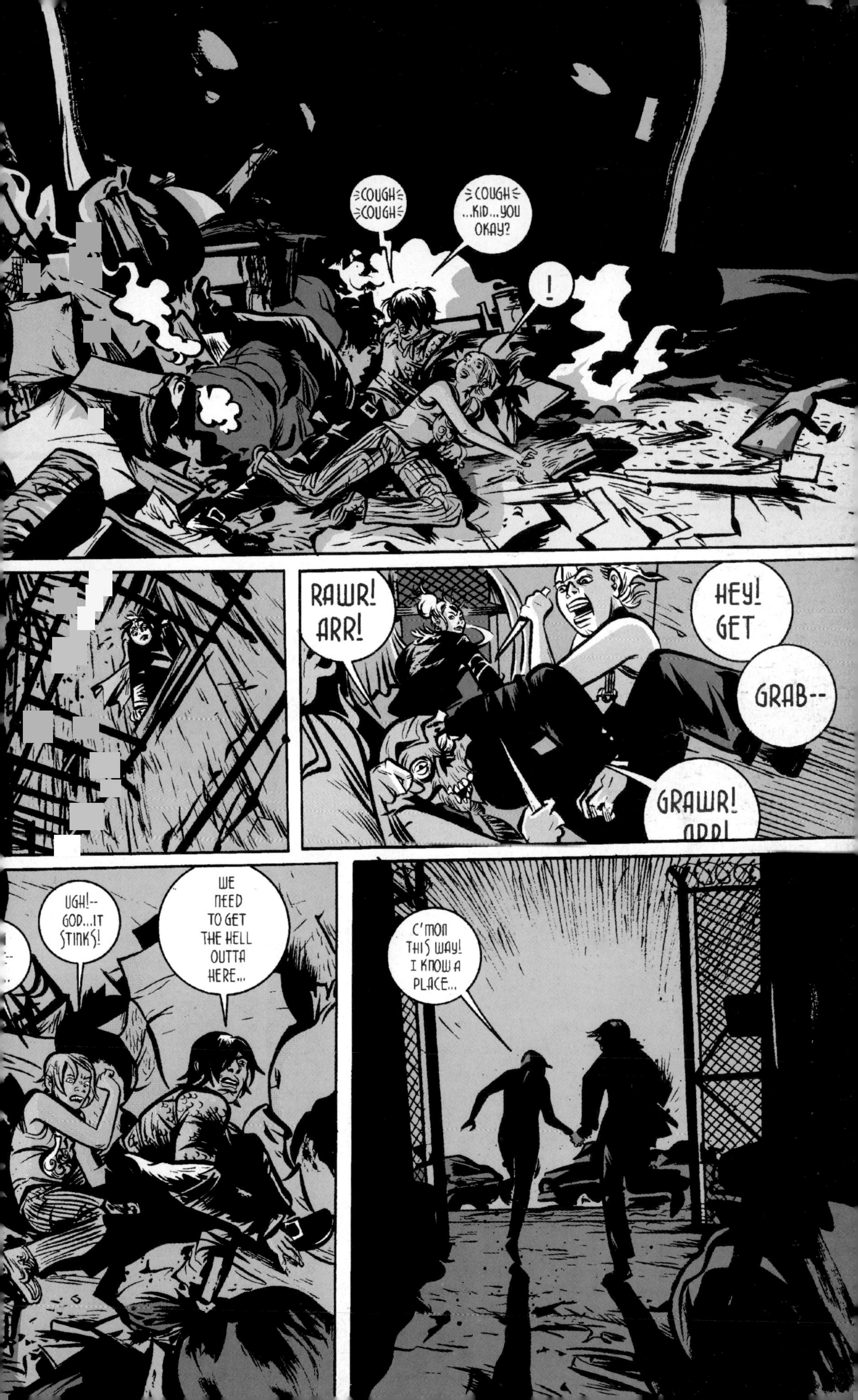
COUGH
COUGH
COUGH
...KID...YOU OKAY?
!
RAWR! ARR!
HEY! GET
GRAB--
GRAWR!
UGH!-- GOD...IT STINKS!
WE NEED TO GET THE HELL OUTTA HERE...
C'MON THIS WAY! I KNOW A PLACE...

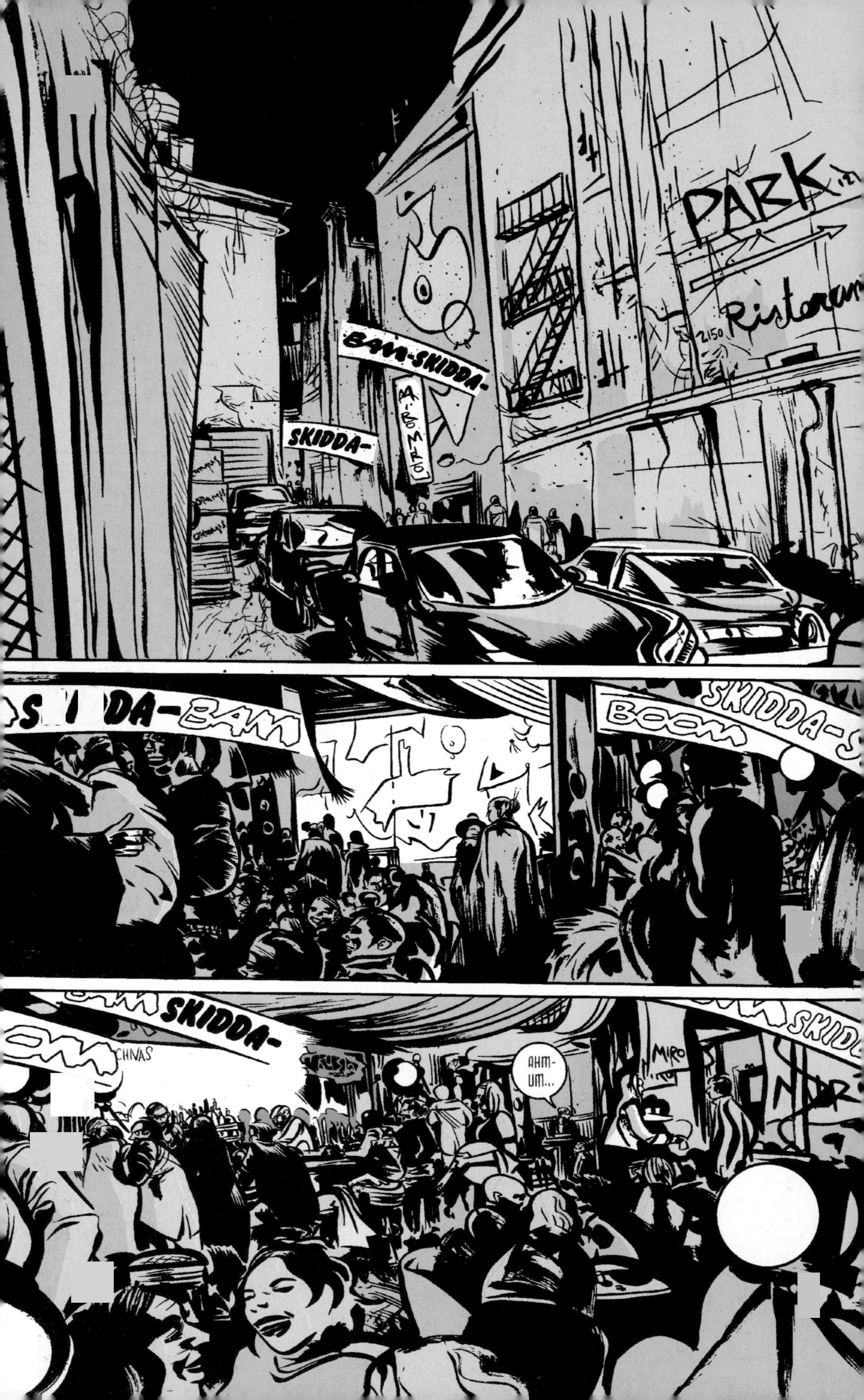
PARK
2150
BAM-SKIDDA-
SKIDDA-
BOOM
SKIDDA-
SKIDDA-
CHIVAS
AHM-UM...
MIRO

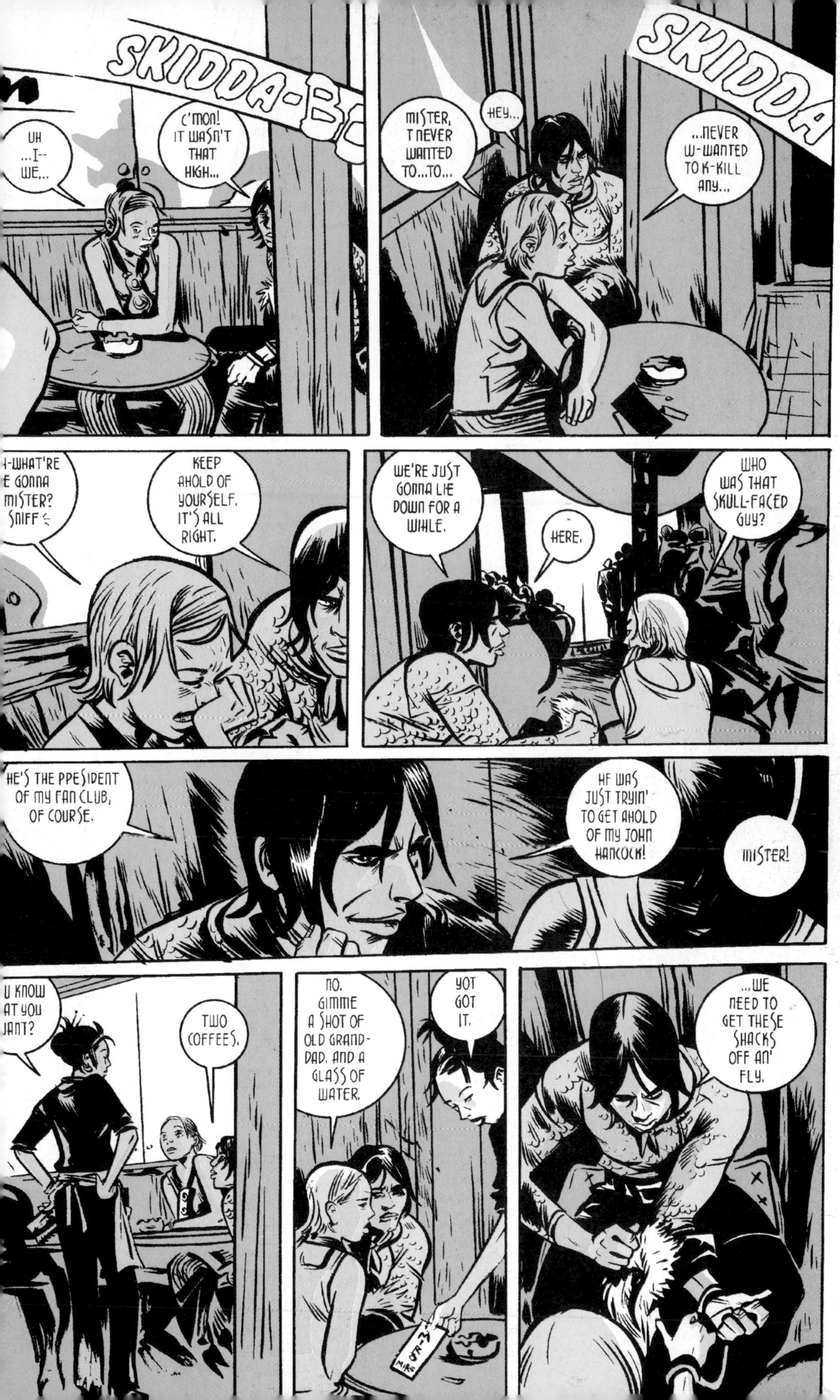
SKIDDA-BO
UH ...I-- WE...
C'MON! IT WASN'T THAT HIGH...
SKIDDA
HEY...
MISTER, I NEVER WANTED TO...TO...
...NEVER W-WANTED TO K-KILL ANY...
-WHAT'RE E GONNA MISTER? SNIFF
KEEP AHOLD OF YOURSELF. IT'S ALL RIGHT.
WE'RE JUST GONNA LIE DOWN FOR A WHILE.
HERE.
WHO WAS THAT SKULL-FACED GUY?
HE'S THE PRESIDENT OF MY FAN CLUB, OF COURSE.
HE WAS JUST TRYIN' TO GET AHOLD OF MY JOHN HANCOCK!
MISTER!
U KNOW AT YOU ANT?
TWO COFFEES.
NO. GIMME A SHOT OF OLD GRAND-DAD, AND A GLASS OF WATER.
YOT GOT IT.
...WE NEED TO GET THESE SHACKS OFF AN' FLY.

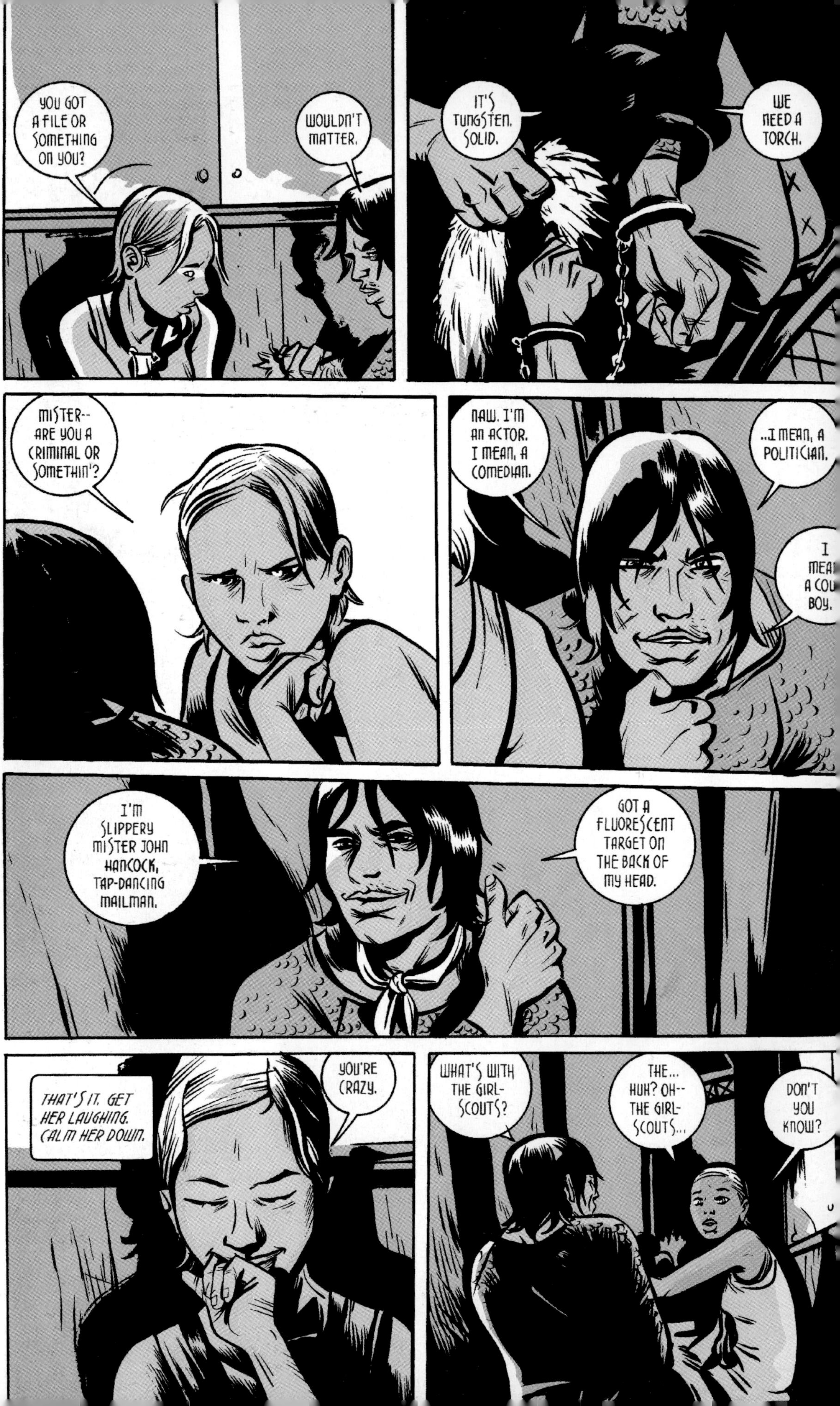
YOU GOT A FILE OR SOMETHING ON YOU?
WOULDN'T MATTER.
IT'S TUNGSTEN. SOLID.
WE NEED A TORCH.
MISTER-- ARE YOU A CRIMINAL OR SOMETHIN'?
NAW. I'M AN ACTOR. I MEAN, A COMEDIAN.
...I MEAN, A POLITICIAN.
I MEA A CO BOY.
I'M SLIPPERY MISTER JOHN HANCOCK, TAP-DANCING MAILMAN.
GOT A FLUORESCENT TARGET ON THE BACK OF MY HEAD.
THAT'S IT. GET HER LAUGHING. CALM HER DOWN.
YOU'RE CRAZY.
WHAT'S WITH THE GIRL-SCOUTS?
THE... HUH? OH-- THE GIRL-SCOUTS...
DON'T YOU KNOW?

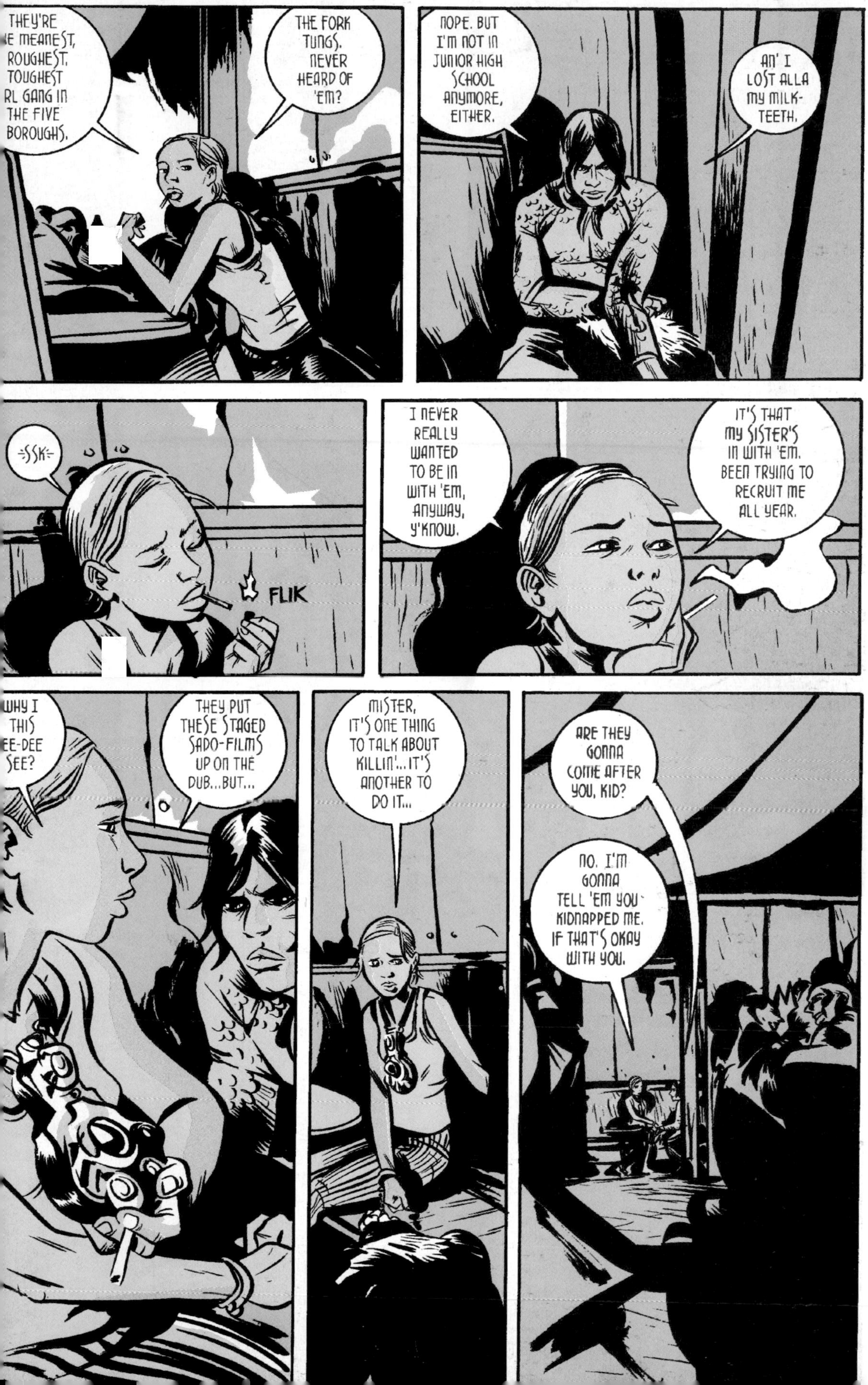
THEY'RE
E MEANEST,
ROUGHEST,
TOUGHEST
RL GANG IN
THE FIVE
BOROUGHS.
THE FORK TUNGS. NEVER HEARD OF 'EM?
NOPE. BUT I'M NOT IN JUNIOR HIGH SCHOOL ANYMORE, EITHER.
AN' I LOST ALLA MY MILK-TEETH.
SSK
FLIK
I NEVER REALLY WANTED TO BE IN WITH 'EM, ANYWAY, Y'KNOW.
IT'S THAT MY SISTER'S IN WITH 'EM. BEEN TRYING TO RECRUIT ME ALL YEAR.
WHY I
THIS
EE-DEE
SEE?
THEY PUT THESE STAGED SADO-FILMS UP ON THE DUB...BUT...
MISTER, IT'S ONE THING TO TALK ABOUT KILLIN'...IT'S ANOTHER TO DO IT...
ARE THEY GONNA COME AFTER YOU, KID?
NO. I'M GONNA TELL 'EM YOU KIDNAPPED ME. IF THAT'S OKAY WITH YOU.

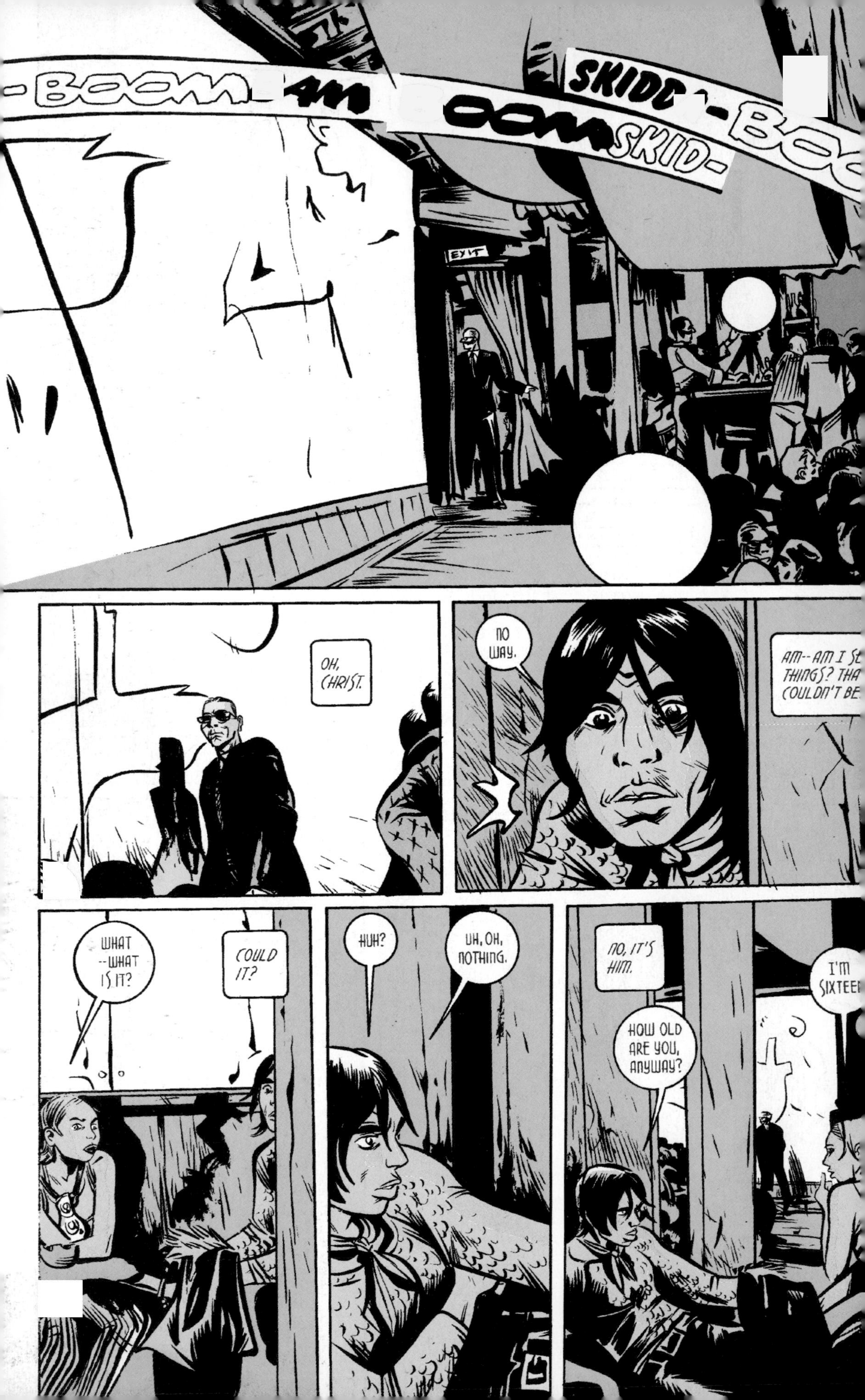
-BOOM
AM
OOM
SKIDD
SKID-
-BOO
OH, CHRIST.
NO WAY.
AM--AM I S
THINGS? THA
COULDN'T BE
WHAT --WHAT IS IT?
COULD IT?
HUH?
UH, OH, NOTHING.
NO, IT'S HIM.
HOW OLD ARE YOU, ANYWAY?
I'M SIXTEE

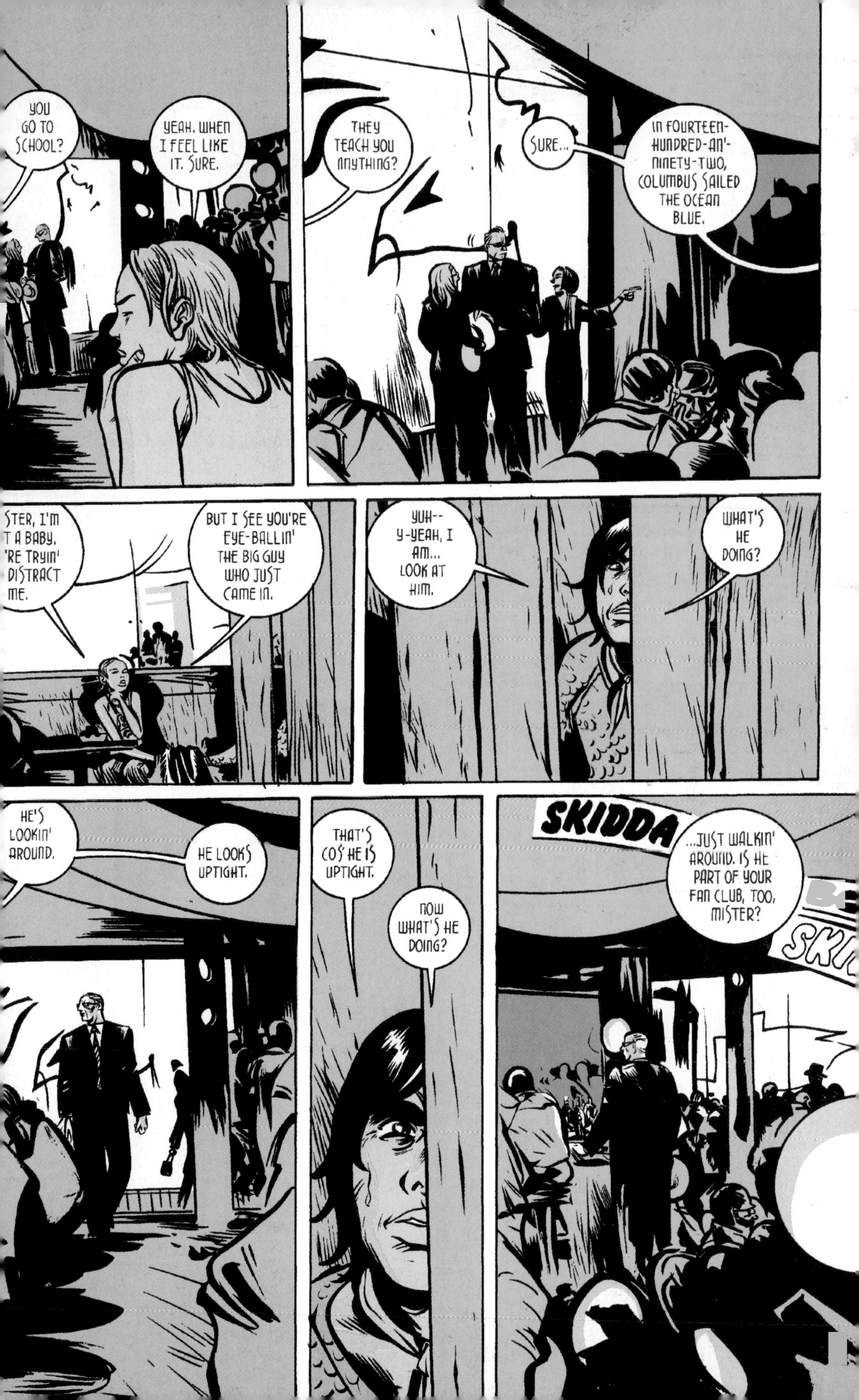
YOU GO TO SCHOOL?
YEAH. WHEN I FEEL LIKE IT. SURE.
THEY TEACH YOU ANYTHING?
SURE...
IN FOURTEEN-HUNDRED-AN'-NINETY-TWO, COLUMBUS SAILED THE OCEAN BLUE.
STER, I'M T A BABY. 'RE TRYIN' DISTRACT ME.
BUT I SEE YOU'RE EYE-BALLIN' THE BIG GUY WHO JUST CAME IN.
YUH-- Y-YEAH, I AM... LOOK AT HIM.
WHAT'S HE DOING?
HE'S LOOKIN' AROUND.
HE LOOKS UPTIGHT.
THAT'S COS' HE IS UPTIGHT.
NOW WHAT'S HE DOING?
SKIDDA
...JUST WALKIN' AROUND. IS HE PART OF YOUR FAN CLUB, TOO, MISTER?

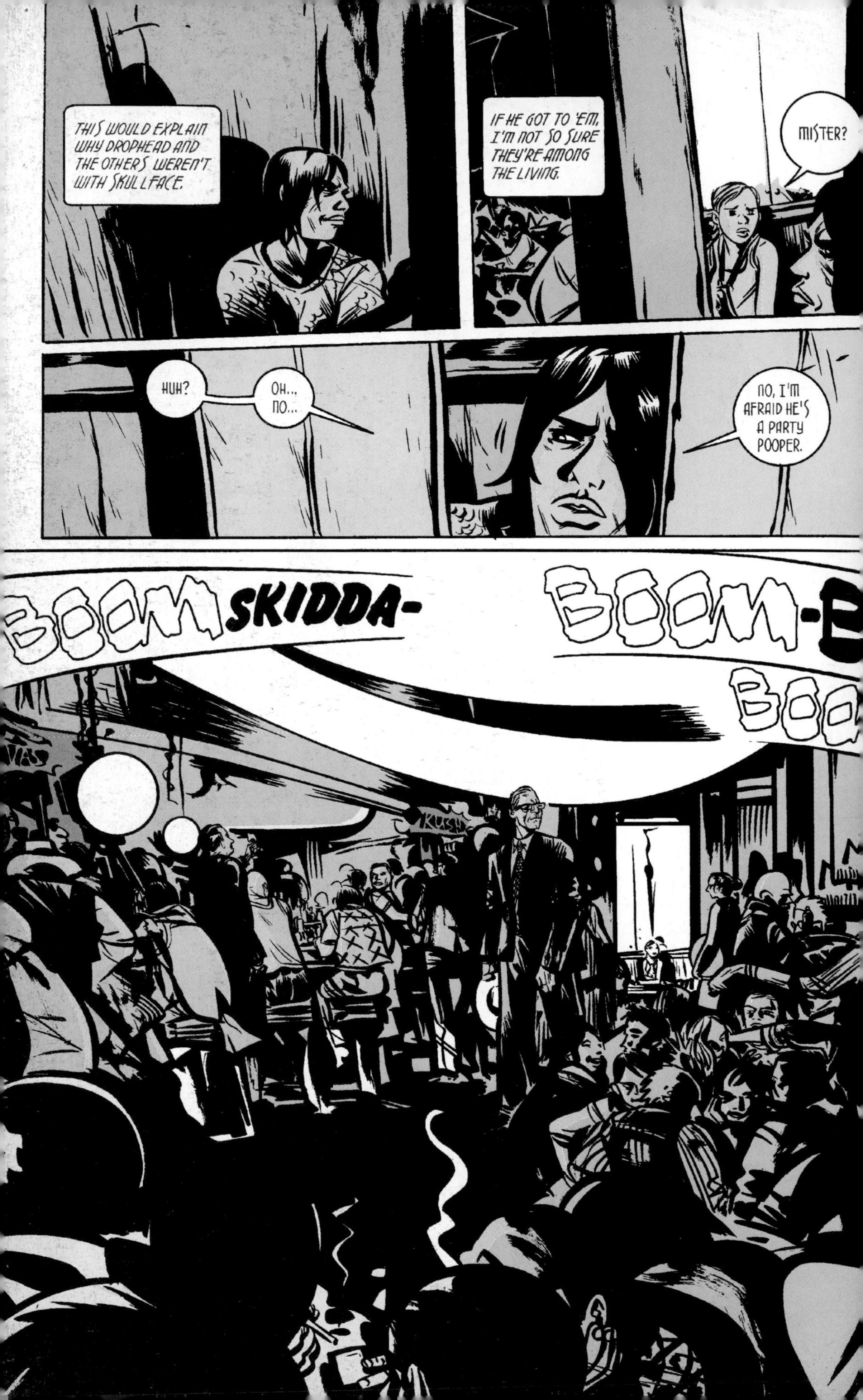
THIS WOULD EXPLAIN WHY DROPHEAD AND THE OTHERS WEREN'T WITH SKULLFACE.
IF HE GOT TO 'EM, I'M NOT SO SURE THEY'RE AMONG THE LIVING.
MISTER?
HUH?
OH... NO...
NO, I'M AFRAID HE'S A PARTY POOPER.
BOOM SKIDDA-
BOOM-B
BOO

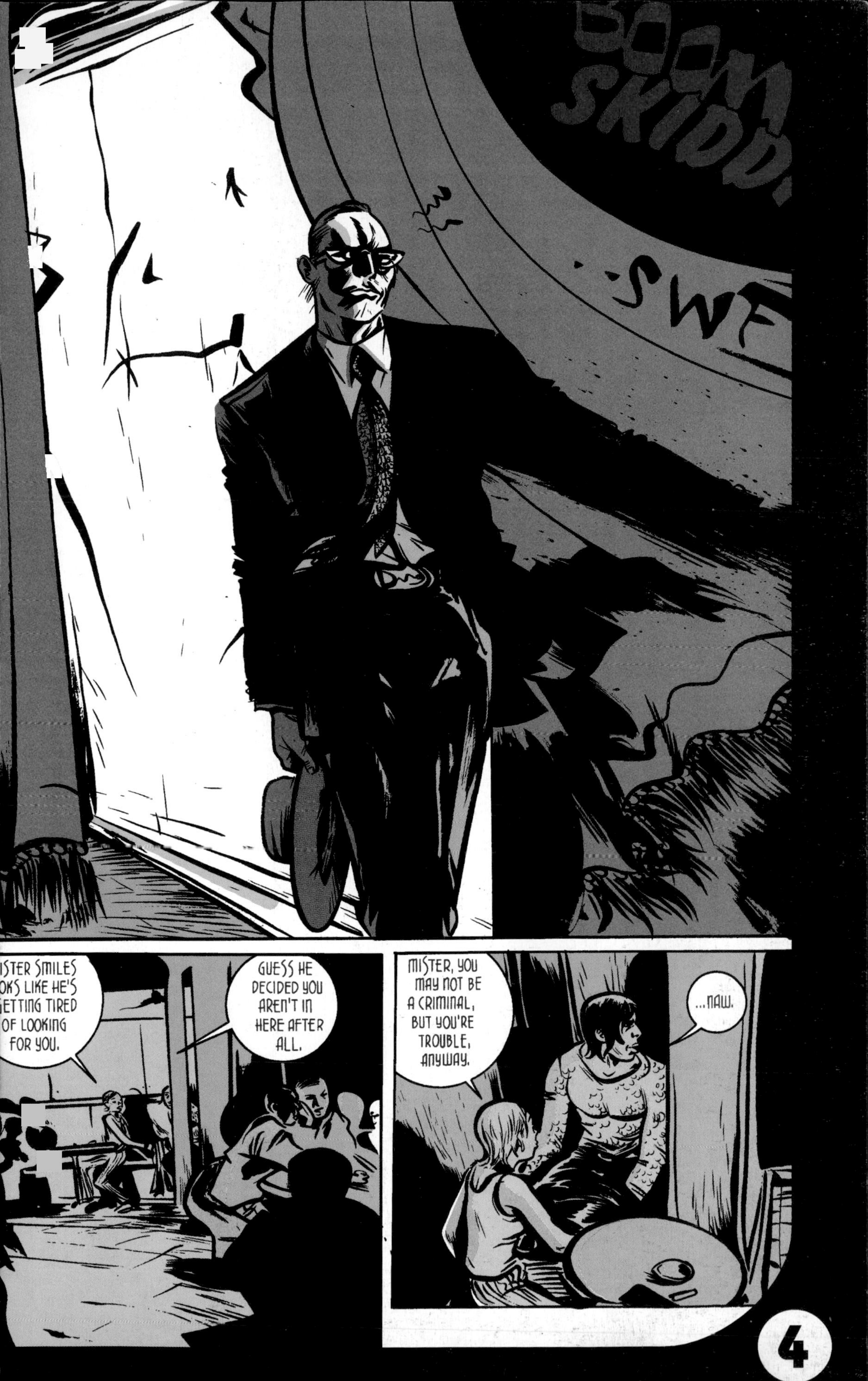
BOOM
SKIDD
SWF
ISTER SMILES OKS LIKE HE'S GETTING TIRED OF LOOKING FOR YOU.
GUESS HE DECIDED YOU AREN'T IN HERE AFTER ALL.
MISTER, YOU MAY NOT BE A CRIMINAL, BUT YOU'RE TROUBLE, ANYWAY.
...NAW.

SKIDDA-**BOOM**

YEAH--YOU MUST HAVE SOME UNLUCKY STARS PILED UP ABOVE YOU...

SHUCKS, KID.

SURE, BET YOU GOT BORN AND TROUBLE WAS RIGHT THERE TO SLAP YOUR BEHIND, HUH, MISTER?

SNIFF

...I COULD GET TO LIKE YOU, MISTER... TROUBLE GOT A GIRLFRIEND?

NAW. I'M A MONK.

SUIT YOUR-SELF.

...HE'S GONE.

NOW U GOTTA SOMETI ABOU THES

I THINK I CAN GET THESE OFF. WHAT'D YA SAY THEY'RE MADE OF?

TUNGSTEN.

HERE YOU GO, COFFEE AND OLD GRAND-DAD.

HEY... THIS'LL SOUND, LIKE, CRAZY, BUT DO YOU HAVE A HACKSAW OR SOME-THIN'?

...MY BOYFRIEND AND I DID THIS BY ACCIDENT.

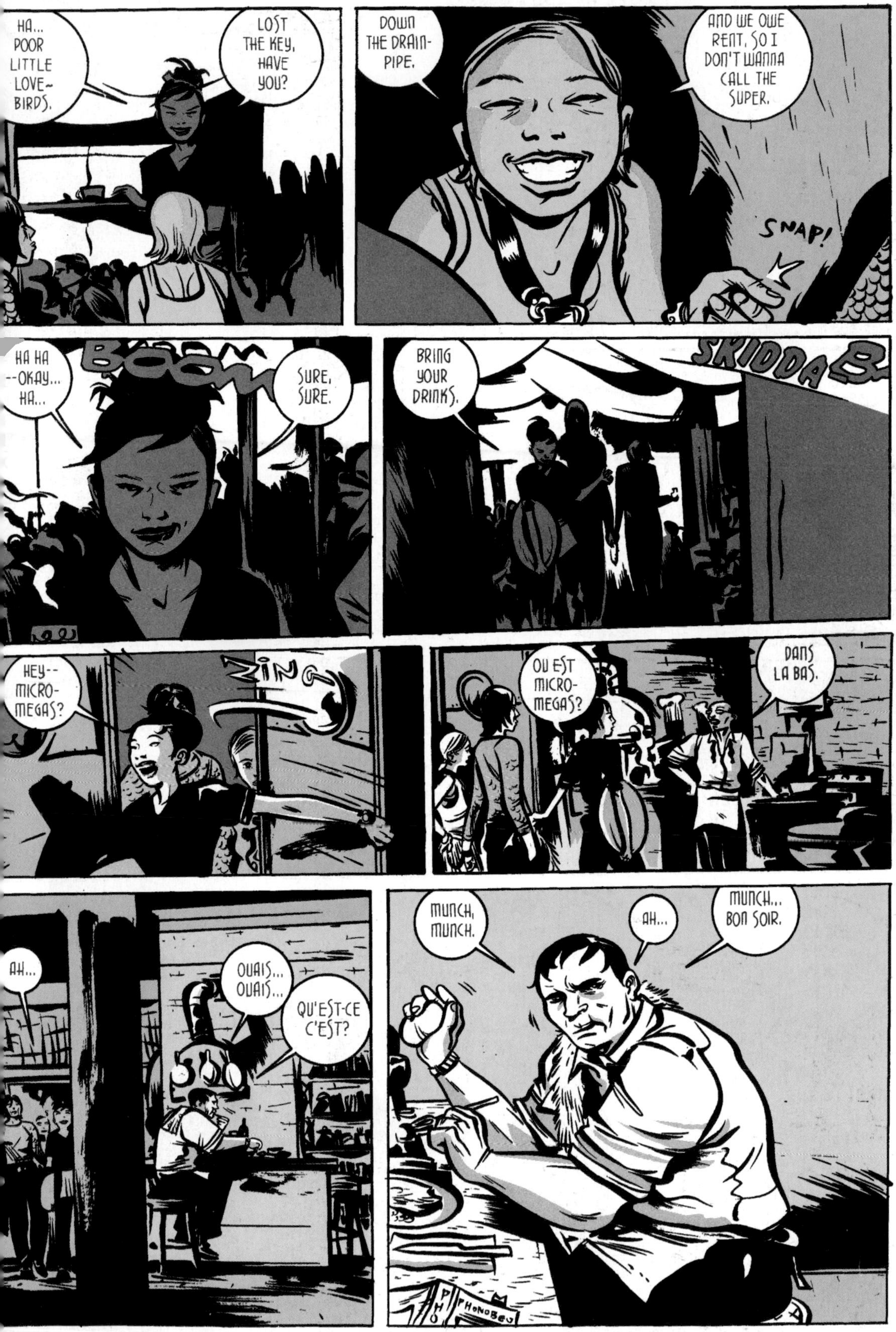
HA... POOR LITTLE LOVE-BIRDS.
LOST THE KEY, HAVE YOU?
DOWN THE DRAIN-PIPE.
AND WE OWE RENT, SO I DON'T WANNA CALL THE SUPER.
SNAP!
HA HA --OKAY... HA...
SURE, SURE.
BRING YOUR DRINKS.
SKIDDAB
HEY-- MICRO-MEGAS?
ZING
OU EST MICRO-MEGAS?
DANS LA BAS.
AH...
OUAIS... OUAIS...
QU'EST-CE C'EST?
MUNCH, MUNCH.
AH...
MUNCH... BON SOIR.

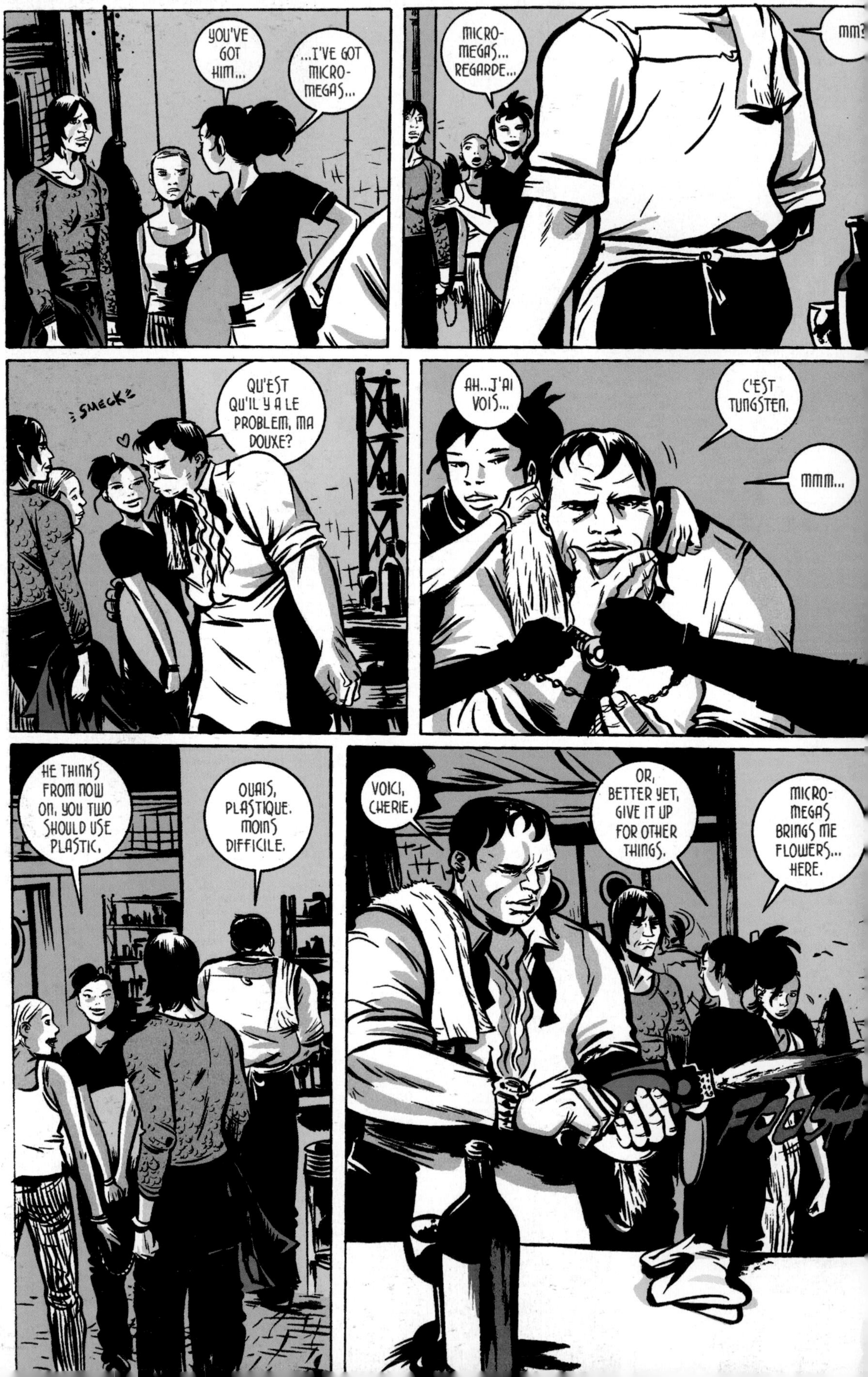

YOU'VE GOT HIM...
...I'VE GOT MICRO-MEGAS...
MICRO-MEGAS... REGARDE...
MM?
SMECK
QU'EST QU'IL Y A LE PROBLEM, MA DOUXE?
AH...J'AI VOIS...
C'EST TUNGSTEN.
MMM...
HE THINKS FROM NOW ON, YOU TWO SHOULD USE PLASTIC.
OUAIS, PLASTIQUE. MOINS DIFFICILE.
VOICI, CHERIE.
OR, BETTER YET, GIVE IT UP FOR OTHER THINGS.
MICRO-MEGAS BRINGS ME FLOWERS... HERE.

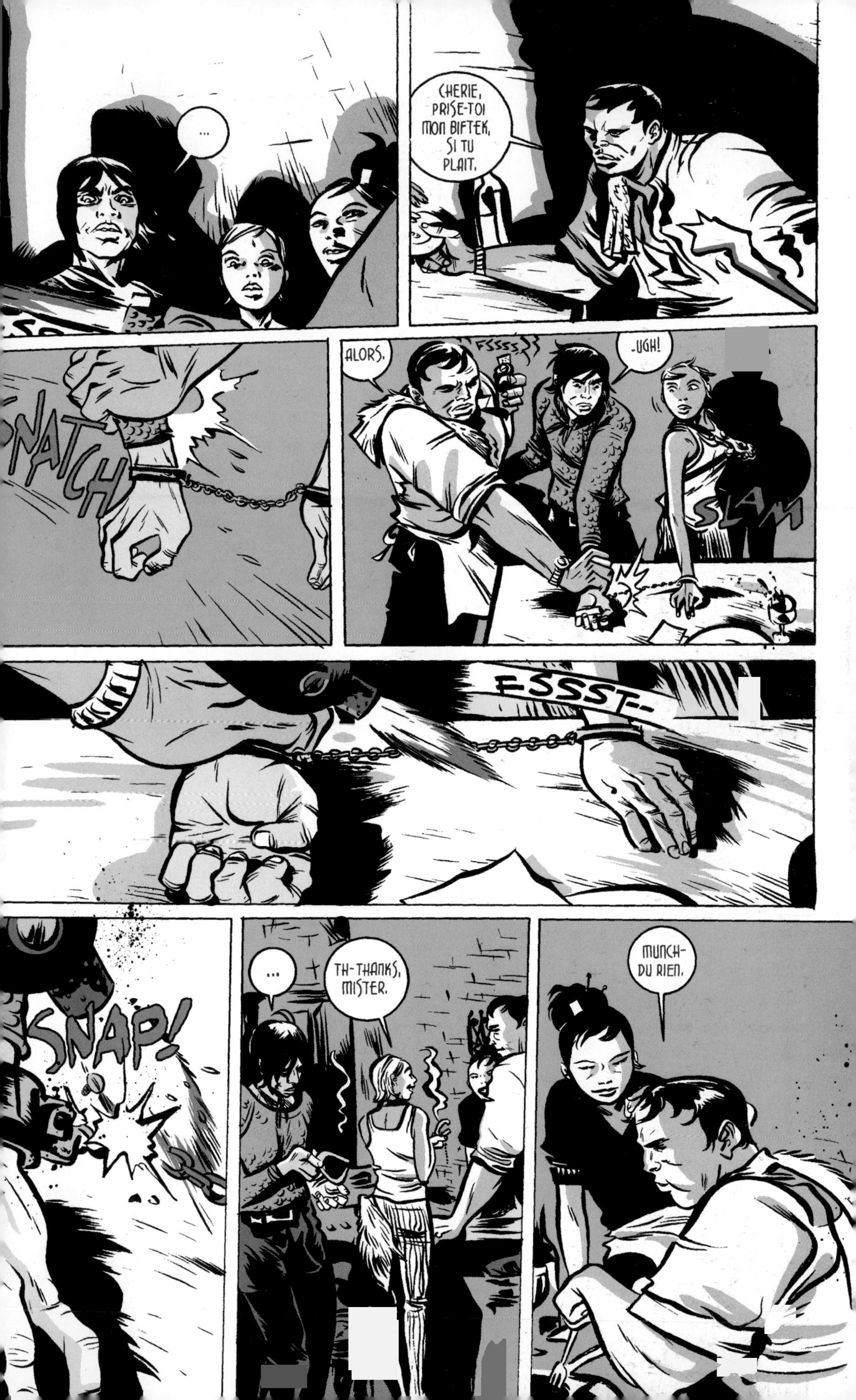
...
CHERIE, PRISE-TOI MON BIFTEK, SI TU PLAIT.
SNATCH
ALORS.
FSSSS
..UGH!
SLAM
FSSST--
SNAP!
...
TH-THANKS, MISTER.
MUNCH-DU RIEN.

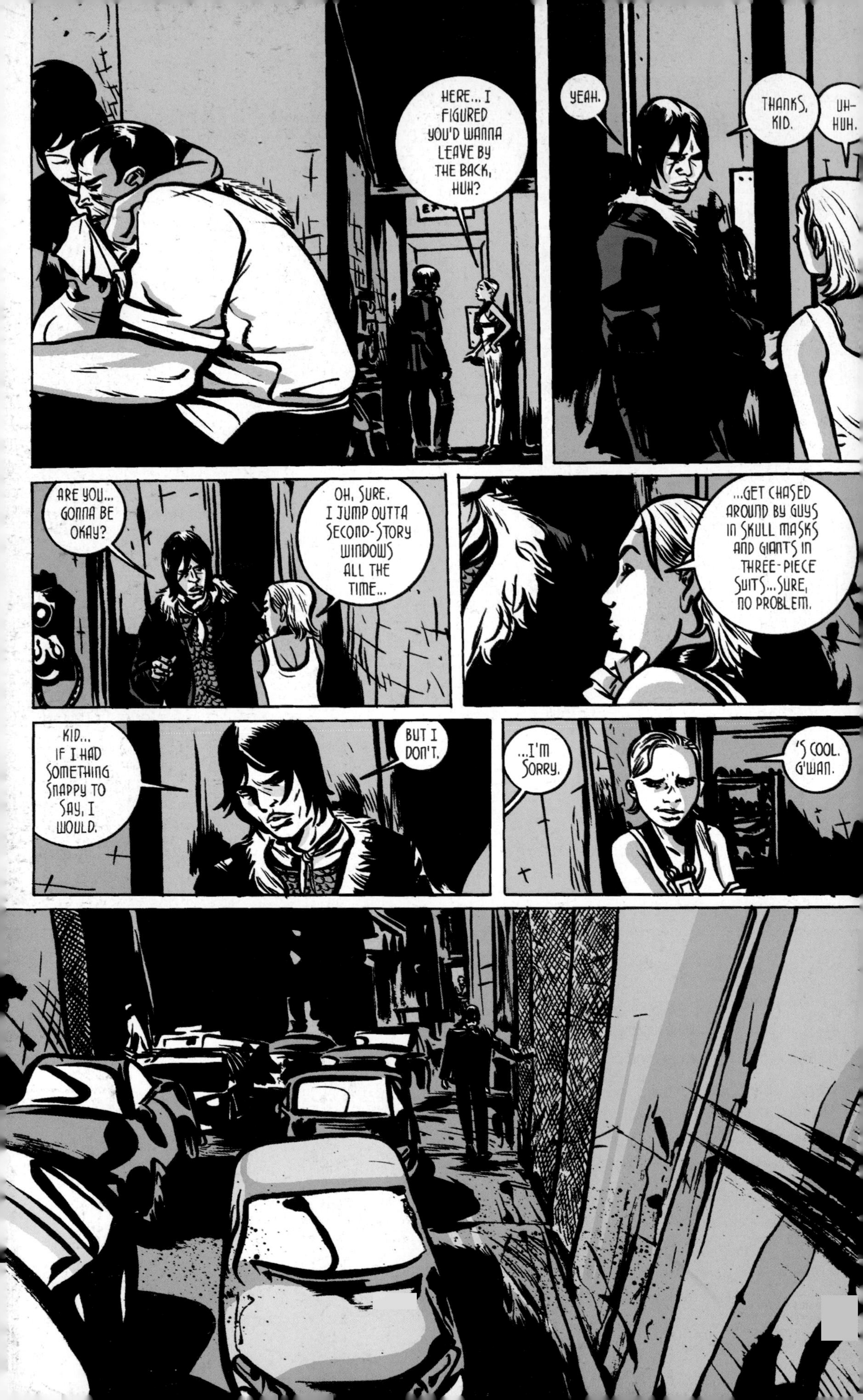

HERE... I FIGURED YOU'D WANNA LEAVE BY THE BACK, HUH?
YEAH.
THANKS, KID.
UH-HUH.
ARE YOU... GONNA BE OKAY?
OH, SURE. I JUMP OUTTA SECOND-STORY WINDOWS ALL THE TIME...
...GET CHASED AROUND BY GUYS IN SKULL MASKS AND GIANTS IN THREE-PIECE SUITS... SURE, NO PROBLEM.
KID... IF I HAD SOMETHING SNAPPY TO SAY, I WOULD.
BUT I DON'T.
...I'M SORRY.
'S COOL. G'WAN.

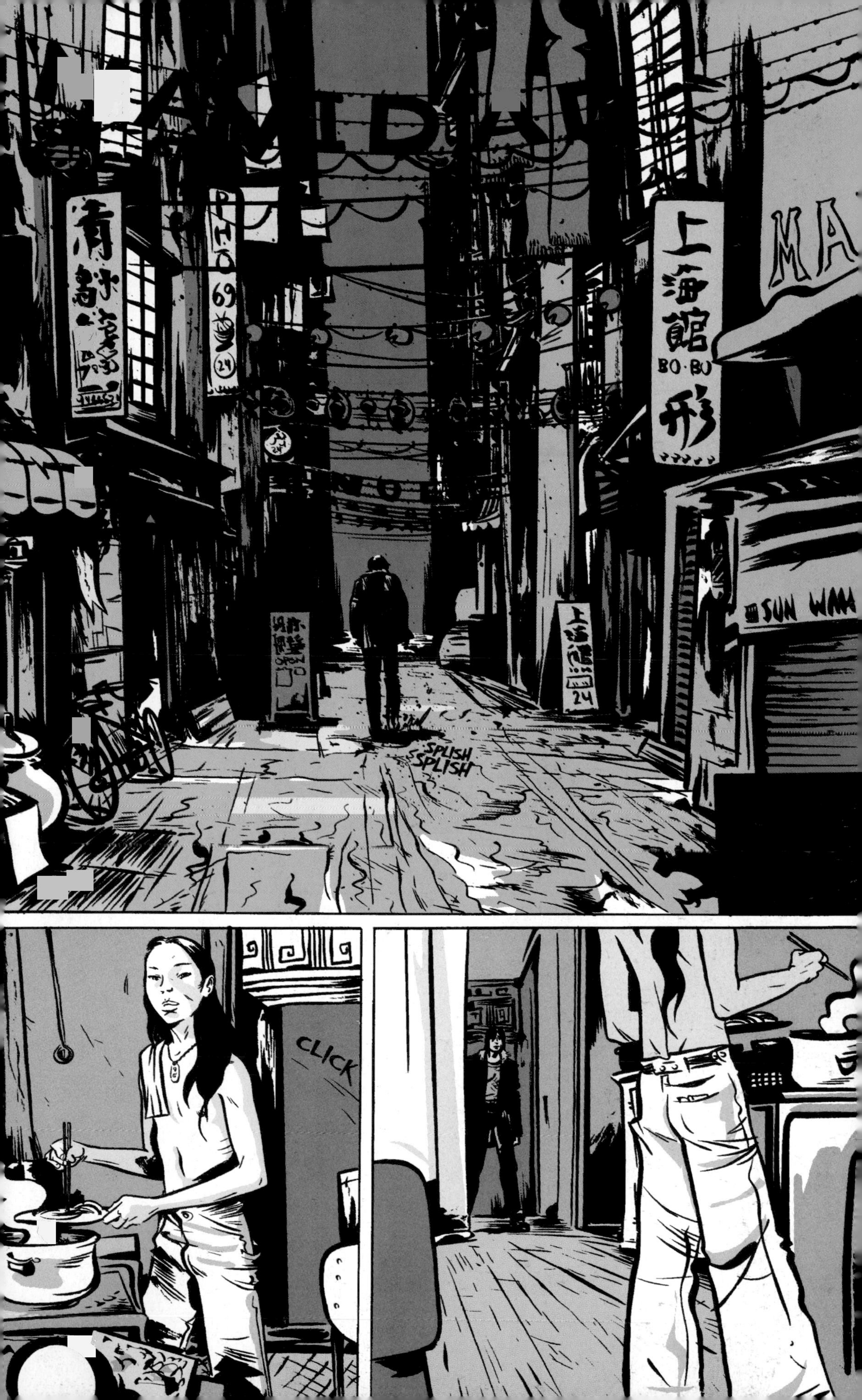
PHO
69
上海館
BO·BU
SPLISH
SPLISH
CLICK

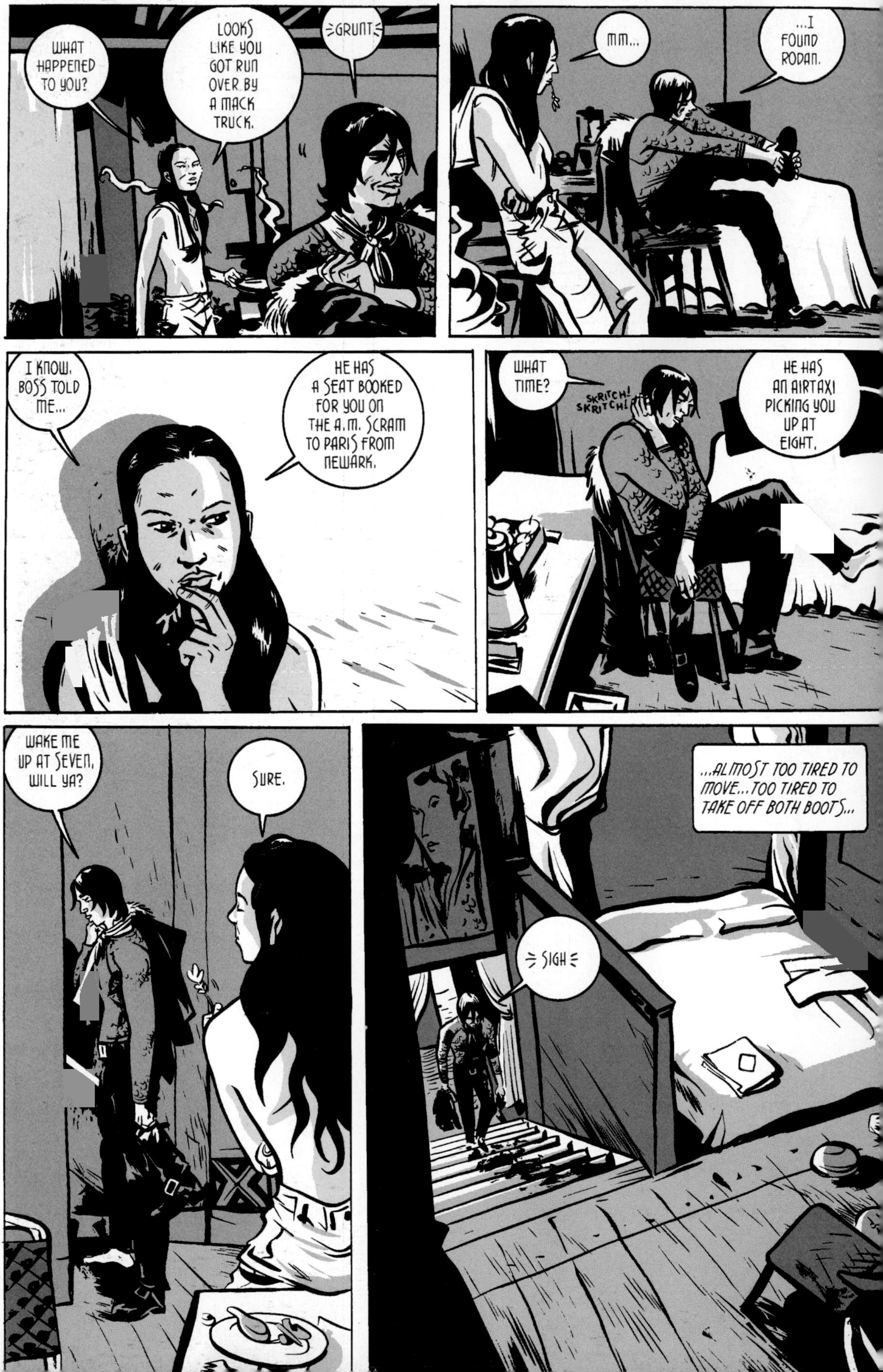
WHAT HAPPENED TO YOU?
LOOKS LIKE YOU GOT RUN OVER BY A MACK TRUCK.
GRUNT
MM...
...I FOUND RODAN.
I KNOW. BOSS TOLD ME...
HE HAS A SEAT BOOKED FOR YOU ON THE A.M. SCRAM TO PARIS FROM NEWARK.
WHAT TIME?
SKRITCH! SKRITCH!
HE HAS AN AIRTAXI PICKING YOU UP AT EIGHT.
WAKE ME UP AT SEVEN, WILL YA?
SURE.
...ALMOST TOO TIRED TO MOVE...TOO TIRED TO TAKE OFF BOTH BOOTS...
SIGH

THE FUNNY PART IS...

...I NEVER DID GET TO USE THE HEAVY LIQUID.

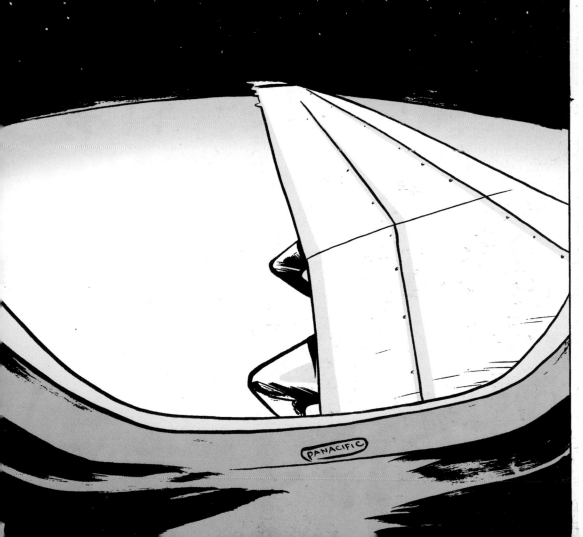

PANACIFIC

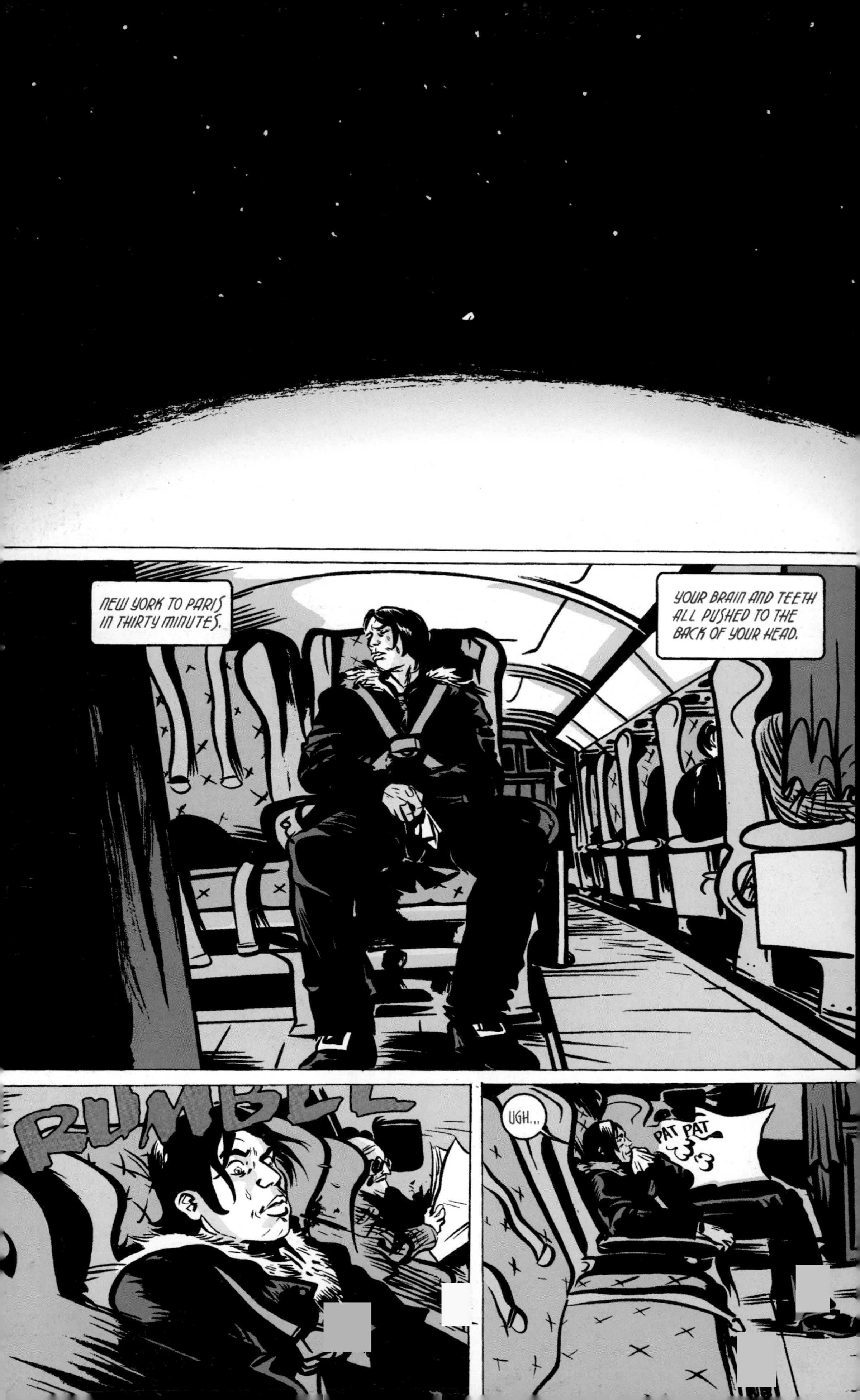
NEW YORK TO PARIS IN THIRTY MINUTES.
YOUR BRAIN AND TEETH ALL PUSHED TO THE BACK OF YOUR HEAD.
RUMBLE
UGH...
PAT PAT

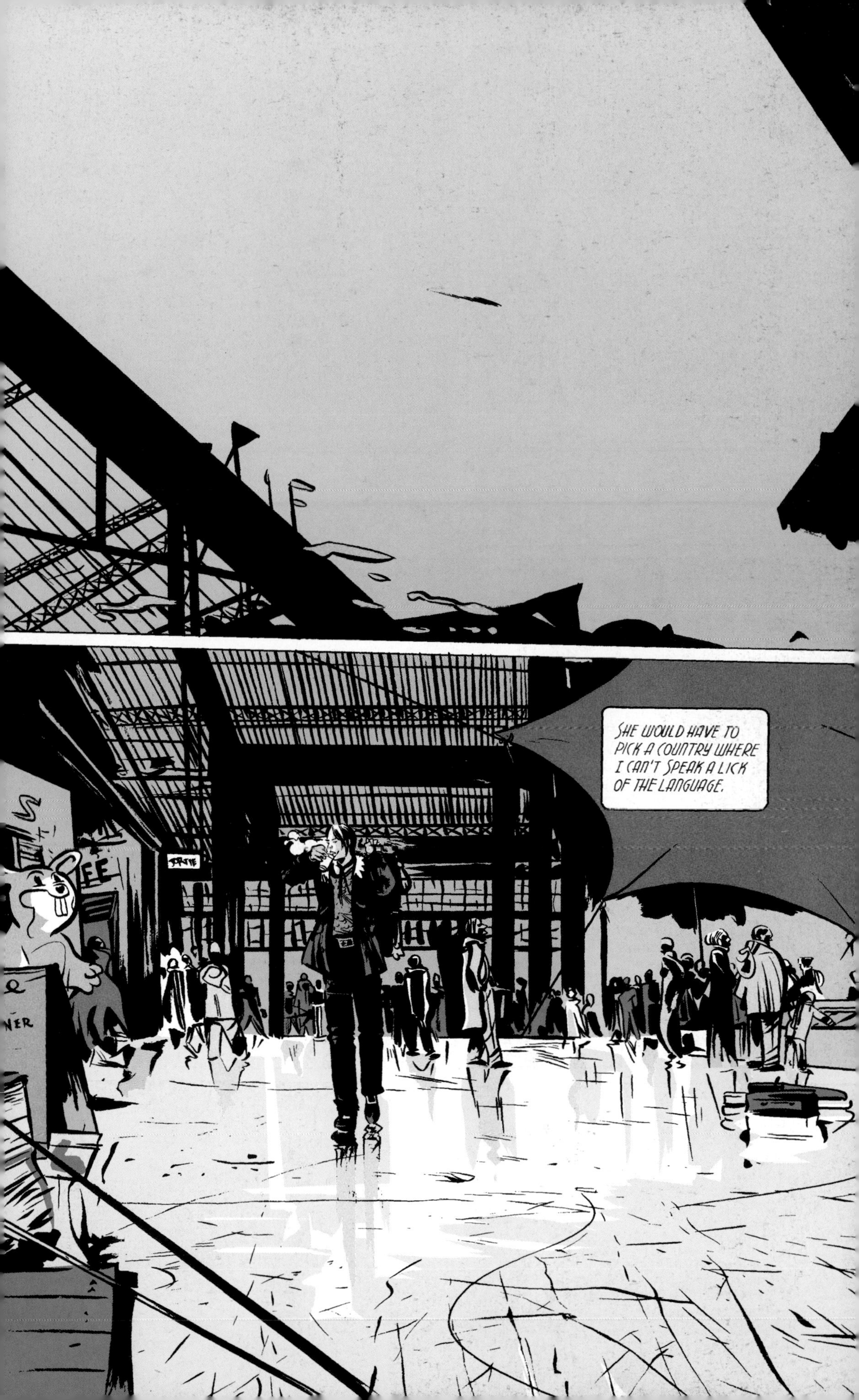
SHE WOULD HAVE TO PICK A COUNTRY WHERE I CAN'T SPEAK A LICK OF THE LANGUAGE.

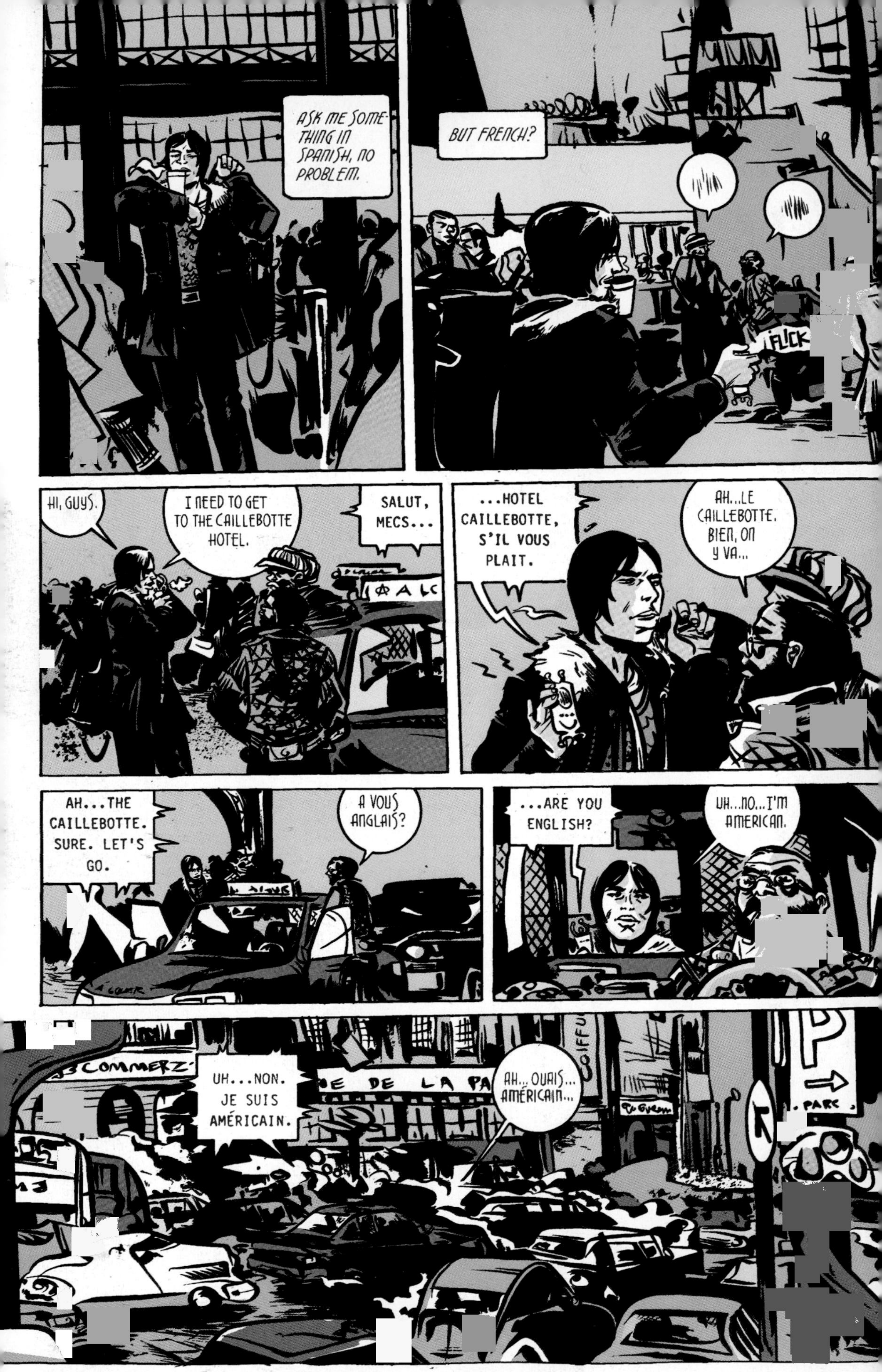
ASK ME SOMETHING IN SPANISH, NO PROBLEM.
BUT FRENCH?
FLICK
HI, GUYS.
I NEED TO GET TO THE CAILLEBOTTE HOTEL.
SALUT, MECS...
...HOTEL CAILLEBOTTE, S'IL VOUS PLAIT.
AH...LE CAILLEBOTTE. BIEN, ON Y VA...
AH...THE CAILLEBOTTE. SURE. LET'S GO.
A VOUS ANGLAIS?
...ARE YOU ENGLISH?
UH...NO...I'M AMERICAN.
COMMERZ
E DE LA PA
UH...NON. JE SUIS AMÉRICAIN.
AH... OUAIS... AMÉRICAIN...
COIFFU
PARC

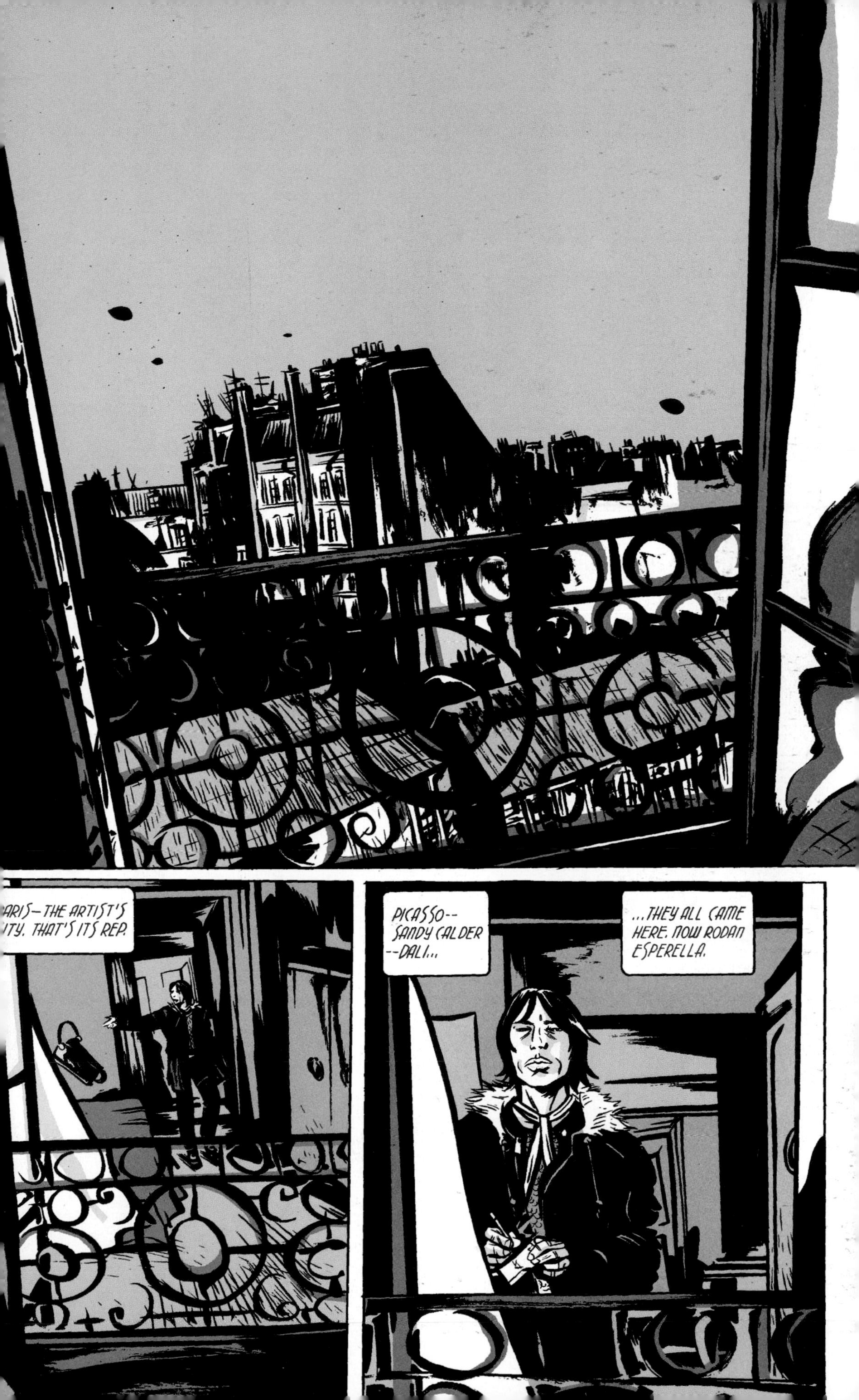
ARIS—THE ARTIST'S
ITY. THAT'S ITS REP.
PICASSO--
SANDY CALDER
--DALI...
...THEY ALL CAME
HERE. NOW RODAN
ESPERELLA.

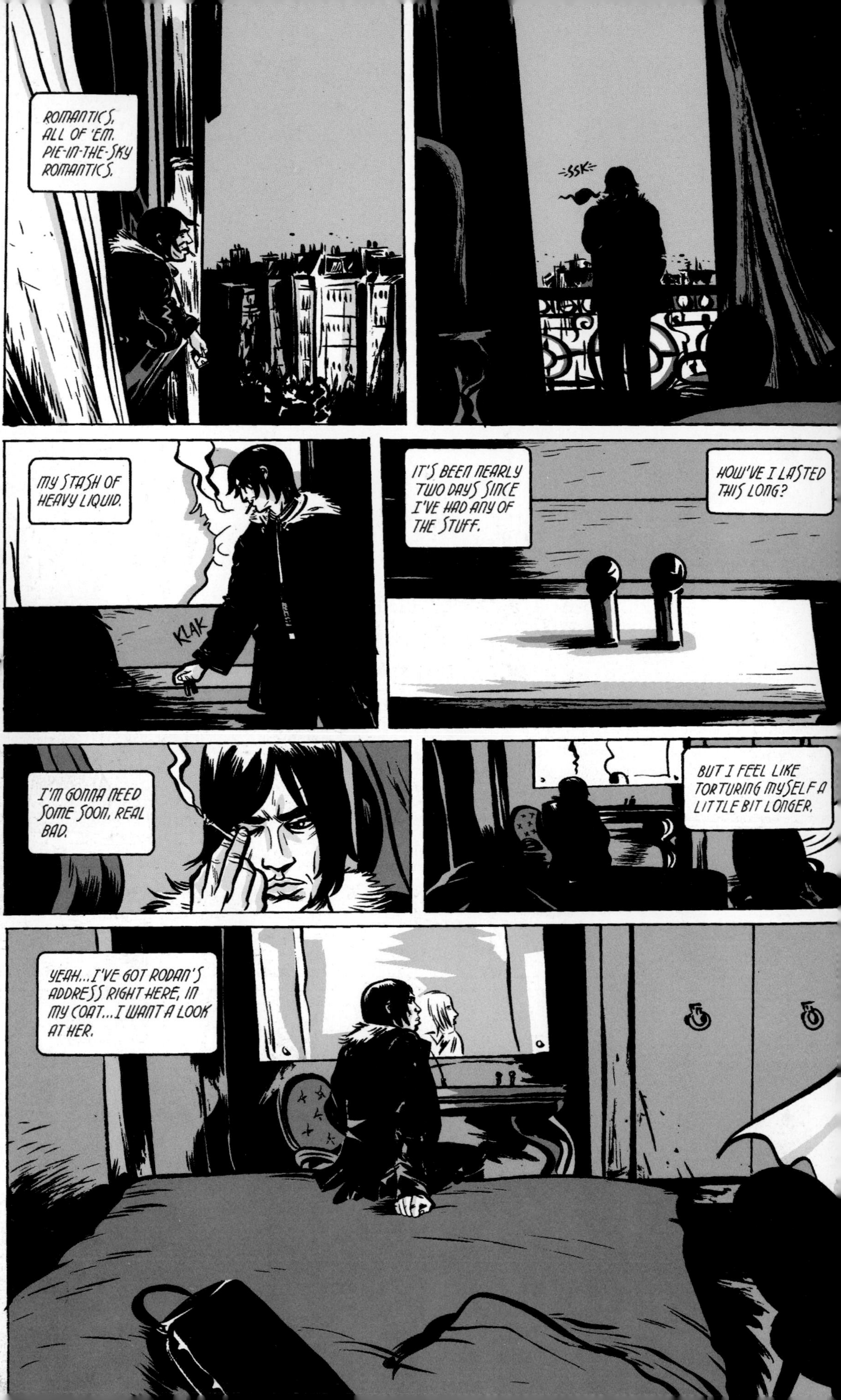
ROMANTICS, ALL OF 'EM. PIE-IN-THE-SKY ROMANTICS.
SSK
MY STASH OF HEAVY LIQUID.
KLAK
IT'S BEEN NEARLY TWO DAYS SINCE I'VE HAD ANY OF THE STUFF.
HOW'VE I LASTED THIS LONG?
I'M GONNA NEED SOME SOON, REAL BAD.
BUT I FEEL LIKE TORTURING MYSELF A LITTLE BIT LONGER.
YEAH... I'VE GOT RODAN'S ADDRESS RIGHT HERE, IN MY COAT... I WANT A LOOK AT HER.

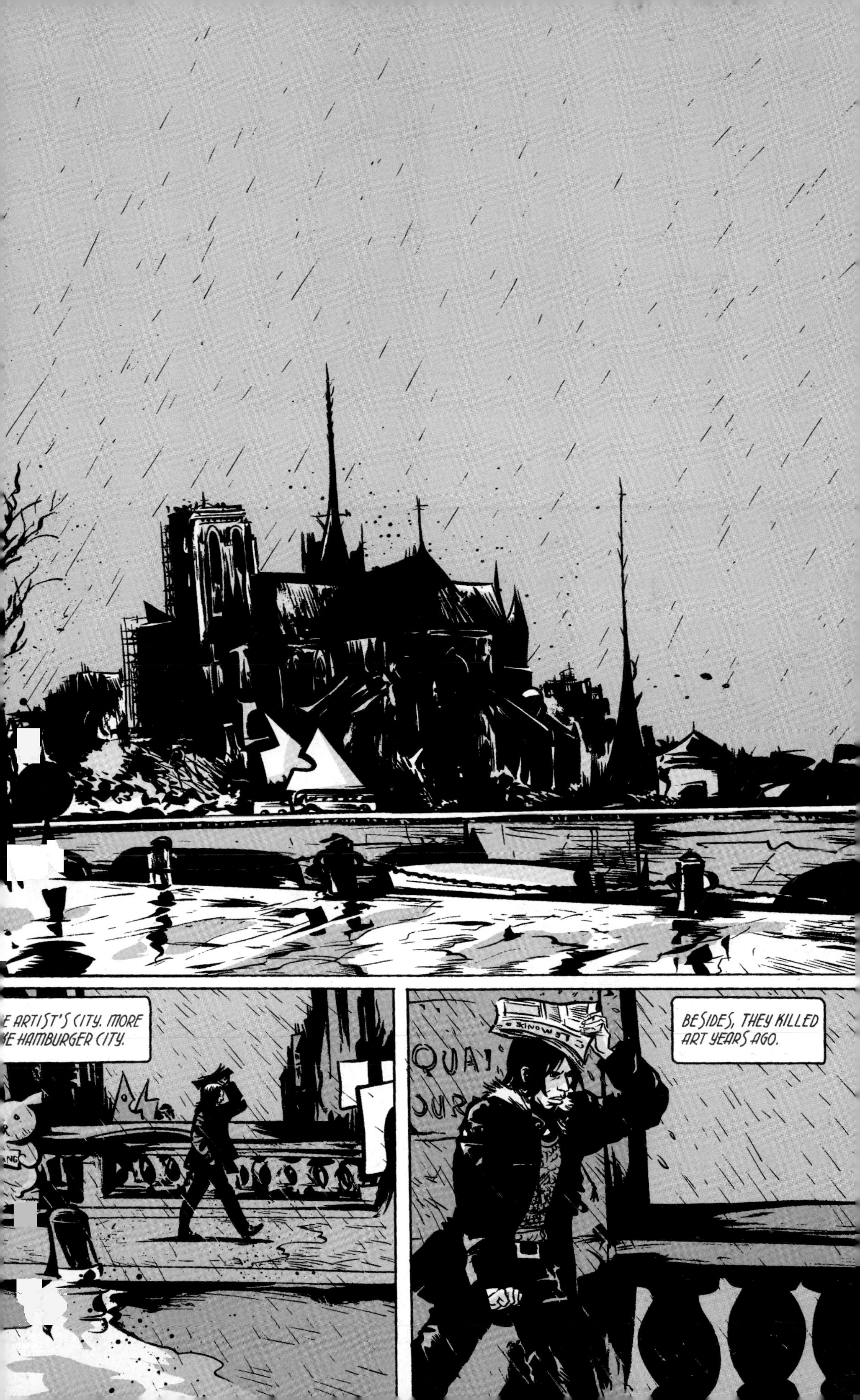
E ARTIST'S CITY. MORE
E HAMBURGER CITY.
QUAI
BESIDES, THEY KILLED ART YEARS AGO.

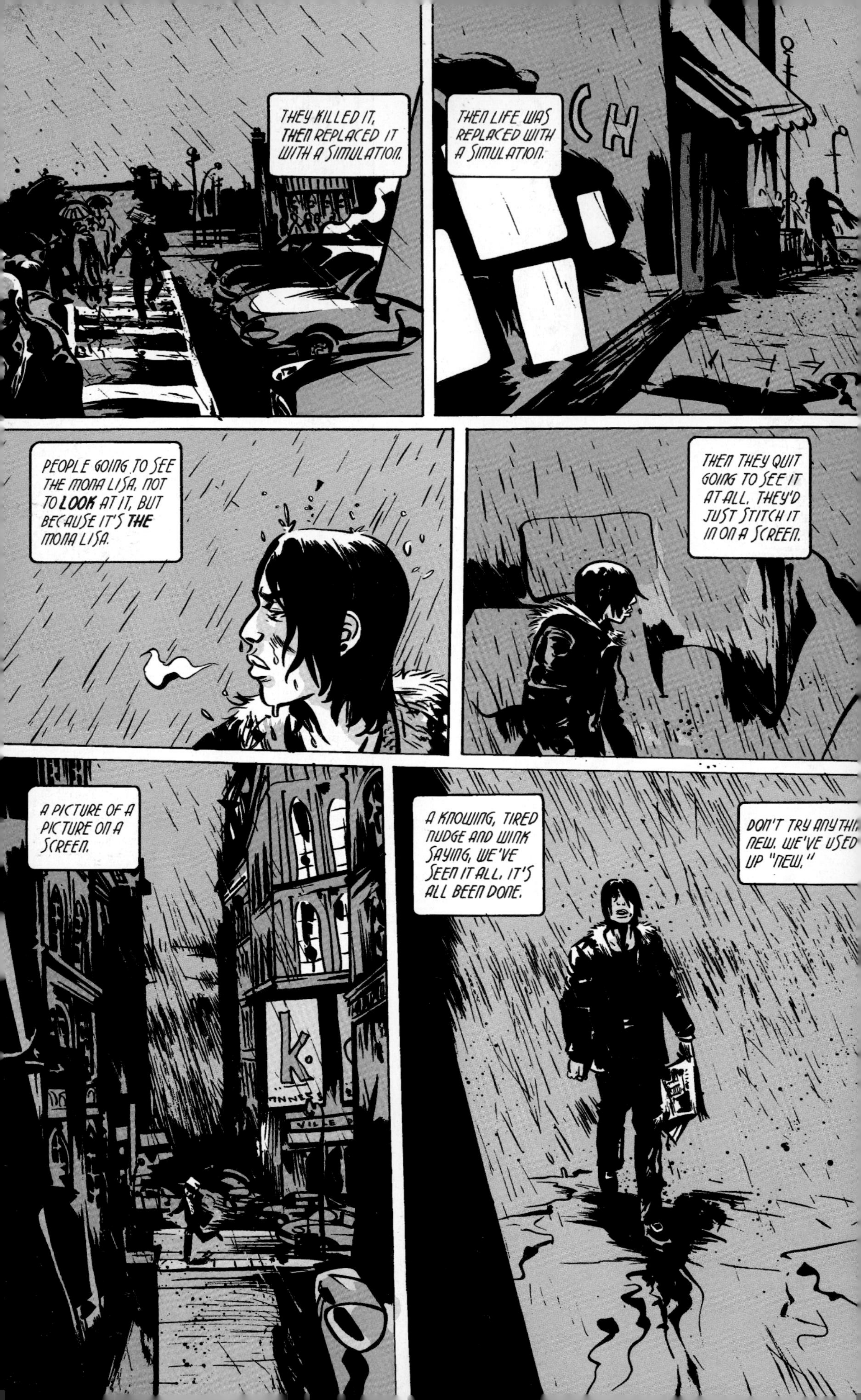
THEY KILLED IT, THEN REPLACED IT WITH A SIMULATION.
THEN LIFE WAS REPLACED WITH A SIMULATION.
CH
PEOPLE GOING TO SEE THE MONA LISA, NOT TO **LOOK** AT IT, BUT BECAUSE IT'S **THE** MONA LISA.
THEN THEY QUIT GOING TO SEE IT AT ALL. THEY'D JUST STITCH IT IN ON A SCREEN.
A PICTURE OF A PICTURE ON A SCREEN.
K
VILLE
A KNOWING, TIRED NUDGE AND WINK SAYING, WE'VE SEEN IT ALL, IT'S ALL BEEN DONE.
DON'T TRY ANYTHI NEW. WE'VE USED UP "NEW."

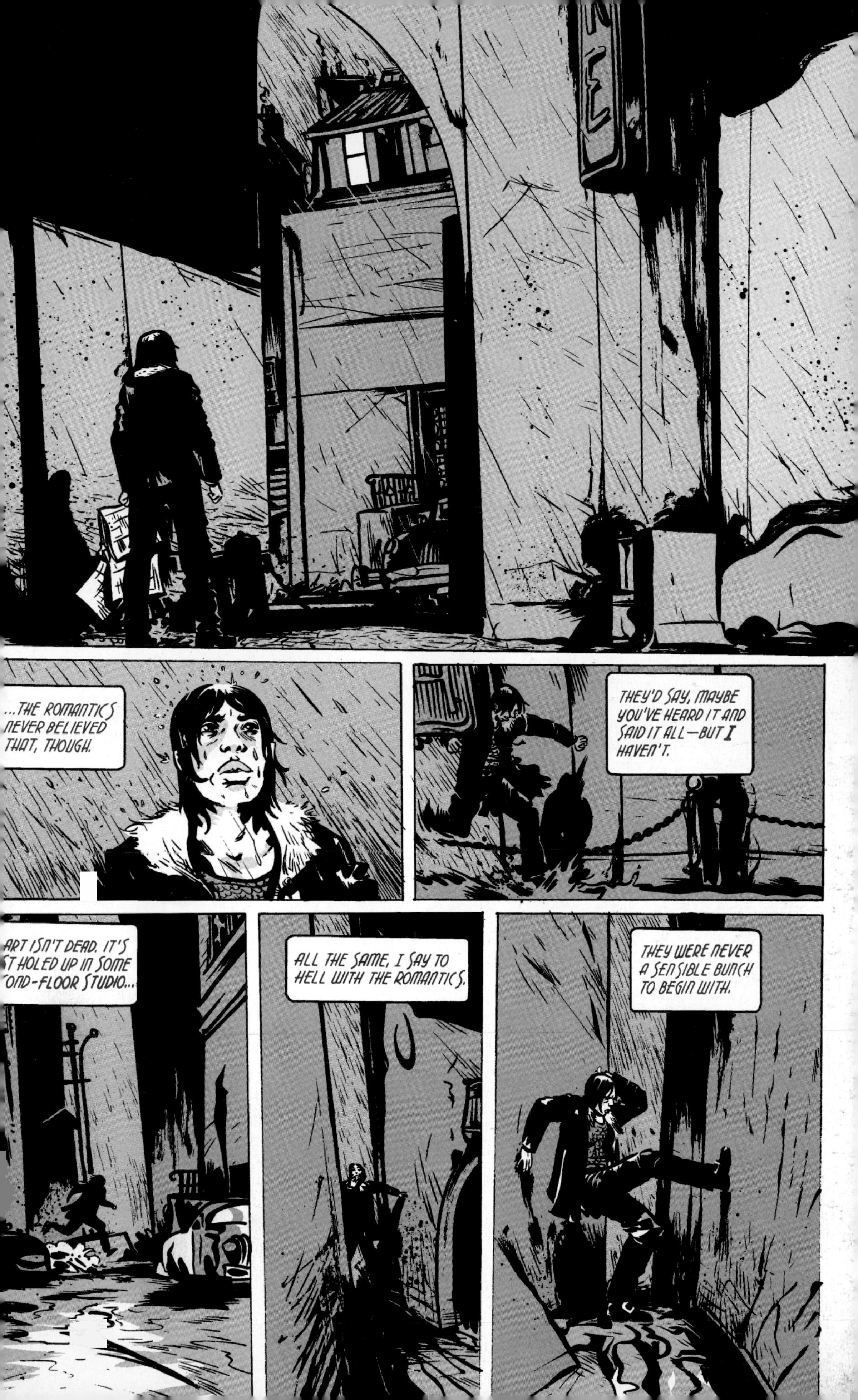
...THE ROMANTICS NEVER BELIEVED THAT, THOUGH.
THEY'D SAY, MAYBE YOU'VE HEARD IT AND SAID IT ALL—BUT I HAVEN'T.
ART ISN'T DEAD. IT'S ST HOLED UP IN SOME OND-FLOOR STUDIO...
ALL THE SAME, I SAY TO HELL WITH THE ROMANTICS.
THEY WERE NEVER A SENSIBLE BUNCH TO BEGIN WITH.

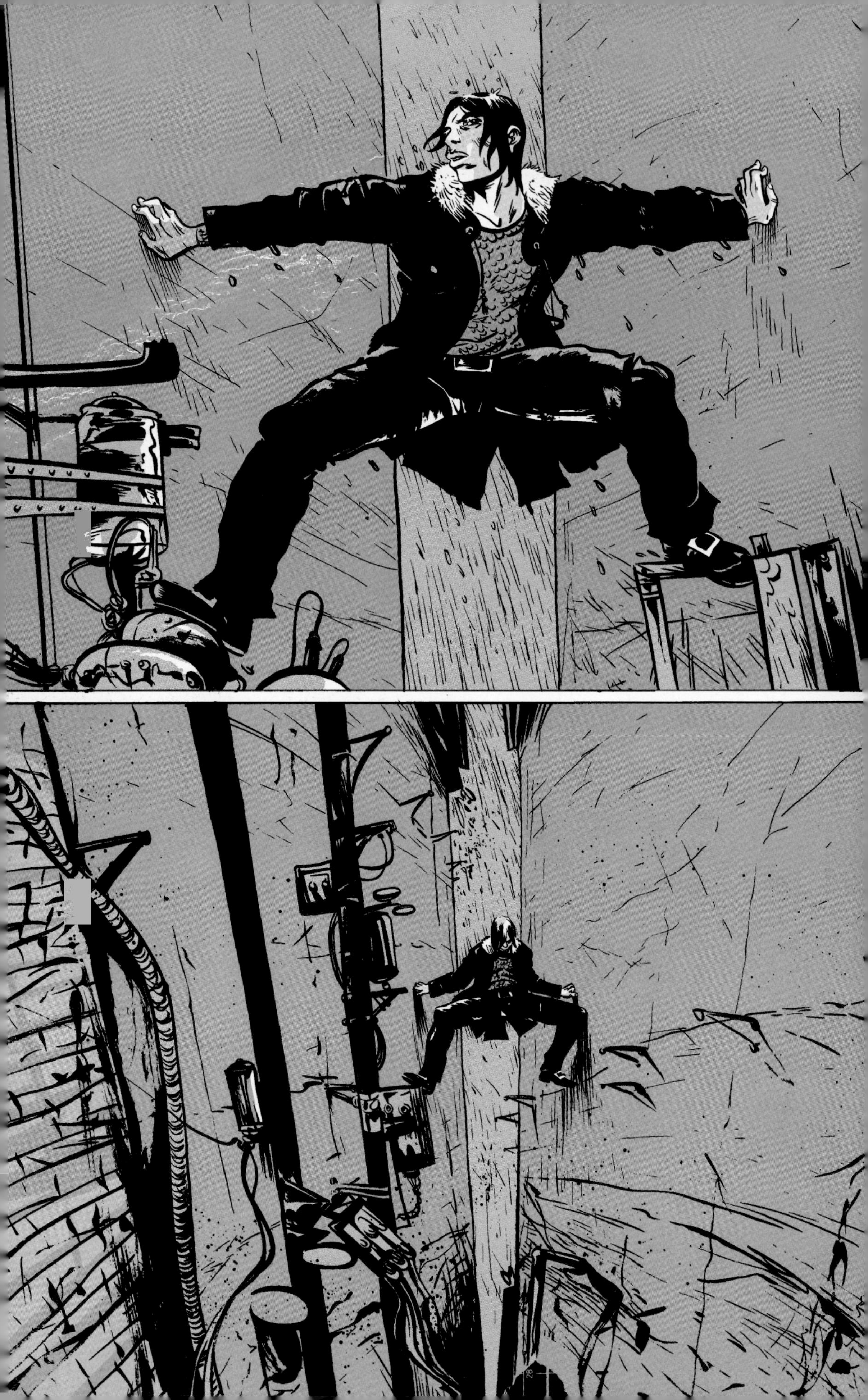

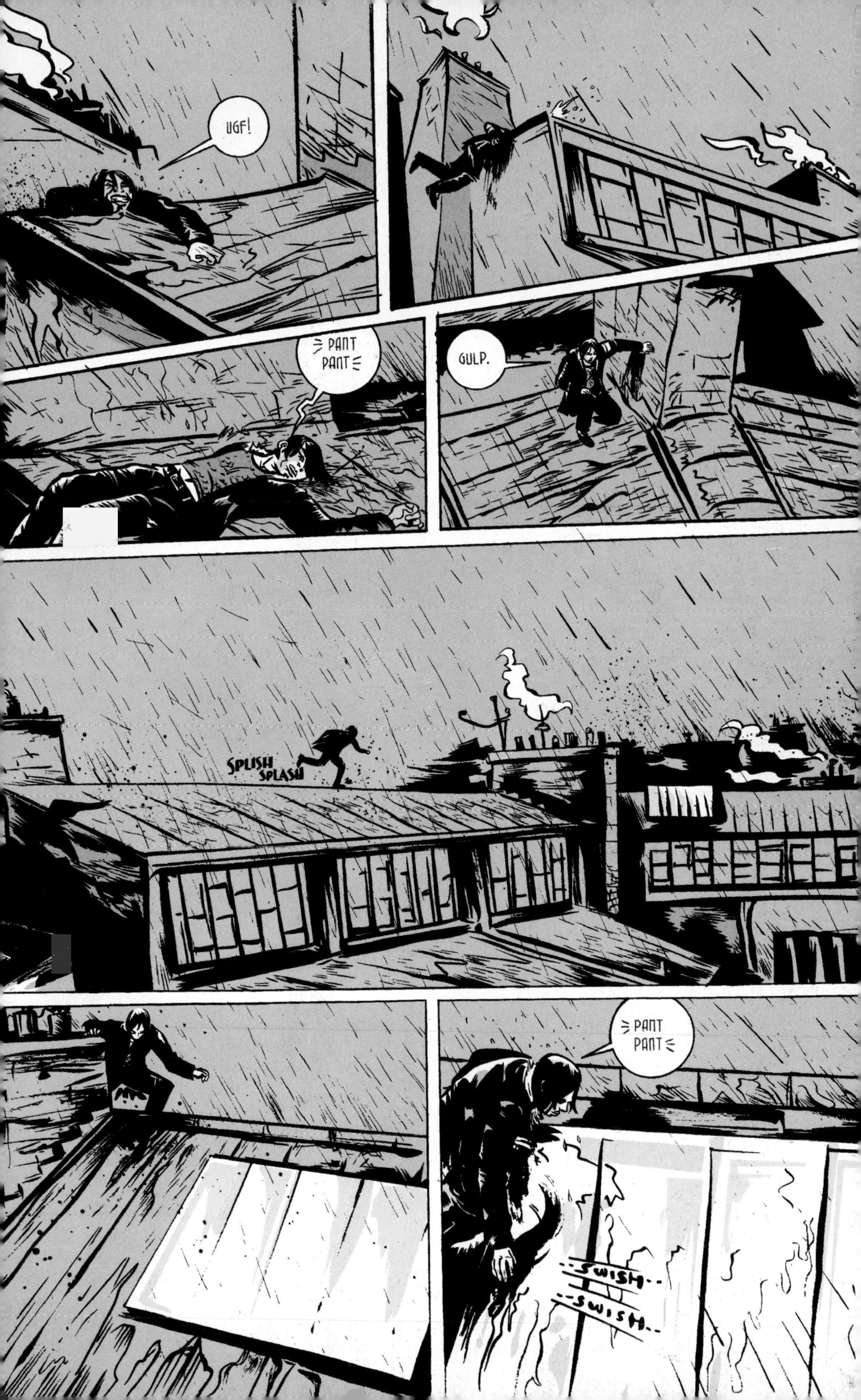
UGF!
PANT PANT
GULP.
SPLISH SPLASH
PANT PANT
SWISH
SWISH

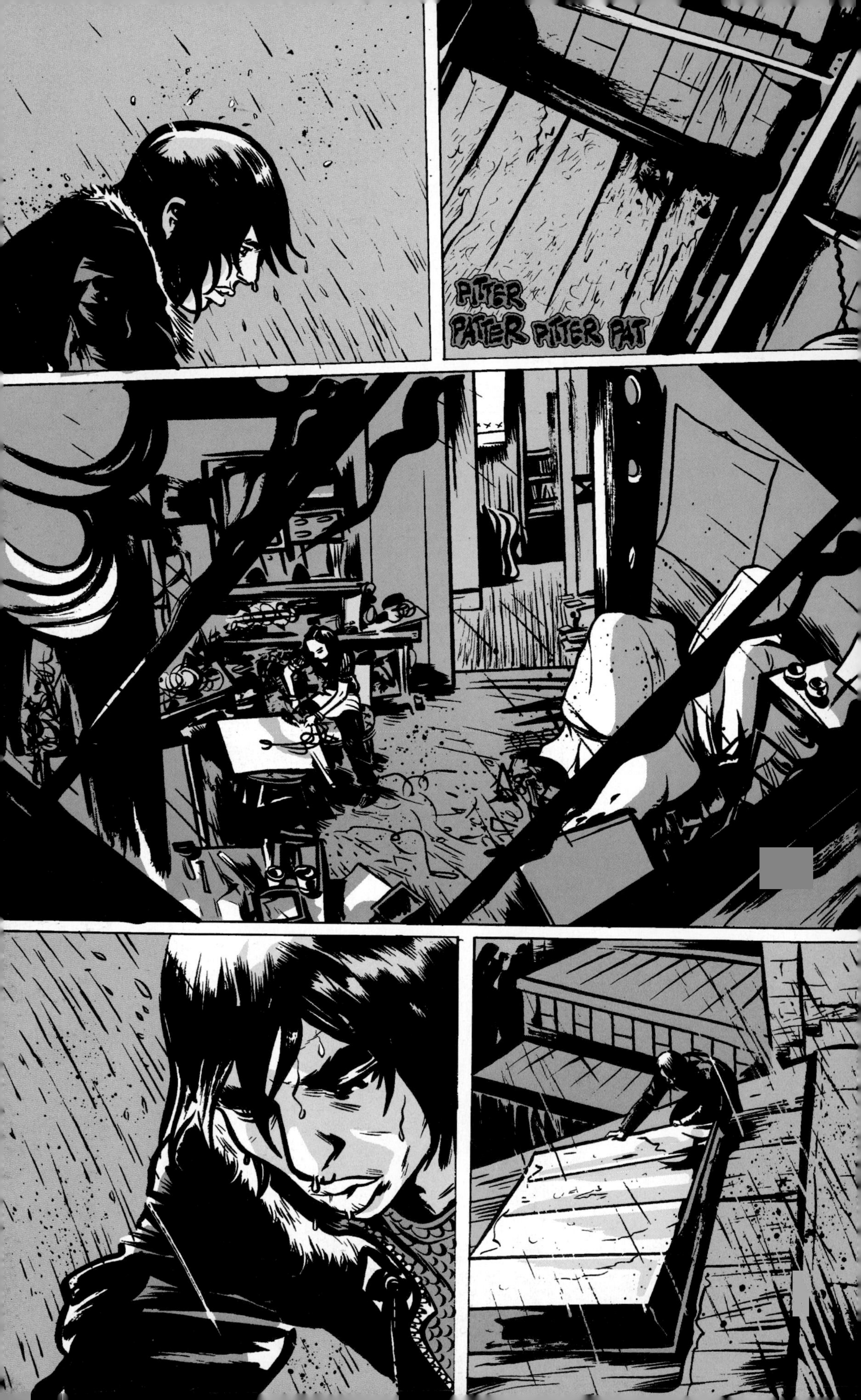
PITTER PATTER PITTER PAT

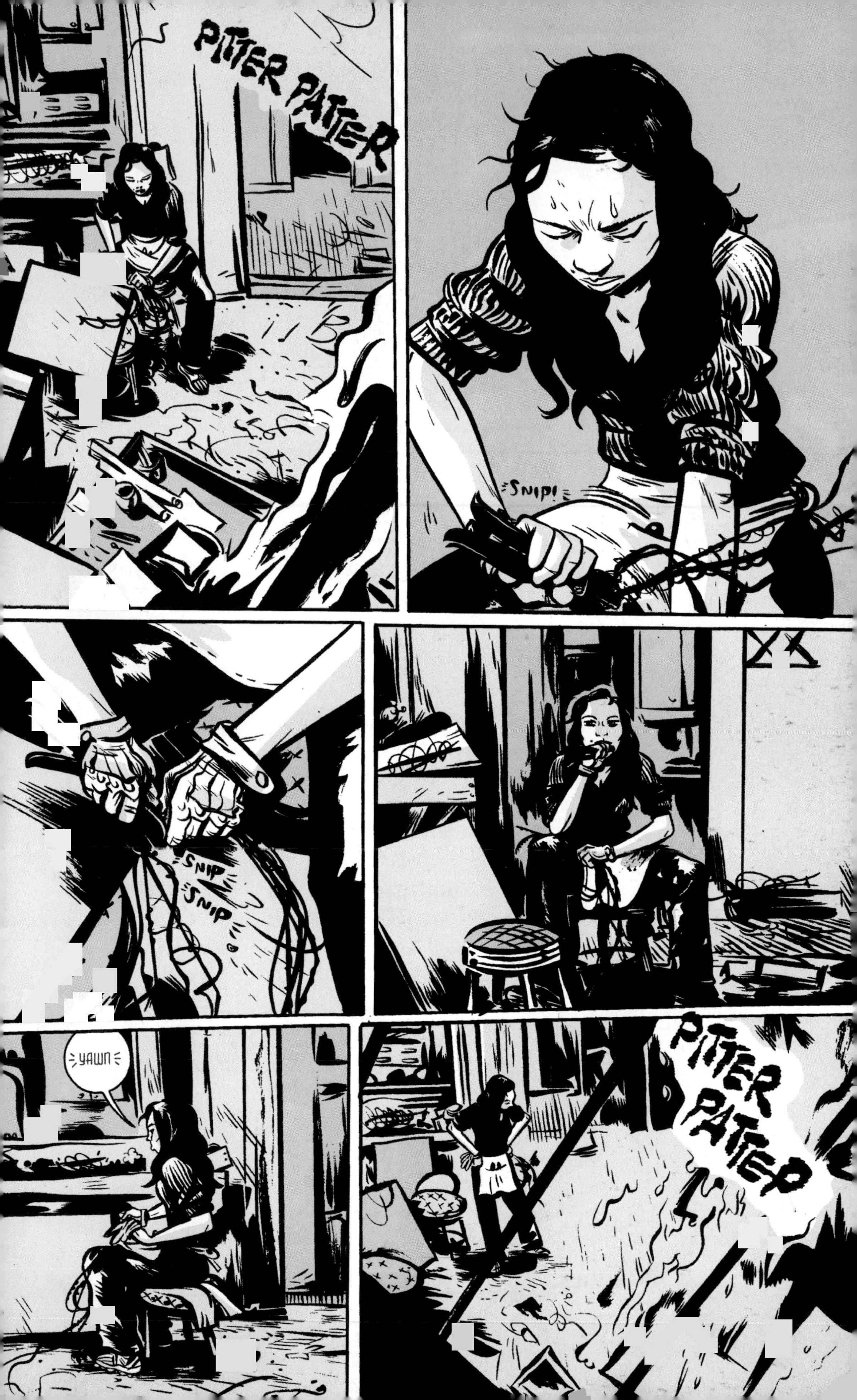
PITTER PATTER
SNIP!
SNIP
SNIP
YAWN
PITTER PATTER

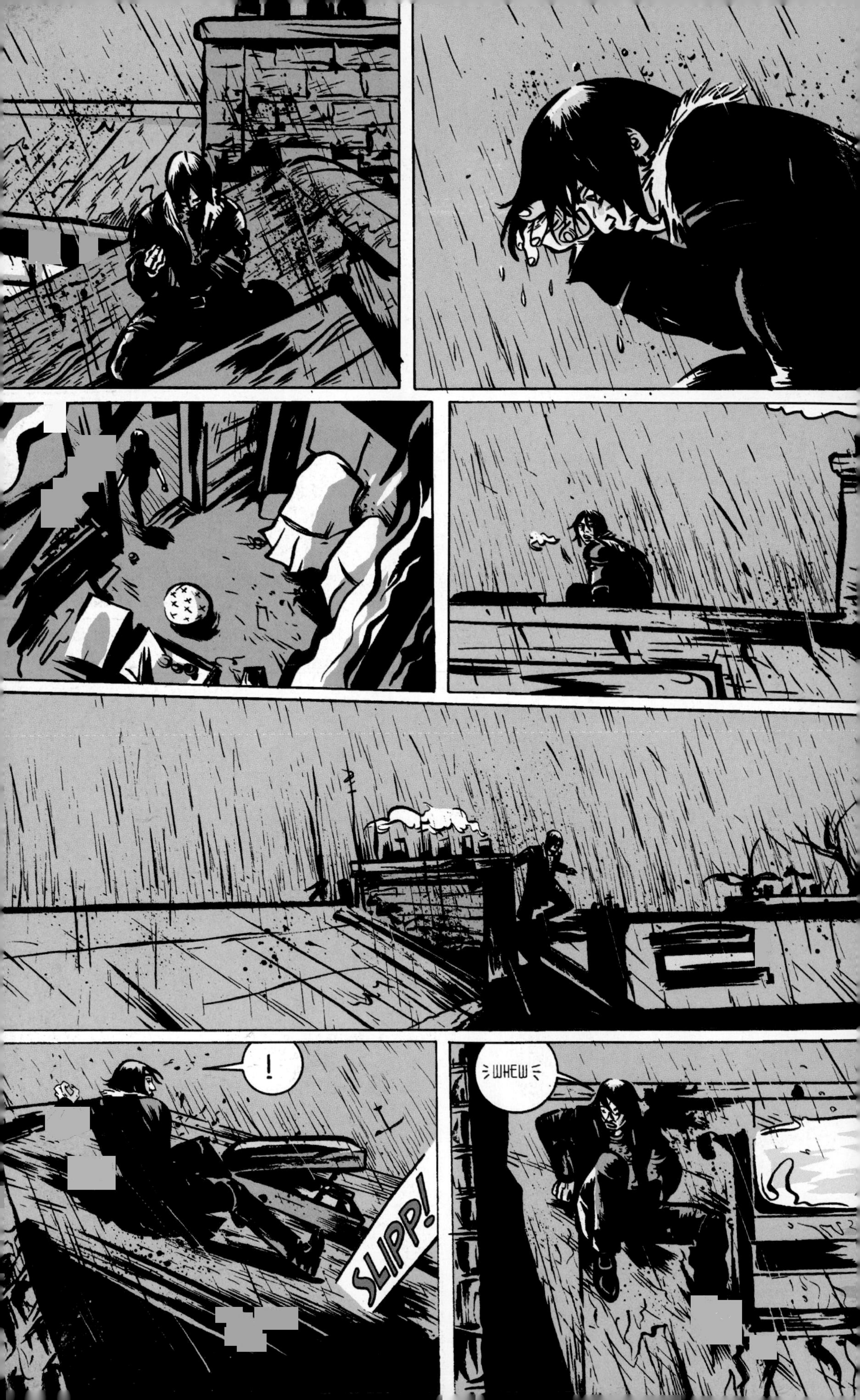
!
SLIPP!
WHEW

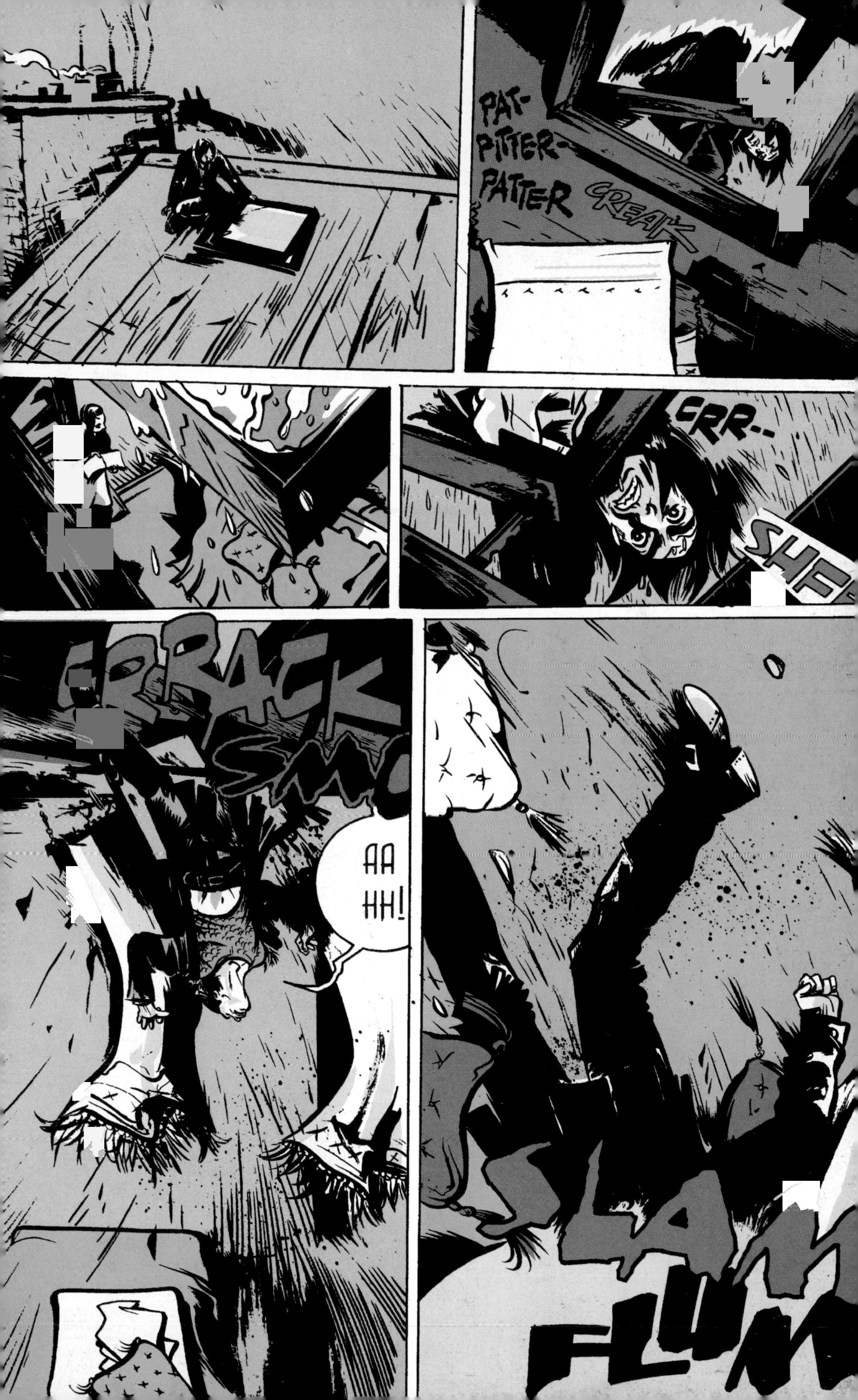
PAT-
PITTER-
PATTER
CREAK
CRR..
AA
HH!

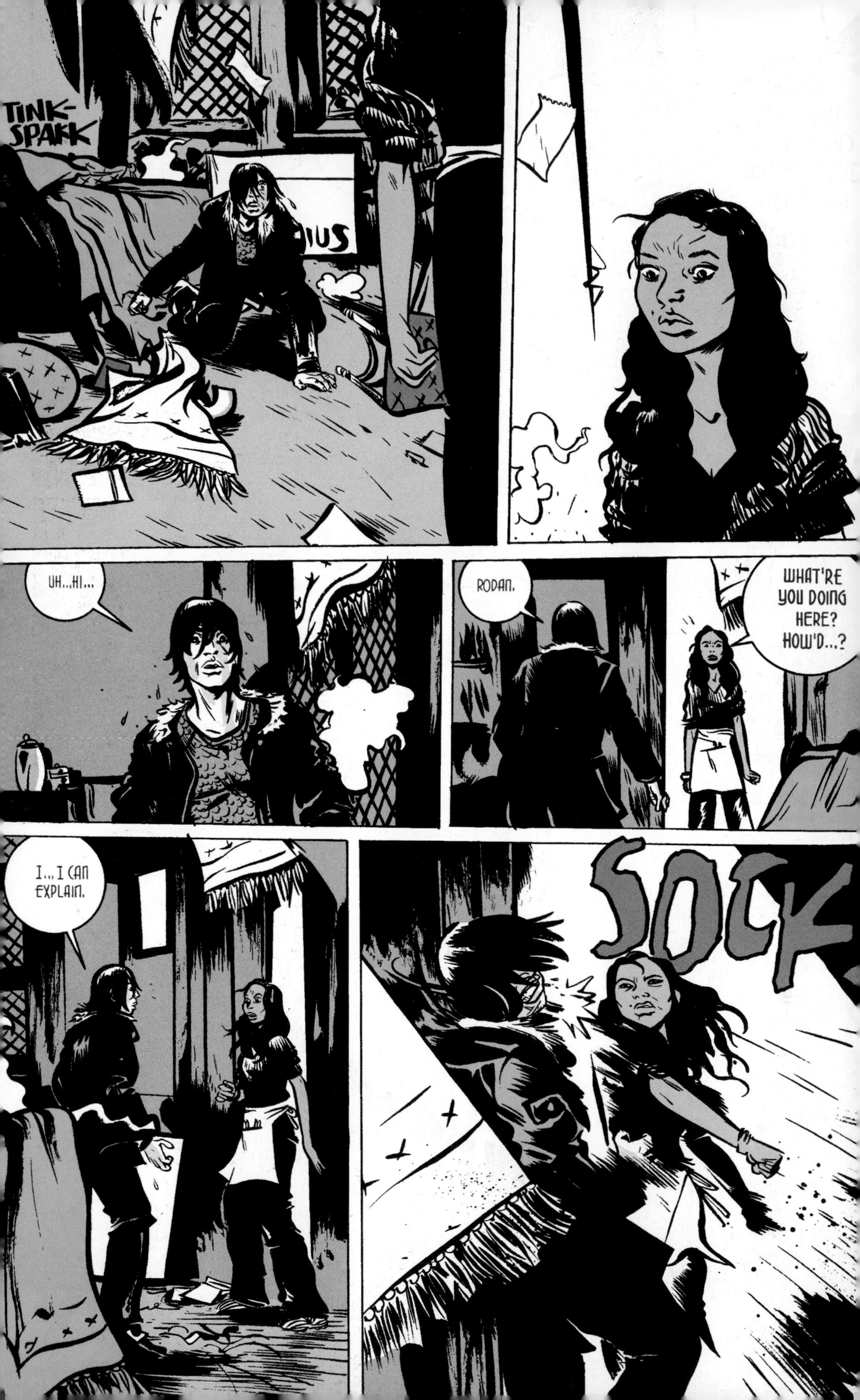
TINK-SPARK
IUS
UH...HI...
RODAN.
WHAT'RE YOU DOING HERE? HOW'D...?
I... I CAN EXPLAIN.
SOCK

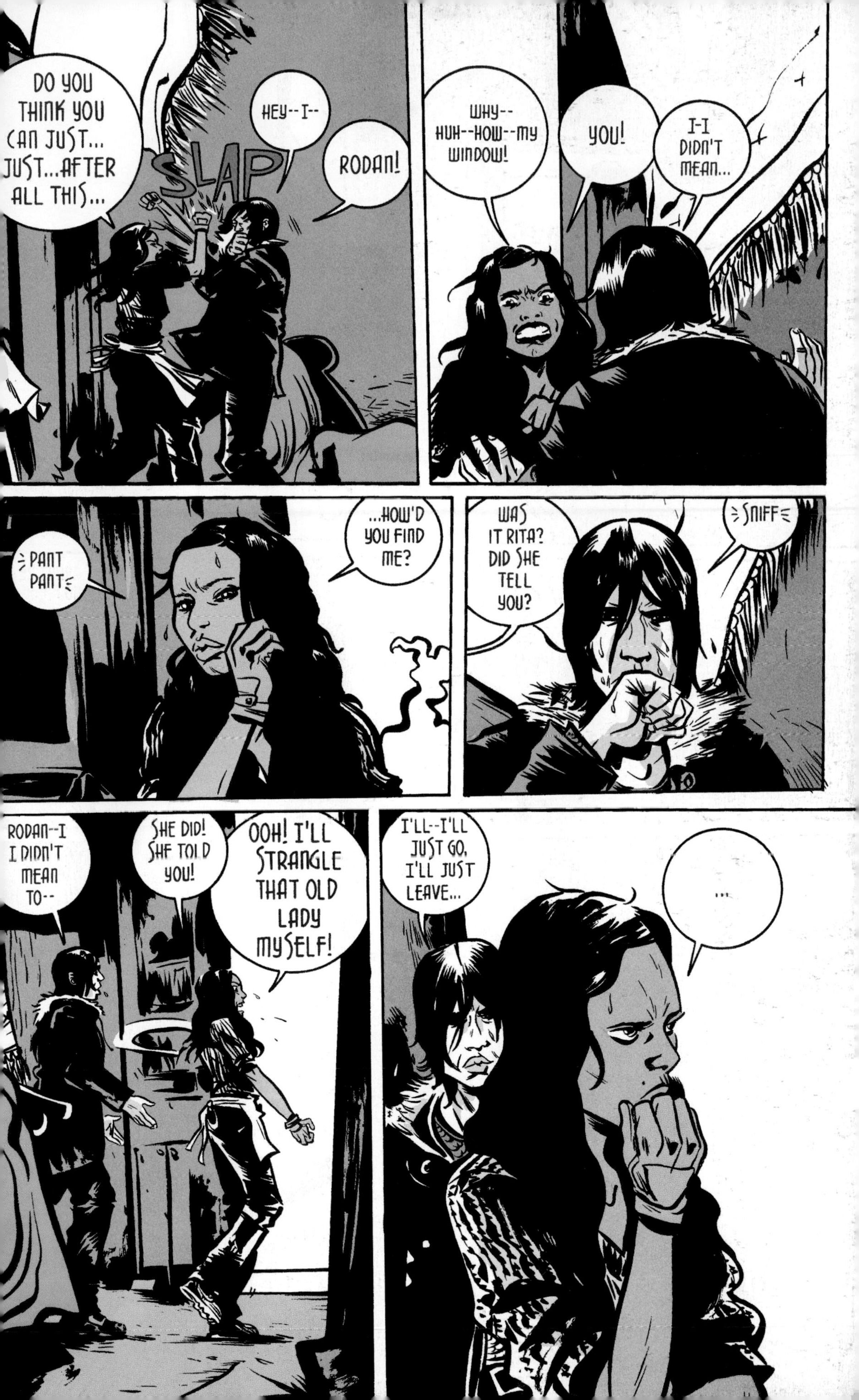
DO YOU THINK YOU CAN JUST... JUST...AFTER ALL THIS...
SLAP!
HEY--I--
RODAN!
WHY--HUH--HOW--MY WINDOW!
YOU!
I-I DIDN'T MEAN...
PANT PANT
...HOW'D YOU FIND ME?
WAS IT RITA? DID SHE TELL YOU?
SNIFF
RODAN--I I DIDN'T MEAN TO--
SHE DID! SHE TOLD YOU!
OOH! I'LL STRANGLE THAT OLD LADY MYSELF!
I'LL--I'LL JUST GO, I'LL JUST LEAVE...
...

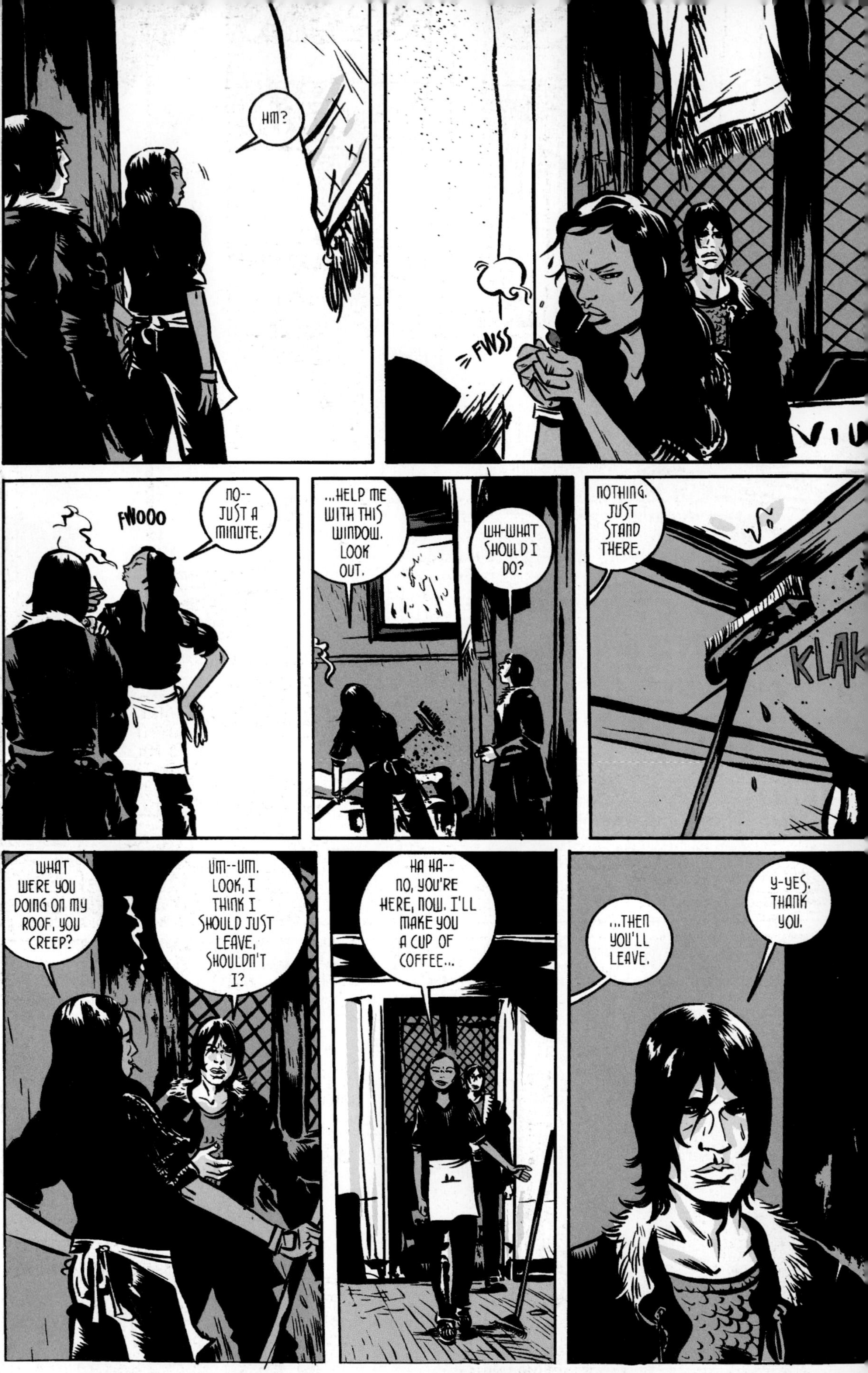
HM?
FWSS
VIU
FWOOO
NO-- JUST A MINUTE.
...HELP ME WITH THIS WINDOW. LOOK OUT.
WH-WHAT SHOULD I DO?
NOTHING. JUST STAND THERE.
KLAK
WHAT WERE YOU DOING ON MY ROOF, YOU CREEP?
UM--UM. LOOK, I THINK I SHOULD JUST LEAVE, SHOULDN'T I?
HA HA-- NO, YOU'RE HERE, NOW. I'LL MAKE YOU A CUP OF COFFEE...
...THEN YOU'LL LEAVE.
Y-YES. THANK YOU.

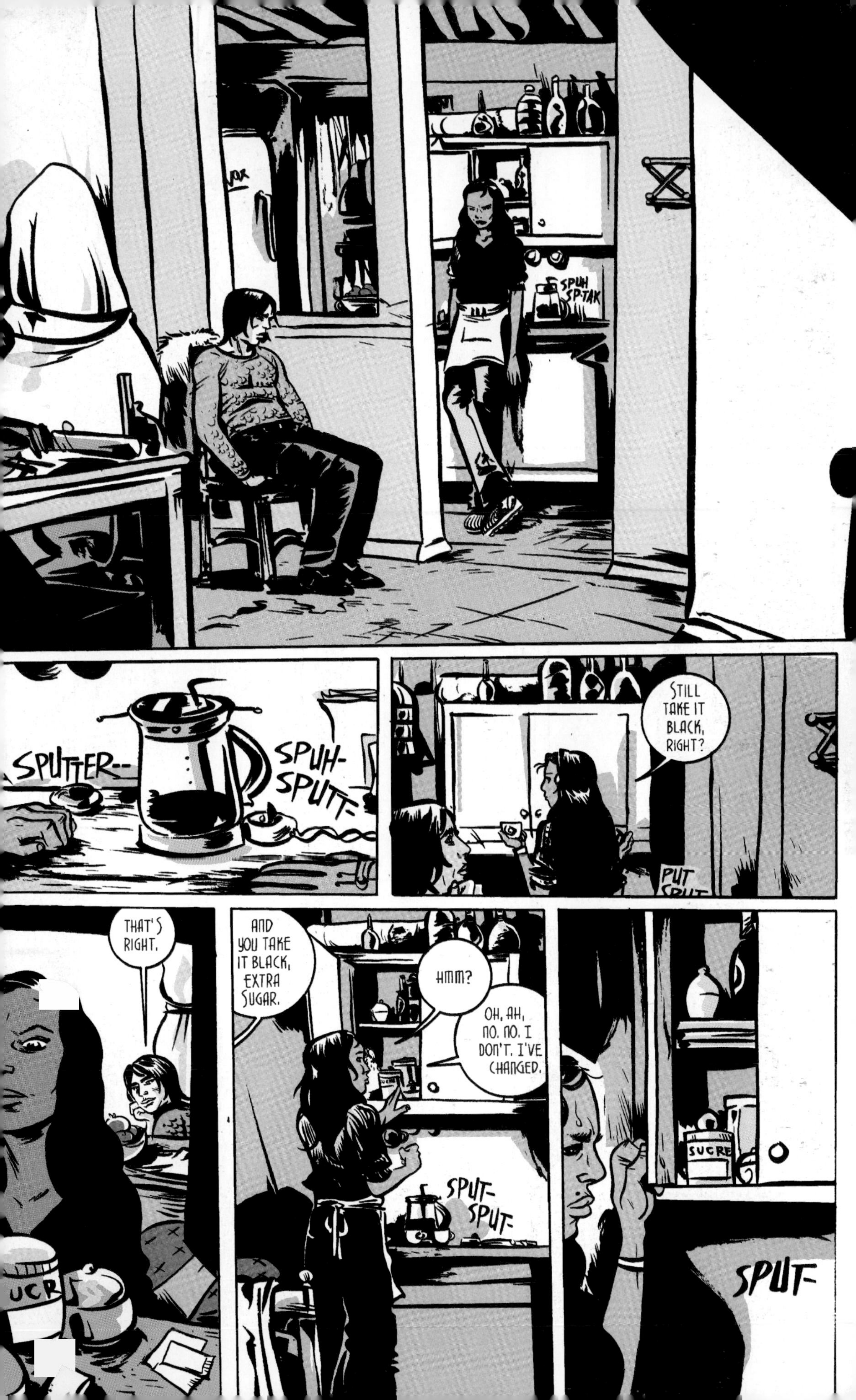
SPUH SP-TAK
SPUTTER--
SPUH-SPUTT-
STILL TAKE IT BLACK, RIGHT?
PUT SPUT
THAT'S RIGHT.
AND YOU TAKE IT BLACK, EXTRA SUGAR.
HMM?
OH, AH, NO. NO. I DON'T. I'VE CHANGED.
SPUT-SPUT-
SUCRE
SPUT-

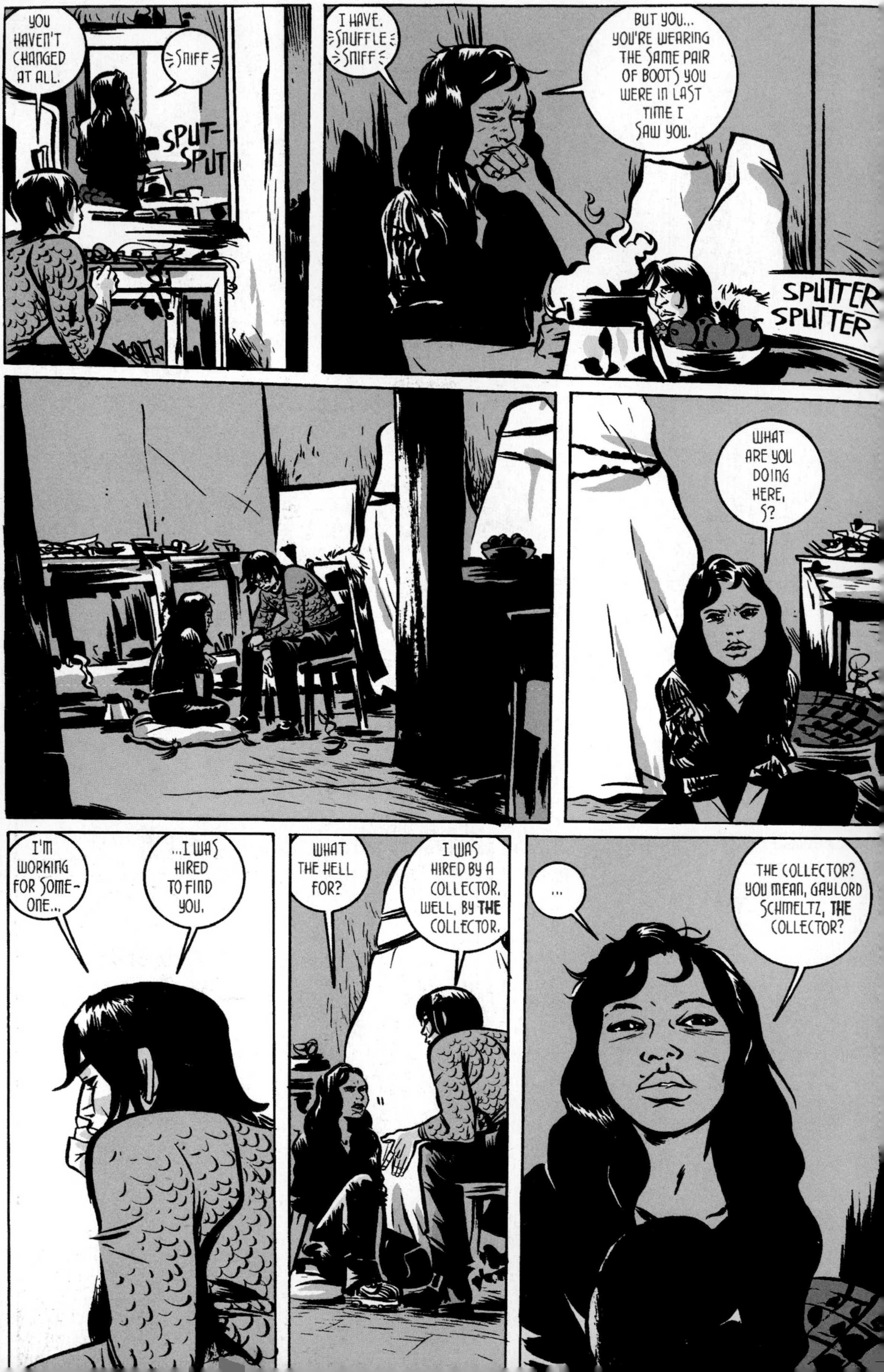
YOU HAVEN'T CHANGED AT ALL.
SNIFF
SPUT-SPUT
I HAVE. SNUFFLE SNIFF
BUT YOU... YOU'RE WEARING THE SAME PAIR OF BOOTS YOU WERE IN LAST TIME I SAW YOU.
SPUTTER SPUTTER
WHAT ARE YOU DOING HERE, S?
I'M WORKING FOR SOME-ONE...
...I WAS HIRED TO FIND YOU.
WHAT THE HELL FOR?
I WAS HIRED BY A COLLECTOR. WELL, BY THE COLLECTOR.
...
THE COLLECTOR? YOU MEAN, GAYLORD SCHMELTZ, THE COLLECTOR?

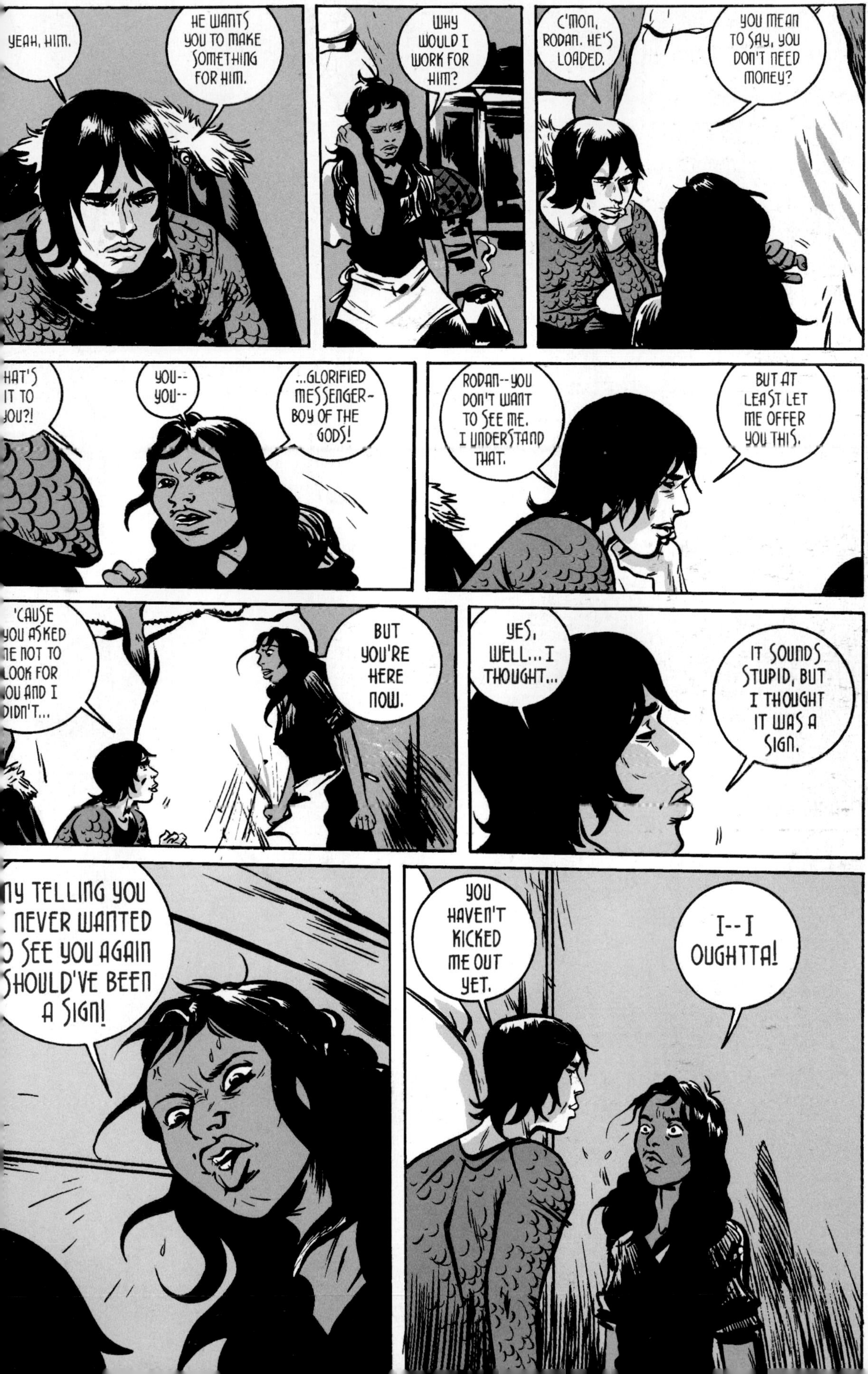
YEAH, HIM.
HE WANTS YOU TO MAKE SOMETHING FOR HIM.
WHY WOULD I WORK FOR HIM?
C'MON, RODAN. HE'S LOADED.
YOU MEAN TO SAY, YOU DON'T NEED MONEY?
HAT'S IT TO IOU?!
YOU-- YOU--
...GLORIFIED MESSENGER-BOY OF THE GODS!
RODAN--YOU DON'T WANT TO SEE ME. I UNDERSTAND THAT.
BUT AT LEAST LET ME OFFER YOU THIS.
'CAUSE YOU ASKED IE NOT TO LOOK FOR OU AND I DIDN'T...
BUT YOU'RE HERE NOW.
YES, WELL...I THOUGHT...
IT SOUNDS STUPID, BUT I THOUGHT IT WAS A SIGN.
IY TELLING YOU NEVER WANTED O SEE YOU AGAIN SHOULD'VE BEEN A SIGN!
YOU HAVEN'T KICKED ME OUT YET.
I--I OUGHTTA!

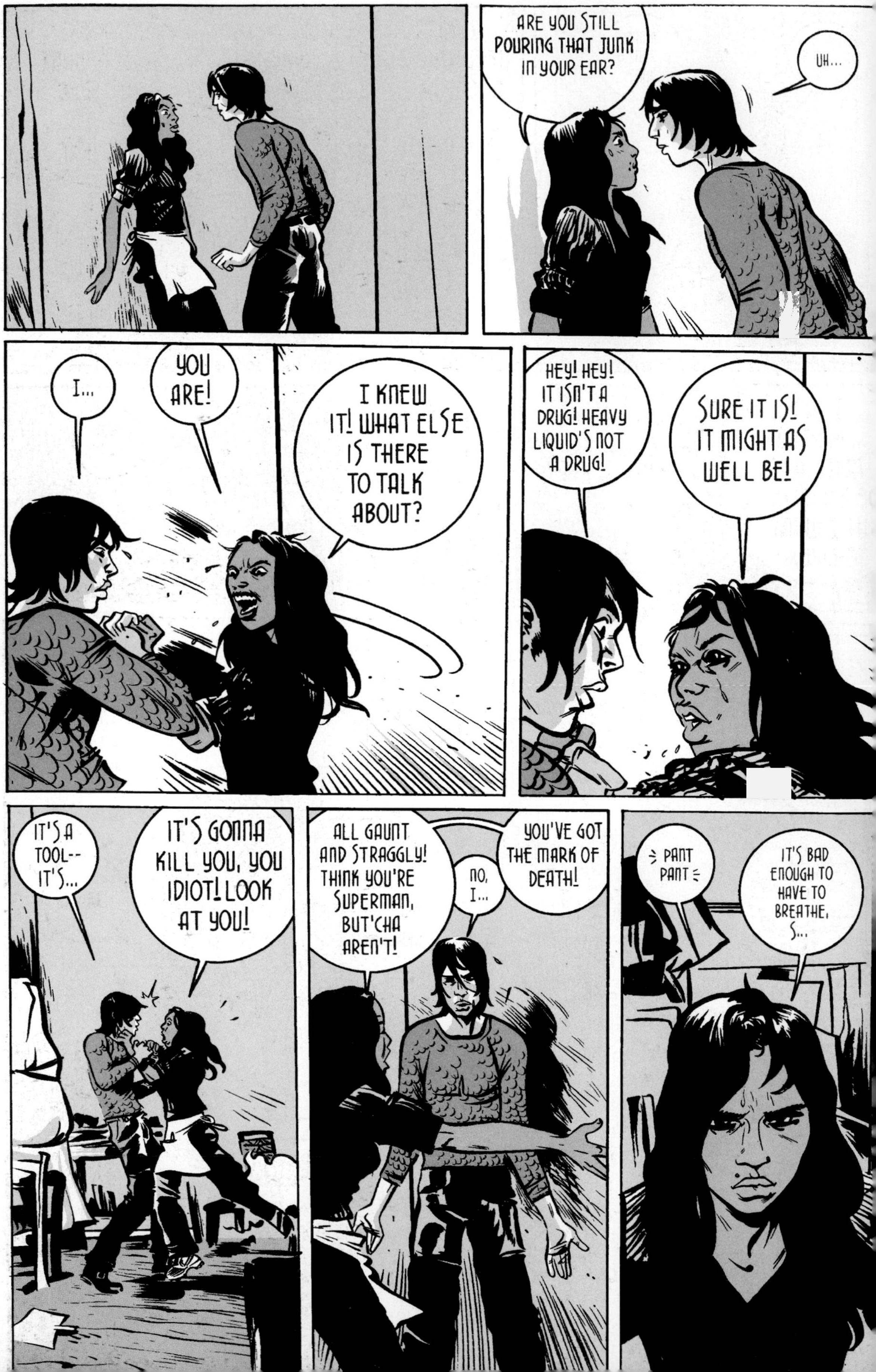

ARE YOU STILL POURING THAT JUNK IN YOUR EAR?
UH...
I...
YOU ARE!
I KNEW IT! WHAT ELSE IS THERE TO TALK ABOUT?
HEY! HEY! IT ISN'T A DRUG! HEAVY LIQUID'S NOT A DRUG!
SURE IT IS! IT MIGHT AS WELL BE!
IT'S A TOOL-- IT'S...
IT'S GONNA KILL YOU, YOU IDIOT! LOOK AT YOU!
ALL GAUNT AND STRAGGLY! THINK YOU'RE SUPERMAN, BUT'CHA AREN'T!
NO, I...
YOU'VE GOT THE MARK OF DEATH!
PANT PANT
IT'S BAD ENOUGH TO HAVE TO BREATHE, S...

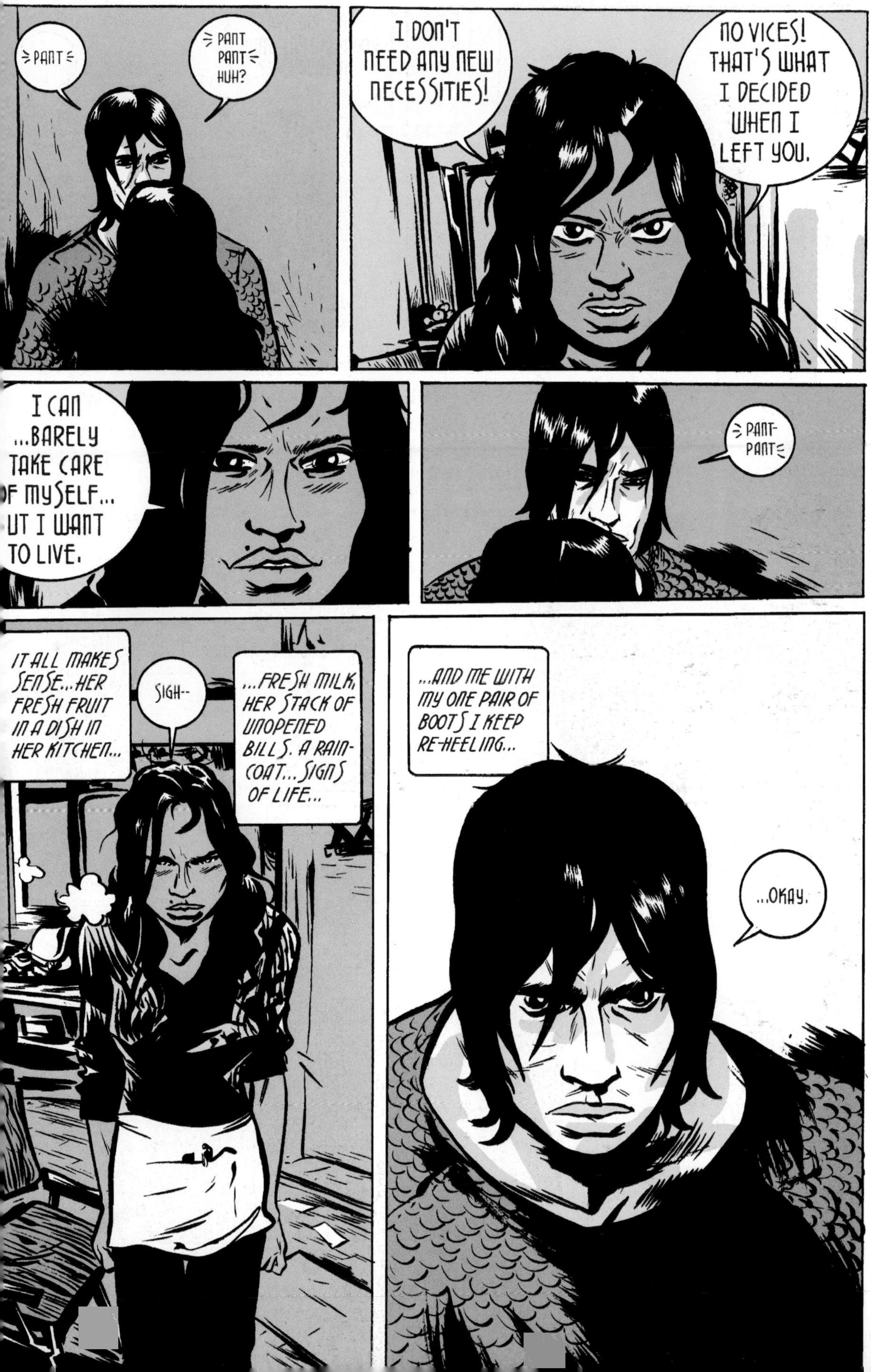
PANT
PANT PANT HUH?
I DON'T NEED ANY NEW NECESSITIES!
NO VICES! THAT'S WHAT I DECIDED WHEN I LEFT YOU.
I CAN ...BARELY TAKE CARE OF MYSELF... BUT I WANT TO LIVE.
PANT- PANT
IT ALL MAKES SENSE...HER FRESH FRUIT IN A DISH IN HER KITCHEN...
SIGH--
...FRESH MILK, HER STACK OF UNOPENED BILLS. A RAINCOAT...SIGNS OF LIFE...
...AND ME WITH MY ONE PAIR OF BOOTS I KEEP RE-HEELING...
...OKAY.

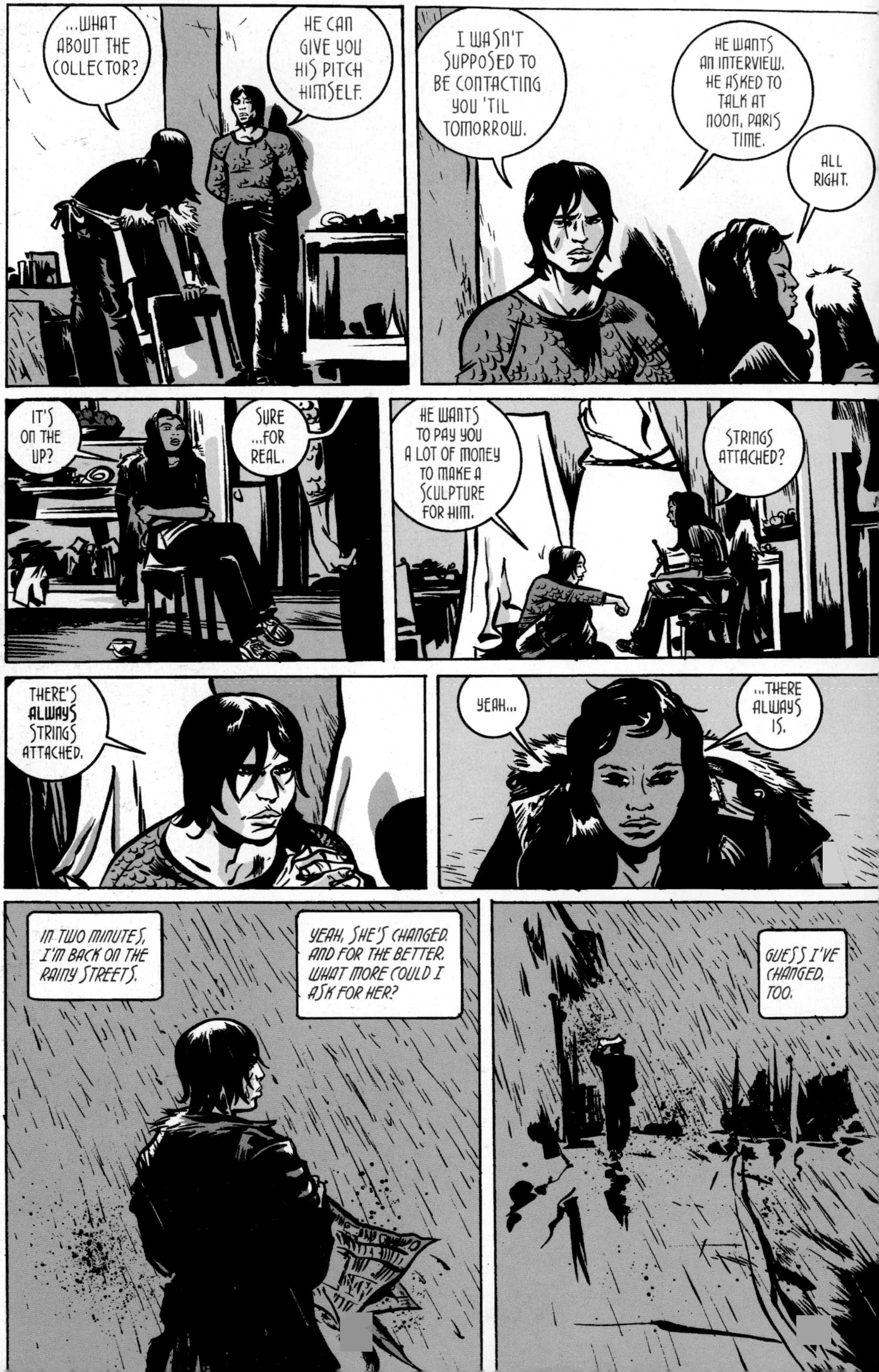
...WHAT ABOUT THE COLLECTOR?
HE CAN GIVE YOU HIS PITCH HIMSELF.
I WASN'T SUPPOSED TO BE CONTACTING YOU 'TIL TOMORROW.
HE WANTS AN INTERVIEW. HE ASKED TO TALK AT NOON, PARIS TIME.
ALL RIGHT.
IT'S ON THE UP?
SURE ...FOR REAL.
HE WANTS TO PAY YOU A LOT OF MONEY TO MAKE A SCULPTURE FOR HIM.
STRINGS ATTACHED?
THERE'S **ALWAYS** STRINGS ATTACHED.
YEAH...
...THERE ALWAYS IS.
IN TWO MINUTES, I'M BACK ON THE RAINY STREETS.
YEAH, SHE'S CHANGED. AND FOR THE BETTER. WHAT MORE COULD I ASK FOR HER?
GUESS I'VE CHANGED, TOO.

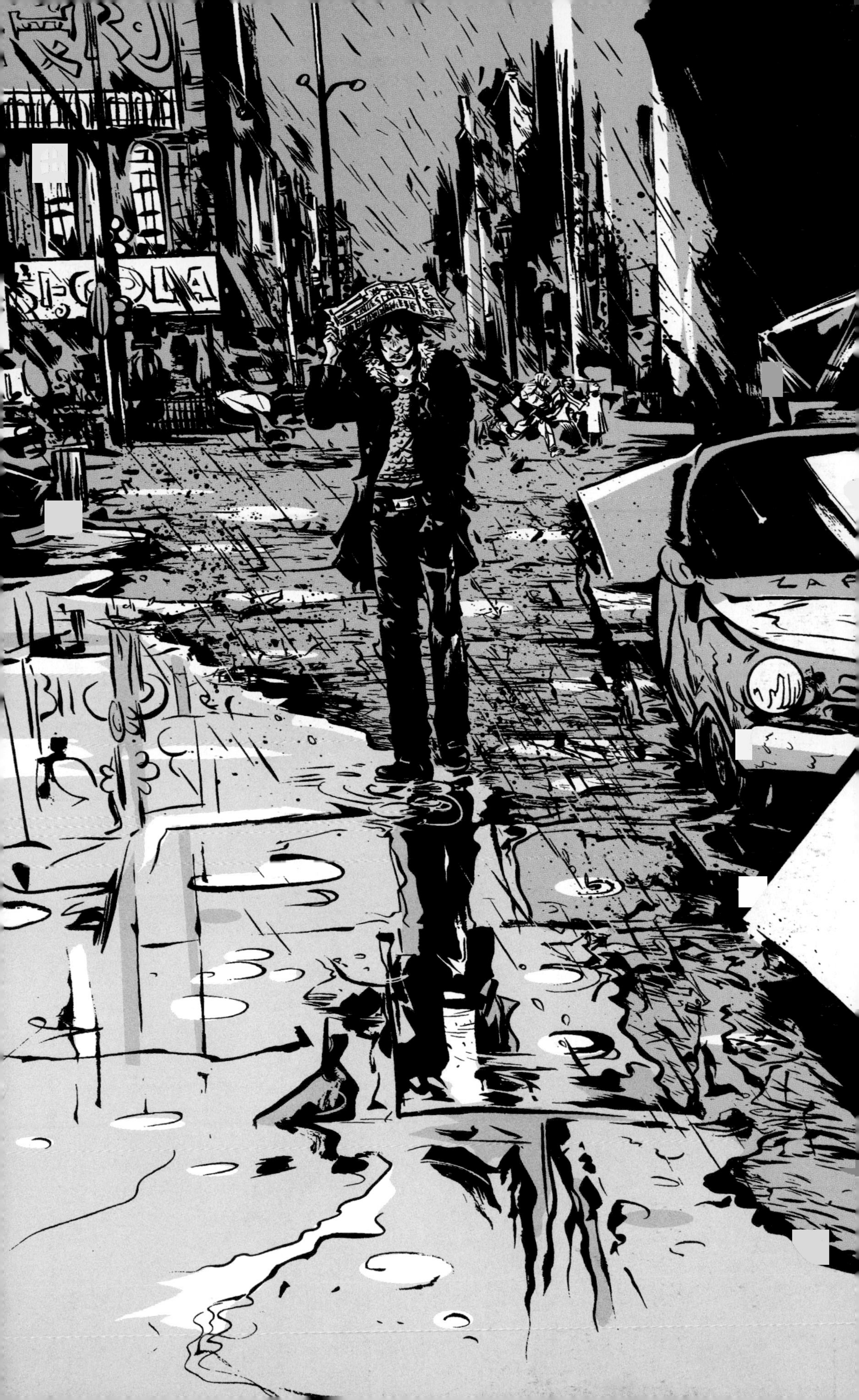

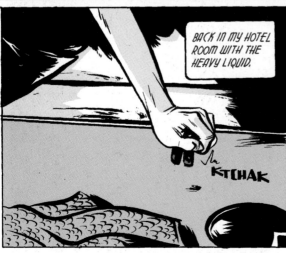

BACK IN MY HOTEL ROOM WITH THE HEAVY LIQUID.

KTCHAK

LUIS AND I FIRST FOUND SOME OF THE STUFF SIX YEARS AGO, BY ACCIDENT, BUT I ALREADY TOLD YOU THAT PART.

WE EVENTUALLY STARTED STEALING IT. WE STOLE A BUNCH FROM THE CLOWNS. BUT THAT DOESN'T MATTER NOW.

AT FIRST, IT WAS JUST FUN--LIKE HAVING A NEW TOY.

LIKE LAVA AT ROOM TEMPERATURE. YOU COULD HOLD IT IN YOUR HAND.

WELL--NOT LITERALLY. IT WAS CAUSTIC, LIKE THE STUFF YOU'D USE TO UNCLOG A PIPE.

...HAD TO WEAR A GLOVE TO HOLD IT. WE KEPT IT IN A RUBBER BAGGIE.

THEN SOMEHOW I GOT THE STUPID IDEA TO HEAT IT UP--JUST TO SEE WHAT WOULD HAPPEN.

THAT'S WHEN MY TROUBLE REALLY STARTED.

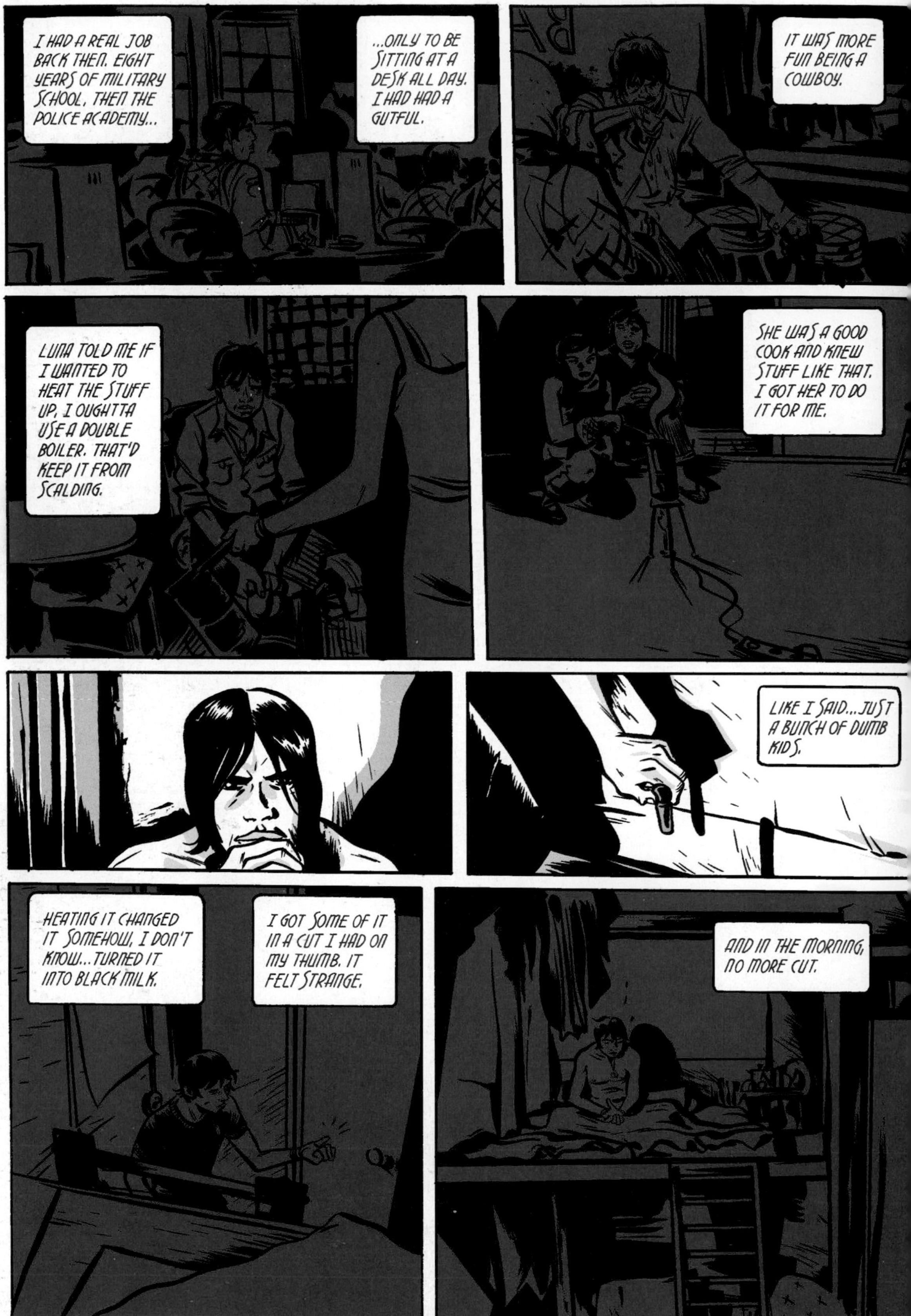
I HAD A REAL JOB BACK THEN. EIGHT YEARS OF MILITARY SCHOOL, THEN THE POLICE ACADEMY...
...ONLY TO BE SITTING AT A DESK ALL DAY. I HAD HAD A GUTFUL.
IT WAS MORE FUN BEING A COWBOY.
LUNA TOLD ME IF I WANTED TO HEAT THE STUFF UP, I OUGHTTA USE A DOUBLE BOILER. THAT'D KEEP IT FROM SCALDING.
SHE WAS A GOOD COOK AND KNEW STUFF LIKE THAT. I GOT HER TO DO IT FOR ME.
LIKE I SAID... JUST A BUNCH OF DUMB KIDS.
HEATING IT CHANGED IT SOMEHOW, I DON'T KNOW... TURNED IT INTO BLACK MILK.
I GOT SOME OF IT IN A CUT I HAD ON MY THUMB. IT FELT STRANGE.
AND IN THE MORNING, NO MORE CUT.

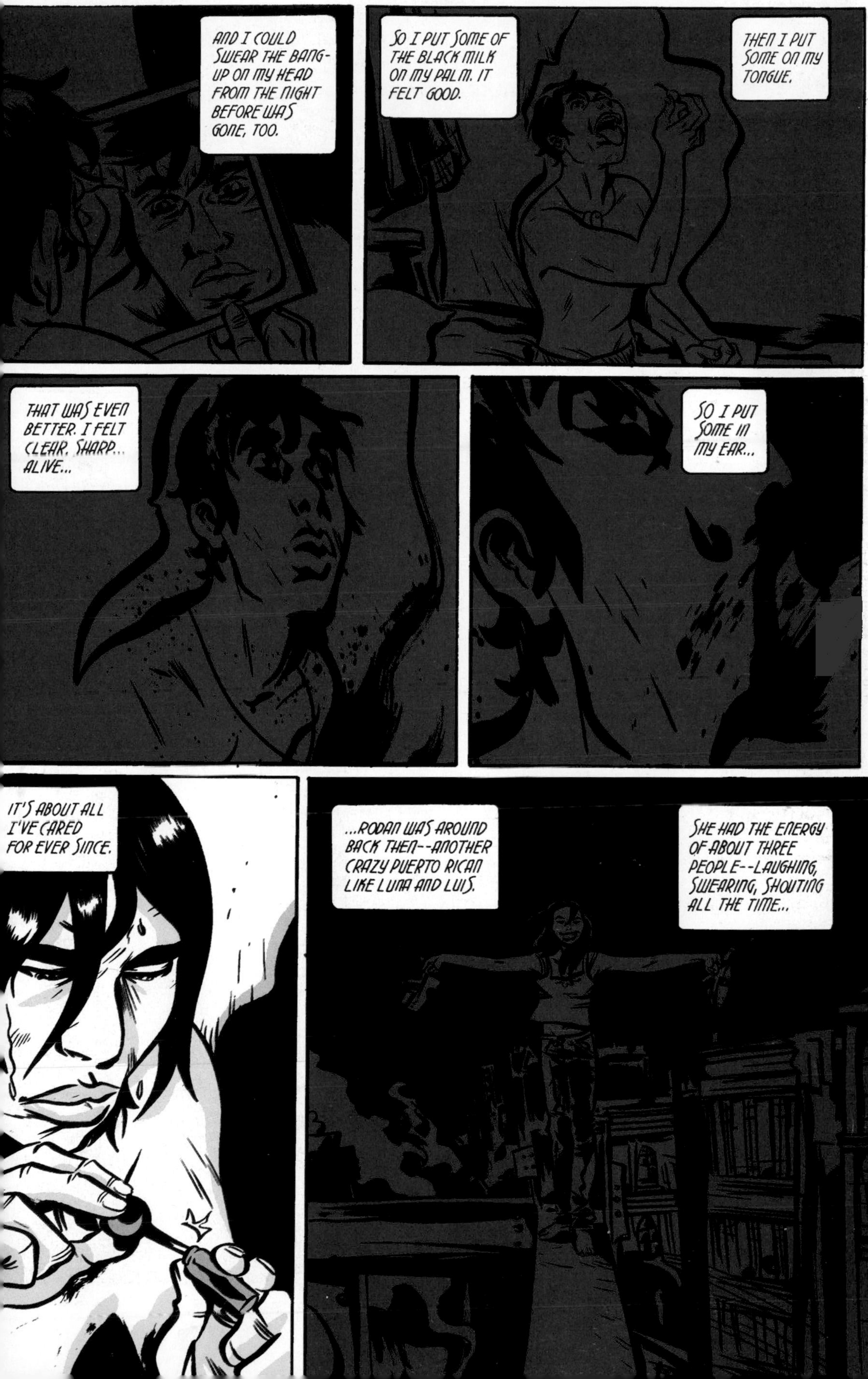
AND I COULD SWEAR THE BANG-UP ON MY HEAD FROM THE NIGHT BEFORE WAS GONE, TOO.
SO I PUT SOME OF THE BLACK MILK ON MY PALM. IT FELT GOOD.
THEN I PUT SOME ON MY TONGUE.
THAT WAS EVEN BETTER. I FELT CLEAR. SHARP... ALIVE...
SO I PUT SOME IN MY EAR...
IT'S ABOUT ALL I'VE CARED FOR EVER SINCE.
...RODAN WAS AROUND BACK THEN--ANOTHER CRAZY PUERTO RICAN LIKE LUNA AND LUIS.
SHE HAD THE ENERGY OF ABOUT THREE PEOPLE--LAUGHING, SWEARING, SHOUTING ALL THE TIME...

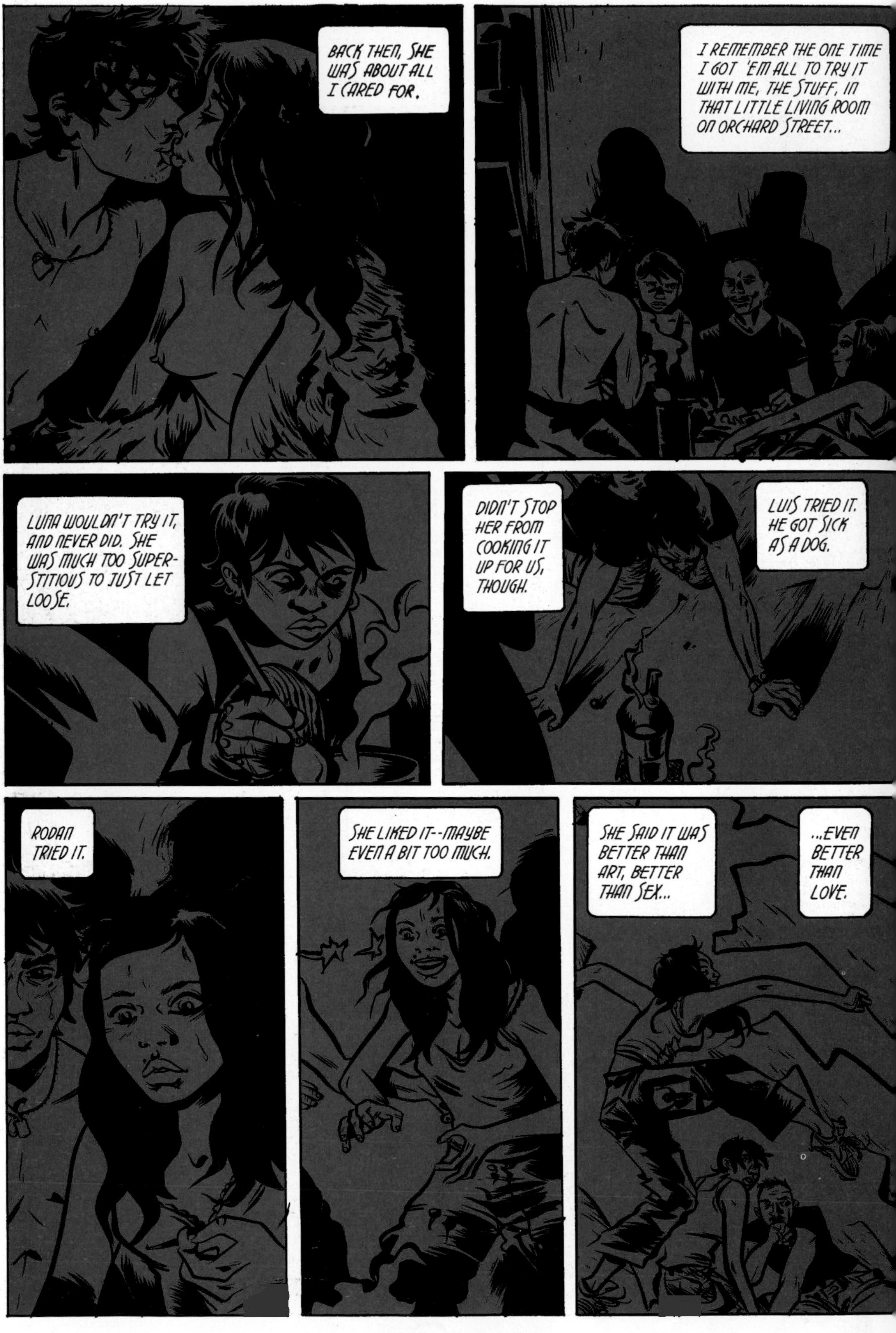
BACK THEN, SHE WAS ABOUT ALL I CARED FOR.
I REMEMBER THE ONE TIME I GOT 'EM ALL TO TRY IT WITH ME, THE STUFF, IN THAT LITTLE LIVING ROOM ON ORCHARD STREET...
LUNA WOULDN'T TRY IT, AND NEVER DID. SHE WAS MUCH TOO SUPER-STITIOUS TO JUST LET LOOSE.
DIDN'T STOP HER FROM COOKING IT UP FOR US, THOUGH.
LUIS TRIED IT. HE GOT SICK AS A DOG.
RODAN TRIED IT.
SHE LIKED IT--MAYBE EVEN A BIT TOO MUCH.
SHE SAID IT WAS BETTER THAN ART, BETTER THAN SEX...
...EVEN BETTER THAN LOVE.

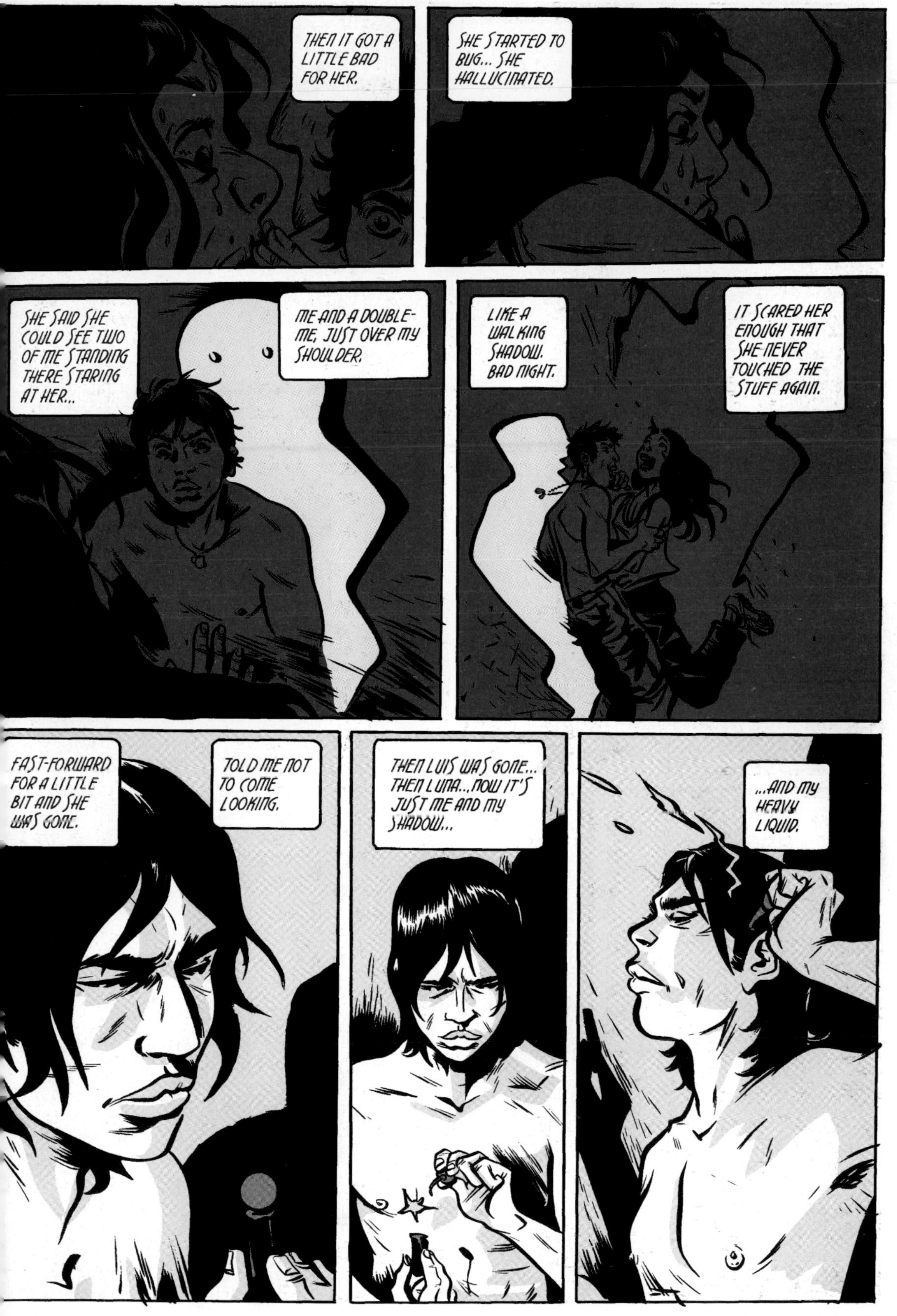

THEN IT GOT A LITTLE BAD FOR HER.
SHE STARTED TO BUG... SHE HALLUCINATED.
SHE SAID SHE COULD SEE TWO OF ME STANDING THERE STARING AT HER...
ME AND A DOUBLE-ME, JUST OVER MY SHOULDER.
LIKE A WALKING SHADOW. BAD NIGHT.
IT SCARED HER ENOUGH THAT SHE NEVER TOUCHED THE STUFF AGAIN.
FAST-FORWARD FOR A LITTLE BIT AND SHE WAS GONE.
TOLD ME NOT TO COME LOOKING.
THEN LUIS WAS GONE... THEN LUNA... NOW IT'S JUST ME AND MY SHADOW...
...AND MY HEAVY LIQUID.

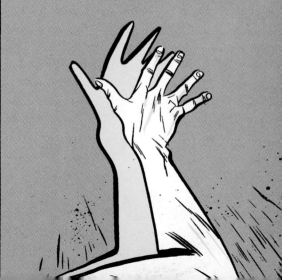

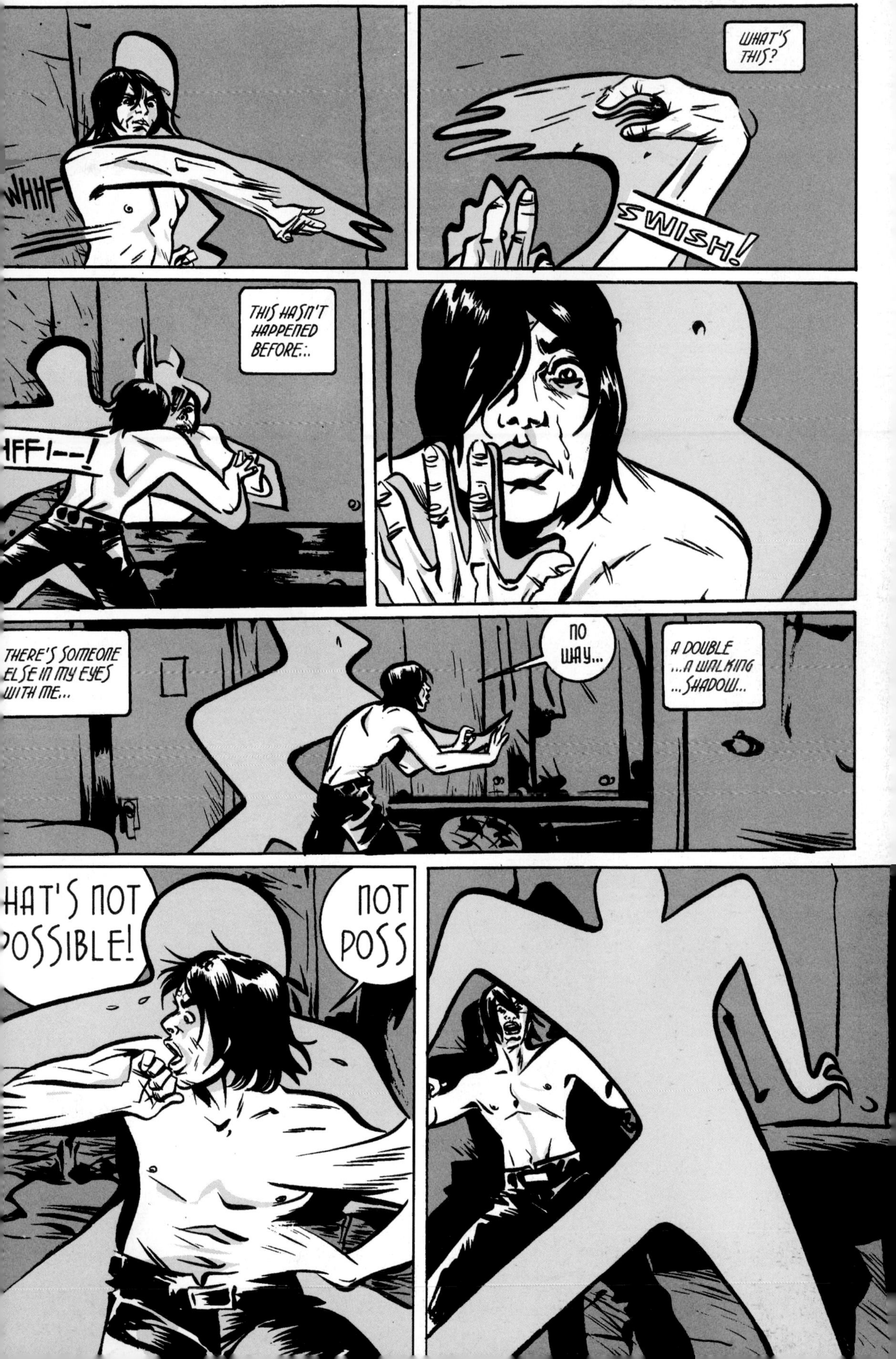
WHHF
WHAT'S THIS?
SWISH!
THIS HASN'T HAPPENED BEFORE:.
HFFI--!
THERE'S SOMEONE ELSE IN MY EYES WITH ME...
NO WAY...
A DOUBLE ...A WALKING ...SHADOW...
HAT'S NOT POSSIBLE!
NOT POSS

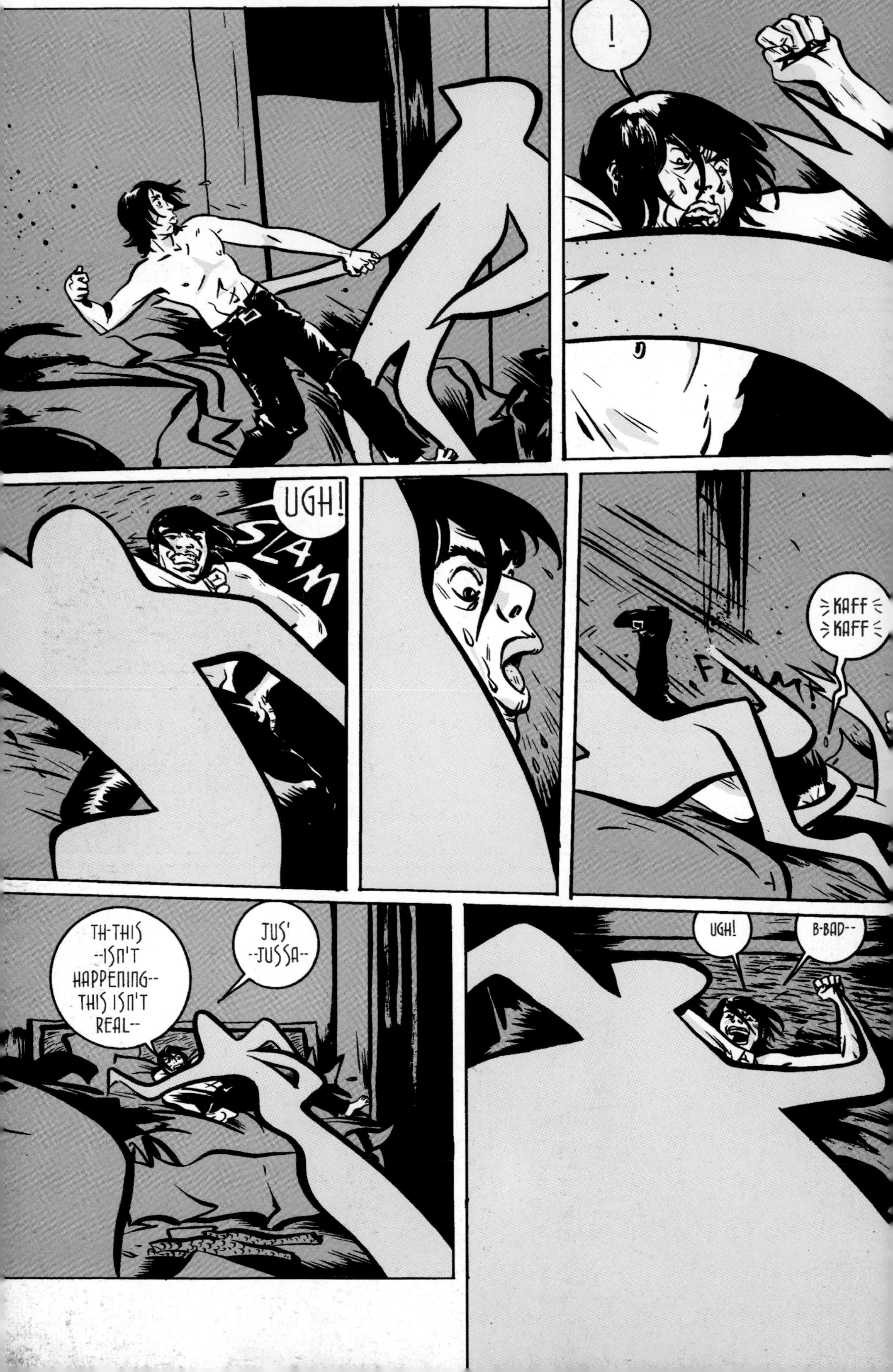
!
UGH!
SLAM
KAFF KAFF
TH-THIS --ISN'T HAPPENING-- THIS ISN'T REAL--
JUS' --JUSSA--
UGH!
B-BAD--

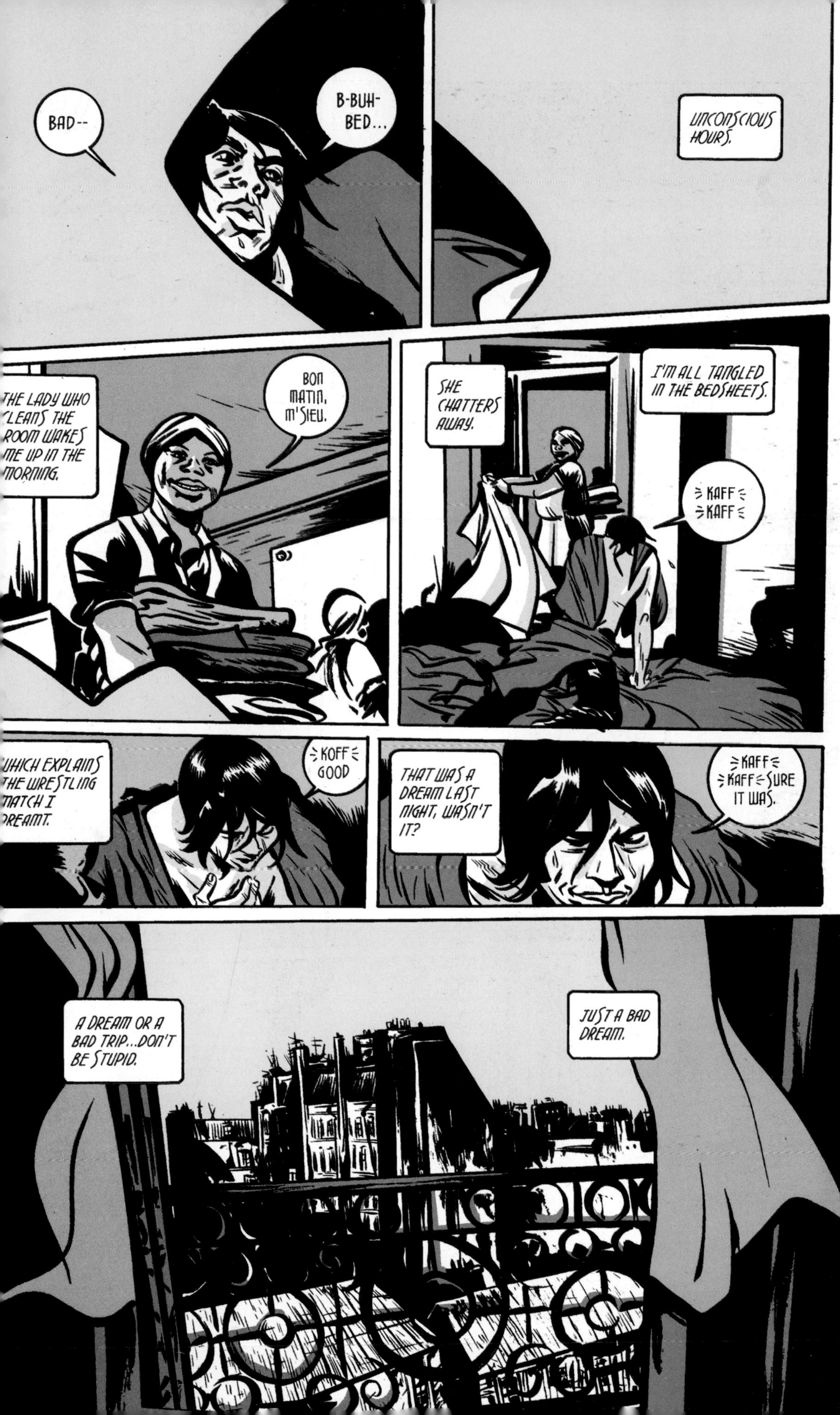
BAD--
B-BUH-BED...
UNCONSCIOUS HOURS.
THE LADY WHO CLEANS THE ROOM WAKES ME UP IN THE MORNING.
BON MATIN, M'SIEU.
SHE CHATTERS AWAY.
I'M ALL TANGLED IN THE BEDSHEETS.
KAFF KAFF
WHICH EXPLAINS THE WRESTLING MATCH I DREAMT.
KOFF GOOD
THAT WAS A DREAM LAST NIGHT, WASN'T IT?
KAFF KAFF SURE IT WAS.
A DREAM OR A BAD TRIP...DON'T BE STUPID.
JUST A BAD DREAM.

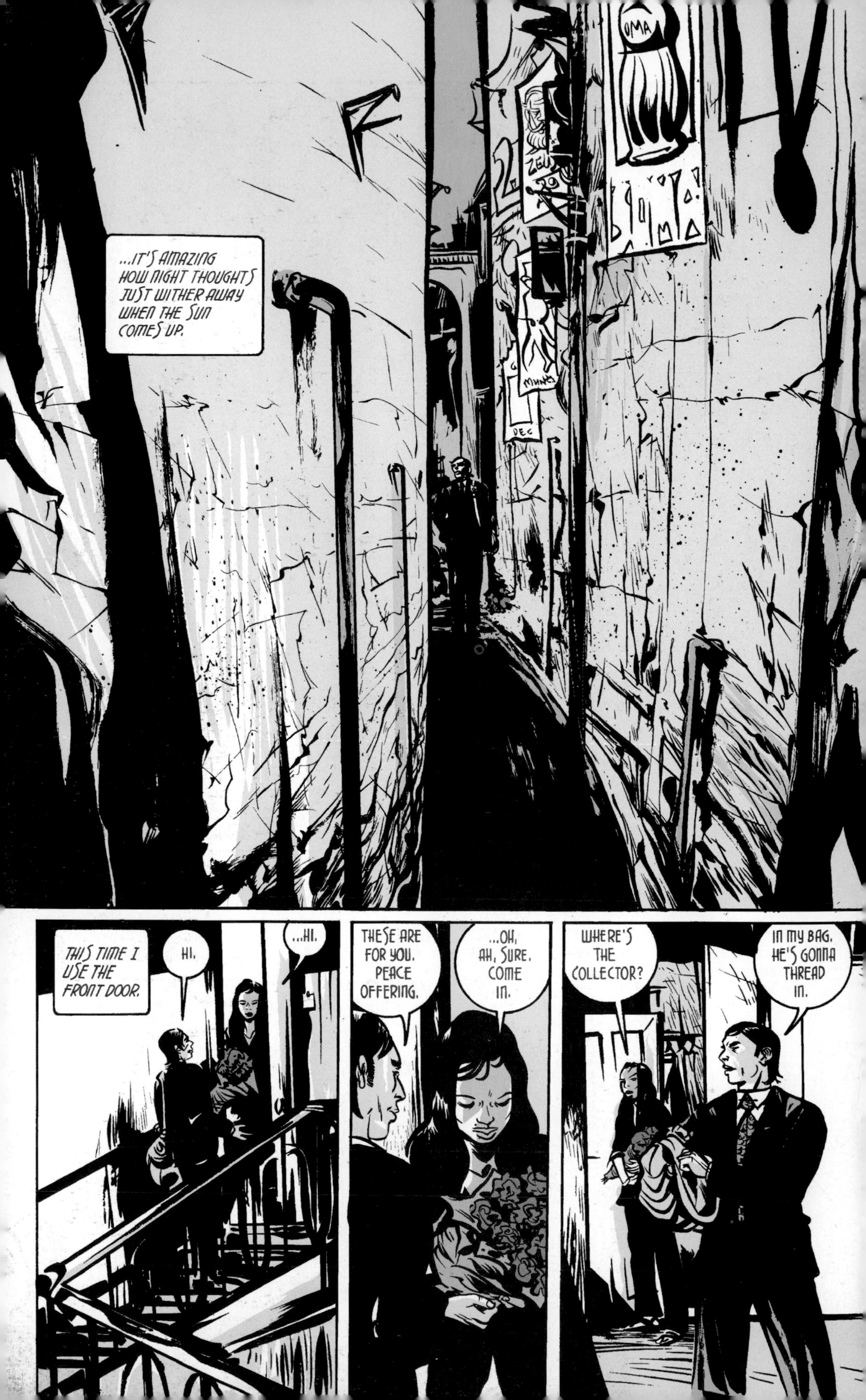

...IT'S AMAZING HOW NIGHT THOUGHTS JUST WITHER AWAY WHEN THE SUN COMES UP.
THIS TIME I USE THE FRONT DOOR.
HI.
...HI.
THESE ARE FOR YOU. PEACE OFFERING.
...OH, AH, SURE. COME IN.
WHERE'S THE COLLECTOR?
IN MY BAG. HE'S GONNA THREAD IN.

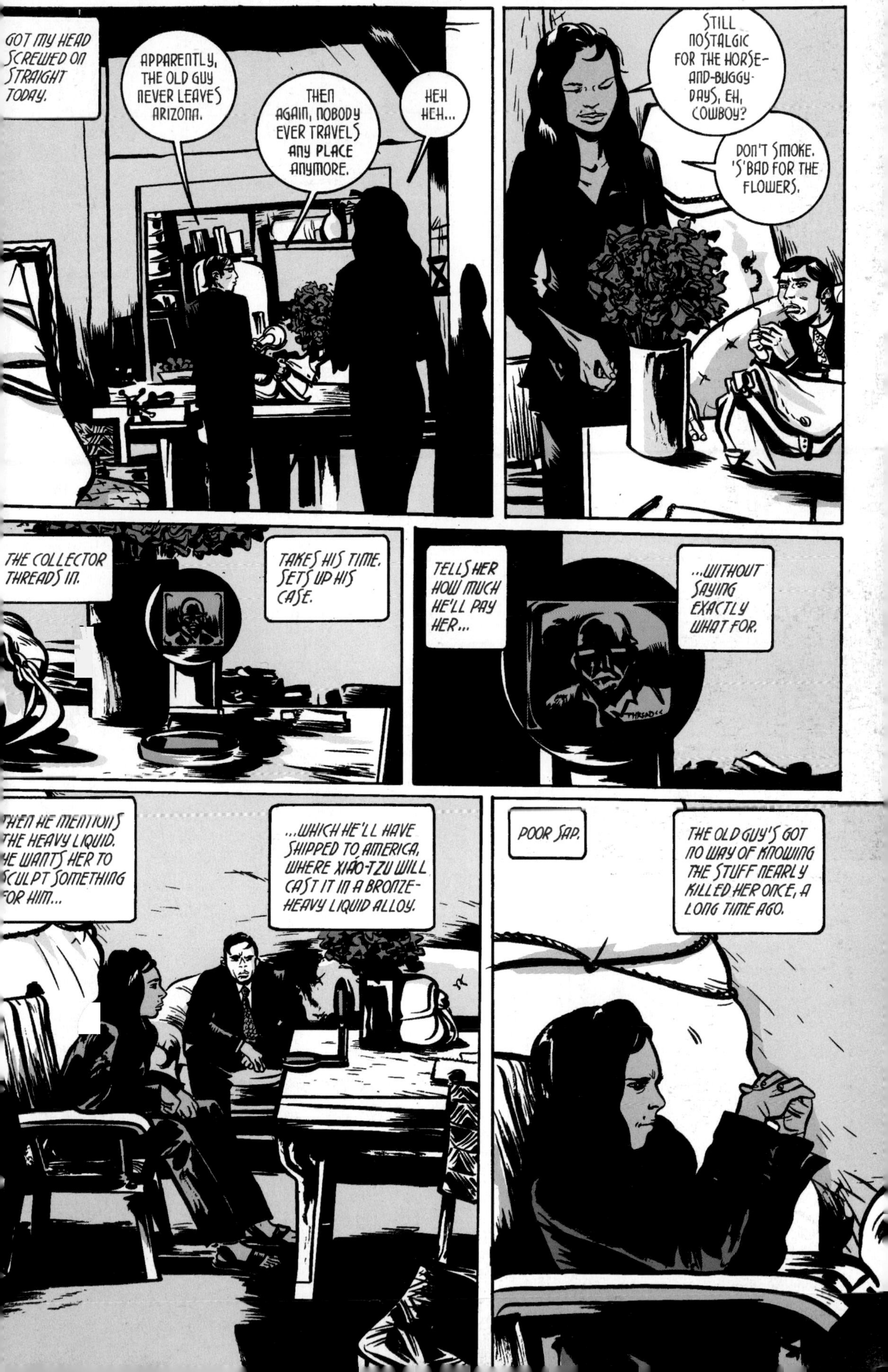

GOT MY HEAD SCREWED ON STRAIGHT TODAY.
APPARENTLY, THE OLD GUY NEVER LEAVES ARIZONA.
THEN AGAIN, NOBODY EVER TRAVELS ANY PLACE ANYMORE.
HEH HEH...
STILL NOSTALGIC FOR THE HORSE-AND-BUGGY-DAYS, EH, COWBOY?
DON'T SMOKE. 'S'BAD FOR THE FLOWERS.
THE COLLECTOR THREADS IN.
TAKES HIS TIME. SETS UP HIS CASE.
TELLS HER HOW MUCH HE'LL PAY HER...
...WITHOUT SAYING EXACTLY WHAT FOR.
THEN HE MENTIONS THE HEAVY LIQUID. HE WANTS HER TO SCULPT SOMETHING FOR HIM...
...WHICH HE'LL HAVE SHIPPED TO AMERICA, WHERE XIÃO-TZU WILL CAST IT IN A BRONZE-HEAVY LIQUID ALLOY.
POOR SAP.
THE OLD GUY'S GOT NO WAY OF KNOWING THE STUFF NEARLY KILLED HER ONCE, A LONG TIME AGO.

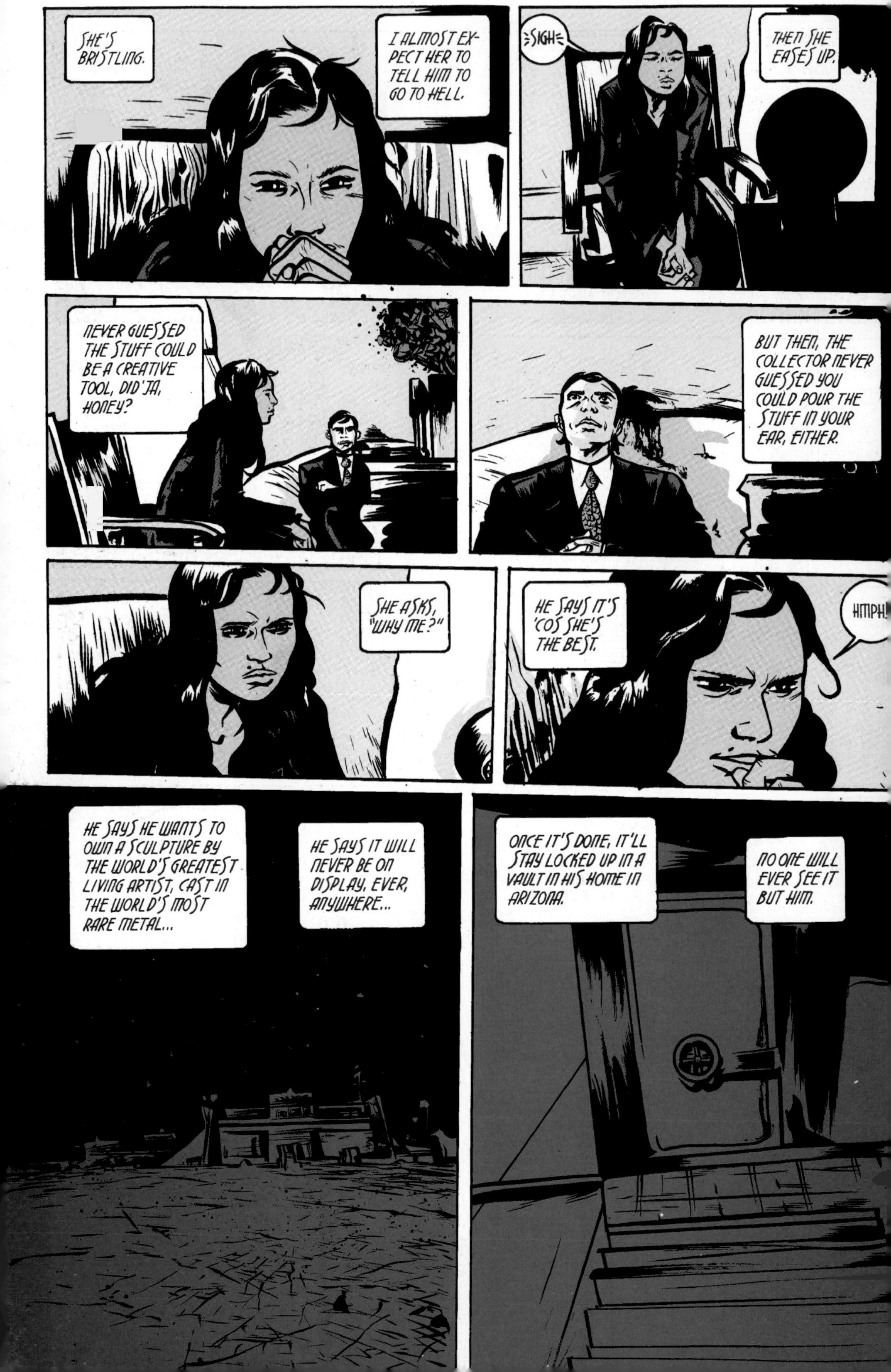
SHE'S BRISTLING.
I ALMOST EXPECT HER TO TELL HIM TO GO TO HELL.
SIGH
THEN SHE EASES UP.
NEVER GUESSED THE STUFF COULD BE A CREATIVE TOOL, DID'JA, HONEY?
BUT THEN, THE COLLECTOR NEVER GUESSED YOU COULD POUR THE STUFF IN YOUR EAR, EITHER.
SHE ASKS, "WHY ME?"
HE SAYS IT'S 'COS SHE'S THE BEST.
HMPH
HE SAYS HE WANTS TO OWN A SCULPTURE BY THE WORLD'S GREATEST LIVING ARTIST, CAST IN THE WORLD'S MOST RARE METAL...
HE SAYS IT WILL NEVER BE ON DISPLAY, EVER, ANYWHERE...
ONCE IT'S DONE, IT'LL STAY LOCKED UP IN A VAULT IN HIS HOME IN ARIZONA.
NO ONE WILL EVER SEE IT BUT HIM.

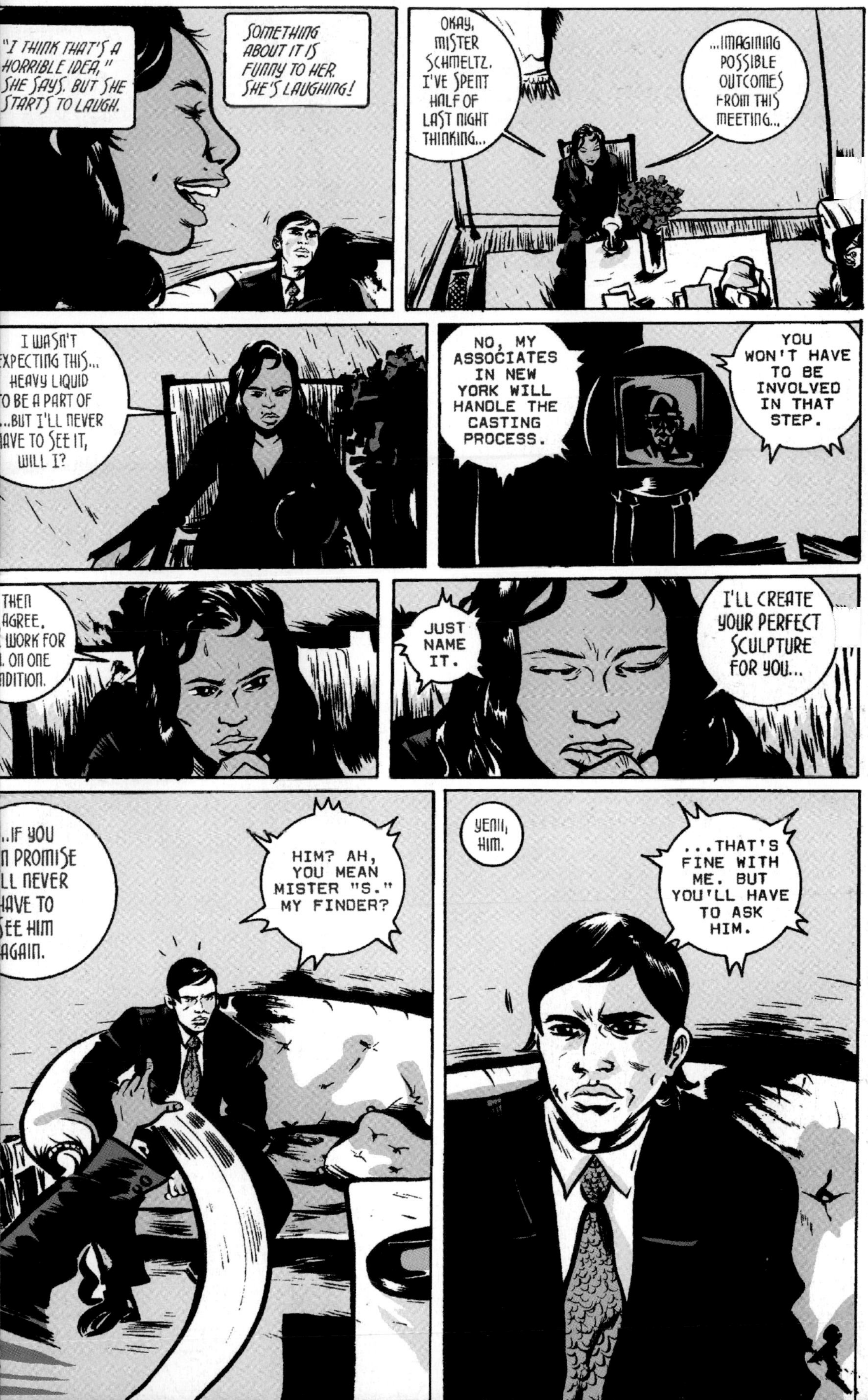
"I THINK THAT'S A HORRIBLE IDEA," SHE SAYS. BUT SHE STARTS TO LAUGH.
SOMETHING ABOUT IT IS FUNNY TO HER. SHE'S LAUGHING!
OKAY, MISTER SCHMELTZ. I'VE SPENT HALF OF LAST NIGHT THINKING...
...IMAGINING POSSIBLE OUTCOMES FROM THIS MEETING...
I WASN'T EXPECTING THIS... HEAVY LIQUID TO BE A PART OF ...BUT I'LL NEVER HAVE TO SEE IT, WILL I?
NO, MY ASSOCIATES IN NEW YORK WILL HANDLE THE CASTING PROCESS.
YOU WON'T HAVE TO BE INVOLVED IN THAT STEP.
THEN AGREE. WORK FOR ON ONE DITION.
JUST NAME IT.
I'LL CREATE YOUR PERFECT SCULPTURE FOR YOU...
...IF YOU PROMISE LL NEVER HAVE TO SEE HIM AGAIN.
HIM? AH, YOU MEAN MISTER "S." MY FINDER?
YEAH, HIM.
...THAT'S FINE WITH ME. BUT YOU'LL HAVE TO ASK HIM.

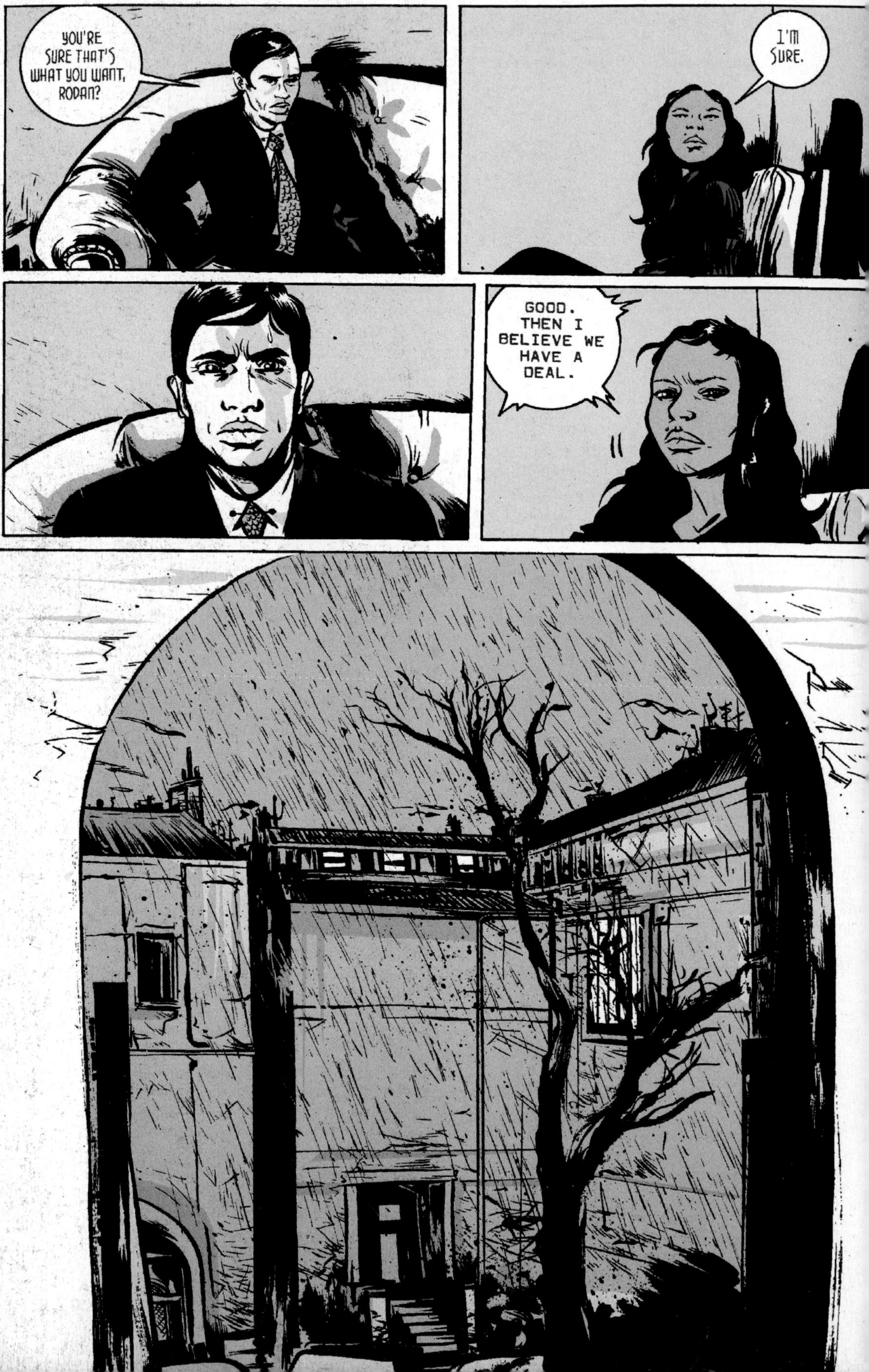
YOU'RE SURE THAT'S WHAT YOU WANT, RODAN?
I'M SURE.
GOOD. THEN I BELIEVE WE HAVE A DEAL.

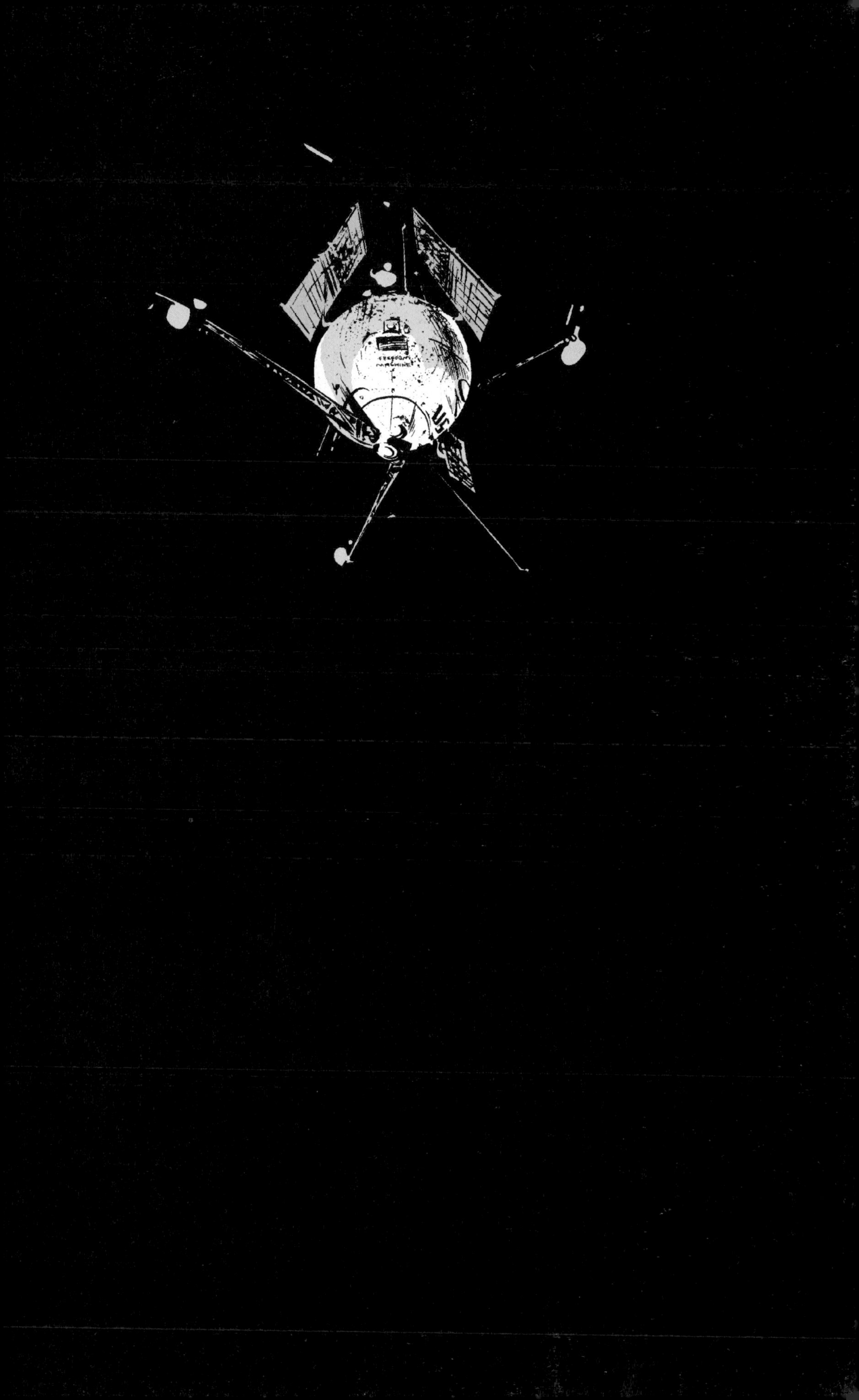

FREEDOM
MACHINE
US

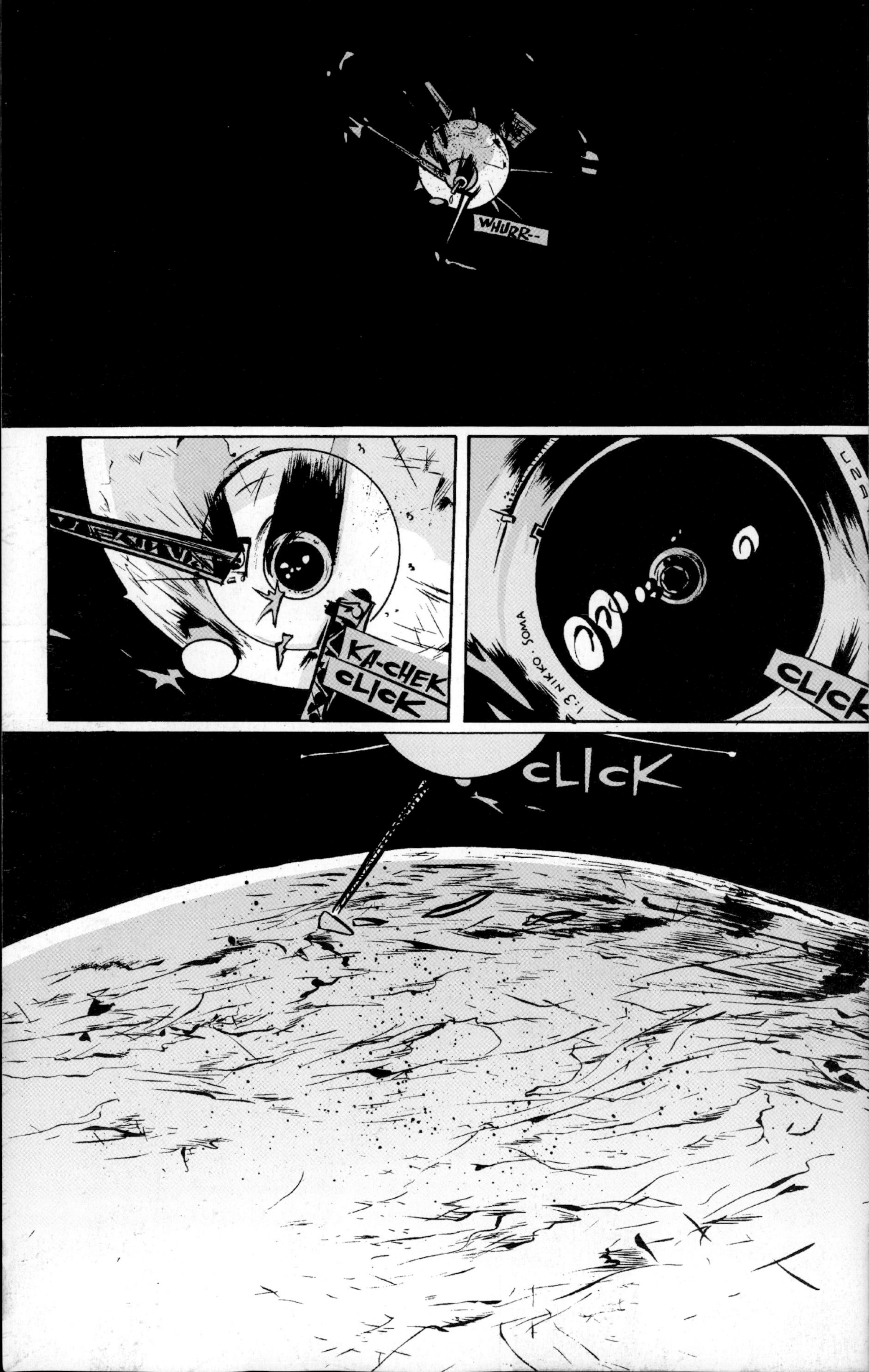
WHURR--
KA-CHEK
CLICK
1:3 NIKKO . SOMA
CLICK
CLICK

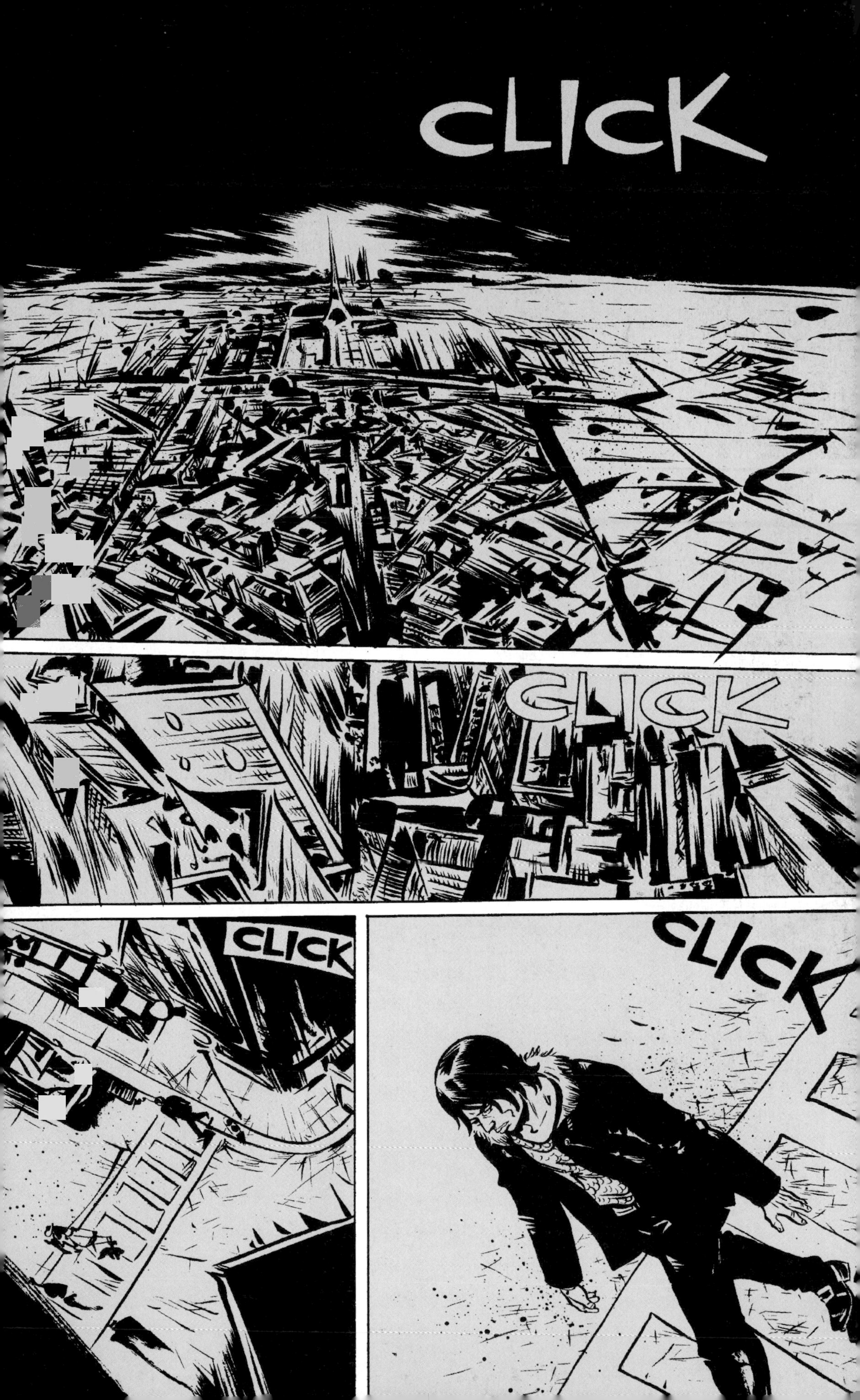
CLICK
CLICK
CLICK
CLICK

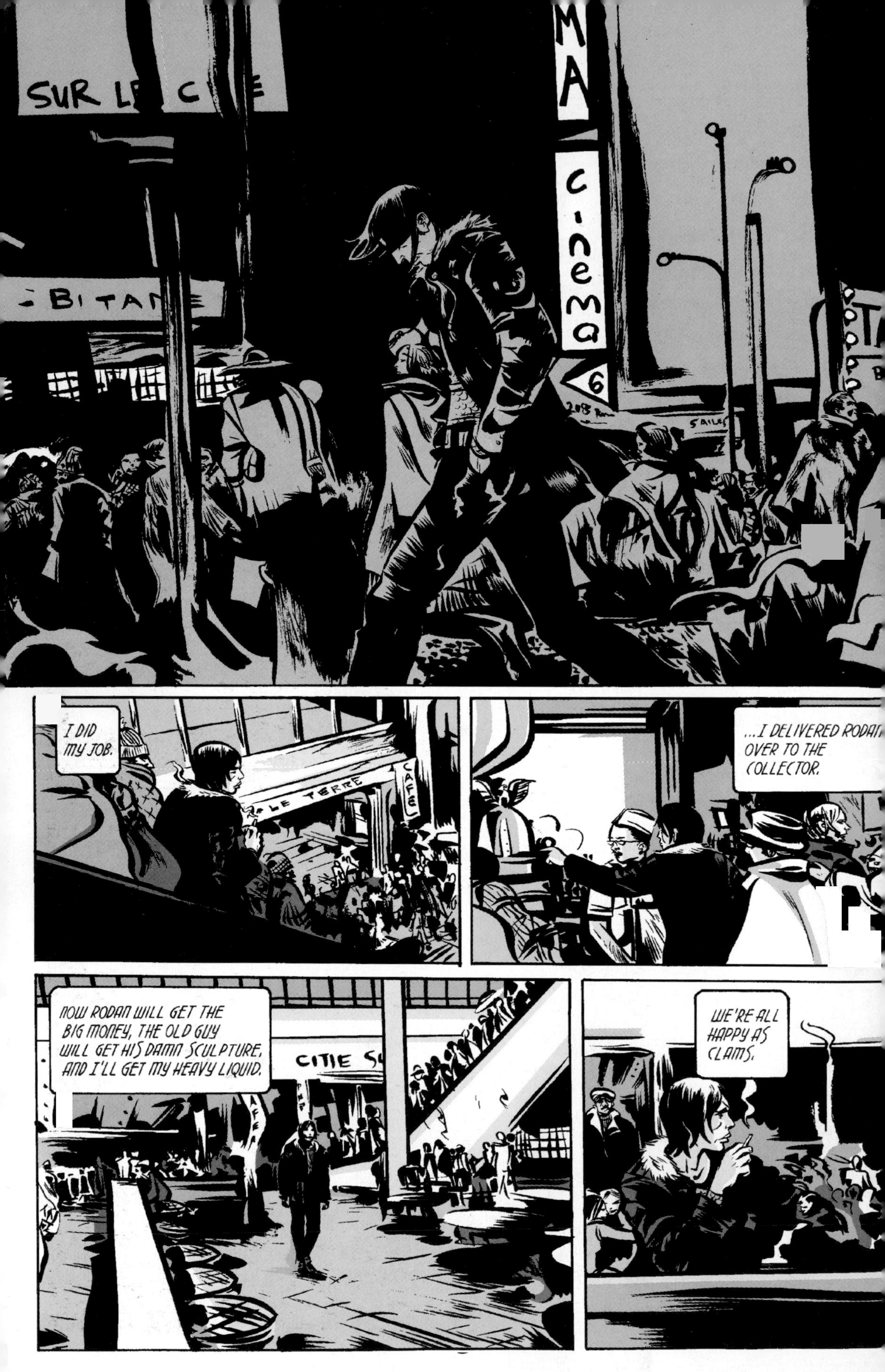
SUR LE C E
BITAN
MA
cinema
6
I DID MY JOB.
LE TERRE
CAFE
...I DELIVERED RODAN OVER TO THE COLLECTOR.
NOW RODAN WILL GET THE BIG MONEY, THE OLD GUY WILL GET HIS DAMN SCULPTURE, AND I'LL GET MY HEAVY LIQUID.
CITIE S
WE'RE ALL HAPPY AS CLAMS.

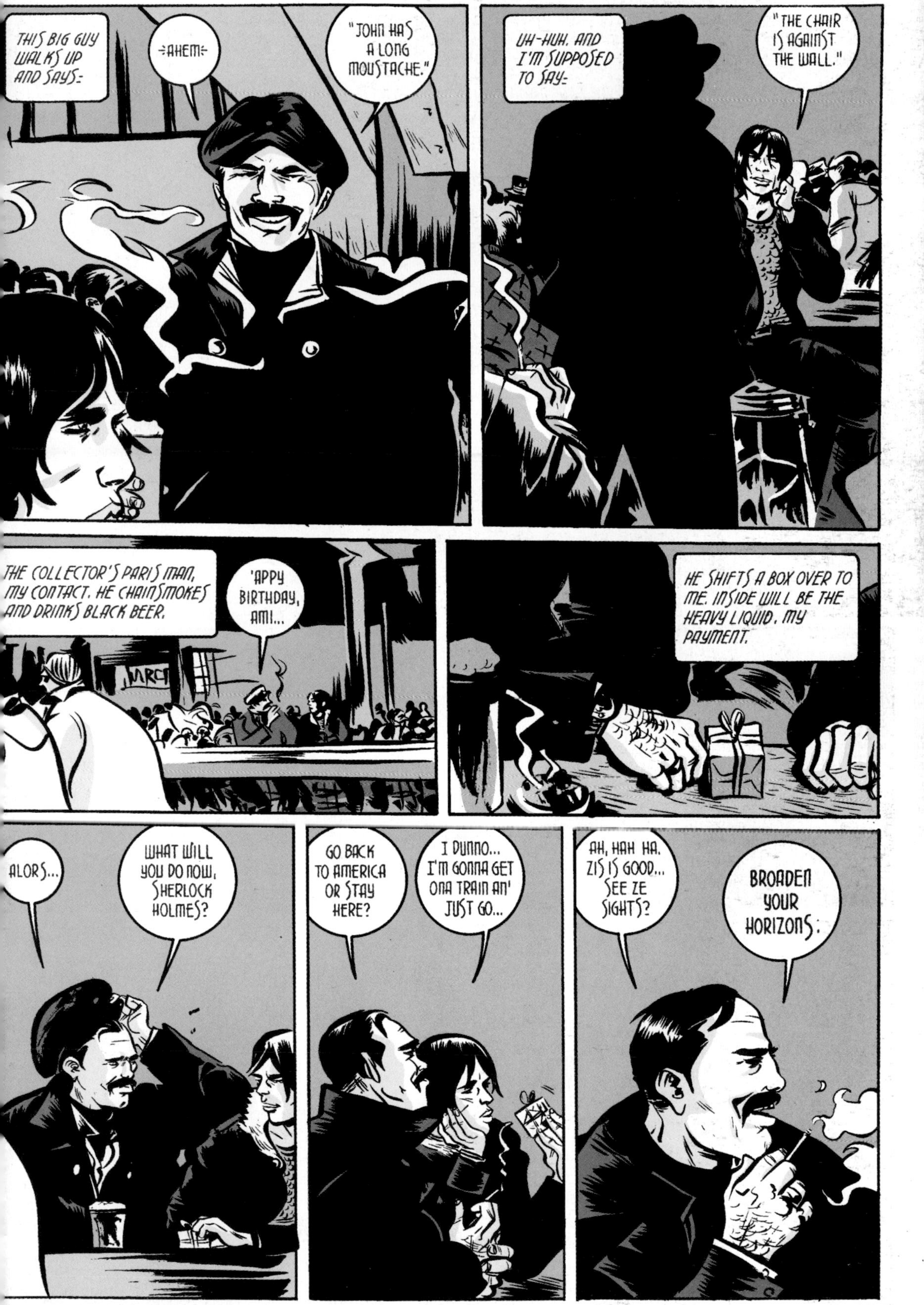
THIS BIG GUY WALKS UP AND SAYS:
÷AHEM÷
"JOHN HAS A LONG MOUSTACHE."
UH-HUH. AND I'M SUPPOSED TO SAY:
"THE CHAIR IS AGAINST THE WALL."
THE COLLECTOR'S PARIS MAN, MY CONTACT. HE CHAINSMOKES AND DRINKS BLACK BEER.
'APPY BIRTHDAY, AMI...
HE SHIFTS A BOX OVER TO ME. INSIDE WILL BE THE HEAVY LIQUID. MY PAYMENT.
ALORS...
WHAT WILL YOU DO NOW, SHERLOCK HOLMES?
GO BACK TO AMERICA OR STAY HERE?
I DUNNO... I'M GONNA GET ONA TRAIN AN' JUST GO...
AH, HAH HA. ZIS IS GOOD... SEE ZE SIGHTS?
BROADEN YOUR HORIZONS:

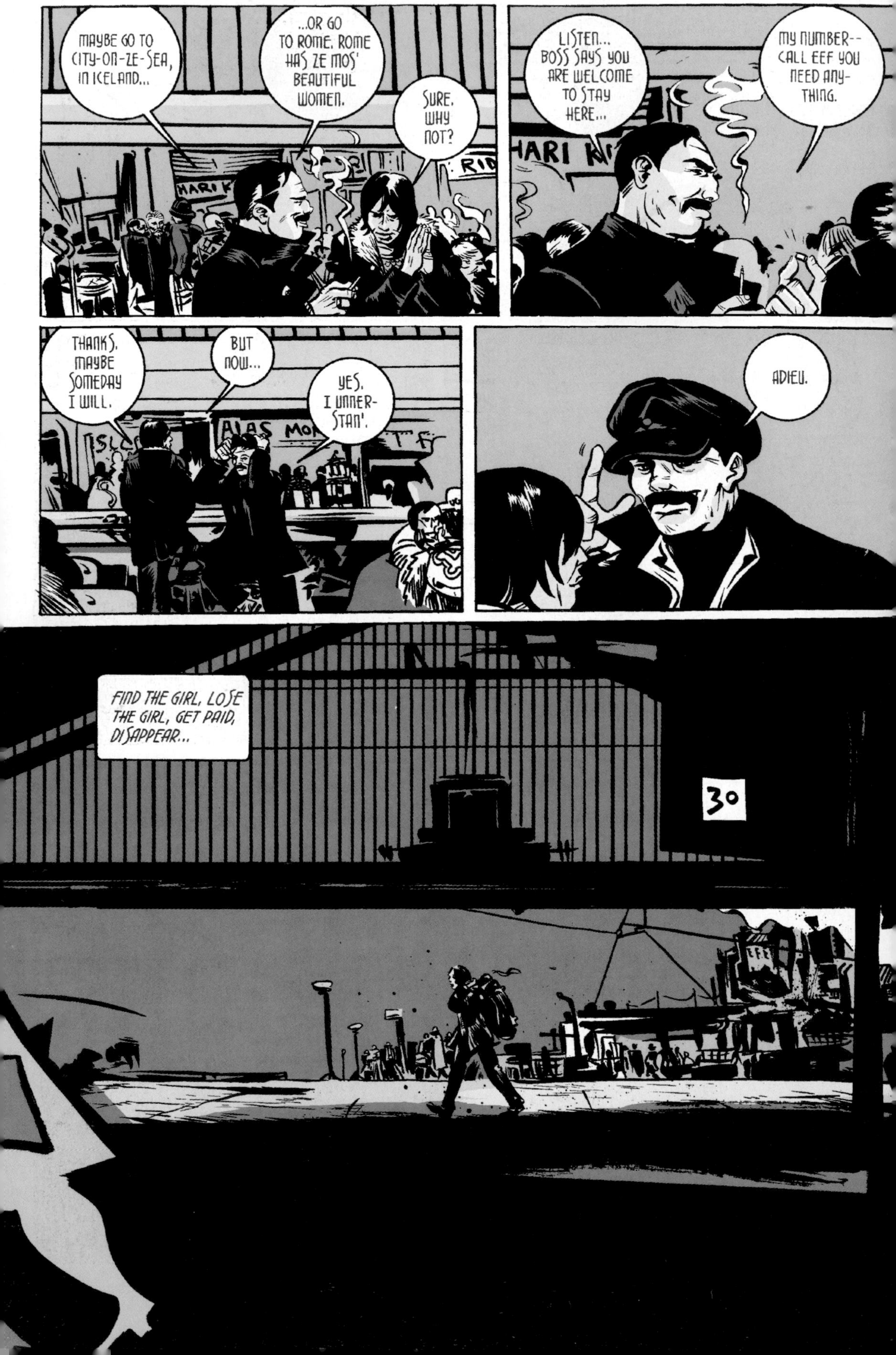
MAYBE GO TO CITY-ON-ZE-SEA, IN ICELAND...
...OR GO TO ROME. ROME HAS ZE MOS' BEAUTIFUL WOMEN.
SURE. WHY NOT?
LISTEN... BOSS SAYS YOU ARE WELCOME TO STAY HERE...
MY NUMBER-- CALL EEF YOU NEED ANY-THING.
THANKS. MAYBE SOMEDAY I WILL.
BUT NOW...
YES. I UNNER-STAN'.
ADIEU.
FIND THE GIRL, LOSE THE GIRL, GET PAID, DISAPPEAR...
30

FADE OFF INTO THE SUNSET, LIKE THE END OF A MOVIE.

...LIKE LUNA.

LUNA...I CAN JUST SEE HER NOW...

...DRINKING RUM IN A WICKER CHAIR, HER TOENAILS PAINTED POPSICLE RED.

LAID OUT LIKE SOME RECLUSIVE MOVIE STAR ON SOME GULFSTREAM BEACH.

SHE WOULDN'T HAVE WANTED TO KEEP A DROP OF THE HEAVY LIQUID WE SPLIT BACK THERE.

NO WAY.

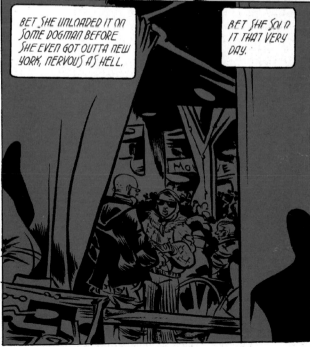

BET SHE UNLOADED IT ON SOME DOGMAN BEFORE SHE EVEN GOT OUTTA NEW YORK, NERVOUS AS HELL.

BET SHE SOLD IT THAT VERY DAY.

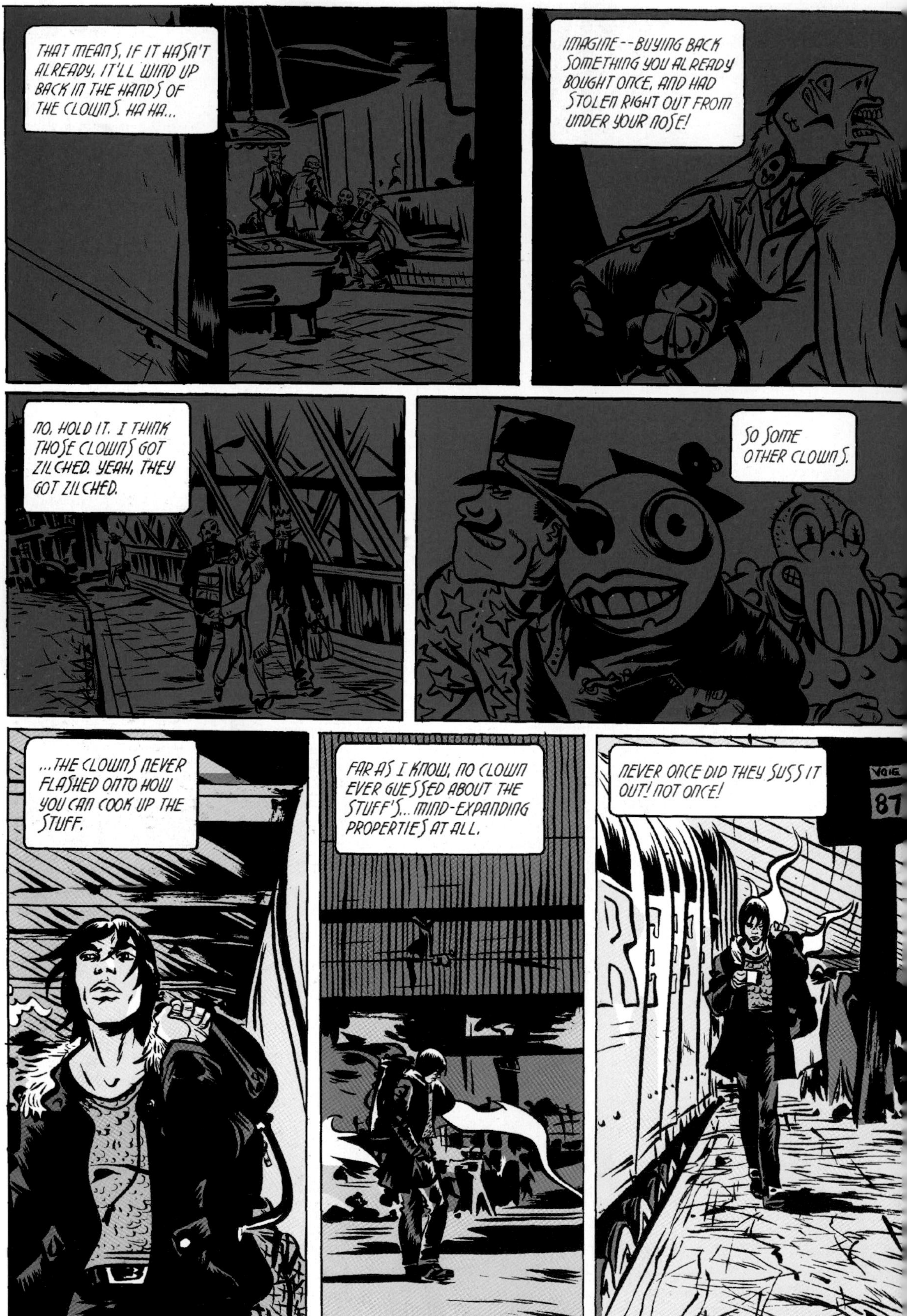
THAT MEANS, IF IT HASN'T ALREADY, IT'LL WIND UP BACK IN THE HANDS OF THE CLOWNS. HA HA...
IMAGINE--BUYING BACK SOMETHING YOU ALREADY BOUGHT ONCE, AND HAD STOLEN RIGHT OUT FROM UNDER YOUR NOSE!
NO, HOLD IT. I THINK THOSE CLOWNS GOT ZILCHED. YEAH, THEY GOT ZILCHED.
SO SOME OTHER CLOWNS.
...THE CLOWNS NEVER FLASHED ONTO HOW YOU CAN COOK UP THE STUFF.
FAR AS I KNOW, NO CLOWN EVER GUESSED ABOUT THE STUFF'S... MIND-EXPANDING PROPERTIES AT ALL.
NEVER ONCE DID THEY SUSS IT OUT! NOT ONCE!
87

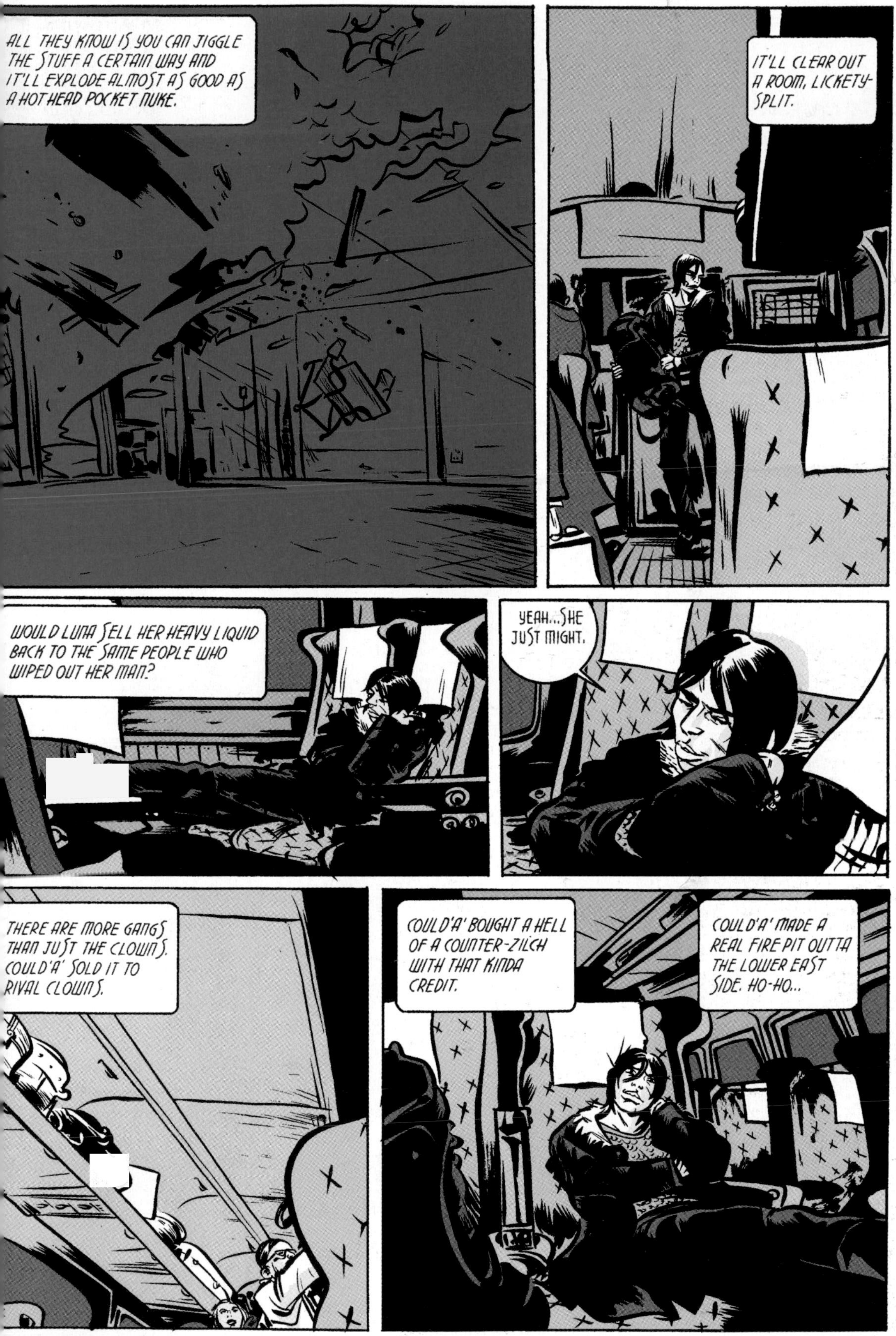
ALL THEY KNOW IS YOU CAN JIGGLE THE STUFF A CERTAIN WAY AND IT'LL EXPLODE ALMOST AS GOOD AS A HOT HEAD POCKET NUKE.
IT'LL CLEAR OUT A ROOM, LICKETY-SPLIT.
WOULD LUNA SELL HER HEAVY LIQUID BACK TO THE SAME PEOPLE WHO WIPED OUT HER MAN?
YEAH...SHE JUST MIGHT.
THERE ARE MORE GANGS THAN JUST THE CLOWNS. COULD'A' SOLD IT TO RIVAL CLOWNS.
COULD'A' BOUGHT A HELL OF A COUNTER-ZILCH WITH THAT KINDA CREDIT.
COULD'A' MADE A REAL FIRE PIT OUTTA THE LOWER EAST SIDE. HO-HO...

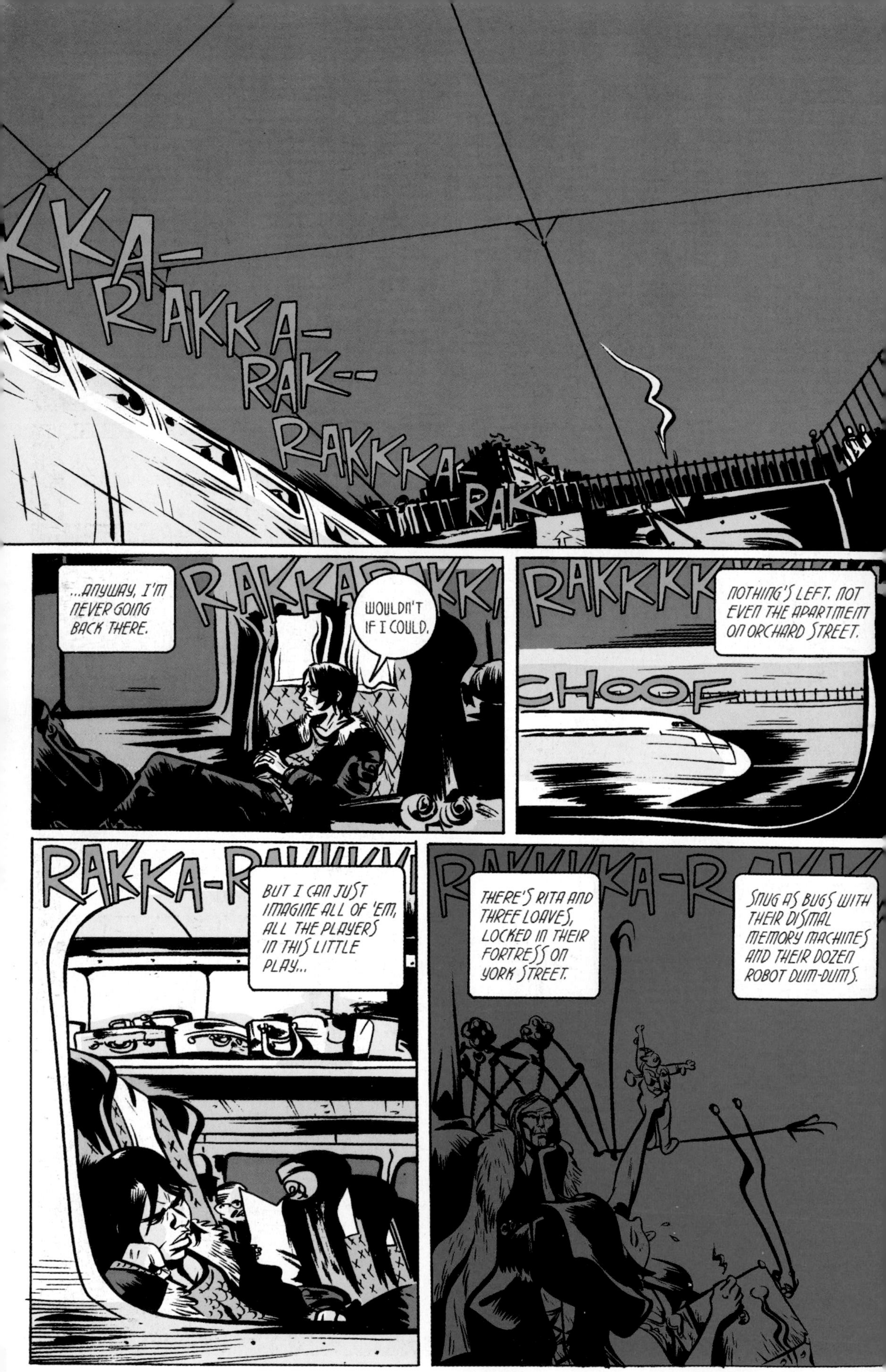
KKA-
RAKKA-
RAK--
RAKKKA-
RAK
RAKKARAKKA
...ANYWAY, I'M NEVER GOING BACK THERE.
WOULDN'T IF I COULD.
RAKKKK
NOTHING'S LEFT. NOT EVEN THE APARTMENT ON ORCHARD STREET.
CHOOF
RAKKA-R
BUT I CAN JUST IMAGINE ALL OF 'EM, ALL THE PLAYERS IN THIS LITTLE PLAY...
KA-R
THERE'S RITA AND THREE LOAVES, LOCKED IN THEIR FORTRESS ON YORK STREET.
SNUG AS BUGS WITH THEIR DISMAL MEMORY MACHINES AND THEIR DOZEN ROBOT DUM-DUMS.

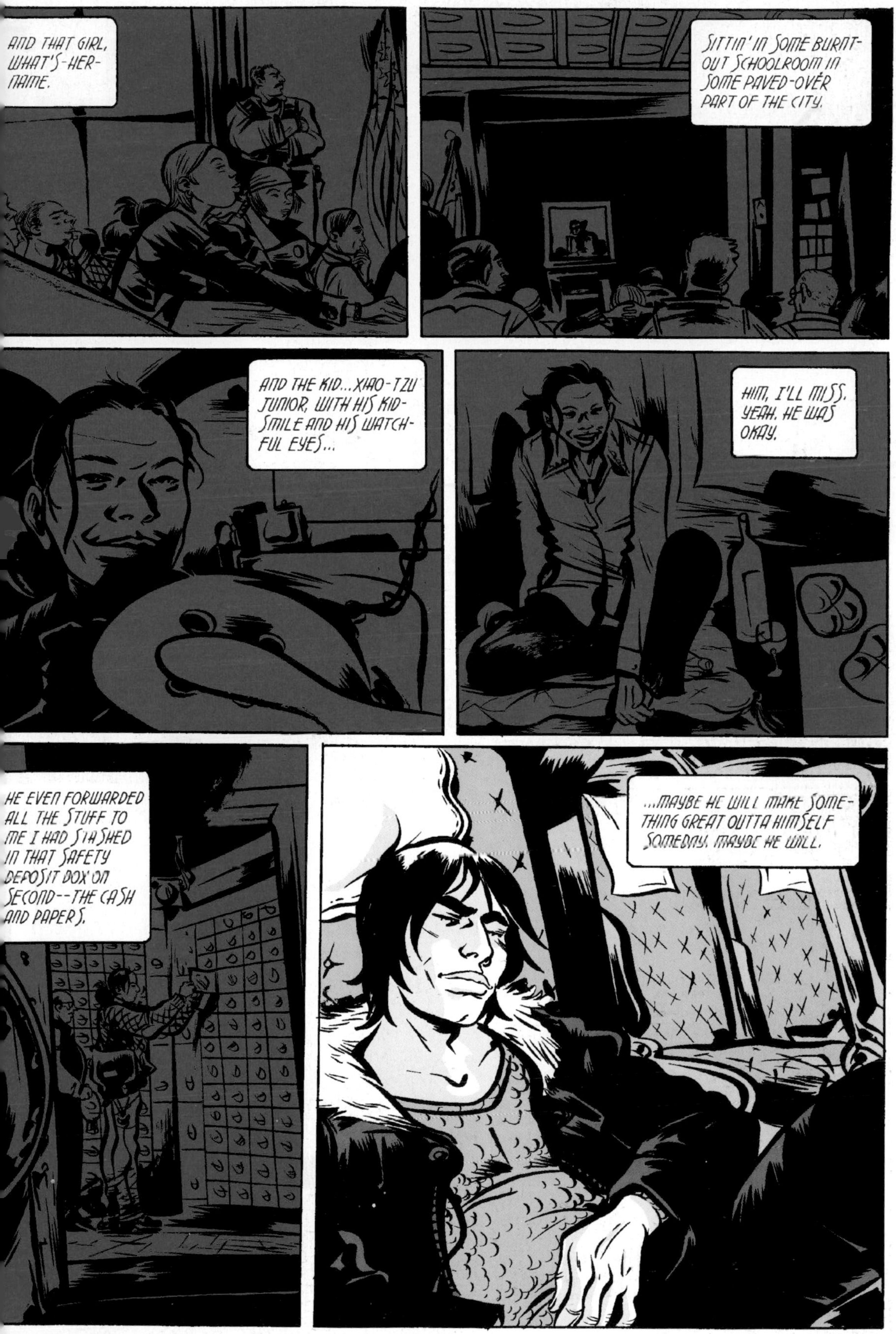
AND THAT GIRL, WHAT'S-HER-NAME.
SITTIN' IN SOME BURNT-OUT SCHOOLROOM IN SOME PAVED-OVER PART OF THE CITY.
AND THE KID...XIAO-TZU JUNIOR, WITH HIS KID-SMILE AND HIS WATCH-FUL EYES...
HIM, I'LL MISS. YEAH. HE WAS OKAY.
HE EVEN FORWARDED ALL THE STUFF TO ME I HAD STASHED IN THAT SAFETY DEPOSIT BOX ON SECOND--THE CASH AND PAPERS.
...MAYBE HE WILL MAKE SOME-THING GREAT OUTTA HIMSELF SOMEDAY. MAYBE HE WILL.

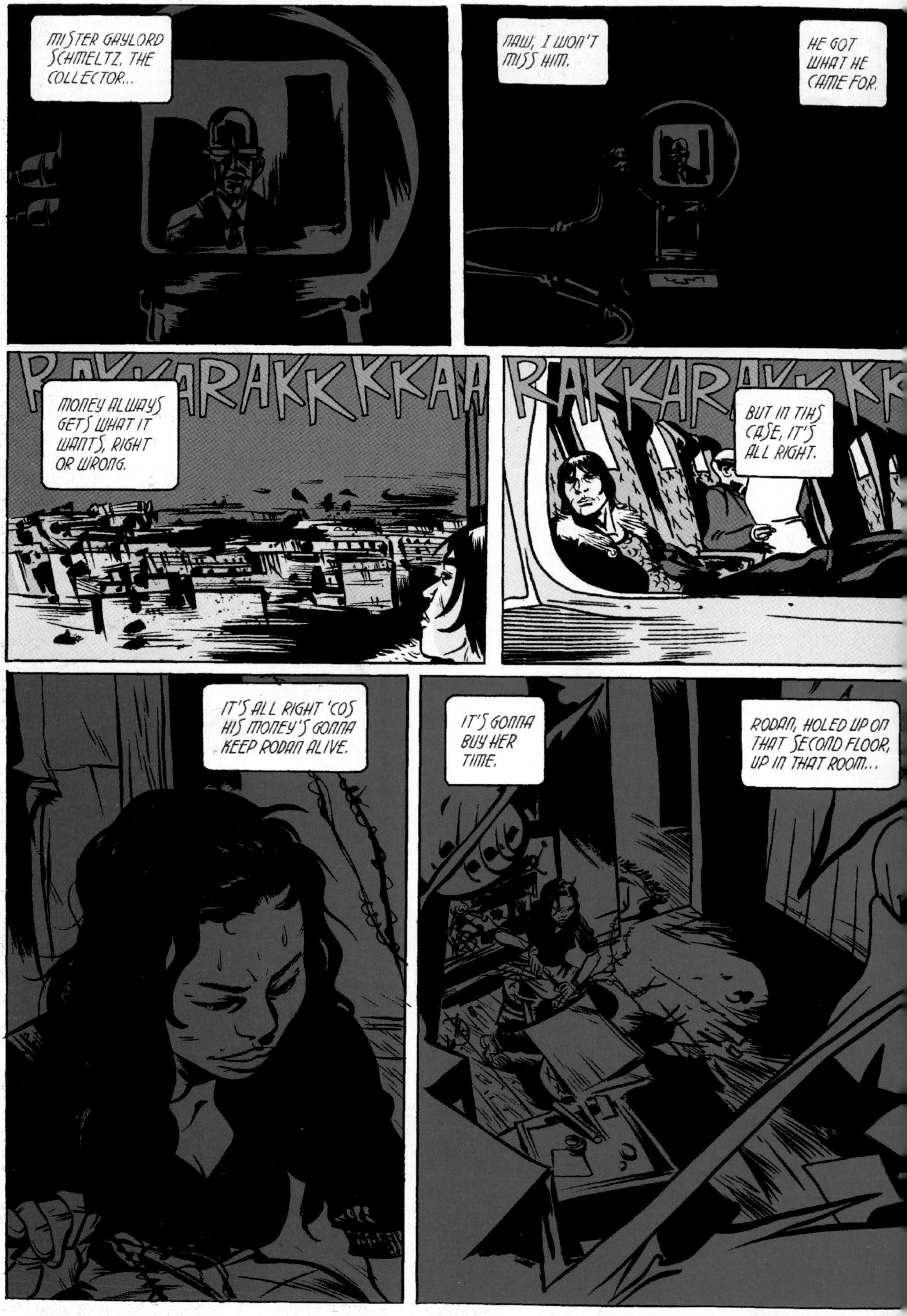
MISTER GAYLORD SCHMELTZ, THE COLLECTOR...
NAW, I WON'T MISS HIM.
HE GOT WHAT HE CAME FOR.
RAKKARAKKKKAA
MONEY ALWAYS GETS WHAT IT WANTS, RIGHT OR WRONG.
BUT IN TIHS CASE, IT'S ALL RIGHT.
IT'S ALL RIGHT 'COS HIS MONEY'S GONNA KEEP RODAN ALIVE.
IT'S GONNA BUY HER TIME.
RODAN, HOLED UP ON THAT SECOND FLOOR, UP IN THAT ROOM...

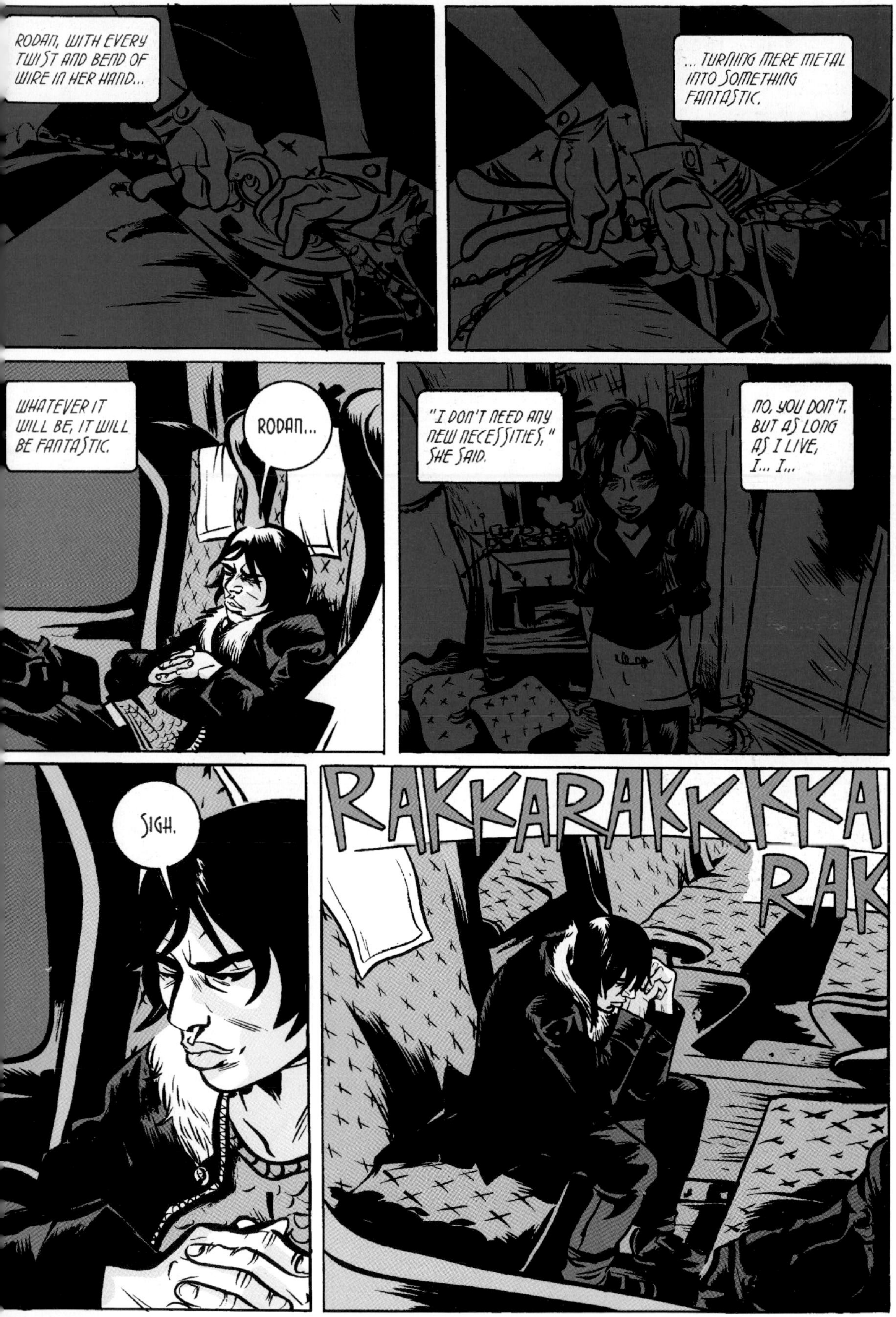
RODAN, WITH EVERY TWIST AND BEND OF WIRE IN HER HAND...
... TURNING MERE METAL INTO SOMETHING FANTASTIC.
WHATEVER IT WILL BE, IT WILL BE FANTASTIC.
RODAN...
"I DON'T NEED ANY NEW NECESSITIES," SHE SAID.
NO, YOU DON'T. BUT AS LONG AS I LIVE, I... I...
SIGH.
RAKKARAKKKKA
RAK

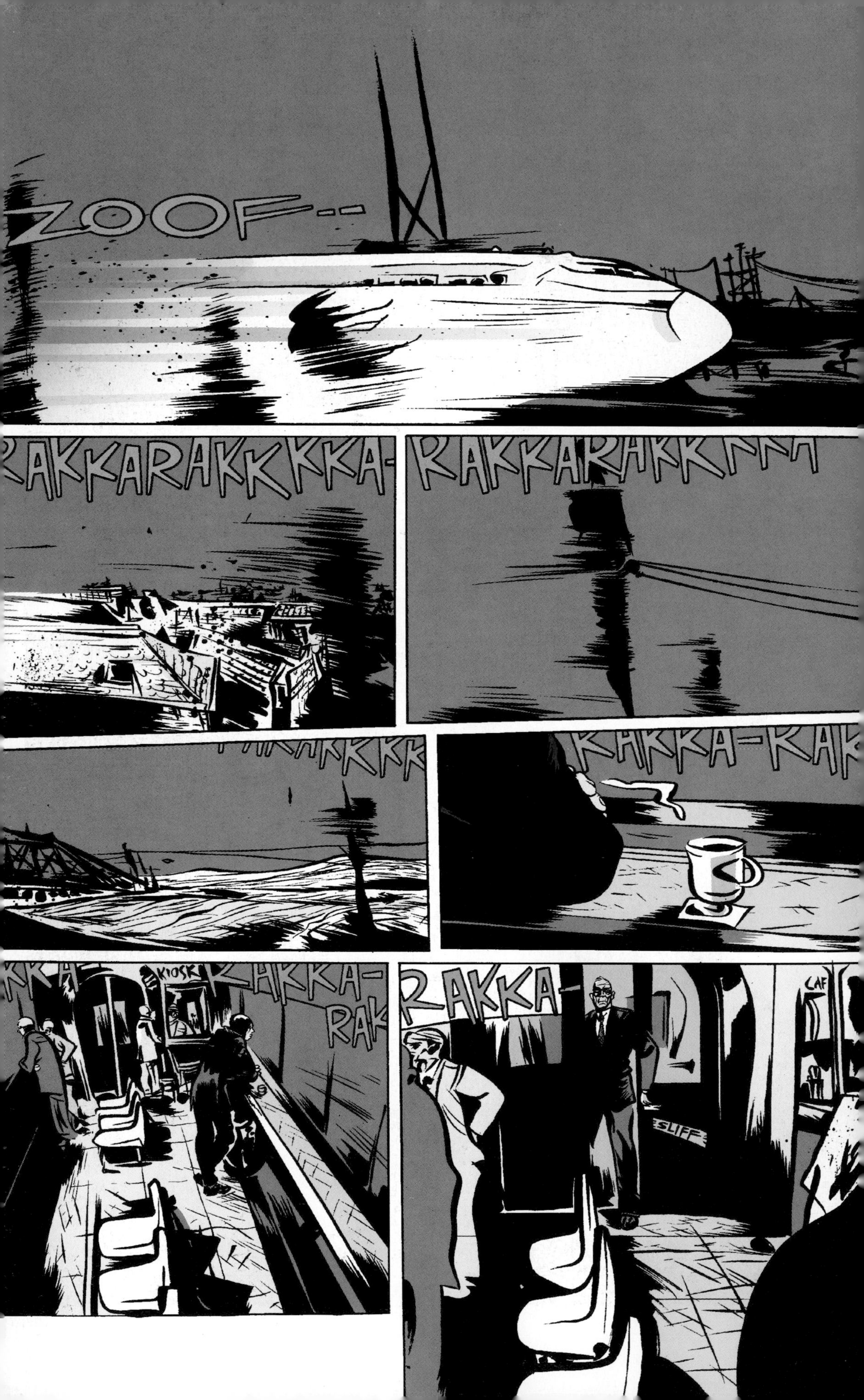
ZOOF--
RAKKARAKKKKA-
RAKKA-RAK
KIOSK
RAKKA-
RAK
RAKKA-
CAF
SLIFF

RAK-RAK-RA

!

OH, NO--NOT HIM--HOW'D--

THE LAST PERSON IN THE WORLD I'D HAVE EXPECTED TO SEE--

--THAT COPPER JULIE FROM BACK HOME...

YOU'RE NOT THE EASIEST GUY IN THE WORLD TO FIND, BUDDY.

POLISHED SHOES, MIDAS CIGARETTES--HE'S JUST ARRIVED. BE COOL, S. COOL.

WOKE UP IN NEW YORK, NOW I'M HERE.

YOU FOUND ME EASILY ENOUGH.

YEAH. BUT I GOT A BILLION-DOLLAR SATELLITE UP THERE WORKING FOR ME TODAY.

YOU'RE IN TROUBLE NOW, S. BE SMOOTH.

ZZK

PLAY THE SHUCK.

GUESS I SHOULD'A' GROWN A BEARD.

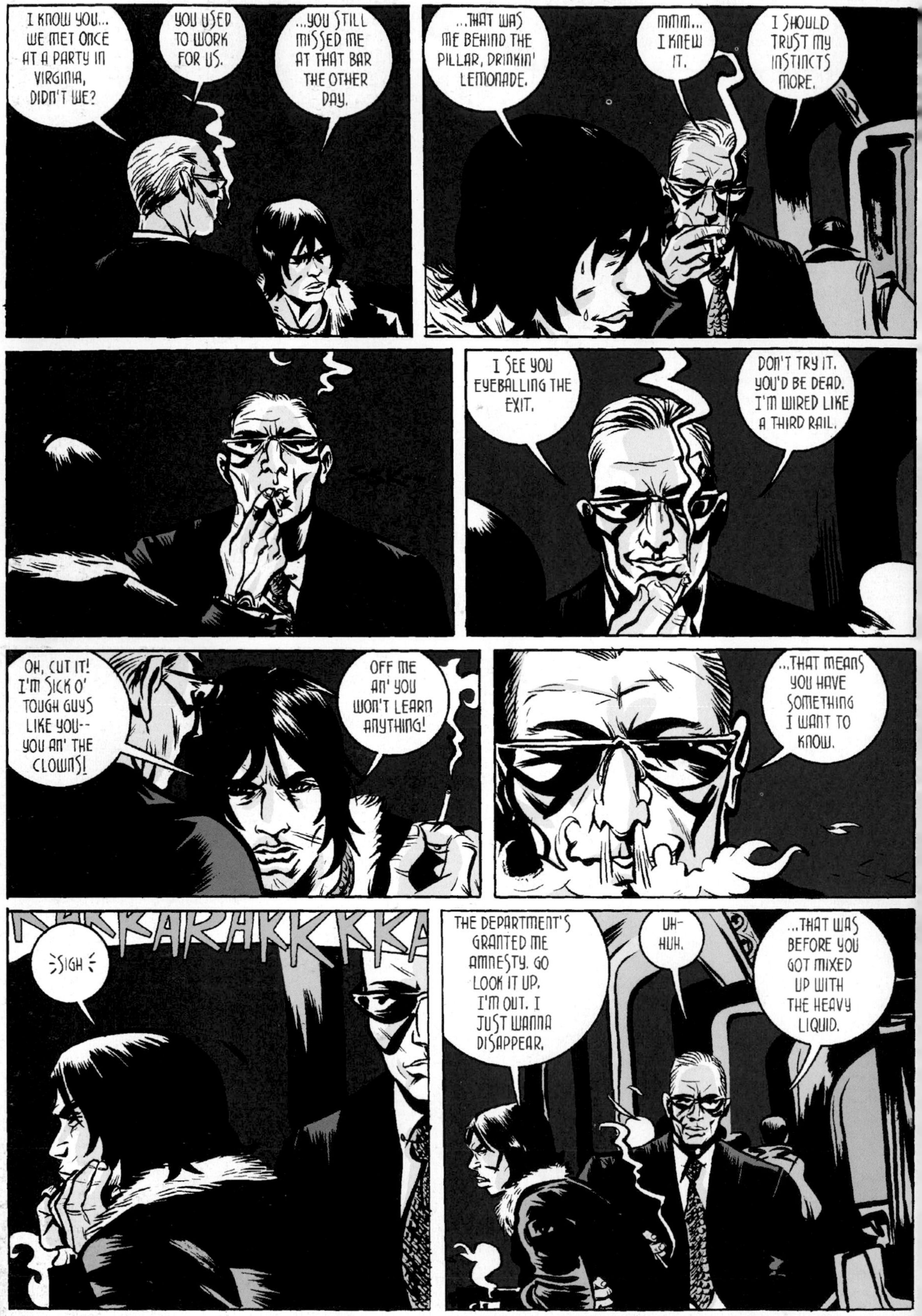
I KNOW YOU... WE MET ONCE AT A PARTY IN VIRGINIA, DIDN'T WE?
YOU USED TO WORK FOR US.
...YOU STILL MISSED ME AT THAT BAR THE OTHER DAY.
...THAT WAS ME BEHIND THE PILLAR, DRINKIN' LEMONADE.
MMM... I KNEW IT.
I SHOULD TRUST MY INSTINCTS MORE.
I SEE YOU EYEBALLING THE EXIT.
DON'T TRY IT. YOU'D BE DEAD. I'M WIRED LIKE A THIRD RAIL.
OH, CUT IT! I'M SICK O' TOUGH GUYS LIKE YOU-- YOU AN' THE CLOWNS!
OFF ME AN' YOU WON'T LEARN ANYTHING!
...THAT MEANS YOU HAVE SOMETHING I WANT TO KNOW.
KRRKARAKKKKA
SIGH
THE DEPARTMENT'S GRANTED ME AMNESTY. GO LOOK IT UP. I'M OUT. I JUST WANNA DISAPPEAR.
UH-HUH.
...THAT WAS BEFORE YOU GOT MIXED UP WITH THE HEAVY LIQUID.

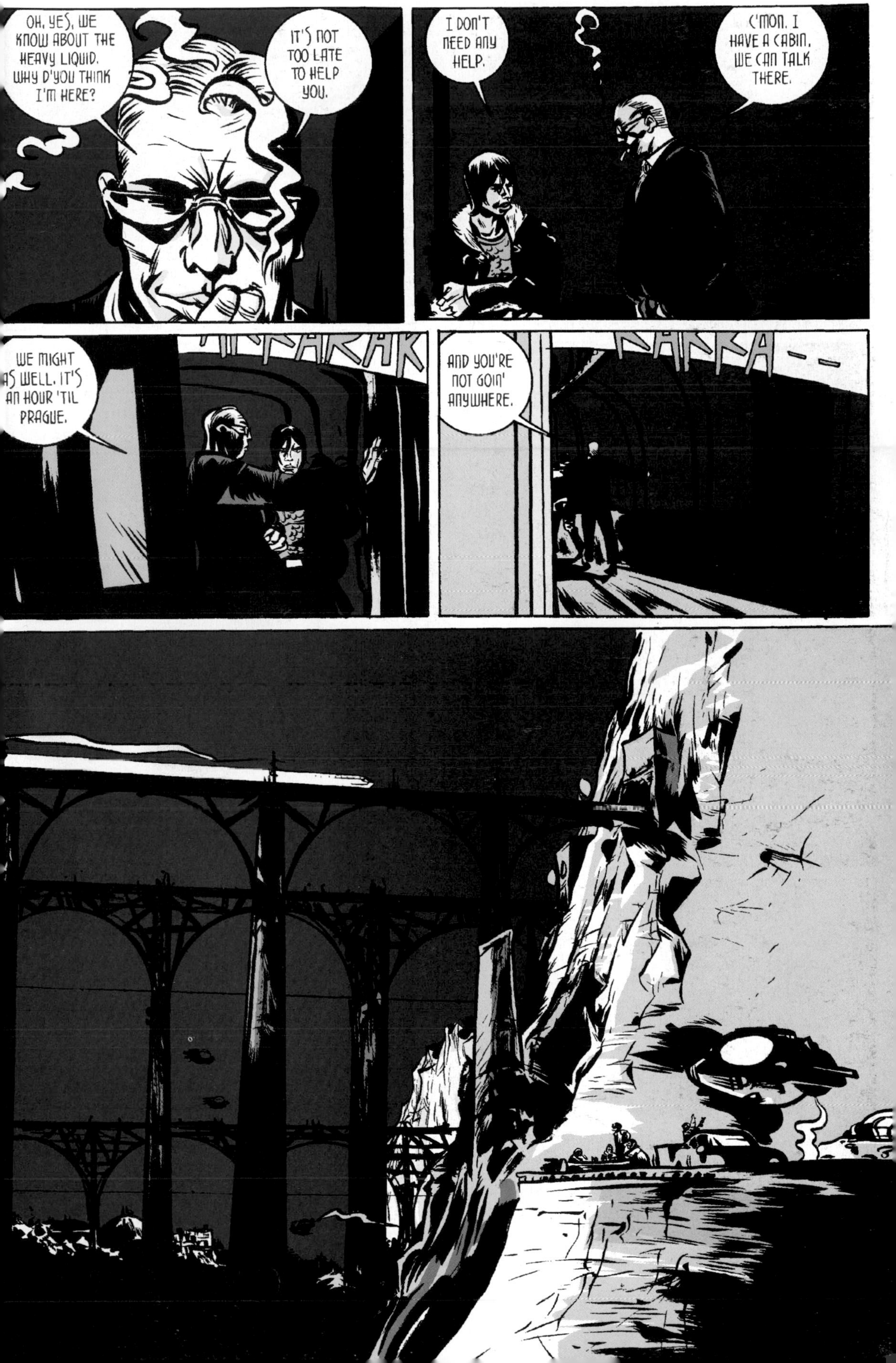
OH, YES, WE KNOW ABOUT THE HEAVY LIQUID. WHY D'YOU THINK I'M HERE?
IT'S NOT TOO LATE TO HELP YOU.
I DON'T NEED ANY HELP.
C'MON. I HAVE A CABIN. WE CAN TALK THERE.
WE MIGHT AS WELL. IT'S AN HOUR 'TIL PRAGUE.
AND YOU'RE NOT GOIN' ANYWHERE.

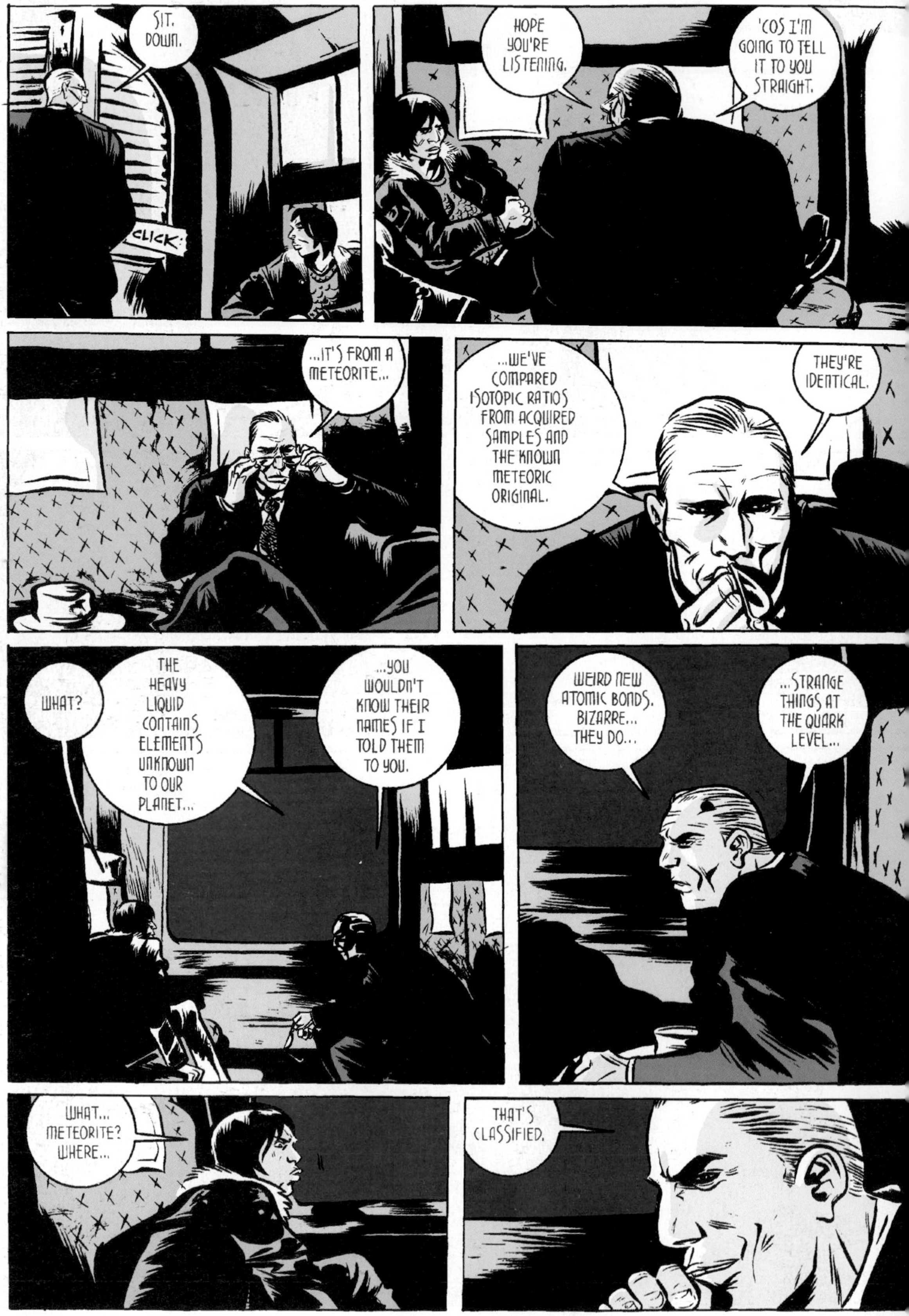
SIT. DOWN.
CLICK
HOPE YOU'RE LISTENING.
'COS I'M GOING TO TELL IT TO YOU STRAIGHT.
...IT'S FROM A METEORITE...
...WE'VE COMPARED ISOTOPIC RATIOS FROM ACQUIRED SAMPLES AND THE KNOWN METEORIC ORIGINAL.
THEY'RE IDENTICAL.
WHAT?
THE HEAVY LIQUID CONTAINS ELEMENTS UNKNOWN TO OUR PLANET...
...YOU WOULDN'T KNOW THEIR NAMES IF I TOLD THEM TO YOU.
WEIRD NEW ATOMIC BONDS. BIZARRE... THEY DO...
...STRANGE THINGS AT THE QUARK LEVEL...
WHAT... METEORITE? WHERE...
THAT'S CLASSIFIED.

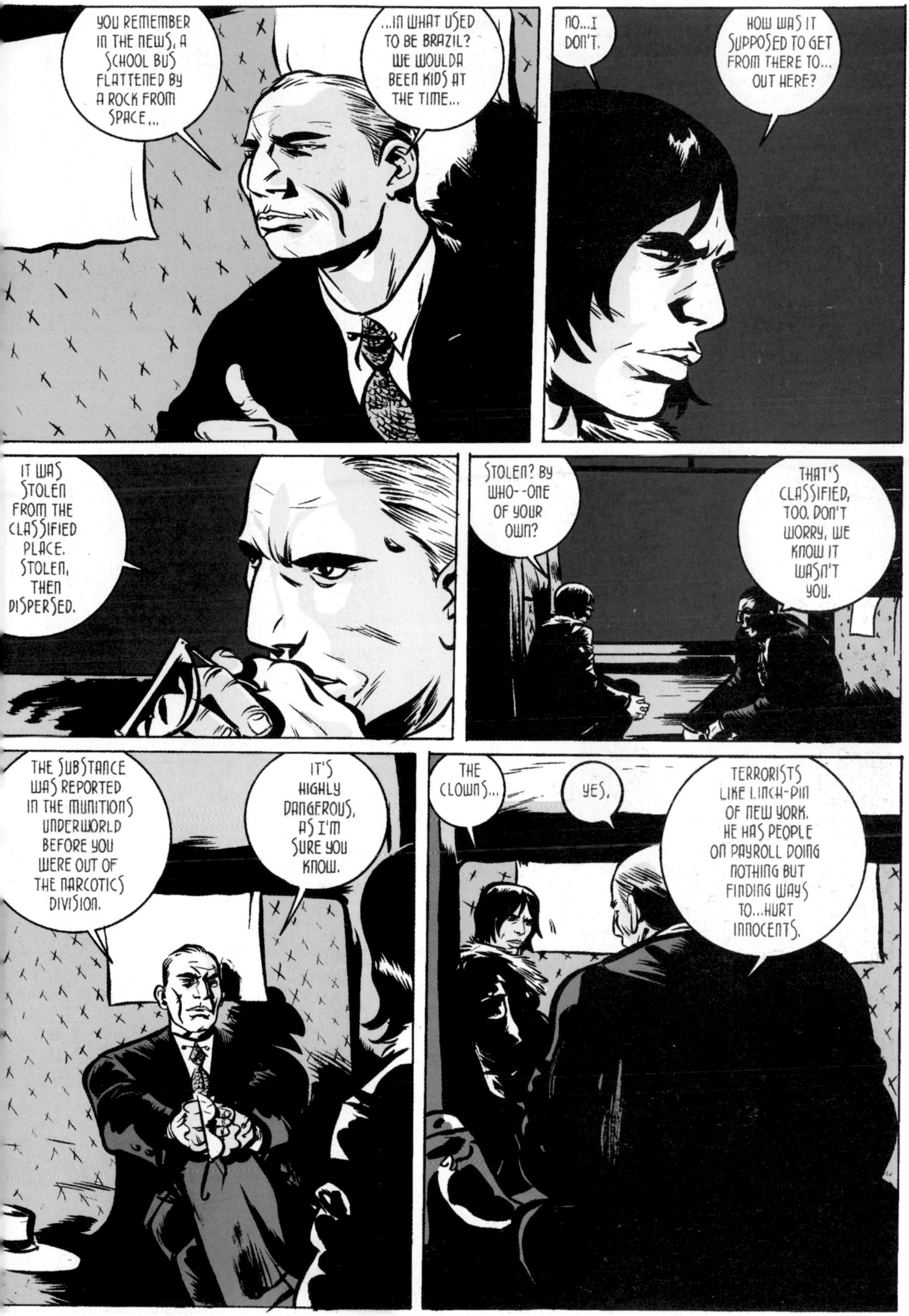
YOU REMEMBER IN THE NEWS, A SCHOOL BUS FLATTENED BY A ROCK FROM SPACE...
...IN WHAT USED TO BE BRAZIL? WE WOULDA BEEN KIDS AT THE TIME...
NO...I DON'T.
HOW WAS IT SUPPOSED TO GET FROM THERE TO... OUT HERE?
IT WAS STOLEN FROM THE CLASSIFIED PLACE. STOLEN, THEN DISPERSED.
STOLEN? BY WHO--ONE OF YOUR OWN?
THAT'S CLASSIFIED, TOO. DON'T WORRY, WE KNOW IT WASN'T YOU.
THE SUBSTANCE WAS REPORTED IN THE MUNITIONS UNDERWORLD BEFORE YOU WERE OUT OF THE NARCOTICS DIVISION.
IT'S HIGHLY DANGEROUS, AS I'M SURE YOU KNOW.
THE CLOWNS...
YES.
TERRORISTS LIKE LINCH-PIN OF NEW YORK. HE HAS PEOPLE ON PAYROLL DOING NOTHING BUT FINDING WAYS TO...HURT INNOCENTS.

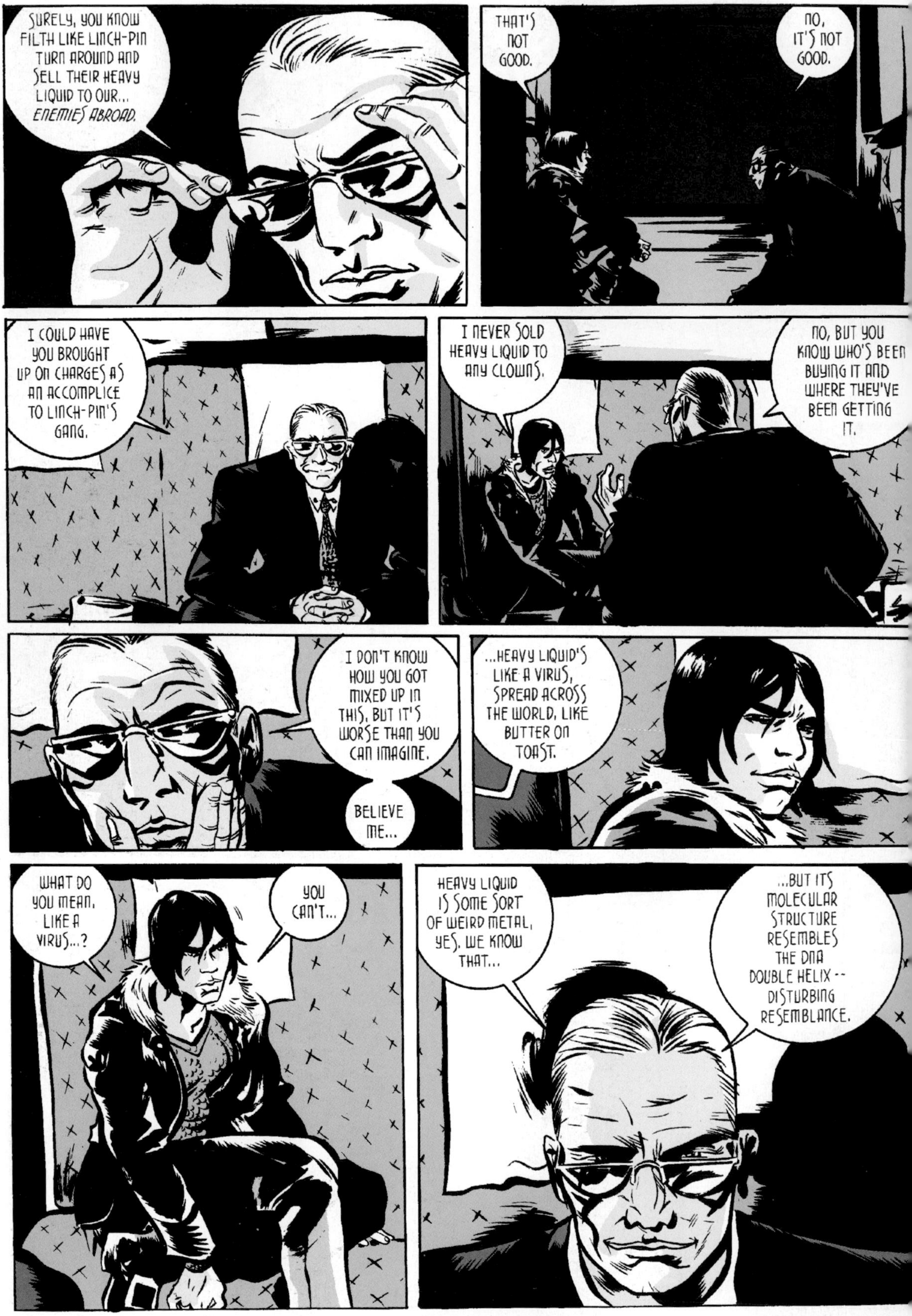
SURELY, YOU KNOW FILTH LIKE LINCH-PIN TURN AROUND AND SELL THEIR HEAVY LIQUID TO OUR... *ENEMIES ABROAD.*
THAT'S NOT GOOD.
NO, IT'S NOT GOOD.
I COULD HAVE YOU BROUGHT UP ON CHARGES AS AN ACCOMPLICE TO LINCH-PIN'S GANG.
I NEVER SOLD HEAVY LIQUID TO ANY CLOWNS.
NO, BUT YOU KNOW WHO'S BEEN BUYING IT AND WHERE THEY'VE BEEN GETTING IT.
I DON'T KNOW HOW YOU GOT MIXED UP IN THIS, BUT IT'S WORSE THAN YOU CAN IMAGINE.
BELIEVE ME...
...HEAVY LIQUID'S LIKE A VIRUS, SPREAD ACROSS THE WORLD, LIKE BUTTER ON TOAST.
WHAT DO YOU MEAN, LIKE A VIRUS...?
YOU CAN'T...
HEAVY LIQUID IS SOME SORT OF WEIRD METAL, YES. WE KNOW THAT...
...BUT ITS MOLECULAR STRUCTURE RESEMBLES THE DNA DOUBLE HELIX -- DISTURBING RESEMBLANCE.

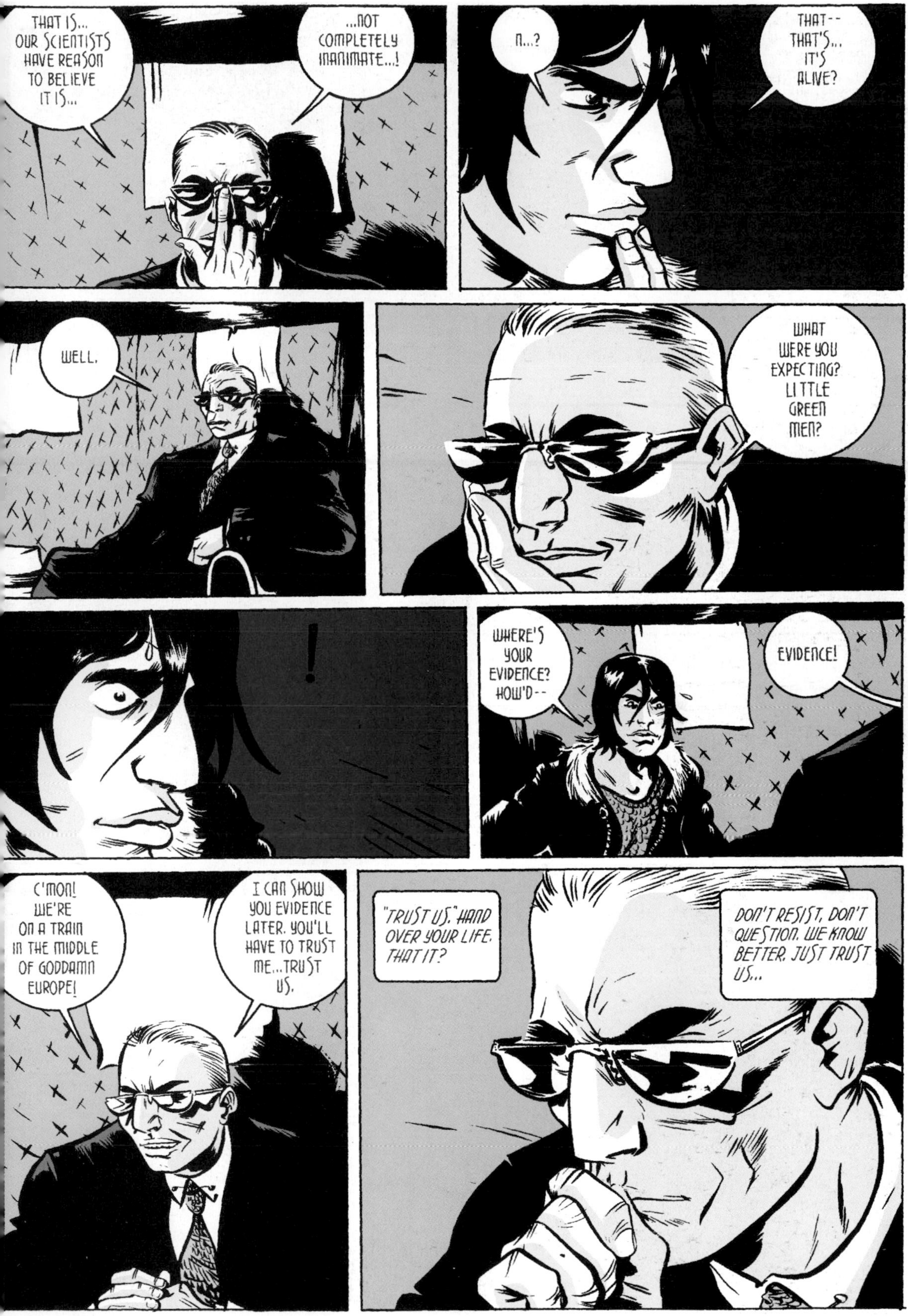
THAT IS... OUR SCIENTISTS HAVE REASON TO BELIEVE IT IS...
...NOT COMPLETELY INANIMATE...!
N...?
THAT-- THAT'S... IT'S ALIVE?
WELL.
WHAT WERE YOU EXPECTING? LITTLE GREEN MEN?
!
WHERE'S YOUR EVIDENCE? HOW'D--
EVIDENCE!
C'MON! WE'RE ON A TRAIN IN THE MIDDLE OF GODDAMN EUROPE!
I CAN SHOW YOU EVIDENCE LATER. YOU'LL HAVE TO TRUST ME...TRUST US.
"TRUST US." HAND OVER YOUR LIFE. THAT IT?
DON'T RESIST, DON'T QUESTION. WE KNOW BETTER. JUST TRUST US...

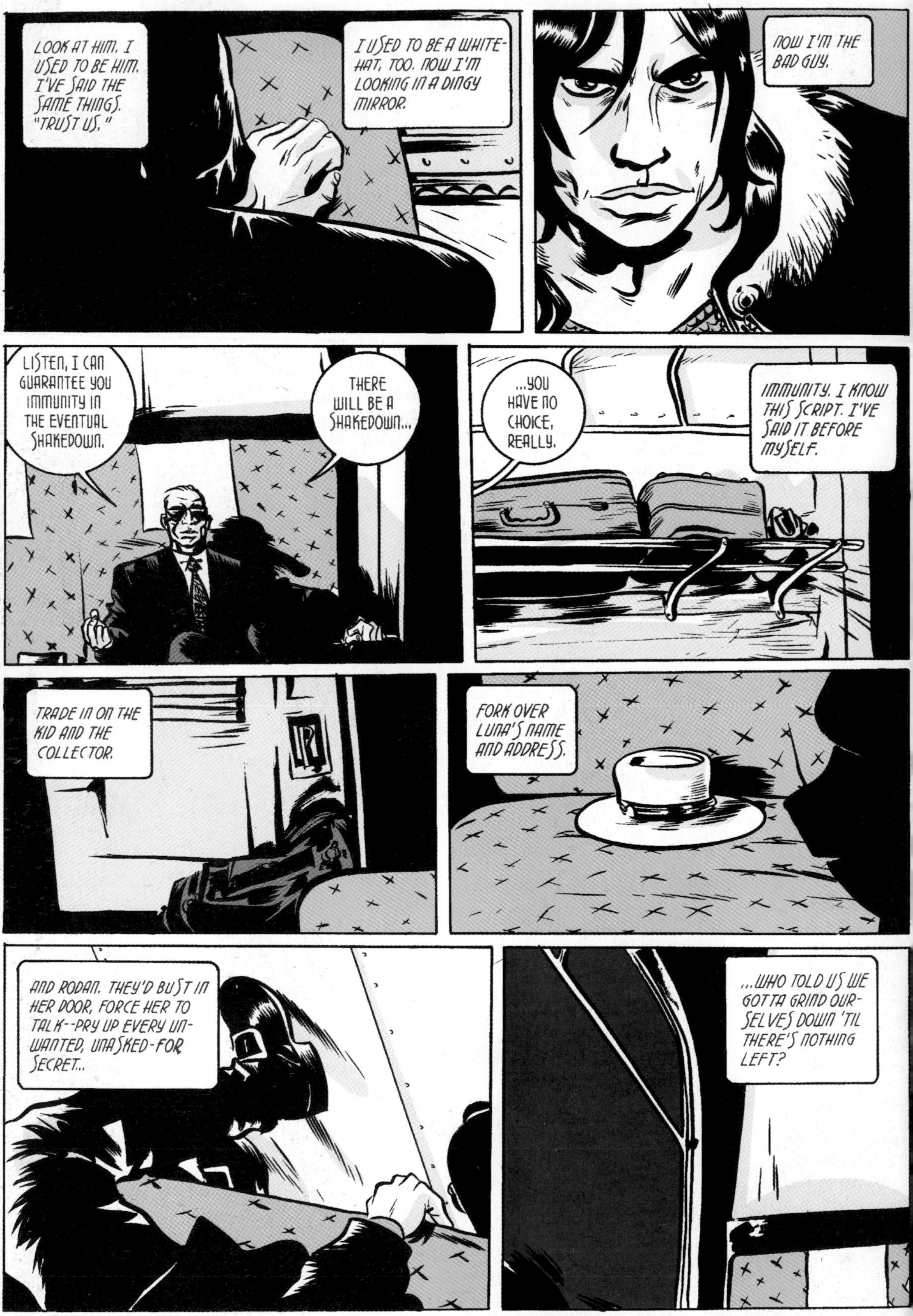
LOOK AT HIM. I USED TO BE HIM. I'VE SAID THE SAME THINGS. "TRUST US."
I USED TO BE A WHITE-HAT, TOO. NOW I'M LOOKING IN A DINGY MIRROR.
NOW I'M THE BAD GUY.
LISTEN, I CAN GUARANTEE YOU IMMUNITY IN THE EVENTUAL SHAKEDOWN.
THERE WILL BE A SHAKEDOWN...
...YOU HAVE NO CHOICE, REALLY.
IMMUNITY. I KNOW THIS SCRIPT. I'VE SAID IT BEFORE MYSELF.
TRADE IN ON THE KID AND THE COLLECTOR.
FORK OVER LUNA'S NAME AND ADDRESS.
AND RODAN. THEY'D BUST IN HER DOOR, FORCE HER TO TALK--PRY UP EVERY UN-WANTED, UNASKED-FOR SECRET...
...WHO TOLD US WE GOTTA GRIND OUR-SELVES DOWN 'TIL THERE'S NOTHING LEFT?

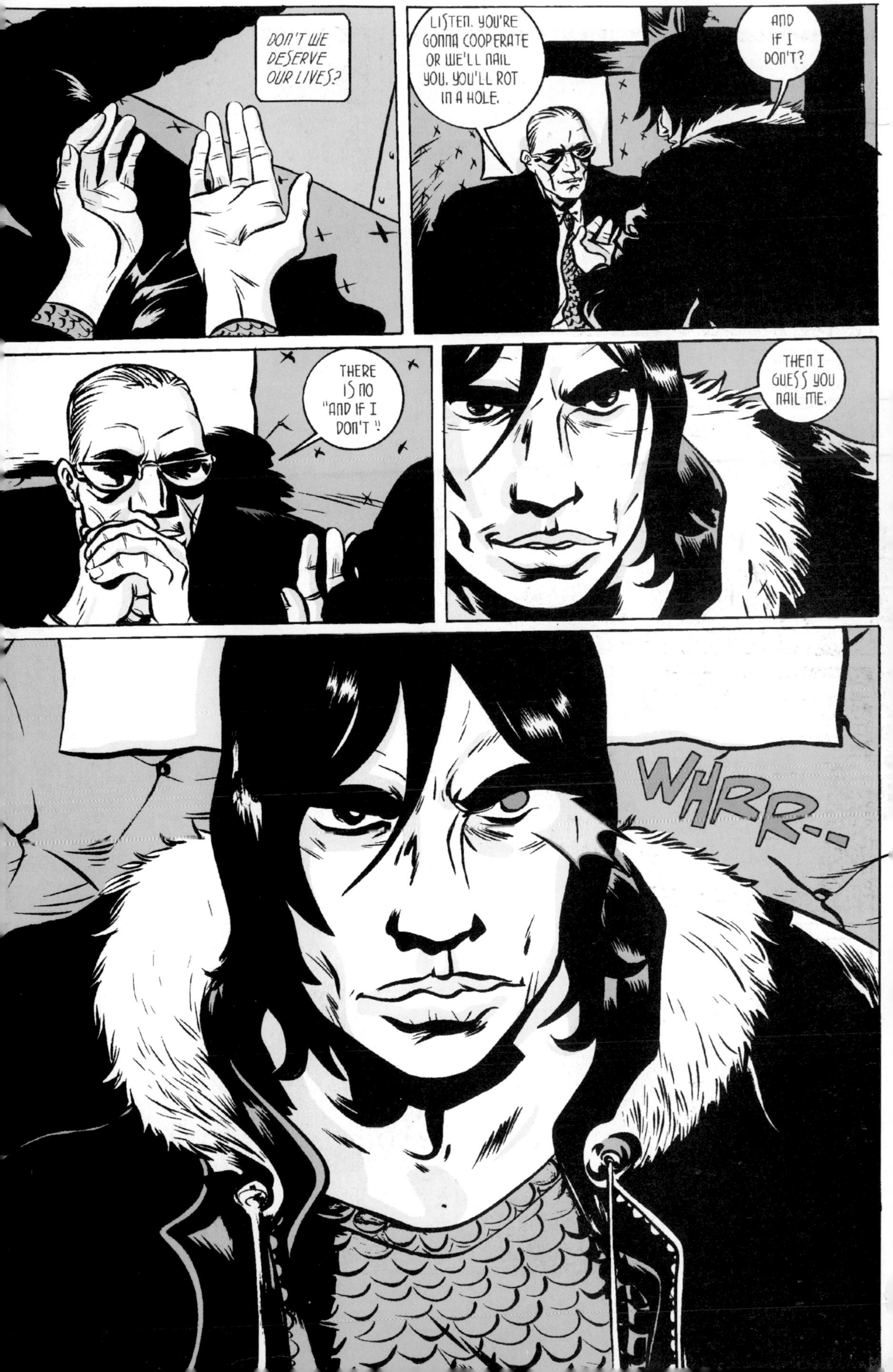
DON'T WE DESERVE OUR LIVES?
LISTEN. YOU'RE GONNA COOPERATE OR WE'LL NAIL YOU. YOU'LL ROT IN A HOLE.
AND IF I DON'T?
THERE IS NO "AND IF I DON'T"!
THEN I GUESS YOU NAIL ME.
WHRR...

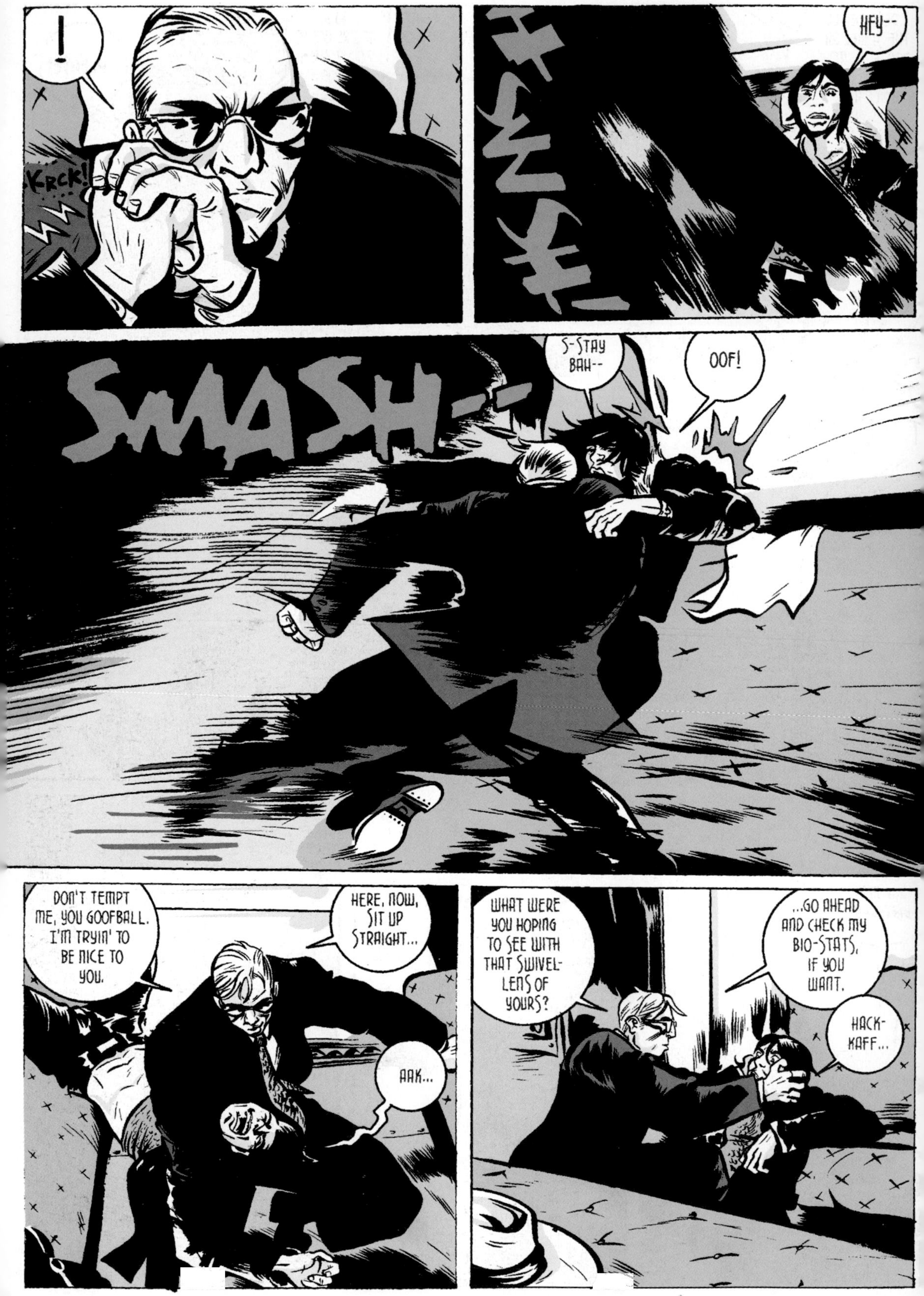
!
KRCK!
HEY--
SMASH--
S-STAY BAH--
OOF!
DON'T TEMPT ME, YOU GOOFBALL. I'M TRYIN' TO BE NICE TO YOU.
HERE, NOW, SIT UP STRAIGHT...
AAK...
WHAT WERE YOU HOPING TO SEE WITH THAT SWIVEL-LENS OF YOURS?
...GO AHEAD AND CHECK MY BIO-STATS, IF YOU WANT.
HACK-KAFF...

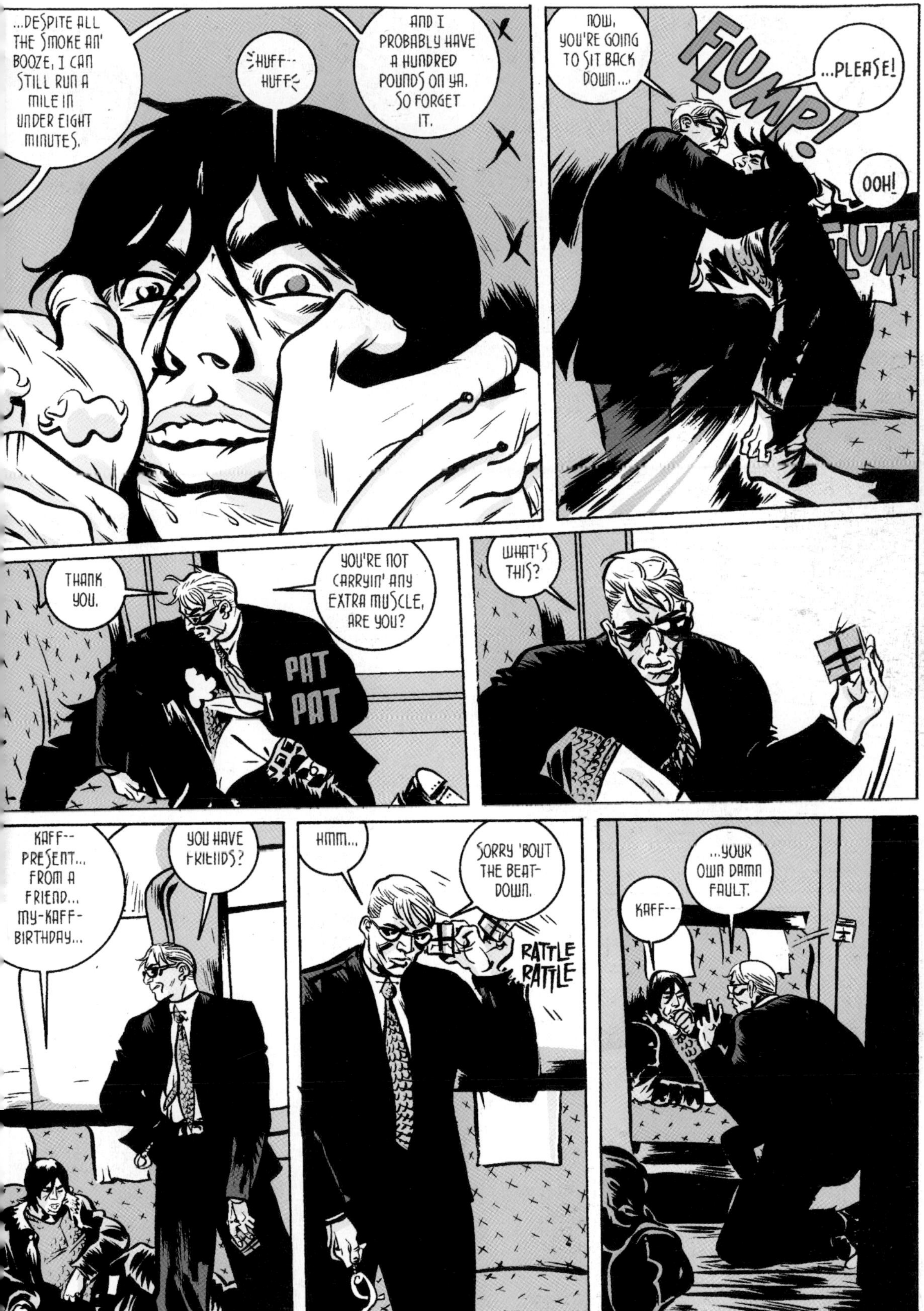
...DESPITE ALL THE SMOKE AN' BOOZE, I CAN STILL RUN A MILE IN UNDER EIGHT MINUTES.
HUFF--HUFF
AND I PROBABLY HAVE A HUNDRED POUNDS ON YA. SO FORGET IT.
NOW, YOU'RE GOING TO SIT BACK DOWN....
FLUMP!
...PLEASE!
OOH!
THANK YOU.
YOU'RE NOT CARRYIN' ANY EXTRA MUSCLE, ARE YOU?
PAT PAT
WHAT'S THIS?
KAFF--PRESENT... FROM A FRIEND... MY-KAFF-BIRTHDAY...
YOU HAVE FRIENDS?
HMM...
SORRY 'BOUT THE BEAT-DOWN.
RATTLE RATTLE
KAFF--
...YOUR OWN DAMN FAULT.

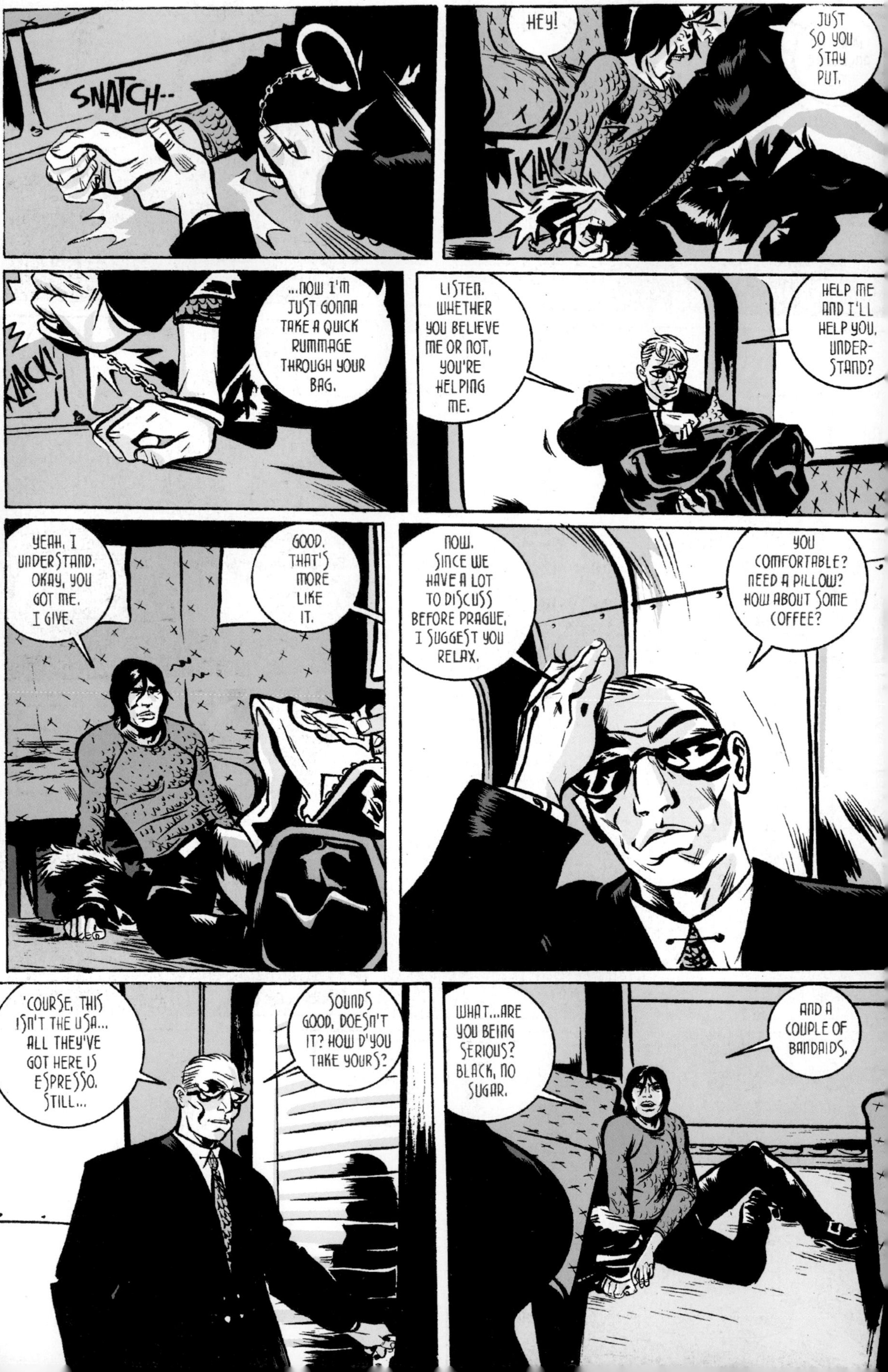
SNATCH--
HEY!
JUST SO YOU STAY PUT.
KLAK!
KLACK!
...NOW I'M JUST GONNA TAKE A QUICK RUMMAGE THROUGH YOUR BAG.
LISTEN. WHETHER YOU BELIEVE ME OR NOT, YOU'RE HELPING ME.
HELP ME AND I'LL HELP YOU, UNDER-STAND?
YEAH, I UNDERSTAND. OKAY, YOU GOT ME. I GIVE.
GOOD. THAT'S MORE LIKE IT.
NOW. SINCE WE HAVE A LOT TO DISCUSS BEFORE PRAGUE, I SUGGEST YOU RELAX.
YOU COMFORTABLE? NEED A PILLOW? HOW ABOUT SOME COFFEE?
'COURSE, THIS ISN'T THE U.S.A... ALL THEY'VE GOT HERE IS ESPRESSO. STILL...
SOUNDS GOOD, DOESN'T IT? HOW D'YOU TAKE YOURS?
WHAT...ARE YOU BEING SERIOUS? BLACK, NO SUGAR.
AND A COUPLE OF BANDAIDS.

DON'T GO ANYWHERE, NOW.

SCREW YOU.

RAKKARAKKKKARAK--

"DON'T GO ANY-WHERE." HA HA.

KAKKAK

...

RAK

I THINK HE REALLY WENT TO GET US COFFEE.

...HMPH!

ARROGANT BASTARD! WHAT KIND OF TRAINING ARE THEY GIVING OUT AT THE U.N.S.T.F. THESE DAYS?

GUESS THAT'S WHAT HE GETS FOR NEVER BEING WRONG.

DIDN'T EVEN LOOK AT MY PRESENT FROM THE PARIS MAN.

THAT WOULD'A' GIVEN HIM A BIG SURPRISE...

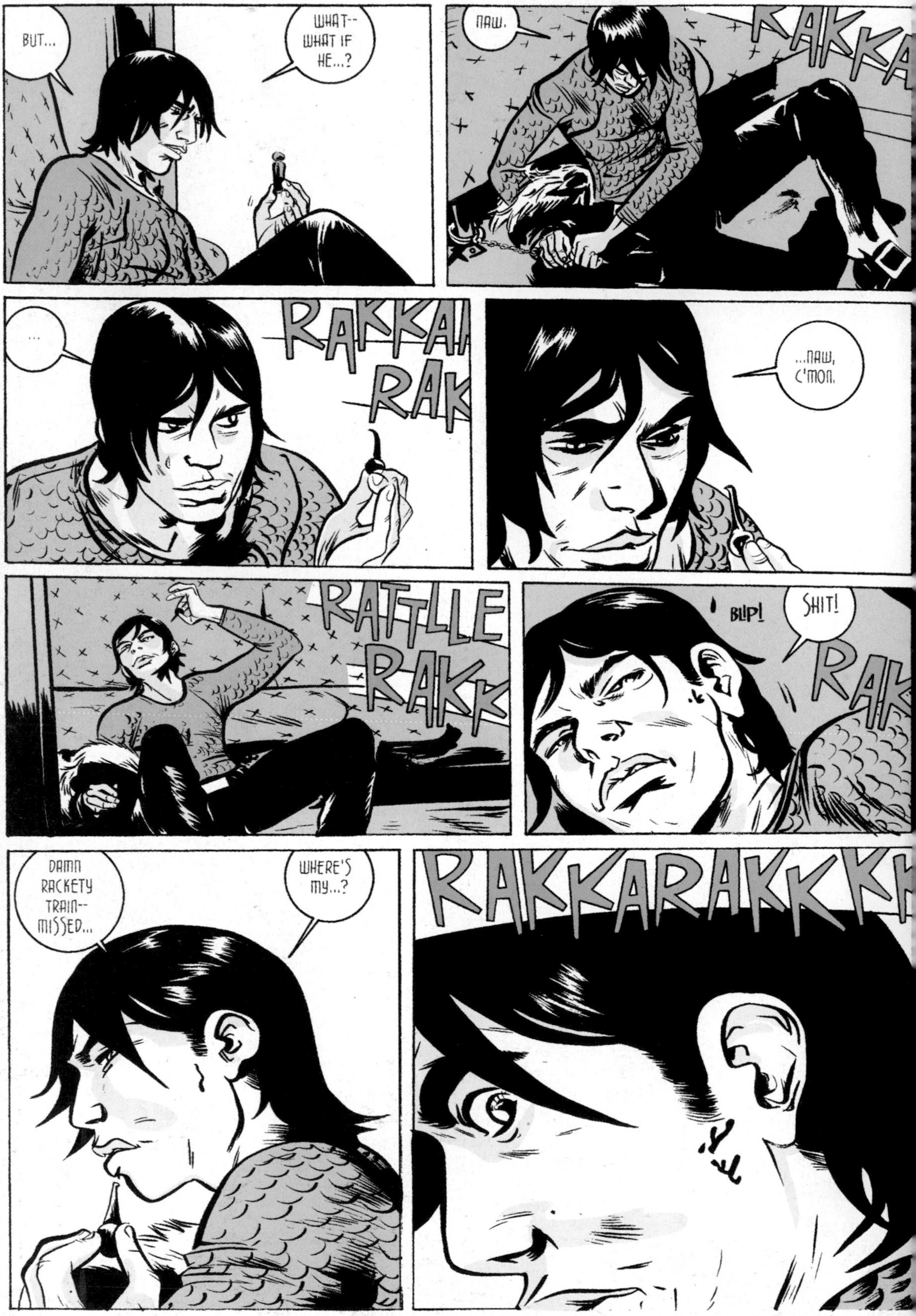
BUT...
WHAT-- WHAT IF HE...?
NAW.
RAKKA
...
RAKKAI
RAK
...NAW, C'MON.
RATTLE
RAKK
BLIP!
SHIT!
RAK
DAMN RACKETY TRAIN-- MISSED...
WHERE'S MY...?
RAKKARAKKK

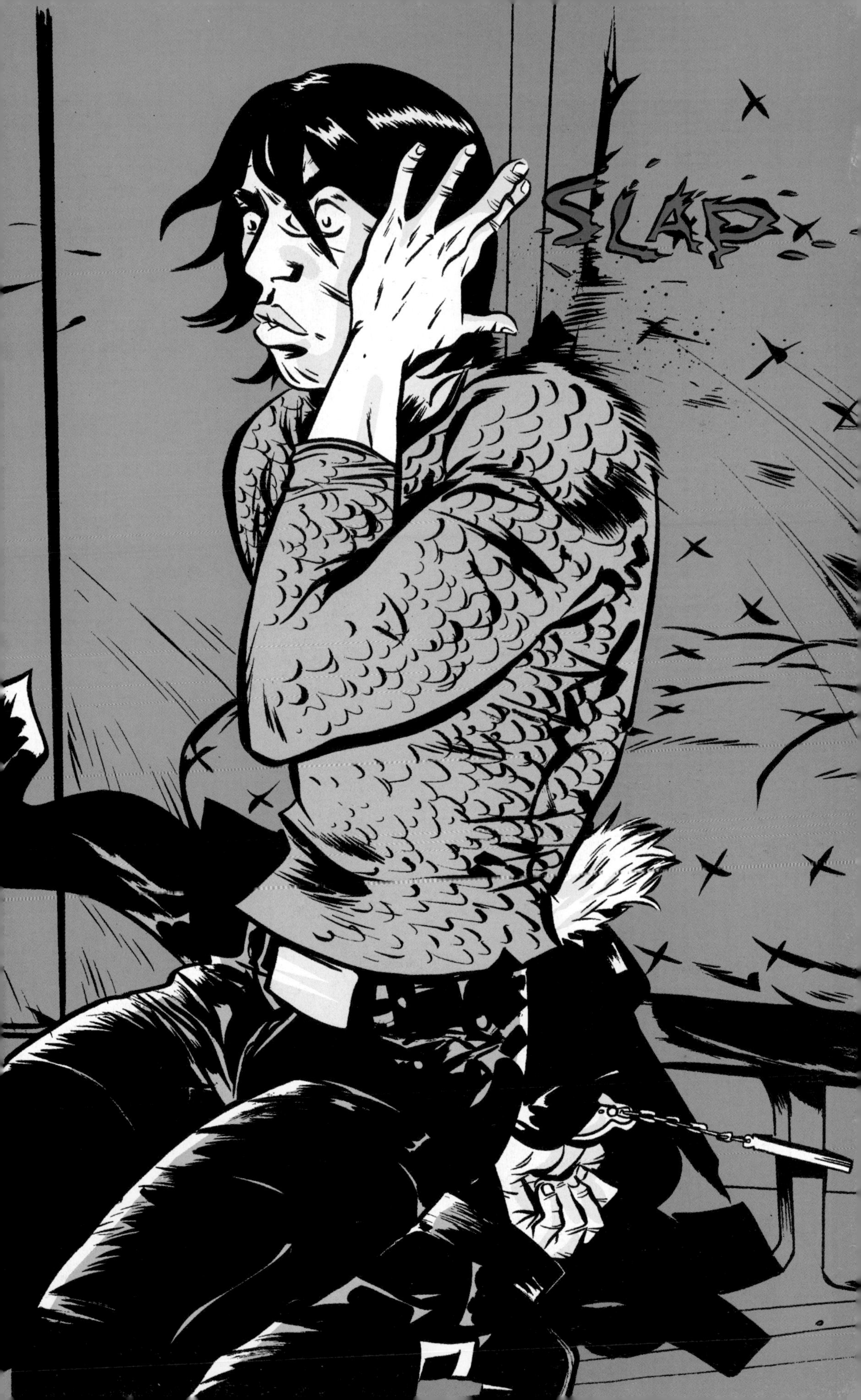
SLAP!

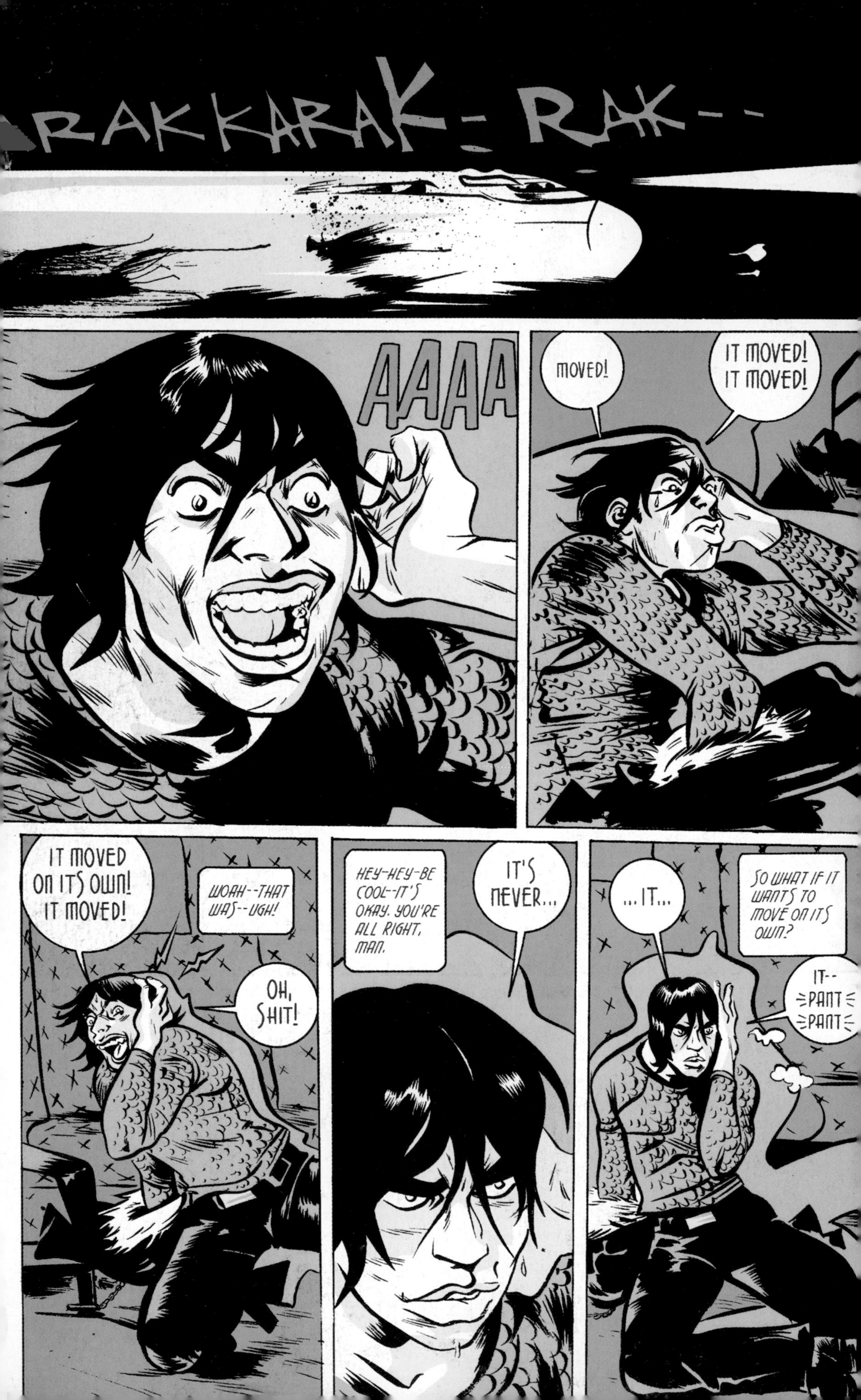
RAKKARAK-RAK--
AAAA
MOVED!
IT MOVED! IT MOVED!
IT MOVED ON ITS OWN! IT MOVED!
WOAH--THAT WAS--UGH!
OH, SHIT!
HEY-HEY-BE COOL--IT'S OKAY. YOU'RE ALL RIGHT, MAN.
IT'S NEVER...
...IT...
SO WHAT IF IT WANTS TO MOVE ON ITS OWN?
IT-- PANT PANT

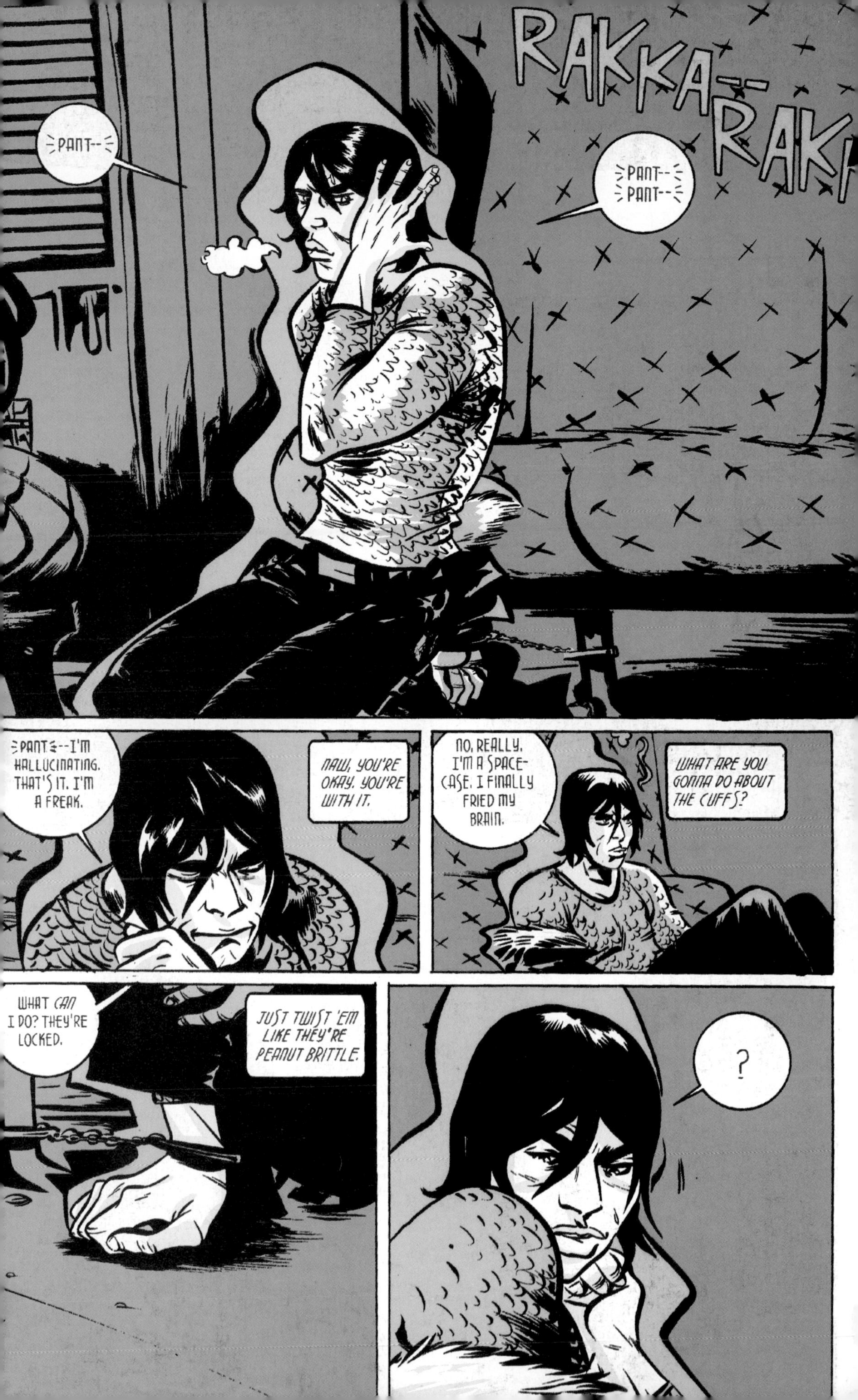
RAKKA--RAKK
PANT--
PANT-- PANT--
PANT--I'M HALLUCINATING. THAT'S IT. I'M A FREAK.
NAW, YOU'RE OKAY. YOU'RE WITH IT.
NO, REALLY, I'M A SPACE-CASE. I FINALLY FRIED MY BRAIN.
WHAT ARE YOU GONNA DO ABOUT THE CUFFS?
WHAT CAN I DO? THEY'RE LOCKED.
JUST TWIST 'EM LIKE THEY'RE PEANUT BRITTLE.
?

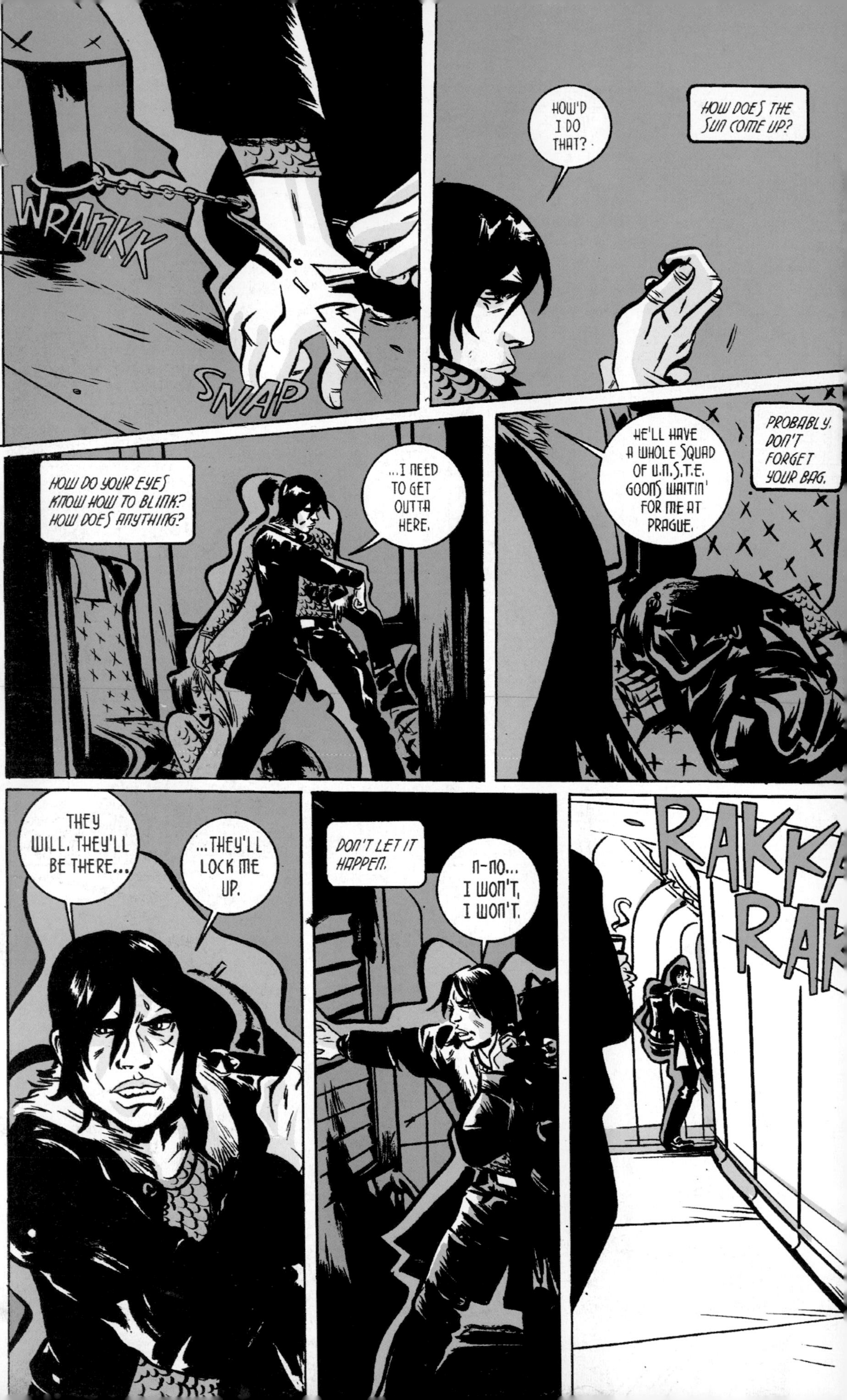
WRANKK
SNAP
HOW'D I DO THAT?
HOW DOES THE SUN COME UP?
HOW DO YOUR EYES KNOW HOW TO BLINK? HOW DOES ANYTHING?
...I NEED TO GET OUTTA HERE.
HE'LL HAVE A WHOLE SQUAD OF U.N.S.T.E. GOONS WAITIN' FOR ME AT PRAGUE.
PROBABLY. DON'T FORGET YOUR BAG.
THEY WILL. THEY'LL BE THERE...
...THEY'LL LOCK ME UP.
DON'T LET IT HAPPEN.
N-NO... I WON'T, I WON'T.
RAKKA
RAK

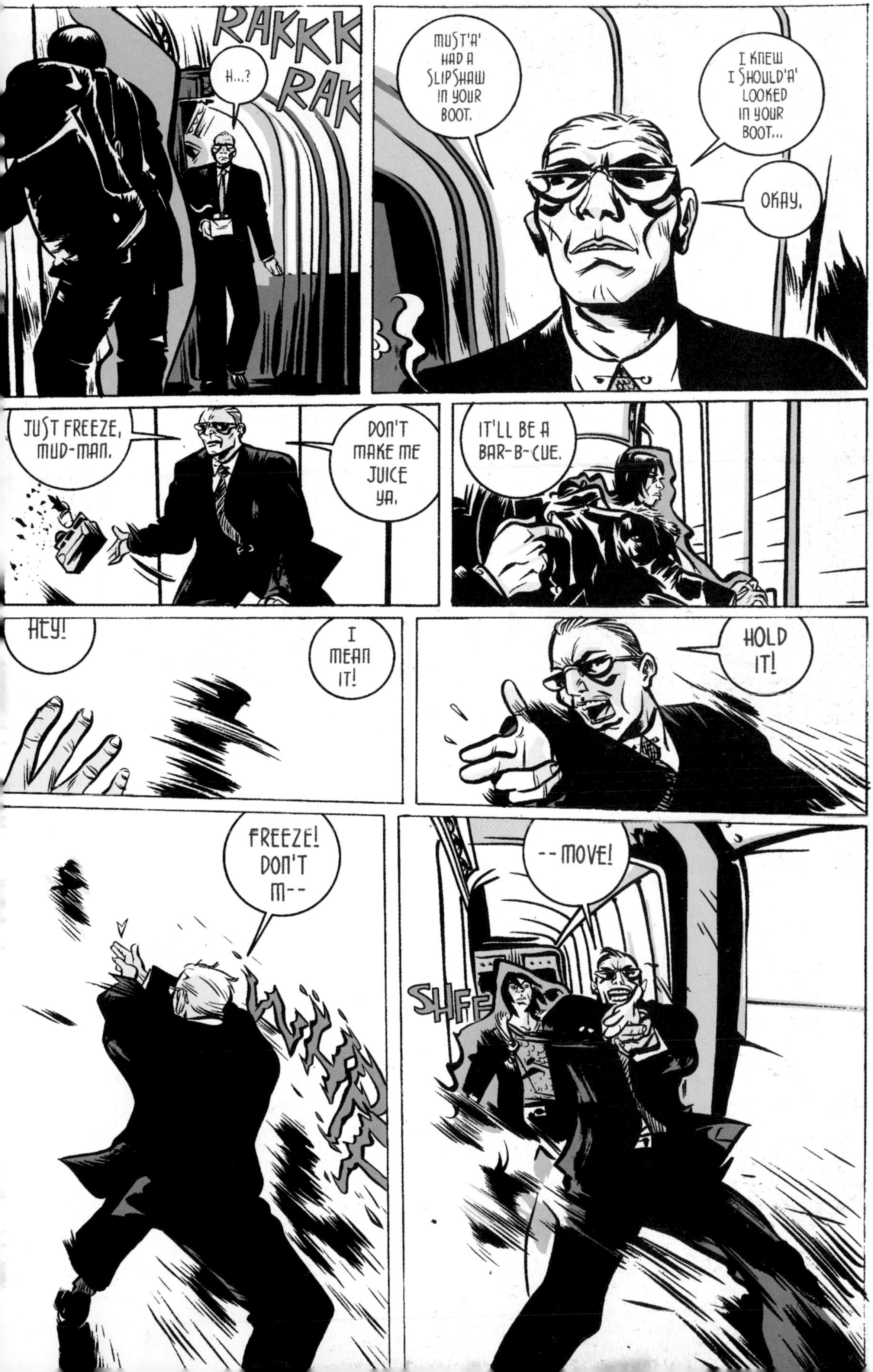
RAKKK
RAK
H...?
MUST'A' HAD A SLIPSHAW IN YOUR BOOT.
I KNEW I SHOULD'A' LOOKED IN YOUR BOOT...
OKAY.
JUST FREEZE, MUD-MAN.
DON'T MAKE ME JUICE YA.
IT'LL BE A BAR-B-CUE.
HEY!
I MEAN IT!
HOLD IT!
FREEZE! DON'T M--
--MOVE!
SHFF

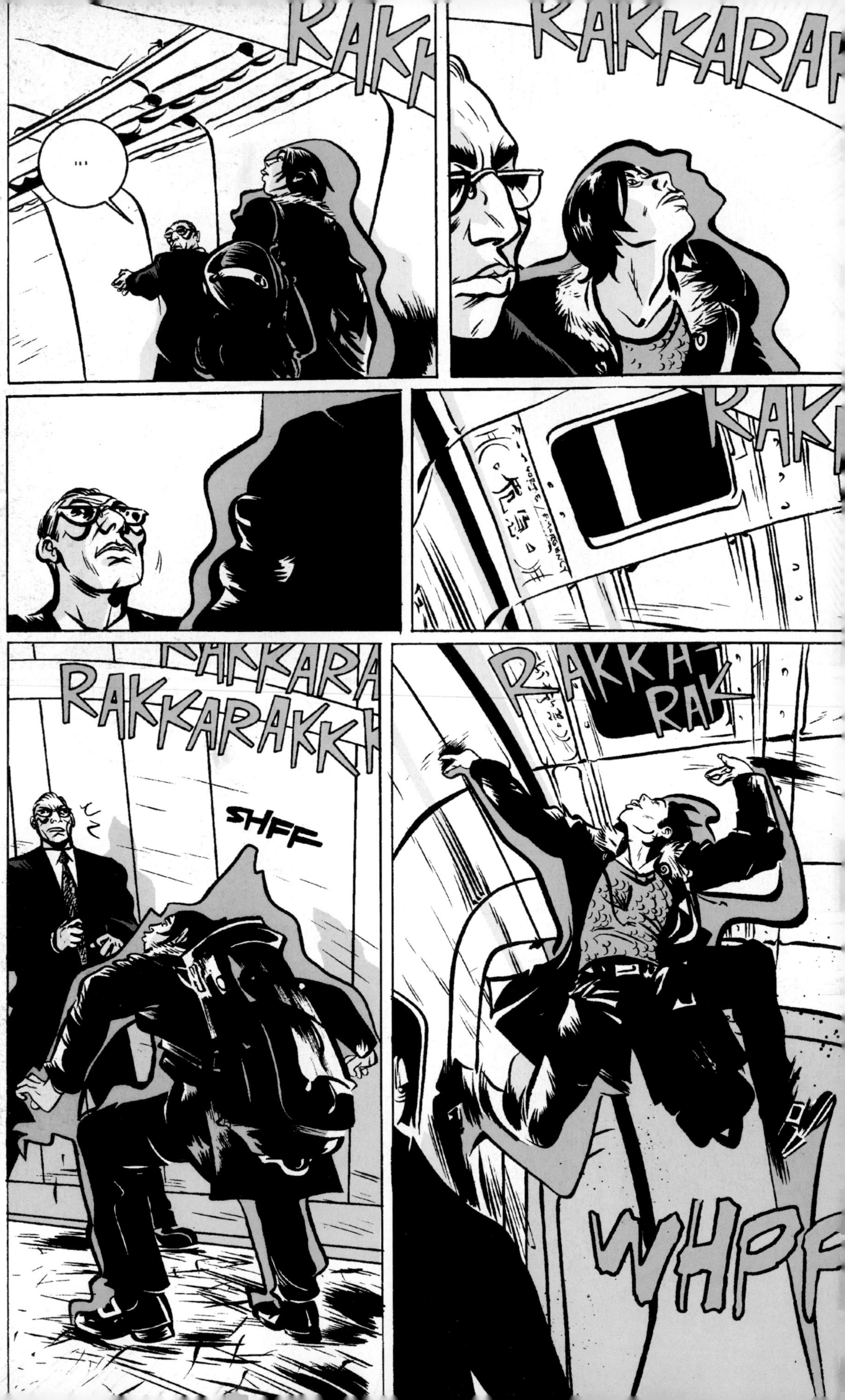
RAKK
...
RAKKARAK
RAK
RAKKARA
RAKKARAKK
SHFF
RAKKA-
RAK
WHPP

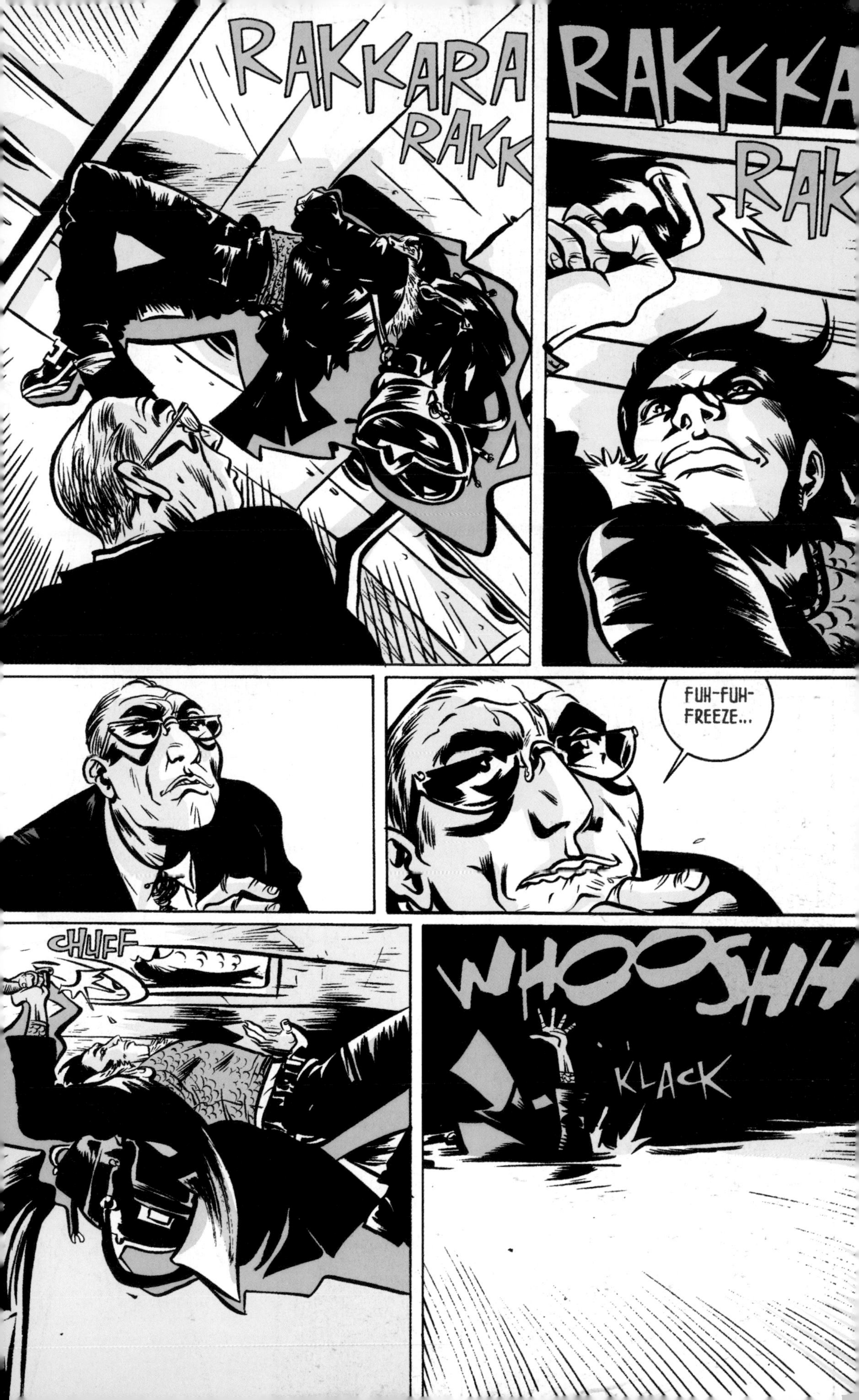
RAKKARA
RAKK
RAKKKA
RAK
FUH-FUH-
FREEZE...
CHUFF
WHOOSHH
KLACK

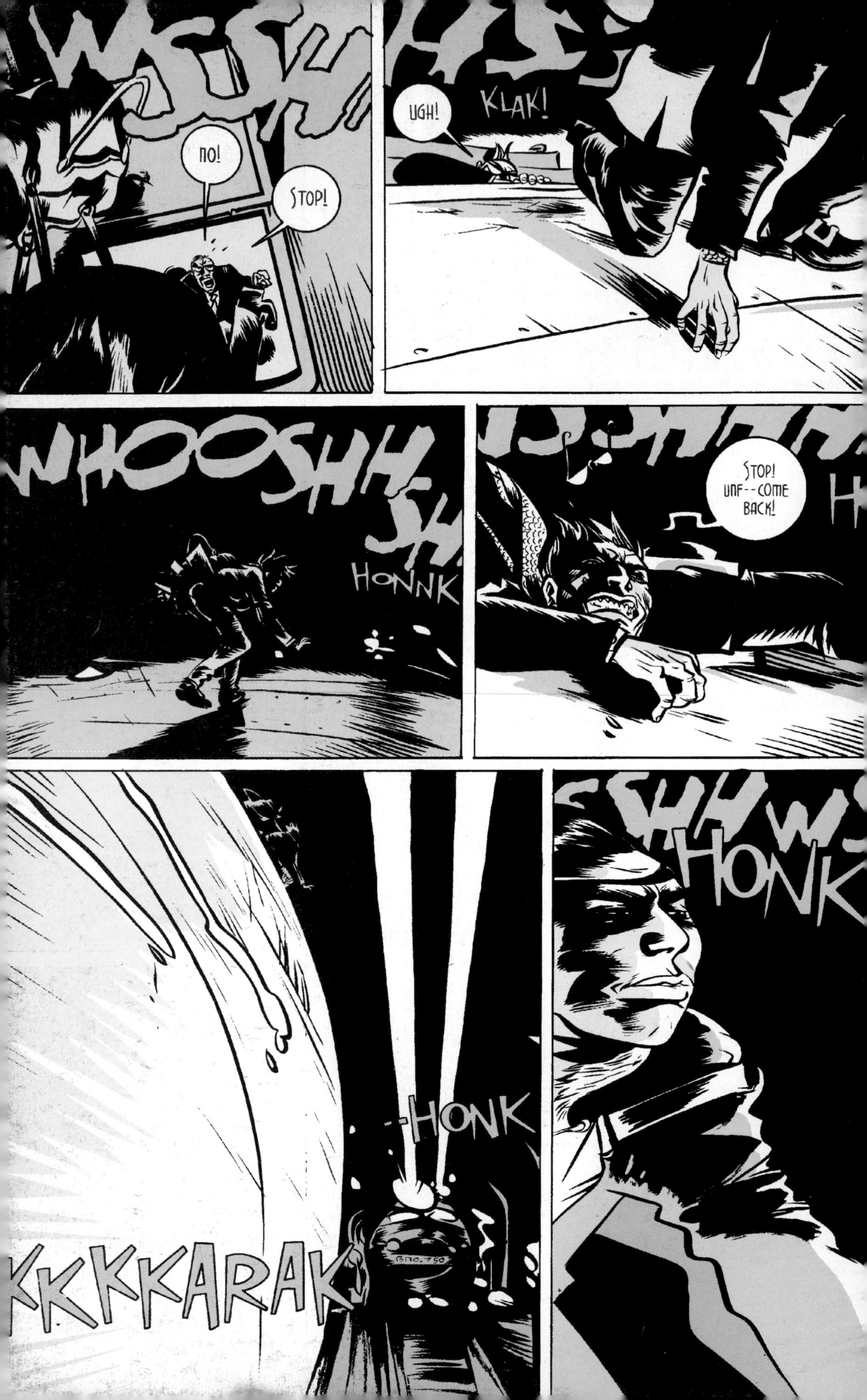
WSSHH
NO!
STOP!
UGH!
KLAK!
WHOOSHH-SHH
HONNK
STOP! UNF--COME BACK!
KKKKARAK
-HONK
HONK
BBO-750

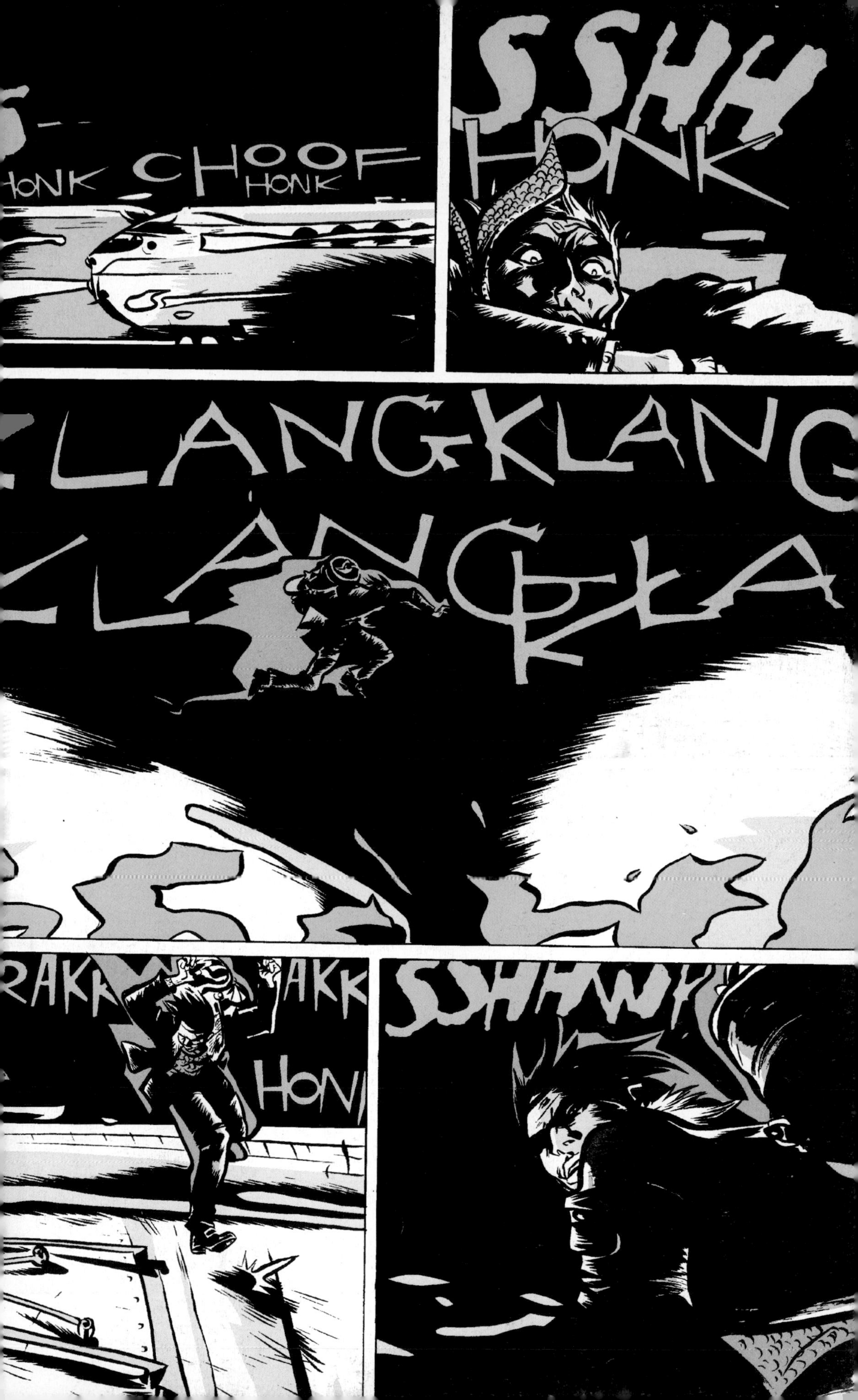
S--
HONK
CHOOF
HONK
SSHH
HONK
KLANGKLANG
KLANG
KLA
RAKK
AKK
HONK
SSHHWH

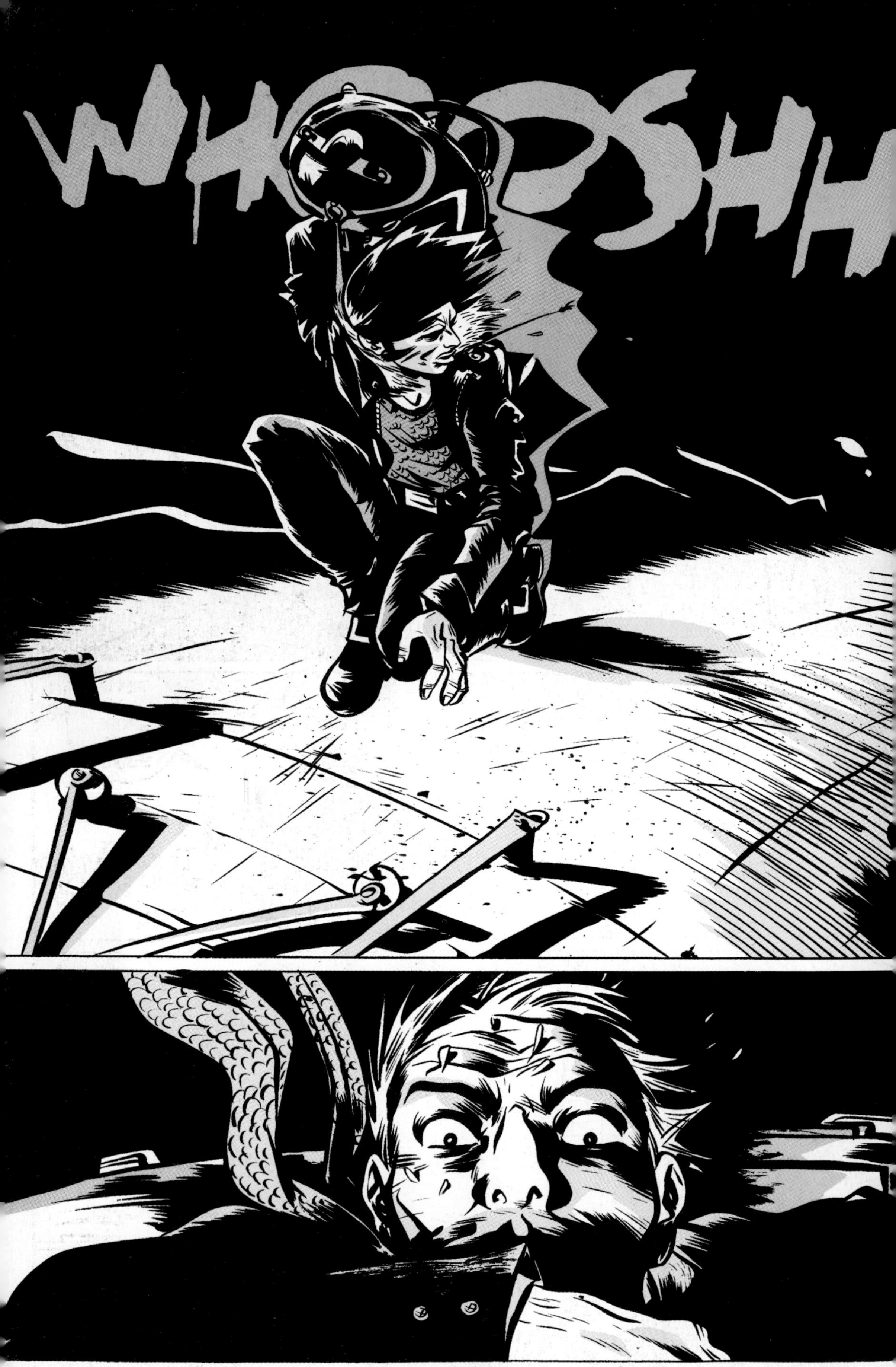
WHOOSHH

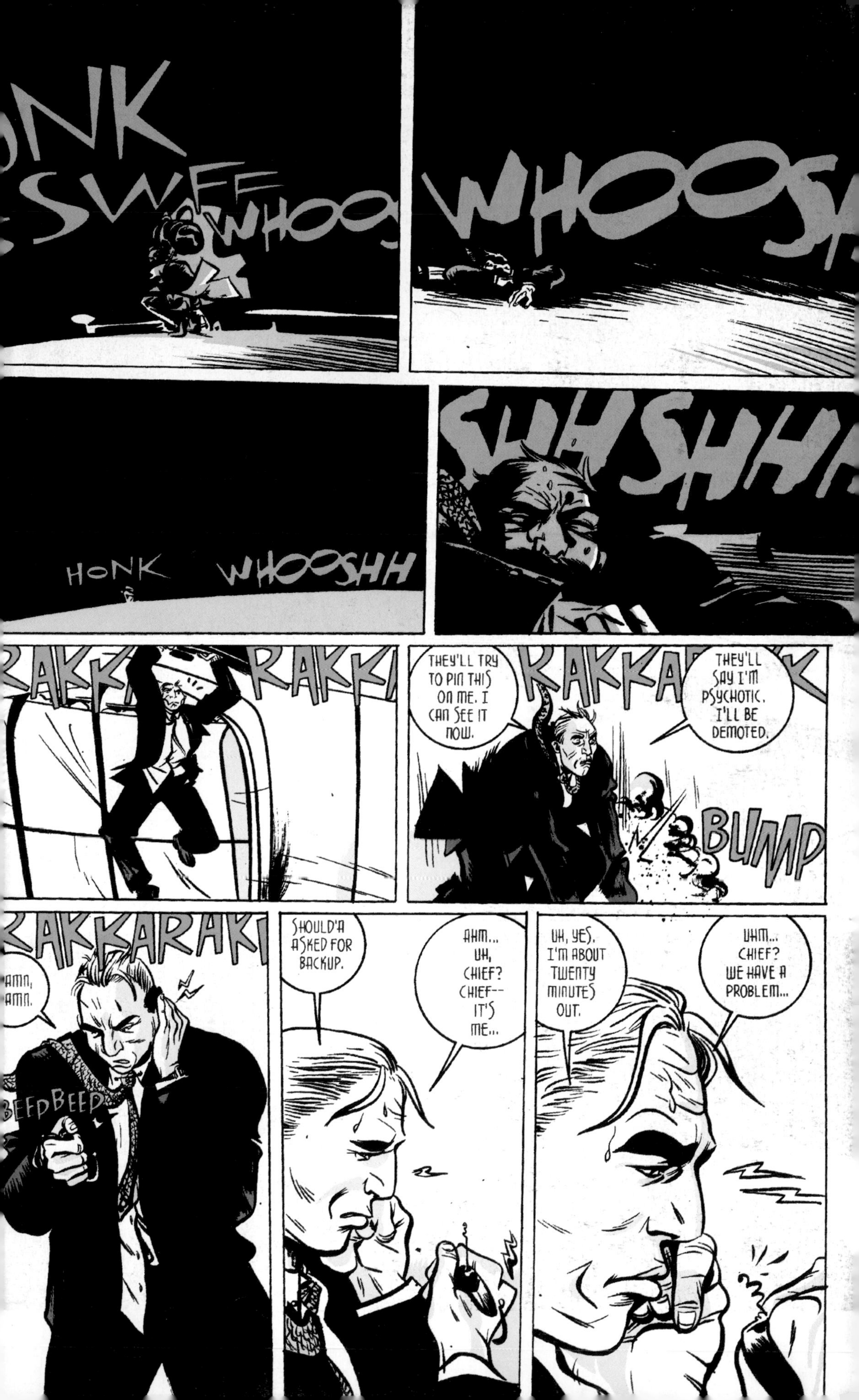
ONK
SWFF
WHOOS
WHOOSH
HONK
WHOOSHH
SHHSHH
RAKKI
RAKKI
THEY'LL TRY TO PIN THIS ON ME. I CAN SEE IT NOW.
RAKKARAK
THEY'LL SAY I'M PSYCHOTIC. I'LL BE DEMOTED.
BUMP
RAKKARAKI
AMN, AMN.
BEEPBEEP
SHOULD'A ASKED FOR BACKUP.
AHM... UH, CHIEF? CHIEF-- IT'S ME...
UH, YES. I'M ABOUT TWENTY MINUTES OUT.
UHM... CHIEF? WE HAVE A PROBLEM...

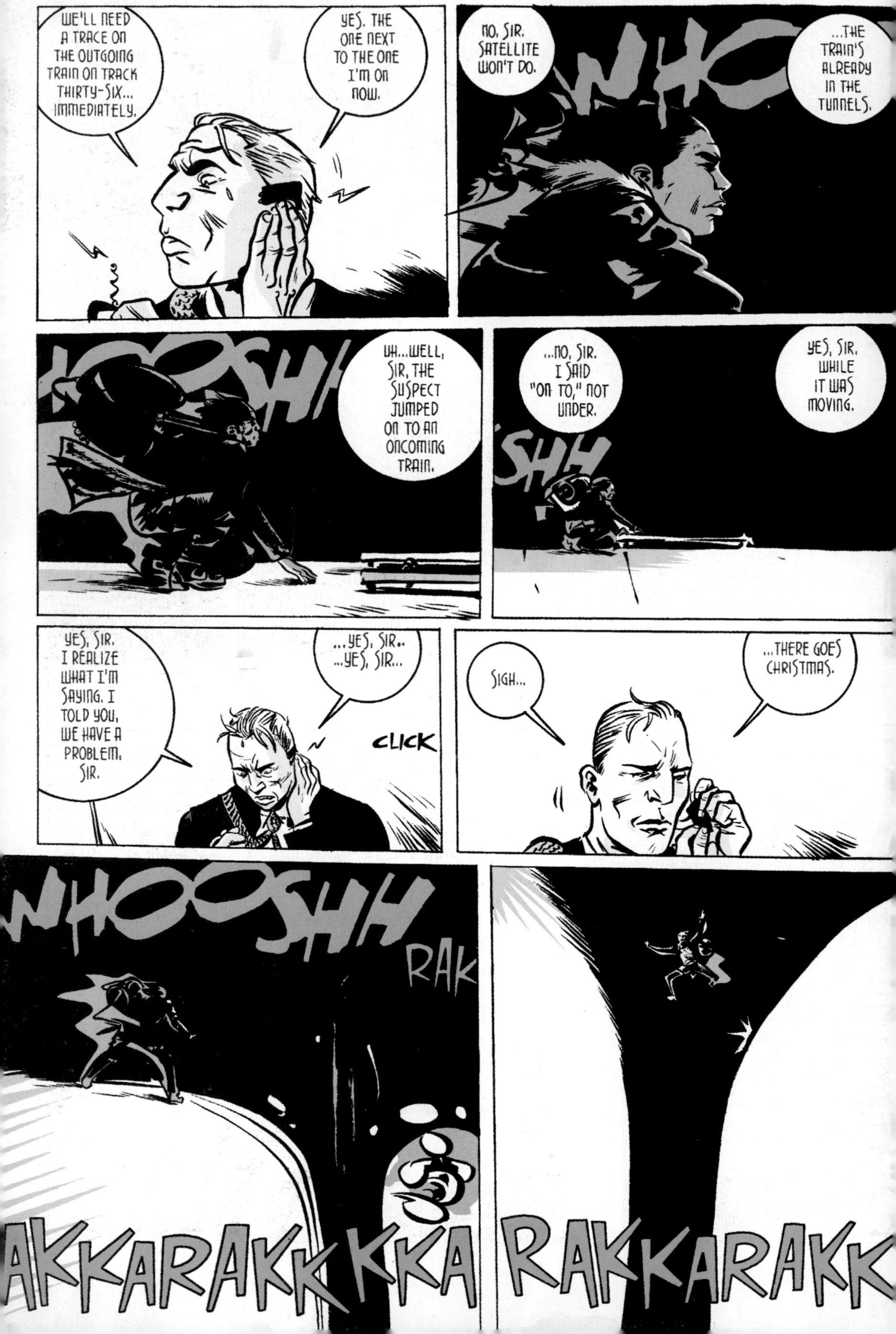
WE'LL NEED A TRACE ON THE OUTGOING TRAIN ON TRACK THIRTY-SIX... IMMEDIATELY.
YES. THE ONE NEXT TO THE ONE I'M ON NOW.
NO, SIR. SATELLITE WON'T DO.
WHO
...THE TRAIN'S ALREADY IN THE TUNNELS.
WHOOSHH
UH...WELL, SIR, THE SUSPECT JUMPED ON TO AN ONCOMING TRAIN.
...NO, SIR. I SAID "ON TO," NOT UNDER.
YES, SIR. WHILE IT WAS MOVING.
SHH
YES, SIR. I REALIZE WHAT I'M SAYING. I TOLD YOU, WE HAVE A PROBLEM, SIR.
...YES, SIR.. ...YES, SIR...
CLICK
SIGH...
...THERE GOES CHRISTMAS.
WHOOSHH
RAK
AKKARAKKKKA
RAKKARAKK

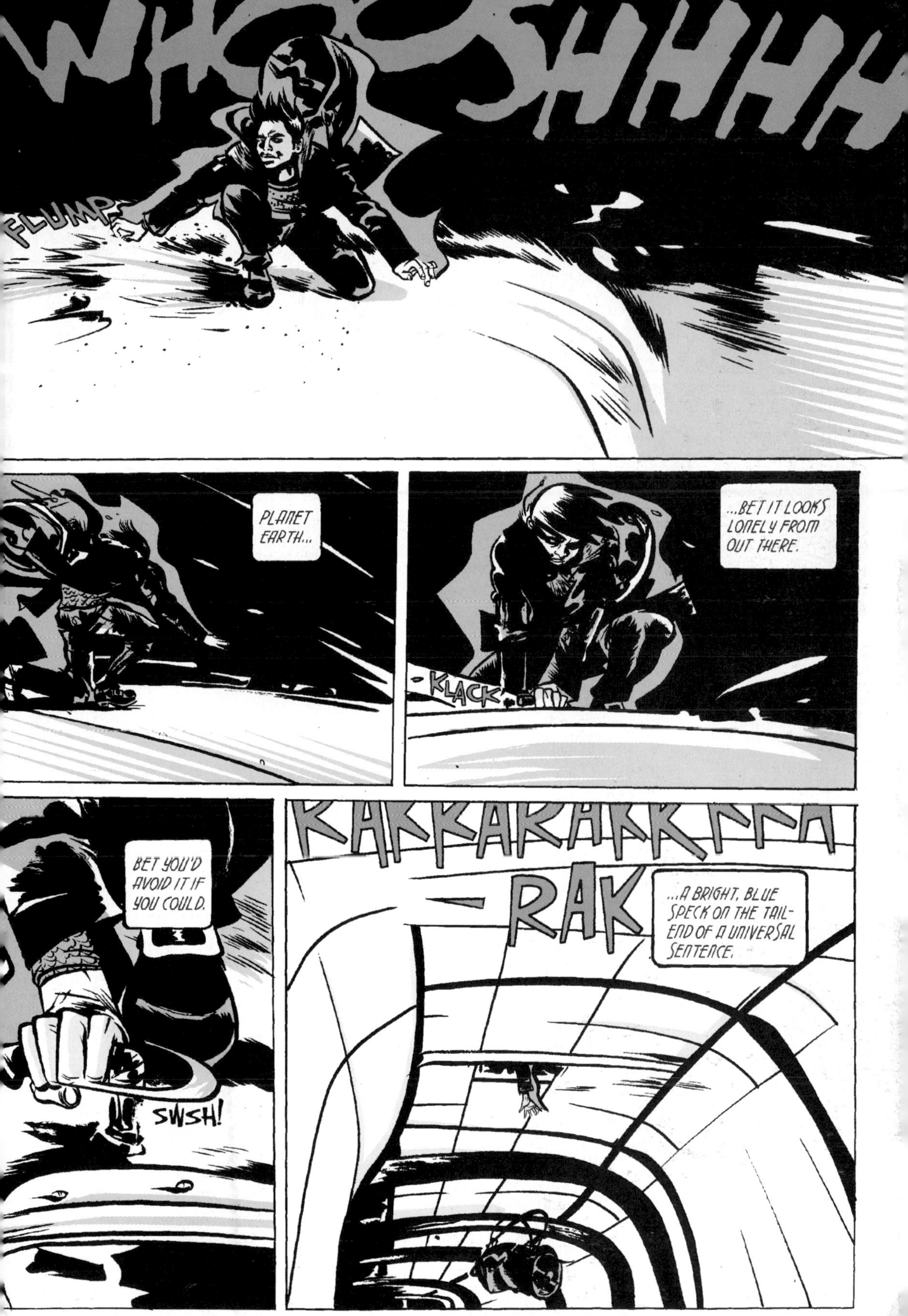
WHOOSHHHH
FLUMP
PLANET EARTH...
...BET IT LOOKS LONELY FROM OUT THERE.
KLACK
BET YOU'D AVOID IT IF YOU COULD.
SWSH!
KAKKAKAKKKKKA
RAK
...A BRIGHT, BLUE SPECK ON THE TAIL-END OF A UNIVERSAL SENTENCE.

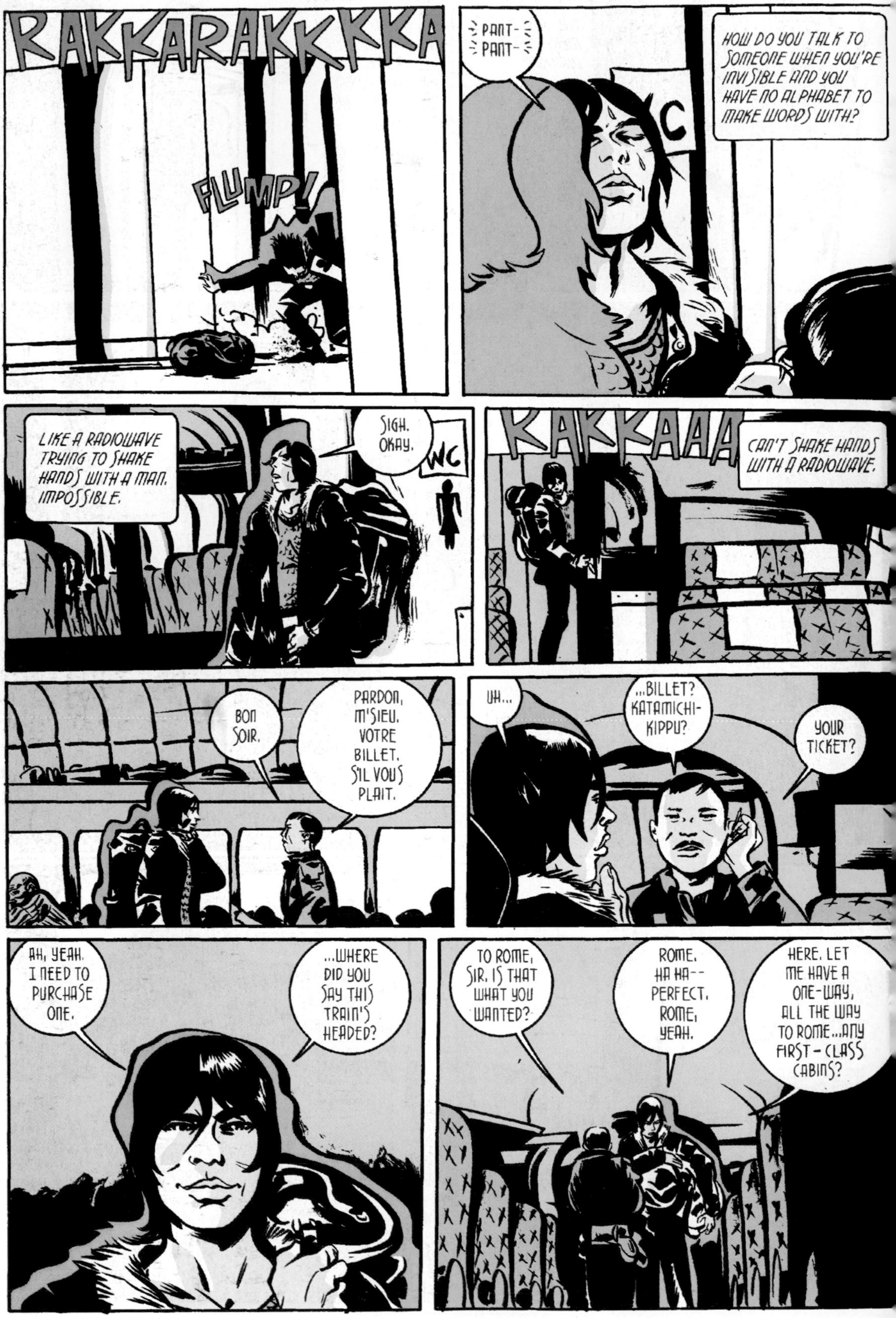
RAKKARAKKKKA
FLUMP!
PANT-
PANT-
HOW DO YOU TALK TO SOMEONE WHEN YOU'RE INVISIBLE AND YOU HAVE NO ALPHABET TO MAKE WORDS WITH?
LIKE A RADIOWAVE TRYING TO SHAKE HANDS WITH A MAN. IMPOSSIBLE.
SIGH. OKAY.
WC
RAKKAAA
CAN'T SHAKE HANDS WITH A RADIOWAVE.
BON SOIR.
PARDON, M'SIEU. VOTRE BILLET. S'IL VOUS PLAIT.
UH...
...BILLET? KATAMICHI-KIPPU?
YOUR TICKET?
AH, YEAH. I NEED TO PURCHASE ONE.
...WHERE DID YOU SAY THIS TRAIN'S HEADED?
TO ROME, SIR. IS THAT WHAT YOU WANTED?
ROME. HA HA-- PERFECT. ROME, YEAH.
HERE. LET ME HAVE A ONE-WAY, ALL THE WAY TO ROME...ANY FIRST-CLASS CABINS?

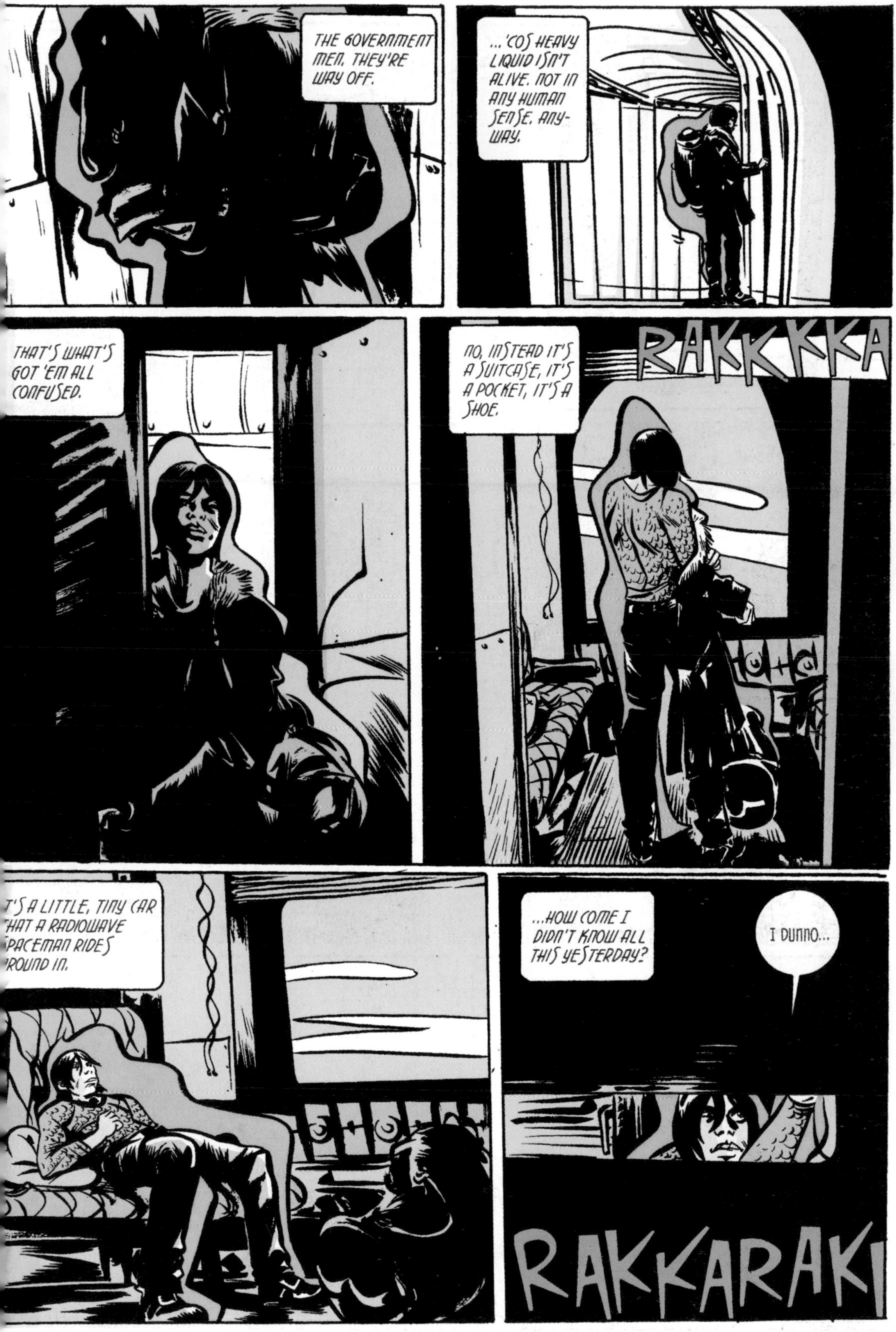
THE GOVERNMENT MEN. THEY'RE WAY OFF.
...'COS HEAVY LIQUID ISN'T ALIVE. NOT IN ANY HUMAN SENSE, ANYWAY.
THAT'S WHAT'S GOT 'EM ALL CONFUSED.
NO, INSTEAD IT'S A SUITCASE, IT'S A POCKET, IT'S A SHOE.
RAKKKKA
T'S A LITTLE, TINY CAR
HAT A RADIOWAVE
PACEMAN RIDES
ROUND IN.
...HOW COME I DIDN'T KNOW ALL THIS YESTERDAY?
I DUNNO...
RAKKARAKI

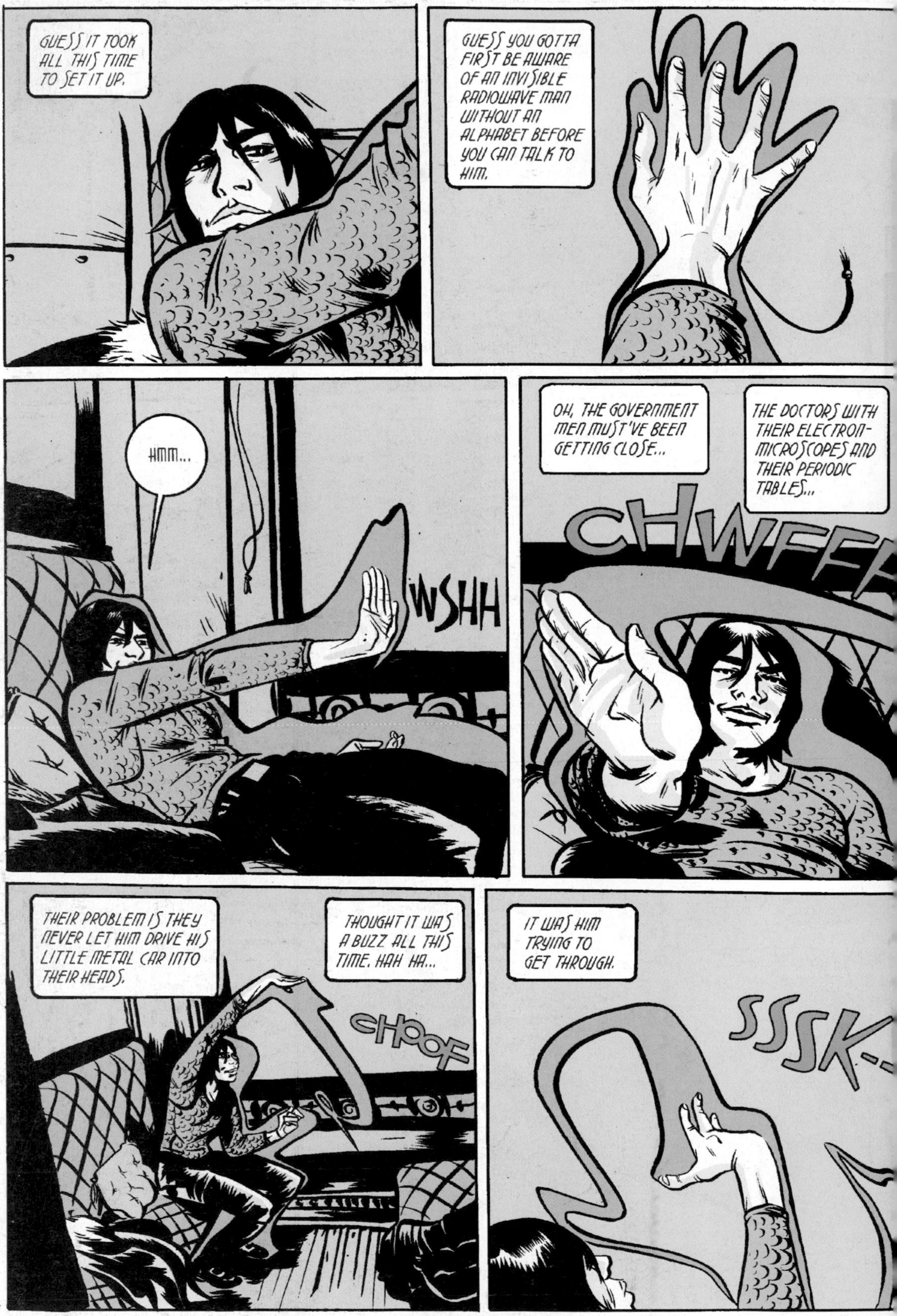
GUESS IT TOOK ALL THIS TIME TO SET IT UP.
GUESS YOU GOTTA FIRST BE AWARE OF AN INVISIBLE RADIOWAVE MAN WITHOUT AN ALPHABET BEFORE YOU CAN TALK TO HIM.
HMM...
WSHH
OH, THE GOVERNMENT MEN MUST'VE BEEN GETTING CLOSE...
THE DOCTORS WITH THEIR ELECTRON-MICROSCOPES AND THEIR PERIODIC TABLES...
CHWFFF
THEIR PROBLEM IS THEY NEVER LET HIM DRIVE HIS LITTLE METAL CAR INTO THEIR HEADS.
THOUGHT IT WAS A BUZZ ALL THIS TIME. HAH HA...
CHOOF
IT WAS HIM TRYING TO GET THROUGH.
SSSK--

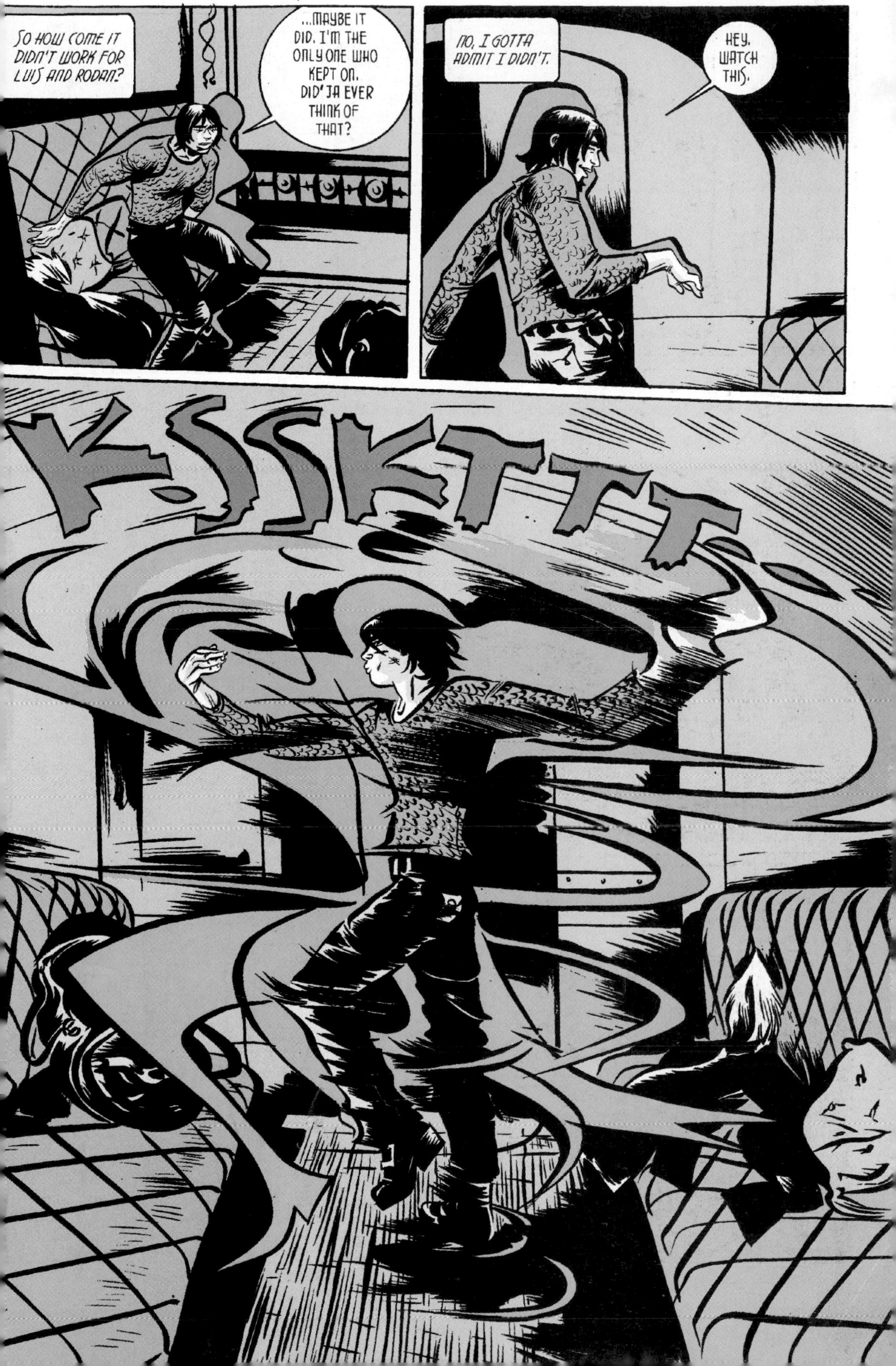

SO HOW COME IT DIDN'T WORK FOR LUIS AND RODAN?
...MAYBE IT DID. I'M THE ONLY ONE WHO KEPT ON. DID'JA EVER THINK OF THAT?
NO, I GOTTA ADMIT I DIDN'T.
HEY. WATCH THIS.
KSSKTTT

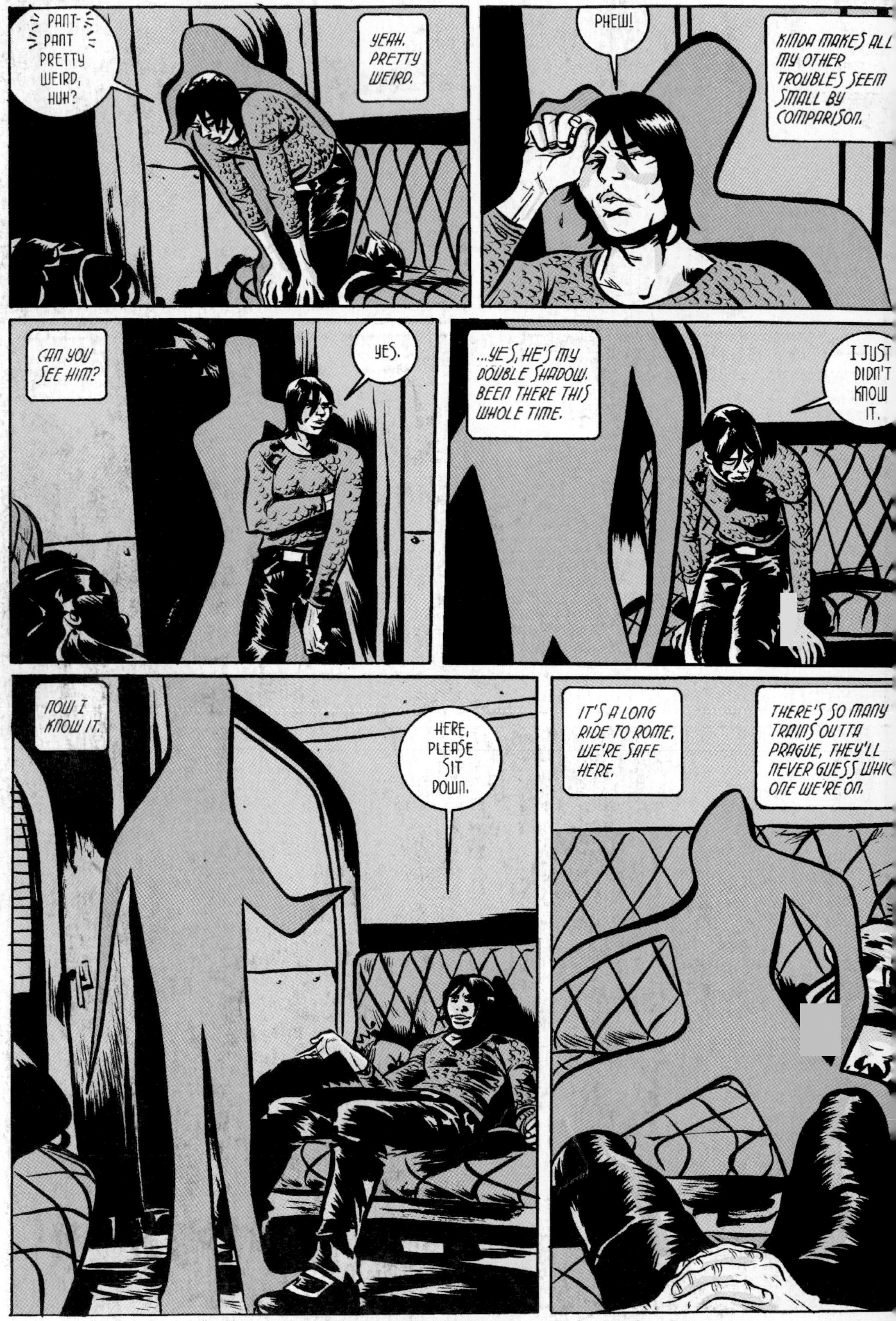
PANT-
PANT
PRETTY
WEIRD,
HUH?
YEAH.
PRETTY
WEIRD.
PHEW!
KINDA MAKES ALL
MY OTHER
TROUBLES SEEM
SMALL BY
COMPARISON.
CAN YOU
SEE HIM?
YES.
...YES, HE'S MY
DOUBLE SHADOW.
BEEN THERE THIS
WHOLE TIME.
I JUST
DIDN'T
KNOW
IT.
NOW I
KNOW IT.
HERE,
PLEASE
SIT
DOWN.
IT'S A LONG
RIDE TO ROME.
WE'RE SAFE
HERE.
THERE'S SO MANY
TRAINS OUTTA
PRAGUE, THEY'LL
NEVER GUESS WHIC
ONE WE'RE ON.

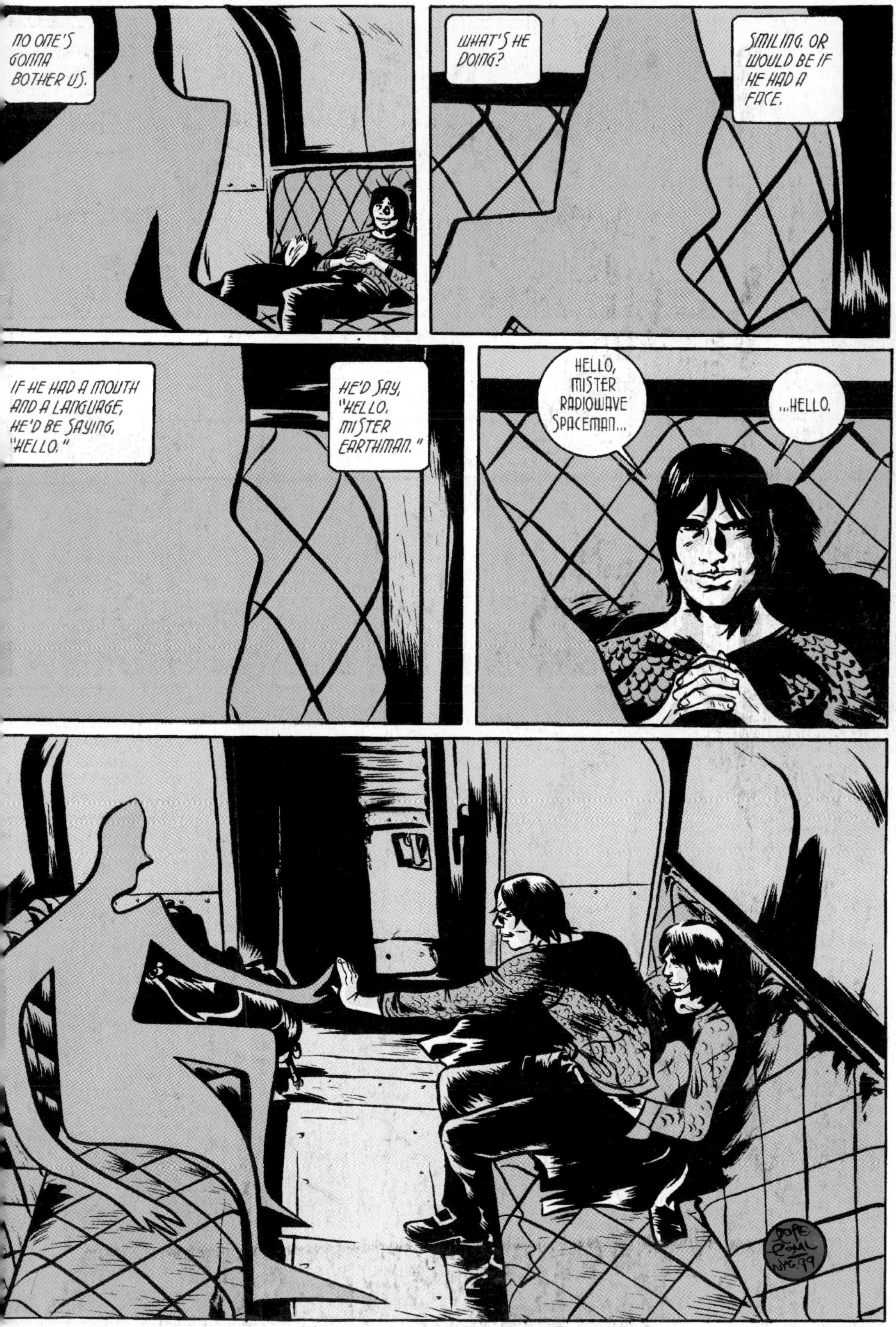
NO ONE'S GONNA BOTHER US.
WHAT'S HE DOING?
SMILING. OR WOULD BE IF HE HAD A FACE.
IF HE HAD A MOUTH AND A LANGUAGE, HE'D BE SAYING, "HELLO."
HE'D SAY, "HELLO. MISTER EARTHMAN."
HELLO, MISTER RADIOWAVE SPACEMAN...
...HELLO.

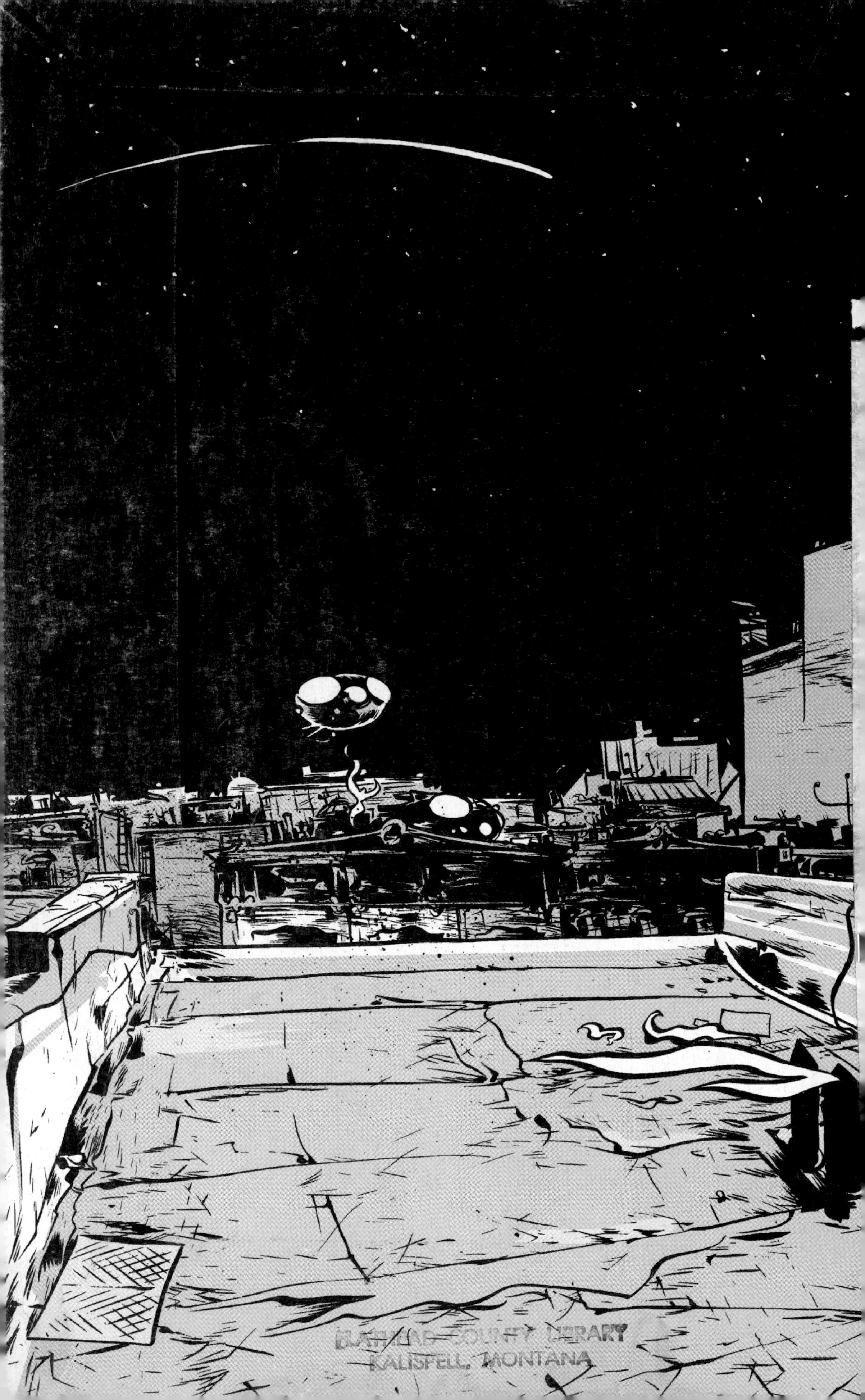